FEDERAL INCOME TAX

Examples and Explanations

FEDERAL INCOME TAX

Examples and Explanations

Joseph Bankman
Professor of Law
Helen L. Crocker Faculty Scholar
Stanford University

Thomas D. Griffith
Professor of Law
University of Southern California

Katherine Pratt
Visiting Associate Professor of Law
Loyola Law School, Los Angeles

LITTLE, BROWN AND COMPANY
BOSTON   NEW YORK   TORONTO   LONDON

Library of Congress Catalog Card No. 95-82170

ISBN 0-316-08040-3

ICP

Published simultaneously in Canada
by Little, Brown & Company (Canada) Limited

Printed in the United States of America

Summary of Contents

Contents

Contents

Contents

Contents

An Introductory Note to Students

If you're considering buying this book, you've probably already purchased a casebook. Most casebooks contain some explanatory text, as well as cases, and those explanations are usually pretty good. (Of course, at least one of us thinks the best explanations are found in the Klein, Bankman casebook.) There are also a number of excellent treatises and student aids on the market.

What this book does — and those other books do not do — is teach the subject through a question-and-answer approach. For each topic, we provide a summary of most of what you will cover in class. You should integrate these summaries with classroom discussion and the reading assigned in your tax course. We then ask a series of questions (called "examples") on each topic and provide you with answers to the questions (called "explanations").

The question-and-answer format is the heart of the book. Although, in practice, many questions do not have clear or simple answers, we have tried to draft discrete questions for which there are clear answers so that you can actively test your grasp of each specific rule or concept. If you can answer the questions correctly, you can be confident that you have mastered the basic rules and concepts covered in the introductory tax course. (Think of it as a "programmed learning" guide to tax rules and concepts.) We have also included numerous policy questions throughout the book.

The book is designed to supplement, rather than supplant, the class and class reading. Although some of the answers to the questions in this book can be gleaned from the topic summaries, other questions can be answered correctly only after you carefully read the Internal Revenue Code and Treasury Regulation sections assigned for the topic. Note that, by deliberately breaking a complex subject into discrete questions, we unavoidably underplay the importance of issue spotting. You must develop issue spotting skills by studying cases, participating in class discussion, and trying to answer more complex "real world" questions. In order to give you an opportunity to answer some complex questions, we have included a diverse sample of actual law school exams, with suggested answers, at the end of the book.

We have tried to include material on just about any topic that might be covered in your tax course. Most tax courses do not cover every topic in this book. For each topic assigned in your course, you can locate the corresponding material in this book by looking at the table of contents in the front of the book or the Code section and topical indexes in the back of the book.

Most of the examples and explanations in this book have been used, in unpublished form, by students for over a decade. The material in this book has been assigned, recommended, or made available to students at many law schools, including UCLA, Capitol, NYU, USC, Loyola (Los Angeles), Miami, and Stanford. Student comments and anonymous reviews of the material have been uniformly favorable. Even those (fortunately few) students who panned our tax classes gave rave reviews to the material that now comprises this book.

Joseph Bankman
Thomas Griffith
Katherine Pratt
January 1996

Acknowledgments

Thanks to all of our students, whose enthusiastic questions prompted us to write these examples and explanations, and to George Demos and the scores of research assistants who worked on this book. Thanks also to Professors William Blatt, Barbara Fried, and Nancy Kaufman for contributing to the sample exam appendix.

FEDERAL INCOME TAX

Examples and Explanations

1

Introduction

The income tax is the largest source of revenue for the federal government. Income tax revenue exceeds $750 billion a year, most of which is collected from individuals. However, over $150 billion a year is collected from corporations, which are generally separate taxpaying entities. The determination of taxable income is similar for individuals and corporations; however, some provisions apply specifically to either individuals or corporations. Moreover, corporations are subject to a maximum tax rate that is just slightly lower than the top rate for individuals. A much smaller amount of income tax is raised from estates and trusts.

Vying with the income tax for the dubious honor of being the greatest federal government revenue-raiser is what is commonly referred to as the social security tax. (Although most of this tax revenue is used to fund social security benefits, a portion of it is used to fund Medicare health benefits.) The social security tax is a payroll tax levied on both employees and employers and is calculated as a percentage of salary income. Other sources of revenue for the federal government include excise taxes on fuel, alcohol, tobacco, firearms, and certain imports, and estate and gift taxes, levied on the transferor (or the estate of the transferor) of significant wealth.

The income tax is also an important source of revenue for state and local governments. In recent years income taxes on individuals, estates, trusts, and corporations have accounted for over a quarter of state and local tax revenues. The determination of taxable income for the purpose of state and local income taxes is for the most part identical to the determination of taxable income under the federal income

1

tax. Knowledge of the federal income tax therefore translates into knowledge of state and local income taxes. Sales and property taxes account for most of the revenue of state and local governments. In recent years each of these taxes has accounted for approximately 35 percent of total revenue. The precise mix of taxes varies from state to state. Some states, for example, have no income tax; other states tax individual income but not corporate income.

A.   Introduction to Terminology and Structure

The starting point in computing a taxpayer's tax liability for the year is the taxpayer's *gross income*. In Chapter 2 we will discuss the concept of gross income at length; for now, note the items expressly included in or excluded from gross income in Internal Revenue Code §§61 and 71-136. (If you look at the table of contents at the front of your Code, you will see a list of the items covered in §§71-136.) Many of the items included in gross income are straightforward; for example, salary from a job is included in gross income. However, a couple of the §61 gross income items are not really "gross" income items.

For example, §61(a)(2) provides that gross income includes "[g]ross income derived from a business." However, in this context, "gross" does not really mean "gross" because a taxpayer's gross income from business means the gross receipts from the business less the cost of the taxpayer's inventory sold. In Chapter 5 we will explore the rules for determining a taxpayer's inventory costs.

Also look at §61(a)(3), which states that gross income includes "[g]ains from dealings in property." Appreciation in the value of property is taxed when the gain is *realized*, for example when the property is sold or exchanged. When a taxpayer sells or exchanges property, the taxpayer must compute the gain or loss she realizes on the disposition of the property. The taxpayer realizes a gain if the taxpayer receives for the property more than the taxpayer's unrecovered investment in the property (in the simplest case, what the taxpayer paid for the property); the taxpayer realizes a loss if the taxpayer receives for the property less than the taxpayer's unrecovered investment in the property. The Code calls the amount the taxpayer receives on the sale or exchange the *amount realized*. §1001(a). The Code calls the taxpayer's unrecovered investment in the property *adjusted basis*. §§1011-1016. So, technically, a taxpayer's realized gain equals the amount realized less the taxpayer's adjusted basis in the property sold, and a taxpayer's realized loss equals the taxpayer's adjusted basis less the taxpayer's amount realized. In other words, a taxpayer's "gross income from dealings in property" is net of the taxpayer's unrecovered investment in the property.

For example, assume that in year one Betsy buys raw land as an investment for $400,000. In year 10, Betsy sells the land for $2 million. Betsy's amount realized is $2 million and her adjusted basis is $400,000, so her realized gain from the sale is $1.6 million. She will include $1.6 million in gross income under §61(a)(3). If Betsy had instead bought property that would decline in value over time, such as an apartment building, she would be allowed to depreciate the property, meaning that she would be allowed to deduct, for purposes of computing the tax she owes, part of the cost of the property each year during the time she owned it. If, for example, Betsy were allowed to take $100,000 of depreciation deductions, her unrecovered investment in the property is no longer $400,000; since she recovered, for tax purposes, $100,000 of her investment through depreciation deductions, her unrecovered investment is $300,000. In this variation her original basis is $400,000, but her adjusted basis is $300,000. §1016. If she sold the apartment building for $2 million, her realized gain on the sale would be $1.7 million.

Not all realized gains from dealings in property are included in gross income. A realized gain is included in gross income only if the gain is also *recognized*. The general rule is that a realized gain is recognized and included in income. §1001(c). However, a realized gain is not recognized if a *nonrecognition* rule in the Code applies to the sale or exchange. There are a number of such nonrecognition rules in the Code. They generally apply to transactions in which the taxpayer has exchanged property but has continued her investment in another form. If one of the specific nonrecognition rules applies to a transaction, the tax on the gain realized in the transaction is deferred until the taxpayer sells the property received in the nonrecognition transaction.

Suppose that Teresa owns land in Hilton Head worth $1 million that is held for investment. Her unrecovered investment in the land, or adjusted basis, is $300,000. She exchanges this land for land in Tampa, worth $1 million, that she will also hold for investment. Teresa's realized gain on the exchange of the Hilton Head property is $700,000, the $1 million amount realized less her $300,000 adjusted basis in the property. However, that gain will not be recognized because the exchange was of like-kind property held for investment so the "like-kind exchange" nonrecognition rule of §1031 applies. (We will consider

§1031 in some detail in Chapter 3.) The realized gain will be deferred until Teresa sells the Tampa property. Teresa's basis in the Tampa land will be $300,000, the basis of the property exchanged for the Tampa property. For now, note that, although Teresa realized a gain on the exchange, the gain is not included in her gross income because it is not recognized.

After computing the taxpayer's gross income, the next step is to compute the taxpayer's adjusted gross income. Section 62 defines *adjusted gross income* as gross income less certain costs of earning income and a hodgepodge of other items, such as alimony paid by the taxpayer.

The next step is to compute the taxpayer's taxable income. Section 63 defines *taxable income* as the taxpayer's adjusted gross income less the sum of (i) the taxpayer's *personal exemptions* plus (ii) the greater of (a) the taxpayer's *standard deduction* or (b) the taxpayer's *itemized deductions*. The personal exemption amount is adjusted each year for inflation and was $2,500 in 1995. A taxpayer is allowed one personal exemption deduction for each of the following: (i) the taxpayer; (ii) the taxpayer's spouse; and (iii) each of the taxpayer's dependents. §151. The standard deduction amount is also adjusted for inflation; in 1995 it was $6,550 for married taxpayers filing a joint return, $5,750 for heads of households, and $3,900 for unmarried individuals. The standard deduction ensures that lower-income taxpayers do not have to pay tax and frees many taxpayers from having to keep records of their itemized deductions. Itemized deductions include all deductions other than the personal exemption deduction and the deductions allowable in computing adjusted gross income under §62. §63(d). For example, itemized deductions include the deductions for state and local income and property taxes, charitable contributions, and home mortgage interest.

Many types of expenses incurred in business or in the production of income (for example, rent and utility bills paid by a business) are deducted in full in the year in which they are incurred. However, if an expense creates an asset that will last beyond the year in which the expense is incurred, the expense cannot be deducted in full in the year in which it is incurred; this type of expense must instead be *capitalized*. If the expense is incurred to purchase an income-producing asset that will be used in the business and has a limited useful life, the taxpayer's expense for the asset is allocated across the years in which the asset is expected to produce income. Each year during the useful life of the asset, the taxpayer will deduct a portion of the cost of the asset, in the form of *depreciation* deductions. If the asset purchased by the taxpayer does not have a limited useful life (for example, raw land), the taxpayer is not permitted to recover her investment in the asset until she sells or exchanges it, at which time the taxpayer's amount realized for the asset is reduced by her adjusted basis in the asset.

After computing the taxpayer's taxable income, the next step is to compute the amount of tax due on the taxpayer's taxable income. Taxable income of individuals is taxed at rates specified in §1(a)-(d) of the Code. The §1 rates are *progressive*, meaning that as the taxpayer's income increases, the rate of tax increases. The rate applicable to the last dollar of income earned by the taxpayer is the taxpayer's *marginal rate*. The taxpayer's *effective rate* is his tax liability for the year divided by his taxable income for the year; it is the same as the taxpayer's average rate. A rate schedule exists for each of four possible filing statutes: married filing a joint return; head of household; individual; and married filing separately. There is also an implicit zero rate since a taxpayer does not owe tax if her taxable income does not exceed the sum of her personal exemptions and standard or itemized deductions. The top nominal rate in §1 is 39.6 percent, but the top rate is really higher because personal exemptions and certain itemized deductions are phased out as a taxpayer's income increases beyond certain threshold amounts. The dollar amounts for the brackets in the §1 rate schedule are indexed annually for inflation. §1(f).

Individuals, estates, and trusts pay a maximum tax rate of 28 percent on long-term *capital gain*, which is gain from the sale or exchange of a capital asset held by the taxpayer for more than a year. §§1(h), 1222. A capital asset is, loosely speaking, an investment asset as opposed to an asset used in an operating business. For example, §1221 provides that inventory and depreciable property used in a business are not capital assets. The characterization of assets as capital or ordinary will be discussed further in Chapter 8 where we will see that this characterization is sometimes difficult to determine. For now, note that high bracket taxpayers pay less tax on capital gain than on ordinary gain, so they prefer to characterize gain as capital. For example, a taxpayer whose marginal tax rate is 36 percent owes $360,000 of tax on $1 million of gain if the gain is ordinary. If the gain is instead capital, the taxpayer will owe $280,000 of tax on the gain, thus saving $80,000 of tax. You can see why the taxpayer would prefer to characterize the gain as capital.

In addition, the progressivity of the income tax encourages high bracket taxpayers to attempt to shift income to family members in lower rate brackets. In Chapter 7 we will consider the congressional and judicial responses to various income shifting techniques employed by taxpayers. For now, note that unearned income (that is, income not from personal services) of a child under age 14 is taxed at the parent's higher tax rate under §1(g), the so-called "kiddie tax." Also note that the income of spouses filing a joint return is aggregated so that attribution of income between the spouses is irrelevant.

Most married couples file jointly because doing so saves them tax. The §1 rates for spouses filing a joint return are the lowest in §1. Married couples with only one income earner pay less tax than they would have if they were not married and each spouse were taxed individually. However, married couples with two income earners pay more tax than they would have if they were not married and each spouse were taxed individually. Why? Because each of the two earners would have benefited from the progressivity of the rates. The added tax owed by two income earners who marry is referred to as the *marriage penalty*.

C corporations are treated as separate taxpaying entities and are taxed at progressive rates specified in §11 of the Code. A C corporation is any corporation that is not an *S corporation*. A corporation is an S corporation only if it meets certain eligibility requirements and elects to be an S corporation. §§1361, 1362. (The names are derived from subchapter designations in the Code: S corporations are subject to the provisions of subchapter S of Chapter 1 of the Code and corporations are generally subject to the provisions of subchapter C of Chapter 1 of the Code.) The special §1(h) 28 percent capital gain rate does not apply to corporate taxpayers. §1201.

After applying the appropriate tax rates to the taxpayer's taxable income, the next step is to reduce the tax due by the credits for which the taxpayer is eligible. A *credit* is a direct reduction in tax. A deduction or exclusion, on the other hand, reduces the taxpayer's taxable income; it reduces the tax due from the taxpayer by an amount equal to the product of multiplying the deduction or exclusion by the taxpayer's tax rate. For example, a $1,000 deduction saves a taxpayer in the 30 percent tax bracket $300 of tax; a $1,000 credit, on the other hand, saves the same taxpayer $1,000 of tax. There are a number of credit provisions in the Code. The most generally applicable is the credit for taxes withheld from the taxpayer's wages. §31. If the taxpayer's credits exceed the taxpayer's tax due, the taxpayer receives a tax refund. If the taxpayer's tax due exceeds the taxpayer's credits, the taxpayer owes tax.

1. Introduction

Our tax system has adopted an *annual accounting period*, so taxpayers must compute the tax they owe each year. The annual accounting period is considered to be an administrative necessity, but it can create unfairness where transactions occur over a period of years. Congress and the courts have fashioned a number of special rules that ameliorate some of the potentially harsh effects of the annual accounting period. For example, §172 provides that a taxpayer with a net operating loss (deductions in excess of gross income) in a given year may use that loss to reduce its taxable income for other years.

For purposes of computing their tax liability, taxpayers use either the *cash method of accounting* or the *accrual method of accounting*. A taxpayer must use the same method of accounting for both tax accounting and financial accounting. §446(a).

Under the cash method of accounting, a taxpayer includes an item of income in the year in which the item is actually or constructively received. Income is constructively received if it is made available to the taxpayer but the taxpayer decides to defer actual receipt of it. For example, suppose that on December 31 of year one a client hands her attorney a check for services already performed. The attorney refuses to accept the check, however, stating that she prefers to be paid in year two. The attorney will be said to have constructively received the check in year one. A cash method taxpayer generally deducts an expense in the year in which it is paid, but must capitalize an expense that creates an asset that lasts longer than the year in which the expense is incurred. (Capitalization is discussed in more detail in Chapter 5.)

The accrual method of accounting is more complex. In general, a taxpayer using this method includes an item of income in the year in which (i) all of the events have occurred that fix the right to receive the income and (ii) the amount of the income can be determined with reasonable accuracy. An accrual method taxpayer deducts an expense when (i) all the events have occurred that establish the fact of the liability, (ii) the amount of the liability can be determined with reasonable accuracy, and (iii) the "economic performance" requirement of §461(h) (which often requires payment before a deduction is allowed) is met.

The following example illustrates the operation of the accrual and cash methods of accounting. Suppose that in December of year one an accrual method taxpayer repairs a computer used by an attorney who is on the cash method of accounting. The cost of the repair is $1,000. The attorney pays for the repair in January of year two. The $1,000 is taken into income by the accrual method taxpayer in year one, the time at which the right to receive the income is fixed and the amount of income can be determined with reasonable accuracy. The repair is deducted as a business expense by the cash method taxpayer in the year of payment — year two.

In many cases, the operation of the cash and (especially) accrual methods of accounting is quite complicated. (Accounting methods are discussed in greater detail in Chapter 3.)

The cash method permits some manipulation of the timing of inclusions and deductions. However, not all taxpayers may use the cash method. Businesses that keep inventories, including wholesalers, retailers, and manufacturers, must use the accrual method. In addition, §448 places limitations on taxpayers using the cash method of accounting. Section 446(b) also provides that if, in the Commissioner's view, the method of accounting used by the taxpayer does not clearly reflect income, the taxpayer's taxable income is computed using the method that the Commissioner thinks more clearly reflects income. Courts give the Commissioner's determination on this issue great deference.

EXAMPLES

1. a. In year one Tad bought a piece of raw land for $75,000. In year 10 Tad sells the land for $300,000. What amount does Tad include in his gross income in year 10?

    b. Suppose that, in year 10, instead of selling the land for $300,000, Tad exchanges the land for Greenacre, a parcel of land in another state. The exchange of like-kind property qualifies for the nonrecognition rule of §1031. At the time of the exchange, Greenacre is worth $300,000. In year 15 Tad sells Greenacre for $500,000. What amount does Tad include in gross income in year 10 and year 15?

    c. Now suppose instead that Tad sells the land in year 10 for $50,000. What amount does Tad include in gross income in year 10?

2. a. In year one Tina, an unmarried individual with no dependents, has $100,000 of gross income, $15,000 of the types of deductions specified in §62, and $7,000 of itemized deductions. The standard deduction for year one is $3,900 and the personal exemption amount for year one is $2,500. What is Tina's year one adjusted gross income? What is her year one taxable income?

1. Introduction

   b. Assume now that Tina's taxable income is $73,000 and that the following rate schedule (which is a fictitious, simplified version of the real §1 rate schedule) applies to unmarried individuals.

If taxable income is:	The tax is:
Not over $23,000	15 percent of taxable income
Over $23,000	$3,450 (15 percent of $23,000) plus 30 percent of the excess over $23,000
Over $115,000	$31,050 ($3,450 plus $27,600, which is 30 percent of the income between $23,000 and $115,000) plus 36 percent of the excess over $115,000.

   Compute the tax due on Tina's $73,000 of taxable income.

   c. How would your answer in part (b) change if Tina's taxable income were instead $125,000?

   d. How, if at all, would your answers in part (a) change if Tina instead has $3,000 of itemized deductions in year one?

3. Is each of the following statements true or false?

   a. Business expenses are always deducted in the year in which they are incurred.

   b. The §1 tax rates are progressive.

   c. A taxpayer's marginal rate is the taxpayer's average rate of tax.

   d. All married and unmarried taxpayers are subject to the same rate schedule in §1.

   e. The maximum tax rate on long-term capital gain is 28 percent for individuals, estates, trusts, and corporations.

   f. Our tax system utilizes an annual accounting period.

   g. Taxpayers are free to choose whether to adopt the cash method of accounting or the accrual method of accounting.

   h. A taxpayer using the cash method of accounting includes an item of income only when it is actually received by the taxpayer.

   i. A taxpayer using the accrual method of accounting generally includes an item of income in the year in which all of the events have occurred that fix the right to receive the income, and the amount of the income can be determined with reasonable accuracy.

EXPLANATIONS

1. a. Tad includes $225,000, which is the realized and recognized gain on the sale. The realized gain equals the $300,000 amount realized on the sale less the $75,000 adjusted basis of the land. §§1001, 1011, 1012. Realized gain is recognized unless otherwise provided in the Code. §1001(c). Gross income includes gains from dealings in property. §61(a)(3).

   b. The realized gain on the year 10 exchange is still $225,000, the $300,000 amount realized less Tad's $75,000 adjusted basis in the land given up in the exchange. §§1001, 1011, 1012. Realized gain is recognized unless a specific nonrecognition rule applies. §1001(c). Here, the §1031 like-kind exchange nonrecognition rule applies, so Tad does not include any of the realized gain in his year 10 gross income. In year 15 Tad's realized gain in the sale of Greenacre is $425,000, the $500,000 amount realized less Tad's $75,000 basis in Greenacre. (Tad's basis in Greenacre, the property received in the year 10 exchange, is the same as the basis of the property Tad gave up in the year 10 exchange, $75,000.) Tad includes that $425,000 of gain in his year 15 gross income. §1001(c). Note that $200,000 of that gain is attributable to appreciation in the value of Greenacre between year 10 and year 15, and the remaining $225,000 of gain is the gain Tad realized in the exchange in year 10 but deferred under §1031.

   c. Zero. Although Tad receives $50,000 in year 10, he has realized a $25,000 *loss* on the land since the amount realized is $50,000 and his basis for the property is $75,000.

2. a. Tina's year one adjusted gross income is $85,000 ($100,000 gross income less $15,000 of §62 deductions). §62. Her taxable income is $75,500—$85,000 adjusted gross income less $9,500, which is the sum of (i) her $7,000 of itemized deductions (which exceed the $3,900 standard deduction) and (ii) her $2,500 personal exemption. §63.

   b. The tax due on $73,000 of taxable income is $18,450—$3,450 (15 percent of $23,000) plus $15,000 (30 percent of the $50,000 in excess of $23,000).

   c. The tax due on $125,000 of taxable income is $34,650—$31,050 plus $3,600 (36 percent of the $10,000 in excess of $115,000).

d. Her taxable income would instead be $78,600 — $85,000 adjusted gross income less $6,400, which is the sum of (i) the $3,900 standard deduction (which exceeds her $3,000 of itemized deductions) and (ii) her $2,500 personal exemption. §63.

3. a. The statement is false. Taxpayers generally deduct business expenses in the year in which the expense is incurred. (The exact timing standard depends on whether the taxpayer uses the cash or accrual method of accounting.) However, if an expense results in the creation of an asset with a useful life that extends substantially beyond the close of the year in which the expense is incurred, the expense must be capitalized, in which case the expense cannot be deducted in full in the year in which the expense is incurred. For example, if the expense is incurred to purchase an asset with a limited useful life, the taxpayer's cost for the property will be deducted over the period of time that the property is expected to be used, in the form of annual depreciation deductions. If the expense is incurred to purchase an asset with an unlimited useful life, such as raw land, the taxpayer recovers her cost for the property only when the property is later sold or exchanged.

b. The statement is true because under §1 a taxpayer's tax *rate* (not just the absolute amount of tax) increases as his taxable income increases.

c. The statement is false. A taxpayer's marginal rate is the tax rate applicable to the last dollar of income earned by the taxpayer. The taxpayer's average tax rate is sometimes referred to as the taxpayer's effective rate. The effective rate equals the tax due from the taxpayer divided by the taxpayer's taxable income.

d. The statement is false. Married taxpayers have two rate schedules, depending on whether they file a joint return or separate returns. There are separate rate schedules for heads of households and unmarried individuals without children. §1(a)-(d).

e. The statement is false. The maximum rate is 28 percent for individuals, estates, and trusts. §1(h). However, the 28 percent maximum rate does not apply to corporations, which are instead taxed on capital gain at their ordinary income rate, which can be as high as 35 percent. §§1201, 11.

f. The statement is true. However, Congress and courts have created a number of special rules that are designed to ameliorate some of the potentially harsh effects of the annual accounting period.

g. The statement is false. Businesses that maintain inventories (manufacturers, wholesalers, and retailers) must use the accrual method of accounting. Section 448 also restricts use of the cash method of accounting. In addition, a taxpayer must use the same method of accounting for both financial and tax purposes. §446(a).

h. The statement is false. A cash method taxpayer includes either an actual receipt or constructive receipt. A taxpayer constructively receives an item of income if the item is made available to the taxpayer but the taxpayer chooses to defer receipt of the item.

i. The statement is true.

B. Time Value of Money and the Value of Deferring Tax

A dollar received today is worth more than a dollar received in the future and a dollar paid today costs more than a dollar paid in the future. The longer the period of deferral, the greater the difference between the present value of an amount and the future value of the amount. The concept that the value of money depends on when it is paid or received is sometimes referred to as the *time value of money*.

You need to understand the concept of time value of money because (i) it is a basic financial concept that your business clients will understand thoroughly and will expect you to understand; (ii) it is essential in determining the benefit of tax deferral; and (iii) it is used in a number of specific Code sections. (For example, one Code provision imputes the amount borrowed in certain loan transactions by discounting the amounts to be paid on the loan to present value.)

Tax lawyers spend much of their time counseling clients on how they can defer the payment of taxes. Deferral of tax is advantageous to a taxpayer because he can invest the deferred tax and earn income on it until it is paid to the government. We can quantify the savings from deferral by determining the amount that would have to be set aside in year one so that the sum of the amount set aside and the earnings on that amount would fund the future tax liability. We would calculate the amount to be set aside by computing the *present value* of the future tax

Table 1-1 Present Value of $1: What a Dollar at the End of a Specified Future Year Is Worth Today

Year	3 percent	4 percent	5 percent	6 percent	7 percent	8 percent	10 percent	12 percent	15 percent	20 percent	Year
1	.971	.962	.952	.943	.935	.926	.909	.893	.870	.833	1
2	.943	.925	.907	.890	.873	.857	.826	.797	.756	.694	2
3	.915	.889	.864	.840	.816	.794	.751	.712	.658	.579	3
4	.889	.855	.823	.792	.763	.735	.683	.636	.572	.482	4
5	.863	.823	.784	.747	.713	.681	.620	.567	.497	.402	5
6	.837	.790	.746	.705	.666	.630	.564	.507	.432	.335	6
7	.813	.760	.711	.665	.623	.583	.513	.452	.376	.279	7
8	.789	.731	.677	.627	.582	.540	.467	.404	.327	.233	8
9	.766	.703	.645	.592	.544	.500	.424	.361	.284	.194	9
10	.744	.676	.614	.558	.508	.463	.386	.322	.247	.162	10
11	.722	.650	.585	.527	.475	.429	.350	.287	.215	.135	11
12	.701	.625	.557	.497	.444	.397	.319	.257	.187	.112	12
13	.681	.601	.530	.469	.415	.368	.290	.229	.163	.0935	13
14	.661	.577	.505	.442	.388	.340	.263	.205	.141	.0779	14
15	.642	.555	.481	.417	.362	.315	.239	.183	.123	.0649	15
16	.623	.534	.458	.394	.339	.292	.218	.163	.107	.0541	16
17	.605	.513	.436	.371	.317	.270	.198	.146	.093	.0451	17
18	.587	.494	.416	.350	.296	.250	.180	.130	.0808	.0376	18
19	.570	.475	.396	.331	.277	.232	.164	.116	.0703	.0313	19
20	.554	.456	.377	.312	.258	.215	.149	.104	.0611	.0261	20
25	.478	.375	.295	.233	.184	.146	.0923	.0588	.0304	.0105	25
30	.412	.308	.231	.174	.131	.0994	.0573	.0334	.0151	.00421	30
40	.307	.208	.142	.0972	.067	.046	.0221	.0107	.00373	.000680	40
50	.228	.141	.087	.0543	.034	.0213	.00852	.00346	.000922	.000109	50

Table 1-2 Future Value of $1: What a Dollar Invested Today Is Worth at the End of a Specified Future Year

Year	3 percent	4 percent	5 percent	6 percent	7 percent	8 percent	10 percent	12 percent	15 percent	20 percent	Year
1	1.03	1.04	1.05	1.06	1.07	1.08	1.10	1.12	1.15	1.20	1
2	1.06	1.08	1.10	1.12	1.14	1.17	1.21	1.25	1.32	1.44	2
3	1.09	1.12	1.16	1.19	1.23	1.26	1.33	1.40	1.52	1.73	3
4	1.13	1.17	1.22	1.26	1.31	1.36	1.46	1.57	1.74	2.07	4
5	1.16	1.22	1.28	1.34	1.40	1.47	1.61	1.76	2.01	2.49	5
6	1.19	1.27	1.34	1.41	1.50	1.59	1.77	1.97	2.31	2.99	6
7	1.23	1.32	1.41	1.50	1.61	1.71	1.94	2.21	2.66	3.58	7
8	1.27	1.37	1.48	1.59	1.72	1.85	2.14	2.48	3.05	4.30	8
9	1.30	1.42	1.55	1.68	1.84	2.00	2.35	2.77	3.52	5.16	9
10	1.34	1.48	1.63	1.79	1.97	2.16	2.59	3.11	4.05	6.19	10
11	1.38	1.54	1.71	1.89	2.10	2.33	2.85	3.48	4.66	7.43	11
12	1.43	1.60	1.80	2.01	2.25	2.52	3.13	3.90	5.30	8.92	12
13	1.47	1.67	1.89	2.13	2.41	2.72	3.45	4.36	6.10	10.7	13
14	1.51	1.73	1.98	2.26	2.58	2.94	3.79	4.89	7.00	12.8	14
15	1.56	1.80	2.08	2.39	2.76	3.17	4.17	5.47	8.13	15.4	15
16	1.60	1.87	2.18	2.54	2.95	3.43	4.59	6.13	9.40	18.5	16
17	1.65	1.95	2.29	2.69	3.16	3.70	5.05	6.87	10.6	22.2	17
18	1.70	2.03	2.41	2.85	3.38	4.00	5.55	7.70	12.5	26.6	18
19	1.75	2.11	2.53	3.02	3.62	4.32	6.11	8.61	14.0	31.9	19
20	1.81	2.19	2.65	3.20	3.87	4.66	6.72	9.65	16.1	38.3	20
25	2.09	2.67	3.39	4.29	5.43	6.85	10.8	17.0	32.9	95.4	25
30	2.43	3.24	4.32	5.74	7.61	10.0	17.4	30.0	66.2	237	30
40	3.26	4.80	7.04	10.3	15.0	21.7	45.3	93.1	267.0	1,470	40
50	4.38	7.11	11.5	18.4	29.5	46.9	117	289	1,080	9,100	50

liability. Students (and practicing lawyers) generally use tables or computers to determine present values or, depending on the nature of the work and size of the client, accept the present value calculations done by the client's accounting staff. For the record, however, the formula for determining present value is as follows:

$$\frac{\text{Present}}{\text{Value}} = \frac{\text{Future Value}}{(1 + r)^n}$$

(r is the interest rate and n is the number of periods of deferral.)

For example, assume that a taxpayer defers a $10,000 tax payment for five years and that the appropriate interest rate is 8 percent. The amount that would have to be set aside in year one in order to fund that future payment is $6,806:

$$\frac{\text{Present}}{\text{Value}} = \frac{\$10,000}{(1 + .08)^5}$$

$$= \frac{\$10,000}{(1.08)(1.08)(1.08)(1.08)(1.08)}$$

$$= \frac{\$10,000}{1.46933}$$

$$= \$6,806$$

The value of deferral can be expressed in another way; it is the equivalent of a reduction in rates. If a taxpayer in the 40 percent bracket owes $10,000 of tax on $25,000 of taxable income, a reduction in the present value of the tax owed to $6,806 is the equivalent of reducing the taxpayer's tax rate to 27 percent (since 27 percent of $25,000 equals $6,806).

The formula for computing the future value of an amount is:

$$\text{Future Value} = \text{Present Value} (1 + r)^n$$

For example, assume a present value of $6,806. That amount will yield a return of 8 percent a year, payable in five years. (No interest will be paid during the five years.) What is the future value, in year five, of the $6,806 present value? It is $10,000:

1. Introduction

$$\text{Future Value} = \$6,806 \, (1.08)^5$$
$$= \$6,806 \, (1.46933)$$
$$= \$10,000$$

Tables 1-1 and 1-2 show the present and future values of $1 at various interest rates and over various periods of time.

Using Table 1-1, we can determine the present value of an amount to be paid in the future if we know the period over which the amount will be discounted and the appropriate interest rate. For example, this table indicates that the present value of $1 to be paid in 40 years, assuming a 5 percent interest rate, is 14.2 cents.

Using Table 1-2, we can determine the future value of $1 if we know the period over which interest will compound and the appropriate interest rate. For example, the table indicates that the future value of $1 invested for 40 years, assuming a 5 percent interest rate, is $7.04.

EXAMPLES

4. Through careful tax planning, Tom, who is in the 40 percent tax bracket, is able to defer a $20,000 tax liability for five years. Assume an annual interest rate of 10 percent a year during that five-year period. Explain the way in which Tom benefits from the deferral of tax, incorporating the concept of present value. (You may use the table in the text above to compute the present value.)

5. Assume a present value of $10,000 and an interest rate of 10 percent a year. What is the future value in five years? (You may use the table in the text above to compute the future value.)

EXPLANATIONS

4. Table 1-1 indicates that the present value of $1 to be paid in five years, assuming a 10 percent interest rate, is 62 cents. The present value of $20,000 to be paid in five years, assuming a 10 percent interest rate, is $12,400 ($.62 multiplied by 20,000). By deferring the $20,000 tax payment for five years, Tom saves $7,600 ($20,000 less $12,400).

   How would we compute the present value using the formula? The future value is $20,000; the interest rate is 10 percent; the number of periods of deferral is five. Therefore, the present

1. Introduction

value of the $20,000 tax payment to be made in five years is $12,418, computed as follows:

$$\text{Present Value} = \frac{\$20,000}{(1 + .1)^5}$$

$$= \frac{\$20,000}{(1.1)(1.1)(1.1)(1.1)(1.1)}$$

$$= \frac{\$20,000}{1.61051}$$

$$= \$12,418$$

(Note that the present value calculated using the table is a little less due to rounding.)

The value of deferral can be expressed in another way; it is the equivalent of a reduction in rates. Tom, who is in the 40 percent bracket, owes $20,000 of tax (presumably on $50,000 of taxable income). Deferring the tax reduces the present value of the tax owed to $12,418, which is the equivalent of reducing Tom's tax rate to 24.84 percent (since 24.84 percent of $50,000 equals $12,418).

5. Table 1-2 indicates that the value in five years of $1 invested today is $1.61, assuming a 10 percent interest rate. The value in five years of $10,000 invested today is $16,100, assuming a 10 percent interest rate.

How would we compute the future value using the formula? The formula for computing the future value of an amount is:

$$\text{Future Value} = \text{Present Value} (1 + r)^n$$

Here the present value is $10,000, r equals 10 percent, and n equals 5, so the future value is $16,051.

$$\text{Future Value} = \$10,000 (1.1)^5$$

$$= \$10,000 (1.1)(1.1)(1.1)(1.1)(1.1)$$

$$= \$10,000 (1.61051)$$

$$= \$16,051$$

(Note that the future value calculated using the table is a little more due to rounding.)

C. Tax Administration and Litigation

The main sources of the tax law are the Internal Revenue Code (the Code) (title 26 of the United States Code) and case law. The tax law is administered by the Treasury Department, which in turn delegates most administrative responsibility to an agency under its authority, the *Internal Revenue Service* (the Service). The person who is the head of the Service is known as the *Commissioner*. One important responsibility of the Treasury and the Service is to provide guidance to taxpayers as to interpretation of the law. This guidance generally is provided in the form of treasury regulations,[1] revenue rulings, and revenue procedures; however, the Service sometimes provides guidance in various other forms (for example, announcements, notices, general counsel memoranda).

Treasury regulations are generally *interpretive regulations*, meaning that they are promulgated under Code §7805, which grants to the Secretary of the Treasury the authority to enforce the provisions of the Code. However, some regulations are instead *legislative regulations*, meaning that the regulations are promulgated pursuant to a specific grant of authority in a particular Code section. See, e.g., §104(e)(4)(A). Congress typically grants authority to issue legislative regulations when a Code provision is incomplete and requires filling in. Regulations are, strictly speaking, not the "law." Instead, they represent the view of the Service as to the meaning of a Code section so a taxpayer may argue that a regulation is invalid. However, courts give interpretive regulations great deference and legislative regulations even more deference; they invalidate regulations only in unusual circumstances.

A regulation is usually issued as a *proposed regulation* so that taxpayers and their counsel may formally comment on the regulation before it is finalized. Proposed regulations are published in the Federal Register. A regulation is also sometimes issued as a *temporary regulation*, meaning that the regulation is not final but taxpayers may rely on it until the *final regulation* is issued. A temporary or final regulation is promulgated in the form of a Treasury Decision. The Treasury Decision includes the text of the regulation and a preamble that gives the name and telephone number of the principal drafter of the regulation.

A *revenue ruling* is the Service's view on a particular issue. The

---

1. Any citation in this book to regulations refers to treasury regulations.

rulings, which are generally short, describe a hypothetical fact pattern, frame an issue, and then give the Service's view as to the correct outcome of the case. *Revenue procedures* generally describe the internal practices and procedures of the Service, but occasionally also address issues that might be characterized as substantive. Both revenue rulings and revenue procedures are officially published in the weekly Internal Revenue Bulletin (IRB); at the end of the year, the IRBs for the year are compiled in the Cumulative Bulletin.

The Service is also frequently willing to rule on the tax consequences of a particular taxpayer's prospective transaction. Such a ruling, referred to as a *private letter ruling*, is not officially published and applies only to the taxpayer who requested the ruling. Private letter rulings are, however, published (in a redacted form, so that the taxpayer's identity is concealed) by commercial publishers. Code §6110(j)(3) provides that private letter rulings may not generally be cited as authority but they can be helpful in practice nonetheless; sometimes they provide the only indication of the Service's position on a particular issue. (At the beginning of each year, the Service issues a revenue procedure in which it states the specific tax issues on which it will not issue a private letter ruling.) A *technical advice memorandum* is similar to a private letter ruling except that the advice is requested after the transaction with uncertain tax consequences has occurred and the taxpayer has been audited.

To many taxpayers the Service is nothing more than the issuer and collector of tax returns (and payments). Our tax system is a *self-assessment* system, meaning that taxpayers compute their own tax liability. However, sometimes the Service audits a taxpayer and determines that the taxpayer owes additional tax (to the taxpayer's horror). For the most part, the Service selects for audit those returns that it believes are most likely to understate tax liability. (Exactly what the Service is looking for, or, to put the issue more concretely, the formula under which returns are selected for audit, is not public knowledge.) Only 1 or 2 percent of returns are audited, so the number of taxpayers who have to suffer through an audit is relatively small. If, at the conclusion of the audit, the revenue agent determines that the taxpayer owes additional tax for the year, the agent will issue a *Revenue Agent's Report* (RAR) and a *30-day letter* in which the agent indicates the amount of the asserted tax deficiency and notifies the taxpayer that she has 30 days to file an administrative appeal of the agent's determination. The taxpayer can also agree that the asserted deficiency is owed and pay that amount. (Once a taxpayer agrees that the asserted deficiency is owed, the taxpayer generally will pay the deficiency as soon as possible because interest runs on the deficiency from the original due date for the return for the tax year audited.)

The Appeals Office of the Service hears the taxpayer's appeal of the revenue agent's determination; although a taxpayer might fear that an office that is part of the Service will just rubber stamp the agent's determination, that is not the case. Appeals officers are (at least in our experience) generally quite reasonable, and, in fact, many cases heard by appeals officers are settled for less than the deficiency asserted by the revenue agent.

If a taxpayer does not resolve a tax controversy in the appeals process or if the taxpayer fails to respond to the 30-day letter, the Service will issue the taxpayer a *statutory notice of deficiency* (also know as a *90-day letter*). The Service must issue the 90-day letter before it can begin collection of the asserted deficiency. The 90-day letter gives the taxpayer 90 days to file a petition in the United States Tax Court and litigate the issue. (The Tax Court is based in Washington, D.C., but the Tax Court judges travel around the country hearing cases.) A taxpayer does not have to pay the asserted tax deficiency to litigate in the Tax Court. If the taxpayer does not file a Tax Court petition during the 90-day period, the Service may begin collection of the asserted deficiency. Tax Court decisions are appealable to the court of appeals for the circuit where the taxpayer resides.

Instead of litigating in the Tax Court, the taxpayer can pay the asserted deficiency and sue for a refund of tax in either the federal district court where the taxpayer resides or the United States Court of Federal Claims, which sits in Washington, D.C. In other words, the taxpayer has a choice of forum. Typically, taxpayers litigate in the Tax Court so they do not have to pay the asserted deficiency while the litigation is pending. However, there are a number of reasons why certain taxpayers might prefer to litigate in a court other than the Tax Court. Taxpayers may choose to litigate in district court because jury trials are available only in that forum. Taxpayers may choose to litigate in the claims court because that court follows the precedent of the Court of Appeals for the Federal Circuit, which may be more favorable to the taxpayer than the precedent of the court of appeals for the circuit where the taxpayer resides, which the Tax Court or district court would follow. (The rule that the Tax Court follows the precedent of the court of appeals for the circuit where the taxpayer resides is sometimes called the *Golsen rule* because the rule was articulated in

Golsen v. Commissioner, 54 T.C. 742 (1970), aff'd, 445 F.2d 985 (10th Cir. 1971).)

The statute of limitations in tax cases is generally three years from the date the return for the year was filed or, if later, the due date for the return. §6501. If the taxpayer omits a substantial amount of income from his return, the statute of limitations is six years. §6501(e). If the taxpayer files a fraudulent return or fails to file a return, there is an open statute of limitations. §6501(c).

If a taxpayer underpays her tax due for a given year, she must pay interest on the tax deficiency from the due date for the return at a statutorily prescribed rate that approximates a market rate of interest. §§6201, 6621. For this reason, taxpayers generally pay any deficiency as soon as they settle a tax controversy. On the other hand, if a taxpayer overpays tax for a given year, the government pays interest on the amount of the overpayment but at a lower rate. §§6611, 6621.

Taxpayers with a tax deficiency may also be subject to a variety of penalties, both civil and criminal. For example, they may be subject to the §6662 accuracy-related penalty if their underpayment of tax is attributable to negligence or one of the other reasons specified in the section. Taxpayers are also subject to §6662 if the understatement of tax is substantial, meaning that it exceeds the greater of (i) 10 percent of the tax actually owed for the year or (ii) $5,000. The §6662 penalty is 20 percent of the portion of the underpayment subject to §6662. Section 6663 also imposes a penalty for fraud equal to 75 percent of the portion of the underpayment attributable to fraud.

EXAMPLES

6. The Internal Revenue Service is part of what cabinet-level department?

7. Is each of the following statements true or false?
   a. Since private letter rulings may not be cited as authority, you should disregard them in doing tax research.
   b. If it is not clear how a recently issued set of regulations applies to a problem that you are researching, you can phone the drafter of the regulations and discuss the issue.
   c. Only around 1 or 2 percent of tax returns are audited.
   d. The Appeals Office of the Service rarely settles cases for less than the deficiency asserted by the revenue agent.

1. Introduction

8. What happens at the conclusion of an audit in which the agent determines that additional tax is owed by the taxpayer, and what are the taxpayer's options at that point?

9. What must happen before a taxpayer can file a petition in the Tax Court?

10. Under what circumstances must the Service send the taxpayer a 90-day letter?

11. Compare the three courts in which one can litigate a tax controversy.

12. Ted lives in San Francisco, which is in the Ninth Circuit. He is litigating a case in the Tax Court that involves the issue of whether a particular item can be excluded from his income for tax purposes. In several earlier Tax Court cases the court ruled that this type of item is not excludable. Two taxpayers appealed the decision of the Tax Court. On appeal the Seventh Circuit affirmed the Tax Court decision in one of the cases, but in the other case the Ninth Circuit reversed and held that the item is excluded from gross income. In Ted's case will the Tax Court apply the prior Tax Court precedent or the Ninth Circuit precedent?

EXPLANATIONS

6. The Treasury Department.

7. a. The statement is false. Although private letter rulings may not be cited, they are still helpful because they can give an indication of the Service's position on the issue discussed in the ruling. In fact, in practice they are sometimes the only source that you can find on an issue.

   b. The statement is true. The name and telephone number of the principal drafter of the regulations is published when the regulations are promulgated. The drafter of the regulations will often be quite helpful in interpreting any aspects of the regulations that are ambiguous.

   c. The statement is true.

   d. The statement is false. Many tax controversies are settled in the appeals process for less than the deficiency asserted by the revenue agent.

8. The agent will send the taxpayer the Revenue Agent's Report and a 30-day letter. The taxpayer can agree with the asserted tax deficiency and pay it. If the taxpayer disagrees, the taxpayer can either

file a protest with the Appeals Office or do nothing. If the tax-payer files a protest, the case will be heard by an appeals officer. If the taxpayer does nothing, the Service will then send the taxpayer a 90-day letter.

9.	The taxpayer must receive a 90-day letter before filing a petition in the Tax Court.

10.	The Service cannot begin collection of the asserted deficiency until it has first given the taxpayer an opportunity to litigate in the Tax Court by sending the taxpayer a 90-day letter. However, if a tax controversy is settled during the audit or appeals process, the Service does not have to send the taxpayer a 90-day letter.

11.	A taxpayer can litigate a tax controversy in the Tax Court, the claims court, or the federal district court for the district in which the taxpayer resides. Taxpayers generally litigate in the Tax Court because a taxpayer does not have to pay the asserted deficiency to litigate there. A taxpayer must pay an asserted deficiency and then sue for a refund in order to be able to litigate in the district court or the claims court. A taxpayer who wants a jury trial must litigate in the district court. Sometimes there is favorable precedent in one court or another, which may affect the decision of where to litigate. The claims court follows the precedent of the Court of Appeals for the Federal Circuit, but the Tax Court and district court follow the precedent of the court of appeals for the circuit in which the taxpayer resides. Tax Court cases and district court cases are heard locally, whereas claims court cases are heard in Washington, D.C.

12.	The Tax Court will follow the Ninth Circuit precedent because Ted resides in the Ninth Circuit. Golsen v. Commissioner, 54 T.C. 742 (1970), aff'd, 445 F.2d 985 (10th Cir. 1971).

# D.	Tax Legislation

Under Article I of the Constitution, tax legislation originates in the House of Representatives (at least formally). The legislation begins in the House Ways and Means Committee, the committee that has jurisdiction over revenue, debt, customs, trade, health, welfare, and social security issues. The committee first conducts hearings at which various witnesses testify. After hearings are concluded, there are "mark-up" sessions during which the tax bill is drafted. Various parties, including the House Legislative Council, the staff of the Joint Committee on Taxation (described below), the Treasury Department, and the staff of the Ways and Means Committee, are involved in drafting the bill. When the Ways and Means Committee has completed the bill, it is sent to the floor of the House with the *House Report*. The House Report explains the existing law and the reasons for making the changes included in the bill. The bill is then debated on the floor of the House under procedural rules that limit amendment of the bill. The House then votes on the bill and, if it is approved, the Senate considers the bill.

In the Senate, the bill begins in the Senate Finance Committee, the committee that has jurisdiction over taxation, foreign trade, health, social security, and other financial matters. The Senate Finance Committee then holds hearings and prepares its version of the bill and the *Senate Report*. The bill then goes to the floor of the Senate for debate and a vote. The procedural rules in the Senate permit numerous amendments to the bill during the floor debate.

If the Senate approves its bill, the House and Senate bills usually go to the Conference Committee, which is made up of a small number of members of the House Ways and Means and Senate Finance Committees. The Conference Committee reaches compromises on the provisions that vary in the House and Senate versions of the bill and sometimes even adds new provisions. The Conference Committee also prepares the *Conference Committee Report* (which is designated by a House Report number).

Both chambers then vote on the conference bill. If both the House and Senate approve the bill, it goes to the President, who either signs or vetoes the bill. The date that the President signs the bill is the *enactment date*. The *effective date* of the various provisions of the bill may be an earlier or later date. The provisions of the new law are then incorporated into the Internal Revenue Code.

After a major tax act is passed, the staff of the Joint Committee on Taxation prepares an explanation of the new law. The Joint Committee on Taxation (JCT), which is made up of a small number of members of the House Ways and Means and Senate Finance Committees, has two main functions: First, it must review and approve or disapprove any large tax refunds; second, the JCT staff assist in drafting tax legislation and prepare the post-enactment explanation of the new tax act, referred to as "The General Explanation of the Revenue Provisions of [the name of the tax act]." Instead of using this cumbersome title, tax lawyers refer to this book as the "Blue Book" because the cover of the book is blue. (If a tax lawyer tells you to check the Blue Book, she may be telling you to look in this book, not in the Uniform System of Citation — the book you probably know as the Blue Book.) The Blue Book does not reprint the new law; instead, it explains the new law. It is not, strictly speaking, legislative history, although many courts treat it like legislative history.

EXAMPLES

13. What is the name of the House of Representatives committee responsible for tax legislation? The Senate Committee?

14. Is each of the following statements true or false?
    a. The legislative history of a tax act includes the House Report, the Senate Report, and the Conference Committee Report.
    b. The effective date of a tax act is the date on which the President signs the bill.
    c. After enactment of a tax act, the text of the act is printed in the Blue Book prepared by the Joint Committee on Taxation.

EXPLANATIONS

13. The House of Representatives committee responsible for tax legislation is the Ways and Means Committee. The Senate committee responsible for tax legislation is the Finance Committee.

14. a. The statement is true.
    b. The statement is false. The enactment date is the date on which the President signs the bill. The effective date of the provisions in the bill may be an earlier or later date than the enactment date.
    c. The statement is false. The Blue Book explains the new law but does not reprint it.

E. Tax Research

Suppose you are confronted with a client's real life tax issue as a law clerk or beginning lawyer, or a friend or relative has a tax problem. The issue may be too specialized or complicated to answer out of your casebook or notes, so you'll have no choice but to research the issue. But how do you proceed? If you're no better prepared than we were as young lawyers, you'll end up wandering around the law library, trying to find the tax section and then looking, more or less at random, through the indexes of the most authoritative-looking volumes. This brief introduction to tax research is designed to give you some idea of how to start your research. We can't give you too much of a head start; every question is different, and the only way to become adept at tax research is to do it. But if you're as at sea as we were as beginning lawyers, you'll be grateful for any help you can get. If you would like more detailed information about how to do federal tax research, we suggest that you consult Federal Tax Research (4th ed.) by Gail Richmond.

The starting place in tax research is the Code, followed closely by case law and administrative pronouncements. How do you locate the relevant sources? There are several ways. First, you can search for relevant sources by looking in the topical index in the front of one of the two federal tax loose-leaf services published by Commerce Clearing House, Inc. (CCH) and Research Institute of America (RIA). (The RIA service is purple with gold lettering; the CCH service is black with gold lettering.) Each service consists of a dozen or so hardcovered three-ring binders that are continuously updated. The index in the front of the service will refer you to particular numbered paragraphs in the main volumes of the service (referred to as "compilation volumes"). The compilation volumes are organized by Code section in numerical order. For each Code section, the services contain the text of the Code section and regulations, an explanation of the law, and annotations of relevant cases, revenue rulings, and other administrative pronouncements.

Another way to locate the relevant sources is to read about your issue in a secondary source that explains the law such as a treatise or journal article. There are many tax treatises, some of which are quite good, and two of which deserve special mention. The five-volume treatise on taxation of individuals, estates, and trusts by Professors Boris Bittker and Lawrence Lokken is superb. It offers the most sophisticated treatment anywhere on some subjects but is well written enough to be intelligible to the novice. Federal Taxation of Corporations and Shareholders, by Professors Boris Bittker and James Eustice is equally impressive. For many years it has been the "bible" of corporate tax lawyers.

The tax portfolios published by the Bureau of National Affairs (BNA) are also frequently quite helpful. The BNA portfolio system consists of a few hundred gray, softcovered, spiral-bound portfolios on the most common tax issues. For example, there is a separate portfolio on Code §1031 that covers exchanges of like-kind property. Each portfolio is a hundred or so pages long and contains textual explanation with citations to relevant authority. At the end of the textual explanation there are sometimes appendixes with relevant statutes, regulations, rulings, and worksheets to aid in tax planning. The portfolios are kept up to date, though not quite as often as the tax services, and are organized according to a largely arbitrary numeric system. However, the subject matter of each portfolio is listed on its spine and you can look up the topic (or Code section if you know what it is) in the index for the portfolios, which is usually shelved immediately after the portfolio binders.

There are also a number of journals that specialize in tax. Tax Notes, a weekly magazine, is a particularly useful starting place for researching recent or proposed legislation or administrative pronouncements, or for finding the "skinny" on important cases. Tax Notes also contains more wide-ranging "thought" pieces (called Special Reports) by leading tax authorities. Other tax journals include the ABA Tax Lawyer, the Journal of Taxation, the Journal of Corporate Taxation, Taxes Magazine, the Tax Law Review, the Florida Tax Review, and the Virginia Tax Review. Tax articles also appear in general law reviews. Tax articles, along with all other legal articles, are indexed in the Guide to Legal Periodicals. In addition, there are two indexes solely for tax articles — one published by CCH and one published by Warren, Gorham & Lamont.

Note that, even if you begin your research by looking in secondary sources that explain the law, you should always read any primary sources (for example, Code sections and cases) cited in the secondary sources. In your memoranda and briefs cite directly to primary authority for a proposition if there is primary authority to support it; do not cite a secondary source that describes a primary source. (Citing secondary authority when primary authority is available is one of the most common mistakes made by novice tax researchers.)

You can also use LEXIS and WESTLAW to do tax research. These databases include the Code, cases, regulations, and various types of administrative pronouncements, including revenue rulings, revenue procedures, private letter rulings, technical advice memoranda, general counsel memoranda, and actions on decision. The databases also include many useful secondary sources such as Tax Notes, the tax law reviews and journals, the daily tax newsletters, and the BNA portfolios. The next time you find yourself at your computer, take a few minutes to browse through the menu for the LEXIS and WESTLAW tax libraries. (The LEXIS library is called "Fedtax" and the WESTLAW library is called "Taxation.") Note that the database libraries include some combined files that are quite useful in practice; for example, the LEXIS combined file called "Rels" includes many different types of administrative pronouncements. Using these combined files can help you do your tax research more efficiently.

Sometimes you'll want to look up a case you know by name rather than cite. You can locate the case cite by using the aptly named CCH Citator, which contains the cite for alphabetically listed case names. That source also contains the names and cites of other cases that cite the case in question. RIA has a similar, though in our opinion much harder to use, citation system. You can also locate the cite by searching in the LEXIS and WESTLAW databases. In order to "Shepardize" the tax cases that you find in your research, you should consult the Citators, or Shepardize the case on-line, because the standard Shepard's you learned to use during your first year of law school does not include citations to Tax Court cases.

There are two types of Tax Court opinions, regular and memorandum. Regular decisions are officially published in the United States Tax Court Reporter (cited as T.C.). Memorandum decisions are not officially published, but are published by commercial publishers. The Chief Judge of the Tax Court decides which opinions are regular opinions and which are memorandum opinions. Memorandum opinions do not have the precedential force of regular opinions although the Tax Court occasionally cites memorandum opinions. Usually one Tax Court judge decides a Tax Court case. However, the Chief Judge of the Tax Court sometimes subsequently decides to have the case decided by the full Tax Court in which the decision is designated as "reviewed by the court." (CCH also publishes United States Tax Cases, sometimes cited as "U.S.T.C.," which are unofficial reprints of federal district court and court of appeals tax cases. We mention this item because, if you were not aware of it, it would be easy to mistake a U.S.T.C. cite for a cite to a regular decision of the Tax Court.) After losing a Tax Court case, the Service often indicates in the Internal Revenue Bulletin whether it *acquiesces* in the decision or not. The acquiescence or nonacquiescence lets the staff of the Service know whether to apply the case or not.

If, in your research, you have found a citation to a revenue ruling or revenue procedure and you would like to look at the item, you can find it in the Cumulative Bulletin. (The Cumulative Bulletin books are grayish-green.) To find the page number on which the revenue ruling or revenue procedure appears, consult the table at the front of the Cumulative Bulletin. Before citing a revenue ruling or revenue procedure, you should check to see whether the revenue ruling or procedure has been *amplified*, *superseded*, or *revoked*. You can check the status of a revenue ruling or revenue procedure in the Citators or the computer databases.

In researching a particular Code provision, you will frequently need to read the legislative history of the Code section. You can search for legislative history in many different sources. In years in which Congress passes a major tax bill, the legislative history of the bill is reprinted in volume three of the Cumulative Bulletin. Our favorite source for legislative history is the series compiled by Professor Bernard Reams. (The voluminous Reams series includes witness testimony as well as committee reports.) Legislative history is also available in the LEXIS and WESTLAW databases.

Service forms and accompanying explanatory booklets on how to fill out the forms are compiled in hardcover, three-ring binders by CCH, BNA, and RIA. The Service accepts photocopies of these (or any other Service forms), so if it is already April 15 and you have lost your individual tax form 1040, don't panic. Just find the appropriate one of the three collections of Service forms and publications; photocopy the relevant form, fill it out, and send it in.

The Service has an automated system through which taxpayers can obtain recorded information on over a hundred tax topics. In addition, the Service will give "live" advice on basic tax questions. The number for the recorded system is listed on the back of the 1040 tax form (the basic individual income tax form); the number to obtain live advice is in your phone book. Unfortunately, if an issue is too difficult for you, it is probably not covered in the recordings and won't (or can't) be answered by the person designated to answer the public queries.

There is one occasion when you are apt to find someone in the Service who will be up to speed on a difficult issue and willing to speak with you about it. If the answer to the question you are researching turns on language in a recently issued regulation, you can call the drafter of the regulation (whose name and phone number are published when the regulations are issued). The drafter of the regulation often will be willing to explain, in an off-the-record manner, what he or she meant by a certain phrase or example.

EXAMPLES

15. You have been asked to research a question concerning the deductibility of educational expenses. Explain how you might use the loose-leaf services to begin your research.

1. Introduction

16. You have been asked to research the question of whether a plaintiff may exclude from income damages received in a suit under the federal age discrimination statute. You have found concise and readable general discussions of the taxation of personal injury recoveries in a BNA Tax Management Portfolio and in the outstanding Bittker and Lokken treatise. You think that you can extrapolate from these general discussions to answer your question. Have you finished your research?

17. How do you check the subsequent history of a revenue ruling?

EXPLANATIONS

15. If you did not know the Code section under which the issue arises, you would begin by looking it up in the topical index for the loose-leaf service. The topical index would indicate the compilation volume paragraph numbers covering your issue. An experienced tax lawyer would know that the issue arises under §162 and go directly to the compilation volume paragraphs that correspond to that section. The compilation volume paragraphs on the issue include the text of the Code section and regulations promulgated under the section, explanatory text, and annotations.

16. No! As good as the Bittker and Lokken treatise and BNA portfolios are, there is no substitute for reading the statute, cases, regulations, and other administrative pronouncements on an issue. Suppose you rely on general language in a treatise or portfolio, but your specific question is directly answered by the statute, regulations, or cases in a way that is either too remote to merit discussion in that or any other text or too recent to have been incorporated into the material updating the secondary service — and in a way that is contrary to the general statements made in the treatise. You have committed M-A-L-P-R-A-C-T-I-C-E. You must always read the applicable statute, cases, regulations, and other administrative pronouncements.

17. Before relying on a revenue ruling, you should always check to see whether the ruling has been amplified, revoked, or superseded. You check the subsequent history of a revenue ruling in a manner similar to "Shepardizing" a case — by looking for citations to the ruling in the Citators or the computer databases.

2
Some Characteristics of Gross Income

As we saw in Chapter 1, in order to compute a taxpayer's tax liability, we must first determine the taxpayer's *gross income*. How does the Code define gross income? Section 61 provides that gross income includes "all income from whatever source derived." Although this circular definition, standing alone, would not help us much, case law and other specific Code provisions have embellished the statutory definition. Early this century, in Eisner v. Macomber, 252 U.S. 189, 207 (1920), income was narrowly defined as "gain derived from capital, from labor, or from both combined." However, in a later case, Commissioner v. Glenshaw Glass, 348 U.S. 426 (1955), income was defined much more broadly to include "all accessions to wealth, clearly realized, and over which the taxpayer has dominion and control." The Code also explicitly provides, in §§61 and 71-136, that certain items are to be included in or excluded from gross income. For example, §61 provides that gross income includes wages, interest, dividends, rents, and gains from dealings in property. In this chapter, we will consider whether a number of specific items are included or excluded for purposes of computing gross income. As we will see, the current law is not entirely coherent.

A. The Haig-Simons Definition of Income

The definition of income adopted in the *Glenshaw Glass* case approximates the ideal definition of income that most tax theorists advocate.

2. Some Characteristics of Gross Income

Under that definition known as the *Haig-Simons* definition of income, income equals the sum of (i) the taxpayer's personal expenditures plus (or minus) (ii) the increase (or decrease) in the taxpayer's wealth. Not everyone agrees that the Haig-Simons definition of income is correct and even supporters admit that full implementation of the definition is impossible. Nonetheless, the Haig-Simons definition provides a widely accepted theoretical benchmark against which we can compare the current tax treatment of specific items.

EXAMPLES

1. Larry's total wealth at the beginning of year one is $10,000. During the next 12 months, Larry earns $35,000 in wages. He spends $20,000 on rent, food, and other consumption items. He deposits $15,000 in a savings account and earns $1,000 in interest on the deposit. At the end of year one, Larry's total wealth is $26,000 ($10,000 wealth at the beginning of the period, $15,000 savings and $1,000 interest). What is Larry's Haig-Simons income for year one?

2. Carolyn's total wealth at the beginning of year one is an acre of land with a fair market value of $15,000. During the year, Carolyn earns $40,000 in salary and spends the entire amount on rent, food, and other consumption items. By the end of year one, the fair market value of Carolyn's land has increased to $25,000.
   a. What is Carolyn's Haig-Simons income for year one?
   b. What part of Carolyn's Haig-Simons income might *not* be subject to tax under current law? Why?

EXPLANATIONS

1. Haig-Simons income is defined as personal consumption plus any change in year-end wealth. Here, Larry consumes $20,000 and increases his year-end wealth by $16,000 ($15,000 savings plus $1,000 interest income), so his Haig-Simons income in year one is $36,000.

2. a. Carolyn's Haig-Simons income in year one is $50,000 ($40,000 personal consumption plus a $10,000 increase in year-end wealth).
   b. The portion of Haig-Simons income that might not be subject to tax under current law is the $10,000 attributable to unrealized property appreciation. In general, gains and losses on property are not taxed until the property is sold or exchanged.

B.   Noncash Compensation: Fringe Benefits

Most people equate income with cash salary. However, noncash ("in-kind") employer-provided benefits such as medical care and life insurance may constitute a significant part of employee earnings. As we will see, the law adopts a neither-here-nor-there approach to fringe benefits. Some forms of fringe benefits are included in gross income in full, some are excluded entirely from gross income, and others are excluded subject to certain requirements and limitations.

Section 61(a)(1) provides that gross income includes "compensation for services," including "fringe benefits." Regulation §1.61-1(a) provides that "[g]ross income includes income realized in any form, whether in money, property or services." Regulation §1.61-2(d)(1) adds: "[I]f services are paid for in property, the fair market value of the property taken in payment must be included in income as compensation." However, the Code contains a number of provisions that exclude from gross income specific noncash fringe benefits, several of which we will consider here.

As we consider each Code section, ask yourself the following questions: (i) Under what circumstances does the Code section apply? (ii) How does the section operate if it applies? (iii) Is the Code section consistent with the Haig-Simons definition of income? (iv) What policy goals are served or disserved by the provision?

1.   *Employer-Provided Meals and Lodging*

Reading: §§61(a)(1), 107, 119; Reg. §1.61-1(a) and -2(d)(1)

We begin our discussion of noncash compensation with an examination of §119, which under certain circumstances allows employees to exclude from income the value of employer-provided meals and lodging. Section 119 is not a terribly significant code provision — it does not affect many taxpayers and the amounts at stake are (relatively) small. Section 119 does, however, offer a useful starting point at which to begin thinking about statutory construction. Section 119 can also be used to explore how the tax law affects economic behavior.

Let's begin by examining the statute. Section 119(a) excludes from income the value of meals if (i) the employer furnishes meals to an employee, her spouse, or her dependents; (ii) the meals are provided for the convenience of the employer; and (iii) the meals are provided on the business premises of the employer. The same section excludes the value of lodging if (i) it is furnished on the business premises by the employer to an employee, her spouse, or her dependents; (ii) it is provided for the convenience of the employer; and (iii) the employee is required to accept the lodging as a condition of her employment.

For purposes of §119, the term *"dependent"* is defined (in §152) to include any U.S. citizen who resides with the taxpayer and who either (i) receives a majority of his support from the taxpayer, or (ii) is treated under the special rules of §152(c)-(e) as having received over half of his support from the taxpayer. Thus, children, parents, and significant others can qualify as dependents if they meet the support test.

Courts have had to clarify some of the other requirements under §119. For example, §119(a) covers meals "furnished" by the employer. Suppose the employer does not itself provide food but instead gives the employee a cash meal allowance. Robert Kowalski was a New Jersey state trooper who, while on call, was required to eat his meals at a public eating place within his assigned area. Kowalski received meal allowances in an amount equal to approximately 19 percent of his cash wages. The Supreme Court held that §119 does not cover amounts reimbursed for meals and that Mr. Kowalski had to include the meal allowance in income. Commissioner v. Kowalski, 434 U.S. 77 (1977).

The decision in *Kowalski* is almost certainly correct. Section 119 was intended to cover situations in which the employee is constrained in his or her choice of food or eating places. Kowalski was not so constrained: The system of reimbursement made it possible for him to choose from a wide range of restaurants. Still, the Court might have more plausibly based its decision on two other grounds: Kowalski was not on the business premises of the employer (he had argued that, for a state trooper, the entire state constituted the employer's business premises) and the reimbursement system did not appear to be instituted for the convenience of the employer.

In other cases, courts have focused more closely on the "business premises" requirement. In some of these cases, courts have held that the employer's business premises include homes that were located near but not on the property where the employer conducted most of its business. For example, in Lindeman v. Commissioner, 60 T.C. 609 (1973), acq. 1975-2 C.B. 2, the Tax Court held that a house across the street from the employer's principal place of business was on the employer's business premises because the employee who lived in the house performed some of his duties in the house. However, in other cases, courts have held the employer's business premises did not include homes near the employer's principal place of business. For example, in Commissioner v. Anderson, 371 F.2d 59 (6th Cir. 1966), cert. denied, 387 U.S. 906 (1967), the court held that the business premises of a motel did not include a home for the motel manager, which was located two blocks from the motel.

Other cases have revolved around the "convenience of the employer" requirement. Generally, a taxpayer can establish that the meals or lodging were provided for the convenience of the employer by showing that the employee is required to be on-call even when the employee is not working. For example, in Benaglia v. Commissioner, 36 B.T.A. 838 (1937), acq. 1940-1 C.B. 1, the manager of a luxury hotel in Hawaii was permitted to exclude the value of meals and lodging provided at the hotel because the manager was required to be on duty continuously. Although the meals and lodging provided were quite valuable, the court concluded that the meals and lodging were provided so that the manager could perform his duties, not as additional compensation.

Who benefits from §119? At first glance, it might appear that favored employees are the sole beneficiaries. Employers, however, who are able to offer tax-free benefits may be able to attract employees at lower salaries. If that is the case, some of the benefit of the statute might be captured by employers. A reduction in labor costs may lead to new entrants and price-cutting in the affected industry. If this occurs, consumers will benefit. Depending upon the economics of the particular industry, then, §119 may benefit employees, employers, consumers, or, most likely, some combination of the three groups. The losers in all of this are the taxpayers who must pay higher taxes to make up for the revenue lost by the §119 exclusion.

It is easy to criticize a provision that benefits an arbitrary class of employees, employers, and consumers. It is difficult, however, to implement a better method of taxing these sorts of in-kind benefits. One possibility would be to tax the employee on the retail value of the benefits so that a manager of a resort who was required to live on the premises for business reasons would be taxed on the retail cost of his room and board. This approach ignores the limitation on the manager's choice of where to eat and sleep. Another possibility would be to tax the manager on the cost of alternative arrangements. This approach requires speculation as to what arrangements the manager would have made and, in any event, ignores the fact that the provided room and board may be more or less desirable than those alternative arrangements. It would be best, perhaps, to tax the employee on his or her subjective valuation of the room and board. As a practical matter, however, that value is impossible to determine.

Section 107 sets forth another specific exclusion for employer-provided lodging. That section states that "ministers of the gospel" may exclude from gross income the value of lodging provided to the minister or the portion of a cash lodging allowance used by the minister to rent a home.

EXAMPLES

3. Donald earns $40,000 a year as the manager of the Sea Air Hotel. Donald also receives free meals and lodging at the hotel. A year-round guest would pay $50,000 for such lodging and food. In order for Donald to perform effectively his duties as hotel manager, it is necessary for him to live at the hotel. Also, Donald's employment contract requires him to reside at the hotel.
   a. Is Donald taxed on the free lodging and meals he receives as hotel manager?
   b. Is Donald taxed if his employer also provides free lodging and meals to Donald's spouse and dependent children?
   c. Suppose that Donald's employment contract provides that he may accept either lodging at the hotel or a salary increase of $5,000. Donald chooses to accept the free lodging. Is Donald taxed on the employer-provided lodging?
   d. Is each of the following statements true or false?
      i. Free food and lodging leaves Donald wealthier than similarly situated persons earning $40,000 a year.
      ii. Nontaxation of food and lodging may lead to compensation arrangements that would otherwise be inefficient.
      iii. Fairness and efficiency require that Donald be taxed on the fair market value of his bed and board, $50,000 per year.
      iv. If we could determine the amount that Donald otherwise would have spent on board and lodging, then it would be fair and efficient to tax Donald on that sum since that is the amount Donald saves each year by virtue of his compensation arrangement.

4. Alice is the manager of the Traveltime Motel. As a condition of her employment, the motel requires her to live in a home, owned by the motel, which is located one-half mile from the motel so that she will be close enough to arrive quickly in an emergency. Alice is on-call 24 hours a day and wears a paging device that enables the motel to contact her at any time. The value of the lodging is $10,000 per year. Is Alice entitled to exclude the value of the lodging under §119?

5. Sally, a police officer, is on duty from 8 A.M. to 4 P.M. each day. Her employment contract requires her to remain on duty during her lunch hour. The police department reimburses Sally for lunch expenses up to a maximum of $5.00 per day. A state statute setting out the terms for employment for police officers provides that the meals are a working condition and not a part of Sally's compensation. Is Sally taxed on the reimbursement?

6. Jack is the president and sole shareholder of the Rustic Inn, Inc., a motel located alongside Interstate 80. The Rustic Inn consists of 80 motel rooms and an adjoining house where Jack and his family live. The phone line and door bell to the motel rings in Jack's house so that he can answer calls and welcome guests 24 hours per day. Most other motels the size of the Rustic Inn have full-time managers who are required to live on the premises. However, most managers of comparable motels are not given accommodations as nice as the house in which Jack and his family live. The motel deducts all expenses associated with the adjoining house, including those (such as utilities) that clearly would be nondeductible for ordinary homeowners. Is Jack entitled to exclude the value of the lodging from his gross income under §119?

EXPLANATIONS

3. a. No. Under §119 the value of any meals or lodging furnished by an employer to an employee is excluded from gross income if (i) such meals and lodging are provided for the convenience of the employer; (ii) the meals are furnished on the business premises of the employer; and (iii) the employee is required to accept such lodging on the business premises as a condition of his employment. These requirements are met here. The convenience of the employer requirement is met, as in *Benaglia*, because Donald must reside at the hotel to perform his duties as the hotel manager.

b. No. The exclusion under §119 extends to meals and lodging provided to an employee's spouse and dependents. §119(a).

c. Yes. Since Donald is no longer required to accept the lodging as a condition of his employment, the exclusion from gross income is not available. §119(a)(2).

d. i. True. Nontaxation of food and lodging leaves Donald wealthier than other individuals with the same monetary income.

ii. True. Suppose the meals and lodging cost the hotel $18,000 per year but are worth only $15,000 to Donald. In the absence of taxes, the hotel obviously would not provide meals and lodging because both parties would be better off if Donald were given an additional $16,000 in cash. But if Donald is in the 40 percent tax bracket and meals and lodging are tax-free, the incentives change. The tax-free meals and lodging worth $15,000 to Donald provide the same benefit as $25,000 in taxable salary. (If Donald's marginal tax rate is 40 percent, the tax on $25,000 is $10,000, leaving Donald with $15,000 of after-tax income.) It costs the hotel $18,000 to provide meals and lodging with a value equal to $25,000 of cash compensation.

iii. False. Taxation of the lodging at fair market value would give Donald an income of $90,000 per year. However, Donald is not as well off as most persons who earn that sum because he is forced to spend $50,000 per year on hotel food and lodging. It would not be equitable to treat Donald the same as other individuals earning $90,000. Said another way, the food and lodging are obviously not worth $50,000 to Donald and it seems unfair to tax him on that sum.

It also may be economically inefficient to tax Donald on the retail value of his meals and lodging. One way to determine whether a tax is inefficient is to ask whether it prevents (or induces) transactions that would be attractive (or unattractive) in a no-tax world. We saw above that the nontaxation of meals and lodging under current law might well be inefficient because it encourages otherwise uneconomical compensation arrangements. Taxation at full retail value would be inefficient for the opposite reason — in some cases it would discourage the parties from sensible compensation arrangements that included meals and lodging.

The provision of meals and lodging might be attractive to both Donald and the hotel in a no-tax world. First, the meals and lodging might cost the hotel a modest amount, say $8,000 per year, but might be worth $13,000 a year to Donald. Second, the hotel might benefit from having Donald easily available during nonworking hours. If the meals and lodging are taxed at the retail value of $50,000, it will no longer make sense for the parties to reach agreements that include this benefit. The tax alone ($20,000, assuming a 40 percent rate) will be greater than its benefit.

iv. Probably false. The meals and lodging may be more or less valuable to Donald than the cost of the alternative arrangements. Donald may not be willing to pay the retail price to live in the hotel, but may still prefer the hotel food and lodging to the food and lodging he would otherwise purchase. Or suppose this issue comes up in the context of someone who pilots a freighter. The employee may find ship's quarters and food *much* less desirable than the food and lodging he or she would otherwise purchase.

How *should* we tax the benefit? The ideal solution would be to tax the meals and lodging at their value to Donald — $13,000 per year. Taxation at that value, often referred to as the good's *shadow price*, would be efficient because a benefit that is attractive in a no-tax world will be equally attractive if taxed at each individual's shadow price. Taxing Donald on the shadow price of the benefit also seems fair since that price represents the amount of cash income Donald would pay for the benefit. The obvious difficulty with this approach is that it is impossible to know the value that Donald puts on the meals and lodging.

Students should note that the subject of efficiency can get quite complicated very quickly. For example, virtually all taxes cause some distortion; the amount of distortion depends not only on the tax itself, but on the interaction among the tax, other taxes, and non-tax economic forces. Moreover, some tax-induced changes in behavior, such as reduced smoking due to an excise tax on tobacco, may be desirable and efficient. Nonetheless, when evaluating particular provisions of the tax law, it is useful to ask yourself whether such provisions distort decisionmaking. In many cases this question can be answered without elaborate analysis and it will be obvious that the change is not justified by any compelling social policy. For example, a law that taxes employer-provided bus passes but does not tax employer-provided parking will distort the decision between use of private automobiles and reliance on mass transit. The result will be that more employees will drive to work than is economically efficient.

4. Probably not. An employee can exclude the value of lodging under §119 only if the employee is required to accept such lodging on the "business premises" of her employer. §119(a)(2). It is unlikely that a home one-half mile from the motel would be considered on the business premises of the motel. See Commissioner v. Anderson, 371 F.2d 59 (3d Cir. 1966), cert. denied, 387 U.S. 906 (1967).

5. Yes. In a number of cases decided in the 1960s, courts held that the business premises of the state police included the entire area under police jurisdiction and thus that state police could exclude meal money under §119. However, in 1978 the Supreme Court put an end to this exclusion, but not by limiting the definition of business premises. Instead, the Supreme Court held that meals purchased with money provided by the state are not "furnished" by the employer, and so do not qualify for the exclusion. Commissioner v. Kowalski, 434 U.S. 77 (1977). The state statute does not determine whether the meals are intended for compensation. §119(b)(1).

6. Here Jack is both an employee of the corporation and its owner. Does that dual role prevent him from qualifying for the §119 exclusion? Probably not. Jack can establish that his residence on the business premises is for the convenience of the employer because he is on-call 24 hours a day and comparable motels require that their managers live on the motel premises. However, the potential for abuse of §119 is great here because Jack can set the conditions of his own employment, as owner of the corporation, and his accommodations are nicer than the accommodations motels generally give their managers. Courts and the Service may carefully scrutinize such potentially abusive arrangements. See

Hatt v. Commissioner, 28 T.C.M. 1194 (1969), aff'd per curiam, 457 F.2d 499 (7th Cir. 1972). However, on these facts, Jack can probably qualify for the §119 exclusion.

2. Employer-Provided Insurance and Health, Accident, and Death Benefits

Reading: §§79, 101, 105, 106, 213

Section 105 excludes from gross income amounts employees receive from their employers as reimbursement for medical expenses and the value of services employees receive under an employer-provided health care plan. The benefits of §105 are conditioned upon the requirement that the employer health care plan not discriminate in favor of highly compensated employees. In general, a health plan will meet the nondiscrimination requirement if the benefits provided to highly compensated employees are also provided to rank and file employees. Section 106 complements §105 by excluding from gross income the value of health and accident insurance premiums paid by the employer to cover employees.

The exclusion for employer-provided health care benefits has the same effect as requiring employees to include in income the value of employer-provided medical care and allowing the employees to take a corresponding deduction for those expenses. In either event, medical costs would be paid out of before-tax dollars. Section 213 does allow a deduction for unreimbursed medical expenses. However, as discussed in Chapter 4, the §213 medical expense deduction is subject to significant limitations, including a floor of 7.5 percent of adjusted gross income. The §§105 and 106 exclusions, together with the §213 deduction, represent a significant, albeit indirect, form of government support for medical expenses.

If an employer buys life insurance for an individual employee and the employee designates the policy beneficiary, the value of the life insurance is income to the employee. Reg. §1.61-2(d)(2)(ii)(a). However, if the employer buys group term life insurance for its employees, the employees can exclude the value of the insurance from gross income, under §79, to the extent that the insurance provides death benefits not greater than $50,000. Section 79 requires that the employer not discriminate in favor of highly compensated employees.

If an employer pays a death benefit to the estate or beneficiary of an employee, the estate or beneficiary can exclude up to $5,000 of the death benefit paid, under §101(b)(1).

EXAMPLES

7. David receives $50,000 of group term life insurance from his employer. He names his long-time companion Fred as beneficiary. Is David subject to tax on the value of the life insurance? If David dies, is Fred taxed on the $50,000 death benefit?

8. a. Larry is paid a cash salary of $25,000 and his employer provides him with health insurance valued at $4,000 per year. The health insurance covers all of Larry's health care costs. How much, if any, of the value of the employer-provided health insurance must Larry include in gross income?

    b. Leslie is paid a cash salary of $29,000 and spends $4,000 on health care. How much, if any, of her health care costs may Leslie deduct?

    c. What is the likely impact of the differential tax treatment of employer-paid and employee-paid medical expenses?

9. Management offers the union representing employees of Xenon Corporation a choice of new salary packages. The first package offers employees additional medical insurance at a cost of $1,000 per employee per year. The second package does not offer additional insurance but provides for a salary bonus of $1,000 per employee. The union polls its employees and discovers that, on the average, $1,000 of insurance is valued by employees at $900; that is, the average employee would be indifferent between receiving $900 in cash and $1,000 of medical insurance.

    a. Assume the employees were not subject to income tax. Will the union accept the package with the insurance or the package with the $1,000 salary bonus?

    b. Assume that both the insurance and the salary increase are subject to income tax and that all employees are in the 30 percent bracket. Will the union accept the package with the insurance or with the $1,000 salary bonus? What will be the after-tax value of the chosen benefit to each employee? How much tax will the government collect? What is the sum of the cash value of the benefit to the employee and the cash value of the taxes raised to the government?

    c. Assume that the salary bonus is subject to income tax but the medical insurance is tax-free, and that all employees are subject to a marginal tax rate of 30 percent. Will the union accept the package with the insurance or the package with the $1,000 bonus? What will the after-tax value of the chosen benefit be to each employee? How much tax will the government collect from each employee? What is the sum of the cash value of the benefit to the employee and the cash value of the taxes raised by the government?

EXPLANATIONS

7. David is not taxed on the value of the term life insurance, and Fred is not taxed on the value of the death benefit if David dies. Section 79 excludes from income the premiums that finance the first $50,000 of group term life insurance coverage. If David dies, Fred will exclude the $50,000 proceeds of the life insurance. §101(a).

8. a. Larry excludes the entire $4,000 of health insurance costs, under §106.
   b. Leslie will be able to deduct her health care costs under §213(a) only to the extent such costs exceed a floor of 7.5 percent of adjusted gross income, here $2,175 if her adjusted gross income is $29,000. She may deduct only $1,825 ($4,000 less $2,175) of her costs.
   c. The fact that individuals who receive employer-provided medical benefits pay less tax than individuals who pay for their own medical care encourages employees to take a portion of their salary in the form of in-kind medical benefits. Employees who must purchase medical insurance with after-tax dollars will pay higher taxes than employees with identical economic incomes who are able to secure tax-free employer-provided medical care.

9. a. The union will prefer the salary bonus.
   b. The union will still prefer the salary bonus. The salary is worth $1,000 before tax and $700 after-tax; the benefit package is worth only $900 before-tax and $630 after-tax. The government will collect $300 per employee. The cash value of the benefit to the employee is $700 and the government raises taxes of $300 for a total benefit of $1,000.
   c. The union will now prefer the insurance. The insurance will return a before-tax and after-tax benefit to each employee of $900; the salary bonus will return an after-tax benefit to each

employee of only $700. The government will not collect any tax so the total benefit will be the $900 benefit to the employee. The tax-induced reduction in value of the total amount of goods and services is called the *deadweight loss* of the tax. Here the deadweight loss associated with the differential tax treatment of a salary bonus and of medical insurance is $100 (the $1,000 value of the bonus as compared to the $900 value of the medical insurance).

3. The Section 132 Exclusion for Miscellaneous Fringe Benefits

Reading: §132; Reg. §§1.132-1, -2, -6, -8; 1.61-21(g)(12)

Thus far we have considered a number of specific exclusion sections, including the exclusions for employer-provided food, lodging, insurance, and health care. What is the tax treatment of other types of fringe benefits? Section 132 covers miscellaneous fringe benefits that are not covered by other specific exclusion sections. Adopted in 1984, it excludes from income the following six categories of benefits: (i) no-additional-cost services; (ii) qualified employee discounts; (iii) working condition fringe benefits; (iv) de minimis fringe benefits; (v) qualified transportation fringe benefits; and (vi) qualified moving expense reimbursements.

Two principal requirements must be met before a benefit qualifies as an excludable *no-additional-cost service*. Not surprisingly, the first requirement is that the benefit constitutes a service that imposes no substantial additional cost on the employer. §132(b)(2). The second requirement is that the service is offered for sale in the ordinary course of the line of business of the employer in which the employee is performing services. §132(b)(1). Thus, a hotel might allow employees free use of otherwise unused hotel rooms. However, due to the line of business limitation, a manufacturing concern could not offer its employees, as a tax-free benefit, hotel rooms it was not using but for which it had paid. The line of business limitation is designed to limit the loss of tax revenue from the exclusion and to prevent conglomerates from receiving an unfair advantage over other firms.

Services provided pursuant to reciprocal written agreements among employers operating similar businesses can qualify for the §132 no-additional-cost service exclusion so long as no employer incurs any substantial additional cost in providing the service. §132(i).

Such reciprocal agreements, for example, might permit an employee of one airline to fly (on a stand-by basis) on another airline at no charge.

The §132(c) test for excluding an *employee discount* varies depending on whether the employee is purchasing goods or services at a discount. An employee purchasing goods can exclude a discount up to the employer's *gross profit percentage.* §132(c)(1)(A). If, for example, an employer sold goods for an aggregate sale price of $100,000 and the employer's aggregate cost of the goods is $60,000, the employer's gross profit percentage is 40 percent, which is $40,000 (the $100,000 aggregate sale price less the $60,000 aggregate cost) divided by the $100,000 aggregate sale price. The employer could offer its employees tax-free discounts of up to 40 percent. An employee purchasing services may exclude a discount of up to 20 percent. §132(c)(1)(B). The exclusion for qualified employee discounts is limited to goods or services sold in the line of business in which the employee is providing services. §132(c)(4).

Both the qualified employee discount exclusion and the no-additional-cost service exclusion are conditioned upon compliance with a nondiscrimination provision. §132(j)(1). This provision, like the nondiscrimination provision governing employer health care plans, generally requires that the benefit be made available to a wide cross section of employees, including non-highly compensated employees. (Under Regulation §1.132-8(f)(1), an employee is a "highly compensated employee" if the employee (i) owns 5 percent or more of the employer, (ii) is paid salary of more than $75,000, (iii) is paid salary of more than $50,000 and is one of the employer's top wage earners, or (iv) is paid more than 150 percent of the amount specified in §415(c)(1)(A), which limits qualified pension plan contributions to $30,000.)

A *working condition fringe benefit* is defined, generally, as an item that could be deducted as a business expense under §162 or §167 if paid directly by the employee. §132(d). Thus, an employee who would be able to deduct the costs of a subscription to a professional journal if she bore those costs herself is not taxed if her employer supplies the journal free of charge. We defer detailed discussion of what constitutes a deductible business expense until later. For now, it may suffice to say that the term includes costs that are ordinary and necessary for one's employment. Some examples include the costs of office furniture and equipment, and meals, lodging, and transportation while the taxpayer is out of town on business trips.

A *de minimis fringe benefit* is defined as any property or service the value of which is so small as to make accounting for it unreasonable or administratively impracticable. §132(e)(1). Regulation §1.132-6(e) lists the following items as examples of de minimis fringe benefits: occasional parties, occasional theater or sporting event tickets, coffee, doughnuts, soft drinks, and local telephone calls. In addition, §132(e)(2) provides a special rule for eating facilities operated by employers for their employees: The eating facility will be treated as a de minimis fringe if (i) it is on or near the employer's business premises and (ii) the revenue from the facility generally equals or exceeds the employer's cost of operating the facility.

Qualified transportation fringe benefits include "qualified parking," transit passes (such as bus passes), and transportation provided in a "commuter highway vehicle" that is used principally to drive employees to and from work. §132(f)(1)(A). *Qualified parking* is defined as parking provided to an employee on or near the business premises of the employer. §132(f)(5)(C). A *commuter highway vehicle* must have a seating capacity of at least six adult passengers (not including the driver) and at least 80 percent of the expected mileage of the vehicle must be incurred in transporting employees (at half-capacity or greater) to and from work. §132(f)(5)(B).

Section 132(f)(2) caps the exclusion for qualified transportation fringe benefits. The limits are indexed for inflation. §132(f)(6). For tax year 1995, an employee could exclude parking only to the extent that the value of the parking did not exceed $160 per month. Rev. Proc. 94-72. (If the cost exceeds the limit, the employee is taxed on the excess.) In the case of transit passes and commuter highway vehicle services, the exclusion for tax year 1995 was limited to $60 per month. Rev. Proc. 94-72.

Qualified moving expense reimbursements are amounts received by an individual from an employer as payment for expenses that would be deductible by the employee as moving expenses under §217 if paid by the employee.

A special rule provides that gross income does not include the value of any *on-premises athletic facility* provided by an employer to employees. §132(j)(4)(A). An on-premises athletic facility must be located on the premises of the employer and operated by the employer. In addition, substantially all the use of the facility must be by employees, their spouses, and their dependent children. §132(j)(4)(B).

The following examples review the rules described above and test your knowledge of other aspects of §132 that should be apparent from a careful reading of the statute.

EXAMPLES

10. Dean, an airline reservation clerk for Friendly Airlines, is allowed to fly free of charge on Friendly Airlines flights. Dean is required to fly on a stand-by basis and is permitted to board only when there otherwise would be unoccupied seats. Is the flight taxable to Dean?

11. Donald works as a salesman for a retailer that sells tools. Donald's employer gives him an airline voucher, good for a round-trip ticket to Hawaii. Donald's employer received the voucher at no cost as part of a promotional effort of the airline. The voucher is subject to seat availability and may be used only when there are otherwise unoccupied seats. Is the flight taxable to Donald?

12. Sarah works as a proofreader for Jones Books, Inc., a successful publishing company. Jones Books owns a jet that can carry 20 passengers. When the jet makes a business trip, there is often additional space on board. The company usually permits employees who are on vacation to "hitch a ride" on the jet if there is extra space available. Jones Books, Inc. flies several of its employees to New York for a business convention and Sarah "hitches a ride" on the flight in order to visit friends. What amount, if any, does Sarah have to include in income as a result of the flight to New York?

13. a. Allison works at the candy counter of the Imperial Theater, a movie theater owned by Globe, Inc. Allison is allowed free midweek admission to films showing at any of the eight Globe theaters in the city if the show is not sold out prior to the time the feature movie begins. Is Allison taxed on the value of the free movie admissions?

    b. How, if at all, would your answer in part (a) change if Allison's spouse and dependent children were also allowed free admission to the films?

    c. How, if at all, would your answer in part (a) change if Allison were a retired former employee of the Imperial Theater rather than a current employee?

    d. How, if at all, would your answer in part (a) change if Allison were a veterinarian working for Hollywood Milk, a dairy owned by Globe, Inc., the owner of the theaters?

    e. Globe, Inc. signs an agreement with a rival theater owner, Johnson Film Exhibitors, Inc. (JFE), under which the movie house employees of either corporation are permitted free midweek admission to films showing at any Globe- or JFE-owned theater if the film is not sold out. Is Allison taxed on her free admissions to JFE theaters?

14. Betty is vice president of Malibu Tanning Centers, Inc., a chain of tanning salons. Officers of the corporation (but not other employees) are permitted to use the facilities at no cost when they are not being used by paying customers. Betty takes advantage of this program by visiting the salon three times a week. Is this fringe benefit taxable to Betty?

15. Albert is a sales clerk at City Sporting Goods. The store's total sales for the prior year were $600,000 and its cost of goods sold was $400,000. Albert wishes to purchase a ski outfit that the store sells to ordinary customers for $240. The store's cost for the ski outfit is $180.

   a. City Sporting Goods permits its employees to purchase goods for their personal use at one-third off the retail price so Albert will be able to purchase the ski outfit for $160. Is the discount taxable income to Albert? If so, what amount is included in his gross income?

   b. Suppose City Sporting Goods permits its employees to purchase goods at one-half off the retail price so that Albert will be able to purchase the ski outfit for $120. Is the discount taxable income to Albert? If so, what amount is included in his gross income?

16. Mary is an accountant for the Eastside Cleaning Service. The business pays housecleaners $5.00 an hour to clean customers' homes. The gross receipts of the business for the year were $500,000 and its total expenses were $450,000. Employees of Eastside are permitted to purchase cleaning services at a 20 percent discount. Mary hires the service to clean her apartment once a week for $40, which is 20 percent less than the ordinary price of $50. Is Mary subject to tax on the $10 discount?

17. Carol is an attorney employed by Bears Investments. The business of Bears is the purchase and sale of stock, bonds, and limited partnership interests in various new businesses. Bears' gross profit percentage is 10 percent. Bears permits its employees to purchase investments at a 5 percent discount. Carol purchases $20,000 of such investments for $19,000. What are the tax consequences to Carol?

18. Jack is the sales manager of Elegant Clothing, Inc., a corporation that runs a chain of men's clothing stores. The corporation permits senior sales managers, the vice president, and the president of the corporation to purchase clothing at a 25 percent discount. In the prior year, the corporation had sales of $5 million and its cost of goods sold was $3 million. Jack purchases $1,000 of clothing for $750. What are the tax consequences to Jack?

19. Joan is an associate for a large law firm. State whether each of the following benefits is excludable as a §132(d) working condition fringe.
    a. Joan travels to New York to take a deposition. The firm pays for her travel, meals, and lodging.
    b. Each day the firm hires a caterer to provide sandwiches and soft drinks for all employees who wish to eat in their offices. Joan takes advantage of this free lunch two or three times a week.
    c. The firm provides Joan with free parking in the office building housing the law firm. It would cost Joan $100 per month to purchase such parking herself.
    d. At Joan's request, the firm buys her a subscription to The Litigation News, a weekly legal magazine. She is the only member of the firm who reads the magazine and, with the firm's permission, she discards the periodical after reading it.

20. Albert says, "In general, the Treasury does not lose revenue by the exclusion of working condition fringe benefits from an individual's gross income. If working condition fringe benefits were included in the individual's gross income, the taxpayer would be able to deduct the same amount as a business expense." Is Albert correct? (Before answering, take a look at §§63 and 67.)

21. a. Ellen works at a small rural law firm. Her employer pays for her dinners, which are delivered to the firm, on those occasional evenings when she has to work late. Is Ellen taxed on the value of the dinners?
    b. Instead of paying for dinners delivered to the firm, the firm gives Ellen a cash meal allowance for her dinners when she works late. Is Ellen taxed on the meal allowance?

22. a. Andy works at a large urban law firm. His employer pays for his dinners, which are delivered to the firm on the five to ten days a month when he works late. Is Andy taxed on the value of the dinners?

    b. Instead of paying for dinners delivered to the firm, the firm gives Andy a cash meal allowance for his dinners when he works late. Is Andy taxed on the meal allowance?

23. Debby works for Ace Accountants. Ace provides free coffee, soda, and donuts to its employees. Is Debby taxed on the value of the refreshments?

24. a. Susan works for Able, Baker & Gonzalez, a large downtown law firm. In order to encourage their attorneys and staff to keep fit, the firm will pay 50 percent of the cost of any health club membership that an employee purchases. The firm reimburses Susan for $500 of a $1,000 fee that she paid for membership in the Downtown Squash and Tennis Club. Can Susan exclude the $500 reimbursement from her income?

    b. What if the law firm instead built exercise facilities on the firm premises for its employees and allowed Susan to use it at no charge?

25. Urban Hospital sets the meal prices at its cafeteria at a level just high enough to cover its operating costs, so the cafeteria meals are considerably less expensive than comparable meals at off-site restaurants. Jane, a doctor at the hospital, saves approximately $20 per week by eating at the cafeteria. Is Jane taxed on the savings?

26. Sam is the general manager of the Mountainview Country Club restaurant. The Club charges an annual membership fee of $500. In addition, the Club charges members $20 per round of golf and $8 per hour of tennis court time. However, employees and their dependents are allowed to use the facilities free of charge. Sam and his wife play tennis at the club two to three times a week. Is Sam taxed on the value of the free court time?

27. Mark is a professional hockey player for the Boston Brawlers. During the off-season Mark lives in Mystic, Connecticut. The Brawlers purchase a membership for Mark in a Mystic health club at a cost of $500 and hire a private trainer at a cost of $1,000 to supervise Mark's workouts. Is Mark taxed on the cost of the club membership and trainer?

28. In each circumstance described below, state whether the value of the transportation-related fringe benefit is taxable to employees receiving the benefit, and, if so, the amount that would be included.

    a. The Arnold Manufacturing Company provides free parking for employees who drive to work. The value of the parking is $160 per month.

b. Betty's Furniture World provides free parking only to its highly compensated employees. The value of the parking is $160 per month.

c. Carol's Cakes reimburses its employees for their monthly job-related parking costs, up to a maximum of $160 per month.

d. Dan's Drapes provides its employees with monthly mass transit passes. The value of the monthly passes is $160 per month.

e. Earl's Enterprises hires a taxi (with a driver) to pick up its top executives and drive them to work. Typically, two or three executives are driven to work in each cab. The value of the cab rides to each executive is $160 per month.

EXPLANATIONS

10. The flight is not taxable to Dean. Under §132(a)(1), an employee may exclude from gross income a fringe benefit that qualifies as a no-additional-cost service. Section 132(b) defines a *no-additional-cost service* as a service provided by an employer to an employee if such service is offered for sale to customers "in the ordinary course of the line of business of the employer in which the employee is performing services" and if the employer incurs no substantial additional cost (including foregone revenue) in providing such services to the employee.

    Dean meets all of these tests. His employer, the airline, is providing the service, is in the business of selling flights to the public, and will incur no substantial additional costs in providing Dean with the seat on the plane since the seat would not otherwise be occupied by a paying customer. If, on the other hand, Dean were permitted to reserve a seat on the flight, he would be taxed on its value because he might displace a paying customer. Reg. §1.132-2(c).

11. The flight is taxable to Donald. A taxpayer may exclude a no-additional-cost service from income only if the taxpayer's employer offers the service to customers. §132(b)(1). Here Donald's employer is a retailer of tools and, quite obviously, does not sell airplane flights to its customers.

12. The flight does not qualify for the §132 no-additional-cost service exclusion. Although the company will not incur any additional expense by allowing Sarah to "hitch a ride," the flight is not a §132 no-additional-cost service because Jones Books, Inc. does not offer airline service for sale to customers in the ordinary

course of its business. §132(b)(1). How much does Sarah have to include in income?

Reg. §1.61-21(g)(12) provides a special valuation rule where most of the passengers on a company airplane are traveling for business and an employee "hitches a ride" on the plane. This special (and admittedly obscure) valuation rule may permit Sarah to exclude the value of the flight. The regulation provides that if at least half of the seats on the employer's airplane are occupied by employee's traveling primarily for the employer's business, the value of the flight to the employee traveling for personal reasons will be deemed to be zero.

13. a. The free passes do not deprive the theater of substantial revenue it would otherwise earn and the theater is in the business of selling seats to movies, so the benefit would qualify as a no-additional-cost service. §132(b)(2).

  b. The tax treatment of the benefit should not change. Under §132(h)(2)(A), the spouse and dependent children of an employee are treated as employees for purposes of both §132(a)(1) (no-additional-cost service) and §132(a)(2) (qualified employee discount).

  c. The tax treatment of the benefit should not change. Under §132(h)(1), an employee who is retired or disabled or a surviving spouse of an employee is treated as an employee for purposes of §132(a)(1) and (2).

  d. Here the free tickets would be taxable to Allison. To qualify for exclusion under §132, the free service must be provided by the line of business in which the employee is performing services. §132(b)(1). This rule is designed to prevent employees of corporations that operate a number of different types of businesses from receiving a wide variety of services on a tax-free basis.

  e. Allison is not taxed on her free admissions to the movie theaters owned by the rival company. Under §132(i), two or more employers are permitted to make a reciprocal agreement for the provision of tax-free no-additional-cost services to their employees. Such agreements must be in writing and neither employer may incur any substantial additional cost (including foregone revenue) in providing such service pursuant to the agreement. If these conditions are met, as they are here, services provided to an employee by any party to such a reciprocal agreement will be treated as though they were provided by the employee's actual employer.

14. Betty is taxed on the use of the tanning salon. The §132 exclusions for no-additional-cost services and qualified employee discounts are available to highly compensated employees only if the nondiscrimination requirement of §132(j)(1) is met. That requirement is not met here because the fringe benefit is not available on substantially the same terms to both highly compensated and non-highly compensated employees.

15. a. None of the discount is taxable. Section 132(a)(2) excludes from income the amount of any "qualified employee discount." In the case of a discount on goods, the discount may be excluded from income only to the extent it does not exceed the gross profit percentage of the price at which property is being offered by the employer to customers. §132(c)(1)(A). *Gross profit percentage* equals:

$$\frac{\text{aggregate sale price} \quad \text{aggregate cost of}}{\text{of goods sold} \quad \text{goods sold}}$$
$$\text{aggregate sale price of goods sold}$$

Said another way, the gross profit percentage is equal to the gross profit on goods sold divided by the aggregate sales price of goods. The calculation must be based on the employer's sales during a representative period. §132(c)(2)(B)(ii).

In this problem, the aggregate sales price of goods sold is $600,000 and the aggregate cost of goods is $400,000. City Sporting Goods' gross profit percentage is 33.33 percent, which is:

$$\frac{\$600,000 - \$400,000}{\$600,000}$$

Albert is given a discount of one-third or 33.33 percent. This discount equals, but does not exceed, the gross profit percentage and otherwise meets the requirements of §132 so the discount will not be taxable to Albert. The amount that the employer paid for the particular item sold to the employee at a discount is irrelevant for purposes of §132.

   b. In this case, Albert's employee discount of 50 percent exceeds the gross profit percentage of 33.33 percent, so Albert is taxed on the excess discount. The maximum permissible discount of 33.33 percent would reduce the price of the ski outfit to $160. Albert paid $120 for the outfit, so he must include the $40 difference in his gross income.

16. No. Section 132(c)(1)(B) defines a qualified employee discount on services as a discount that does not exceed 20 percent of the price at which the service is offered to customers. The employer's profit percentage and cost of providing the service are irrelevant. Here the discount provided to Eastside employees equals but does not exceed 20 percent, so Mary may exclude the value of the discount from her gross income.

17. Carol must include the $1,000 in her gross income. Discounts on property held for investment (as well as discounts on real property) are not excludable from income. §132(c)(4).

18. Jack must include the $250 discount in his gross income because the discount does not meet the requirements of §132. As in the case of no-additional-cost services, employee discounts provided to highly compensated employees are excluded from gross income only if the discount is provided on substantially the same terms to both highly compensated and non-highly compensated employees. §132(j)(1). The discount offered by Elegant Clothing, Inc. is only available to employees who are probably highly compensated employees within the definition of Regulation §1.132-8(f)(1), so the discount fails the nondiscrimination requirement.

19. a. The payment of the expenses of the New York trip are excludable as a working condition fringe under §132(a)(3). Working condition fringes are defined in §132(d) as property or services provided to an employee to the extent that the employee would have been able to take a §162 or §167 deduction had the employee paid for the services or property. Section 162 allows taxpayers to deduct all the "ordinary and necessary" expenses paid or incurred during the taxable year in carrying on any trade or business. Section 167 allows taxpayers to take depreciation deductions for wear and tear on property used in a trade or business or held for the production of income.

If Joan had paid these travel expenses herself, she would have been able to deduct the expense under §162, so the payment of the items by her employer will be considered a working condition fringe. Trade or business expenses and depreciation are considered in more detail in later sections of this book. It is worth noting here, however, that Joan's employer would be permitted to deduct only 50 percent of the cost of Joan's meals. See §274(n).

b. The free meals do not qualify as a §132(d) working condition fringe because an employee buying her own lunches would not be able to deduct the cost of lunches under these circumstances. However, if the law firm provides the free meals so that the lawyers in the firm work through lunch and bill more hours, the meals are probably provided "for the convenience of the employer" so Joan could exclude the value of the meals under §119.

c. Joan would not be able to deduct the cost of parking if she purchased it herself, so the payment would not be excludable as a working condition fringe. The value of the free parking would be excludable, however, as a qualified transportation fringe under §132(f)(1)(C).

d. Joan would be able to deduct the cost of the subscription as a business expense under §162 if she purchased it herself, so the cost is excludable as a working condition fringe under §132.

20. No. The exclusion is more valuable than the corresponding business expense deduction for most taxpayers. First, certain employee business expenses are deductible only if a taxpayer itemizes deductions. §63. Second, employee business expenses generally are deductible only to the extent they exceed 2 percent of the taxpayer's adjusted gross income. §67.

21. a. Ellen is not taxed on the value of the dinners. If the meals furnished to Ellen at the law firm are provided for the convenience of the employer (so that Ellen will work late), the meals qualify for the §119 exclusion. In the alternative, Ellen can exclude the meals as a §132(e) de minimis fringe because the meals are provided only occasionally and to allow her to extend her normal work hours. Reg. §1.132-6(d)(2)(B).

b. Ellen can exclude the meal money, which qualifies as a de minimis fringe because the meals are provided only occasionally and so that she can extend her normal work hours. §132(e) and Reg. §1.132-6(d)(2)(B).

22. a. Andy is probably not taxed on the value of the dinners. It is not totally clear whether the meals would qualify as a de minimis fringe, under §132(e), because the meals have probably been provided more than occasionally. However, even if the meals are not within §132(e), Andy can exclude the value of the

meals under §119 if the meals are furnished "for the convenience of the employer" (for example, so that Andy will work late).

b. It is uncertain whether Andy will be permitted to exclude the value of the dinners from his gross income. Cash meal allowances do not qualify for the §119 exclusion. Commissioner v. Kowalski, 434 U.S. 77 (1977). However, the meals may qualify for exclusion as a §132(e) de minimis fringe. Section 132(e) defines a de minimis fringe as a property or service the value of which is so small (taking into account the frequency with which similar fringes are provided to the employer's employees) as to make accounting for it unreasonable or administratively impracticable.

Regulation §1.132-6(d)(2)(B) states that meal money qualifies as a de minimis fringe benefit if it is reasonable and satisfies three conditions. First, the meal money must be provided only on an occasional basis. Second, it must be provided because overtime work necessitates an extension of the employee's normal work schedule. Third (and somewhat repetitively), the meal money must be provided to enable the employee to work overtime.

The application of these provisions to these facts raises more questions than answers. Is the providing of one or two meals per week "occasional"? What is Andy's "normal workday"? If Andy works late once per week and spends $10 per meal, the annual amount of employer-provided meal money will be approximately $500. Is $500 a small amount? Would it be unreasonable or administratively impracticable to record each meal payment? Would it be relevant whether the firm keeps such records for purposes of billing clients?

Regulation §1.132-6(b)(1) provides that if an employer provides a free meal to one employee on a daily basis, the value of the meals is not de minimis even though with respect to the entire work force the meals are provided infrequently. On the other hand, the regulation states that where it would be "administratively difficult" to determine frequency with respect to individual employees, the frequency with which the fringes are provided to employees in general is considered rather than the frequency with which the individual employees receive them. Reg. §1.132-6(b)(2).

As a practical matter, Andy may be able to justify taking a

"reporting position" on his return that excludes the meal money from income. However, the Service and some courts might take the position that Andy receives meals more than "occasionally" and that the meals cannot be excluded as a §132(e) de minimis fringe.

23. No. The value of the refreshments is small and it would be administratively difficult to keep track of each individual's consumption, so the refreshments qualify for exclusion as a §132(e) de minimis fringe. Reg. §1.132-6(e)(1).

24. a. The $500 payment is taxable to Susan. Reg. §1.132-6(e)(2) states that membership in a private country club or athletic facility will not qualify as a de minimis fringe.

    b. If the law firm built exercise facilities on firm premises for its employees, Susan would not have to include in her income the value of the use of those facilities. §132(j)(4)(B)(iii).

25. No. Section 132(e)(2). Note that, even if the hospital gave Jane free meals in the hospital cafeteria, she would probably still be able to exclude the value of the meals under §119.

26. Sam will be taxed on the fringe benefit if his use of the court deprives the club of revenue it might have obtained from members. Thus, Sam's use is likely to be tax-free only if he uses the court on a stand-by (rather than on a reservation) basis, so that his use can qualify as a no-additional-cost fringe benefit. §132(a)(1), §132(b).

    Use of the tennis courts is not tax-free as an on-premises athletic facility under §132(j)(4) because that exclusion only applies where substantially all the use of the facility is by employees of the employer, their spouses, and their dependent children. §132(j)(4)(B)(iii).

27. No. These costs would be excluded as a working condition fringe since training costs are ordinary and necessary business expenses of a professional athlete. If training were not an ordinary and necessary expense in his profession, Mark would be taxed on these fringe benefits.

28. a. The free parking is nontaxable as a qualified transportation fringe under §132(f)(1)(C). Note that §132(f)(2) limits the value of free parking to $155 per month but, for tax year 1995, that figure was inflation adjusted upward to $160.

    b. The free parking still is nontaxable as a qualified transportation fringe under §132(f)(1)(C). The nondiscrimination requirement applies only to no-additional-cost services and qualified employee discounts. §132(j)(1).

c. The free parking again is nontaxable as a qualified transportation fringe under §132(f)(1)(C). Section 132(f)(3) provides that free parking may be provided directly or through cash reimbursement.

d. Section 132(f)(2) limits the excludable value of transit passes to $60 per month. (Although §132(f)(6) provides that the §132(f)(2) limit is to be adjusted for inflation, Rev. Proc. 94-72 indicates that the 1995 limitation was still $60.) The employees who receive these transit passes must include the monthly cost in excess of the limit. Note that the amount of tax-free benefit available through the use of transit passes is much lower than the amount of tax-free benefit available through employer-provided or subsidized parking.

e. The top employees are taxed on the full value of the cab ride. In order to qualify as a commuter highway vehicle (i) the vehicle must have a seating capacity of at least six adults (not including the driver) and (ii) at least 80 percent of the mileage must be incurred in transporting employees to and from work and on trips during which at least one-half the seats are filled with employees. §132(f)(5)(B). Neither condition is met here. Note that, even if the cab qualified as a commuter highway vehicle, only part of the $160 per month value could be excluded. §132(f)(2).

C. Imputed Income

Almost everyone agrees that persons ought to be taxed on increases in wealth realized through wages. But what about increases in wealth realized through non-market transactions? If the individual who spends his salary on food and lodging is subject to tax, should the individual who grows his own food and builds his own home be subject to tax as well? As a practical matter, the answer to the latter question is "No." Taxation of imputed income raises seemingly insurmountable problems of valuation and liquidity and may be objectionable for other reasons. Do we really want a system that monitors whether we clean our home ourselves (rather than employ a maid or cleaning service) and then taxes us on the value of our housekeeping efforts?

Nonetheless, nontaxation of imputed income raises equity and efficiency problems. As noted in the questions below, one effect is to encourage persons to provide services in the home rather than accept "formal" jobs outside the home.

EXAMPLES

29. Xavier receives $12 per hour working as an accountant. He can save $10 an hour by cleaning his own home rather than hiring a cleaning service. Xavier likes (or dislikes) cleaning as much as accounting.
    a. In a tax-free world, will Xavier clean his own house or will he work as an accountant?
    b. If Xavier is taxed on the value of both his accounting and his cleaning at a 30 percent rate, will he clean his own house or will he work as an accountant?
    c. If Xavier's accounting income is taxed at a 30 percent rate but his imputed income from cleaning his own home is not subject to tax, will he clean his own house or will he work as an accountant?

30. Larry has $200,000. He can use the money to purchase a home and an automobile. Alternatively, Larry can invest the money at 8 percent interest and use the interest income ($16,000 per year) to rent an equivalent home and an automobile. Assume Larry is in the 30 percent tax bracket. What should he do?

31. Denise, who is taxed at a marginal rate of 30 percent, is offered $12 per hour to work on Saturday. Denise values her weekend leisure at $10 per hour. Will she work on Saturday?

32. Which, if any, of the following provide untaxed imputed income?
    a. Ownership of a home
    b. Ownership of a pound of flour
    c. Ownership of a tuxedo
    d. Ownership of an automobile
    e. Driving oneself to work
    f. Filling out a tax return without the aid of an accountant

33. Sheila, who has worked for Xenon Corporation for 10 years, accepts a new job with Yaba Corporation. The jobs differ in only one significant respect: Xenon is located in an industrial area and the office in which Sheila worked has poor lighting and ventilation. Yaba offered Sheila an attractive, comfortable office with a beautiful view. Sheila regards her new office as a valuable benefit

of her new job. Indeed, Sheila regards her new environment as equal to a $5,000 per year pay increase. Is Sheila taxed on the improvement in her working environment?

34. Reconsider the forms of imputed income discussed in examples 29-33 above. Can you think of any ways to directly or indirectly tax such income? Are there any other measures that might offset the distortion and unfairness caused by nontaxation of such income?

EXPLANATIONS

29. a. Xavier will work as an accountant and earn an extra $2 per hour.

b. Xavier would still choose to work as an accountant. The $12 per hour he earns, less the tax of 30 percent, yields $8.40 per hour after-tax. The $10 per hour he earns cleaning his own home yields only $7 per hour after-tax.

c. Xavier will clean his own home and earn $10 an hour tax-free. Work as an accountant will pay Xavier only $8.40 per hour ($12 less 30 percent tax) after-tax.

30. Larry should purchase the home and car. Unlike interest income, the imputed rental value of the home and car are not taxed. If Larry earns $16,000 per year of taxable interest and uses that amount to rent an equivalent home and car, he'll find himself with an additional tax burden of $4,800 per year.

31. No. If she works on Saturday, she will earn only $8.40 an hour ($12 less 30 percent tax), $1.60 less per hour than the imputed value of her leisure. Note that Denise would choose to work on Saturday if both income and leisure were taxed or if neither income nor leisure were taxed.

32. All choices except (b) involve untaxed imputed income. The rental value of an owner-occupied home is not taxed. Similarly, an individual who owns a tuxedo or an automobile is not taxed on its rental value. Flour, on the other hand, does not produce imputed rent. Unlike a home or a tuxedo, flour is consumed when it is used. Driving oneself to work and doing one's own tax return produce untaxed imputed income from services.

33. No. The move to a more attractive office clearly enriches Sheila. As stated in the example, Sheila's welfare is improved as much as it would be by a $5,000 raise. However, this kind of employer-

provided fringe benefit is treated as a form of imputed income and it is not subject to tax because of valuation, reporting, and other problems. The nontaxation of imputed income does not depend on the existence of a statutory exclusion.

34. We could directly tax imputed income from home ownership by determining the rental value of the home and taxing the home-owner on that amount. (In fact, that approach was taken as recently as the Civil War!) We could do the same for automobile ownership. On the zanier side, we might indirectly tax the imputed income one receives from leisure by levying excise (or sales) taxes on leisure-related goods and services (for example, television sets, tennis balls, ski lift tickets), or by subjecting leisure-related businesses to an additional layer of income tax. That way, to return to example 31, Denise might end up (indirectly) paying a tax whether she works or not. (But what could we do about Sheila or those persons who obtain imputed income from a walk in the park? Or from daydreaming?)

   Somewhat more realistically, we could remove the distortion and inefficiency caused by the nontaxation of household services by allowing individuals who accept jobs paying taxable wages to deduct the cost of obtaining household services. In example 29 we could allow Xavier to deduct the cost of hiring a cleaning service or a child care provider. That would allow Xavier to earn tax-free income equal to the cost of the provided household services. If Xavier provided the services himself, he would have tax-free imputed income. Alternatively, Xavier could accept a formal job and the taxable income he receives that is used to pay for the household services would be offset by the deduction for those services. If Xavier earns $12 per hour, $10 of which goes to pay for child care and cleaning services, then Xavier would have gross income of $12, offset by a $10 deduction, for a taxable income of $2. In effect, the money used to pay household services would be tax-free.

   We could remove the distortion illustrated by example 30 by allowing individuals who rent to deduct their rental payments. That way, Larry ends up with no taxable income from his $200,000 investment whether he purchases the car and home or invests his funds and uses the taxable interest from the investment to rent the car and home.

   There is no practical way to eliminate the distortion illustrated in example 31. Although, as noted above, we can attempt to tax leisure indirectly by taxing leisure-related goods and services, it is impossible to remove the distortion completely. We can't very well allow individuals to deduct from wages the value of the leisure they could have received tax-free.

D. Windfalls, Gifts, Scholarships, Prizes, and Transfer Payments

1. *Windfalls*

Early in this century, the term "income" was narrowly defined in cases as the gain from capital, from labor, or from both combined. See, e.g., Eisner v. Macomber, 252 U.S. 189 (1920). However, in a later case, Commissioner v. Glenshaw Glass, 348 U.S. 426 (1955), the Supreme Court expanded the definition of income to include any "undeniable accessions to wealth, clearly realized, and over which the taxpayers have dominion and control." Applying this definition of income, the Supreme Court held that Glenshaw Glass had to include in its gross income punitive damages it received in settlement of an antitrust lawsuit.

The *Glenshaw Glass* case is cited narrowly for the proposition that taxpayers must include in income any windfalls they receive, and broadly for its expansive definition of income. The *Glenshaw Glass* definition of income is consistent with the Haig-Simons definition of income. Under this definition it is irrelevant whether the taxpayer, through the provision of her labor or capital, "earned" the income; instead, what matters is whether receipt of the item increased the taxpayer's wealth.

Cesarini v. United States, 296 F. Supp. 3 (N.D. Ohio 1969), aff'd per curiam, 428 F.2d 812 (6th Cir. 1970), is another famous case involving the receipt of a windfall by a taxpayer. The lucky taxpayer in *Cesarini* bought an old piano for $15 at an auction and later discovered almost $4,500 in cash hidden in the piano. The court held that the cash was income to the taxpayers in the year in which they found it, citing *Glenshaw Glass*, as well as a revenue ruling and treasury regulation, both of which provided that a taxpayer must include the value of "treasure trove" in income in the year in which the taxpayer discovers it and reduces it to possession. Note, however, that the circumstances in *Cesarini* should be distinguished from situations in which a taxpayer discovers that something that he had bought was worth more than he originally paid for it. In the latter situation the taxpayer would not have an income inclusion until the property was sold or exchanged — in other words, until the gain was "realized." (For more on the realization requirement, see Chapter 3 of this book.)

EXAMPLES

35. a. In year one, Ellie pays $300 for an antique dresser at an estate sale. In year three, as Ellie is refinishing the dresser, she finds that one of the dresser drawers has a false back. When she removes the false back, she discovers antique gold coins worth $10,000. Does Ellie have to include the value of the coins in income, and, if so, in which year?

   b. Assume that, in year three, instead of finding the coins, Ellie discovers that the dresser is a rare antique, worth $10,000. Later, in year five, Ellie sells the dresser for $12,000. What amounts, if any, does Ellie have to include in income, with respect to the dresser, in years three and five?

EXPLANATIONS

35. a. Ellie must include $10,000 in income in year three, the year in which she discovers the coins and reduces them to possession. Cesarini v. United States, 296 F. Supp. 3 (N.D. Ohio 1969), aff'd per curiam, 428 F.2d 812 (6th Cir. 1970) and Reg. §1.61-14.

   b. Ellie does not have an income inclusion in year three, the year in which she discovers that the dresser is worth $10,000, because the gain has not yet been realized. In year five, in which Ellie sells the dresser for $12,000, she realizes and recognizes $11,700 of gain because the $12,000 amount realized exceeds her $300 basis in the dresser by that amount. §§1001(a), (b), and (c), and 1012. Under §61(a)(3), Ellie must include in gross income the $11,700 of gain from dealings in property.

2. Gifts and Bequests

Reading: §§102, 1015

If we applied *Glenshaw Glass* and the Haig-Simons definition of income to gifts, what would be the tax consequence to the donee of a gift? The gift would increase the donee's wealth, so the donee would have to include the gift in income (and the donor might be allowed a corresponding deduction for the gift). However, we have not adopted this approach: Instead, §102 provides that a donee excludes gifts from income.

Gifts are generally included in the donor's tax base (that is, the donor generally cannot deduct the gift) and excluded from the donee's base instead of being excluded (that is, deducted) from the donor's tax base and included by the donee. This tax treatment is best justified, perhaps, on the grounds that most gifts are made to family members. It makes sense in such circumstances to treat the family as a single taxable unit and ignore both the nominal decline in the donor's wealth and the corresponding increase in the donee's wealth.

Even if gifts are made to donees outside the family, the rule requiring inclusion of the gift in the donor's base is generally easier to administer than requiring inclusion in the donee's base. Consider, for example, the tax treatment of 10,000 commuters each giving a subway panhandler a dollar. It is much easier to collect tax on the $10,000 from the donors, by leaving that amount in their tax base, than it would be to collect it from the donee panhandler. Note, however, that, if the donor is in a higher tax bracket than the donee (which is often the case), more tax is owed under the current approach than would be owed if the donee were taxed on the gift.

What about gifts of appreciated or depreciated property? If, at the time of transfer, the fair market value of the property is equal to or greater than the basis of the property in the hands of the donor, the rule is simple: The donee takes the donor's basis. Suppose, for example, that Mother owns a piece of property. She paid $20 for the property so that is her basis in the property under §1012. Mother gives Daughter the property after it has appreciated in value to $50. At the time of the gift, the property has "built-in gain" of $30 (because the $50 value of the property exceeds Mother's $20 basis by $30). Instead of taxing Mother on the $30 pre-gift appreciation in the property, that gain is deferred until Daughter sells the property. This is accomplished by assigning Daughter a basis in the property equal to Mother's basis of $20. If Daughter then sells the property for $50, she will realize the $30 of gain that was inherent in the property at the time of the gift. §1015(a).

If the property has declined in value in the hands of the donor so that the fair market value of the property at the time of transfer is less than the donor's basis in the property, the rule is more complicated.

For the purpose of determining *gain* on a subsequent disposition of the property by the donee, the donee again takes the donor's basis. However, for the purpose of determining *loss* on a subsequent disposition of the property by the donee, the donee takes a basis equal to the fair market value of the property at the time of transfer. §1015(a). To illustrate the operation of this rule, suppose Mother gives property worth $10, with a $20 basis, to Daughter. If Daughter sells the property for $10, she realizes no loss because, for the purpose of determining loss, the property has a basis equal to its $10 fair market value at the time of transfer. Now suppose that Daughter sells the property for $15. For the purpose of determining loss, Daughter has a basis of $10 and so realizes no loss. For the purpose of determining gain, Daughter inherits a basis of $20 and so realizes no gain. Thus, Daughter realizes neither gain nor loss on the sale.

In other words, if a taxpayer sells property that she received as an inter vivos gift (that is, not as a bequest), compute her gain or loss from the sale of the property as follows: First, if at the time she received the gift, the fair market value of the property transferred was greater or equal to the donor's basis, the donee takes the donor's basis. On a subsequent disposition of the property by the donee, she has gain to the extent that her amount realized on the sale exceeds her basis.

Suppose, on the other hand, the property declined in value in the donor's hands so that the property had a basis greater than its fair market value at the time the donee received the gift (that is, the property had "built-in loss"). On a subsequent disposition of the property by the donee, first apply the "gain rule" and give the donee the same basis as the donor. If that produces a gain to the donee, you have finished your calculations. If that calculation does not produce a gain, apply the "loss rule" and give the donee a basis in the property equal to its fair market value at the time of transfer. The donee realizes the amount of loss that results from that calculation. If, as was the case in the preceding paragraph, the gain rule does not produce a gain and the loss rule does not produce a loss, the donee realizes neither gain nor loss on the sale.

If a beneficiary receives a gift as a bequest on the death of the donor, the beneficiary excludes the gift from income, again under §102. However, under these circumstances the beneficiary's basis will not be determined under §1015. The special basis rule of §1014 will instead apply. Property acquired by reason of death takes a basis in the hands of the beneficiary equal to its fair market value on the date of the decedent's death (or, as provided in §2032A, six months after the decedent's death). §1014(a)(1). The date-of-death basis rule means that the appreciation of the property during the decedent's lifetime will *never* be taxed. The date-of-death rule thus encourages individuals to retain appreciated property until their death, but to sell before death any property that has declined in value. Some commentators have described the tax-free step-up in basis of appreciated property at death as the single largest loophole in the Code. However, when Congress repealed the §1014 rule in 1976, there was such an uproar that the provision repealing §1014 was itself repealed, leaving the §1014 tax-free basis step-up rule intact.

Neither §102 nor any other Code section defines the term *gift*. The Supreme Court, however, has defined a gift as a transfer that stems from the "detached and disinterested" generosity of the donor. Commissioner v. Duberstein, 363 U.S. 278 (1960). The *Duberstein* test, which focuses on the donor's state of mind, is subject to a number of exceptions.

For example, §102(c), enacted in 1986, explicitly provides that a transfer from an employer to an employee cannot be a gift. Thus, unless some other Code exclusion (for example, §132(e) or §74(c)) applies, even the rare transfer to an employee that arises from an employer's "detached and disinterested" generosity is taxable compensation to the employee. (If an employer occasionally gives employees inexpensive gifts, such as Christmas turkeys, the employees may still be able to exclude the value of the gifts as a §132 de minimis fringe. Employees can also exclude the value of certain achievement awards from their employers, under §74(c).)

What if a taxpayer receives tips from customers? Can the tips be characterized as gifts for purposes of §102? Regulation §1.61-2(a)(1) specifically provides that tips that constitute compensation for services must be included in gross income. What if it is not clear that the tips were compensation for services? In Olk v. United States, 536 F.2d 876 (9th Cir.), cert. denied, 429 U.S. 920 (1976), the issue was whether a craps dealer at a casino could exclude the tips (in the form of "tokes") he received from gamblers. The district court in the case found that the tokes were not given as compensation for services, but were instead given by gamblers as a result of "impulsive generosity" or "superstition." Applying the *Duberstein* test, the court concluded that the dealer could exclude the tokes as gifts. However, the court of appeals reversed the district court, concluding that the gamblers' generosity was not "detached and disinterested" and that tokes were not gifts within

§102. (The court was also not convinced that the transfers were non-compensatory since the tokes were received by the taxpayer as a result of being employed as a dealer.)

EXAMPLES

36. On his 39th birthday, Steven receives a $10,000 gift from his mother, and (as luck would have it) a $15,000 bequest distributed from his late aunt's estate. Is Steven required to include the gift or bequest in income?

37. Carol gives Doug a parcel of land. The parcel has a basis in Carol's hands of $50,000; however, the fair market value of the parcel is only $40,000.
    a. Doug sells the parcel the next year for $60,000. Determine Doug's realized and recognized gain or loss on the sale.
    b. Doug sells the parcel the next year for $35,000. Determine Doug's realized and recognized gain or loss on the sale.
    c. Doug sells the parcel the next year for $45,000. Determine Doug's realized and recognized gain or loss on the sale.

38. Ms. Moneybags gives her daughter 1,000 shares of Xenon stock. Ms. Moneybags paid $10,000 for the stock, which is worth $100,000 at the time of the transfer.
    a. Assume the gift is made while Ms. Moneybags is still alive. What is her daughter's basis in the stock?
    b. Assume the stock is transferred upon Ms. Moneybags's death. What is her daughter's basis in the stock?

39. a. Ski resort owner Max Mogul contracts with Home Builders, Inc. to plan and complete a new lodge for his resort. The owners and principal employees of Home Builders, Inc. are architect Amy and contractor Ken. The lodge is completed on schedule. Max Mogul pays Home Builders, Inc. the agreed price for the work and gives both Amy and Ken non-transferable gift certificates for $1,000 ski outfits from the shop at his ski resort. As Mr. Mogul hands them the gift certificates, he tells them that the certificates are in appreciation for the excellent quality of their work. Are Amy and Ken taxed on the value of the gift certificates? Is it relevant to inquire whether Max Mogul deducted the cost of the certificates as a business expense?
    b. Assume instead that Amy and Ken are Max Mogul's employees. In addition to paying them their normal salaries for the work

that they did on the lodge, he gives them the gift certificates. Are Amy and Ken taxed on the value of the gift certificates?

40. New York City taxi driver Tom takes Fred to the airport. Fares are set by city ordinance and cannot be raised by agreement of the parties. However, taxi drivers are allowed to accept unsolicited tips. Fred pays the fare and gives Tom a $5 tip. Is Tom taxed on the tip?

41. Lawyer Leslie sends each of her clients a $40 bottle of wine each Christmas. Are the clients taxed on the value of the wine? Is the cost of the wine deductible to Leslie?

42. Under current law, donees exclude gifts received from income and donors cannot generally deduct the gifts they make. Assume that §102 is amended to provide that donees have to include gifts in income.

a. Why might such a change be justified?

b. What practical problems might be posed by a law that taxed all gifts as income?

EXPLANATIONS

36. No. Gifts and bequests are excluded from the recipient's gross income. §102(a).

37. a. This example illustrates the special §1015 basis rule and the calculation of gain or loss on the sale of property that was received as a gift by donee Doug. Here the $40,000 value of the property was less than donor Carol's $50,000 basis at the time of the transfer, so, for the purpose of determining *loss*, the donee inherits a basis equal to the value of the property at the time of the transfer, in this case $40,000. §1015(a). The property is sold for $60,000, so Doug recognizes no loss. For the purpose of determining *gain*, Doug inherits Carol's basis of $50,000. The property is sold for $60,000, so Doug realizes and recognizes $10,000 of gain. §§1001 and 1015(a).

b. Doug's $35,000 amount realized is less than Doug's $50,000 basis in the property, so there is no gain. Is there a loss? The $40,000 value of the property was less than its $50,000 basis at the time of transfer, so, for the purpose of determining loss, the donee has a basis equal to the value of the property at the time of transfer, in this case $40,000. The property is sold for $35,000, so the donee, Doug, realizes and recognizes a $5,000 loss ($40,000 basis less the $35,000 amount realized). §§1001 and 1015(a).

c. Doug's $45,000 amount realized is less than his $50,000 basis in the property, so there is no gain on the sale. The $40,000 value of the property was less than its $50,000 basis at the time of transfer, so, for the purpose of determining loss, the donee has a basis equal to the value of the property at the time of transfer, in this case $40,000. The property is sold for $45,000, so there is no loss on the sale.

38. a. The daughter will receive a carryover basis of $10,000 in the stock. §1015(a). (Note that since the value of the property exceeds the donor's basis in the property at the time of the transfer, we do not have to worry about the special rule under which a different basis is used for calculating gain and loss.)

b. The daughter's stock basis will be stepped up to the $100,000 value at the date of the decedent's death. §1014(a).

39. a. The issue presented here is whether the gift certificates are gifts for tax purposes. In Commissioner v. Duberstein, 363 U.S. 278 (1960), the Supreme Court defined a gift for income tax purposes as a transfer made out of "detached and disinterested generosity." The taxpayer in that case regularly provided a list of potential customers to a metal manufacturer. The manufacturer provided the taxpayer with a new Cadillac. The Cadillac was unsolicited and, apparently, unexpected. The Court held that the transfer was intended as compensation for past service or an inducement for future service and, therefore, was taxable to the transferee.

The transfer here is also business-related and might be regarded as compensation for past services. Amy and Ken's argument for gift characterization will be helped if there is no prospect of ongoing work for the ski resort. And while the treatment of the transaction by the payor is not dispositive, Amy and Ken's argument for gift characterization will also be helped if the gift certificates are not deducted by Max Mogul as a business expense.

If the certificates are not treated as a gift, the receipt of the certificates will constitute income to Ken and Amy. But how much income should the two recognize? The certificates are not transferable. It may be that neither Ken nor Amy skis or wants to purchase ski outfits. In somewhat analogous circumstances, courts have taxed recipients of nontransferable property on amounts substantially less than the retail value of the property. See, e.g., United States v. Drescher, 179 F.2d 863 (2d Cir. 1950), cert. denied, 340 U.S. 821 (1950); Turner v. Commissioner, 11 T.C.M. 604 (1952).

If the certificates were transferable, Ken and Amy would recognize income equal to the lesser of the retail price of the certificates or, if the certificates were sold, the amount realized upon sale. See McCoy v. Commissioner, 38 T.C. 841 (1962), acq. 1963-2 C.B. 5 (where a game show contestant won a car and immediately sold it to a dealer at wholesale, the contestant was required to include in income the wholesale, not retail, value of the car). The obvious difficulty in determining how much income is recognized upon the receipt of the certificates might well lead a court to give Amy and Ken the benefit of the doubt and treat the receipt of the certificates as a gift.

   b. Since Amy and Ken are Max Mogul's employees, the transfers cannot be excluded as gifts. §102(c). (However, Amy and Ken might be able to exclude all or a part of the value of the gift certificates under §132 or §74.)

40. Tom might argue that the tip constitutes a nontaxable gift under the *Duberstein* standard because it is made out of Fred's detached and disinterested generosity. Tom would point out that no tip is required and that Fred has nothing to "gain" by the tip since it is unlikely that Fred will ever again choose Tom's taxi.

Not surprisingly, the government has always regarded tips as taxable compensation. Reg. §1.61-2(a)(1). The government's position has been upheld by the courts. Courts have held that there is an "element of compulsion" in tipping and that tips are intended as recompense for past services. See Killoran v. Commissioner, 709 F.2d 31 (9th Cir. 1983); Roberts v. Commissioner, 176 F.2d 221 (9th Cir. 1949) (both cases holding that taxi drivers must include tips in gross income). The fact that tips are regarded as compensation by the recipient, though irrelevant under the *Duberstein* test (which looks to the state of mind of the donor), forms an implicit basis for taxation in many of the cases. See, e.g., Olk v. United States, 536 F.2d 876 (9th Cir. 1976), cert. denied, 429 U.S. 920 (1976).

41. Section 274(b)(1) allows Leslie a business deduction for the first $25 per year of untaxed gifts made to each client. How does one determine the scope of the §274(b)(1) business gift exception? In practice, the exception appears to apply only to small gifts given

to customers in an effort to bolster goodwill. Leslie's purchase appears to fit within the scope of the §274(b) business gift exception; the first $25 of the $40 cost of each bottle of wine would be deductible and the customers would not be taxed on the full value of the wine.

42. a. The justification for including the value of gifts in income is that recipients are enriched by gifts. We tax individuals on other forms of enrichment, such as salary or investment return, so why not levy a tax on enrichment realized through gifts? Indeed, it seems odd to tax increases in wealth that require effort (such as wages) but to exclude an increase in wealth that for the most part is "unearned" and determined largely by relationship to those who are financially successful.

   If we taxed recipients on the value of gifts, would we have to give donors a deduction? If so, the result would be a net loss for the Treasury since donors are generally in higher tax brackets than recipients. Henry Simons, the economist who, along with Robert Haig, is credited with the Haig-Simons definition of income, didn't think taxing the donee required giving the donor a deduction. Simons argued that for donors giving was a form of consumption and should be no more deductible than the cost of an expensive meal.

   b. Most gifts are between family members, and a law that taxed donees on all gifts would be impossible to administer. Would we tax a child on the value of food and lodging provided by his parents? A teenager on her allowance? A 20-year-old on the value of a used car received as a gift? Would the exchange of Christmas presents generate tax liability all around?

   We could get around some of these problems, at least, by requiring taxation only on gifts above a certain threshold amount. We could adopt, for example, a system similar to that used for estate and gift tax purposes and treat gifts as a taxable event only to the extent that the value of the gifts exceeded a certain floor. (The federal estate and gift tax system, which taxes transfers of property, is separate from the federal income tax. The estate and gift tax system applies to donors. Under that transfer tax system, a donor incurs no liability on the first $10,000 transferred each year to each donee. §2503(b).)

   On a more theoretical level, a system that treated the transfer of funds between family members as a taxable event seems somewhat odd, perhaps because in many ways we regard the family as a single unit for tax purposes.

3. *Scholarships, Prizes, and Awards*

Reading: §§74, 117

Until 1954 courts cited the forerunner of §102 for the proposition that scholarships and some prizes and awards could be excluded from income. Since 1954 the Code has contained specific provisions governing the tax treatment of these items. In 1986 the exclusions for these items were substantially curtailed. Section 117 now excludes only "qualified scholarships" received by "degree candidates." A student is a *degree candidate* if she is a primary, secondary, undergraduate, or graduate student. Prop. Reg. §1.117-6(c)(4). A scholarship is *qualified* to the extent that it covers the student's tuition and required fees, books, and supplies. §117(b). Students must include in income scholarships that cover other expenses such as room and board. The term *scholarship* includes both cash scholarships and tuition reductions (for example, tuition reductions for in-state students at state universities). Prop. Reg. §1.117-6(c)(3)(i).

The exclusion for qualified scholarships does not apply to the extent that the scholarship is compensation for services, including teaching and research. §117(c). Does that exception to the exclusion apply to athletic scholarships? The answer may depend on the terms of the scholarship. If continued participation in the sport is required as a condition of retaining the scholarship, §117(c) would appear to apply. On the other hand, if the scholarship is not conditioned on the student continuing to play the sport, §117(c) would not apply. On a more practical level, the Service has, to date, not taken the position that athletic scholarships are within the §117(c) exception to the exclusion for qualified scholarships.

Section 74(a) provides that gross income includes amounts received as prizes or awards. There are limited exceptions, in §§74(b) and (c), for prizes transferred directly to charities and for certain employee achievement awards.

EXAMPLES

43. Donna attends Private University. During the year, Donna spends (i) $10,000 on tuition, (ii) $1,000 on books and supplies, and

(iii) $8,000 on room and board. Donna, a National Merit Scholar, receives a $19,000 scholarship designed to cover all of the above expenses. What portion, if any, of the scholarship is taxable to Donna?

44. Eastern Law School uses second- and third-year law students as teaching assistants in its first-year legal writing program. Many of the students hired as teaching assistants already are receiving scholarships from the Law School for part of their tuition. The Law School is considering giving all students selected as teaching assistants full tuition scholarships. Student teaching assistants who had previously received partial tuition scholarships would instead receive a full tuition scholarship. Discuss the tax consequences of this plan.

EXPLANATIONS

43. Section 117 excludes from gross income scholarships covering tuition and required fees, books, supplies, and equipment at non-profit schools. Thus, Donna excludes from gross income the portion of the scholarship that she spent on tuition and required books and supplies, $11,000. However, Donna must include in gross income the portion of the scholarship that she spent on room and board, $8,000.

44. As noted in the explanation for example 43 above, students exclude from gross income tuition scholarships. However, the exclusion does not apply to scholarships conditioned upon the performance of teaching, research, or other services, which students must include in gross income. §117(c). If the school replaces the old partial scholarships with full tuition teaching stipend scholarships, the students will have to pay more tax than they would have to pay if the school instead gives them (i) partial scholarships that are not conditioned on performing services and (ii) taxable teaching stipend scholarships only to cover the tuition not covered by the nontaxable partial scholarship.

4. Transfer Payments

Federal tax payments reduce an individual's wealth but such payments are not deductible, of course, in determining federal tax liability (think about it). Government expenditures for items that benefit the public, on the other hand, may increase an individual's wealth. Is an individual's increased wealth due to such expenditures taxable? Generally speaking, the answer is no. Individuals are not taxed on the indirect increase in wealth due to government-supplied highways, education, and the like. (But if such expenditures increase the value of a taxpayer's assets, then the individual will be taxed on the increase when the assets are sold.)

The tax treatment of direct transfers from government is more complicated and varies from program to program. For example, welfare payments are nontaxable. Rev. Rul. 76-144. On the other hand, unemployment insurance is fully taxable. §85. Why are these transfers treated differently? The legislative history of §85 and other Congressional and Treasury reports draw a distinction between (i) payments that provide subsistence benefits to families living in poverty and (ii) payments that are the equivalent of wages: The former are generally excluded from gross income, but the latter are generally included in gross income.

The tax treatment of social security payments is annoyingly complex. Taxpayers with incomes of $25,000 or less ($32,000 for married taxpayers filing joint returns) do not have to include any of their social security benefits in gross income. Taxpayers with incomes over $25,000 ($32,000 for joint returns), but not over $34,000 ($44,000 for joint returns), include 50 percent of their social security benefits in gross income. Taxpayers with incomes of $34,000 or more ($44,000 for joint returns) include 85 percent of their social security benefits in gross income. Phase-ins of the 50 percent and 85 percent inclusion percentages (which are too byzantine to warrant a detailed explanation here) prevent a sudden increase in tax liability when the threshold amounts are reached. (The rationale for the 85 percent inclusion percentage is that only around 15 percent of the benefits payable to social security recipients are attributable to nondeductible employee contributions to social security.)

EXAMPLES

45. Jill, a single taxpayer, is a retired bank executive with an adjusted gross income of $80,000 per year from investments. She also receives $10,000 per year in social security payments. What portion, if any, of the social security payments is subject to tax?

46. Shannon receives state and federal welfare payments of $6,000. Shannon's adjusted gross income for the year is $10,000. What portion, if any, of the welfare payments are subject to tax?

EXPLANATIONS

45. Jill is well above the $34,000 adjusted base amount for an individual return, so she has to include in gross income $8,500 (85 percent) of the $10,000 social security benefits she receives. §86(a)(2) and (c).

46. Shannon will not have to include any of the $10,000 welfare payments in gross income. Rev. Rul. 76-144.

E. Selected Recovery of Capital Issues: Partial Sales, Annuities, Insurance Policies, Life Estates, and Remainder Interests

A person who buys property for $100 and sells the same property for $120 is taxed on a profit of $20 — the remaining $100 of sales proceeds is excluded from taxable income as recovery of the taxpayer's invested capital. The recovery of capital rule that applies to the above situation is intuitively obvious. In other cases, however, the recovery of capital rules can be quite complex. Here we cover four recovery of capital rules — partial sales, annuities, insurance policies, and life interests. Other recovery of capital rules are covered elsewhere in this book. (For example, the rules governing depreciation are discussed in Chapter 5, and the installment sale rules are discussed in Chapter 3.)

1. Partial Sales

Reading: §§61, 1001; Reg. §1.61-6

The term *partial sale* is defined, for our purposes, as a sale of a portion of property currently held by a taxpayer. For example, a person may purchase 10 acres of land for $100,000 and sell one of those acres the next year for $20,000. The applicable recovery of capital rule requires the taxpayer to allocate basis to the acre sold, based on the relative value of the sold and unsold portions of the property at the time of purchase. Thus, if all acres were equally valuable at the time of purchase, each acre would receive one-tenth of the total basis, or $10,000. If, at the time of purchase, the acre sold was worth 20 percent of the amount paid for the property, it would receive a basis of 20 percent of the aggregate basis, or $20,000. For those who like formulas, the rule can be expressed as follows:

$$\text{The basis of the parcel sold} = \text{the total basis of all of the parcels} \times \frac{\text{the value of the parcel sold}}{\text{the total value of all of the parcels}}$$

(Note that this simplified formula assumes that there are no upward adjustments to basis for improvements to the property or downward adjustments to basis for depreciation taken with respect to the property. If there were such adjustments, they would have to be taken into account.)

In certain rare circumstances, taxpayers have been allowed to ignore the allocation rule stated above and treat the entire proceeds of a partial sale as tax-free recovery of capital. For example, in Inaja Land Co. v. Commissioner, 9 T.C. 727 (1947), acq. 1948-1 C.B. 2, the taxpayer owned riverfront property that was damaged by the actions of an upstream user. The taxpayer threatened legal action and ultimately reached settlement with the tortfeasor. Under that settlement the taxpayer received approximately $50,000 and, in exchange, gave the upstream user certain rights with respect to the land. The Tax Court allowed the taxpayer to treat the proceeds from the sale of those rights as tax-free recovery of capital. In effect, the taxpayer was allowed to allocate basis first to the rights sold up to the sales proceeds. In so ruling, the Tax Court was no doubt influenced by two facts: First, basis allocation in the case would have been difficult, and, second, the sale was involuntary.

EXAMPLES

47. Sally purchases four acres of land for $40,000. She later sells the north acre for $30,000. How much gain or loss does Sally realize on the sale of the land?

48. David pays $250,000 for a 10-acre parcel of land. A few years later, the government condemns a tiny strip of David's parcel upon which it places power lines. The government agrees that it will remove the power lines when they are replaced by underground power lines. It is unclear when the power lines will be removed from his property. David receives $20,000 of compensation for the condemned strip of property. Discuss the proper tax treatment of the proceeds.

EXPLANATIONS

47. Reg. §1.61-6(a) requires Sally to allocate her $40,000 purchase price among the four acres based on the relative value of each acre. If the acres were equally valuable, each acre would receive a $10,000 basis and Sally's gain would be $20,000. If the north acre were as valuable as the other three acres combined, the north acre would receive a $20,000 basis and Sally's gain would be $10,000. In other words, Sally's gain or loss would depend upon the extent to which her $40,000 basis was allocable to the land that was sold. Sally cannot allocate the entire $40,000 basis to the portion of the land sold because these facts are distinguishable from the facts of Inaja Land Co. v. Commissioner, 9 T.C. 727 (1947), acq. 1948-1 C.B. 2 (where allocation of the basis according to the value of the sold and unsold interests was particularly problematic).

48. As noted in the explanation for example 47 above, the basis of property sold in a partial sale generally is determined by allocating some portion of the basis to the portion of property sold. That allocation is based on the value of the land at the time of purchase. If, for example, at the time of purchase, the parcel sold represented one-fiftieth of the total value of the property, then one-fiftieth of the total basis of the land will be allocated to the parcel sold. However, where the parcel is involuntarily "sold" through government action, and the parcel sold is not susceptible to easy valuation, at least one court has treated the entire sale proceeds as tax-free recovery of basis. See Inaja Land Co. v. Commissioner, 9 T.C. 727 (1947), acq. 1948-1 C.B. 2.

2. Annuities

Reading: §72

An *annuity* is a contract that provides for a series of payments in return for a fixed sum. Annuities are often purchased to ensure sufficient funds for a financially stable retirement. For example, an individual may pay an insurance company (the usual purveyor of annuities) $100,000 in return for annual payments of $10,000, ending upon the death of the purchaser/annuitant. Assume that, at the time of purchase, the annuitant is expected to live 15 years and that the payments begin immediately after purchase, so that the annuitant is expected to receive $150,000. The difference between the cost and the expected return represents interest. The insurance company will have the use of the $100,000 for many years. It will earn interest on that sum, and some or all of that interest will be passed on to the annuitant in the form of annual payments. Assume also that the annuitant is still alive at the end of the first year, at which time she receives the $10,000. How should that sum be taxed?

There are several possible basis recovery methods. One approach, the *basis first* method, would treat each payment as a tax-free recovery of capital until the entire $100,000 investment in the annuity is recovered. (You will recognize this method as the allocation method used in Inaja Land Co. v. Commissioner, 9 T.C. 727 (1947), discussed in the unit on partial sales.) The rationale for the basis-first rule would be that the annuitant may die before year 10 and therefore never show a profit on the contract. Under this approach, the first $10,000 payment would be tax-free. After the annuitant recovered her $100,000 investment in the annuity, all remaining payments would be fully taxed.

Another approach, the *income first* method, would treat all payments as income to the extent of any income set aside for the policyholder in the insurance company's policyholder reserves. The insurance-company will invest the annuitant's $100,000 and earn a return on it. Assume that the insurance company loans the $100,000 to a borrower who will pay the insurance company 15 $10,000 payments. The investment will fund the 15 $10,000 annuity payments to be made by the insurance company to the annuitant. Each of the 15 level $10,000 payments has two components: first, interest on the outstanding balance of the loan, and, second, a partial payment of the principal on the loan. (In other words, the principal would be "amortized," so that the 15 $10,000 payments would repay the $100,000 of principal on the loan, as well as interest on the loan.) Most of the early $10,000 payments would be interest, but over time the interest component of the $10,000 payment would decrease and the principal repayment component would increase. Under this approach, the interest would start out high, then decrease over time, and the principal repayment would start out low and increase over time. In other words, in the annuity context, most of the early payments to the annuitant would be income and most of the later payments to the annuitant would be received tax-free as basis recovery.

A third approach, the *pro rata* method, would allocate a pro rata portion of the taxpayer's $100,000 investment to each of the 15 payments. Under this approach, the income and basis-recovery portions of each $10,000 payment would be constant.

The basis-first method would be the most favorable to an annuitant because it provides the maximum possible deferral of the income from the annuity. The income-first approach would be the least favorable to an annuitant because it defers basis recovery and accelerates the income from the annuity. The pro rata approach is less favorable than the basis-first approach but more favorable than the income-first approach.

The Code adopts the pro rata method for annuities. Section 72(a) provides that gross income includes annuity payments. However, §72(b) provides that the taxpayer may exclude from each annuity payment the product of the payment multiplied by the *exclusion ratio*, which, in turn, equals the cost of the annuity contract divided by the expected return on the annuity contract. In our example, the exclusion ratio would be 2/3 ($100,000 cost/$150,000 expected return). Two-thirds of each $10,000 payment, or $6,666.67, which is treated as recovery of capital, is excluded under §72(b). The remaining one-third of each payment, $3,333.33, which is treated as gain, is included under §72(a).

If the taxpayer lives for exactly her life expectancy of 15 years, she will recover tax-free $6,666.67 in each of the 15 years, for a total recovery of $100,000 — which is exactly what she invested in the contract. If the taxpayer outlives her life expectancy, all of each subsequent annuity payment must be included in income. If the taxpayer dies "early," her estate will be able to deduct the difference between the aggregate amount excluded from income under §72(b) and the cost of the contract. Put differently, the estate will be able to deduct her "unrecovered" basis.

Individuals often purchase annuities that do not provide for any payments for many years. For example, payments may begin at retirement. The tax treatment of such "deferred annuities" is the same as outlined above: An exclusion ratio is determined by dividing the cost of the contract by the expected return; a portion of each payment, equal to the exclusion ratio multiplied by the payment, is treated as recovery of capital.

The tax treatment of deferred annuities is quite favorable. If an annuitant lives to life expectancy, the annuity payments will exceed the annuity cost. The difference represents interest. The longer the period of deferral, the greater the interest return on the taxpayer's annuity investment. The beneficiary of a deferred annuity pays no tax on this interest until the receipt of the annuity payments. In contrast, an individual who decides to save for retirement by earning interest on amounts invested in a savings account or other interestbearing investment must pay an annual tax on any interest earned (even if the taxpayer does not withdraw the interest).

The favorable treatment of deferred annuities has given rise to several tax avoidance schemes. For example, at one time, individuals could use annuities to build up interest income tax-free and then borrow the increase in value in the policy. Typically, the loan was made by the annuity company and secured by the annuity. Under the general rules applicable to loans, no tax would be paid on receipt of the loan proceeds. (Loans are discussed in more detail later in this chapter.) This tax avoidance scheme is no longer available. Under current law, amounts borrowed on a loan secured by an annuity policy are treated as taxable income to the extent that (due to the build-up of interest) the value of the policy has risen as the payout date approaches. §72(e). In addition, unless the recipient is age $59\frac{1}{2}$ or older, a 10 percent tax penalty applies to such amounts. §72(q). Thus, as a practical matter, deferred annuities are desirable only for those individuals who are willing to "lock up" their money until retirement.

EXAMPLES

49. Barbara, who is 88 years old, pays $4,000 for an annuity that, should Barbara live to her five-year life expectancy, will pay her $5,000 ($1,000 per year for five years). Assume this sum reflects a return on Barbara's investment of 8 percent. (The actual return is a bit less — 7.93 percent.) How much of the first $1,000 payment does Barbara include in income?

50. Tom agrees to loan Peter $4,000 for five years. The loan will be amortized with five $1,000 payments. (In other words, a portion of each payment constitutes repayment of part of the principal so that, after five years, the principal has been fully repaid. Each payment also includes interest on the principal still outstanding.) Assume that the loan bears interest at 8 percent. (The actual interest rate is slightly lower — 7.93 percent.) How much of the first $1,000 payment does Tom include in income?

51. Compare the tax treatment of the annuity and the loan in examples 49 and 50. Which is more favorable to the annuitant/lender?

52. Dan paid $4,000 for an annuity that pays $1,000 per year for life. At the time of the purchase, Dan has a life expectancy of five years. Dan actually lives to collect on the annuity for 10 years. How much of the $1,000 payment in year six is treated as recovery of capital?

53. In year one, Steven, who is 70 years old and has a life expectancy of 10 years, purchases a deferred annuity for $2,000. Under the annuity contract, Steven receives nothing during years one through five, but will be paid $1,000 a year, beginning in year six, until he dies.

    a. Steven receives five $1,000 payments on the annuity, then dies, as expected, at age 80. How much of the first payment constitutes income to Steven?

    b. Steven dies at age 78 and therefore receives only three $1,000 payments. Discuss the tax treatment of the payments.

54. Tracy, who is 45 years old, is interested in assuring herself of retirement income. Stan is an agent for a company that sells deferred annuities. Stan tells Tracy that for $100,000 his company will provide her with an annuity contract that pays $50,000 a year for life, beginning at age 65. Tracy is expected to live until age 83, so that if she lives to life expectancy, she will receive total payments of $900,000. Stan informs her that that number represents an annual return of 8 percent. "Big deal," replies Tracy. "I can earn 8 percent on long-term government bonds; I can probably average about that on deposits with my local bank. Why should I buy the deferred annuity?" What is the best answer to Tracy's question?

55. At age 39, rock star Roger records a hit record that generates large royalties and leads to a lucrative concert schedule. A few months shy of his 40th birthday, Roger pays $100,000 for a deferred annuity that will pay him (i) nothing for slightly over 20 years, and (ii) beginning when Roger is 60 years old, $50,000 a year for the rest of his life. Roger is expected to live until age 78, so the annuity is expected to provide Roger with 18 annual payments of $50,000 each, for a total return of $900,000. The expected return of $900,000 represents an 8 percent annual before-tax return on Roger's initial $100,000 investment. Under §72(b)(1), Roger's exclusion ratio will be $100,000/$900,000, or 1/9 (11.11 percent). Thus, he will exclude $5,556 (rounding a little) of each $50,000 payment and include the rest of each payment. (Said another way, he will recover 1/18th of his $100,000 investment, or $5,556, from each of the 18 expected $50,000 payments.) Suppose, however, that when Roger is 58 years old, the annuity company loans him $50,000. Assume that the loan is nonrecourse and is secured

only by Roger's right to future payments on the annuity. What is the tax treatment of the loan proceeds?

EXPLANATIONS

49. Section 72 allows Barbara to recover a percentage of each payment equal to her exclusion ratio as tax-free recovery of capital. A taxpayer's exclusion ratio is defined as the total cost of the contract divided by the expected return. Here the cost of the contract is $4,000 and the expected return is $5,000, so Barbara's exclusion ratio is $4,000/$5,000 or 80 percent. Thus, 80 percent of each $1,000 payment, or $800, will be treated as recovery of capital. §72(b). Only the remaining $200 of each of those installments will be treated as income. §72(a). Note that, for an annuity with level payments, the effect of §72 will be to allow the taxpayer to recover her cost in equal increments over the expected number of payments.

50. $320. This is an example of a common self-amortizing level payment loan — the kind of loan you may enter into when you buy a car or home. Each $1,000 payment has two components: (i) interest on the outstanding balance and (ii) repayment of part of the loan principal. Over time the portion of the payment that represents interest will decrease and the portion of the payment that represents principal repayment will increase. Here, the first year's interest would be $320 (8 percent of $4,000). The last year's interest would be only $75. (The actual return is 7.93 percent. However, we have assumed that the return is 8 percent, to simplify the explanation, so an adjustment to correct the numbers is required in the last year.)

Beginning balance, year one	$4,000
Interest at 8 percent	320
Reduction of principal/Recovery of capital	680
Beginning balance, year two	3,320 (4,000 − 680)
Interest at 8 percent	266
Reduction of principal/Recovery of capital	734
Beginning balance, year three	2,586 (3,320 − 734)
Interest at 8 percent	207
Reduction of principal/Recovery of capital	793

Beginning balance, year four	$1,793 (2,586 − 793)
Interest at 8 percent	143
Reduction of principal/Recovery of capital	857
Beginning balance, year five	936 (1,793 − 857)
Interest at 8 percent	75
Reduction of principal/Recovery of capital	936 ($925 + $11 adjustment required by 8 percent interest assumption)

51. The annuity is more favorable to the annuitant/lender. Income from an annuity is determined as a constant portion of each payment. Under a level-payment loan, early payments contain a relatively large portion of interest; later payments contain relatively little interest. In example 49 above, the first $1,000 annuity payment received by Barbara is characterized as $800 of capital recovery and $200 of income, whereas in example 50 above, the first $1,000 loan payment received by Tom is characterized as $680 of capital recovery and $320 of income. Taxpayers, of course, generally prefer to defer recognition of income as long as possible, so they would consider the annuity tax treatment to be more favorable than the loan tax treatment.

52. None of the payment in year six is treated as recovery of capital. The cost of the annuity is $4,000 and the annuity is expected to return five payments of $1,000 for a total of $5,000. Under §72, the $4,000 cost is recovered on a pro rata basis during the expected payout period. Here, the expected payout period is five years, so one-fifth of the capital, or $800, is treated as recovery of capital during the first five payments. (The exclusion ratio is 80 percent, which represents the $4,000 investment in the contract divided by the $5,000 expected return. §72(b)(1).) After the fifth payment, all of the subsequent payments are income because the taxpayer has already recovered his $4,000 investment in the annuity. §72(b)(2). Here, Dan must include in income the entire $1,000 year six payment. (If the annuitant dies before his capital is recovered, the amount of unrecovered capital may be claimed as a loss. §72(b)(3).)

53. a. An annuity that provides the beneficiary with no payments
       for a period of time following purchase is called a deferred
       annuity. A deferred annuity is taxed in the same manner as
       any other annuity: Cost is recovered pro rata from each ex-
       pected payment; the portion of each payment that is not allo-
       cated to cost is income. Here, the cost of the annuity is
       $2,000 and there are five expected payments. Thus, one-fifth
       of the cost, or $400, is recovered tax-free in each payment.
       (The exclusion ratio is 40 percent, which represents the
       $2,000 investment in the contract divided by the $5,000 ex-
       pected return. §72(b)(1).) Each payment consists of $400 of
       capital recovery ($1,000 payment multiplied by the 40 per-
       cent exclusion ratio) and $600 of income.

    b. The first three payments are treated under the rule described
       immediately above. There are five expected payments, so one-
       fifth of the total cost is recovered from each payment. At the
       end of the third payment, Steven will have recovered $1,200
       of his total $2,000 cost. If Steven had lived to life expectancy,
       he would have recovered the remaining $800 as part of the
       fourth and fifth $1,000 payments. Steven does not live to life
       expectancy, so his estate will deduct the $800 of unrecovered
       basis on his final tax return. §72(b)(3). Ultimately, then, net
       income of $1,000 is recognized on Steven's investment:
       $1,800 of income ($600 per year for three years) less a deduc-
       tion of $800 when Steven dies. This is as it should be since
       the difference between the amount Steven received from the
       annuity ($3,000) and the amount Steven paid for the invest-
       ment ($2,000) is $1,000.

54. The tax treatment of the deferred annuity will be much more
    favorable than the tax treatment of the other investments Tracy is
    considering. Suppose that Tracy can earn 8 percent simply by
    leaving her money in a savings account and that she lives to life
    expectancy. Suppose, further, that if Tracy leaves her money in a
    savings account, she will want to withdraw $50,000 per year,
    starting at age 65. (In other words, assume that she withdraws
    the same amounts that the annuity contract would have paid, at
    the same times that the annuity contract would have paid it.) In
    that case, both the savings account and the deferred annuity will
    offer identical before-tax returns, and the total income recognized
    on each investment will be $800,000.

If Tracy invests in the savings account, she will be taxed on the growth in the account. If, in the year in which she deposits her $100,000 into the savings account, she earns $8,000 of interest, she will have to include that interest in income. If Tracy invests in the deferred annuity, the value of her investment will also increase by $8,000 during the first year of the investment. However, Tracy will not have to include any income (or pay any tax) on that increase until payments begin. And even after payments begin, the annuity recovery of capital rules will defer recognition of income. Thus, the annuity provides Tracy with a substantial deferral of the tax liability on her investment. There may be nontax reasons, however, why Tracy does not want to tie up her money in a deferred annuity.

55. This example is most easily understood if the deferred annuity is seen as a type of savings account: an investment of $100,000 that earns 8 percent a year. Obviously, the value of the investment increases each year; after 20 years, the value of the account is sufficient to pay out $50,000 a year for 18 years. As noted in example 54, the deferred annuity is taxed more favorably than a savings account because the annual increase in value of the annuity is not taxed until the proceeds are withdrawn.

At one time, taxpayers could combine the favorable treatment of a deferred annuity with the liquidity of a savings account by borrowing against the annuity. So long as the amount borrowed did not exceed the investment in the annuity, the loan proceeds were tax-free. Today, the tax treatment of such loans is far less favorable. First, such loans are taxable to the extent of the increase in the value of the policy. Thus, if the $100,000 invested by Roger in the contract has increased by more than $50,000 in the intervening 20 years, the entire loan will be treated as taxable income. §72(e). (In this case, if the annuity provides a return of 8 percent per year, the value of the contract after 20 years will be almost $400,000, so the entire loan will be treated as taxable income.) In addition, there is a special 10 percent penalty on "premature distributions" from annuity contracts. §72(q). Generally speaking, a premature distribution is any non-periodic payment made to a recipient who is not at least age $59\frac{1}{2}$. So Roger will pay tax on the $50,000 and will also pay a penalty tax of $5,000. The unfavorable treatment of such loans is designed to ensure that annuities are used for retirement security rather than simply as a tax-favored means of investment.

3. Life Insurance

Reading: §101

Life insurance policies may be divided into two broad categories: term and whole life. As the name implies, *term insurance* provides protection for a specific term, almost always a single year. If the insured dies within the year, the policy pays a specified amount to the designated beneficiary. If the insured does not die during the year, the insurer retains the premium, or policy cost. Quite obviously, then, a term insurance policy represents a gamble, which is "won" by the purchaser only if the insured dies. The cost of the gamble depends on the age and health of the insured. A 25-year-old male, for example, may be able to purchase $250,000 of term insurance for only a few hundred dollars a year. The same policy purchased by a 65-year-old male will cost many times more.

One might expect that the purchase of an insurance policy would be treated like an equally risky investment in the stock market: In the event of death, a tax would be levied (presumably on the estate of the insured-purchaser) on the difference between the cost of the policy and the amount paid out. If the insured does not die, a loss would be allowed equal to the cost of the policy. In fact, an individual who purchases a policy on her own life and lives out the term of the policy is not allowed to deduct the cost of the policy as a loss. On the other hand, no tax is levied on the "profit" from a policy. Instead, under §101, the beneficiary receives the insurance proceeds tax-free.

A *whole life insurance* policy provides protection for the entire life of the insured. Generally, a whole life policy requires annual premiums. However, the amount of the annual premium in a whole life policy does not increase with the age of the insured. Thus, a 25-year-old might purchase a policy that provides $250,000 of coverage in return for an annual premium of $2,000 a year.

The purchase of a whole life insurance policy also represents a gamble of sorts. If the 25-year-old who purchases the policy described above dies after a single year, the policy will represent a profitable gamble. The purchase of a whole life policy represents a form of savings as well. The amounts paid to beneficiaries under a whole life policy always exceed the expected premiums received by the insurance company. That is because, if the insured lives to life expectancy, the insurance company will be able to invest the premiums paid in early years and earn interest from the investment.

Assume, in the example above, that the 25-year-old insured lives to be 80. The insurance company will keep the first $2,000 premium paid by the 25-year-old for 55 years. At an interest rate of 5 percent, the insurance company will be able to earn over $27,000 of income on that first $2,000 premium alone. Some portion of the income is returned to the beneficiary in the form of payments that exceed the premiums paid. In cases in which the insured lives exactly to life expectancy, there is no mortality gain or loss, so the excess of the amounts paid to beneficiaries over the premiums paid by the insured represents interest income.

Even though its savings component distinguishes a whole life policy from a term policy, the proceeds of a whole life policy qualify for the same exclusion under §101 as the proceeds of a term policy. This makes a whole life policy a tax-favored form of investment. An individual who places $2,000 per year in a savings account and gives that sum, together with interest, to her children upon her death will pay tax on the annual interest income. The same individual who purchases a whole life policy and lives to life expectancy earns, in effect, the same interest, but is not taxed.

EXAMPLES

56. Assume you invest $100 in a one-year term life insurance policy. If you die within the year, how will the proceeds be taxed to your beneficiaries? If the policy does not pay off (because you do not die), can you take a loss on the $100 that you invested in the policy?

57. On what grounds might one criticize the present treatment of whole life insurance? Can you think of any way you might defend the current treatment?

EXPLANATIONS

56. If you die, the proceeds will be tax-free to your beneficiaries under §101. You are not permitted to deduct the cost of the policy if you live.

57. Whole life insurance is, as the name implies, insurance that provides benefits regardless of when the insured dies — the coverage

extends over the "whole life" of the insured. If the insured lives to life expectancy, the return on a whole life policy is considerably greater than its cost. For example, a 30-year-old might pay a single premium of $20,000 for a whole life policy that pays her beneficiaries $300,000 upon her death. The $300,000 represents about a 6 percent return on the original investment, a return that is perhaps most appropriately characterized as interest. In effect, the insurance company is borrowing money and repaying the loan, plus interest, at the time of the death of the insured. Neither the insured nor the insurance company is taxed on this interest as it accrues, and the proceeds are tax-free to the beneficiaries. In contrast, had the insured put $20,000 in the bank, allowed the interest to accumulate, and bequeathed the account to her beneficiary upon her death, she would have been subject to tax on the annual interest as it was earned. Thus, as compared to the treatment of other investments, the annual returns on which are taxable, the purchase of a whole life insurance policy is tax-favored. One might argue that life insurance should not be tax-favored, relative to other forms of savings.

One could defend the present treatment on the grounds that we ought to encourage wage earners to provide for dependents in the event of (timely or untimely) death. One might also argue that the treatment of life insurance is no more tax-favored than investments that appreciate in value but do not return annual interest or dividends and are given at death to one's beneficiaries. Such investments benefit from the step-up in basis at death rule of §1014 and can be sold by the beneficiary tax-free. To illustrate the similar tax treatment of life insurance and this latter sort of investment, imagine that, instead of purchasing a whole life insurance policy for $20,000, the taxpayer described above pays $20,000 for rare coins. If the rare coins appreciate by 6 percent per year, their value at the time of the taxpayer's death (assuming she lives to life expectancy) will be about $300,000 (the same amount as the death benefit of the insurance policy). Under §1014, the property will have a fair market value basis in the hands of the taxpayer's beneficiaries and can be sold immediately after acquisition without recognizing any taxable gain. This produces precisely the same tax result as the purchase of the whole life insurance policy. Another possible justification for the favorable tax treatment of life insurance is that the life insurance companies make long-term investments with the premiums they are paid and that such investments provided a needed source of capital.

4. *Gambling Winnings and Losses*

Reading: §165(d)

A person who makes a risky investment in, say, land, is taxed on any gain and — subject to some restrictions discussed at a later point in this book — is allowed to deduct any loss. Someone who makes a risky investment in life insurance, on the other hand, is not taxed on gain and cannot deduct loss. What about someone who makes a risky investment on a horse race? Losses from wagering transactions are deductible only to the extent of the gains from such transactions. §165(d). Thus, net gambling winnings are taxed, but net gambling losses are nondeductible. The reason for this is that gambling losses are conceptualized as consumption, that is, as the price paid for the enjoyment of gambling.

5. *Life Estates and Remainder Interests*

Reading: §102

Recovery of capital issues, no matter how complicated, usually involve only a single taxpayer. Occasionally, however, a question arises as to the allocation of capital and income between two (or more) persons. For example, suppose that Mother leaves $1 million in her will, with the interest earned on the $1 million to go to Daughter during Daughter's life, and the $1 million to go to Granddaughter upon Daughter's death. In the language of bequests, Daughter is said to have a life interest; Granddaughter is said to have a remainder interest.

Assume that, at the time of Mother's death, Daughter's life expectancy is 20 years and the prevailing interest rate is 8 percent. The total amount expected to be paid out under the will is then $2.6 million — Daughter will receive $80,000 a year ($1 million times 8 percent) for 20 years, or $1.6 million, and Granddaughter will receive $1 million. The basis of the bequest is $1 million and the income earned on the bequest is $1.6 million. Under §102(b), the entire basis goes to the person who is granted the remainder interest—in this example Granddaughter. Daughter has no basis in her annual payout, so she pays tax on the entire $80,000 a year.

The rule that all of the basis goes to the remainder interest is subject to one exception. If both the life and remainder interest are sold at the same time, then for purposes of determining gain on the sale, each interest receives a basis equal to its fair market value at the time of the bequest.

The treatment of interests that are split over time may seem intuitively obvious. After all, Daughter is simply getting the interest income on the original bequest—the $1 million is going to Granddaughter. Suppose, though, that Mother had left two separate bequests, one to Daughter in the form of an annuity that paid out $80,000 a year until Daughter's death, and one to Granddaughter in the form of an interest bearing account that was calculated to yield $1 million in principal and interest at the time of Daughter's death.

Under the interest and life expectancy assumptions stated above, the value of the annuity would be about $800,000; the value of the amount left to Granddaughter would be about $200,000. Had the bequests taken this explicitly separate form, Daughter would receive a separate basis in her annuity of $800,000 under the date-of-death basis rule of §1014. The difference between this basis and the $1.6 million received would be taxed as gain. Granddaughter, on the other hand, would receive a basis in her remainder interest equal to its value upon receipt of $200,000. The difference between the $200,000 and the $1 million in the account upon Daughter's death (assuming the sum were left to accumulate interest until Daughter's death) would be taxable as interest income.

To summarize: In situations where a bequest is split into life and remainder interests, the entire basis is allocated to the remainder interest and all of the income from the life interest is taxable. Basis is allocated between the two interests in accordance with their respective fair market values in only one situation: where both the remainder and life interest are sold concurrently.

EXAMPLES

58. Dr. Dean leaves $5 million in trust for her husband and her niece. The husband receives all of the income from the trust during his lifetime; thereafter, the property is distributed to the niece. At the time of the gift, the $5 million is expected to earn $2 million in interest before the husband's death. The present value of the

husband's interest is $1 million. The present value of the niece's interest is $4 million.

    a. Assume the husband receives exactly $2 million from the trust. How much of that sum is excluded from income as recovery of capital?

    b. How much of the $5 million basis is allocated to the niece's remainder interest?

59. Dr. Dale dies. His will provides for a distribution of $1 million to his wife, Willa, and $4 million to his daughter, Donna. Willa invests the $1 million in an annuity that is expected to return a total of $2 million over her life. Donna invests the $4 million in the bank where it is expected to earn $1 million of interest prior to Willa's death.

    a. How much basis is allocated to the bequest to Willa? To the bequest to Donna?

    b. Assume Willa (the wife) receives exactly $2 million from the annuity. How much of that sum does Willa include in income?

EXPLANATIONS

58. a. No portion of the sum is excluded from income as recovery of capital because the husband receives no basis in his life interest. §102(b).

    b. The niece receives the entire $5 million basis.

59. a. Willa receives a basis of $1 million; Donna receives the remaining $4 million basis.

    b. She includes in income $1 million — the difference between the proceeds of $2 million and her $1 million basis.

       Note that this transaction is economically equivalent to the transaction described in example 58. The tax consequences, however, are quite different.

F. Annual Accounting

Reading: §§61, 111, 172, 441, 1341

The income tax is based on annual accounting. For nearly all individuals, the taxable year is the calendar year, beginning on January 1 and ending on December 31. On the other hand, corporations frequently have taxable years that begin and end on a different date. A corporation that runs a professional sports franchise, for example, may have a taxable year that ends just after the close of its season. Thus, a major league baseball team might adopt a taxable year that begins on November 1 and ends on October 31.

The convention of annual accounting is necessary for practical and administrative reasons. If unmodified, however, the convention could lead to unfair results. For example, a newly formed company might lose $100,000 in its first year of operation and earn $100,000 in the following year. Strictly applied, the annual accounting convention would require the company to pay tax on its second year income of $100,000 even though the company has broken even during its first two years. In fact, however, the company can take advantage of the net operating loss provisions of §172.

Under §172, a net operating loss suffered in any year can be carried back to the previous three taxable years. The taxpayer files an amended return for the prior year reducing its income for that year by the loss carryback. This amended return produces a refund for the taxpayer. Any loss not used up in offsetting income from prior years can be carried forward and applied against income from the next 15 years. If the company prefers, it can forgo the loss carryback and simply carry the loss forward. (A company might choose to forgo the carryback if tax rates were low in the past, but are expected to rise in the future.)

The mechanics of the net operating loss rules are quite complex. Basically, a loss carryback is applied first against income from the earliest eligible prior year; any loss left after reducing operating income to zero in that year is applied against income from the next earliest year, and so on. Loss carryforwards are applied first against income recognized during the first year following the loss; any loss left over is applied against income recognized during the following year, and so on. In the example above, the company has no prior income and so would apply its first year loss against its second year income. After application of the net operating loss carryforward, the company would have no second year income and thus would pay no tax in year two. The net operating loss rules apply to individuals as well as corporations, although salaried employees cannot have an operating loss and the interaction of the net operating loss rules with the regime of personal deductions can be quite complex.

The convention of annual accounting is subject to a number of other rules and exceptions. For example, imagine that two taxpayers claim ownership over the same stream of income. Under the so-called *claim of right* doctrine, the taxpayer who has possession of the income is taxed on the income despite the dispute. North American Oil Consolidated v. Burnet, 286 U.S. 417 (1932). If this taxpayer later is forced to give up this income, an adjustment in her tax liability will be needed. The adjustment is not made on the return for the year in which the amount was included. Instead, the adjustment takes the form of a deduction in the year in which the income is repaid. United States v. Lewis, 340 U.S. 590 (1951).

What happens if the taxpayer's tax bracket in the year in which the amount is repaid is lower than it was in the year in which the taxpayer included the amount? In these circumstances, allowing the taxpayer to take a deduction in the year of repayment will not make the taxpayer whole for the extra tax that the taxpayer paid in the year in which the amount was included. Section 1341 addresses this problem. If the requirements of that section are met (for example, if the amount of the deduction exceeds $3,000), the taxpayer will reduce her *tax liability* (not income) in the year of repayment by the reduction in tax that would have occurred in the year in which the income was included had the taxpayer not included that amount. This reduction in tax is taken in lieu of the deduction.

If, on the other hand, the taxpayer's tax bracket is lower in the year of inclusion than in the year of repayment, §1341 allows the taxpayer to deduct the amount repaid, in the year of repayment, despite the fact that the deduction saves the taxpayer more than she paid in tax when the item was included in the earlier year.

Suppose, for example, that under the claim of right doctrine, a taxpayer includes $20,000 in year one. The taxpayer, who is in the 40 percent bracket, pays $8,000 of tax on that amount. In year two, the taxpayer, who is now in the 30 percent bracket, is forced to return the disputed funds. The taxpayer is allowed a deduction in year two for the $20,000 repaid in that year. The deduction, which would save the taxpayer $6,000 in year two, would not make the taxpayer whole for the $8,000 of tax that the taxpayer paid in year one. However, §1341 allows the taxpayer to reduce her year two tax liability by $8,000, which is the reduction in tax that would have occurred in year one (the year in which the income was included) had the taxpayer not included that amount.

If the taxpayer had instead been in the 30 percent bracket in year one and the 40 percent bracket in year two, §1341 would allow the taxpayer to deduct the $20,000 in year two for a tax savings of $8,000, despite the fact that the taxpayer paid only $6,000 of tax on the $20,000 inclusion in year one.

The so-called *tax benefit rule* provides another exception to the annual accounting rule. The term "tax benefit rule" is used for two separate rules: one that requires the taxpayer to include an item in income (the *inclusionary tax benefit rule*), and the other that permits a taxpayer to exclude an item that would otherwise be included in income under the inclusionary tax benefit rule (the *exclusionary tax benefit rule*). Both branches of the tax benefit rule have their origins in case law, but the exclusionary tax benefit rule has also been codified in §111.

The inclusionary tax benefit rule triggers an inclusion whenever an event occurs that is fundamentally inconsistent with a tax benefit recognized in an earlier year. Hillsboro National Bank v. Commissioner, 460 U.S. 370 (1983). Suppose, for example, that a taxpayer with $200,000 of adjusted gross income donates $10,000 to a college in year one. As discussed later in this book, the taxpayer would be able to deduct the charitable contribution. Suppose that the college is forced to give up operations in year two and returns the money to the taxpayer at that time. The taxpayer's receipt of the $10,000 in year two is inconsistent with the charitable deduction taken by the taxpayer in year one. Thus, the taxpayer must "give back" the year one deduction by including $10,000 of income in year two.

However, the exclusionary tax benefit rule of §111(a) permits a taxpayer to exclude the recovered item in the later year to the extent that it did not reduce the taxpayer's tax liability in the earlier year. Continuing our example, if the charitable contribution did not reduce the taxpayer's tax liability in year one, she may exclude the $10,000 in year two. For example, a charitable contribution would not reduce an individual's tax liability if the taxpayer had no taxable income in the year in which the deduction would have been taken.

Both the §1341 and tax benefit rules apply where a return was correct at the time that it was filed, but a *subsequent* event renders it incorrect. Compare this situation with one in which a return is incorrect at the time it was filed, but the mistake is not discovered until after the return was filed. For example, a taxpayer might discover in year two that she had incorrectly added a column of figures in calculating her taxable income for year one. In that situation, the taxpayer would file an *amended return*, for year one, which serves as a *claim for refund* for the tax she overpaid in that year. Most taxpayers supplement this claim for refund with a brief explanation of the grounds on which the refund is sought. If the Service denies the taxpayer's claim for refund, the taxpayer may file a suit for refund in either the district court or the United States Court of Federal Claims. A claim for refund must generally be filed within three years from the date the return was filed. §6511(a). (A return filed before the due date for the return is deemed filed on the due date. §6513(a).) However, if the taxpayer makes a payment of tax after filing a return (for example, as a result of the Service asserting that the taxpayer owes additional tax for that year), the period for filing the claim for refund may be longer. §6511(a).

EXAMPLES

60. In May of year one, college roommates Allison and Zelda devise a new computer word-processing program. The program is powerful but unwieldy and is rejected by software distributors. After graduation, Allison enters law school and loses interest in the program. Zelda continues to work on the project and eventually manages to make the program "user friendly." The program is successfully marketed; Zelda receives $10,000 per year in royalties during years three through five for a total of $30,000. Zelda is in the 40 percent bracket during those three years.

    In year six, Allison sues Zelda for 50 percent of all program royalties. In December of year seven, a jury finds for Allison and awards her a $30,000 payment, which represents a one-third interest in the royalties Zelda received for years three through five plus a one-third interest in all future program royalties. Zelda, who is in the 30 percent bracket in year seven, pays Allison the $30,000 late in December of year seven. The deadline for filing an appeal in the case is February 28 of year eight, but Zelda does not file an appeal.

    a. Advise Allison on how the $30,000 she receives from Zelda should be treated for tax purposes.

    b. Advise Zelda on how the $30,000 payment to Allison should be treated for tax purposes. Should she file an amended return for years three through five?

61. Larry suffers an uninsured business theft loss of $20,000 in year one. He deducts the loss in year one, but recovers the stolen property in year two.

    a. Assume that Larry is in the 15 percent tax bracket in year one and the 40 percent tax bracket in year two. Must Larry report the $20,000 as income in year two?

    b. Assume that Larry is in the zero percent tax bracket in year one and the 40 percent tax bracket in year two. Must Larry report the $20,000 as income in year two?

62. In year one David contributes $10,000 to charity. David neglects to list this contribution on his year one tax return, which he files on April 15 of year two. After filing the return for year one, David does not pay any additional tax for that year. David does not discover his $10,000 mistake on the year one return until February of year five. Is each of the following statements true or false?

   a. If the charitable contribution would reduce his year one tax payment, David may file an amended return for year one and claim a refund.

   b. David may not file an amended return for year one and claim a refund because the statute of limitations has run.

   c. Instead of filing an amended return for year one, David may report the charitable contribution on his year five return.

EXPLANATIONS

60. a. Allison will include the $30,000 in year seven, the year in which she received the funds under a "claim of right," despite the fact that she might have to return the $30,000 to Zelda if the case were reversed on appeal. North American Oil Consolidated v. Burnet, 286 U.S. 417 (1932).

   b. If Zelda deducts the $30,000 in year seven, the deduction would reduce her taxes in year seven by $9,000 ($30,000 deduction multiplied by her 30 percent tax rate). Zelda paid $12,000 of tax ($30,000 multiplied by her 40 percent tax rate) on the royalties when they were included in years three through five. Said another way, if, in those three years, she had excluded the $30,000 from her gross income, she would have paid $12,000 less in taxes. This $12,000 reduction in her tax liability that would have occurred had she not included the items in years three through five exceeds the $9,000 that she would save in taxes in year seven if she deducted the $30,000. Therefore, Zelda will reduce her tax liability for year seven by $12,000 instead of deducting the $30,000 payment. §1341.

   Zelda cannot amend her returns for years three through five because the return was correct at the time it was filed, but was rendered incorrect by a subsequent event. United States v. Lewis, 340 U.S. 590 (1951). However, the effect of §1341, saving her $12,000 in tax in year seven, is almost the same as allowing her to amend the returns for years three through five and receive a $12,000 refund. (They are not exactly the same because the government has to pay interest on refunds owed to taxpayers, but does not have to pay interest on Zelda's $12,000 tax reduction under §1341.)

61. a. Yes. Recovery of the stolen item is inconsistent with the $20,000 theft deduction taken in year one. Under the inclusionary tax benefit rule, Larry must give the year one tax benefit back by including the $20,000 in income in year two. Hillsboro National Bank v. Commissioner, 469 U.S. 370 (1983). Note that, although Larry's tax benefit from the deduction was only $3,000 (15 percent of $20,000) in year one, he will be required to pay an additional $8,000 (40 percent of $20,000) in tax in year two; unlike §1341, the tax benefit rule does not generally take into account any changes in the taxpayer's bracket between the year in which the item is deducted and the year in which it is included. In other words, §1341 is a more precise error correction device than the tax benefit rule.

   b. No. Larry received no tax benefit from the $20,000 deduction in year one. Under the exclusionary tax benefit rule, he may exclude the $20,000 item recovered in year two. §111.

62. Statement (a) is correct and statements (b) and (c) are false. A taxpayer generally may file a claim for refund anytime within three years of the time of filing. §6511(a). (Since David did not pay any additional tax for year one after filing the return, the "two-years-from-payment" rule in §6511(a) does not apply.) February of year five is within three years of the date on which the year one return was filed, April 15 of year two, so David's claim for refund is not barred by the statute of limitations. Thus, statement (a) is correct and statement (b) is false.

   David, an individual, is a cash method taxpayer. He must report the charitable contribution deduction on the return for the year in which the contribution was made, here, year one. The failure to take the deduction was a mistake at the time the return was filed, so David cannot take it on his year five return. Statement (c) is therefore false.

G. Personal Injury Recoveries

Reading: §104; Reg. §1.104-1(c)

Compensatory payments for personal injuries or sickness are generally excluded from gross income under §104(a). This exclusion applies both to recoveries under workers' compensation acts and to damages received (whether by suit or by settlement agreement) "on account of personal injury." Until recently, courts deciding whether a recovery was excludable under §104 have focused primarily on the definition of the term "personal injury." However, a recent Supreme Court case stressed that the "on account of" requirement must also be satisfied for the §104 exclusion to apply. Commissioner v. Schleier, 115 S. Ct. 2195 (1995).

How is the term *personal injury* defined? In common parlance, the term usually refers to an injury without a clear business nexus or business consequences. For tax purposes, however, whether something is a personal injury depends on the taxpayer's claim to recompense. In order for the personal injury exclusion to apply, the claim must be a tort-type claim, not a contract claim. Reg. §1.104-1(c). Tort-type claims include claims for physical harm and nonphysical wrongs such as infliction of emotional distress. If the taxpayer's claim is tort-like, compensatory damages received by the taxpayer "on account of" the personal injury are excludable.

The distinction between tort and contract claims is somewhat artificial, and courts have sometimes struggled to determine whether certain types of claims are sufficiently tort-like to qualify for the exclusion. For example, in United States v. Burke, 112 S. Ct. 1867 (1992), the issue was whether the taxpayer could exclude amounts received on account of sex discrimination. The court looked to the remedial scheme in the sex discrimination statute (Title VII of the Civil Rights Act of 1964) to determine whether the claim was tort-like. The statute provided for back pay and injunctive relief, but did not provide for other types of damages which are generally included in the remedial scheme of tort statutes (for example, other types of compensatory damages and punitive damages), so the court concluded that the sex discrimination claim was not sufficiently "tort-like" for the personal injury exclusion to apply. In 1991, after the facts in *Burke* arose, the Title VII sex discrimination statute was amended to provide for additional remedies; thus, certain claims for intentional discrimination under the amended statute would probably be treated as tort-like.

In a more recent case, Commissioner v. Schleier, 115 S. Ct. 2195 (1995), the Supreme Court considered whether age discrimination claims under the Age Discrimination in Employment Act (ADEA) were tort-like. The ADEA remedial scheme provides only for back pay and liquidated damage awards. The majority concluded that ADEA liquidated damages do not serve a compensatory function, but are instead punitive in nature. Despite the fact that the ADEA remedial scheme includes punitive damages, the majority held that the remedial scheme is not tort-like because it does not provide for a broad array of compensatory damages.

The majority opinion also stated that, even if a taxpayer's claim is sufficiently tort-like to be treated as a personal injury claim, the taxpayer's recovery is excludable under §104 only if the damages are received "on account of" that personal injury. For example, if a taxpayer injured in an auto accident by a tortfeasor receives compensatory damages for the taxpayer's medical expenses, lost wages, and pain and suffering, the damages are fully excludable because they are received on account of the injury. However, the majority concluded that the taxpayer in the *Schleier* case did not receive his back pay award "on account of" personal injury. The majority conceded that age discrimination might potentially cause both personal injury (for example, pain and suffering similar to that suffered by a taxpayer injured in an auto accident) and loss of wages, but concluded that back pay awards under ADEA are determined without regard to personal injury.

What if a personal injury leads to a business loss? Are the damages excludable under §104? The Service has argued (in the context of a defamation action) that, although damages for an injury to personal reputation are excludable under §104, damages for an injury to business reputation are taxable. This view was rejected by the Ninth Circuit in Roemer v. Commissioner, 716 F.2d 693 (1983). In *Roemer*, the taxpayer received payments from a credit bureau for defamatory statements about his character, which led to a substantial reduction in income from the taxpayer's insurance business. The Ninth Circuit held that, even though the damage was largely to the taxpayer's business, qualification for exclusion under §104 depended on the nature of the taxpayer's claim (not on the nature of the damages received). Since, under state law, defamation was a personal injury claim, the taxpayer was entitled to the §104 exclusion.

Schleier may have revived the business versus personal distinction put to rest in *Roemer*. How would a case like *Roemer* be decided after *Schleier*? Even though the taxpayer's claim would be tort-like, the taxpayer's recovery would not be excludable unless it was received "on account of " personal injury. The majority opinion in *Schleier* indicates that, unless the facts resemble the auto accident tort example in the opinion, damages will not be considered received on account of personal injury if they are for economic injury (for example, business income or wages lost as a result of the tort) instead of noneconomic injury (for example, pain and suffering). Thus, it appears that *Schleier* is inconsistent with the decision in *Roemer*.

The personal injury exclusion does not apply to recoveries for medical expenses already deducted under §213 (which permits a personal deduction for medical expenses exceeding 7.5 percent of a taxpayer's adjusted gross income).

Interest earned on damages received is taxable under §61(a)(4), but if payments are received over a period of years, the entire recovery is excluded from income — even if the payments include implicit interest as compensation for the delay. §104(a)(2) (parenthetical). This disparity in tax treatment creates an incentive to pay the award over time (usually in a structured settlement) instead of in a lump sum.

Does the exclusion apply to punitive damages received by a taxpayer on account of personal injury? Section 104(a)(2) states that the personal injury damage exclusion applies to "any" damages received. However, a 1989 amendment to §104(a) specifically provides that punitive damages received in cases not involving physical injury are not excludable under §104(a)(2). It is not clear whether a negative inference can be drawn from the 1989 amendment that punitive damages are excludable in cases that do involve physical injury. Since 1984 the Service has taken the position that punitive damages cannot be excluded. Rev. Rul. 84-108 (revoking Rev. Rul. 74-45, in which the Service earlier ruled that punitive damages were excludable). Some courts have held that the exclusion applies to punitive damages, while other courts have held that it does not. See, e.g., Horton v. Commissioner, 100 T.C. 93 (1993), aff'd, 33 F.3d 625 (6th Cir. 1994) (allowing exclusion of punitive damages) and Reese v. United States, 28 Cl. Ct. 702 (1993), aff'd, 24 F.3d 228 (Fed. Cir. 1994) (requiring inclusion of punitive damages in a case involving nonphysical injury prior to the 1989 amendment). Due to this split in authority, it is unclear whether punitive damages in cases that do involve physical injury are excludable. However, the *Schleier* majority opinion analysis of the "on account of " requirement indicates that such punitive damages may not be excludable.

The tax treatment of damages received on account of personal injury is far more favorable than the treatment of recoveries for business injuries. Compensation received for a business injury is taxed according to the nature of the loss. If the compensation is received for lost profits, for example, the recovery will be taxed as ordinary income. If the compensation is received for the destruction of a capital asset, then capital gains treatment will apply. Damages received on account of personal injury, on the other hand, are in some circumstances excluded from income even if they are based on lost wages.

Should personal injury recoveries be excluded from taxation? To answer this question, it is useful to consider separately four types of recoveries: (i) recoveries for medical expenses; (ii) recoveries for lost wages; (iii) recoveries for pain and suffering; and (iv) punitive damages.

Medical expense recoveries present the strongest case for tax-free treatment. The medical expense recovery places the injured person in the same financial position that she would have occupied had she not been injured. It seems fair, then, that she should pay the same amount of tax. This can be achieved by excluding the medical expense recovery from the tax base.

Recoveries for lost wages, on the other hand, replace funds that would have been taxed if the person had earned them by working. Taxing lost wage recoveries places the person recipient in the same financial position that she would have occupied had she been able to work.

The proper taxation of recoveries for pain and suffering is controversial. Supporters of tax-free treatment argue that pain and suffering recoveries compensate the injured person for the loss of imputed income from good health. Since the imputed income from good health would not have been taxed, damages received for the loss of good health also should not be taxed. Advocates of taxing pain and suffering recoveries argue that an individual's tax burden should depend on her financial position, not on her psychic well-being. Pain and suffering damages compensate an injured person for a non-monetary loss and place the recipient in a better financial position than she would have occupied had she not been injured. An individual who receives pain and suffering damages has a greater financial ability to pay and thus should bear a higher tax burden.

Punitive damages represent a windfall gain to the recipient and thus present a strong case for taxation. The best argument for tax-free treatment is that excluding punitive damages from taxation will encourage taxpayers to file suit.

EXAMPLES

63. Lucy assaulted Dan. Dan sustained severe injuries and filed a civil suit against Lucy. After a trial, Dan is awarded $10,000 for pain and suffering, $10,000 for medical expenses, $12,000 for lost wages, and $25,000 for punitive damages. What are the tax consequences to Dan?

64. Martin, a longshoreman, injured his back while unloading a crate at the docks. He was on duty at the time, performing tasks pursuant to his employment contract. He was compensated $10,000 for his medical expenses and lost wages under the Longshoremen's and Harbor Workers' Compensation Act. What portion, if any, of his recovery is excludable?

65. a. Ken Kanter, a teacher, is fired for criticizing the school's staff and administration. He sues the school, claiming that his First Amendment rights had been violated. He settles with the school for $50,000, an amount equal to his lost wages. What are the tax consequences to Mr. Kanter?

    b. How would Mr. Kanter be taxed if he received an additional $20,000 in punitive damages?

66. Mary Morse files suit under federal civil rights statutes against her employer, the Smithtown Board of Education, for sex discrimination in their pay policies. The court awards her $50,000 for the back pay that she would have earned if she had not been the victim of unlawful discrimination. What are the tax consequences of the award to Ms. Morse?

67. The Bannister Badgers, a college basketball team, are defeated in the conference championship game. In a column in the local paper the next day, sports columnist Sam Scandal writes that the team lost because the coach, Fred Walker, "threw" the game in exchange for $10,000. Coach Walker files a $500,000 defamation lawsuit against Scandal, claiming that Scandal's allegations have cost him the respect of his family and peers and reduced his expected off-the-court earnings (from endorsements, speaking engagements, and teaching at summer basketball camps) by $200,000. Two days before the trial is scheduled to begin, Walker agrees to settle the case in exchange for $150,000.

    a. How might Coach Walker argue the award is excludable?

    b. How should Coach Walker's attorney draft the settlement agreement to strengthen his client's case for exclusion of the award?

    c. *Should* the award be taxed as a matter of tax policy?

68. Albert, a locksmith, hires Betty to repair the leaking roof of his store during his annual two-week vacation in August. When Albert returns from his vacation, he learns that Betty has not completed the repair as agreed. Albert sues for breach of contract, claiming lost profit of $30,000 due to a delay in reopening. Albert states that his reputation as a reliable businessman will be injured by his failure to reopen on schedule. Prior to trial, the case is settled for $20,000. How will the recovery be taxed to Albert?

69. Jack is a teacher at Pleasantville High School. The terms of his contract provide that he will receive paid sick leave for up to 15 days per year and that unused days will carry over to future years. In his ninth year of teaching, Jack suffers a skiing accident and misses 12 weeks of work. Fortunately, he has accumulated substantial sick leave and thus he receives his full salary of $500 per week (for a total of $6,000) during his illness. Is Jack taxed on the $6,000 he received?

70. In year one, Marna receives a $10,000 settlement for a personal injury she suffered. She invests the $10,000 for 10 years, earning $20,000 of interest on it. What are the tax consequences to Marna in years one through ten?

71. a. Pablo is injured by Mr. Negligent in an auto accident. Pablo's estimated damages are $10,000. Pablo accepts Mr. Negligent's offer to settle the suit with monthly payments totaling $30,000 over the next 10 years. In order to meet his legal obligation to provide Pablo with monthly payments for the next 10 years, Mr. Negligent purchases an annuity contract from Helping Hands Insurance Company for $10,000, naming Pablo as the beneficiary. Mr. Negligent retains rights of ownership of the annuity, including the right to change the beneficiary. What are the tax consequences to Pablo in years one through ten?
    b. Assume the same facts as above, except that Mr. Negligent buys an annuity from an insurance company that will make the required monthly payments. Mr. Negligent pays $10,000 for the annuity, but Pablo has all rights of ownership. What are the tax consequences to Pablo in years one through ten?

In each of the following examples, assume (i) that the taxpayers are subject to a flat 30 percent rate on their taxable income and (ii) that their taxable income equals their adjusted gross income.

72. Albert and Betty each earn $100,000 per year. Betty is injured in an automobile accident, incurs $5,000 of medical expenses, and receives a $5,000 damage payment. Albert and Betty have no other medical expenses.
    a. How much does Albert have to live on after paying his taxes?
    b. How much does Betty have to live on after paying her taxes and medical expenses if her medical expense recovery is taxed?
    c. How much does Betty have to live on after paying her taxes and medical expenses if her medical expense recovery is not taxed?
    d. What do the answers to parts (a) through (c) suggest about the proper tax treatment of medical expense recoveries?

73. Carl and Debby each earn $5,000 per month. Carl works 12 months and earns $60,000. Debby is injured in an automobile accident and cannot work for a month. She works for 11 months and earns $55,000. Debby receives a $5,000 recovery for her lost wages.
    a. How much does Carl have to live on after paying his taxes?
    b. How much does Debby have to live on after paying her taxes if her lost wage recovery is taxed?
    c. How much does Debby have to live on after paying her taxes if her lost wage recovery is not taxed?
    d. What do the answers to parts (a) through (c) suggest about the proper tax treatment of lost wage recoveries?

74. Ed earns $60,000 per year. Flora earns $50,000 per year. Flora is injured in an automobile accident and receives a $10,000 recovery for pain and suffering.
    a. How much does Ed have to live on after paying his taxes?
    b. How much does Flora have to live on after paying her taxes if her pain and suffering recovery is taxed?
    c. How much does Flora have to live on after paying her taxes if her pain and suffering recovery is not taxed?
    d. What do the answers to parts (a) through (c) suggest about the proper tax treatment of pain and suffering recoveries?

75. Greta earns $80,000 per year and Harry earns $60,000 per year. Harry receives $20,000 in punitive damages from a local newspaper that published an article defaming his character.
    a. How much does Greta have to live on after paying her taxes?
    b. How much does Harry have to live on after paying his taxes if the punitive damages are taxed?

      c. How much does Harry have to live on after paying his taxes if the punitive damages are not taxed?

      d. What do the answers to parts (a) through (c) suggest about the proper tax treatment of punitive damages?

76. Most plaintiffs in personal injury actions retain their attorneys on a contingency basis. Typically, the attorney receives one-third of any damage award. What are the implications of this arrangement for the proper taxation of personal injury awards?

EXPLANATIONS

63. Damages received for pain and suffering, lost wages, and medical expenses on account of personal injury or sickness are all excludable under §104. Thus, Dan can exclude the $10,000 award for pain and suffering, the $10,000 award for medical expenses, and the $12,000 award for lost wages. However, it is not clear whether Dan can exclude the $25,000 punitive damage award. Although §104(a)(last sentence) specifically provides that punitive damages received for nonphysical injury are definitely not excludable, it is not clear whether punitive damages on account of physical injury are excludable. The Service takes the position that punitive damages are not excludable. Rev. Rul. 84-108. It is not clear which way a court would rule on the issue because there is conflicting case law on the question of whether punitive damages that do not fall within the 1989 amendment language are excludable. Compare Horton v. Commissioner, 100 T.C. 93 (1993), aff'd, 33 F.3d 625 (6th Cir. 1994) (allowing exclusion of punitive damages) and Reese v. United States, 28 Cl. Ct. 702 (1993), aff'd, 24 F.3d 228 (Fed. Cir. 1994) (requiring inclusion of punitive damages in a case involving nonphysical injury prior to the 1989 amendment). The *Schleier* majority opinion analysis of the "on account of" requirement indicates that punitive damages may not be excludable even if received in a case involving physical injury.

64. The entire $10,000 will be excludable from Martin's gross income. Amounts that are received by an employee under a workers' compensation act or under a statute that provides compensation to employees for personal injuries or sickness sustained in the course of employment are excludable from gross income. The Longshoremen's and Harbor Workers' Compensation Act is a workers' compensation act. Reg. §1.104-1(b).

65. a. Mr. Kanter may exclude the recovery if he receives it "on account of personal injury." This example demonstrates the difficulty in defining "personal injury" and determining when a recovery is received "on account of" a personal injury.

    A court would have to decide whether Mr. Kantor's claim is sufficiently tort-like to qualify for the exclusion. Reg. §1.104-1(c). In the case upon which this fact pattern is based, the court held that the settlement was based on tort-type rights and thus the settlement amount was excludable under §104(a)(2). Bent v. Commissioner, 835 F.2d 67 (3d Cir. 1987).

    However, Mr. Kantor must also satisfy the second requirement for exclusion, which was stressed in the *Schleier* case: that the recovery is received "on account of" the personal injury. In *Schleier*, the majority concluded that the taxpayer's lost wages were caused by his age or being discharged, not by a personal injury — so the back pay damages were not received on account of personal injury. The majority noted that, under the ADEA remedial scheme, a back pay award is determined without regard to whether the taxpayer experienced pain and suffering or some other form of personal injury. Here it is unclear whether a court would conclude that Mr. Kantor's lost wages were caused by the personal injury.

    b. Mr. Kanter would be taxed on any punitive damages received. The treatment of punitive damages in this case is clear because the case involves nonphysical injury. §104(a) (last sentence).

66. As in the previous example, this fact pattern illustrates the problems in clearly defining a personal injury. This fact pattern is based on United States v. Burke, 112 S. Ct. 1867 (1992). In *Burke*, the court had to determine whether sex discrimination claims, under Title VII of the Civil Rights Act of 1964, were sufficiently tort-like to warrant exclusion. The remedial scheme of the statute provided for lost wages and injunctive relief, but did not provide for other compensatory damages or punitive damages. Remedial schemes in tort statutes generally include the type of remedies omitted from the sex discrimination statute, so the court held that the claims were not sufficiently tort-like to qualify for exclusion. However, after the facts in *Burke* arose, the sex discrimination statute was amended to provide for additional remedies. Following the amendment, certain sex discrimination claims under the federal civil rights statute are probably tort-like. However, since

the sex discrimination award was solely for lost wages, a court might conclude that the recovery was not received "on account of" personal injury. Commissioner v. Schleier, 115 S. Ct. 2195 (1995). The recovery is excludable only if it is received "on account of" personal injury.

67. a. Coach Walker would argue that the award constitutes damages received on account of personal injury and therefore is excludable under §104. He would argue that the damages received compensate for pain and suffering, not lost wages. He would also take the position that the recovery should be tax-free even if it represents compensation for lost income on the grounds that defamation is a personal injury. This latter position is supported by Roemer v. Commissioner, 716 F.2d 693 (9th Cir. 1983) in which the court held that where a taxpayer's claim is a personal injury claim, the recovery will be tax-free even if it represents lost profits on the taxpayer's business. However, the *Schleier* majority opinion indicates that, even if the taxpayer's claim is tort-like, a recovery for lost wages is not received "on account of" a personal injury unless the facts in the case resemble the auto accident tort example in the opinion — which they do not in this example.

   b. Coach Walker's attorney should draft a settlement agreement that states that the $150,000 payment is compensation for Walker's pain and suffering. The reference to the pain and suffering claim and the lack of any reference to lost wages might make it more difficult for the Service to argue that some or all of the award should be taxed.

   c. Coach Walker would have been taxed on his earnings, so it seems reasonable to tax him on compensation for the loss of those earnings. Walker's "ability to pay" taxes seems to be the same whether he receives income from his own earnings or as compensation for lost earnings.

   With respect to compensation received for emotional pain and suffering, some individuals might argue that Walker should not be taxed because he is only being placed in the same situation that he would have been in if he had not been defamed. This position is similar to that taken in Solicitor's Opinion 132, 1-1 C.B. 92 (1922), which held that compensatory damages for certain personal injuries were not income because they did not represent gain or profit.

Under general tax principles, however, gain is equal to the amount received less the taxpayer's basis. Calculating a sensible basis for human capital is extremely difficult; it is simply not possible to determine whether Walker has received an amount in excess of his basis. Perhaps we could arbitrarily give human capital a basis equal to its fair market value. Recovery of damages to human capital would therefore never exceed basis and never be taxed. Such a rule would be consistent with the view that someone who has suffered personal injury and who has (at best) simply been "made whole" by a damage award should not be taxed. On the other hand, a taxpayer who receives a damage award for non-pecuniary losses is better off financially than a similarly situated taxpayer who suffered no injury and receives no award. Since the injured taxpayer receiving the damage award has a greater financial ability-to-pay than the uninjured taxpayer, perhaps he should pay higher taxes.

Because it is difficult to distinguish between injury to human capital and lost profits and to tax human capital in a consistent manner, it may be reasonable to take the approach of the court in *Roemer* and simply not tax personal injury awards. One problem with this approach is that it may create an incentive for taxpayers to recharacterize business receipts, which would otherwise be taxable, as personal injury awards.

Aside from the conceptual "human capital" problems raised by personal injury awards, are there any other reasons to exclude the damages received? Although most property transactions are voluntary, in personal injury cases the taxpayer plaintiff has involuntarily entered into the transaction giving rise to the damage award. In addition, we might feel sorry for personal injury victims and want them to be able to keep all of their recovery. However, if that is the justification for the exclusion, is it fair to deny a deduction to the *more* unfortunate taxpayer who is injured but does not recover damages?

68. Albert will be taxed on the entire $20,000 recovery. Albert's claim appears to be for breach of contract rather than for a "tort-like" personal injury, so the §104 exclusion does not apply.

69. Jack is taxed on the full $6,000. The $6,000 is not a personal injury recovery because it does not arise out of tort or tort-like rights. Reg. §1.104-1(c). The payment is not workers' compensa-

tion because it does not arise out of an occupational injury or sickness. Reg. §1.104-1(b).

70. Marna excludes the $10,000 settlement in year one under §104(a)(2). However, Marna will pay tax on the $20,000 of interest earned on her investment in years one through ten.

71. a. Section 104(a)(2) allows the taxpayer to exclude amounts received for personal injuries "whether as lump sums or as periodic payments." Pablo may exclude all of the monthly payments received in settlement of the suit despite the fact that $20,000 of the $30,000 payments represent interest on the original $10,000 settlement. Compare the tax treatment of Marna, in example 70 above, who had to include the $20,000 of interest on her invested damages.

    b. In this case, Pablo is receiving, in effect, an annuity in year one as settlement for his damages. Since Pablo has full control over the annuity, he will be treated as if he received a $10,000 personal injury recovery, which is excludable under §104, and purchased the annuity himself. Pablo would then be taxed on the monthly payments received under the standard rules governing the taxation of annuities. Rev. Rul. 79-220.

72. a. Albert has taxable income of $100,000 and pays a 30 percent tax of $30,000. He has no medical expenses. Thus, Albert has $70,000 to live on after paying taxes and medical expenses.

    b. If Betty's $5,000 medical expense recovery is taxed, she will have taxable income of $105,000 and pay a 30 percent tax of $31,500. She has $5,000 in medical expenses. Thus, Betty will have $68,500 to live on after paying taxes and medical expenses.

    c. If Betty's $5,000 medical expense recovery is not taxed, she will have taxable income of $100,000 and pay a 30 percent tax of $30,000. She has $5,000 in medical expenses. Thus, Betty will have $70,000 to live on after paying taxes and medical expenses.

    d. Betty's income is $5,000 greater than Albert's, but she has $5,000 of additional medical expenses. Albert and Betty appear to have a similar ability to pay and should bear the same tax burden. This can be achieved by excluding the medical expense recovery from taxation.

73. a. Carl has taxable earnings of $60,000 and pays a 30 percent tax of $18,000. Thus, Carl has $42,000 to live on after paying taxes.

    b. If Debby's $5,000 lost wage recovery is taxed, she will have taxable income of $60,000 and pay a 30 percent tax of $18,000. Debby will have $42,000 to live on after paying taxes.

    c. If Debby's $5,000 lost wage recovery is not taxed, she will have taxable income of $55,000 and pay a 30 percent tax of $16,500. Debby will have $43,500 to live on after paying taxes.

    d. Carl and Debby each have $60,000 of income and there is no evidence that their needs are different. Carl and Debby appear to have a similar ability to pay and should bear the same tax burden. This can be achieved by taxing the lost wage recovery.

74. a. Ed has taxable earnings of $60,000 and pays a 30 percent tax of $18,000. Thus, Ed has $42,000 to live on after paying taxes.

    b. If Flora's $10,000 pain and suffering recovery is taxed, she will have taxable income of $60,000 and pay a 30 percent tax of $18,000. Flora will have $42,000 to live on after paying taxes.

    c. If Flora's $10,000 pain and suffering recovery is not taxed, she will have taxable income of $50,000 and pay a 30 percent tax of $15,000. Flora will have $45,000 to live on after paying taxes.

    d. The answer is not clear. On the one hand, Ed and Flora each have $60,000 of income and there is no evidence that their needs are different. Since Ed and Flora appear to have a similar ability to pay, they should bear the same tax burden. This can be achieved by taxing the recovery for pain and suffering. On the other hand, Flora is worse off than Ed because she has endured a lot of pain and suffering ($10,000 worth, according to the court). This nonfinancial loss doesn't affect Flora's financial ability to pay taxes, but it might justify subjecting her to a lower tax burden.

75. a. Greta has taxable earnings of $80,000 and pays a 30 percent tax of $24,000. Thus, Greta has $56,000 to live on after paying taxes.

    b. If Harry's $20,000 of punitive damages is taxed, he will have taxable income of $80,000 and pay a 30 percent tax of $24,000. Harry will have $56,000 to live on after paying taxes.

    c. If Harry's $20,000 of punitive damages is not taxed, he will have taxable income of $60,000 and pay a 30 percent tax of $18,000. Harry will have $62,000 to live on after paying taxes.

   d. Greta and Harry each have $80,000 of income and there is no evidence that their needs are different. Thus, Greta and Harry appear to have a similar ability to pay and should bear the same tax burden. This can be achieved by taxing the punitive damages.

76. If a plaintiff must give one-third of her recovery to her attorney, then she will not be fully compensated for her loss. This makes the case for tax-free treatment stronger. Consider, for example, an individual in the 30 percent tax bracket who receives a lost wage recovery of $10,000. The individual must pay $3,333 in attorneys' fees on the lost wage recovery, leaving $6,667 for himself before taxes. If the $6,667 recovery is taxed, the individual will pay a tax of $2,000, leaving only $4,667 for himself. If the taxpayer had not been injured, he would have paid a tax of $3,000 on the additional $10,000 he would have earned, leaving $7,000 for himself. Excluding the lost wage recovery from taxation is desirable if the goal is to leave the injured individual in a position similar to the one that he would have occupied if he had not been injured.

H. Transactions Involving Loans and Income from Discharge of Indebtedness

Reading: §§61(a)(12), 108, 1011, 1012, 1016;
Reg. §1.1001-2(a)(3)

An individual is not taxed on amounts that he borrows on the theory that the obligation to repay the loan offsets the amount received. In other words, the loan does not increase the taxpayer's net worth. Similarly, an individual does not receive a deduction for amounts used to repay a loan.

Although the repayment of a loan generally has no tax consequences, if a loan is discharged for less than the amount owed, the borrower must include in income the amount of the discount (the amount owed less the amount paid to discharge the debt). §61(a)(12). There are two reasons why lenders might discharge debt for less than the amount owed. First, if the taxpayer is financially troubled and cannot repay the debt, the lender may discharge the debt for the amount that the borrower can pay. Second, if the interest rate on the debt is lower than the current market interest rate, the lender may make money by letting the borrower pay back less than the full amount owed, then relending the money at a higher interest rate.

For example, suppose an individual borrows $100,000 from a bank, at a 10 percent rate of interest, with an obligation to repay the loan over a 30-year period. If interest rates rise to 15 percent, the bank might be willing to discharge the debt for an immediate payment of less than $100,000 since the amount repaid could be reloaned at 15 percent. If the loan were discharged for a payment of $90,000, the borrower would recognize *discharge of indebtedness income* of $10,000. §61(a)(12).

What if, instead, interest rates stay at 10 percent and the lender discharges the $100,000 debt for $90,000 because the borrower is financially troubled and cannot repay the full $100,000? The taxpayer has $10,000 of debt discharge income, but may be able to exclude it under §108(a). A financially troubled taxpayer can exclude discharge of indebtedness income if the taxpayer has filed a bankruptcy petition. §108(a)(1)(A) and (d)(2). If the taxpayer has not filed a bankruptcy petition, the taxpayer can exclude the discharge of indebtedness income only to the extent of the taxpayer's insolvency (the taxpayer's liabilities less the value of the taxpayer's assets) at the time of the debt discharge. §108(a)(1)(B), (a)(3), and (d)(3). Continuing our example, if the taxpayer's liabilities exceed the value of her assets by $6,000 at the time of the discharge, she could exclude $6,000 of the $10,000 of debt discharge income, leaving her $4,000 to include under §61(a)(12).

Section 108 also provides several other specific rules that may permit a taxpayer to exclude discharge of indebtedness income, including the following: Section 108(e)(5) provides that if the seller of property takes back debt on the property sold (so-called *purchase money* debt) and later reduces the purchaser's debt, the reduction in the debt is treated as a purchase price adjustment; it does not create discharge of indebtedness income that has to be included under §61(a)(12). Section 108(e)(2) also provides that the discharge of a liability does not result in discharge of indebtedness income to the extent that the liability would have been deductible had it been paid. Thus, the discharge at a discount of a liability to pay compensation to an employee will not result in any discharge of indebtedness income to the employer since the compensation paid would have been deductible by the employer (under §162, as an ordinary and necessary business expense).

Beyond §108, other exceptions to the debt discharge inclusion rule may permit the taxpayer to exclude the debt discount. For example, if a lender and borrower disagree about the amount owed and the borrower ultimately pays the lender less than the amount that the lender said was owed, the difference between the amount the lender said was owed and the amount the borrower pays does not have to be included in income. Sobel, Inc. v. Commissioner, 40 B.T.A. 1263 (1939). In addition, if a lender cancels the debt at a discount as a gift to the borrower, the borrower does not have to include the discount in income. §102.

If a taxpayer is relieved of a nonrecourse liability in connection with the disposition of encumbered property, the consequences are not determined under §§61(a)(12) and 108; instead, the debt relief is included in the taxpayer's amount realized for the purpose of computing her gain or loss realized in the property transaction. Realized gain equals the amount realized less the adjusted basis of the property (and loss equals the adjusted basis less the amount realized). §1001(a). Amount realized equals the cash received by the taxpayer plus the value of any other property received by the taxpayer. §1001(b).

In the case of nonrecourse debt incurred to acquire or improve the property, the rationale for this rule is as follows: The debt relief is included in the taxpayer's amount realized because the debt will have been included in the taxpayer's basis for the property when the taxpayer acquired the property. Crane v. Commissioner, 331 U.S. 1 (1947) and Reg. §1.1001-2(a). The amount realized includes the debt relief even if the encumbered property is worth less than the amount of debt at the time the taxpayer disposes of the property. Commissioner v. Tufts, 461 U.S. 300 (1983).

Consider the following example, which illustrates the "symmetry" principle: In year one, an individual purchases real estate worth $200,000 with $50,000 of his own funds and $150,000 of proceeds from debt that is secured by the property. Under §1012 and the *Crane* case, the taxpayer's basis in the property is $200,000 (the sum of the cash plus the debt proceeds). Assume the taxpayer takes $70,000 of depreciation deductions on the property in years one through ten and, in year ten, sells the property for $10,000 in cash. The purchaser also assumes the $150,000 of debt on the property. The taxpayer's adjusted basis in the property equals $130,000 ($200,000 basis less $70,000 of depreciation deductions). §§1011 and 1016. Under §1001 and the *Crane* case, the taxpayer's amount realized equals $160,000 ($10,000 of cash received by the taxpayer plus $150,000 of debt relief) and the taxpayer's gain realized thus equals $30,000 ($160,000 amount realized less $130,000 adjusted basis). The value of the encumbered property at the time the taxpayer sells the property is irrelevant: Even if the property is worth only $140,000 at the time of the sale, the taxpayer will include the full $150,000 of debt relief in income. Commissioner v. Tufts, 461 U.S. 300 (1983).

The debt relief is included in amount realized based on the symmetry theory: The $150,000 of debt was included in the taxpayer's basis for the property, permitting the taxpayer to take depreciation deductions on the property in excess of the taxpayer's cash investment in the property, so the debt relief should be included in amount realized on the sale of the property. (If the debt were included in basis but not in amount realized, the taxpayer would realize a $120,000 loss on the sale, measured by the difference between the $130,000 adjusted basis and the $10,000 cash received on sale. This, together with the $70,000 depreciation deductions, would yield a taxable loss of $190,000. The taxpayer's actual economic loss, however, would only be $50,000, the cash invested in the property.)

The upshot of *Crane* and *Tufts* is that taxpayers can trade current depreciation deductions on encumbered property, the basis of which has been increased to reflect debt used to purchase the property, for deferred gain on the later disposition of the property. This treatment benefits taxpayers because it permits them to defer taxes. However, there is a limitation on the general rule of including the debt in basis: If taxpayers "inflate" their basis (in order to claim larger depreciation deductions) by claiming nonrecourse debt far in excess of the value of the property, the taxpayer's basis for the property may not include all or a portion of the debt. (See Chapter 5 of this book for a more detailed discussion of this limitation on including debt in the basis of property.) If that basis limitation applies, the symmetry approach requires that, on the subsequent disposition of the encumbered property, the taxpayer's amount realized reflect the debt relief only to the extent that the taxpayer's basis included the debt. Reg. §1.1001-2(a)(3). Continuing the earlier example, if the special limitation just described permitted the taxpayer to include in basis only $100,000 of the $150,000 debt when he bought the property in year one, then only $100,000 of the $150,000 of the debt relief in year 10 would have been included in the taxpayer's amount realized. Reg. §1.1001-2(a)(3).

There is one exception to this approach. Suppose a taxpayer purchases property for cash and then many years later uses the property as security for a loan to finance personal consumption or to pay an unrelated business expense. In that event, the basis of the property will not include the debt. Nonetheless, the amount realized on the subsequent sale of the property will include the relief of that nonrecourse debt because the taxpayer extracted the loan proceeds from the property. In these circumstances, the general rule set forth in *Crane* and *Tufts*—that the amount realized includes relief of nonrecourse debt—still applies.

What if a family member transfers encumbered property to another family member as a gift and the donee assumes the donor's debt? Does *Crane* apply to the donor's debt relief? In Diedrich v. Commissioner, 457 U.S. 191 (1982) the donors gave family members "net" gifts, meaning that the donees agreed to pay the donors' gift tax liability that arose as a result of making the gifts. The court held that the transaction was partly a gift and partly a sale because the donees assumed the donors' gift tax liability, citing both *Crane* and Old Colony Trust Co. v. Commissioner, 279 U.S. 716 (1929) (where a taxpayer had to include in income a debt that his employer paid on his behalf). In *Diedrich*, the donors' gain from the sale portion of the transfer equaled their amount realized as a result of the debt relief less their entire basis in all of the assets transferred. (In other words, even though the transaction was treated as part gift and part sale, the donors were not required to allocate their basis between the sale and gift portions of the transfer.)

EXAMPLES

77. a. Bob borrows $10,000 in year one and uses the proceeds to finance a ski trip. Is Bob taxed on the $10,000 he receives from the lender?

    b. Bob earns $100,000 in year two and uses $10,000 of the money to repay the loan. What are the tax consequences to Bob of repayment of the loan in year two?

78. In year one, Linda borrows $200,000 from a bank. The term of the loan is 30 years; the interest rate on the loan is 11 percent. In year two, interest rates skyrocket to 15 percent. The bank decides it would rather have $150,000 to lend out at 15 percent than a $200,000 loan on which it earns only 11 percent. The bank tells Linda that if she will pay them $150,000 immediately, they will forgive the loan. Linda pays the bank $150,000 in year two. What are the tax consequences to Linda of repayment of the loan in year two?

79. a. In year one, Donald borrows $100,000 from a bank. The 10 percent interest on the loan is payable annually and the principal is to be repaid 10 years later. In year 10, Donald notifies the bank that he cannot repay the full $100,000 of principal. After some negotiations, the bank agrees to discharge the debt for $85,000. Immediately before the discharge, Donald has $300,000 of debt and $290,000 of assets; after the discharge, he has $200,000 of debt and $205,000 of assets. What are the tax consequences to Donald in year 10?

    b. How, if at all, would your answer in part (a) change if Donald filed a bankruptcy petition before discharging the bank debt?

80. Jill purchases a television from Nat's Department Store on an installment plan requiring her to pay Nat's $100 a month for 12 months (for a total of $1,200) plus interest. One week later, Jill sees an identical set for sale at another store for $1,000. Jill complains and Nat agrees to reduce the amount Jill owes to $1,000. What are the tax consequences to Jill of Nat reducing the debt by $200?

81. Ralph writes his neighbor, Sam, a check for $1,000. Sam builds a fence between their yards with the $1,000 Ralph gave him plus $1,000 of his own money. When Ralph later asks Sam to repay the $1,000, Sam refuses, claiming that Ralph had earlier promised to pay half of the cost of constructing the fence. Ralph denies making such a promise and insists on repayment, but ultimately agrees to discharge the debt for $600. What are the tax consequences to Sam of Ralph reducing the debt by $400?

82. In year one, Lawrence loans his sister, Shantelle, $5,000. In year two, Lawrence forgives the debt as a birthday present to Shantelle. What are the tax consequences to Shantelle in year two?

83. Ted owes $1,000 to Valerie. Valerie agrees to discharge the debt in exchange for Ted's baseball card collection. Although Ted originally bought the cards for $50, they are now worth $1,000. What are the tax consequences to Ted of this transaction?

84. Dan purchases Greenacre from Emily, giving her a 10-year $100,000 purchase money nonrecourse note bearing 12 percent interest, in exchange for the property. Dan's note requires him to pay Emily $12,000 interest per year and to repay the principal of $100,000 in a balloon payment at the end of the 10th year. Four years later, Dan sells Greenacre to Frank for $20,000 cash and assumption of the $100,000 debt.

    a. What are the tax consequences to Dan on the sale?

    b. What is Frank's basis in Greenacre?

85. Harry owns Blackacre with an adjusted basis of $100,000 and a fair market value of $700,000. The property is subject to a mortgage of $500,000. (Harry's original basis in Blackacre included the entire $500,000 of debt.) Carol wishes to purchase the property subject to the mortgage. How much cash will she pay for the property? What will be her basis in the property? How much gain will Harry realize and recognize on the sale?

86. John purchases an apartment building in year one for $100,000 cash and a $900,000 nonrecourse note. In years one through five, John takes $170,000 of total depreciation on the building. In year five, the apartment rental market collapses, the property declines in value to $850,000, John defaults on the note, and the nonrecourse lender seizes the apartment building. At the time of the default, John still owes $900,000 on the nonrecourse note.

    a. How much gain or loss does John realize and recognize in year five?

    b. In part (a) when the apartment building is repossessed by the bank in year five, the full $900,000 nonrecourse note is included in the amount realized. Is there an alternative tax treatment that might make sense? If so, what is it?

    c. Assume now that property was worth only $500,000 in year one, but John "inflated" the nonrecourse debt in order to increase his depreciation deductions. Under certain case law involving tax shelters, he might not get full basis credit for the nonrecourse debt. Assume that John's basis in year one is limited to $600,000 (the sum of (i) the nonrecourse debt up to the $500,000 value of the property plus (ii) the $100,000 cash invested). How, if at all, does the application of the special basis limitation rule change the answer in part (a) above?

EXPLANATIONS

77. a. Bob is not taxed because his receipt of cash is balanced by an offsetting liability to repay the loan.

    b. The repayment of loan principal is not deductible. The nondeductibility of loan repayment is a necessary corollary of the exclusion of loan proceeds.

78. Under §61(a)(12), Linda includes discharge of indebtedness income of $50,000 (the $200,000 owed less the $150,000 paid to

discharge the debt). This makes sense because the discharge of the $200,000 liability for $150,000 increases her net worth by $50,000.

79. a. The discount on the debt is $15,000 ($100,000 owed less the $85,000 paid to discharge it). Donald can exclude $10,000 of the discount under §108, but must include the other $5,000 of discount under §61(a)(12). Since Donald has not filed a bankruptcy petition, he can exclude the $15,000 of discharge of indebtedness income only to the extent of his $10,000 insolvency immediately before the debt discharge ($300,000 liabilities less the $290,000 value of his assets). §108(a)(1)(B), (a)(3), and (d)(3). The remaining $5,000 of debt discharge income must be included under §61(a)(12).

   b. Donald can exclude the entire $15,000 of debt discharge income because the discharge occurs in a bankruptcy proceeding. §108(a)(1)(A) and (d)(2). The fact that debt discharge income is treated more favorably in bankruptcy cases than in out-of-court workouts creates an incentive to file a bankruptcy petition before discharging debt instead of restructuring the debt out-of-court.

80. The $200 reduction in Jill's purchase money liability by the seller, Nat, is treated as a nontaxable reduction in the purchase price of the television. §108(e)(5).

81. Sam will not have to include the $400 discount on the debt, because the original $1,000 liability was disputed. Sobel, Inc. v. Commissioner, 40 B.T.A. 1263 (1939).

82. Shantelle does not have to include the $5,000 discount on the debt. Lawrence forgave the debt out of "detached and disinterested generosity," so the debt forgiveness is an excludable §102 gift. Commissioner v. Duberstein, 363 U.S. 278 (1960).

83. Ted is giving Valerie property worth $1,000 to discharge his $1,000 debt, so the transaction does not result in any debt discharge income. However, when a taxpayer pays a debt with appreciated property, the taxpayer must realize and recognize the gain on the transferred property. Here, Ted will recognize $950 of gain ($1,000 amount realized less $50 basis) on the transfer of the cards.

84. a. Dan's basis includes the $100,000 he borrowed to purchase the property. §1012 and Crane v. Commissioner, 331 U.S. 1

(1947). Relief of the indebtedness is included in amount realized, so the amount realized is $120,000 ($20,000 cash received plus $100,000 of debt relief). Crane v. Commissioner, 331 U.S. 1 (1947); §1001(b); Reg. §1.1001-2(a). Dan's realized gain equals $20,000 ($120,000 amount realized less $100,000 basis). §1001(a). His $20,000 realized gain is recognized under §1001(c).

b. The assumption of indebtedness is included in the basis of the property, under *Crane*, so Frank's basis is $120,000 ($20,000 cash plus $100,000 of debt assumed).

85. Carol will pay $200,000 in cash for the property subject to the $500,000 mortgage because the gross value of the property is $700,000. Her basis in the property will be $700,000 ($200,000 cash paid plus the $500,000 of debt). §1012 and *Crane*. Harry's amount realized equals $700,000 ($200,000 of cash received plus $500,000 of debt relief) and his basis is $100,000, so he realizes and recognizes $600,000 of gain on the sale. *Crane*, Reg. §1.1001-2(a)(1), and §1001(a)-(c).

86. a. John realizes and recognizes $70,000 of gain ($900,000 amount realized less $830,000 adjusted basis) in year five. John's adjusted basis in the apartment building is $830,000 ($1 million basis less the $170,000 depreciation taken). John's amount realized includes the full $900,000 of debt relief despite the fact that the property is worth only $850,000 at the time of the foreclosure. Commissioner v. Tufts, 461 U.S. 300 (1983).

John's out-of-pocket loss on the apartment building is the $100,000 of his own funds that he used to purchase the property. However, he was permitted to take $170,000 of depreciation deductions on the building. In other words, for tax purposes he was treated as having lost $170,000, when he really only lost $100,000. Thus, the $70,000 difference between his out-of-pocket loss and the tax losses that he took should be included in income, which it is.

b. In Commissioner v. Tufts, 461 U.S. 300 (1983), the Supreme Court held that the full amount of nonrecourse debt relief is included in amount realized even if the property is worth less than the debt owed at the time of the discharge. An alternative approach would be to (i) treat the value of the property at the time of the discharge as the amount realized and (ii) treat any discharge of indebtedness in excess of the value of the property as regular debt discharge income. In other words, this approach would separate the gain or loss from the property transaction from the income from debt discharge.

If this approach is applied to the facts of part (a), John would be treated as if he had sold the property for $850,000 and then used that amount to discharge the $900,000 nonrecourse loan. Since John's adjusted basis in the property is $830,000, John would realize and recognize $20,000 of property-related gain. In addition, since he discharged the $900,000 debt for $850,000, he would recognize $50,000 of discharge of indebtedness income, which might qualify for exclusion under §108. Justice O'Connor advocates this approach in her concurring opinion in *Tufts*. The different approaches taken by the *Tufts* majority and Justice O'Connor would frequently produce different tax results since (i) the property transaction might produce gain or loss, which might be capital or ordinary in character, and (ii) the debt discharge transaction would produce ordinary income, which might be excluded under §108.

c. John inflated his nonrecourse debt, so only $500,000 of the $900,000 of nonrecourse debt was included in basis in year one. Under the symmetry approach, only $500,000 of the $900,000 of debt relief in year five is included in John's amount realized. *Crane, Tufts*, and Reg. §1.1001-2(a)(3). John's realized and recognized gain equals $500,000 less his adjusted basis. His adjusted basis, in turn, equals his $600,000 basis less the depreciation that he took on that basis. Since the basis is reduced from $1 million to $600,000 in this part of the example, the depreciation taken here in years one through five will be less than the $170,000 of depreciation taken in part (a) of the example. If, for example, five years of depreciation on the $600,000 basis would equal $100,000, John's adjusted basis would be $500,000 and his gain or loss on the sale would be zero. This would make sense since John's $100,000 out-of-pocket loss equals the $100,000 of depreciation deductions he had claimed prior to the foreclosure.

I. Tax-Exempt Bonds

Section 103 provides that taxpayers may exclude the interest they receive on certain state, municipal, and other bonds. Tax-exempt bonds bear a lower rate of interest than taxable bonds; nonetheless, people invest in tax-exempt bonds because the interest on them is not taxed.

To illustrate, assume that the interest rate on taxable bonds is 10 percent and the rate on comparable tax-exempt bonds is 7 percent. The after-tax return on either type of bond would be equal for a taxpayer in the 30 percent tax bracket; if the taxpayer invests $1,000 in a taxable bond and earns annual interest of $100, the tax on that interest is $30 (30 percent of $100), leaving the taxpayer with $70, the same after-tax amount that the taxpayer could earn on a $1,000 investment in the tax-exempt bond. The $30 of pre-tax interest that the investor loses by investing in the tax-exempt bond is referred to as a *putative tax*.

If all taxpayers were in the 30 percent bracket, the exemption would simply shift the $30 of tax that the federal government would have collected to the state or local entity that issued the bonds. However, some taxpayers are taxed at higher rates. Consider, for example, a taxpayer in the 40 percent bracket who invests $1,000 in either a taxable or tax-exempt bond; if the taxpayer invests $1,000 in a taxable bond and earns annual interest of $100, the tax on that interest is $40 (40 percent of $100), leaving the taxpayer with $60, but if the taxpayer invests the $1,000 in a tax-exempt bond, the taxpayer earns $70 after-tax. If this taxpayer invests in the tax-exempt bond, the taxpayer pays a putative tax of $30 instead of an actual tax of $40. In other words, the federal government has given up $40 of tax to transfer $30 to the state or local entity; the extra $10 goes to the taxpayer. (Compare a taxpayer in the 40 percent bracket who earns $100 of wages and would have to pay $40 of tax on the wages.) Many individual investors are in the top tax brackets, so the exemption has been criticized as an inefficient form of federal subsidy to state and local governments.

3

Problems of Timing

Timing issues play a central role in tax planning. Taxpayers generally prefer to defer income and accelerate deductions because tax deferral is valuable to them. Even if the tax paid in a later year is, in absolute terms, the same amount that would have been paid in the earlier year, absent deferral, deferring the tax saves the taxpayer money. For example, assume that Yvette can structure a pending transaction in two ways. If she structures the transaction one way, she will have to include $50,000 of income in year one. If she structures the transaction the other way, she will have to include the $50,000 of income in year 10. Assume that Yvette is in the 40 percent tax bracket in years one and 10, so that she would owe $20,000 of tax on the income regardless of the year in which it is included.

   If Yvette can defer the $20,000 of tax for 10 years, she can invest the $20,000 and earn income on it. If, for example, she invests it in bonds that earn 10 percent (after-tax) a year, she will earn $20,000 ($2,000 per year of interest for 10 years) on the invested amount. Permitting Yvette to defer the $20,000 of tax for 10 years is thus comparable to a 10-year, interest-free $20,000 loan to Yvette from the federal government. The tax deferral has the effect of reducing Yvette's tax rate on the $50,000 of income. With the deferral, Yvette pays $20,000 of tax in year 10. How much money would Yvette have to invest in year one if she wanted the investment to grow to $20,000 by year 10 — and fund the tax payment due in that year? Assume that Yvette could earn 10 percent (after-tax) on funds invested in years 1 through 10. If Yvette invests $7,711, and earns 10 percent a year on that investment for 10 years, the $7,710 investment grows to $20,000 by year 10. If Yvette pays the $20,000 tax in year one, her tax rate is 40 percent. On the other hand, if Yvette pays the $20,000 tax in year 10, it costs her only $7,710 in year one; in other words, the deferral reduces Yvette's tax rate from 40 percent to 15.42 percent ($7,710/ $50,000).

In this chapter we will examine various timing rules that determine when taxpayers include certain items of income and deduct certain expenses. First, we will consider several rules that determine when gains and losses from property transactions are taken into account by taxpayers. As we will see, appreciation or decline in the value of property is not taxed until it is "realized." In addition, taxpayers can, in some circumstances, temporarily defer their realized gains. However, subject to a very small number of exceptions (for example, the §1014 basis step-up rule, which permanently excludes pre-death appreciation in property), taxpayers cannot permanently defer their property gains. Second, we will examine the rules that apply to transfers incident to divorce, including a rule that defers gain realized on the transfer of appreciated property incident to divorce. We will also consider the tax treatment of alimony and child support. Third, we will consider the differences between the cash and accrual methods of accounting and discuss the tests for determining when taxpayers using each method include income and deduct expenses. We will also review the original issue discount rules, which require both cash and accrual taxpayers to use economic accrual concepts to determine when the interest on certain loans is included and deducted. Fourth, we will compare the income tax with consumption and value added taxes since the choice of the tax base is related to the timing rules adopted by the tax system.

A. Gains and Losses from Investment in Property

1. *Realization of Gains and Losses*

Reading: §1001; Reg. §1.1001-1(a)

If the tax law adopted and applied the Haig-Simons definition of income in its purest form, persons would be taxable on their annual increase in wealth. An individual holding appreciated property would be taxed in the year the appreciation occurred, for example, rather than in the year the property is sold. A tax system based strictly on the Haig-Simons definition of income would have the virtue of treating all increases in wealth in a uniform manner. However, such a tax regimen would raise serious liquidity and valuation problems. In light of these problems, our tax system defers the tax on appreciation until it is "realized." Eisner v. Macomber, 252 U.S. 189 (1920).

Realization is a term of art that does not have a single, all-encompassing definition. Sometimes it will be obvious when realization has occurred. For example, a sale of property for cash is obviously a realization event. In other cases, the time of realization will be less clear. For example, suppose that in year one a taxpayer buys land and leases it to a tenant for 10 years. In year two, the tenant constructs a valuable new building on the property. In year 11, the taxpayer sells the land with the building. In which year does the taxpayer realize gain from the new building on the property? In Helvering v. Bruun, 309 U.S. 461 (1940), the Supreme Court held that a lessor realized gain from improvements made by the tenant upon termination of the lease. (However, Congress later enacted §§109 and 1019, which defer the gain from tenant improvements realized by a lessor on the termination of a lease, provided that the improvements were not a form of rent.)

Although the Code does not define the term "realization," Regulation §1.1001-1(a) provides that gain or loss is realized when property is exchanged for cash or other property "differing materially either in kind or in extent." In Cottage Savings Association v. Commissioner, 499 U.S. 554 (1991), the Supreme Court held that exchanged properties are "materially different" if they "embody legally distinct entitlements." In *Cottage Savings*, a savings and loan association exchanged a group (or "pool") of residential mortgages that had declined in value for another pool of residential mortgages. For bank regulation purposes, Cottage Savings did not have to report the loss on the mortgage pool given up in the exchange because the mortgage pools were "substantially identical" (within the meaning of federal bank regulations). However, for tax purposes, Cottage Savings took the position that the loss was realized on the exchange of the mortgage pools. The Supreme Court concluded that the exchanged mortgage pools embodied legally distinct entitlement (since, for example, the obligors on the mortgages varied between the two pools) and that the exchange was thus a realization event for tax purposes.

2. *Recognition of Gains and Losses*

Realized gains and losses are taken into account, for purposes of computing the taxpayer's gross income, only to the extent that they are also "recognized." Section 1001(c) provides that realized gains and losses are recognized unless otherwise provided in the Code. A number of *nonrecognition* rules are scattered throughout the Code. If a nonrecognition rule applies to a transaction, the taxpayer's realized gain or loss from the transaction will be deferred (in whole or in part). Nonrecognition rules apply to some (but not all) of the many situations in which a taxpayer shifts her investment from one piece of property to another piece of property of a similar character. For example, assume that a taxpayer exchanges land in Houston held for investment for land in Austin that she will also hold for investment. Although the exchange is a realization event, the taxpayer is simply continuing her investment, so it may make sense to defer her gain realized on the exchange of the Houston property until she sells the Austin property. Section 1031, the first nonrecognition rule that we will consider, does just that.

a. Like-Kind Exchanges

Reading: §§1001, 1031; Reg. §§1.1031(a)-1,
1.1031(a)-2, 1.1031(d)-2

Section 1001(c) provides that realized gains and losses are recognized unless otherwise provided in the Code. Sections 1031 through 1044 provide a series of nonrecognition rules that apply in certain property transactions. A number of other nonrecognition rules are scattered throughout the rest of the Code. Section 1031 provides for nonrecognition of gain or loss realized on the exchange of trade or business or investment property for like-kind property that will also be used in the taxpayer's trade or business or held for investment. Section 1031 is not elective; if the requirements of the section are met, it applies.

In practice, the great majority of §1031 like-kind exchanges involve exchanges of real property for two reasons. First, §1031 does not apply to many other types of property exchanges, including exchanges of inventory, stocks, bonds, notes, other securities or evidences of indebtedness, partnership interests, beneficial interests in trusts, or contract rights. §1031(a)(2). Second, administrative rulings and regulations treat all real property, developed or undeveloped and commercial or residential, as like-kind, making it relatively easy to qualify real property exchanges for §1031. See, e.g., Reg. §1.1031(a)-1(b) (which provides that the term *like-kind* refers to "the nature and character of the property and not to its grade or quality"). Nonsimultaneous exchanges even qualify for §1031, provided that the requirements of §1031(a)(3)(A) and Regulation §1.1031(k)-1 are met. Thus, most real estate may be exchanged for other real property without recognition, provided, of course, that the real property is held for investment or for productive use in a trade or business. (However, if real estate is held for sale to customers, an exchange of that property would not qualify for §1031 nonrecognition. §1031(a)(2).)

Section 1031 does not eliminate the gain realized in the §1031 exchange; instead, it defers the gain by assigning the property received in the §1031 exchange a basis such that, if the property received were sold immediately after the exchange, the taxpayer would realize gain in an amount equal to the amount of gain realized in the §1031 exchange that went unrecognized under §1031. Section 1031(d) thus provides that a taxpayer's basis in the property received in the §1031 exchange equals the taxpayer's basis in the property given up in the exchange. §1031(d). For example, suppose Bill owns Blackacre, which has a basis of $80 and fair market value of $200, and Carla owns Greenacre, which has a basis of $50 and a fair market value of $200. If Bill and Carla exchange properties, Bill's realized gain in the exchange is $120 ($200 amount realized less $80 basis) and Carla's realized gain is $150 ($200 amount realized less $50 basis), but neither will recognize their realized gain. §1031(a). Bill's basis in the new property, Greenacre, is $80, Bill's basis in the property given up, Blackacre. §1031(d). If Bill sells Greenacre immediately after the exchange, he will realize and recognize $120 of gain ($200 amount realized less $80 basis), which makes sense since Bill's realized but unrecognized gain from the exchange of Blackacre was $120. Said another way, on the sale of Greenacre, the property received in the §1031 exchange, Bill will realize and recognize the $120 of deferred gain from the §1031 exchange. In similar fashion, Carla's basis in Blackacre is $50, her basis in the property given up, Greenacre. If Carla sold Blackacre right after she received it, she would realize and recognize the $150 of gain that she realized but did not recognize in the §1031 exchange of Greenacre.

The nonrecognition rule of §1031(a)(1) provides that no gain is recognized on qualifying like-kind exchanges provided the property is exchanged *solely* for other like-kind property. However (as is true under other nonrecognition sections) "solely" does not really mean

3. Problems of Timing

"solely." Section 1031 applies even if the taxpayer receives both like-kind property (called *permitted property* because the taxpayer is permitted to receive it without recognition) and other property or money (called *boot* or *nonpermitted property*). If a taxpayer receives boot in a §1031 exchange, any gain realized is recognized up to the value of boot received in the §1031 exchange. §1031(b). Said another way, gain recognized equals the lesser of (i) the gain realized in the exchange or (ii) the fair market value of the boot received. If the taxpayer realizes a loss in a §1031 exchange, the loss is not recognized even if the taxpayer receives boot in the exchange. §1031(c). If gain is recognized on a like-kind exchange, the basis of the like-kind property received in the exchange is equal to (i) the basis of the property given up, (ii) less the fair market value of the cash or other boot (for example, appreciated stock) received, (iii) plus the gain recognized. §1031(d). A taxpayer's basis in noncash boot received is its fair market value. §1031(d). The party paying boot adds the boot to the basis of the property acquired in the exchange.

Suppose, for example, that Emma exchanges Seaview, which has a basis of $80 and a fair market value of $100, for $5 in cash and Mountainview, like-kind property that has a fair market value of $95. Emma's realized gain on the exchange is $20, which is the $100 amount realized ($95 of property plus $5 of cash) less the $80 basis of the property. Had Emma exchanged Seaview solely for like-kind property, she would not have recognized any of the realized gain. Here, under §1031(b), Emma recognizes gain of $5, the amount of the cash boot. Emma's basis in Mountainview is $80 ($80 substituted basis less $5 boot received plus $5 of gain recognized). §1031(d). Mountainview has a value of $95. If Emma sells Mountainview immediately after the exchange, she will recognize another $15 of gain. In the §1031 exchange, only $5 of the $20 of realized gain was recognized, so Emma should and will realize $15 of gain on the sale of Mountainview.

Why, in this example, did we add and subtract the same amount, $5, from Emma's basis for Mountainview? Recall that §1031(d) provides that the basis of the like-kind property received in the exchange is equal to (i) the basis of the property given up, (ii) less the fair market value of the cash or other boot received, (iii) plus the gain recognized. Students often ask: Can we just forget about the second and third terms in this formula because they cancel each other? In our example, we subtracted the $5 of boot received and added the $5 of gain recognized as a result of receipt of that boot—so Emma's basis in

Mountainview is ultimately the same as her $80 basis in the property given up, Seaview. The second and third terms in the basis formula do cancel each other out if (i) the taxpayer realizes a gain in the §1031 exchange and (ii) the taxpayer's realized gain exceeds the amount of boot received in the exchange; in those circumstances, the gain recognized will equal the amount of boot received. However, the second and third terms in the basis formula will not cancel each other if either (i) the realized gain is less than the amount of boot received or (ii) the taxpayer realizes a loss in the §1031 exchange; in those circumstances, the gain recognized will not equal the amount of boot received.

To illustrate, assume that Emma instead exchanges Seaview for $25 in cash and Lakeview, which is worth $75. Emma's realized gain is $20, the $100 amount realized ($75 of property plus $25 cash) less $80 basis, all of which is recognized because she receives $25 of boot. Her recognized gain is not $25; although she receives $25 of boot, the recognized gain is limited to the $20 of gain realized in the exchange. Emma's basis in Lakeview is $75 (Emma's $80 basis in Seaview less $25 boot received plus $20 gain recognized). (Note that the second and third terms do not cancel each other.) Lakeview has a value of $75. If Emma sells Lakeview immediately after the exchange, she will realize no gain or loss on the sale. This makes sense because Emma's $20 of gain realized in the §1031 exchange has already been fully recognized.

Like-kind exchanges sometimes involve properties subject to debt. In that case, any *net* reduction in debt due to the exchange is treated as cash received and, thus, boot for purposes of determining the gain recognized in the exchange. A taxpayer's net debt relief equals (i) any liability that the taxpayer gave up in the exchange less (ii) the sum of (a) any liability that the taxpayer assumed in the exchange plus (b) any cash that the taxpayer *paid* in the exchange. Suppose, for example, that Paul owns Swampview, which has a basis of $175 and is subject to a mortgage of $150. Swampview's gross fair market value, determined without regard to the debt, is $290 (so the value, net of the debt, is $140). Paul exchanges Swampview for Oceanview, which has a fair market value of $220 and is subject to an $80 mortgage. Paul's realized gain is $115; it is determined by adding the debt relief of $150 and the $220 gross value of property received and subtracting from that sum Paul's $175 basis in the property given up and the $80 of debt assumed in connection with the property received. Reg. §1.1031(d)-2. How much boot has Paul received? Paul's net debt relief equals $70 (the $150 liability Paul gave up less the $80 liability

3. Problems of Timing

Paul assumed), so Paul is treated as having received $70 of boot in the exchange. Thus, Paul recognizes $70 of the $115 gain realized in the exchange. His basis for Oceanview is $175 (the $175 basis of property given up, plus $70 gain recognized, less $70 net debt relief boot received). Reg. §1.1031(d)-2. If Paul sold Oceanview for $220 immediately after the exchange, Paul would realize $45 of gain, which makes sense since Paul has already recognized $70 of the $115 gain realized in the §1031 exchange.

EXAMPLES

1. State whether the following exchanges would qualify as like-kind exchanges under §1031.
   a. Improved commercial rental real estate in New York City is exchanged for undeveloped investment property in Vail, Colorado.
   b. Corporate stock in Xenon Corporation is exchanged for corporate stock in Yaba Corporation. Both corporations produce medical equipment.
   c. A real estate developer exchanges unimproved lots in Santa Barbara, which were held for development and sale to customers, for unimproved oceanfront property in Oregon, which will also be developed and sold to customers.

2. Alice owns Blackacre, investment property that has a fair market value of $100,000 and basis of $40,000. Bob owns Whiteacre, investment property that has a fair market value of $100,000 and a basis of $80,000. Alice and Bob exchange their properties and hold the property received for investment. What are the tax consequences of the exchange to Alice and Bob?

3. Carol owns a used Ford truck with a fair market value of $1,500 and a basis of $800. Doug owns a used GM truck with a fair market value of $1,000 and a basis of $400. Both Carol and Doug use their trucks exclusively in their businesses. Carol and Doug exchange their trucks and Doug pays Carol $500. Both trucks are still used exclusively in their businesses. What are the tax consequences of the exchange to Carol and Doug?

4. a. Emily owns Greenacre, investment property with a fair market value of $200,000 and a basis of $120,000. Fred owns Whiteacre, investment property with a fair market value of $180,000 and a basis of $80,000. Emily and Fred exchange

3. Problems of Timing

their properties and Fred pays Emily $20,000. What are the tax consequences of the exchange to Emily and Fred?

b. How, if at all, would the consequences to Emily change in part (a) if her basis in Greenacre were $185,000 instead of $120,000?

5. George owns Gulfview, investment property with a fair market value of $100,000 and a basis of $150,000. Harriet owns Pineacre, investment property with a fair market value of $90,000 and basis of $50,000. George and Harriet exchange their properties and Harriet pays George $10,000 in cash. What are the tax consequences of the exchange to George and Harriet?

6. Juan borrows $60,000 and uses the proceeds, together with $40,000 of his own funds, to purchase investment property, Ranchview, for $100,000. Juan's debt is nonrecourse and is secured by Ranchview. Samantha owns Cityview, investment property that has a value of $240,000 and basis of $150,000 and is not subject to any debt. Juan and Samantha exchange their properties. At the time of the exchange, Ranchview is still subject to the $60,000 of debt. Absent that debt, Ranchview would have a fair market value of $300,000; the value net of the debt is $240,000. What are the consequences of the exchange to Juan and Samantha?

7. Alice acquired Blackacre, which she held for investment, in exchange for $20,000 of her own funds and $80,000 that she borrowed. The $80,000 of debt is nonrecourse and is secured by Blackacre. Bob owns Whiteacre, investment property with a $50,000 basis. Whiteacre is subject to a $70,000 mortgage. Alice exchanges Blackacre for Whiteacre. At the time of the exchange (i) Whiteacre has a gross value (without taking into account the debt) of $95,000 and a net value (taking into account the debt) of $25,000; (ii) Blackacre has a gross value of $105,000 (without taking into account the debt) and has a net value (taking into account the debt) of $25,000; and (iii) all of the $80,000 debt on Blackacre and the $70,000 debt on Whiteacre is still outstanding. What are the tax consequences of the exchange to Alice and Bob?

8. Emily owns Riverview, investment property, with a gross value of $110,000 and basis of $100,000, which is subject to $20,000 of debt (so that the net value of the property is $90,000). Fred owns Mountainview, investment property with a value of $60,000 and basis of $40,000. Emily and Fred exchange their properties and

3. Problems of Timing

Fred pays Emily $30,000. What are the tax consequences of the exchange to Emily and Fred?

EXPLANATIONS

1. a. Section 1031 applies to the exchange. Regulation §1.1031(a)-1(b) treats improved realty and unimproved realty as "like-kind." If both properties are held for productive use in a trade or business or for investment, §1031 applies to the exchange.
   b. Section 1031 does not apply to the exchange of stock. §1031(a)(2)(B). It is irrelevant that the two corporations manufacture the same products.
   c. Section 1031 does not apply to the exchange of the lots because they are "stock in trade or other property held primarily for sale." §1031(a)(2)(A).

2. Alice realizes gain of $60,000 ($100,000 amount realized less $40,000 basis) and Bob realizes gain of $20,000 ($100,000 amount realized less $80,000 basis). However, neither one recognizes any gain because the exchange is within §1031 and there is no boot involved in the exchange. §1031(a). Alice's basis in Whiteacre is her basis in the property given up in the exchange, $40,000. Bob's basis in Blackacre is his basis in the property given up, $80,000. §1031(d).

3. The exchange qualifies for §1031. The trucks are "like-kind" because they are in the same asset class for purposes of determining depreciation deductions. Reg. §1.1031(a)-2. Carol realizes gain of $700 and receives boot of $500. In a §1031 exchange, realized gain is recognized up to the amount of boot received, so Alice recognizes a gain of $500. §1031(b). Carol's basis in the GM truck received is $800 (her $800 basis in the property given up, plus $500 of gain recognized on the exchange, less $500 of boot received). Following the exchange, Carol owns a truck, with a basis of $800 and value of $1,000, plus $500 of cash. If she sold the GM truck immediately after receiving it, she would realize $200 of gain ($1,000 amount realized less $800 basis) on the sale. She has already recognized $500 of the $700 of gain realized on the exchange of the Ford truck, so it is appropriate that she has $200 of potential gain in the GM truck she received in the exchange.

   Doug realizes a gain of $600 on the exchange, but does not recognize any gain because he does not receive any boot.

§1031(a). Doug's basis in the property received is $900 (his $400 basis in the GM truck he gave up plus the $500 of cash he paid). §§1031(d) and 1012. Doug now owns a truck with a basis of $900 and a FMV of $1,500. If he sold the Ford truck immediately after receiving it, he would realize $600 of gain ($1,500 amount realized less $900 basis) on the sale. He has not recognized any of the $600 of gain realized on the exchange of the GM truck, so it is appropriate that he has $600 of potential gain in the Ford truck he received in the exchange.

4. a. Emily's realized gain in the exchange is $80,000 — $200,000 amount realized ($180,000 of property plus $20,000 of cash) less $120,000 basis. That realized gain is recognized up to the amount of boot received, here $20,000, so Emily will recognize $20,000 of gain on the exchange. §1031(b). Emily's basis in Whiteacre is $120,000 (her $120,000 basis in Greenacre, plus the $20,000 of gain she recognizes on the exchange, less the $20,000 of boot she receives in the exchange). §1031(d). If Emily sold Whiteacre immediately after she received it in the exchange, she would realize $60,000 of gain ($180,000 amount realized less $120,000 basis). This is appropriate because she has already recognized $20,000 of the $80,000 of gain realized on the §1031 exchange.

Fred's realized gain in the exchange is $100,000 — $200,000 value of Greenacre less $100,000 ($80,000 basis plus $20,000 of cash Fred paid). Reg. §1.1031(d)-2. Fred's recognized gain is zero because he receives no boot in the exchange. Fred's basis in Greenacre is $100,000 — his $80,000 basis in Whiteacre plus the $20,000 of cash he paid. §1031(d) and Reg. §1.1031(d)-2. If Fred sold Greenacre immediately after he received it in the exchange, he would realize $100,000 of gain ($200,000 amount realized less $100,000 basis). This is appropriate because he will not have recognized any of the $100,000 of gain realized on the §1031 exchange.

  b. Emily's realized gain in the exchange is $15,000 — $200,000 amount realized ($180,000 of property plus $20,000 of cash) less $185,000. Although Emily receives $20,000 of boot, the gain recognized is limited to her realized gain, so Emily's recognized gain is $15,000. §1031(b). Emily's basis in Whiteacre is $180,000 (her $185,000 basis in Greenacre, plus the $15,000 of gain she recognizes on the exchange, less the $20,000 of boot she receives in the exchange). §1031(d). If Emily sold Whiteacre immediately after she received it in the exchange, she would realize no gain or loss ($180,000 amount realized less $180,000 basis). This is appropriate because she has already recognized all of the $15,000 of gain realized on the §1031 exchange.

5. George realizes a loss of $50,000 ($150,000 basis less $100,000 amount realized), but does not recognize that loss despite the fact that he received $10,000 of boot. §1031(a) and (c). George's basis in Pineacre will be $140,000 (his $150,000 basis in Gulfacre, plus his gain recognized of $0, less the $10,000 of boot he received). Pineacre is worth $90,000. If George sold Pineacre immediately after the exchange, he would realize a $50,000 loss. This makes sense because he has not recognized any of the $50,000 loss that he realized in the exchange.

Harriet realizes a gain of $40,000, but recognizes no gain because she receives no boot. Her basis in Gulfview is $60,000 ($50,000 from Pineacre plus $10,000 of cash). Since Gulfview has a value of $100,000, this preserves the $40,000 of potential gain that Harriet had in Pineacre prior to the §1031 exchange.

6. Juan's realized gain on the exchange is $200,000 — $300,000 amount realized ($240,000 of property plus $60,000 of debt relief) less $100,000 basis ($40,000 cash investment plus $60,000 of nonrecourse debt, under *Crane*). Reg. §1.1031(d)-2. Juan recognizes gain equal to the lesser of (i) the gain realized or (ii) the boot received. Net relief from indebtedness is treated as boot for purposes of §1031. Reg. §1.1031(d)-2. In this exchange Juan gave up a $60,000 liability and did not assume any liability, so his net debt relief, which is treated as boot, is $60,000. Thus, Juan recognizes gain of $60,000. Juan's basis in Cityview is $100,000 (his $100,000 basis in Ranchview, plus the $60,000 of gain recognized, less the $60,000 of boot received). Cityview is worth $240,000. If Juan sold it immediately after the exchange, he would realize $140,000 of gain ($240,000 amount realized less $100,000 basis), which makes sense since he will have already recognized $60,000 of the $200,000 of gain realized on the §1031 exchange.

On the exchange, Samantha realizes $90,000 of gain — $300,000 amount realized less $210,000 basis plus adjustments ($150,000 basis plus $60,000 debt on Ranchview). She will not recognize any of it because she does not receive any boot in the exchange. §1031(a). Samantha's basis in Ranchview is $210,000 — her $150,000 basis in Cityview plus the $60,000 debt she assumed. Reg. §1.1031(d)-2. Cityview is worth $300,000. If Samantha sold it immediately after the exchange, she would realize $90,000 of gain ($300,000 amount realized less $210,000 basis), which makes sense since she will not have recognized any of the $90,000 of gain realized on the §1031 exchange.

7.   Alice's realized gain in the exchange is $5,000 — $175,000 amount realized ($95,000 of property plus relief of the $80,000 of indebtedness on Blackacre) less $170,000 basis plus adjustments ($100,000 basis plus the $70,000 of debt on the new property, Whiteacre). Alice receives net debt relief of $10,000 ($80,000 liability on Blackacre, the property she gave up, less $70,000 liability on Whiteacre, the property she received in the exchange). That $10,000 of net debt relief is boot and her recognized gain is $5,000. (Even though she receives $10,000 of boot, her recognized gain cannot exceed her realized gain, here $5,000.) Alice's basis in Whiteacre is $95,000 (her $100,000 basis in Blackacre, less the $10,000 of net debt relief, plus the $5,000 of gain recognized). Reg. §1.1031(d)-2. Whiteacre is worth $95,000. If Alice sold it immediately after receiving it, she would not realize any gain or loss, which makes sense since she will have already recognized all of the $5,000 of gain realized in the §1031 exchange.

Bob's realized gain on the exchange is $45,000 — $175 amount realized ($105,000 of property plus relief of the $70,000 of indebtedness on Whiteacre) less $130,000 basis plus adjustments ($50,000 basis plus the $80,000 of debt on the new property, Whiteacre). Bob does not have any net debt relief because he gave up a $70,000 liability and assumed an $80,000 liability. Since he receives no boot in the exchange, he does not recognize any of the realized gain. Bob's basis in Blackacre is $60,000 (his $50,000 basis in Blackacre, plus the $80,000 liability on Blackacre, less the $70,000 liability on Whiteacre). Reg. §1.1031(d)-2. Whiteacre is worth $105,000. If Bob sold it immediately after receiving it, he would realize $45,000 of gain, which makes sense since Bob will not have recognized any of the $45,000 of gain realized in the §1031 exchange.

8.   Emily's realized gain on the exchange is $10,000 — $110,000 amount realized ($60,000 of property, plus $30,000 of cash, plus

135

relief of $20,000 of debt on Riverview) less $100,000 basis. Emily receives $50,000 of boot — $30,000 of cash boot plus $20,000 of net debt relief. Thus, she recognizes $10,000 of gain, which is the lesser of (i) the $10,000 realized gain and (ii) the $50,000 boot received. Her basis in Mountainview is $60,000 — her $100,000 basis in Riverview, plus $10,000 of gain recognized, less the $50,000 of boot she received. Mountainview is worth $60,000. If she sold it immediately after receiving it, she would not realize any gain or loss, which makes sense since she will have already recognized all of the $10,000 of gain realized in the §1031 exchange.

Fred's realized gain on the exchange is $20,000 — $110,000 amount realized (the value of Riverview) less $90,000 basis plus adjustments ($40,000 basis, plus $20,000 of debt assumed on Mountainview, plus $30,000 of cash Fred paid). Reg. §1.1031-2(d). Fred will not recognize any gain on the exchange because he receives no boot. His basis in Riverview is $90,000 — his $40,000 basis in Mountainview, plus $20,000 of debt assumed on Riverview, plus $30,000 of cash Fred paid. Riverview is worth $110,000. If Fred sold it immediately after receiving it, he would realize $20,000 of gain, which makes sense since Bob will not have recognized any of the $20,000 of gain realized in the §1031 exchange.

b. Other Nonrecognition Rules

Reading: §§121, 1033, 1034

A number of other Code sections also provide for nonrecognition in certain types of property transactions. Section 1033 applies to involuntary conversions of property on which gain is realized. (The section does not apply to losses realized on involuntary conversions.) Section 1033(a)(2) provides that a taxpayer may elect to not recognize gain realized on the involuntary conversion of property into cash due to theft, fire, or condemnation, provided that the taxpayer reinvests the cash in property that is similar or related in use to the lost property. Thus, §1033 would permit a taxpayer to avoid recognition of gain realized where an appreciated building was lost due to an earthquake, the taxpayer received insurance proceeds on the destroyed building, and the insurance proceeds were used to construct a similar building. If some of the proceeds are not reinvested in similar use property,

§1033 provides a rule that is similar to the boot gain recognition rule in §1031; realized gain is recognized to the extent that proceeds are not reinvested in similar use property. The basis of the new similar use property is equal to the cost of the similar use property less any gain realized on the involuntarily converted property that was not recognized. §1033(b) (last sentence). (This basis formula is the equivalent of the sum of the basis of the lost property, plus any additional cash or debt invested in the new property, plus any gain recognized on the involuntary conversion transaction, less any proceeds not reinvested in the similar use property.)

Suppose, for example, that an apartment building with a fair market value of $750,000 and a basis of $500,000 is destroyed in a fire and that the building owner receives an insurance payment of $750,000. The building owner realizes a gain of $250,000 on the conversion. If he reinvests all of the $750,000 in similar use property and makes an election under §1033, he will not recognize any of the $250,000 of realized gain. However, if he does not reinvest the entire $750,000 in similar use property, he will recognize gain in an amount equal to the lesser of (i) the $250,000 of realized gain or (ii) the portion of the proceeds that were not reinvested in similar use property. If the owner purchases a new apartment building for $650,000, for example, he will recognize gain of $100,000, the amount of the insurance proceeds he does not reinvest. His basis in the new building would in that case be $500,000 — the $650,000 purchase price of the new building less the $150,000 of gain that was realized in the conversion but not recognized. (Equivalently, we could calculate the basis as the $500,000 basis in the destroyed building plus the $100,000 gain recognized less the $100,000 proceeds that were not reinvested in similar use property.)

Another nonrecognition rule, §1034, applies to sales of personal residences. Section 1034 provides that a taxpayer does not recognize gain realized on the sale of a principal residence if, within a period beginning two years before the date of the sale and ending two years after the date of the sale, the taxpayer purchases a new principal residence and the price of the new residence equals or exceeds the adjusted sales price of the old residence. §1034(a). The "adjusted sales price" of the old residence is equal to the price at which the old residence is sold, less broker's fees and certain other costs of preparing the old residence for sale. What if the new residence costs less than the adjusted sales price of the old residence? Section 1034 follows the approach of other nonrecognition sections, such as §§1031 and 1033: Gain realized on the sale of the old residence is recognized to the extent that the new residence costs less than the adjusted sales price of the old residence. The basis of the new residence is equal to the purchase price of the new residence less any gain that was realized but not recognized on the sale of the old residence. §1034(e).

Section 121 also benefits some homeowners on the sale of a principal residence. However, instead of deferring tax, as the nonrecognition rule of §1034 does, §121 allows qualifying taxpayers to permanently exclude up to $125,000 of gain on the sale of a principal residence. In order for the §121 exclusion to apply, the following requirements must be met: (i) the taxpayer must be age 55 or older, (ii) the taxpayer must have owned the residence and used it as her principal residence for at least three of the five years preceding the sale, and (iii) the taxpayer must make an election to apply the section. §121(a). (Spouses must make the election jointly. §121(c).) A taxpayer can exclude gain under §121 only once in her lifetime. §121(b). Sections 121 and 1034 can both apply to the sale of a principal residence. If both sections apply to a sale, for purposes of determining the consequences under §1034 the amount realized from the sale of the old residence is reduced by the amount of gain excluded under §121. §121(d)(7).

EXAMPLES

9. Linda's warehouse burned down. It had a basis of $250,000 and an estimated fair market value of $400,000. Describe the tax consequences to Linda of the alternative transactions below. (Assume that each of the transactions qualifies as an involuntary conversion under §1033 and that Linda elects nonrecognition treatment.)

   a. She receives $400,000 from insurance and uses the proceeds to purchase a new warehouse for $400,000.

   b. She receives $400,000 from insurance and uses the proceeds to purchase (i) a new warehouse for $300,000 and (ii) a race horse for $100,000.

   c. She receives $300,000 from insurance, borrows an additional $100,000, and uses the $400,000 of insurance and debt proceeds to purchase a new warehouse.

   d. She receives nothing from insurance, borrows $400,000, and uses the debt proceeds to purchase a new warehouse for $400,000.

     e. She receives $400,000 from insurance, purchases a new warehouse for $220,000, and keeps the rest of the money.

10. In year one, Zachary sells his principal residence for $150,000 (which is both the amount realized and the "adjusted sales price" of the residence). His basis in the residence prior to the sale is $100,000. In year two, Zachary purchases a new principal residence. What are the tax consequences to Zachary of the sale of the residence in year one and the purchase of a new principal residence for each of the following alternative amounts?
     a. Zachary pays $150,000 for the new principal residence.
     b. Zachary pays $130,000 for the new principal residence.
     c. Zachary pays $175,000 for the new principal residence.

EXPLANATIONS

9.   a. Linda's realized gain is $150,000 ($400,000 amount realized less $250,000 basis), but she does not recognize any of that gain. Her basis in the new warehouse is $250,000 (the $400,000 purchase price for the new warehouse less the $150,000 of gain realized but not recognized on the conversion). §1033(a)(2)(A) and (b) (last sentence).

    b. Linda's realized gain is $150,000 ($400,000 amount realized less $250,000 basis). The nonrecognition rule of §1033 applies only to the extent that the amount received from the involuntary conversion is used to purchase similar-use replacement property. §1033(a)(2)(A). Here, Linda spends $100,000 of the proceeds on a racehorse, which is not similar-use property, so she recognizes $100,000 of gain. She will have a $100,000 basis in the racehorse, under §1012. Her basis in the new warehouse is $250,000 — the $300,000 purchase price of the new warehouse less the $50,000 of gain that was realized but not recognized on the conversion. §1033(a)(2)(A) and (b) (last sentence).

    c. Linda's realized gain is $50,000 ($300,000 amount realized less $250,000 basis). Linda uses all of the proceeds to acquire similar-use property, the new warehouse, so she does not recognize any gain on the conversion. Her basis in the new warehouse is $350,000 — the $400,000 purchase price of the new warehouse less the $50,000 of gain that was realized but not recognized. §1033(a)(2)(A) and (b) (last sentence).

    d. Linda realizes a loss of $250,000 ($250,000 basis less zero amount realized). Section 1033 does not apply to realized losses. Her realized loss may or may not be deductible under §165 (discussed in Chapter 4). Linda's basis in the new warehouse is $400,000. §1012 and *Crane*, 331 U.S. 1 (1947).

e. Linda's realized gain is $150,000 ($400,000 amount realized less $250,000 basis). The nonrecognition rule of §1033 applies only to the extent that the amount received from the involuntary conversion is used to purchase similar-use replacement property. §1033(a)(2)(A). Here, Linda does not spend $180,000 of the insurance proceeds on similar use property, so she recognizes all of the $150,000 realized gain. Her basis in the new warehouse is $220,000 (the $220,000 purchase price of the new warehouse less zero realized but unrecognized gain). §1033(a)(2)(A) and (b) (last sentence).

10. a. Zachary's realized gain on the sale of the principal residence is $50,000 ($150,000 amount realized less $100,000 basis). Zachary recognizes no gain on the exchange since (i) he purchases a new principal residence within two years of the sale of his previous principal residence and (ii) the $150,000 adjusted sales price of the old residence does not exceed the $150,000 Zachary paid for the new residence. §1034(a). Zachary's basis in the new residence is $100,000 (the $150,000 purchase price of the new residence less the $50,000 of gain that was realized but not recognized on the sale of the old residence). §1034(e). The new residence is worth $150,000. If Zachary sold it immediately after buying it, he would realize $50,000 of gain, which makes sense since that is the amount of realized gain that was not recognized on the sale of the old residence in year one.

b. Zachary's realized gain on the sale of the principal residence is $50,000 ($150,000 amount realized less $100,000 basis). Zachary purchases a new principal residence within two years of the sale of his previous residence. However, the $150,000 adjusted sales price of the old residence exceeds the $130,000 amount Zachary paid for the new residence by $20,000, so Zachary will recognize $20,000 of the realized gain. Zachary's basis in his new residence is equal to $100,000 (the $130,000 cost of the new residence less the $30,000 of gain that was realized but not recognized on the sale of the old residence). The new residence is worth $130,000. If Zachary sold it immediately after buying it, he would realize $30,000 of gain, which makes sense since that is the portion of the $50,000 of realized gain that was not recognized on the sale of the old residence in year one.

c. Zachary's realized gain on the sale of the principal residence is $50,000 ($150,000 amount realized less $100,000 basis). Zachary recognizes no gain on the exchange since (i) he purchases a new principal residence within two years of the sale of his previous principal residence and (ii) the $150,000 adjusted sales price of the old residence does not exceed the $175,000 Zachary paid for the new residence. §1034(a). Zachary's basis in the new residence is $125,000 (the $175,000 purchase price of the new residence less the $50,000 of gain that was realized but not recognized on the sale of the old residence). §1034(e). The new residence is worth $175,000. If Zachary sold it immediately after buying it, he would realize $50,000 of gain, which makes sense since that is the amount of realized gain that was not recognized on the sale of the old residence in year one.

B. Transfers Incident to Marriage and Divorce

Reading: §§71, 215, 62(a)(10), 1041

Transfers made pursuant to marriage and (more commonly) divorce raise a number of interesting tax issues. For example, suppose pursuant to a divorce Leslie gives Sandy property with a basis of $10,000 and a fair market value of $30,000. Should Sandy be taxed on the fair market value received? And what about Leslie? Should Leslie receive a deduction equal to the basis of the property? Or should Leslie be treated as if the property were sold and the proceeds used to purchase freedom from a bad marriage? Should it matter whether the property was community property or Leslie's separate property?

In United States v. Davis, 370 U.S. 65 (1962), reh'g denied, 371 U.S. 854 (1962), the Supreme Court held that a transfer of appreciated property incident to a divorce was a realization event to the transferor. In effect, the Court held that the exchange of property for freedom from marriage was similar to the exchange of property for services or other non-like-kind property and so was taxable. The holding in *Davis* did not apply, however, to a transfer between divorcing spouses of property held as community property. The *Davis* decision was subject to a great deal of criticism both for its view of divorce settlements and the distinction it set up between community property and noncommunity property states.

Eventually the holding in *Davis* was overturned by statute. Section 1041 now provides that no gain or loss is recognized by either party on the transfer of property to (i) a spouse or (ii) a former spouse, provided that the transfer is incident to divorce. (The holding in *Davis* may still apply, however, for property transferred in anticipation of marriage.) As is customary in nonrecognition provisions, §1041 provides that the transferee assumes the transferor's basis in the property. Thus, in the above example neither party would recognize gain or loss, and Sandy would receive a $10,000 basis in the property received.

Transfers of cash made incident to divorce do not raise realization issues and might therefore be dealt with elsewhere in this book. However, in order to provide a more unified view of transfers incident to divorce, we will discuss these transfers here. Payments of cash made incident to divorce are treated as either *alimony* or *child support payments*. Alimony payments are included in the income of the payee and are deducted from the payor's gross income. On the other hand, child support payments are not deductible by the payor or includible by the payee. §§71, 215, 62(a)(10).

In order to qualify as alimony, a payment must meet the following tests. First, as noted above, it must be made in cash. §71(b)(1). (As described above, §1041, not §71, applies to noncash transfers incident to divorce.) Second, the payment must be made pursuant to a written divorce or separate maintenance agreement or decree. §71(b)(1)(A), (2). Third, the payor and payee must live in separate households. §71(b)(1)(C). Presumably, this provision is intended to prevent couples from using divorce to obtain the benefits of income splitting, as described below in an example. Fourth, the payment must not be for child support. §71(c)(1). Any payments that end when a child dies or reaches a certain age (for example, age 18) will be characterized as child support payments. §71(c)(2). Fifth, the payment obligation must not continue after the death of the payee spouse. §71(b)(1)(D). Sixth, §71(f) provides, generally, that payments are treated as alimony only to the extent they are substantially equal in the first three years in which alimony payments are made.

Payments that are "front loaded" in this three-year period are recharacterized as property settlements. In effect, §71(f) requires "recapture" of any disproportionately high amounts of alimony (referred to in §71 as *excess alimony payments*) paid in the first two years. The excess alimony paid in years one and two is recaptured by requiring the payor spouse to include it in income in year three; the spouse who receives the alimony deducts the same amount from gross income in year three. In practice you will not usually have to compute the amount of excess alimony payments under §71(f) because divorce lawyers typically structure the alimony as level payments to avoid triggering §71(f).

How are excess alimony payments calculated under §71(f)? First, we determine the excess payments for the *second* year in which alimony payments are made. §71(f)(4). The excess payments for this year equal (i) the alimony payments made in the second year less (ii) the sum of (a) the alimony payments made in the third year of payment plus (b) $15,000. Second, we determine the excess payments for the *first* year in which payments are made. §71(f)(3). The excess payments for this year equal (i) the alimony payments made in the first year less (ii) the sum of (a) $15,000 plus (b) the average alimony payment made in the second and third years (which is computed after reducing the second-year payment by any portion of that payment treated as an excess payment under §71(f)(4)).

For example, suppose an alimony schedule provides for the payment of $100,000 in the first and second years and $20,000 thereafter. In years one and two, the payor spouse deducts the $100,000 of alimony from gross income and the payee spouse includes it in income. In year three, the payor spouse deducts the $20,000 of alimony from gross income and the payee spouse includes it in income.

Is this payment schedule subject to §71(f)? In order to answer that question, we must determine whether there will be excess alimony payments in the first and second years of payment. First, we determine the excess payments for the *second* year in which payments are made. §71(f)(4). The excess payment for this year equals $65,000 (the $100,000 second year alimony payment less $35,000, which is the sum of the $20,000 year three alimony payment plus $15,000). Second, we determine the excess payments for the *first* year in which payments are made. §71(f)(3). The average alimony payment in years two and three is $27,500, which is the average of (i) the $20,000 year three payment and (ii) the $35,000 year two payment, net of excess payments (that is, the $100,000 second year payment less the $65,000 portion of that payment that is treated as an excess payment under §71(f)(4)). The excess payment for the first year thus equals $57,500 (the $100,000 first year alimony payment less $42,500, which is the sum of $15,000 plus the $27,500 average alimony payment made in the second and third years). In year three, the payor spouse includes and the payee spouse deducts $122,500 (the sum of the $65,000 year two excess payment plus the $57,500 year one excess payment). §71(f)(1). In other words, of the $200,000 of "alimony" paid in years one and two, (i) $77,500 is treated as alimony and (ii) the other $122,500 is recharacterized in year three and is not treated as alimony. If all this seems a bit much, keep in mind that in practice divorce lawyers structure alimony payments so that the payments do not trigger §71(f).

There are a number of exceptions to the recapture rules of §71(f). §71(f)(5). For example, §71(f) does not apply if the alimony payments cease because the payee spouse remarries or dies. In addition, §71(f) does not apply if the alimony schedule provides that for at least three years the payee spouse is to receive a fixed percentage of (i) income from a business or property or (ii) compensation from employment or self-employment.

The intuitive justification for the §71(c) child support exception and the §71(f) recapture provisions is that alimony is a periodic payment for the support of the recipient spouse. A payment that is received all up front or continues after the death of the recipient spouse (for example, through her estate) is thus more in the nature of a property settlement, which is not deductible by the payor or includible by the payee when paid.

If a payor spouse has much higher income than the payee spouse, §§71 and 215 permit the divorcing spouses to shift income from the high-income payor spouse to the low-income payee spouse. Consider the following example. Assume that the following rate schedule (which is a fictitious, simplified version of the real §1 rate schedule) applies to all parties:

If taxable income is:	The tax is:
Not over $23,000	15 percent of taxable income
Over $23,000	$3,450 (15 percent of $23,000) plus 30 percent of the excess over $23,000
Over $115,000	$31,050 ($3,450 plus $27,600, which is 30 percent of the income between $23,000 and $115,000) plus 36 percent of the excess over $115,000

3. Problems of Timing

Assume that Charlie agrees to pay Shannon $15,000 a year pursuant to a divorce decree. The payment will constitute alimony under §71. Assume that, without taking the alimony into account, Charlie has taxable income of $50,000 a year and is in the 30 percent rate bracket, and Shannon has taxable income of $8,000 a year and is in the 15 percent rate bracket. Taking into account the alimony, Shannon has $23,000 of income, so that she is still in the 15 percent rate bracket. §71(a). She will owe $2,250 of tax on the $15,000 of alimony she receives. Charlie deducts the $15,000 he pays Shannon, reducing his income to $35,000. §215(a). He is still in the 30 percent rate bracket. The $15,000 deduction reduces Charlie's taxes by $4,500 (30 percent of $15,000). The alimony increases Shannon's tax by $2,250, but decreases Charlie's tax by $4,500. Thus, the alimony saves Charlie more in tax than it costs Shannon. The net tax on the alimony payments is *negative* $2,250!

Section 71 also contains an elective provision that allows parties to treat what otherwise would be characterized as alimony as a property settlement. §71(b)(1)(B). Thus, in lieu of alimony, which is deductible to the payor and taxable to the payee, the parties can opt for the nonrecognition treatment of property settlements. The parties cannot, however, treat what otherwise would be characterized as a property settlement as alimony.

EXAMPLES

11. Carla gives Don stock with a basis of $5,000 and a fair market value of $50,000. State the tax consequences under the following assumptions.
    a. The stock was held by Carla and Don as community property and is given to Don incident to a divorce.
    b. The stock was held by Carla as separate property and is given to Don incident to divorce.
    c. The stock was held by Carla as separate property and is given to Don as part of an antenuptial agreement. In return, Don waives any right to alimony or property upon divorce.

12. Which of the following characteristics will prevent a series of payments from being characterized as alimony?
    a. The payments are equal but last only three years.
    b. The payments are made under a separate maintenance agreement prior to divorce.

3. Problems of Timing

    c. Upon the death of the payee spouse, the payments continue and so may be passed by will to the payee's beneficiaries.

13. a. Ed will pay Fiona $70,000 of alimony in years one and two, and $30,000 a year thereafter. What are the tax consequences to Ed and Fiona, in years one, two, and three, of the alimony payments?

    b. How, if at all, would the answer in part (a) change if the amounts Ed paid Fiona were calculated by applying a fixed percentage to Ed's employment compensation?

    c. How, if at all, would the answer in part (a) change if Ed will pay Fiona $56,667 a year in years one through three?

In answering examples 14 through 16, assume that the following rate schedule (which is a fictitious, simplified version of the real §1 rate schedule) applies to all parties:

If taxable income is:	The tax is:
Not over $23,000	15 percent of taxable income
Over $23,000	$3,450 (15 percent of $23,000) plus 30 percent of the excess over $23,000
Over $115,000	$31,050 ($3,450 plus $27,600, which is 30 percent of the income between $23,000 and $115,000) plus 36 percent of the excess over $115,000

14. Xavier agrees to pay Yvonne $40,000 a year as alimony, pursuant to a divorce decree. Assume that, without taking the alimony into account, Xavier has taxable income of $100,000 a year and is in the 30 percent rate bracket, and Yvonne has taxable income of $13,000 a year and is in the 15 percent rate bracket.
    a. How much tax will Yvonne pay on the alimony payment?
    b. How much will Xavier save by making the alimony payment?

15. Eloise and Fabian hold as community property shares of stock in two corporations, Hibasis Inc. and Lobasis Inc. The Hibasis stock has a basis of $20,000 and a fair market value of $20,000. The Lobasis stock has a basis of $10,000 and a fair market value of $20,000. Eloise and Fabian plan to get divorced. After the divorce Eloise is expected to have annual taxable income, deter-

mined without regard to extraordinary income from property, of $25,000 a year; Fabian is expected to have annual taxable income of only $5,000 a year. Eloise and Fabian agree that Fabian should receive one of the two blocks of stock in addition to annual alimony. Advise Eloise and Fabian on how the divorce agreement should be structured.

16. George and Helen decide to divorce. In future years George expects to have taxable income, determined without regard to the treatment of alimony, of $60,000; Helen expects to have taxable income, determined without regard to the treatment of alimony, of $10,000. George and Helen own undeveloped land that has a basis of $50,000 and a fair market value of $50,000. George and Helen have tentatively decided that Helen should receive either (i) the undeveloped land or (ii) alimony of $10,000 a year for six years, which has a present value of $50,000. Advise the parties on how they might structure the divorce settlement.

EXPLANATIONS

11. a. Don does not recognize any gain on the receipt of the stock and Carla cannot deduct the stock transferred. Don's basis in the stock is the old $5,000 basis in the stock. §1041.

   b. Under the holding in *Davis*, Carla would have recognized gain on the transfer because the stock was held as separate property. Under current law, however, the result is the same as described in part (a); no gain is recognized on the receipt of stock and the basis remains unchanged. §1041.

   c. Section 1041 provides for the nonrecognition of gain upon transfer to either (i) a spouse or (ii) a former spouse, incident to divorce. If the property is transferred after marriage, §1041 applies. However, if the property is transferred prior to marriage, §1041 would not apply. The transaction would probably be treated as a sale in which appreciated property was used to acquire marital rights. The purchaser of the rights (here, Carla) would be treated as if the stock were sold and the sale proceeds used to acquire the marital rights Don gave up in the agreement. Don would then have a basis in the stock equal to its value on the date of the transfer, $50,000. See Farid-Es-Sultaneh v. Commissioner, 160 F.2d 812 (2d Cir. 1947) (where a transfer of appreciated property to a wife pursuant to an antenuptial agreement was treated as a sale of inchoate marital rights by the wife, who then received a fair market value basis in property).

12. Under §71(f), payments that would otherwise qualify as alimony but are too "front loaded" are recharacterized as property settlements. However, that section only applies to that portion of the payments that are "front loaded" in the first three years. A payment that is substantially equal during the first three years will not run afoul of §71(f). Thus, the condition described in part (a) will not prevent alimony treatment. The same is true of the condition described in part (b); parties need not be divorced so long as there is a written agreement as to separate maintenance and the other requirements of §71 are met. The condition described in part (c) will prevent alimony treatment. §71(b)(1)(D).

13. a. In years one and two, Ed deducts the $70,000 of alimony from gross income and Fiona includes it in income. In year three, Ed deducts the $30,000 of alimony from gross income and Fiona includes it in income. Do the year one or year two payments include "excess alimony payments" that are subject to the recapture rule of §71(f)? In order to determine the recapture amount under §71(f), we must calculate the excess alimony payments for years one and two.

     First, we calculate the excess payments for the *second* year in which payments are made. §71(f)(4). The excess payment for this year equals $25,000 — the $70,000 second-year alimony payment less $45,000, which is the sum of the $30,000 year three alimony payment plus $15,000.

     Second, we determine the excess payments for the *first* year in which payments are made. §71(f)(3). The average alimony payment in years two and three is $37,500, which is the average of (i) the $30,000 year three payment and (ii) the $45,000 year two payment, net of excess payments (that is, the $70,000 second year payment less the $25,000 portion of that payment that is treated as an excess payment under §71(f)(4)). The excess payment for the first year thus equals $17,500 — the $70,000 first-year alimony payment less $52,500, which is the sum of $15,000 plus the $37,500 average alimony payment made in the second and third years.

     In year three, Ed includes and Fiona deducts $42,500, which is the sum of the $25,000 year two excess payment plus the $17,500 year one excess payment. §71(f)(1). In other words, of the $140,000 of "alimony" paid in years one and two (i) $97,500 is treated as alimony and (ii) the other $42,500 is recharacterized in year three and is not treated as alimony.

b. The answer is the same, except that the §71(f) recapture rule would not apply since the payments were computed by applying a fixed percentage to Ed's employment compensation. §71(f)(5)(C).

c. The answer is the same except that the §71(f) recapture rule would not apply because the payments during years one through three are level. Divorce lawyers often use level payments in the first three years to avoid triggering §71(f).

14. a. Yvonne includes the alimony in income and pays $10,500 of tax on it. §71(a). Without the alimony, she would have had $13,000 of taxable income and would have paid $1,950 (15 percent of her $13,000 income). With the alimony, she has $53,000 of taxable income and pays tax of $12,450 — $3,450 plus $9,000 (which is 30 percent of the $30,000 of income over $23,000). (In other words, $10,000 of the alimony is taxed at the 15 percent rate and the other $30,000 is taxed at the 30 percent rate.) The tax on the $40,000 of alimony is $10,500.

b. Xavier deducts the $40,000 of income. With or without the alimony payment, Xavier is in the 30 percent rate bracket. A $40,000 deduction will reduce Xavier's taxes by $12,000 (30 percent of $40,000). Thus, the alimony saves Xavier more in tax than it costs Yvonne. The net tax on the alimony payments is negative $1,500.

15. If, after the divorce, the Hibasis stock were sold, there would be no gain realized on the sale (because the value of the stock equals its basis), regardless of who owned it. If Eloise receives the Lobasis stock in the divorce and then sells it, she will have to pay tax on the gain at a 30 percent rate. On the other hand, if Fabian receives the Lobasis stock in the divorce and then sells it, he will have to pay tax on the gain at only a 15 percent rate. Thus, the combined tax burden of the parties will be minimized if Fabian receives the Lobasis stock. Fabian can be compensated for the tax liability involved in accepting Lobasis stock through payment of additional alimony, if necessary.

16. The transfer of land would have no tax consequences. §1041. The alimony will be deductible to George and included in

income by Helen. However, since George is in a higher tax bracket than Helen, George will save more from the deduction than Helen will pay in additional tax. George is in the 30 percent tax bracket so will save $18,000 (30 percent of $60,000) by deducting the alimony. Helen is in the 15 percent tax bracket so will pay only $9,000 (15 percent of $60,000) upon receipt of the alimony. Structuring the payment as alimony will result in a net tax savings of $9,000. The savings could be left entirely to George or, more likely, split between the parties through an additional transfer. For example, suppose Helen agreed to accept taxable alimony on the condition that she receive an additional property worth $12,000. The $12,000 would more than offset the $9,000 of tax Helen must pay on the alimony, but would be only two-thirds of the $18,000 of tax George would save by deducting the alimony.

C.   Installment Sale and Open Transaction Reporting

Reading: §§453, 453A, 453B

There are several alternative approaches that could be used to determine the tax consequences to a seller on the sale of property in exchange for a series of payments to be made in the future. In order to illustrate these different approaches, consider the following hypothetical: Suppose Catherine owns property with a basis of $100,000 and a fair market value of $500,000. She sells the property to Bob for $500,000. Under the terms of the sales contract, Bob does not have to pay the full $500,000 immediately. Instead, he is required to pay $100,000 a year for five years. In addition, he must make annual payment of interest, at a market rate, on the unpaid balance of the installments. In the first year, Catherine receives $100,000 of the $500,000 sales price owed her. (She also receives interest, which we will ignore for the remainder of this hypothetical.)

Catherine might argue that the first $100,000 payment of principal should be treated as tax-free recovery of her $100,000 basis. Under this "basis first" approach, Catherine would not recognize any gain until she recovers her basis; the remaining payments would be taxable in full. Another approach would tax Catherine on the full $400,000 of realized gain in the year of the sale — even though she receives only a quarter of that amount. A third approach would treat a pro rata share of each principal payment as recovery of capital and the remaining share of each principal payment as gain.

Congress has adopted the last approach. Section 446(c) provides that taxpayers may adopt the following accounting methods: (i) cash method, (ii) accrual method, and (iii) any other special accounting method permitted by the Code. (We will discuss the cash and accrual methods later in this chapter.) Section 453 provides a special accounting method for reporting gain from the sale of property in exchange for deferred payments. Under §453(c), a seller first determines the overall ratio of the gain to the sales price in order to determine what portion of each payment should be included as gain from the sale. Here Catherine has $400,000 of gain and a $500,000 sales price, so the ratio is 400,000/500,000 (or 4/5 or 80 percent). Next, the seller determines the annual inclusions of gain from the sale by multiplying any installment payment (other than interest) received during the year by the ratio determined under §453(c). Catherine receives $100,000 each year, so her annual gain inclusion is $80,000 (80 percent of the $100,000 payment she receives). Thus, she will include 80 percent (or 4/5) of each payment as gain from the sale.

Using the §453 terms of art, the gross profit ratio is the ratio of the *gross profit* to the *contract price*. §453(c). The gross profit is (i) the *selling price* (ii) less the seller's adjusted basis in the property sold. Reg. §15A.453-1(b)(2). The selling price is the amount to be paid by the buyer (other than interest). Id. If the property sold is subject to a liability that is assumed by the buyer, for the purpose of computing the §453(c) ratio, the selling price includes the amount of the debt. Id. The contract price is the selling price less the debt assumed by the buyer. Id. Even though it might make sense to treat the debt relief like a cash payment in year one, that approach is not generally used. Instead §453 spreads the gain from debt relief in the same way that the rest of the gain is spread. However, if the debt assumed or taken subject to exceeds the seller's basis in the property sold, the liability in excess of the basis is treated as a cash payment in the year of the sale. Reg. §15A.453-1(b)(3)(i).

To illustrate the operation of §453 where the property sold is encumbered, consider the following example: Suppose Lee owns property with a basis of $300,000 and a gross fair market value of $700,000. The property is encumbered by a $200,000 mortgage, so the value of the property net of the liability is $500,000. He sells the property to George for $500,000 and assumption of the mortgage. George will pay Lee $100,000 a year for the next five years, but nothing in the year of the sale. (George will also pay interest, but disregard it in this example.) How much gain does Lee include when he receives each of the five $100,000 payments from George? Lee's gross profit is $400,000 — the $700,000 selling price (which includes both the $500,000 of installment payments to be made and the $200,000 of debt George assumed) less her $300,000 basis. The contract price is $500,000 ($700,000 selling price less $200,000 of debt assumed by Bob). The gross profit percentage is 80 percent ($400,000 gross profit/$500,000 contract price). Lee will include $80,000 of gain when he receives each $100,000 payment from George, for a total inclusion of $400,000 over the five installments. This makes sense since Lee's total gain realized on the sale is $400,000.

Under what circumstances does §453 apply? Section 453 applies automatically to a sale of property if the seller realizes a gain on the sale and at least one payment for the property will be received by the seller after the close of the taxable year of the sale. §453(a) and (b). However, taxpayers can elect out of §453 and recognize the entire gain in the year of the sale. §453(d). (Presumably, taxpayers will so elect only when the taxpayer faces an unusually low tax bracket in the year of sale.) Section 453 does not apply to sales of personal property by taxpayers who regularly sell personal property on the installment plan, such as department stores, and sales of real property by taxpayers who hold real property for sale to customers in the ordinary course of business, such as real estate developers. §453(b)(2), (l)(1). Section 453 also does not apply to the sale of publicly traded stocks or securities. §453(k). (Taxpayers who do not qualify for §453 must include the full gain in the year of sale — even if the payments are to be made over a period of many years.) Finally, §453 does not apply if the seller realizes a loss on the sale.

What if the total amount of the deferred payment on the sale is uncertain at the time of the sale? Can the taxpayer then use the "basis first" approach instead of §453? In Burnet v. Logan, 283 U.S. 404 (1931), the Supreme Court held that a taxpayer who sold stock in a mining company in exchange for cash and payments that were to be based on the amount mined in the future could adopt an *open transaction* (basis first) approach to report the gain from the sale. Since the amount to be received in the future was not ascertainable, Mrs. Logan was permitted to recover all of her basis first, then include all amounts received after she had recovered her basis. However, §453(j)(2), enacted in 1980, and various regulations promulgated after the *Logan* decision now require sellers receiving contingent payments to apply

§453 in the year of the sale and preclude open transaction reporting except in extraordinary cases. See, e.g., Reg. §§15A.453-1(c) and 1.1001-1(a). Regulation §15A.453-1(c) provides three special rules for determining the timing of basis recovery and gain inclusion where the amount paid for property is contingent: First, if a maximum payment for the property can be determined, that amount is treated as the selling price for the purpose of computing the §453 inclusion ratio. Second, if a maximum payment cannot be determined, but the number of years over which payments will be made can be determined, the taxpayer's basis is allocated equally over that period. Third, if neither a maximum payment nor time period for payment can be determined, the taxpayer recovers basis equally over 15 years.

Although §453 reporting is not as beneficial to taxpayers as the "basis first" approach, it is much more beneficial to taxpayers than the third possible approach, which would require taxpayers to include gain in the year of the sale even if no payments were to be received in the year of the sale. The deferral of tax under §453 is like an interest-free loan from the government to the taxpayer in an amount equal to the tax on the gain realized in the sale. However, the tax benefits of §453 are limited by several provisions. For example, if the installment payments exceed $5 million, the taxpayer will have to pay the government interest on the tax liability deferred under §453. §453A(a)(1). In addition, §453A(d) provides that if an installment obligation is pledged as security for a loan, the proceeds of the loan will, in some circumstances, be treated as a payment on the installment obligation, triggering an inclusion under §453.

EXAMPLES

17. a. Barbara owns Blackacre, which has a value of $40,000 and basis of $10,000. On January 1 of year one, Barbara sells Blackacre to Susan for $40,000; Susan will pay Barbara $10,000 a year in years two through five (plus a market rate of interest on the unpaid balance). How much gain from the sale, if any, does Barbara include in years one and two?

    b. How, if at all, would your answer in part (a) change if, instead of making the four $10,000 payments, Susan paid Barbara the entire $40,000 sale price at the end of the fifth year?

18. Alice owns Whiteacre, which has a gross value of $10,000 and basis of $7,000 and is subject to a $6,000 mortgage (so the value, net of the mortgage, is $4,000). Alice sells Whiteacre to Bob,

who takes Whiteacre subject to the mortgage and agrees to pay Alice $1,000 immediately and an additional $1,000 per year for the next three years (plus interest). What are the tax consequences to Alice?

19. Carol sells her mineral rights in certain land to the Douglas Mining Corporation. Her basis in the mineral rights is $10,000. Douglas agrees to pay her $5,000 immediately plus an additional amount depending on how much ore is mined in the future. The parties estimate that payments are likely to vary in amount from $1,250 to $2,000 per year and that mining is likely to continue for eight to ten years. In year two Carol receives a payment of $1,500.

   a. Under the open transaction approach adopted in Burnett v. Logan, how much of the payments received in years one and two would Carol have to include in income?

   b. How much income would Carol report from the payments received in years one and two if the method of allocating basis stated in the §453 regulations were adopted?

   c. What alternative method of allocation might be fairer than either of the two methods above?

EXPLANATIONS

17. a. Section 453 applies because Barbara has sold property at a gain and will receive at least one payment after year one, the year of the sale. §453(a) and (b)(1). Barbara's gross profit is $30,000 ($40,000 selling price less her $10,000 basis). The contract price is $40,000. The gross profit percentage is 75 percent ($30,000 gross profit/$40,000 contract price). Thus, Barbara must include 75 percent of each payment she receives. §453(c). In year one Barbara does not receive any payment, so she does not have to include any of the gain. In year two Barbara must include $7,500, which is 75 percent of the $10,000 payment she receives in that year. By the fourth payment, in year five, Barbara's four $7,500 inclusions will total $30,000, her total gain realized on the sale of Blackacre.

   b. The gross profit percentage is the same as in part (a), 75 percent. As in part (a), Barbara does not have to include any of the $30,000 gain in year one because she receives no payment in that year. The answer changes for years two through five. Here, since Barbara does not receive any payments in years two through four, she will not include any gain in those years. In year five Barbara will include $30,000 of gain (75 percent of the $40,000 payment she receives in year five). Said another way, Barbara reports her entire gain in the year in which she receives the entire deferred payment for the property.

18. Alice's gross profit is $3,000 ($10,000 selling price — which includes the debt — less her $7,000 basis). §453(c) and Reg. §15A.453-1(b)(2). The contract price is $4,000 ($10,000 selling price less the $6,000 debt Bob took subject to). Reg. §15A.453-1(b)(2). The gross profit percentage is 75 percent ($3,000 gross profit/$4,000 contract price). Alice will include $750 (75 percent of each $1,000 payment received) in each of years one through four. §453(c). (Even though it might make sense to treat the debt relief like a cash payment in year one, that approach is not adopted unless the mortgage assumed by the buyer exceeds the seller's basis in the property sold. Reg. §15A.453-1(b)(3)(i).)

19. a. Under the open transaction, or basis first, approach, Carol would not report any gain until the amounts received exceed her basis, $10,000. Carol receives total payments of $6,500 ($5,000 plus $1,500) in years one and two. Thus, she would not have to include any income in those years.

    b. Where payments are contingent, Regulation §15A.453-1(c) requires the taxpayer to calculate the inclusion amount, under §453(c), based on an assumption that the maximum possible payments will be received. In this case, that would require Carol to assume that $2,000 per year will be received for 10 years, for a total of $25,000 (including the $5,000 year one payment). Carol's gross profit is $15,000 ($25,000 selling price less $10,000 basis) and the contract price is $25,000, so the gross profit percentage is 60 percent ($15,000/$25,000 or 3/5). In year one Carol must include $3,000 (60 percent of the $5,000 payment she receives in that year). In year two Carol must include $900 (60 percent of the $1,500 payment she receives in that year).

    c. A fairer approach might be to attempt to estimate the most likely total payments rather than the maximum. In this case, total contingent payments are expected to fall between $10,000 (eight years at $1,250 per year) and $20,000 (10 years at $2,000 per year). You might choose a number somewhere in between, say $15,000. Then the total expected payment would be

$20,000 for a gain of $10,000, so $10,000/$20,000 or 50 percent of each payment would be gain. Thus, $2,500 of gain would be reported in year one and $750 in year two. Although this approach seems more accurate and reasonable than the Treasury approach, it would make it easier for the taxpayer to underestimate total expected payments and thus underreport gain in the early years.

Note that if the Treasury's allocation method is adopted and the taxpayer receives less than the maximum expected amount, the taxpayer will have basis remaining after all payments have been received. At that point she will take a loss deduction for her unrecovered basis. Similarly, if the taxpayer receives more than the expected amount, her basis will be used up before all installment payments have been made and all of the final payments received will be included as gain.

D. Original Issue Discount

Reading: §§1271-1278

A borrower must pay a lender interest on principal borrowed in order to compensate the lender for the borrower's use of the lender's funds while the loan is outstanding. *Compound interest* is determined by applying the interest rate on the debt to the sum of (i) the amount originally loaned plus (ii) any interest on the debt that has already accrued but has not been paid. (In other words, the unpaid, accrued interest increases the principal owed.) *Simple interest* is interest paid on only the amount originally loaned. Interest can be either (i) stated explicitly or (ii) unstated and implicit. *Original issue discount* (OID) is the term for unstated interest on debt, determined at the time the debt is issued. To illustrate the concepts of stated interest and unstated interest, consider the following examples.

In year one Sherry places $377 in a bank savings account that pays interest every six months. (In other words, the interest is compounded semiannually.) The annual interest rate is 10 percent, compounding semiannually. The interest in the first six months of year one is $18.85. This amount is the product of 5 percent semiannual interest (the annual 10 percent rate/two compounding periods in each year) multiplied by the $377 of principal. If that interest is not withdrawn, the balance in the account after the first six months is increased to $395.85 ($377 original principal plus $18.85 of interest for the first six months). The interest in the second six months of year one is $19.80 (5 percent semiannual interest on $395.85 principal). This increases the balance to $415.65 ($395.85 plus $19.80 of interest for the second six months of year one). Mary includes $38.65 ($18.85 plus $19.80) of interest in year one even if she leaves it in the bank. §61(a)(4). In this example, the bank is paying Mary 10 percent annual stated interest, compounding semiannually, on the balance in her savings account. (This is the economic equivalent of paying Mary 10.25 percent annual interest, compounding annually.) The semiannual interest calculations are carried out until the 10th year in the chart below. *Note that the dollar amount of interest grows every six months despite the fact that the 5 percent interest rate is constant because the constant interest rate is being applied to an ever-increasing principal balance.*

	Beginning balance	Semiannual 5 percent interest	Ending balance
Year 1: 1st 6 months	$377	$18.85	$395.85
Year 1: 2d 6 months	395.85	19.80	415.65
Year 2: 1st 6 months	415.65	20.78	436.43
Year 2: 2d 6 months	436.43	21.82	458.25
Year 3: 1st 6 months	458.25	22.91	481.16
Year 3: 2d 6 months	481.16	24.06	505.22
Year 4: 1st 6 months	505.22	25.26	530.48
Year 4: 2d 6 months	530.48	26.52	557
Year 5: 1st 6 months	557	27.85	584.85
Year 5: 2d 6 months	584.85	29.24	614.09
Year 6: 1st 6 months	614.09	30.70	644.79
Year 6: 2d 6 months	644.79	32.24	677.03
Year 7: 1st 6 months	677.03	33.85	710.88
Year 7: 2d 6 months	710.88	35.54	746.42
Year 8: 1st 6 months	746.42	37.32	783.74
Year 8: 2d 6 months	783.74	39.18	822.92
Year 9: 1st 6 months	822.92	41.15	864.07
Year 9: 2d 6 months	864.07	43.20	907.27
Year 10: 1st 6 months	907.27	45.36	952.63
Year 10: 2d 6 months	952.63	47.63	1,000*

(* Due to rounding amounts in the chart, the balance plus interest in the last year is a little over $1,000.)

Now consider another example. Mary purchases a bond from BigCo for $377. The bond does not provide for annual cash payments of interest or principal, but is redeemable in 10 years for $1,000. (Such bonds are often referred to as *zero coupon bonds* because there is zero stated interest on the debt.) What is the tax treatment of the $623 difference between the amount Mary paid for the bond, $377, and the $1,000 amount that she will receive at maturity in 10 years? One approach would be to treat the $623 as property gain when the bond matures, just as if Mary had bought a parcel of land for $377 and sold it 10 years later for $1,000. Mary would not have to pay tax on such gain until year 10, and the gain would qualify as capital gain and be taxed at low rates. (For a discussion of capital gains, see Chapter 8.) The other approach would be to treat the $623 as interest income. Current law adopts the second approach; the $623 will be treated as interest income.

The $623 that Mary earns on the BigCo bond is governed by the OID rules in the Code. The unstated interest, or OID, on a debt instrument equals (i) the *stated redemption price at maturity* of the debt instrument (the amount payable under the debt instrument less any stated interest that is paid at least annually) less (ii) the *issue price* of the debt instrument, which is generally the amount of cash the bond-holder paid for the debt. §§1273(a) and (b). The stated redemption price at maturity of Mary's BigCo bond is $1,000, the amount payable at maturity. §1273(a)(2). The issue price of the bond is $377, the amount Mary paid for it. §1273(b). The OID on Mary's BigCo bond is thus $623 (the $1,000 stated redemption price at maturity less the $377 issue price).

The $623 of OID on the bond is then allocated over the 10-year period during which the bond is outstanding. Here again, there are two possible approaches. One approach would be to allocate the $623 of OID equally over the 10 years so that Mary would include $62.30 per year of interest for 10 years. The other approach (called either the *constant-yield to maturity method* or the *economic accrual method*) is to tax Mary in the same way that Sherry is taxed on her savings account, by requiring her to include amounts of interest that increase each year — because the interest inclusion is calculated by applying a constant rate of interest to a balance that keeps increasing to reflect prior accrued but unpaid interest. The implicit interest rate, referred to as the *yield-to-maturity*, on the bond is 10 percent, compounding semiannually — because $377 invested at 10 percent annual interest, compounding semiannually, would grow to $1,000 in 10 years. (The implicit interest rate for a given issue price and redemption amount can be determined by a formula that is "hard wired" into programmable calculators and comes with computer spreadsheet programs. Lawyers will seldom, if ever, be required to calculate the yield-to-maturity of a debt instrument.)

Mary must compute her OID inclusion for each six-month period during which she owns the bond. §1272(a)(1), (3), and (5). Her OID inclusion for each semiannual period is the product of multiplying (i) the yield-to-maturity, which is 5 percent for each semiannual period, by (ii) the *adjusted issue price* of the bond. §1272(a)(1) and (3). The adjusted issue price is (i) the issue price of the bond plus (ii) any unstated interest that has already accrued on the bond but not been paid to the bondholder. §1272(a)(4). In our example, the issue price of the bond is $377, the amount Mary paid for the bond. The OID for the first six-month period in year one equals $18.85 (5 percent semiannual interest on $377). The OID for the second six-month period in year one is $19.80 — 5 percent semiannual interest on the $395.85 adjusted issue price ($377 issue price plus the $18.85 of accrued but unpaid interest from the first six-month period). In year one Mary includes the total OID for year one, $38.65, as interest. §1272(a)(1). If you refer back to the chart on page 157 from our first example, you will see that Mary's OID inclusions on the BigCo bond track the interest inclusions from Sherry's savings account. The OID that Mary must include each year is added to her basis for the bond so that when she receives the $1,000 at maturity she realizes no gain or loss on the redemption. Reg. §1.1272-1(g). If the issuer, BigCo, does not pay the full redemption amount due to bankruptcy or some other event, Mary will recognize a capital loss equal to the difference between her basis at that time and the amount received. §§1271(a)(2) and 1221.

Mary, an individual, is a cash method taxpayer. Cash method taxpayers include items of income in the year in which they receive the item of income. Reg. §1.451-1. (The cash method of accounting is discussed later in this chapter.) Why do the OID rules require Mary to include annual interest income if she is not going to receive any interest until year 10? To answer that question, we have to consider the treatment of the OID to BigCo, the issuer of the bond. BigCo, like all corporate bond issuers, is an accrual method taxpayer. If we did not have the OID rules, cash method individual bondholders would not have to include unstated interest until the maturity date for the bond, but, under the accrual method, corporate issuers would deduct the unstated interest as it accrues economically (that is, as we just described in the above example with Mary) in each of the 10 years. In order to avoid this asymmetry in the timing of OID interest income and deductions, the OID rules put both issuers and bondholders on the same accounting method, the accrual method, for the purpose of determining OID interest deductions and inclusions. §§1272(a)(1) and 163(e)(1) and (2). (Of course, we could also avoid the asymmetry by allowing cash method bond purchasers to defer recognition of interest income until payment, and putting the accrual method issuers on the cash method so that interest could not be deducted until payment.)

The application of the original discount rules is not limited to the purchase or issuance of zero coupon bonds for cash — the rules also apply to certain property sales. Suppose, for example, that Xavier owns property with a basis of $100,000 and a fair market value of $377,000. If Xavier sells the property and purchases 1,000 10-year zero coupon BigCo bonds that pay $1,000 each upon redemption, the tax treatment is obvious: Xavier will recognize $277,000 gain on the property sale, and then, under the OID provisions, will recognize interest income as described above. In other words, he will include $623,000 of interest over the 10 years and the interest will be allocated over each of the 10 years using the constant yield-to-maturity method described above. Would the result change if Xavier sold the property in exchange for a single $1 million payment in 10 years?

Xavier might hope that the entire $1 million payment would be characterized as proceeds from the sale of property. The gain in that case would be capital gain, which is taxed at a lower rate than other income. §1(a)-(d) and (h). The transaction might also qualify for installment sales treatment, which, as we discuss in the following section, would defer taxation until payment in year 10. Instead, under the OID rules the transaction will effectively be divided into two separate tax transactions: The first transaction, the property transaction, is Xavier's sale of his property for the 10-year zero coupon BigCo bonds. Xavier's gain from the sale may be capital gain and may qualify for the installment sale method, described in the following section, in which case the tax on the gain would be deferred until payment is made in year 10. The second transaction is the debt transaction. Xavier must include in income the interest that accrues on the bond in each of the 10 years the bond is outstanding.

How does the tax law determine the exact amount of interest income and property sale proceeds? If no interest is stated on the debt instrument issued in exchange for property, the payments to be made on the debt instrument are discounted to present value using the *applicable federal rate* (AFR). §1274(b). The AFR is set monthly by the Treasury, pursuant to §1274(d), to reflect prevailing interest rates on U.S. government bonds. (If the stated principal on debt issued in exchange for property does not exceed the amount specified in §1274A(b), adjusted for inflation—for example, $3,523,600 for tax year 1995—the rate used in the OID calculations cannot exceed 9 percent. §1274A(a), (b), and (d); Rev. Rul. 95-10). The unstated interest on the debt instrument equals the gross amount of payments to be made on the debt instrument less the present value of those payments. §§1273(a)(1) and (b)(4), and 1274(a) and (b)(1). Assume that the AFR is 10 percent, compounding semiannually. (Disregard §1274A(a) to simplify the example and keep it comparable to our earlier two examples.) The present value of $1 million received in 10 years, discounted at 10 percent, compounding semiannually, turns out to be $377,000, so the $623,000 difference between the $1 million amount to be paid and the $377,000 present value of that payment is treated as OID interest. §§1273(a)(1) and (b)(4), and 1274(a) and (b)(1). In other words, Xavier will include interest in each of the 10 years that the bond is outstanding based on the constant yield-to-maturity method described above. His OID interest inclusion in year one is $38,650 ($18,850 of OID for the first six months of year one plus $19,800 of OID for the second six months of year one). Note that, in this process, we have imputed the amount for which Xavier's property was exchanged in year one, $377,000. For the purpose of determining his gain from the property transaction, this $377,000 amount will be treated as the amount realized in the property transaction. Reg. §1.1001-1(g). Xavier's gain from the sale of the property is thus $277,000 ($377,000 amount realized less his $100,000 basis in the property).

Section 1274 does not apply to (i) sales of principal residences, (ii) sales in which payments are not deferred for more than six months, and (iii) certain sales of farmland. §1274(c). In addition, if debt issued in exchange for property is publicly traded, or the property for which the debt is exchanged is publicly traded (for example, traded stock), we do not use §1274 to impute an issue price for the debt, in order to calculate the OID on the debt. §1274(c). Instead, the issue price of the debt is the value of the property in exchange for which the debt is issued, so the OID on the debt equals the stated redemption price at maturity of the debt less the value of the property exchanged for the debt. §1273(a) and (b)(3).

3. Problems of Timing

Moreover, the OID rules have no effect on property sales that require at least annual interest payments provided that the stated interest rate on the debt at least equals the AFR. §§1273(a)(2), (b)(4), 1274(c)(1) and (2); Reg. §1.1274-1(b)(ii). However, if the debt bears stated interest at a rate that at least equals the AFR, but that interest is not payable until maturity, the debt will have OID in an amount equal to the stated interest payable at maturity. §§1273(a)(1), (a)(2), (b)(3), 1274(a)(1). The holder and issuer of the debt will thus have to include and deduct the interest each year using the constant yield-to-maturity method described above.

Section 1274 also does not apply to a sale if the total payments to be made on a debt instrument exchanged for property are not at least $250,000. §1274(c)(3)(C). However, §483 may still apply to such a debt instrument. Section 483, like §1274, determines the amount of unstated interest on a debt instrument issued for property by comparing the payments to be made on the debt and the present value of the payments to be made (again discounting the payments at the AFR). §483(b). However, §483, unlike the OID rules, does not require accrual of the unstated interest, calculated using the constant yield-to-maturity method. Instead, the holder and issuer of the debt instrument report the unstated interest under their normal methods of accounting (despite the fact that this results in asymmetrical treatment of the interest where the holder is a cash method taxpayer and the issuer is an accrual method taxpayer). Reg. §1.483-1(a)(2)(ii).

EXAMPLES

20. At the beginning of year one, Abe pays $1,000 for a three-year zero-coupon BigCo bond, which will pay Abe $1,340 at maturity, in three years, and nothing before then. The constant interest rate necessary to produce $1,340 at the end of three years on a $1,000 investment is 10 percent, compounding semiannually, so the yield-to-maturity on the bond is 10 percent compounding semiannually. What are the tax consequences to Abe and BigCo in year one?

21. a. Bernice sells business property with a basis of $400,000 to Carl in exchange for one payment of $1.34 million to be made in three years. The applicable federal rate is 10 percent, compounding semiannually. Applying this rate, the present value of the $1.34 million payment due in three years is $1 million. What are the tax consequences to Bernice?

3. Problems of Timing

    b. How, if at all, would your answer in part (a) change if Bernice had exchanged her property for $1 million payable in three years, and six semiannual interest payments of $50,000 each?

EXPLANATIONS

20. The bond has $340 of OID ($1,340 stated redemption price at maturity less $1,000 issue price — what Abe paid for the bond). §1273(a)(1), (2), (b). The $340 of OID will be allocated over the three-year term of the debt using the constant yield-to-maturity method. §§1272(a)(1) and 163(e). The OID for the first six months is $50 — 5 percent (the semiannual interest rate) of the issue price of the bond, $1,000. §1272(a)(1) and (3). The OID for the second six months is $52.50 — 5 percent of the $1,050 adjusted issue price of the bond (the issue price plus prior OID). §1272(a)(1), (3), and (4). The OID for year one equals $102.50 ($50 plus $52.50). Abe will include and BigCo will deduct $102.25 of interest in year one. §§1272(a)(1) and 163(e). The chart below shows the amount of OID allocated to each six-month period during the three-year term of the debt.

	Beginning balance	Semiannual 5 percent interest	Ending balance
Year 1: 1st 6 months	$1,000	$50	$1,050
Year 1: 2d 6 months	1,050	52.50	1,102.50
Year 2: 1st 6 months	1,102.50	55.13	1,157.63
Year 2: 2d 6 months	1,157.63	57.88	1,215.51
Year 3: 1st 6 months	1,215.51	60.78	1,276.29
Year 3: 2d 6 months	1,276.29	63.81	1,340*

(* Due to rounding amounts in the chart, the sum of the beginning balance plus interest in the last year is a little over $1,340.)

21. a. The transaction will be split into two transactions for tax purposes: (i) a property transaction and (ii) a debt transaction. First consider the tax consequences of the debt transaction. The debt does not bear any stated interest. However, it does have unstated interest. The stated redemption price at maturity is $1,340,000. §1273(a)(2). The issue price of the debt is the $1 million present value of the payment to be made in three years, discounting at the 10 percent AFR. §§1273(b)(4) and

163

1274(a)(2) and (b). There is $340,000 of OID on the debt ($1,340,000 stated redemption price at maturity less $1 million issue price). The $340,000 of OID will be allocated over the three-year term of the debt using the constant yield-to-maturity method. §§1272(a)(1) and 163(e). The OID for the first six months is $50,000 — 5 percent (the semiannual interest rate) of the $1 million issue price of the debt. §1272(a)(1) and (3). The OID for the second six months is $52,500 — 5 percent of the $1,050,000 adjusted issue price of the debt (the issue price plus prior OID). §1272(a)(1), (3), and (4). The OID for year one thus equals $102,500 ($50,000 plus $52,500). Bernice will include $102,500 of interest in year one. §1272(a)(1). She will also include $113,000 of OID in year two and $124,500 of OID in year three. (See the chart above in the previous explanation for an illustration of the computations in years two and three.)

Now consider the tax consequences of the property transaction. Bernice's gain realized on the property transaction is $600,000 — $1 million amount realized (which is the present value of the payment to be made, discounting at the 10 percent AFR) less her $400,000 basis in the property. §1001; Reg. §1.1001-1(g). Bernice may qualify for installment reporting of the gain (discussed earlier in this chapter), in which case she would not be taxed on the $600,000 of gain until the year three payment is made. §453(c).

b. The OID rules do not apply to the debt transaction because the debt bears stated interest, payable at least annually, at the 10 percent annual rate. §§1273(a)(2), (b)(4), 1274(c)(1) and (2); Reg. §1.1274-1(b)(ii). (Since the interest is payable semiannually, the interest does not compound.) Bernice includes the interest when she receives it.

E.   The Cash Method of Accounting

Reading: §§61, 83, 451(a); Reg. §§1.451-1(a), 1.446-1(c)(1)(i), 1.451-2

Taxpayers who use the cash method of accounting generally must include an item of income when they receive it. §451(a). Inclusion is required whether the item of income is received in the form of cash, property, or services. Reg. §1.446-1(c)(1)(i). Cash method taxpayers generally deduct an item of expense when it is paid. Reg. §1.446-1(c)(1)(i). However, where the payment of an expense creates an asset with a useful life that extends substantially beyond the close of the year in which the expense is incurred, the cash method taxpayer cannot simply deduct the entire expense; instead, the expense must be capitalized. (For a discussion of capitalization and depreciation of business assets, see Chapter 5.)

Under the general inclusion rule stated above, a cash method taxpayer who sells property on December 1, year one, and is paid on that day will include the gain from the sale in income in year one. Can the taxpayer defer inclusion until year two by arranging to defer receipt of the year one payment until year two? No, he cannot because a cash method taxpayer is deemed to have received an item if it is *constructively received*. In other words, a cash method taxpayer includes on the earlier of actual or constructive receipt. Reg. §§1.451-1(a), 1.446-1(c)(1)(i). An item of income is constructively received if it is made available to the taxpayer, so that he could receive it, but he chooses not to receive it. Reg. §1.451-2. Under the doctrine of constructive receipt, the taxpayer in our example will be deemed to have received income in year one, the year in which the payment was made available to him, even if he defers actual receipt of the payment until year two.

On the other hand, if the original sale contract had provided for payment to be made in year two, the constructive receipt doctrine will not apply because under the terms of the contract the taxpayer has no right to the payment until year two. Courts will not "look through" the contract to determine whether the payment date was insisted upon by the taxpayer or his purchaser. If the taxpayer qualifies for the installment method, described in the preceding section, inclusion of the gain would be deferred until year two.

The doctrine of constructive receipt, and the point that constructive receipt can be avoided through contract, both apply to payment for services as well as goods. Thus, an employee whose salary is made available to her on December 1, year one, must recognize taxable income in year one, even if she does not pick up her paycheck until year two. On the other hand, an employee who contracts ahead of time to be paid on January 1, year two, will not include the income until year two. In other words, an employee can defer compensation income if she enters into the deferral agreement before she earns the income. Rev. Rul. 60-31 (which describes several deferred compensation arrangements and explains why each of them would or would not result in income deferral). (Note that, in deferred compensation arrangements such as those described in the ruling, the employer will not be able to deduct the compensation until the employee includes it. §404(a)(5).)

The doctrine of constructive receipt is closely related to the *economic benefit doctrine*, which is the product of case law. Under the economic benefit doctrine, a cash method taxpayer recognizes income as soon as a payor irrevocably sets aside funds for the taxpayer in a manner that prevents the payor's creditors from being able to reach the amount set aside. See, e.g., Pulsifer v. Commissioner, 64 T.C. 245 (1975). Inclusion is required despite the fact that the cash method taxpayer has not actually received the amount set aside. However, if the funds set aside for the taxpayer's benefit can be reached by the payor's creditors, the taxpayer does not have to include the funds set aside. Suppose, for example, that in year one a cash method taxpayer, Teresa, renders services for her employer in exchange for the employer transferring $20,000 to an irrevocable trust with Teresa as the sole beneficiary. If the employer's creditors could not reach the trust assets (if, for example, the employer later defaulted on its debts), Teresa will have to include the $20,000 in year one despite the fact that she has not received the money. On the other hand, she can defer inclusion of the $20,000 set aside in year one if the employer's creditors can reach the funds set aside. In addition, the economic benefit doctrine does not require inclusion in year one if the employer makes an unsecured promise to pay her the $20,000 in year two instead of transferring the funds to the trust. Rev. Rul. 60-31.

Deferring compensation by contract, in the manner discussed above, has two drawbacks. First, the employee runs the risk that the employer will not be able to make the deferred payment when it is due. If the employer and employee structure the deferred compensation so that the employee does not run the risk of nonpayment, the employee will not be able to defer the income. Second, an employer cannot deduct deferred compensation until the employee includes it, so the tax advantage gained by deferral of the employee's income is offset by the loss of the employer's deduction. §404(a)(5). In most cases, therefore, deferral of compensation by contract is not desirable. Occasionally, however, such deferral is advantageous. One well-publicized industry where deferral is common is professional athletics. Professional sports teams often lose money and so are in the zero percent tax bracket. Such teams are often owned, however, by wealthy individuals, and so are unlikely to default on contractual obligations. An employee of such a team can defer compensation without fear of default and the team can give up its tax deduction without cost. For this and other reasons, compensation for professional athletes is frequently deferred by contract.

The two drawbacks of deferring income by contract can be avoided if the deferred compensation takes the form of a qualified pension or profit-sharing plan. Under such a plan, funds are set aside (usually through a trust or annuity contract) for the irrevocable benefit of employees. The employer is able to deduct the current payment and the employee is not taxed on the contributions, or the interest earned on the contributions, until she receives the funds upon retirement or separation from service. A form of qualified retirement plan can be utilized by self-employed persons: The amounts set aside can be deducted from business earnings and are not taxable until withdrawn.

Why doesn't all deferred compensation take the form of qualified retirement plans? One reason is that such plans must comply with certain nondiscrimination provisions designed to ensure retirement coverage for low-paid employees. In general, if an employer provides high-paid employees with retirement benefits equal to, say, 10 percent of their annual salary, the employer must provide low-paid employees with retirement benefits equal to 10 percent of their salary. Another reason is that the amount that can be set aside for an employee in a qualified retirement plan is subject to statutory limits. §415. Finally, high penalties apply if the employee withdraws her interest in such plans prior to retirement or separation from employment. See, e.g., §72(t). Thus, such plans cannot be used to defer compensation for only a year or two.

An employee who wishes to set aside money for retirement can also establish her own individual retirement account (IRA). The employee can deduct up to $2,000 a year in contributions to such an account. The deduction is unavailable, however, to employees who are covered under a qualified retirement plan and have adjusted gross income above a certain amount. A slightly higher limit ($2,250) and a similar set of restrictions apply to plans established by married couples. No tax is levied on the contributions, or the interest earned on the contributions, until the amounts are withdrawn. Penalties apply for withdrawals prior to retirement. Employees who are unable to deduct their IRA contributions (because they are covered by a qualified retirement plan and have a relatively high adjusted gross income) may still wish to establish an IRA because the interest earned on the nondeductible contributions is not taxed until it is withdrawn.

EXAMPLES

22. In year one Andrew, a cash method taxpayer, sells real property, which has a basis of $40,000, to Roberta for $100,000. Under which, if any, of the following circumstances would the doctrines of constructive receipt or economic benefit require that Andrew be taxed on his property gain in year one?

   a. The sale closes on December 1, year one. On that date, the property is transferred to Roberta and she sends Andrew a certified check for the sale proceeds. Andrew does not accept the certified check until January 1, year two.

   b. During the sale negotiations, Roberta tells Andrew that she would prefer to close the deal and receive the property on December 1, year one. However, Andrew counters that for tax reasons he does not want the sale to close until January 1, year two. Roberta agrees to time the transaction as Andrew prefers. On January 1, year two, the property is transferred to Roberta, she gives Andrew a certified check for the sale proceeds, and he cashes the check.

   c. During the sale negotiations, Roberta tells Andrew that she would prefer to close the deal and receive the property on December 1, year one. Andrew would like to defer the tax on the gain until year two. However, he is not sure whether Roberta will still be able to make the $100,000 payment in year two, so he would like for her to actually make the payment in year one. They work out a compromise. On December 1, year one, Andrew transfers the property to Roberta and she places the $100,000 of sale proceeds in an irrevocable trust, naming Andrew the sole beneficiary of the trust. Roberta's creditors cannot reach the trust assets. The $100,000 in the trust will be distributed to Andrew on January 1, year two.

23. On January 1, year one, executive Ellen and BigCo sign an employment contract that contains the following terms: Ellen agrees to work for BigCo from January 1, year one, to December 31, year one. BigCo agrees to pay Ellen $5,000 a month during year one. BigCo also agrees to pay Ellen $36,000 on January 30, year two. In order to fund the year two payment to Ellen, BigCo agrees to purchase an annuity contract that will pay BigCo $36,000 on January 30, year two. Is Ellen taxed on the $36,000 deferred payment in year one? Can BigCo deduct the cost of the annuity in year one?

3. Problems of Timing

24. Is each of the following statements true or false?
    a. An employer currently can deduct amounts set aside for employees in a qualified profitsharing or pension plan.
    b. Amounts contributed to a qualified profitsharing or pension plan by an employer will be currently taxable to the employees because the employer's creditors cannot reach the amounts contributed.
    c. An employer may adopt a qualified pension or profitsharing plan that covers only a few "key" employees.
    d. Withdrawals from qualified profitsharing or pension plans prior to retirement or separation from employment are subject to substantial penalties.
    e. An employee who is covered by a qualified pension or profitsharing plan cannot establish an IRA.

EXPLANATIONS

22. a. Andrew will be taxed on the gain in year one, under the constructive receipt doctrine. He constructively received the sale proceeds in year one because the check was made available to him in year one but he chose not to receive it until year two. §451(a), Reg. §§1.451-1(a), 1.446-1(c)(1)(i), and 1.451-2.
    b. Andrew will not be taxed on the gain in year one. The contract did not permit Andrew to receive payment in year one. The constructive receipt doctrine does not apply because the sale proceeds were not made available to Andrew in year one. Reg. §1.451-2. The fact that the contractual deferral of payment benefits Andrew and was his idea is irrelevant. In situations such as this, the tax law will not rewrite a contract to eliminate a tax benefit to one of the parties.
    c. Andrew must include the property gain in year one. Roberta transferred the sale proceeds in year one to an irrevocable trust with Andrew as the sole beneficiary, and the trust assets were beyond the reach of Roberta's creditors. Under the economic benefit doctrine, Andrew will be treated as though he received in year one the $100,000 that was transferred to the trust. Pulsifer v. Commissioner, 64 T.C. 245 (1975). Note that §453 does not defer inclusion of the gain until year two because the transfer here of $100,000 to the trust is treated as a "payment" under §453. Reg. §15A.453-1(b)(3).

23. Under the doctrine of economic benefit, the deferred payment would be taxable in year one only if it were funded and irretrievably dedicated to Ellen in a manner that secured it from BigCo's creditors. Here, the purchase of the annuity should guarantee that BigCo will have funds with which to make the deferred payment. However, there is no guarantee that BigCo will use the funds to pay Ellen. Moreover, because BigCo is the beneficiary of the annuity contract, the contract is an asset of BigCo and is probably subject to the claims of its creditors. As a result, the doctrine of economic benefit does not require Ellen to include the deferred payment in year one. See Rev. Rul. 60-31. (Similarly, Ellen has received only an unfunded, unsecured promise to pay $36,000 in year two, which is not "property" subject to §83, which is discussed in the next section of this book.) Because Ellen does not take the deferred payment into income in year one, BigCo cannot receive a deduction for the payment in year one. §404(a)(5).

24. a. True. An employer may deduct qualified pension or profit-sharing plan contributions in the year in which the contributions are made.
    b. False. Employees are not taxed on amounts contributed on their behalf to qualified pension or profitsharing plans until those amounts are withdrawn.
    c. False. A plan will not qualify for tax-favored treatment unless it covers low-paid, as well as high-paid, employees.
    d. True. Premature withdrawals from a qualified retirement plan are subject to immediate taxation and to a 10 percent "penalty" tax under §72.
    e. False. Any individual may establish an IRA. However, contributions to an IRA are deductible only for those individuals who are not covered by a qualified pension or profitsharing plan or who are covered by such a plan but have an adjusted gross income below a certain amount. §219.

F. Section 83 Transfers

Reading: §§83, 421, 422; Reg. §§1.83-3, -7, 1.61-2(d)(2)

Some of the case law that established the economic benefit doctrine has been supplanted by the enactment of §83, which applies to compensatory transfers of property. For example, if an employer irrevocably transfers cash or property to a trust for the employee's benefit, and the trust assets are beyond the reach of the employer's creditors, §83 requires the employee to include the amounts set aside in the year in which they are transferred to the trust. §83(a) and Reg. §1.83-3(e). However, transfers outside the employment context are not subject to §83 and may be subject to the economic benefit doctrine.

Section 83 applies to transfers of property in connection with the performance of services. (Although §83 applies to service providers, which would include employees and independent contractors, assume for the purposes of this explanation that the compensatory transfer is made to an employee.) For purposes of §83, the term "property" does not include money or an unfunded, unsecured promise to pay money in the future, but it does include real and personal property or a beneficial interest in assets transferred to a trust or escrow account if the assets are beyond the reach of the transferor's creditors. Reg. §1.83-3(e). Under §83(a), the employee must include income from the transfer in the first year in which the transferred property vests, which means that it is either *transferable* or no longer *subject to a substantial risk of forfeiture*. Rights in the transferred property are subject to a substantial risk of forfeiture if the person's rights in the property are conditioned on the future performance of substantial services by the employee. §83(c)(1). Rights in property are transferable only if the employee can transfer the property to someone else who would not be subject to a substantial risk of forfeiture (which does not generally happen if the employee is subject to a substantial risk of forfeiture). §83(c)(2). The amount included under §83(a) is (i) the value of the transferred property *at the time that it vests* less (ii) the amount (if any) that the employee paid for the property. Since the amount included is compensation for services, it is taxed at ordinary income rates, not the special capital gain rate. The employee's basis in the property is the value of the property at the time of inclusion under §83. Reg. §1.61-2(d)(2). The employer deducts the compensation only when the employee includes it. §83(h).

Section 83(a) does not apply if an employee makes an election under §83(b). If a §83(b) election is made, the employee includes, in the year in which the property is transferred, (i) the value of the property *at the time of the transfer* less (ii) the amount (if any) that the employee paid for the property. Throughout this book, we stress that

taxpayers prefer to defer income. Why would a taxpayer make a
§83(b) election? Because, under some circumstances, making a §83(b)
election will save the taxpayer money. Amounts included under either
§83(a) or (b) constitute ordinary income so do not qualify for the
special capital gain rate. However, appreciation in the property following the §83 inclusion does qualify for the special capital gain rate
(assuming that the property transferred, which is often stock, is a
capital asset). If §83(a) applies, at the time of vesting the employee
will be taxed at ordinary rates on all appreciation in the property. If
§83(b) applies, the employee will be taxed (i) in the year of the transfer, at ordinary income rates on the difference between the value of the
property and the amount the employee paid for it, and (ii) on sale of
the property, at the capital gain rate, on the appreciation in the property after the transfer to the employee. In effect, a taxpayer making a
§83(b) election is betting that the cost of accelerating the §83 ordinary
income inclusion will be more than made up by the tax savings from
converting ordinary income on the appreciation in the property into
capital gain.

The following example will illustrate the §83 rules. In year one, a
start-up company called Minicomp is recruiting Steve, a young computer wizard. Minicomp cannot afford to pay Steve as much cash
compensation as he wants, but offers to let him buy 100 shares of
Minicomp stock, which has a value of $200,000 ($2,000 a share), for
$100,000. If Steve works for Minicomp until the end of year five, he
can keep the stock. If Steve leaves Minicomp before the five years are
up, he must sell the stock back to Minicomp for $100,000. Steve
accepts their offer, goes to work for Minicomp, and buys the stock in
year one. At the end of year five, Steve is still working for Minicomp
and the stock that he bought has appreciated in value to $2.1 million.
When the stock vests, Steve sells it for $2.1 million. (Assume that
Steve's tax rate in years one through five is 40 percent.)

Section 83 applies to the transfer of the stock to Steve. The stock
is transferred in connection with the performance of services because
Steve was allowed to buy the stock at a discount. Reg. §1.83-1(f).
Steve's rights in the stock are subject to a substantial risk of forfeiture
because retention of the stock is conditioned on Steve working for
Minicomp for five years. §83(c)(1). If Steve does not make a §83(b)
election in year one, §83(a) will apply. In year one, there is no inclusion because the stock is nontransferable and subject to a substantial
risk of forfeiture. §83(a). However, in year five, the year in which the
stock vests, Steve will have an income inclusion of $2 million, which is

3. Problems of Timing

(i) the $2.1 million value of the stock at the time that it vests less (ii) the $100,000 amount that Steve paid for the stock in year one. He will owe $800,000 of tax (40 percent of the inclusion because it is ordinary income) in year five.

If Steve makes a §83(b) election in year one, he will include in year one $100,000, which is (i) the $200,000 value of the stock at the time of the transfer less (ii) the $100,000 that he paid for the stock. He will pay $40,000 of tax (40 percent of the inclusion, which is ordinary income) in year one. His basis in the stock is $200,000, the value of the stock at the time of inclusion. In year five, when the stock vests, §83(a) does not apply. §83(b)(1) (flush language). When Steve sells the stock, he will realize a capital gain of $1.9 million ($2.1 million amount realized less the $200,000 basis in his stock). Assume that the capital gain rate is 28 percent. He will pay $532,000 of tax (28 percent of $1.9 million), in year five. Summarizing these results, Steve will either (i) apply §83(a) and pay $800,000 of tax in year five or (ii) make a §83(b) election and pay $40,000 in year one and $532,000 in year five. Assume that the present value of the $800,000 year five amount is $497,000 and the present value of the $532,000 year five amount is $330,000. By making the election, Steve saves $127,000, which is $497,000 less $370,000 ($40,000 plus $330,000).

Special rules apply under §83 if an employee receives *stock options*, instead of stock. A stock option gives the employee the right to buy stock of the employer at a specified price (referred to as the *strike price* or *exercise price*). For example, an employee of Growth Company may be given the right to buy Growth Company stock at $10 a share at any time during the next five years. The value of such an option depends on the current and future value of the stock. (Although the value of the option depends in part on other factors as well, we will disregard those other factors for now.) If Growth Company stock now sells for $12 a share, the employee can exercise the option, buying the stock for $10 a share, then sell it for $12 a share, making a $2 a share profit. If, as in this example, the stock price exceeds the exercise price, the option is said to be *in the money*. Even if the stock now sells for $8 a share, the option has value because the stock price may rise above $10 a share during the five-year period of the option. If, as in this variation of the example, the stock price is less than the exercise price, the option is said to be *out of the money*.

The §83 tax treatment of the grant and exercise of a stock option depends on whether the option has a readily ascertainable fair market value; §83 applies to the grant of an option with a readily ascertainable fair market value, but does not apply to the grant of an option that does not have a readily ascertainable fair market value. §83(e)(3). Why does §83 make this distinction? If we permitted an employee to make a §83(b) election on the grant of an option that does not have a readily ascertainable fair market value, the employee may understate the value of the option to reduce or eliminate the tax cost of making the §83(b) election. (Of course, an employee receiving stock in a closely held corporation, instead of an option, might also underestimate the value of the stock, but the potential for valuation understatement is even worse with options, which have only small value if they are out of the money. It would be more difficult to take the position that the stock has only a nominal value.) The §83(b) election would then permit the conversion of the appreciation in the stock after the grant of the option into capital gain, at little or no tax cost. This potential for abuse in the valuation of options is reduced if the option has a readily ascertainable value, so §83 draws a distinction between options with and without a readily ascertainable fair market value.

Regulation §1.83-7 provides that the value of an option is generally not ascertainable unless the option is actively traded on an established securities market. An option that is not actively traded has an ascertainable fair market value if the taxpayer can establish that several conditions are satisfied; however, taxpayers generally cannot satisfy these conditions.

Section 83 does not apply to the grant of an option that does not have a readily ascertainable fair market value; instead, §83(a) and (b) will apply to the subsequent transfer of stock on the exercise of the option. §83(e)(3); Reg. 1.83-7(a). If the option is sold, instead of being exercised, §83 applies to the money or property received for the option. Reg. §1.83-7(a).

If an option has a readily ascertainable fair market value, §83(a) and (b) apply to the grant of the option. Reg. §1.83-7(a). If such an option is not subject to a substantial risk of forfeiture, the employee is taxed on the value of the option in the year of receipt. §83(a). In effect, the employee is treated as if she had received cash and used it to purchase the stock option. If the employee later exercises the option and purchases the stock, §83 does not apply to the transfer of the stock on exercise. §83(e)(4). The employee's basis in the stock received on exercise is the sum of (i) the amount she included in income under §83(a) on receipt of the option plus (ii) the price she pays for the stock when she exercises the option. Reg. §1.61-2(d)(2). If the employee does not exercise the option (because the stock price is below the option price), she can, subject to certain limitations, deduct the amount previously taken into income. §§1234, 1211. The rationale for the deduction is that the employee has acquired an asset, the stock option, that has become worthless. In keeping with this rationale, the deduction may be limited by the capital loss limitations discussed in Chapter 8.

The following example illustrates the §83 rules for options with a readily ascertainable fair market value. On January 1, year one, Frank receives a stock option in High Company stock. The option allows Frank to purchase 100 shares of stock at $10 a share at any time during the next five years. The option is nonforfeitable and is a type of option that is traded on an established securities market. The price of High Company stock on January 1, year one, is $10 a share. The option is valuable because (i) if the stock rises to, say, $15 a share, Frank will be able to buy the stock for $5 less than its value and (ii) if the stock price does not rise above $10, or falls, Frank loses nothing. Assume that the value of the option on January 1, year one, is $100 ($1 for every share of stock Frank can purchase under the option). Frank is taxed as if he had in year one received $100 cash and purchased the stock options. In other words, he has an ordinary income inclusion of $100 in year one and a $100 basis in the option. On January 1, year two, High Company stock has risen in value to $25 a share, and Frank exercises the option, paying $10 a share for 100 shares, for a total of $1,000. Frank receives a basis in the stock of $1,100 ($100 included in year one plus $1,000 paid for the stock in year two on exercise), or $11 a share. If Frank now sells the stock for $25 a share, or $2,500, he will recognize $1,400 of gain. This makes sense: The stock option has made Frank $1,500 richer — he paid only $1,000 for stock he sold for $2,500. Frank recognizes $1,500 total gain, $100 upon receipt of the option and $1,400 upon sale of the stock.

If retention of an option with an ascertainable value is conditioned on the employee continuing to work for the employer for some specified period of time, the option is subject to a risk of forfeiture. In that case the employee is not taxed in the year in which the option is granted; instead, the employee is taxed, in the year in which the restriction lapses, on the value of the option at the time of inclusion. If the fair market value of an option is expected to increase greatly between the time it is granted and the time the risk of forfeiture will lapse, the employee might benefit from making a §83(b) election.

3. Problems of Timing

There is one final twist to the tax treatment of stock options: Section 83 does not apply to so-called *incentive stock options* (ISO). An ISO is an employee stock option that satisfies certain conditions set forth in §422. Employees are not taxed on the grant or exercise of an ISO. §421(a). A taxpayer's basis for stock received on the exercise of an ISO equals the amount paid for the stock on exercise. If an ISO had to be included in income, the stock basis would be increased by the amount included in income; not taxing an ISO therefore decreases the basis for the stock and increases the gain realized on the subsequent sale of the stock. Nonetheless, ISOs are advantageous to employees because they defer tax. On the other hand, the employer receives no deduction for the issuance of an ISO. §421(a)(2). Under many plausible assumptions, the disadvantageous treatment of ISOs to the employer outweighs the advantageous treatment of ISOs to the employee. The issuance of ISOs can actually increase the parties' combined tax burden.

As is perhaps obvious, the tax treatment of stock options is quite complex; indeed, the above discussion ignores some hard issues and is incomplete in other ways. Even experienced tax attorneys find this area of the law requires careful attention to detail.

EXAMPLES

25. a. In year one Biotech Breakthroughs Inc. (BB Inc.) hires Anna. Anna receives year one compensation of $300,000. In addition, BB Inc. gives her BB Inc. stock worth $100,000, for which she pays nothing. If Anna works for BB Inc. until the end of year five, she can keep the stock. If Anna leaves BB Inc. before the five years are up, she has to give the stock back to BB Inc. In year five Anna is still working for BB Inc. and her stock is worth $1 million. What are the tax consequences to Anna and BB Inc. of the transfer of the stock?

    b. What tax advice would you give Anna if you are her lawyer in year one?

26. On January 1, year one, Gary receives a stock option to purchase up to 10 shares of Sybex Company stock for $20 a share. The Sybex options are publicly traded, so Gary's option has a readily ascertainable value. The option is nonforfeitable and may be exercised at any time during the next 10 years. The value of Sybex Company stock on January 1, year one, is $20 a share. Which, if any, of the following statements are true?

3. Problems of Timing

    a. Gary is taxed in year one on the fair market value of the option on the date he received it, January 1, year one.

    b. Gary includes no income upon receipt of the option because the exercise price of the option is as high as the stock price and so the option has no value.

    c. Sybex Company may deduct the value of the option in the year in which Gary exercises the option and purchases stock.

    d. If the Sybex options were not traded, Gary would be taxed, in year one, on the fair market value of the option on the date he received it, January 1, year one.

27. On January 10, year one, Harriet receives a stock option to purchase 1,000 shares of Tirex Company stock for $10 a share. The option cannot be exercised prior to January 10, year three, and is forfeited if Harriet should voluntarily terminate her employment prior to that time. The option has an ascertainable fair market value. How much income does Harriet include, in years one and three, as a result of the grant of the option?

28. On January 1, year one, Irene receives a stock option to purchase 1,000 shares of HiLo Company stock for $300 a share. On that date the value of HiLo Company stock is $290 a share. The option is nonforfeitable, has an ascertainable value of $30,000 ($30 a share), and may be exercised at any time during the next five years. Irene exercises the option on January 1, year four, when the stock is worth $400 a share. On March 1, year six, Irene sells her 1,000 shares of HiLo Company stock for $500 a share, or $500,000.

    a. How much, if any, income does Irene include upon receipt of the stock option in year one?

    b. How much, if any, income does Irene include upon exercise of the stock option in year four?

    c. How much income does Irene include upon sale of the HiLo Company stock in year six?

29. On January 1, year one, John receives a stock option to purchase 1,000 shares of Uber Company stock for $10 a share. The option is a qualified incentive stock option within the definition of §422. On January 1, year three, John exercises the option; the price of Uber Company stock at that time is $50 a share. On January 2, year three, John sells the Uber Company stock for $50 a share.

    a. How much, if any, income does John recognize upon receipt of the option?

3. Problems of Timing

    b. How much, if any, income does John recognize upon sale of the stock?

    c. What are the tax consequences to Uber Company?

EXPLANATIONS

25. a. Section 83 applies to the transfer of the stock to Anna. The stock is transferred in connection with the performance of services because Anna paid nothing for the stock. Reg. §1.83-1(f). Anna's rights in the stock are subject to a substantial risk of forfeiture because retention of the stock is conditioned on Anna working for BB Inc. for five years. §83(c)(1). If Anna does not make a §83(b) election in year one, §83(a) will apply. In year one there is no inclusion because the stock is non-transferable and subject to a substantial risk of forfeiture. §83(a). However, in year five, the year in which the stock vests, Anna will have an income inclusion of $1 million, which is the $1 million value of the stock at the time that it vests. (Anna did not pay anything for the stock.) Anna will pay tax on that inclusion at her ordinary income rate.

    If Anna makes a §83(b) election in year one, she will include in year one $100,000, which is (i) the $100,000 value of the stock at the time of the transfer less (ii) the amount that she paid for the stock, zero. She will pay tax on that amount at her ordinary income rate. Her basis in the stock will be $100,000, the value of the stock at the time of inclusion. In year five, when the stock vests, §83(a) will not apply. §83(b)(1) (flush language). If Anna later sells the stock, she will realize a capital gain in an amount equal to the value of the stock at the time of the sale less her $100,000 basis in the stock.

    b. I would advise Anna to consider whether she should make a §83(b) election in year one. Anna has two choices. She can either (i) apply §83(a) and pay tax in year five, at ordinary income rates, on the value of the stock in year five, or (ii) make a §83(b) election and pay tax (a) in year one, at ordinary income rates, on the $100,000 value of the stock and (b) at the lower capital gain rate tax on the appreciation over years one through five. If she is in the 40 percent bracket in year one, she would owe $40,000 of tax on the $100,000 inclusion. If the BB Inc. stock will appreciate substantially during years one through five, making the election would allow her to convert a large amount of ordinary income, which would be taxed at ordinary income rates, into capital gain taxed at a lower rate. (In addition, if she does not sell the stock in year five, she can defer the capital gain until she sells the stock.) If the present value of converting the ordinary income in year five into capital gain is more than $40,000, she should consider making the election.

26. a. True. An employee is taxed on the grant of stock options if the options have an ascertainable value and are nonforfeitable. §83(a) and Reg. §1.83-7. The amount included is the value of the option on the date the employee received it (less any amount that the employee paid for the option, here zero). §83(a).

   b. False. Although the exercise price is as high as the current stock price, the option is still valuable. If the stock rises in value, Gary can exercise the option and buy the stock for less than its value. If the stock price falls or remains constant, Gary loses nothing.

   c. False. Under §83, the treatment of the employer and employee is symmetrical. Gary includes income under §83 in the year in which the option is granted, year one, so Sybex Company receives a deduction in that same year. §83(h).

   d. False. Nontraded options do not generally have a readily ascertainable fair market value and §83 does not apply to the grant if an option does not have a readily ascertainable fair market value. Gary would instead be taxed on the exercise of the option. §83(e)(3); Reg. §1.83-7(a).

27. Section 83 applies to the option because it has an ascertainable value. However, the option is forfeitable until year three, so Harriet will not have to include any income in year one as a result of the grant of the option. §83(a). In year three, when the risk of forfeiture lapses, Harriet will include income in an amount equal to the value of the option on the date that the restriction lapses. If the option is not very valuable upon receipt but Harriet believes that it will be quite valuable on January 10, year three, she will probably want to make a §83(b) election. If she makes the election, she will include in year one the value of the option on the date she receives it. Section 83 would then not apply in year three when the restriction lapses. §83(b) (flush language).

28. a. Section 83 applies to the option because it has an ascertainable value. The option is nonforfeitable, so Irene will have to include the $30,000 value of the option in year one, the year in which the option is granted. §83(a).
    b. The option has an ascertainable value, so §83 does not apply to the exercise of the option. §83(e)(4). Irene has no inclusion in year four.
    c. Irene includes $170,000 of gain ($500,000 amount realized less her $330,000 basis in the stock) in year six. Irene included $30,000 upon receipt of the option. This gives her a $30,000 basis in the option. When she exercises the option, her basis in the option is transferred to the shares. Her basis for the stock also includes the price she paid for the stock when she exercised the option, $300,000 ($300 a share). Thus, her total basis is $330,000.

29. a. John includes no income upon receipt of an incentive stock option.
    b. John recognizes $40 per share upon sale of the stock—the difference between the exercise price of $10 and the sale price of $50. Note that since John included no income upon receipt of the stock option, he has no basis in the option, so his basis for the stock is limited to the amount he paid for the stock on exercise of the option.
    c. Uber Company receives no deduction at any time.

G. The Accrual Method of Accounting

Reading: §§446, 448, 451, 456, 461; Reg. §§1.451, 1.461

Earlier in this chapter we saw that taxpayers using the cash method of accounting must generally include income in the year in which they receive it. (Of course, this rule is limited by the doctrines of constructive receipt and economic benefit, and the special rules that apply to various forms of deferred compensation.) In contrast, taxpayers using the accrual method include items of income "when all the events have occurred that fix the right to receive [the] income and the amount thereof can be determined with reasonable accuracy." Reg. §1.451-1(a).

The accrual method of accounting is generally thought to be a more accurate measure of income and expense than the cash method of accounting, so most companies use the accrual method to keep their books. Companies using the accrual method of accounting to keep their books must use the accrual method for tax purposes. §446(a). Regulation §1.446-1(c)(2)(i) also provides that companies that sell merchandise must use the accrual method. In addition, some taxpayers are required to use the accrual method because §448 prevents them from using the cash method.

As a simple example illustrating the difference between the cash and accrual methods of accounting, assume that an automotive repair shop performs services for a customer in November, year one. The customer and the shop agree that the bill for the services will be $100. The shop bills the customer in December, year one, and the customer pays the bill in year two. If the repair shop is on the accrual method, it will include the $100 of income in year one. It is in that year that the *all events test* is met; the events needed to establish the right to income (the provision of services) have occurred, and the amount of income can be determined with reasonable accuracy. In contrast, if the repair shop is on the cash method of accounting, it will not include the $100 of income until year two. Most students will agree that the accrual method more closely tracks the time at which the income is in fact earned.

Suppose, instead, that a customer pays $100 in December, year one, for services to be rendered in January, year two. Under generally accepted accounting principals (GAAP), which govern accounting for nontax purposes, an accrual method taxpayer would not include prepaid income for services until the services were performed. Thus, under GAAP, the $100 of income would be included in year two, not year one; the fact that the accrual method business receives cash prior to that time is irrelevant. However, in American Automobile Association v. United States, 367 U.S. 687 (1961), reh'g denied, 368 U.S. 870 (1961), the Supreme Court concluded that tax accounting does not have to follow GAAP. The issue in that case was whether the taxpayer had to include, in year one, dues paid by members in year one for services to be provided in year two. The taxpayer argued that the all events test was not met until the services were provided in year two and that GAAP would not require inclusion until year two. The Court held that for tax purposes prepaid income is taxable in the year received by an accrual method taxpayer, despite the fact that GAAP would defer inclusion until a later year. The decision in the *American Automobile Association* case effectively requires an accrual method taxpayer to use the cash method for prepaid income. There is a sort of "heads government wins, tails taxpayer loses" aspect to this rule. When an accrual method taxpayer performs services before receiving cash, he is taxed as soon as he performs services. Under the all events test, the liability is fixed as soon as the services are rendered. However, when the taxpayer receives cash before performing services, he is taxed as soon as he receives cash.

The one-sided rule established by the *American Automobile Association* case has been limited by subsequent developments. Soon after the decision was announced, Congress enacted §456, which permits membership organizations to include prepaid dues ratably as services are performed. Thus, the holding in *American Automobile Association* no longer requires the American Automobile Association to include prepaid dues in the year received. Perhaps more importantly, the Service has exercised its administrative discretion to allow an accrual method taxpayer who receives payment in one year, for services to be rendered in the following year, to defer inclusion of income until the services are provided. This deferral of prepaid income for services applies only if the contract for services provides that all services must be performed by the end of the year following payment. Rev. Proc. 71-21. Similarly, Regulation §1.451-5 permits limited deferral of prepaid income for goods. Finally, some, though by no means all, courts have rebelled at the seeming unfairness of the *American Automobile Association* holding and have found ways to allow accrual method taxpayers to defer inclusion of income until the provision of services. See, e.g., Artnell Co. v. Commissioner, 400 F.2d 981 (7th Cir. 1968) (where a baseball team was permitted to defer inclusion of prepaid season ticket sales until the year in which the games were to be played since the time for future performance was relatively certain). Accrual method taxpayers who do not fall within one of the statutory or administrative exceptions and who do not find a sympathetic court will be subject to the holding in *American Automobile Association* and taxed on prepaid income in the year in which they receive it.

The standard for deduction under the accrual method is similar to the standard for including an item in income; deduction is allowed only when all events have occurred to determine the fact of liability and the amount of the liability can be determined with reasonable accuracy. Reg. §1.461-1(a)(2). This standard may be illustrated by again considering the company that provides repair services for a client in November of year one and is paid in January of year two. The appropriate time for the client to receive a deduction (assuming that the repair is a business expense) is year one, the year in which the liability is fixed and determinate.

The application of the all events test to payments to be made far in the future raises difficult questions. For example, suppose someone is injured on company grounds, and the company agrees to pay the victim $10,000 a year for 25 years. At a 10 percent discount rate, the present value of the obligation is about $100,000. The company could fund the obligation by setting aside $100,000 today, or by making future payments that total $250,000. Interpreted literally, the all events test seems to allow the company to deduct the entire $250,000 in the year of settlement. After all, the liability is fixed and determinate, and there is no provision that requires taxpayers to reduce this sort of deduction to present value. If the expense is deductible, and the company is in the 40 percent combined state and federal income tax rate, the deduction will save the company $100,000 in taxes (40 percent of $250,000). That is equal to the amount the company must set aside to pay the obligation. In effect, the company's tort liability has been paid by the government.

This loophole could have been closed by limiting the amount deductible under the all events test to the present value of the future obligation. However, Congress instead chose to adopt §461(h), which provides that an accrual method taxpayer cannot deduct a future expense unless the all events test has been met *and economic performance* has occurred. In the case of a deferred payment in settlement of a tort liability, §461(h)(2)(C) provides that economic performance does not occur until the liability is paid. Thus, in the above example the company gets no deduction in the year of settlement, but may deduct the $10,000 annual payments when they are made.

Section 461(h) also applies more generally to limit deductions for future expenses in connection with services and properties received by the taxpayer or provided by the taxpayer. For example, suppose a company sells a piece of machinery and, as part of the sale, obligates itself to service the machinery once a year for three years. The cost of servicing the machinery, even if determinate, cannot be deducted until economic performance occurs, which is at the time that the machinery is actually serviced.

Section 461(h)(3) and Regulation §1.461-5(b)(1) provide an exception to the §461(h) economic performance requirement. Under this exception (generally referred to as the *recurring item exception*), an item may be deducted notwithstanding the absence of economic performance, provided that the following conditions are satisfied:

   i. the all events test is otherwise met;

   ii. the item is recurring in nature and the taxpayer consistently reports the item in accordance with the all events test;

iii. economic performance with respect to the item occurs by the earlier of (a) the date that the taxpayer files a timely return for that year (taking into account any extensions of the time to file) or (b) eight and a half months following the close of the tax year in which the deduction is taken; and

iv. the item is either (a) not material or (b) accruing the item under the all events test provides better matching of income and expense than the economic performance standard would provide.

To illustrate this exception, consider the following example. Circuit Town Appliances, an accrual method taxpayer, always gives an unconditional one-year money-back guarantee on the television sets it sells. Circuit Town receives an extension of the time to file its tax return for year one, so that the return is due on September 15, year two. During year one, 100 customers request a refund of $500 each, for total refunds due of $50,000. Although Circuit Town takes awhile to process the refunds, it pays them all in year two, before September 15. Circuit Town may take a year one deduction for the $50,000 of refunds paid in year two because the requirements of the recurring item exception are met: First, the all events test is met for the deduction in year one because in that year the refund liability is fixed and determinate. Second, the appliance store would likely have a recurring deduction for refunds. Third, economic performance (that is, payment of the refunds) occurs by the date that the taxpayer files a timely return for year one. Fourth, the deduction for the refunds is better matched with the income from the sale of the televisions if the deduction is taken in year one, the year in which the all events test is met, instead of year two, the year in which economic performance occurs. Thus, Circuit Town may take a deduction in year one for the $50,000 of refunds paid in year two. Reg. §1.461-5(e), example 1.

Section 461(h) is a poorly drafted, cumbersome provision of uncertain scope. The description of §461(h) here oversimplifies and is meant only to provide a rough guide as to the major features of that provision.

EXAMPLES

30. Office Cleaners Inc. and Accountants Inc. are both accrual method taxpayers. In each of the following situations, state the

3. Problems of Timing

year in which Office Cleaners Inc. includes income and the year in which Accountants Inc. receives a deduction.

   a. Office Cleaners Inc. provides office cleaning services for Accountants Inc. in November, year one, and is paid for those services in January, year two.

   b. Office Cleaners Inc. agrees to, and does, provide a fixed and determinate amount of office cleaning for Accountants Inc. in January, year two. Accountants Inc. prepays the cleaning expense in December, year one.

31. Ventana Ranch Inc., an accrual method taxpayer, is an exclusive health spa in Southern California. In year one, 50 people each pay the spa $20,000 for the right to use the spa facilities for five years. How does Ventana Ranch Inc. report the income received for GAAP and tax accounting purposes?

32. On December 31, year one, Consumers Inc., an accrual method taxpayer, sells a television set to Joe's Bar. As part of the sale, Consumers Inc. agrees to service the television set for four years. Consumers Inc. has determined that the average cost of providing such service will be $10 a year, for a total expected cost of $40

   a. May Consumers Inc. deduct the $40 cost in year one?

   b. Assume, instead, that the service contract provided on the purchase of a television set requires Consumers Inc. to provide only a one-time service check of the television at any time during the first two months of year two. The contract covers only the labor cost of the person performing the service. Consumers Inc. has determined that its cost for providing the service in year two is $20. May Consumers Inc. deduct the $20 expense in year one?

EXPLANATIONS

30. a. Office Cleaners Inc. must include income in year one, the year in which the services were performed and the liability became fixed. Accountants Inc. will receive a deduction in that same year.

   b. Under the holding in *American Automobile Association*, Office Cleaners Inc. would be required to include the prepaid income in the year in which it receives the payment, year one. However, Rev. Proc. 71-21 allows taxpayers to defer inclusion of prepaid amounts until the income is "earned" through the provision of services. In order to qualify for the deferral provided

3. Problems of Timing

in the revenue procedure, the contract for services must require that all of the services be provided by the close of the year following payment. Here, the office cleaning will be provided in year two, so Office Cleaners Inc. may defer inclusion of the service income until year two.

Accountants Inc. may or may not be able to deduct the expense of office cleaning in year one. The all events test is met in year one since the liability for cleaning expenses is fixed and determinate in that year. However, Accountants Inc. cannot deduct the expense until the economic performance requirement of §461(h) is also met. With respect to services to be provided to the taxpayer, economic performance occurs when the services are provided, so economic performance occurs in year two. §461(h)(2)(A)(i). Section 461(h)(1) precludes Accountants Inc. from deducting the expense in year one. However, if the expense qualifies for the §461(h)(3) recurring item exception, Accountants Inc. may deduct the expense in year one. Here, Accountants Inc. should be able to satisfy the first three parts of the recurring item exception test, but it may or may not be able to satisfy the last requirement. (In order to satisfy this requirement, Accountants Inc. has to show that the expense is not material or that allowing the deduction in that year results in better matching of income and expense.)

31. Under GAAP, Ventana Ranch will include the prepaid income as it is earned over the five-year period. However, for tax purposes, Ventana Ranch Inc. must include the full $1 million in year one. This transaction falls within the ambit of *American Automobile Association* and does not qualify for any of the exceptions. Note that §456 provides an exception to the rule that prepayments must be taken into income in the year received. However, that section applies only to "membership organizations." A *membership organization*, as defined in §456(e)(3), is an organization that is organized without capital stock and which cannot distribute earnings to any member. Thus, §456 does not apply to most corporations, but does apply to organizations such as a local Automobile Association or the Sierra Club.

32. a. No. Section 461(h) provides that an accrual method tax-payer cannot deduct an item until the later of (i) satisfaction of the all events test or (ii) economic performance. Section 461(h)(2)(B) provides that, where liability arises from the

186

provision of services by the taxpayer, economic performance occurs when the services are provided. Hence, Consumers Inc. will be able to deduct the cost of the service contract only as it provides service. (However, the recurring item exception of §461(h)(3) *might* permit Consumers Inc. to take a year one deduction for the expense of services provided prior to the date in year two on which it files its year one tax return. See, e.g., Reg. §1.461-5(e), example 1.)

b. Under §461(h)(2)(B), economic performance occurs in year two, as Consumers Inc. provides the services. However, the recurring item exception of §461(h)(3) might permit Consumers Inc. to take a year one deduction for all or a part of the expense of the services provided in year two. How do we apply the four-part recurring item exception test here?

   i. Is the all events test met in year one with respect to the $20 expense paid in year two? In one sense, liability to perform the year two service check is fixed and determinate in year one, because Consumers Inc. has obligated itself to perform services that will cost it $20 to perform. However, the all events test may not be met in year one because customers may not avail themselves of the "free" service call. The all events test would then be met when the customers request the service. If customers actually request service prior to the close of year one, and the service is provided in year two, the recurring item exception may permit Consumers Inc. to take a year one deduction for the year two cost of those services requested in year one. See, e.g., Reg. §1.461-5(e), example 1.

   ii. The expense must be recurring in nature. Here, the service liability is likely recurring since it is included on the sale of each television set.

   iii. Economic performance must occur before the earlier of (i) the date on which the taxpayer files its timely tax return (taking into account any extensions of the time to file) or (ii) eight and a half months after the close of year one. §461(h)(3)(A)(ii) and Reg. §1.461-5(b)(ii). Here economic performance occurs no later than February 28, year two, so this requirement is met.

   iv. Consumers Inc. would have to establish that the $20 cost is either not material or that allowing a year one deduction results in better matching of income and expense than allowing a year two deduction. Consumers Inc. may or may not be able to establish this last requirement. We would need more facts in order to determine whether part of the year two expense may be deducted in year one under the recurring item exception.

H. Alternative Tax Bases: Consumption Tax and Value Added Tax

Recall that under a Haig-Simons based income tax, a person is subject to an annual tax on net accretion to wealth — whether spent or saved. As we have seen earlier in this chapter, appreciation in assets is not taxed until gain is realized on the sale or other disposition of the assets. The realization requirement represents a departure from the Haig-Simons ideal, but facilitates administration of the income tax. The tax treatment of other forms of saving also deviates from the Haig-Simons ideal. For example, savings held in qualified retirement plans are not taxed until they are withdrawn by the taxpayer.

Our tax system's various departures from the Haig-Simons ideal have led some commentators to suggest that we repeal the income tax and replace it with a consumption tax. The tax base is computed differently under an income tax and consumption tax. A pure Haig-Simons based income tax would require a taxpayer to pay tax each year on her net accretion to wealth, whether she spent it or saved it. (Said another way, the base is the taxpayer's change in wealth plus personal consumption.) In contrast, under a consumption tax, an individual is taxed only on her personal consumption. For these purposes, the term *personal consumption* refers to expenditures for non-business-related necessities such as food, clothing, and lodging, and for non-business-related luxuries such as entertainment and travel.

The most direct way to implement a consumption tax would be to tax an individual on gross income but allow a deduction for income that is invested. The net income that is left will be the amount spent for personal consumption. This form of consumption tax is sometimes referred to as a *cash flow consumption tax.* Under a cash flow consumption tax, an individual who earns $200,000, puts $30,000 of that amount in the bank, and uses the remainder for consumption would pay tax on a base of $170,000. (If we adopted a cash flow consumption tax, the tax rates would likely continue to be progressive.) The taxpayer's tax liability would be the same if, instead of saving $30,000 in the bank, she used that sum to purchase stock. For consumption tax purposes, savings and investments are treated the same. Indeed, under a consumption tax, the term "savings" is a synonym for investment.

Suppose in the above example the individual sold her $30,000 investment or withdrew her savings and spent the proceeds on personal consumption. Under a cash flow consumption tax, the individual would be taxed on the proceeds in the year the funds were consumed. (This result can also be reached by applying the concepts of basis and realization. Since the individual will have already deducted the cost of her investment, her adjusted basis is zero. The entire sales proceeds are therefore taxable.)

Somewhat complex issues can arise under a cash flow consumption tax with respect to purchases of consumer durables. For example, if an individual buys an automobile for $20,000, it would be wrong to treat the transaction as $20,000 of consumption in the year of purchase because the automobile has a useful life of several years. The correct approach is to treat the rental value of the automobile as consumption. The proper treatment under a consumption tax, then, is to treat amounts used to purchase an automobile as an investment (and thus not included in income) and then tax the purchaser on the rental value each year. The problem with such a scheme is its complexity. A similar problem arises with housing.

A roundabout way of achieving something very similar to a consumption tax would be to levy a tax on the entire Haig-Simons income but then to exempt the yield from any property purchased with that income. This type of tax system is often referred to as a *yield exemption consumption tax*. Suppose, for example, an individual received $100,000 in wages in year one and invested $50,000 in stocks, which she sold in year two for $60,000. Under a yield exemption consumption tax, the individual would receive no deduction in year one but instead would pay tax on her full Haig-Simons income of $100,000. In year two, however, the entire return from the sale of stock would be tax-free. Similarly, had the individual left $50,000 in a bank account in year one, the deposit would have yielded no current deduction but the interest earned on the account would be tax-free. The yield exemption form of consumption tax is less advantageous than the cash flow form of consumption tax when the investment is made, but more advantageous when the investment is sold. Under plausible assumptions, the advantages and disadvantages offset each other.

As may be obvious from the above descriptions, the treatment of savings and investments under a consumption tax is extremely favorable. Under a cash flow consumption tax, the full amount of the investment or saving is currently deductible. Under a yield exemption consumption tax, no tax is ever levied on the return to savings or investment. A consumption tax is often supported on the rationale that it would encourage saving and investment. A consumption tax is often opposed on the rationale that it would benefit the wealthy, who account for a disproportionate amount of the nation's savings and investment.

As an alternative to the consumption taxes described above, some people have suggested replacing or supplementing the federal income tax with a *value added tax*, often referred to by its acronym, VAT. As its name implies, a VAT is levied on the value added to goods and services by those who manufacture, distribute, and sell those goods or services. Each link in the chain of production pays a tax equal to the difference between its costs of materials and its sales proceeds. The following example may help illustrate the operation of a VAT. Suppose that a mining company sells $100,000 of processed iron ore to a widget manufacturer. The manufacturer processes the ore into widgets and sells the widgets to retailers for $250,000. The retailers sell the widgets for $300,000. Assume the rate of the VAT is 10 percent. Here, the mining company has added $100,000 in value — the difference between its cost of goods (0) and its sales ($100,000). The mining company would owe $10,000 of VAT (10 percent of $100,000 value added) on the sale of the ore to the manufacturer. The manufacturer has also added $150,000 in value — the difference between its cost of goods ($100,000) and sales ($250,000). It would owe $15,000 of VAT (10 percent of $150,000) on the sale of the widgets to the retailers. The retailers have added $50,000 in value — the difference between their cost of goods ($250,000) and sales ($300,000). They would owe $5,000 of VAT (10 percent of $50,000 value added) on the sales to customers.

A VAT is a form of a sales tax; the effect of a VAT is virtually identical to the state and local sales taxes most of us are familiar with — a tax collected by the retailer on the sales price of goods. The only real difference is that a VAT is collected piecemeal from the links of the chain of production, while a sales tax is collected solely from the retailer. The similarity of these two forms of sales taxes is evident from the above example. The total amount subject to the VAT is $300,000. That amount is also the retail price of the goods and the amount that would be subject to tax under the form of sales tax those of us in this country are more familiar with. Ultimately, both a VAT and a retail sales tax increase the cost of goods to consumers, as those in the chain of production pass some of the tax on in the form of higher prices.

The consumption tax described above can also be thought of as a form of sales tax since it applies only to the extent an individual purchases goods and services. One significant difference between a consumption tax and a retail sales tax or a VAT is that a consumption tax can be levied at different rates for taxpayers with differing amounts of consumption. For example, someone who spends $20,000 a year might pay a tax of 10 percent on consumption while someone who spends $200,000 a year might pay a tax of 40 percent on consumption.

It is interesting to compare, in a necessarily summary fashion, the relative strengths of an income tax and the other above-mentioned taxes. As noted above, the retail sales tax, VAT, and consumption tax all tax purchases of goods rather than savings and investment. For this reason, most commentators believe a shift away from an income tax and toward these taxes would increase savings, though the amount of increase is hotly debated. The anticipated increase in savings leads many to favor such consumption-based taxes. For different reasons, the exemption of savings is also seen as the biggest disadvantage of these taxes. In any given year, those with high incomes account for nearly all savings; those with low incomes often "dissave," dipping into savings to pay the expenses of ordinary life. In the short run, at least, the exemption of savings from taxation benefits only high income taxpayers. As compared to an income tax, a retail sales tax, VAT, or consumption tax is therefore regressive, raising a greater proportion of revenue from those who, it is argued, can least afford it.

EXAMPLES

33. Barbara is a junior partner at a large San Francisco law firm. Her year one taxable income is $200,000. She spends three-quarters of her earnings; the other quarter is placed in various stocks and money market accounts. What is her year one Haig-Simons taxable income? Her year one taxable income under a cash flow consumption tax? Her year one taxable income under a yield exemption consumption tax?

34. State whether the current tax treatment of each of the following items is more consistent with an income tax defined under the Haig-Simons definition of income or a consumption tax.

3. Problems of Timing

   a. Money market interest, which is included in income as it is earned
   b. Individual retirement accounts. Taxpayers generally deduct their IRA contributions when they are made and are taxed on the proceeds in the account when the funds are withdrawn (usually at retirement).
   c. Appreciation in property
   d. A whole life insurance policy that costs $10,000 and pays out $50,000

35. At the beginning of year one, Alice has $10,000 of savings. During year one, Alice earns $30,000 in wages and $1,000 in interest, which she spends on her daily expenses. At the end of the year she takes an around-the-world vacation that costs an additional $13,000. To finance the vacation, she withdraws $5,000 from her savings account and borrows an additional $8,000. Calculate Alice's year one tax base under a Haig-Simons income tax and under a consumption tax.

36. Bob earns $50,000 in wages in year one. He saves $10,000 of his year one wages and spends the other $40,000. In year two he also earns $50,000 in wages and earns $1,000 on his $10,000 of savings. During year two Bob consumes all of his year two income and all of his savings from year one. Calculate Bob's tax base, in years one and two, under a Haig-Simons income tax and under a consumption tax.

37. Briefly compare a VAT and an income tax.

EXPLANATIONS

33. Under the Haig-Simons definition, income equals accretions to wealth, whether spent or saved (or, said another way, income is the accretion to wealth left at the end of the year plus the amounts consumed during the year). Here, during year one, wealth increases by $200,000 of wages. Total year one Haig-Simons income, therefore, equals $200,000. (Under the alternate definition given above, net accretion to wealth left at the end of the year is $50,000 and personal consumption is $150,000, so income is $200,000.) Under a cash flow consumption tax, year one income equals personal consumption. Here $150,000 is consumed, so Barbara would have to pay tax on a base of $150,000. A yield exemption consumption tax uses the same definition of income as

192

a Haig-Simons income tax, so Barbara would have to pay tax on $200,000. However, under a yield exemption tax, the proceeds on Barbara's $50,000 of investments would be tax-free.

34. a. Under current law, a taxpayer receives no deduction when amounts are placed in a money market account and is taxed on the annual accretion to wealth attributable to such amounts. This is consistent with an income tax under the Haig-Simons definition of income.

   b. Under a consumption tax, all savings are deductible from gross income, and the amounts saved are taxed when withdrawn and used for personal consumption. Thus, the treatment of IRAs is consistent with a consumption tax.

   c. The current treatment of property appreciation is not equivalent to either the Haig-Simons income tax or a consumption tax. It is not equivalent to a pure income tax because annual accretion to wealth accrued on property is not taxed until the property is sold. It is not equivalent to a cash flow consumption tax because the investment is not deductible. It is not equivalent to a yield exemption consumption tax because the proceeds are taxable. In fact, the current treatment of appreciation in property falls somewhere between the income and consumption tax bases. Property appreciation is treated more favorably than it would be under a pure income tax because taxation of annual accretion to wealth is deferred until realization (the timing of which is usually within the taxpayer's control). On the other hand, property appreciation is treated less favorably than it would be under a yield exemption consumption tax because the annual accretion to wealth is eventually taxed. It is also treated less favorably than it would be under a cash flow consumption tax because a taxpayer cannot deduct the amount she invests in the property.

   d. The treatment of the insurance is consistent with a yield exemption consumption tax. The investment is not deductible but, as discussed in Chapter 2, the return on the investment is tax-free.

35. Alice's consumption can be calculated as follows: $31,000 consumed in daily living and $13,000 consumed on the vacation. Thus, her year one tax base under a consumption tax is $44,000.

   Alice's change in wealth is −$13,000 because she has $5,000 less savings and has incurred an $8,000 debt. The sum of her

   −$13,000 change in wealth and $44,000 of consumption is
   $31,000. Thus, Alice's year one tax base under an income tax is
   $31,000.

36. Under a Haig-Simons income tax, Bob has a tax base of $50,000
    ($10,000 increase in wealth plus $40,000 consumption) in year
    one and $51,000 ($61,000 personal consumption plus −$10,000
    change in wealth) in year two. Under a consumption tax, Bob has a
    base of $40,000 in year one and $61,000 in year two.

37. Under an income tax, an individual is taxed both on the portion
    of income she spends and the portion of income she saves or
    invests. A VAT applies only to sales of goods or services so that no
    tax is collected on that portion of income that is saved. As a result,
    many feel that the shift from an income tax toward a VAT would
    increase savings. One perceived downside of a shift toward a VAT
    is that a VAT is more regressive than an income tax since it does
    not cover savings and in any given year high income individuals
    account for virtually all savings.

4

Personal Deductions, Exemptions, and Credits

The deductions, exemptions, and credits examined in this chapter are called *personal* because they are largely unrelated to the cost of earning income. Personal deductions, exemptions, and credits often are designed to reflect differences in ability to pay. This is the primary function, for example, of the deduction for extraordinary medical expenses and the exemption for dependents. Other personal deductions and credits are designed to encourage certain forms of behavior. Section 170, for example, provides a deduction for charitable contributions.

Section A of this chapter introduces the standard deduction, examines some of the issues surrounding personal and dependent exemptions, and briefly describes personal credits. Sections B through F look at the deductions for extraordinary medical expenses, casualty losses, charitable contributions, home mortgage interest, and state and local taxes.

A. Introduction

Reading: §§32, 63(b), 67, 68, 151, 152

Personal deductions are subtracted from adjusted gross income in determining taxable income. A taxpayer may take either (i) *itemized* personal deductions or (ii) a *standard deduction*. §63(b). What qualifies as an itemized personal deduction is the subject of this chapter. To anticipate, the largest itemized deductions are the home mortgage interest deduction and the deduction for state and local taxes.

An otherwise qualifying itemized deduction may be lost entirely or in part due to two statutory limits. First, itemized deductions other than the ones listed in §67(b) are allowed only to the extent they exceed 2 percent of the taxpayer's adjusted gross income. §67(a). Fortunately, all major itemized deductions — including all the itemized deductions discussed later in this chapter — are listed in §67(b) and are not subject to the 2 percent floor. The only deductions of any significance that are subject to the 2 percent floor are those for unreimbursed employee business expenses and certain investment-related fees such as the cost of subscribing to the Wall Street Journal or renting a safe deposit box to store securities.

Second, §68 imposes an overall limitation on itemized deductions for taxpayers with adjusted gross income in excess of the "applicable amount," which is defined in §68(b). The applicable amount for 1995, adjusted for inflation, was $114,700. Rev. Proc. 94-72. If §68 applies, the taxpayer's itemized deductions (other than the deductions listed in §68(c)) are reduced by the lesser of (i) 3 percent of the taxpayer's adjusted gross income in excess of the applicable amount or (ii) 80 percent of the taxpayer's itemized deductions. §68(a). For example, if a taxpayer has $514,700 of adjusted gross income and $50,000 of itemized deductions, §68 reduces the taxpayer's itemized deductions by the lesser of (i) $12,000 (3 percent of the $400,000 of adjusted gross income in excess of the $114,700 applicable amount) or (ii) $40,000 (80 percent of the taxpayer's itemized deductions). Thus, §68 limits the taxpayer's itemized deductions to $38,000 ($50,000 itemized deductions less the $12,000 reduction under §68).

Section 63(c)(2) sets forth the standard deduction amounts, which are adjusted annually for inflation. §63(c)(4). For the 1995 tax year, the inflation adjusted standard deduction was $3,900 for an unmarried taxpayer and $6,550 for a married couple filing a joint return. Rev. Proc. 94-72. (In addition, §63(f) provides small additional inflation adjusted standard deductions for the elderly and the blind.) For most taxpayers who are not paying interest on a home mortgage, the standard deduction will generate a larger deduction than would itemized deductions.

Personal exemptions are also subtracted from a taxpayer's adjusted gross income and may be taken in addition to itemized deductions or the standard deduction. §63(b), (d). Each taxpayer receives a *personal exemption* and an additional *dependent exemption* for each dependent. §151(b), (c). Although §151 provides that the exemption amount for both personal and dependent exemptions is $2,000, that amount is adjusted for inflation under §151(d)(4)(A). For the 1995 tax year, the personal and dependent exemption amount was $2,500. Rev. Proc. 94-72.

The rules for determining who is a *dependent* for purposes of the exemption are surprisingly complex. In general, a dependent must receive more than half of his or her support from the taxpayer taking the exemption and must be either a relative (including blood relatives, step-relatives, and in-laws) or a member of the taxpayer's household. §152(a). Even if an individual otherwise qualifies as a dependent, a dependent exemption can be taken only if the dependent (i) earned less than the exemption amount or (ii) was a child of the taxpayer and was either under age 19 or was a full-time student under age 24. §151(c).

Personal and dependent exemptions are phased out for taxpayers with high incomes. If a taxpayer's adjusted gross income exceeds the "threshold phaseout amount," the taxpayer's personal exemptions are reduced 2 percent for each $2,500 increment (or fraction thereof) of adjusted gross income in excess of the threshold phaseout amount. §151(d)(3). The threshold phaseout amounts provided in §151(d)(3) are adjusted for inflation under §151(d)(4)(B). For 1995 the threshold phaseout amount was $172,050 for married taxpayers filing a joint return and $114,700 for unmarried taxpayers. Rev. Proc. 94-72. Consider the following example: Assume that Jack and Jill, married taxpayers who file a joint return, have one child who qualifies as a dependent. In 1995 they are entitled to three $2,500 exemptions (one each for Jack, Jill, and the child), which total $7,500. Their 1995 adjusted gross income is $200,000, so it exceeds the threshold amount by $27,950. How many increments of $2,500 are there in the $27,950 amount? There are 11.18 increments ($27,950/$2,500) and a partial increment is treated as a full increment, so there are 12 increments for purposes of computing the phaseout. Their $7,500 exemption amount will be reduced 2 percent for each of the 12 increments, or 24 percent. This will reduce their total exemption to $5,700 — $7,500 less $1,800 (24 percent of $7,500).

The income-based limitations on personal deductions and exemptions increase the progressivity of the tax system by limiting the exemptions to those who (arguably) need them the most. On the other hand, the phaseouts increase the complexity of an already (too) complex tax system.

Unlike deductions and exclusions, which reduce a taxpayer's taxable income, tax credits reduce a taxpayer's tax liability on a dollar-for-dollar basis. Thus, for a taxpayer in the 30 percent marginal tax bracket, a $100 deduction reduces taxable income by $100 and reduces tax liability by $30. A $100 credit, by contrast, would reduce tax liability by $100.

Perhaps the most significant credit premised on "ability to pay" concerns is the earned income credit, designed to reduce the tax burden on low income workers. If the credit amount exceeds the taxpayer's tax liability, the excess amount is refundable. As the taxpayer's income increases, the credit is phased out. The precise calculation of the credit is complex and subject to frequent modification. We suggest students just skim the following brief (!) description of its operation.

The §32 credit equals the credit percentage of an eligible taxpayer's earned income up to the earned income amount. §32(a)(1). For tax year 1995, the *credit percentage* was (i) 34 percent if the taxpayer had one qualifying child, (ii) 36 percent if the taxpayer had two or more qualifying children, and (iii) 7.65 percent if the taxpayer had no qualifying children. §32(b)(1)(B). *Earned income* includes wages, salaries, tips, and any other employment compensation and income from self-employment, but does not include pensions or annuities. §32(c)(2). The amount of earned income that may be taken into account, for purposes of computing the credit, is limited to the "earned income amount." §32(a)(1). For tax year 1995, the *earned income amount* was (i) $6,160 if the taxpayer had one qualifying child, (ii) $8,640 if the taxpayer had more than one qualifying child, and (iii) $4,100 if the taxpayer had no children. §32(b)(2)(A), (i)(1) and Rev. Proc. 94-72. In 1995 the maximum earned income tax credit for a taxpayer with one qualifying child was thus $2,094 (the 34 percent credit percentage multiplied by the $6,160 earned income amount). The maximum credit for a taxpayer with more than one qualifying child was $3,110 (the 36 percent credit percentage multiplied by the $8,640 earned income amount). For taxpayers with no qualifying children, the maximum credit was $314 (the 7.65 percent credit percentage multiplied by the $4,100 earned income amount). In addition, the earned income credit is subject to a complex phaseout that ensures that the benefits of §32 go only to the "working poor."

Sound complicated? It is. Few taxpayers could hope to determine the §32 credit without an accountant or tax lawyer — a luxury those eligible for the credit are unlikely to be able to afford. Fortunately, for the working poor who file returns, the amount of the credit can be and is calculated automatically by the Service in their computerized review of returns.

Section 22, another ability-to-pay credit, provides a credit for taxpayers who either are at least 65 years old or are retired because of permanent and total disability. The maximum credit is $750 (15 percent of $5,000) for unmarried taxpayers or married taxpayers where only one spouse qualifies for the §22 credit. §22(c)(2)(A)(i). If married taxpayers both qualify for the credit and file a joint return, the maximum credit is $1,125 (15 percent of $7,500). §22(c)(1)(A)(ii). The credit is reduced if the taxpayer receives certain types of government pension, annuity, or disability payments. §22(c)(1) and (3). The credit is also subject to phaseout based on the taxpayer's adjusted gross income. §22(d).

EXAMPLES

1. Peter and Martina are married and have three children. Each child receives more than half of his or her support from them. The youngest, Alex, age 13, lives at home and earns $4,000 per year as a child actor in advertisements. Alex is adopted. Betsy, age 16, lives with her aunt in New York so that she can attend a special high school for young musicians. Carl, age 21, lives with a friend in an apartment two miles from his parents' home. Carl earns about $5,000 per year as a member of a struggling rock band. Peter and Martina file a joint return.
   a. How many personal and dependent exemptions may be taken by Peter and Martina?
   b. How, if at all, would your answer in part (a) change if Carl were a part-time student at the local community college?
   c. Suppose that Martina and Peter also paid more than half of the support for Anna, Martina's niece. Anna, who lives in New York with her mother, Martina's sister, earns no income during the year. May Peter and Martina take a dependent deduction for Anna?

2. Debby's best friend, Emily, is disabled in a skiing accident. Debby invites Emily to live with her and provides more than half of her support. Emily's income drops to less than the exemption amount. Will Debby be entitled to a dependent exemption for Emily?

3. Mom's daughter Greta, age 22, is attending law school. Her annual expenses are $20,000 for tuition and books, $10,000 for food and lodging, and $5,000 for other expenses. Greta meets these expenses as follows:

$18,000	Scholarship from the law school
$ 4,000	Summer earnings
$ 3,000	Student loans
$10,000	Support from Mom

Will Mom be entitled to a dependent exemption for Greta?

4. Lee and Juanita, married taxpayers who file a joint return, have two children who both qualify as dependents. Their 1995 adjusted gross income is $294,551. What is the total amount of their 1995 personal exemptions?

EXPLANATIONS

1. a. They may take two personal exemptions, one each for Peter and Martina, and two dependent exemptions, one each for Alex and Betsy. They may not take a dependent exemption for Carl. Children, including legally adopted children, qualify as dependents under §152(a) if they receive over half their support from their parents. Under §151(c), a taxpayer is entitled to an exemption for each dependent (i) whose gross income is less than the exemption amount *or* (ii) who is a child of the taxpayer and is either under age 19 or a student under age 24. There is no requirement that the children live at home.

   Peter and Martina are entitled to the exemption for Alex, even though he earns more than the exemption amount, because he is under 19. They also are entitled to the exemption for Betsy, even though she lives with her aunt, because they pay for over half her support. However, they are not entitled to the exemption for Carl because he is over age 19, is not a student, and earns more than the exemption amount.

   b. No. "Student" is defined in §151(c)(4)(A) to include only full-time students.

   c. Yes. The term "dependent" includes a niece of the taxpayer who receives more than half of her support from the taxpayer. §152(a)(6).

2. Yes. Under §152(a)(9), a nonrelative can be a dependent if she lives in the home of the taxpayer as a member of the household and receives over half of her support from the taxpayer.

3. Yes. Mom may exclude the value of the scholarship in determining whether she has provided more than half of Greta's support. §152(d). Greta's total support excluding the scholarship is $17,000. Mom's $10,000 contribution is more than half of this amount, so Mom is entitled to claim Greta as a dependent.

4. Lee and Juanita are entitled to four $2,500 personal exemptions, which total $10,000. However, the exemptions will be reduced under the phaseout provision of §151(d)(3). Their 1995 adjusted gross income is $294,551, so it exceeds the $172,050 threshold amount by $122,501. How many increments of $2,500 are there in the $122,501 amount? There are 49.0004 increments ($122,501/$2,500) and a partial increment is treated as a full increment, so there are 50 increments for purposes of computing the phaseout. Their exemption amount is reduced by 2 percent for each of the 50 increments, so their exemption amount is reduced by 100 percent. In other words, their exemption amount is zero. This problem demonstrates that, in 1995, the phaseout completely eliminated the personal exemptions for married taxpayers with adjusted gross income of over $294,550. For unmarried taxpayers, the exemption was completely phased out if adjusted gross income exceeded $237,200.

B. Casualty Losses

Reading: §165; Reg. §§1.165-1, 1.165-7, 1.165-8

A taxpayer can deduct *net personal casualty losses* (personal casualty losses less personal casualty gains) to the extent that the aggregate losses during the taxable year exceed 10 percent of the taxpayer's adjusted gross income, after reducing each loss by $100. §165(h). Personal casualty losses are losses of "property not connected with a trade or business or a transaction entered into for profit if such losses arise from fire, storm, shipwreck, or other casualty, or from theft." §165(c)(3). Losses of property used in a business or profit-seeking activity are deductible whether or not they are due to casualty or theft. §165(c)(1)-(2).

The rationale for the personal deduction for casualty losses can be illustrated by the following example. Suppose Martha, a young San Francisco lawyer, receives a $5,000 end-of-year bonus from her law firm and uses the money to purchase a set of fine china. One day after the purchase, the china is destroyed in an earthquake. Supporters of the casualty deduction contend that Martha is in the same economic position after the earthquake that she would have been in had she never received the bonus and purchased the china. A casualty loss deduction thus is necessary to ensure that her taxable income accurately reflects her "ability to pay." Opponents of the casualty loss deduction point out that Martha could have avoided a loss by purchasing earthquake insurance or, perhaps, by taking additional measures to protect the china. If she decided not to purchase such insurance or to take such care, they argue, the government should not subsidize part of her loss through a tax deduction.

Under current law, a casualty loss deduction is permitted only to the extent that the loss is not reimbursed by insurance or otherwise. §165(a). In general, the deduction is permitted in the taxable year in which the loss occurs or, in the case of theft, in the taxable year in which the taxpayer discovers the loss. Reg. §§1.165-1(d)(1) and 1.165-8(a)(1)-(2). If the taxpayer has a claim for reimbursement of a casualty loss, the loss may not be deducted until the taxable year in which the amount that will be reimbursed can be ascertained. Reg. §1.165-1(d)(2).

In some circumstances, a taxpayer may have gain from a personal casualty. For example, assume that a taxpayer's basis in lost property is $50,000, but the taxpayer receives $75,000 from the insurance company because the property was insured for its replacement cost. The taxpayer will recognize $25,000 of gain on the involuntary conversion (assuming that the nonrecognition rule of §1033 is inapplicable). If a taxpayer's personal casualty gains exceed the taxpayer's personal casualty losses, the personal casualty gains and losses are treated as capital gains and losses. §165(h)(2)(B). In these circumstances, the personal casualty loss would not be an itemized deduction; instead it would offset the taxpayer's capital gain from the personal casualty. §165(h)(4)(A). If, on the other hand, the taxpayer's personal casualty losses exceed the taxpayer's personal casualty gains, the net personal casualty loss is an itemized deduction. (However, this itemized deduction is not subject to the limitations of §§67 and 68. §§67(b)(3), 68(c)(3).)

The amount of a casualty loss is determined by comparing the fair market value of the damaged property before and after the casualty. Reg. §1.165-7(a)(2)(i) and (b)(1). However, the loss cannot exceed the taxpayer's adjusted basis in the property. §165(b) and Reg. §1.165-7(b)(1). (The amount of the loss claimed as a deduction reduces the taxpayer's basis in the damaged property. Reg. §1.165-1(c)(1).) In addition, the loss from each casualty is allowed only to the extent that it exceeds $100. §165(h)(1). Since 1982 the deduction for net personal casualty losses (personal casualty losses in excess of personal casualty gains) has also been limited to the net casualty losses that exceed 10 percent of the taxpayer's adjusted gross income. §165(a)(2)(A). Thus, a deduction is provided only for losses that have a substantial impact on a taxpayer's financial well-being, distinguishing casualty losses from the ordinary mishaps of daily life. The 10 percent threshold simplified the Code by effectively eliminating the deduction for most losses. However, casualty losses continue to raise interesting theoretical issues.

If a taxpayer's loss of personal property is caused by an event other than fire, storm, shipwreck, or theft, the taxpayer may deduct the loss only if it was caused by a *casualty*. §165(c)(3). Defining the term "casualty" presents difficult line-drawing problems. The Service's position is that only an event that is both "sudden" and "unusual and unexpected" qualifies as casualty. Rev. Rul. 72-592. For example, the Service has taken the position that termite damage does not qualify as a casualty loss because it is not sudden. Rev. Rul. 63-232. The "unusual and unexpected" requirement is illustrated in Dyer v. Commissioner. 20 T.C.M. (CCH) 705 (1961), where the taxpayer claimed a casualty loss deduction for a $100 vase that was destroyed by a cat suffering a fit. The Tax Court denied the deduction because breakage of household goods by a family pet is not unexpected.

Courts do not always apply the "sudden" and "unusual and unexpected" standard consistently. This inconsistency is illustrated in numerous decisions involving casualty loss deductions for lost or destroyed diamond rings. Compare, e.g., Keenan v. Bowers, 91 F. Supp. 771 (E.D.S.C. 1950) (where the taxpayer was denied a casualty loss deduction for a diamond ring that was wrapped in a tissue and mistakenly flushed down a toilet) with Carpenter v. Commissioner, 25 T.C.M. (CCH) 1186 (1966) (where the taxpayer was allowed a casualty loss deduction for a diamond ring that had been left in a glass of ammonia and water for cleaning and was later poured into the kitchen sink and destroyed by the garbage disposal).

A taxpayer may take a casualty loss deduction for property destroyed due to the taxpayer's negligence. However, a casualty loss deduction is not allowed if the loss is caused by gross negligence or a willful act by the taxpayer. See, e.g., Blackman v. Commissioner, 88 T.C. 677 (1987), aff'd without opinion, 867 F.2d 605 (1st Cir. 1988) (where the taxpayer was denied a casualty loss deduction for his destroyed home because of his gross negligence in failing to put out the fire he started) and Reg. §1.165-7(a)(3)(i) (denying a casualty loss deduction if the loss is due to the willful act or negligence of the taxpayer).

EXAMPLES

5.   In year one the contents of Susan's rented apartment are destroyed by a fire. Susan suffers a $20,000 loss from the destruction of her personal belongings in the fire. The property lost had a basis of $35,000. Susan's year one adjusted gross income is $100,000.

   a. If Susan had no renter's insurance, how much of her $20,000 loss is deductible?

   b. How, if at all, would your answer in part (a) change if Susan had renter's insurance that covered $8,000 of her loss?

6.   In year one Jack has adjusted gross income of $40,000. On March 1, year one, his car is stolen. Jack's basis in the car is $20,000, but it is worth only $5,000. On July 1 a flood in his apartment destroys his stereo, worth $500, and television set, worth $200. Jack has a $1,000 basis in the stereo and a $800 basis in the television. Jack will not be reimbursed for the stolen car or the lost stereo and television. How large a casualty deduction is Jack entitled to take in year one?

7.   In year one Mickey, who has adjusted gross income of $50,000, loses a painting worth $12,000 in a storm. Mickey's basis in the painting is $10,000. The painting was not insured. How large a casualty deduction will Mickey be entitled to take in year one?

8.   In year one Nell's uninsured car is destroyed in a flood. Prior to the flood, the car had a basis of $8,000 and a fair market value of $7,000. Nell's year one adjusted gross income is $20,000.

   a. How large a casualty deduction is Nell allowed if the car is her personal car?

   b. How large a deduction is Nell allowed if the car was used exclusively in her business?

9.   a. In year one Maria, who has an adjusted gross income of $100,000, loses her home and her car in an earthquake. From

various insurance policies, she recovers $250,000 for the loss of her home, which has an adjusted basis of $220,000. Her car, which has an adjusted basis of $15,000 and is worth $10,000, is uninsured. How much is her casualty loss deduction in year one?

b. How, if at all, would your answer in part (a) change if Maria's basis in her home at the time of the earthquake is instead $243,000?

c. How, if at all, would your answer in part (b) change if, at the time of the earthquake, Maria's car is worth $35,000 and her basis in the car is $40,000?

Assume, for purposes of the problems below, that the losses incurred are not reimbursed by insurance or otherwise and that the casualty losses stated already take into account the $100 and 10 percent of adjusted gross income floors.

10. Tim suffered a $15,000 loss when his sailboat was destroyed in a storm. Briefly state the arguments for and against allowing Tim a deduction for the loss.

11. Buck lost his home in a flash flood on January 20 of year one. It was unclear whether Buck had let his insurance policy lapse. After the insurance company refused his claim, Buck filed a lawsuit against the company seeking payment. In which year or years can Buck take a casualty loss deduction?

12. Tim keeps a snowmobile at his vacation cabin in the mountains. Tim's snowmobile was stolen on October 15 of year one, but Tim did not discover the theft until January 15 of year two. In which year or years can Tim take the casualty loss deduction for the stolen snowmobile?

13. Pyro lit a bonfire in his living room. He mistakenly believed that he could contain the fire because when he was young he was a boy scout. He was wrong and suffered a $30,000 loss. Is Pyro's loss deductible?

14. a. Giovanni suffers a $7,000 loss when his kitchen floor suddenly collapses due to termite damage. Is Giovanni's loss deductible?

b. Would your answer change if Giovanni's kitchen floor collapsed when his furnace exploded?

15. Wendy's car suffers $5,000 of damage due to her negligent driving. Is her loss deductible?

16. Bill suffers a $4,000 loss due to his negligent driving. Bill has auto insurance, but decides not to file a claim because he does not want his rates raised. Can Bill still deduct his loss?

17. In each of the following cases, determine whether Dusty will be allowed a casualty loss deduction for the loss of his wedding ring:
    a. The ring slips off his finger while he is skiing.
    b. The ring is lost when he runs into a tree while skiing.
    c. Dusty wraps his ring in tissue and puts it on his night stand. His wife flushes the tissue with the ring down the toilet.
    d. The ring is inadvertently dropped into the kitchen sink and is destroyed by the garbage disposal.
    e. A burglar steals the ring.
    f. The ring is lost when a friend accidentally slams a car door on Dusty's finger.

18. Donna's uninsured automobile was destroyed in a stock car race. Can Donna deduct the loss?

EXPLANATIONS

5. a. Susan will be allowed a $9,900 casualty loss deduction. Susan's adjusted gross income is $100,000. A taxpayer is allowed a deduction for net personal casualty losses (reduced by $100) in excess of 10 percent of adjusted gross income. §165(c)(3) and (h). Susan's personal casualty loss is $20,000. That amount is first reduced by $100, to $19,900. §165(h)(1). Susan's adjusted gross income is $100,000 and 10 percent of that amount is $10,000. Thus, she can deduct $9,900 ($19,900 loss less $10,000). §165(h)(2)(A).
    b. Susan will be allowed a $1,900 casualty loss deduction. A deduction is permitted for casualty losses only to the extent that they are not reimbursed. If Susan lost $20,000 in the fire and was reimbursed for $8,000, her loss is reduced to $12,000. That amount is further reduced by $100, to $11,900. §165(h)(1). Her deduction is thus $1,900 — $11,900 less $10,000 (10 percent of her adjusted gross income). §165(h)(2)(A).

6. Jack is allowed a $1,500 casualty loss. Losses resulting from the same event are combined for purposes of the $100 floor, so the flood generates a $700 loss that exceeds the $100 floor by $600. Reg. §1.165-7(b)(4). The amount of the theft loss is the $5,000 value of the car since this amount is less than Jack's basis in the car. §165(b) and Reg. §1.165-7(b)(1) and (3) (example 2). The

loss from the car theft exceeds the floor by $4,900, so the total loss from the two events is $5,500. Ten percent of Jack's $40,000 adjusted gross income is $4,000. Jack is allowed a casualty loss of $1,500 ($5,500 loss less $4,000). §165(c)(3), (h)(1), (2).

7. Mickey is allowed a $4,900 casualty loss. The amount of a casualty loss is $10,000, which is the lesser of the $12,000 value of the painting destroyed or Mickey's $10,000 basis in the painting. That $10,000 loss is reduced by $100 to $9,900. Mickey is allowed to deduct $4,900, which is $9,900 less $5,000 (10 percent of his $50,000 adjusted gross income). §165(c)(3), (h)(1) and (2).

8. a. Nell is allowed a $4,900 casualty loss. The amount of the casualty loss is the $7,000 value of the car destroyed since this amount is less than Nell's adjusted basis. After taking into account the $100 and 10 percent of AGI floors, Nell would be able to deduct $4,900, which is $6,900 ($7,000 less $100) less $2,000 (10 percent of her $20,000 adjusted gross income).

    b. Business losses, which are taken under §165(c)(1) rather than §165(c)(3), are not subject to the $100 and 10 percent floors imposed by §165(h). Nell would be allowed a business loss of $8,000, the adjusted basis of the car. Taxpayers whose personal property is totally destroyed in a casualty are allowed a loss equal to the lesser of the basis or the fair market value of the property. On the other hand, taxpayers whose business property is totally destroyed are allowed a loss equal to the adjusted basis of the property even if that basis is greater than the fair market value of the property. Reg. §1.165-7(b)(1).

9. a. Maria would not be allowed an itemized deduction for her losses. Instead, she would have a $30,000 capital gain and a $9,900 capital loss. §165(h)(2)(B), (3), and (4)(A). Maria has a personal casualty gain of $30,000 on her home because the $250,000 of insurance proceeds received for her home exceed her $220,000 basis in the home by $30,000. §165(h)(3)(A). Maria also has a personal casualty loss of $9,900 on her car ($10,000 less $100) since the $10,000 value of the car is less than her $15,000 basis in the car. If casualty gains exceed casualty losses, the gains are treated as capital gains and the losses are treated as capital losses. Therefore, Maria would have a $30,000 capital gain and a $9,900 capital loss.

§165(h)(2)(B). In other words, the casualty loss would not be allowed as an itemized deduction.

b. Maria is not allowed a casualty loss deduction and does not have to include her casualty gain in income. If Maria's basis in her home is $243,000, her casualty gain is reduced to $7,000 ($250,000 insurance proceeds less her $243,000 basis in her home). Maria's casualty loss on the car is still $9,900. Maria thus has a $2,900 net personal casualty loss. This net casualty loss does not exceed 10 percent of her $100,000 adjusted gross income, so she will not be allowed to take a deduction in year one for the net loss. §165(h)(2)(A). However, she is permitted to net the loss (up to the amount of the gain) against the gain, so she will not have to include the gain. §165(h)(4)(A).

c. Maria is allowed a $17,900 personal casualty loss deduction. §165(c)(3) and (h). As in part (b), Maria's personal casualty gain is $7,000. Her personal casualty loss here is $34,900 ($35,000 value of the lost car less $100). Thus, Maria has a net personal casualty loss of $27,900 ($34,900 personal casualty loss less $7,000 personal casualty gain). She is allowed to deduct $17,900 ($27,900 net casualty loss less $10,000, which is 10 percent of her $100,000 adjusted gross income). §165(h)(2)(A).

10. The basic argument in favor of granting Tim a deduction is as follows: A casualty loss represents a reduction in wealth just like a loss of income. If Tim makes $50,000 and suffers a $15,000 casualty loss, he is in the same financial position as a person who makes $35,000 and suffers no damage. Thus, he should bear the same tax burden as a person who makes $35,000. This can be achieved by allowing Tim a casualty loss deduction.

The basic arguments against granting Tim a deduction are as follows: It is difficult to draw the line between extraordinary, unforeseeable losses and random but predictable losses. Perhaps the loss due to the storm ought to be considered one of the costs of owning a boat, just as the costs of plumbing repairs or the replacement of a worn out furnace are considered nondeductible costs of home ownership. Most individuals probably consider the risk of storm damage as one of the predictable costs of boat ownership and insure against the risk. Free partial insurance in the form of a tax deduction from the government would discourage the purchase of private insurance, since the casualty loss deduction is lost to the extent that an individual is reimbursed through insurance. The free partial insurance provided by a casualty loss deduction also subsidizes individuals who engage in risky activities and, accordingly, may reduce their incentives to take care of their property.

11. A casualty deduction is not permitted for any loss that reasonably might be reimbursed. §165(a). Thus, Buck will not be permitted a casualty loss deduction until the taxable year in which it becomes clear how much reimbursement, if any, he will receive. This is likely to be the year in which the lawsuit is settled or adjudicated. Reg. §1.165-1(d)(2)(i).

12. Losses due to theft are deductible in the taxable year in which they are discovered. Thus, Tim is allowed a theft loss deduction in year two. §165(e).

13. Pyro's loss is probably not deductible. A taxpayer is not allowed a deduction for casualty losses suffered through his own willful act or gross negligence. Losses caused by a taxpayer's ordinary negligence, however, may be deducted. Pyro's actions probably constitute a willful act or gross negligence and thus he would not be allowed a deduction for any portion of his loss. See Blackman v. Commissioner, 88 T.C. 677 (1987), aff'd without opinion, 867 F.2d 605 (1st Cir. 1988). See also Reg. §1.165-7(a)(3)(i), which states that a taxpayer is entitled to a casualty loss for damage to his automobile that results from his faulty driving, but not for damage that is due to a willful act or willful negligence.

14. a. Giovanni will probably not be allowed a casualty loss deduction. The Service contends that a casualty loss deduction is only permitted for "sudden" losses like those caused by the fires, storms, and shipwrecks explicitly listed in §165(c)(3). Since termite damage occurs over a period of years, the Service has taken the position that it is not deductible as a casualty loss. Rev. Rul. 63-232. Courts generally do not treat termite damage as a deductible casualty loss, reasoning that such damage does not occur "suddenly" enough, but over a period of many years. United States v. Rogers, 120 F.2d 244 (9th Cir. 1941); Fay v. Helvering, 120 F.2d 253 (2d Cir. 1941); Dodge v. Commissioner, 25 T.C. 1022 (1956).

    b. Giovanni is allowed a casualty loss deduction. The damage caused by an exploding furnace is a casualty because it meets the "suddenness" requirement.

15. Yes. Although damages caused by willful negligence are not deductible, casualty loss deductions are permitted for damages resulting from ordinary negligence. Reg. §1.165-7(a)(3)(i).

16. No. An insured taxpayer must file a timely claim with his insurance company in order to qualify for the casualty loss deduction. §165(h)(4)(E).

17. a. The ring cases demonstrate that the suddenness requirement can lead to differing results depending upon whether there is the "intervention of any sudden or destructive force." Stevens v. Commissioner, 6 T.C.M. (CCH) 805 (1947). Dusty probably cannot deduct this loss because there is no intervening destructive force. Stevens v. Commissioner, 6 T.C.M. (CCH) 805 (1947) (where the taxpayer was denied a casualty loss deduction for a ring lost in muddy water while the taxpayer was duck hunting).

    b. Dusty will probably be allowed to deduct the loss because the skiing accident is a sudden, destructive force. Kielts v. Commissioner, 42 T.C.M. (CCH) 238 (1981) (where the taxpayer was allowed a deduction where it appeared that a diamond fell out of its ring setting because of a sudden blow to the ring).

    c. Here there is no sudden, destructive force. In a similar case, the court denied the deduction. Keenan v. Bowers, 91 F. Supp. 771 (E.D.S.C. 1950).

    d. On similar facts, a court permitted the deduction. Carpenter v. Commissioner, 25 T.C.M. (CCH) 1186 (1966).

    e. The deduction would be allowed as a loss due to theft. §165(c)(3).

    f. The deduction probably would be allowed because the slamming door was sudden and destructive. See White v. Commissioner, 48 T.C. 430 (1967), acq. 1969-2 C.B. xxv.

18. No. Crashes are not unexpected in automobile racing. Priv. Ltr. Rul. 8227010.

C. Extraordinary Medical Expenses

Reading: §§105, 106, 213; Reg. §1.213-1(e)

Under §213(a), a taxpayer can deduct amounts spent on medical care for the taxpayer and the taxpayer's spouse and dependents to the extent that the medical expenses exceed 7.5 percent of the taxpayer's adjusted gross income. The 7.5 percent limitation makes the medical deduction available only to a small portion of taxpayers. On the other hand, medical benefits provided by an employer are fully excluded from an employee's income. §§105(b) and 106. The exclusion has the same effect as (i) requiring the employee to include the employer-provided benefits then (ii) allowing the employee to deduct 100 percent of the expense. Thus, the taxation of medical expenses paid by a taxpayer is much less favorable than the treatment of employer-provided medical benefits.

The argument in favor of the medical deduction is similar to the argument for the casualty deduction: A taxpayer who becomes ill and incurs substantial medical expenses is in a similar financial situation as a healthy taxpayer with a lower salary. Thus, a medical deduction is needed to ensure that the two taxpayers bear the same tax burden. The argument against the medical deduction is that private insurance is available for most illnesses, so if an individual chooses to forego such insurance there is no reason for the government to provide it through the tax code. Moreover, it is often difficult to distinguish between deductible "medical" expenses and other nondeductible forms of consumption that improve the health of taxpayers or simply make them feel better. Finally, the medical deduction seems to invite claims that border on the fraudulent.

Medical care generally is defined as amounts paid for the "diagnosis, cure, mitigation, treatment, or prevention of disease, or for the purpose of affecting any structure or function of the body." §213(d)(1)(A). If an expense improves the health of the taxpayer, but is not directed at curing or preventing a disease, it is nondeductible. Reg. §1.213-1(e)(1)(ii) (last sentence). For example, if a doctor tells a patient who is not sick but is overweight to join a gym, the cost of the gym membership is nondeductible even though exercise significantly improves the health of the patient. Rev. Rul. 79-151 (where the taxpayer was denied a medical expense deduction for the cost of a weight reduction program, despite the fact that it had been recommended by the taxpayer's doctor). Or, if a doctor tells a patient who is showing signs of stress to take a vacation, the cost of the vacation is not a "medical" expense even if it improves the patient's health. If a taxpayer incurs costs for a medical item (other than over-the-counter drugs) not specifically recommended by her doctor, she may be able to deduct the cost of the item, but will have a difficult time establishing that she bought the item primarily for medical reasons. See, e.g., Rev. Rul. 76-80 (where the taxpayer was denied a deduction for the cost of a vacuum cleaner, allegedly purchased for health reasons, because the vacuum was not specifically recommended by her doctor and she could not establish that she had bought it primarily for medical care).

Amounts spent on property improvements for medical purposes are deductible only to the extent that the cost of the improvement exceeds the increase in the value of the property. Reg. §1.213-1(e)(1)(iii). For example, if a taxpayer, on the advice of his doctor, installs a home swimming pool that costs $50,000 and adds $40,000 to the value of his home, the taxpayer's medical expense deduction is limited to $10,000. Reg. §1.213-1(e)(1)(iii). However, even that deduction will not be allowed if the taxpayer has access to a nearby pool. Evanoff v. Commissioner, 44 T.C.M. (CCH) 1394 (1982) (where a medical expense deduction for a home pool was not allowed because, but for a personal religious objection to boys swimming in the same pool with girls, the taxpayer's daughter could have used the nearby community pool). In addition, if a home pool built for medical reasons is extravagantly expensive, the taxpayer will not be permitted to deduct the entire difference between the cost of the pool and the value it adds to the home; instead, the taxpayer is allowed to deduct only the average cost of a home pool less the value added to a home by such a pool. Ferris v. Commissioner, 582 F.2d 1112 (7th Cir. 1978) (where a taxpayer who needed to use a pool for medical reasons was not allowed to deduct all of the $194,660 cost of adding an elaborate luxury pool to her home). The Service has ruled that certain improvements made to the taxpayer's residence to accommodate a sick or impaired member of the taxpayer's household do not improve the value of the residence. For example, the ruling states that installing ramps, railings, and hardware, and modifying doorways, hallways, stairs, electrical outlets, and kitchen cabinets do not generally improve the value of a personal residence. Rev. Rul. 87-106.

If an expense is for cosmetic surgery, §213 allows a deduction for the expense only if the surgery is necessary to correct a congenital deformity or a deformity arising from injury or disease. §213(d)(9). The costs of insulin and prescription drugs are deductible, but no deduction is allowed for over-the-counter drugs. §213(b). Deductible medical expenses also include the costs of medical insurance, hospital lodging, and transportation incurred "primarily for and essential to medical care." §213(d)(1). However, the cost of lodging while away from home for the primary purpose of obtaining medical care by a physician in a licensed hospital or equivalent medical care facility is deductible only up to $50 per night, and then only if the lodging is not lavish and has no significant element of personal pleasure, recreation, or vacation. §213(d)(2). If medical treatment is available where the taxpayer lives, but the taxpayer chooses to travel to another area (for example, a resort area) to receive the care, the costs of traveling to receive the care are not deductible. Reg. §1.213-1(e)(1)(iv). In addition, if a taxpayer travels on a doctor's orders to a more hospitable climate, the costs of travel may be deductible, but the costs of meals and lodging are nondeductible even if the taxpayer sees a doctor from time to time in the area visited. Polyak v. Commissioner, 94 T.C. 337 (1990).

The costs of institutional care are deductible if the principal reason for institutionalization is to provide the patient medical care. Reg. §1.213-1(e)(1)(v)(a). However, if the primary reason for the institutional care is not medical, then the costs of the institutional care are deductible only to the extent that the costs are specifically attributable to medical care. For example, if a taxpayer's spouse is put in a nursing home for personal, not medical, reasons, the taxpayer is allowed a deduction only to the extent of the cost of any medical care provided by the nursing home. Reg. §1.213-1(e)(1)(v)(b). In addition, if a sick spouse stays at home and sends her children away to boarding school to facilitate her recovery, the costs of the boarding school are not deductible. Ochs v. Commissioner, 195 F.2d 692 (2d Cir.), cert. denied, 344 U.S. 827 (1952).

Although educational costs are not generally deductible, the cost of special schooling designed to rehabilitate an ill or disabled individual is deductible as a medical expense. Reg. §1.213-1(e)(1)(v)(a). For example, the cost of a special school where Braille is taught to blind students is a deductible medical expense. Id. A taxpayer is also allowed a deduction for the extra cost of Braille books and the costs of a seeing eye dog or human guide for a blind person. Reg. §1.213-1(e)(1)(iii), Rev. Rul. 75-318, and Rev. Rul. 64-173.

EXAMPLES

19. a. In year one Randy receives $96,000 in salary and $4,000 worth of medical benefits under an employee health plan. Is Randy taxed on the $4,000 value of the medical benefits?
    b. Assume, instead, that Randy receives $100,000 in salary from his employer and spends $4,000 on §213 medical expenses. Is

Randy allowed a deduction for the $4,000 of medical expenses he pays in year one?

20. a. Betty's adjusted gross income is $50,000. If Betty spends $6,000 on medical expenses qualifying under §213, what portion of those expenses would be deductible?

    b. How, if at all, would your answer in part (a) change if Betty were reimbursed for her medical expenses by an insurance company?

21. Susan says: "Even if medical expenses should be deductible, a deduction should be permitted only to the extent that the expenses exceed a certain floor." What is the best argument for a floor on medical deductions?

For the remaining examples in this section, assume that the expenses exceed the 7.5 percent of adjusted gross income floor.

22. Which of the following can be deducted as medical expenses under §213?

    a. Psychotherapy for a successful, but nervous, comedy director

    b. Hair transplants for a balding opera singer

    c. Cosmetic surgery to improve the appearance of a lawyer born with a harelip

    d. Extra large doorways, ramps, and an elevator for a banker confined to a wheelchair

    e. Membership in an aerobics studio for a former smoker whose family has a history of heart disease

    f. Braces for a taxpayer's daughter

23. a. Robert's daughter, Celia, is blind. In the current year he spends $10,000 on tuition for a school for the blind, $5,000 on a seeing eye dog, and $600 on Braille books. An ordinary private school would cost $6,000 and a regular printed edition of the books would cost $200. How much of these expenditures qualify as medical expenses subject to §213?

    b. Assume that, instead of sending Celia to a school for the blind, Robert sends Celia to public school and pays someone $10,000 a year to accompany and guide Celia while she is at school. Is the $10,000 cost of Celia's human guide deductible under §213?

24. Jerry, a Maine resident, has a chronic respiratory infection. His doctor recommends that he spend a few weeks in a warm and dry climate. Jerry flies to New Mexico for three weeks. While in New Mexico he sees a doctor twice for checkups. His expenses are as

follows: $500 for the plane ticket, $1,500 for lodging, $800 for meals, and $200 for doctor's fees. Which of these expenses, if any, qualify as deductible medical expenses under §213?

25. a. George suffered injuries in an automobile accident, and his doctor recommended swimming as a form of therapy. In keeping with the style of his Beverly Hills estate, George paid $250,000 for the construction of an elaborate swimming pool with marble tiles and a waterfall. The pool increased the value of the house by $100,000. An average swimming pool costs about $50,000 and would increase the value of the home by $30,000. How much, if any, of the cost of the swimming pool would be deductible?

    b. How, if at all, would your answer in part (a) change if the Beverly Hills community pool is two blocks from George's mansion and George can swim there?

26. Jackie suffered injuries from an automobile accident and was hospitalized for seven days. During that time, she paid $53,000 for a private suite in the best hospital in town, nursing care, medical tests, X rays, and the care of the best (and most expensive) doctors. The average cost for a seven day hospital stay in a non-private room with average doctors is $10,000. How much of Jackie's hospital bills are deductible?

27. Which of the following can be deducted as medical expenses under §213?

    a. The cost of aspirin taken to relieve arthritis pain at the advice of a physician

    b. The costs of a vasectomy or legal abortion undertaken solely for contraceptive purposes

    c. The costs of a babysitter hired to enable an individual to visit a doctor

    d. The costs of an annual medical examination

    e. The costs of attending a clinic to stop smoking

28. Pam is a busy executive who is suffering from stress related to her job. At the advice of her psychiatrist, she joins a private tennis club. During year one, she spends $2,000 for court time, $1,000 for lessons, and $800 on tennis clothing and equipment. Are any of these expenses deductible?

29. Without consulting a doctor, Linda purchases a humidifier and air cleaner to help relieve a sinus condition. Are the expenses deductible under §213?

30. Marion's son, James, has performed poorly in school and has been

difficult to control at home. On the recommendation of a psychiatrist, Marion enrolls James in a military school with a highly structured environment. Are the costs of the military school tuition, room, and board deductible under §213?

31. John, a Vermont resident suffering from an unusual illness, is advised by his doctor to get help from Dr. Xerxes, a specialist in Seattle. He flies to Seattle and receives outpatient medical care for a month. John rents a hotel room close to the hospital and visits the hospital for treatment every other day. His expenses are: $800 for the plane ticket, $1,350 for the hotel ($45 per night), and $750 for food ($25 per day). What portion of these expenses can John deduct under §213?

32. After a car accident that left Alice paralyzed from the waist down, she buys a custom made van specifically designed to accommodate her impairment. The van enables Alice to maintain her mobility and independence. Is any portion of the van's cost deductible?

33. While in Oregon with her mother, eight-year-old Yolanda, a California resident, is seriously injured in a car accident and admitted to a Portland hospital. She remains in intensive care and undergoes three operations over the next six weeks until she can be moved back to Los Angeles. On the recommendation of the doctor, Yolanda's mother, Anne, stays at a Portland hotel during Yolanda's treatment. Are Anne's lodging expenses deductible?

EXPLANATIONS

19. a. No. Medical benefits provided by an employer are excluded from income. §§105, 106.

    b. No. Under §213(a), medical expenses are deductible only to the extent such expenses exceed 7.5 percent of adjusted gross income. Randy's adjusted gross income is $100,000, so only medical expenses in excess of $7,500 would be deductible.

20. a. Betty is allowed a $2,250 §213 deduction. Betty can deduct her medical expenses only to the extent that they exceed $3,750, which is 7.5 percent of her $50,000 adjusted gross income. §213(a). Thus, she can deduct $2,250 ($6,000 medical expenses less the $3,750 floor).

    b. Only uncompensated expenses are deductible under §213(a), so Betty would not be able to deduct any amount of the reimbursed medical expenses.

21. The basic argument for permitting a deduction for medical expenses is that such expenses are involuntary expenditures that reduce wealth much like a reduction in income. This is similar to the argument in favor of allowing a casualty loss deduction. However, nearly all taxpayers incur some low level of medical expenses. If a deduction were permitted for all medical expenses without a floor, it would be necessary for all taxpayers to keep track of these costs. Since most taxpayers would receive a deduction of a similar amount, a general reduction in the tax rate would have the same impact as the deduction. Thus, it might be argued, a medical deduction should be permitted only for extraordinarily high medical expenses.

22. a. Costs of psychiatric treatment are deductible under §213. Reg. §1.213-1(e)(1)(ii).

   b. The costs of cosmetic surgery are deductible only if the surgery is performed to repair a congenital defect or a defect caused by an accident or deforming disease. §213(d)(9). Baldness is not considered to be a disease, so the costs of these hair transplants are not deductible.

   c. This cost is deductible. The costs of cosmetic surgery are deductible if the surgery is performed to repair a congenital defect. §213(d)(9).

   d. Capital improvements to property for qualifying medical purposes are deductible to the extent that the cost of the improvements exceeds the value that the improvements add to the home. Ramps and extra large doorways presumably add no value to a home and thus are fully deductible. Rev. Rul. 87-106. The elevator is deductible to the extent its cost exceeds the value it adds to the home. Reg. §1.213-1(e)(1)(iii).

   e. Not deductible. Expenses that help a person who is not "ill" maintain or improve his health are not deductible. Reg. §1.213-1(e)(1)(ii).

   f. Deductible. Dental work is considered a medical expense under §213. Reg. §1.213-1(e)(1)(ii). A taxpayer can deduct the medical expenses of his or her spouse and dependents. §213(a).

23. a. The special school tuition and the cost of the seeing eye dog are fully deductible. Reg. §1.213-1(e)(1)(iii) and (v)(a). The cost

of an ordinary school is irrelevant. Reg. §1.213-1(e)(1)(v)(a). The cost of Braille books is deductible to the extent that the cost exceeds that of the regular printed editions, so Robert is allowed to deduct $400 of the costs of the books. Rev. Rul. 75-318.

b. The Service has ruled that the cost of such a companion is deductible under §213 because it is designed to "alleviate the child's physical defect of blindness." Rev. Rul. 64-173.

24. Only the cost of the transportation and the doctor's fees qualify as medical expenses under §213. The cost of food and lodging while away from home for medical treatment is not deductible unless the taxpayer is residing at a licensed hospital or equivalent facility. Thus, Jerry may only deduct the $500 for the plane ticket and the doctor's fees. Reg. §1.213-1(e)(1)(iv). The fact that Jerry visited a doctor while in New Mexico makes no difference since the main purpose of the trip was to stay in an area with a better climate. Polyak v. Commissioner, 94 T.C. 337 (1990).

25. a. In the case upon which these facts are based, the court held that costs above those that are necessary to produce a functionally adequate swimming pool are not incurred for medical care. The taxpayer probably is not limited to buying the cheapest pool, but it is unclear how much more than the minimum may be spent and still be considered deductible. Assuming it is necessary for George to have a pool at his home, George probably would be allowed to deduct at least $20,000, the average cost of a pool less the increase in property value from such a pool. See Ferris v. Commissioner, 582 F.2d 1112 (7th Cir. 1978).

b. George would likely be denied any deduction for the cost of his home pool since he can swim in the nearby community pool. In Evanoff v. Commissioner, 44 T.C.M. (CCH) 1394 (1982), the court denied a deduction for the cost of building a pool where the taxpayer could have used the nearby community swimming pool for $250 a year. The taxpayers decided to build a pool because their religion forbade their daughter from swimming in the same pool as boys. The court held that this reason made the expenditure personal in nature, not medical, and therefore not deductible.

26. The cost of conventional medical care at hospitals, including food and lodging costs, is fully deductible even if the taxpayer pays

more than is necessary for adequate care. Therefore, Jackie may deduct the full $53,000. Reg. §1.213-1(e)(1)(v).

27. a. Not deductible. Only prescription drugs and insulin are deductible. §213(b).

b. Deductible. Rev. Rul. 73-201.

c. Not deductible. Costs of child care are considered personal expenses, even if incurred to enable an individual to receive medical treatment. Ochs v. Commissioner, 195 F.2d 692 (2d Cir.), cert. denied, 344 U.S. 827 (1952).

d. Deductible. Costs of an annual diagnostic checkup are deductible even though they are not designed to treat a specific illness. Reg. §1.213-1(e)(1)(ii).

e. Not deductible. The costs of attending a smoking clinic, weight loss clinic, or health club are not deductible because such activities are designed to maintain general health rather than to alleviate an illness. Rev. Ruls. 79-151 and 79-162. Certain weight loss programs for obese individuals, however, might qualify for a deduction if obesity is considered to be a disease. Priv. Ltr. Rul. 8004111.

28. No. Expenses that improve the general health of an individual are not deductible. Reg. §1.213-1(e)(1)(ii). Thus, the taxpayer must meet a heavy burden of proof to deduct the expenses of ordinary personal activities, like tennis, that provide general health benefits. In this case, Pam's stressed condition might not qualify as a mental defect or disease for purposes of §213. Even if her condition is viewed as an illness, she will probably not be able to establish that tennis is needed to reduce her stress since running or other less expensive forms of exercise might provide her with the same benefits. See Altman v. Commissioner, 53 T.C. 487 (1969) (where the taxpayer was denied a deduction for his costs of playing golf, despite the fact that the taxpayer's doctor had recommended that the taxpayer play golf as treatment for his emphysema).

29. Yes, if she can establish that she bought the items primarily for medical care. A doctor's recommendation is not required for an expense to be deductible under §213. In this case, the purchase of the humidifier and air cleaner is designed to relieve a medical condition and thus should be deductible. Although a doctor's recommendation is not required under §213, it may enable a taxpayer to demonstrate that a medical purpose underlies an

expense that normally would be considered personal such as the construction of a swimming pool. Here, Linda can take a deduction for the cost of the humidifier and air cleaner if she can establish that she purchased those items primarily for her medical care. See, e.g., Rev. Rul. 76-80 (where the taxpayer was denied a deduction for the cost of a vacuum cleaner, allegedly purchased for health reasons, because it was not specifically recommended by her doctor and she could not establish that she had bought it primarily for medical care).

30. Probably not. Private school tuition generally is deductible only if the school treats a specific medical problem such as blindness or deafness. Reg. §1.213-1(e)(1)(v). See also Fay v. Commissioner, 76 T.C. 408 (1981); Grunwald v. Commissioner, 51 T.C. 108 (1968).

31. John can deduct the full amount of the plane ticket since it is transportation primarily for and essential to his medical care. §213(d)(1)(B). Under §213(d)(2), a taxpayer can also deduct up to $50 per night for lodging away from home in situations where he travels to receive outpatient medical care. Since John receives medical care at the hospital of Dr. Xerxes and there is no significant element of recreation in his trip, he can deduct the $45 per day cost of the hotel room. John gets no deduction, however, for any amount spent on meals.

32. Alice can deduct the cost of the van to the extent that it exceeds the cost of a comparable ordinary automobile. Reg. §1.213-1(e)(1)(iii). See also Rev. Rul. 70-606.

33. The expenses probably are deductible up to $50 per night. In the letter ruling on which this question is based, the hospital requested that parents of minor patients in intensive care remain nearby. Priv. Ltr. Rul. 8516025. The Service noted that the "transportation costs of a family member traveling with the taxpayer have been allowed as a medical expense deduction where the presence of the family member was necessary to enable [the] taxpayer to obtain medical care." Transportation costs include associated lodging, subject to a $50 per day limitation. Although Anne did not incur any actual transportation expenses because she was already in Portland, her lodging expenses should remain deductible since they were necessary for her daughter's medical treatment.

D. Charitable Contributions

Reading: §§170, 501, 6115, 6662(e) and (h)

An itemized deduction for charitable contributions is permitted under §170(a)(1). Charitable contributions are defined in §170(c) as contributions to or for the use of certain listed nonprofit enterprises:

    i. the United States government, a state government or any other political subdivision of the United States, including local governments and United States territories if the contribution is made for exclusively public purposes. §170(c)(1).

    ii. a charitable corporation, trust, community chest, fund, or foundation if the organization is operated exclusively for religious, charitable, scientific, literary, or educational purposes, or to foster national or international amateur sports competition. §170(c)(2).

    iii. a fraternal order or lodge, but only if the gift is to be used exclusively for charitable purposes. §170(c)(4).

    iv. an organization of war veterans or a non-profit cemetery company or corporation. §§170(c)(3), (5).

    Contributions to an organization are not deductible, however, if any part of the net earnings of the donee organization benefit any private shareholder or individual or if the donee organization attempts to influence legislation or political campaigns. §170(c)(2)(C) and (D).

    Section 170 determines the extent to which donors may deduct contributions to charitable organizations. Sections 501-528 determine the tax treatment of charities receiving contributions. Section 501 generally exempts from tax the organizations listed in §501(c). The §501(c) list of organizations is substantially broader than the list of organizations in §170(c). Business leagues, labor unions, and non-profit recreational clubs, for example, can qualify for tax-exempt status under §501(c), but donors contributing to those organizations generally cannot qualify for a charitable contribution deduction under §170(c). On the other hand, if donors' contributions qualify for the §170 charitable contribution deduction, the organization receiving the contribution will almost always qualify for tax-exempt status under §501. Qualifying exempt organizations are not taxed on income from contributions, fees for services related to their charitable purpose, and income from passive investments. §501(a), (b). However, if an exempt organization earns income from a business that is unrelated to the organization's charitable purpose, the exempt organization is taxed on the income from that business. §§501(b) and 511-514. In addition, exempt status will be denied any §501(c)(3) organization that engages in racial discrimination. Bob Jones University v. United States, 461 U.S. 574 (1983) (holding that the test for exempt status includes a requirement that the organization serve a public purpose and not operate in a manner that is contrary to public policy).

A §170 deduction for the full amount contributed is allowed only if the donor receives no substantial benefit from the contribution. Ottawa Silica Co. v. United States, 699 F.2d 1124 (Fed. Cir. 1983). If the donor receives a substantial benefit as a result of the contribution, for purposes of §170 the donor's contribution is reduced by the benefit received. For example, if a charity hosting a fund-raising dinner charges $300 for a dinner that has a value of $50, a donor paying $300 for a ticket to the dinner would be entitled to deduct only $250 ($300 paid to the charity less the $50 value of the dinner), even if the donor decided not to attend the dinner. Rev. Rul. 67-246. What constitutes a "substantial" benefit? In *Ottawa Silica*, the Federal Circuit Court of Appeals stated that benefits received by a donor are "substantial" if the benefits received by the donor "are greater than those that inure to the general public from transfers for charitable purposes." 699 F.2d at 1131 (citing Singer Co. v. United States, 449 F.2d 413, 423 (Cl. Ct. 1971)). Ottawa Silica had donated real property for a high school to a school district that qualified as a §170(c)(1) organization. The plans for the new high school required the school district to construct two access roads to the new school. These access roads provided a benefit to Ottawa Silica because the company owned much of the land in the area around the proposed new school and intended to develop it. The court held that the increase in value of the land that Ottawa Silica did not contribute constituted a substantial benefit to the company, so it was not allowed a §170 deduction for the land contributed.

Section 170(l) sets forth a special rule that applies where a donor makes a contribution to a college or university and the contribution gives the donor the right to buy preferred seating tickets for athletic events at the school. In these circumstances, the donor's deduction is limited to 80 percent of the contribution. §170(l)(1).

The Service has ruled that fixed payments to churches or synagogues for pew rents, dues, or to attend specific services are deductible under §170 despite the fact that the contribution would appear to confer a specific benefit on the donor. Rev. Rul. 70-47. On the other hand, in Hernandez v. Commissioner, 490 U.S. 680 (1989), reh'g denied, 492 U.S. 933 (1989), members of the Church of Scientology were denied a deduction for amounts "donated" to the church for "training" and "auditing." A member could not receive these services without paying a donation that was set by a schedule, so the majority concluded that the payment for these services was "a quintessential quid pro quo exchange" and was thus not deductible under §170. Justices Scalia and O'Connor dissented, noting the Service's long-standing practice of allowing deduction of fixed payments to churches. The Service later issued Rev. Rul. 93-73, in which it reversed the position it had previously taken and stated that it would allow deductions for amounts "donated" to the Church of Scientology. See also §6115(b).

A donor may contribute services, cash, or property to a §170(c) charity. The tax consequences of the contribution to the donor under §170 turn, in part, on the type of contribution made by the donor. If a donor contributes her services, she will not be allowed a §170 deduction for the services. Reg. §1.170A-1(g). However, her unreimbursed expenses incurred in rendering those services (other than child care expenses) are deductible. Id. Child care expenses incurred to enable the taxpayer to donate charitable services are considered nondeductible personal expenses. Rev. Rul. 73-597.

If a taxpayer contributes cash, the §170 deduction is subject only to the general deduction limitations in §170(b)(1)(A), (B), and (2), which limit a taxpayer's charitable contribution deduction to a percentage of the taxpayer's "contribution base" (generally the taxpayer's adjusted gross income). Taxpayers typically make their charitable contributions to the common types of charities listed in §170(b)(1)(A) (so-called "A" charities). A taxpayer's §170 deduction for a contribution to an "A" charity is limited to 50 percent of the taxpayer's adjusted gross income in that year. Any contribution in excess of that limitation is carried forward five years and may be taken in those years as a charitable contribution. §170(d). If a taxpayer makes a contribution to one of the less common types of charities listed in §170(b)(1)(B) (so-called "B" charities), a less favorable limitation rule applies.

The §170 deduction for corporate taxpayers is limited to 10 percent of the corporation's taxable income, determined without regard to its charitable contributions and certain other items (such as net operating loss carrybacks and the §243 deduction for dividends received by a corporate taxpayer that is a shareholder in another corporation). §170(b)(2). In addition, several other special rules in §170 apply to determine a corporate taxpayer's §170 deduction. See, e.g., §170(a)(2), (c)(2), (d)(2), and (e)(3).

Donors of appreciated property deduct the *value* of property they contribute, despite the fact that neither the taxpayer nor the exempt organization will ever pay tax on the appreciation in the property. However, this extremely favorable tax treatment of contributions of appreciated property to charities is limited by a series of special rules in §170(e) and (b)(1)(C) and (D). First, if the property contributed would have produced ordinary income or short-term capital gain had it been sold (because the property is not a capital asset or has not been held by the donor for at least a year), the donor may deduct only her adjusted basis in the contributed property. §170(e)(1)(A). (For a discussion of the distinction between ordinary assets and capital assets, and between short-term and long-term capital gain, see Chapter 8.) Consider the following example, which illustrates the §170(e)(1)(A) limitation. Assume that Lonnie, an art dealer, owns a painting worth $20,000 that he bought for $3,000. If Lonnie donates the painting to an art museum, his §170 deduction will be limited to $3,000, his basis in the painting, because the painting would have produced ordinary income if Lonnie, a dealer in art, had sold it.

Second, even if a sale of the contributed property by the donor would have produced long-term capital gain, the donor's §170 deduction is limited to the donor's adjusted basis in the property if either (i) the contributed property is tangible personal property (for example, works of art, antiques, stamp or coin collections, and books) and the donee charity's use of the property is unrelated to the organization's charitable purpose or (ii) the property is donated to certain private foundations. §170(e)(1)(B). For example, assume that Connie, a professional actress, bought a painting for $10,000 in year one. By year 10, Connie's painting had appreciated in value to $300,000. In year 10, when Connie has adjusted gross income of $800,000, she contributes the painting to her church. Connie's year 10 §170 deduction is limited to $10,000, her basis in the painting, because the painting is tangible property and the use of the painting by the church is not related to its charitable purpose. If Connie instead gives the painting to an art museum, the §170(e)(1)(B) limitation does not apply because the charity's use of the painting is related to its exempt purpose. (However, her deduction is then subject to the §170(b)(1)(C) limitation, described below.)

Third, if a donor contributes property that would have produced long-term capital gain had the donor sold it, and neither of the §170(e) limitations described above applies, the limitation of §170(b)(1)(C) will generally apply to the contribution. If the donor contributes the property to an "A" charity, as is generally the case, her §170 deduction for the contribution is limited to 30 percent of her adjusted gross income. §170(b)(1)(C)(i). Any excess contribution is carried forward for five years. §170(b)(1)(B). The donor can elect to apply §170(e) instead of the 30 percent of adjusted gross income limitation. §170(b)(1)(C)(iii). If this election is made, the donor's §170 deduction is limited to the donor's basis in the contributed property. (A donor may want to make this election if the value of the contributed property exceeds 30 percent of the taxpayer's adjusted gross income and the basis of the property is the same as or not much less than the value of the contributed property.) Again, a less favorable limitation applies to contributions of capital gain property to "B" charities, such as private foundations. §170(b)(1)(D).

For example, assume that Ronnie bought a piece of raw land, as a long-term investment, for $20,000 in year one. In year 10, he contributes the land (which is still held for investment), to a university, which is an "A" charity. The land is worth $300,000 at the time of the contribution. Ronnie's year 10 adjusted gross income is $700,000. A sale of the land by Ronnie would have produced long-term capital gain, so §170(e)(1)(A) does not apply. Section 170(e)(1)(B) does not apply either because (i) the land is not tangible personal property and (ii) Ronnie did not give the land to a private foundation listed in §170(e)(1)(B)(ii). However, §170(b)(1)(B) will limit Ronnie's year 10 §170 deduction to $210,000, which is 30 percent of his $700,000 adjusted gross income. The $90,000 excess contribution ($300,000 contribution less $210,000 allowed as a deduction in year one) is carried forward to the next tax year.

Despite these limitations, the charitable contribution deduction rules are very favorable to taxpayers who contribute appreciated property to charities. Aggressive taxpayers trying to gain the tax benefit of large charitable contribution deductions often claim inflated values for the property contributed. Thus, the valuation of appreciated property contributed to a charity is an issue that is frequently litigated. For example, in Isbell v. Commissioner, 44 T.C.M. (CCH) 1143 (1982), the taxpayer claimed a $15,000 deduction (which was later increased to $50,000 on an amended return) on the charitable contribution of a damaged Han dynasty jar that was valued at $800 by a government expert and was sold by the charity in an auction for $360! Congress and the Service have taken several steps to curb overvaluation of appreciated property contributed to charities.

Section 6662 imposes an "accuracy-related" penalty for valuation overstatement if a taxpayer claims that the value of property contributed to a charity is two or more times the actual value of the property. The penalty is 20 percent of the tax deficiency that results from the valuation overstatement (provided that the deficiency is at least $5,000 for an individual). §6662(e). If a taxpayer claims a value that is four or more times the actual value of the property, the penalty is 40 percent of the deficiency related to the overstatement. §6662(h).

In addition, a taxpayer who deducts a charitable contribution in excess of $250 must be able to substantiate the contribution with a written acknowledgment from the charity donee. §170(f)(8). If donors receive something of benefit (other than intangible religious benefits) in exchange for their contributions, §6115 also requires donee charities to provide donors with an estimate of the value of property received by the donors in the exchange, if the contribution exceeds $75. In addition, if a donor contributes property (other than publicly traded securities) valued at more than $5,000 and the donee charity sells it within two years of the date of contribution, the donee must file a special return with the Service giving them information about the donor, the contribution, and the subsequent disposition of the property. §6050L.

If a taxpayer makes a donation to charity using a credit card, for tax purposes the contribution occurs at the time that the charge is incurred, not when the charge is later paid by the taxpayer. Rev. Rul. 78-38.

A complete discussion of the complex rules on charitable contribution is beyond the scope both of this book and, we suspect, of most introductory courses in income taxation. In the questions that follow, we will explore the basic structure of the charitable contribution deduction rules and a few of the more important details.

EXAMPLES

34. State whether contributions to the following individuals or organizations are deductible.
    a. The City of Los Angeles, California
    b. Harvard University
    c. The Girl Scouts
    d. The Elks Club
    e. The Lutheran Church
    f. The Republican Party

    g. A homeless individual living at a government shelter

    h. A local professional basketball team

    i. The City of Bombay, India

    j. A private university that has a racially discriminatory admissions policy

35. a. In year one Bridget has $100,000 of adjusted gross income and contributes $38,000 to the Red Cross. She makes no other contributions during the year. How much does she deduct under §170 in year one?

    b. How, if at all, would your answer in part (a) change if Bridget is instead Bridget Inc., a corporation, with $100,000 of taxable income?

36. The Metropolis Children's Center provides aid to abused and runaway children.

    a. Suppose that the Children's Center receives $10 million in contributions during the taxable year. On what amount of contributions will the Center have to pay tax?

    b. Suppose that the Children's Center operates a chain of greeting card stores that earn $5 million per year. On what amount of that income will the Center be taxed?

    c. Assume that the Children's Center invests $10 million in corporate stock and bonds and earns $1 million in interest and dividends. On what amount of those earnings will the Center be taxed?

37. If an organization is exempt from taxation on contributions, are such contributions to the organization necessarily deductible by the donor?

38. Maria purchases two seats to an all-star concert to benefit the homeless. The seats cost $200 each. Similar seats at concerts not benefiting charitable organizations cost $30 each. Maria tells her friends that she would have paid $200 each for the seats even if the proceeds were not for the benefit of charity.

    a. How much of the $400 cost of the concert tickets is deductible?

    b. Would your answer in part (a) change if the only reason Maria purchased the tickets was to aid the charity and she never attended the concert?

39. Pasqual donated $2,000 to Grunt University's athletic program, which has one of the top college football teams in the United States. Anyone who donates $2,000 or more to the program is made a member of the Grunters Club, which permits the member

to purchase two season tickets in a preferred section at the 50-yard line for $300 each. Individuals who are not members of the Grunters Club can purchase season tickets at the same price, but the seats are much less desirable. How much of the $2,000 contribution may Pasqual deduct?

40. Bill's son has applied for admission to Posh College, a private college. One week after Bill makes a large donation to the college, his son is accepted for admission. Is the donation deductible under §170?

41. Cindy, a gym teacher, volunteered to work for a week with handicapped children at an athletic event sponsored by a charitable organization. Cindy spent $40 on transportation to the event and paid $100 for child care to enable her to attend. If Cindy had been paid her normal fee for her services, she would have received $500. What amount can Cindy deduct as a charitable contribution?

42. Bill owns a sporting goods store. If Bill contributes inventory (shoes, baseballs, and so forth) with an adjusted basis of $600 and fair market value of $1,000 to a public charity, how much can he deduct under §170?

43. Carlos bought stock in year one for $1,000. In year three, when the stock is worth $10,000, he donates the stock to Alma Mater Law School. Carlos has $100,000 of adjusted gross income in year three. How much gain does Carlos realize on the contribution and how much does he deduct under §170 in year three? If Carlos is subject to a 30 percent marginal tax rate, what is the after-tax cost to Carlos of donating the stock instead of selling it and using the proceeds for personal consumption?

44. Jin owns a Chinese snuff bottle from the 19th century that she found in a trunk in her attic. Jin is in the 30 percent tax bracket and has adjusted gross income of $100,000.
    a. What would be the tax consequence to Jin if she sells the bottle for $1,000?
    b. What would be the tax consequence to Jin if she donates the bottle to a museum, for inclusion in their porcelain collection, and establishes that the value of the bottle is $3,000 at the time of her contribution? Will Jill be wealthier here, or in part (a) above?
    c. How, if at all, would your answer in part (b) change if Jin instead donates the bottle to a hospital?

d. Assume the facts in part (b), except that Jin, in a fit of naive optimism, claimed on her year one return that the bottle was worth $20,000, when it was actually worth $3,000. If the Service later challenges the valuation, and Jin fails to establish that the value of the bottle exceeded $3,000 in year one, what are the tax consequences to her?

45. Larry, a caterer who happens to be a good judge of modern art, buys a painting in March of year one for $10,000. In December of year one, he donates the painting to a contemporary art museum. Two qualified independent appraisers value the painting at $28,000 at the time of contribution. Larry's year one adjusted gross income is $200,000. How much can he deduct as a year one charitable contribution?

46. In year one Kevin bought raw land as an investment. He paid $80,000 for the property. In year three, when the land is worth $95,000, he contributes it to his church. The church will not use the land in its activities, but expects to sell the property within the next several years to raise funds for a renovation of other church property. Kevin's adjusted gross income in year three is $200,000. How much can Kevin deduct under §170 in year three?

47. Robert, a real estate developer in Phoenix, Arizona, contributes to the city of Phoenix the streets and sewers of a residential subdivision he is developing. The city will maintain the streets and sewers after the contribution. May Robert deduct the value of the streets and sewers as a charitable contribution?

48. In December, year one, Elizabeth phones the AIDS Project of Los Angeles and charges a $1,000 donation to the organization on her Mastercard. She pays that charge in March, year two. In which year is Elizabeth allowed to deduct her contribution?

49. Mona says: "It costs a low income taxpayer more to make a donation to charity than it costs a high income taxpayer." Is Mona correct? Explain.

50. Ned says: "The charitable deduction is unfair because it treats taxpayers who donate money to charity more favorably than it treats taxpayers who donate their own services. Taxpayers who donate money can deduct the amount donated, but taxpayers who donate services can't deduct the value of their services." Is Ned correct? Explain.

EXPLANATIONS

34. a. Deductible. Section 170(c) sets forth the list of the organizations to which deductible contributions may be made. This list includes a political subdivision of a state or territory of the United States. §170(c)(1). The City of Los Angeles is a political subdivision of the State of California.

   b. Deductible. A charitable deduction is permitted for contributions to organizations operated exclusively for educational purposes. §170(c)(2)(B). Colleges and universities clearly fall within this provision.

   c. Deductible. The Girl Scouts qualify as an organization devoted to charitable purposes under §170(c)(2)(B).

   d. The answer depends on how the money is to be used. The Elks Club qualifies as a "domestic fraternal society" under §170(c)(4). Contributions made to such organizations are considered charitable contributions only if the contribution is to be used *exclusively* for religious, charitable, scientific, literary, or educational purposes, or for the prevention of cruelty to children or animals. §170(c)(4). Thus, general contributions to such organizations usually are not deductible. It is common, however, for fraternal societies to establish separate funds devoted exclusively to charitable purposes and contributions to such funds are deductible.

   e. Deductible. Contributions to religious organizations are within §170(c)(2)(B).

   f. Not deductible. A political party does not qualify as a charitable organization under any of the provisions of §170(c). Moreover, an organization otherwise qualifying for deductible contributions under §170(c)(2) as devoted exclusively to charitable purposes will lose its qualification if it participates or intervenes in any political campaign on behalf of or in opposition to any candidate. §170(c)(2)(D).

   g. Not deductible. Contributions to particular individuals, even if needy, are not deductible. A contribution to the shelter, however, would be deductible. §170(c)(2)(B).

   h. Not deductible. A professional basketball team is not a charitable organization under §170(c).

   i. Not deductible. Contributions to foreign governments and political subdivisions of foreign governments are not listed in §170(c), so such contributions are not deductible.

j. Not deductible. The Supreme Court has read the test for tax-exempt status under §501(c) to include a requirement that the organization serve public policy and not act in a manner contrary to public policy. In Bob Jones University v. United States, 461 U.S. 574 (1983), the majority held that an organization that maintains a policy of racial discrimination cannot qualify for tax-exempt status under §501(c). The §170(c) test would most likely be interpreted to include a similar requirement.

35. a. All of it is deductible because it does not exceed the 50 percent of adjusted gross income limitation in §170(b)(1)(A), which applies because the cash was donated to an "A" charity.

b. Bridget Inc. may deduct only $10,000 in year one. A corporation is permitted to deduct contributions only to the extent of 10 percent of its taxable income, so Bridget Inc.'s year one deduction is limited to $10,000. §170(b)(2). The $28,000 excess contribution is carried forward. §170(d)(2).

36. a. The Center will not be taxed on any of the contributions. Under §501(a), contributions received by organizations described in §501(c) or (d) are exempt from taxation. The Metropolis Children's Center falls within the description of §501(c)(3) as a corporation organized and operated exclusively for charitable purposes.

b. The Center will be taxed on all of the income from the stores. Under §§511-514, income from business operations that are unrelated to an organization's tax-exempt purpose is subject to tax. The $5 million would constitute "unrelated business taxable income" and would be subject to tax in its entirety. §501(b).

c. The Center will not be taxed on any of the investment earnings. "Passive investment income" earned from investments such as stocks, bonds, and annuities is not considered unrelated business taxable income and thus is not subject to tax when received by a charity. §512(b).

37. No. Some nonprofit organizations, such as political parties, pension plans, labor unions, and social clubs, are tax-exempt under §501(c), but donations to those organizations do not qualify for the §170 deduction.

38. a. $340. A taxpayer who purchases tickets to a concert or other event will be permitted a deduction in an amount equal to the difference between the amount contributed and the fair market

value of the tickets. Maria contributed $400 and received tickets worth $60, so she may deduct only $340 as a charitable contribution. The subjective value of the tickets to Maria is irrelevant. Rev. Rul. 67-246.

b. Even if Maria does not attend the concert, she would be permitted to deduct only $340 if she retained the tickets. Rev. Rul. 67-246. However, if Maria refused the tickets or returned them to the charitable organization, then she would be permitted to deduct the full $400.

39. $1,600. A taxpayer is allowed a §170 deduction only to the extent that the taxpayer did not receive a benefit in return for the donation. A special rule exists, however, for contributions in return for the right to purchase tickets to athletic events. Under §170(l), if a contribution by an individual to a college or university otherwise would be deductible, but the individual receives the right to purchase tickets to an athletic event in return for the contribution, then 80 percent of the amount donated will be deductible. Thus, Pasqual may deduct 80 percent of $2,000 or $1,600.

40. If, as appears to be the case, his son was admitted because of the contribution, then Bill received something of value for his gift and it would not be deductible. On the other hand, if his son's acceptance did not depend on the donation, then a charitable deduction probably would be allowed. See, e.g., Rev. Rul. 83-104.

41. $40. A taxpayer cannot deduct the value of the services donated to a charity. Reg. §1.170A-1(g). (On the other hand, a taxpayer is not taxed on the imputed value of those services.) A taxpayer can deduct unreimbursed expenses incurred in connection with services performed for charitable organizations. However, child care expenses incurred to enable the taxpayer to donate charitable services are considered nondeductible personal expenses. Rev. Rul. 73-597. Thus, only the $40 spent on transportation expenses is deductible.

42. The §170 deduction for a contribution of ordinary income property is limited to the donor's adjusted basis in the contributed property, so Bill can deduct only $600. §170(e)(1)(A). Ordinary income property is any property that would have produced ordinary income had the donor sold it. This includes inventory held for sale in the taxpayer's trade or business.

43. Carlos realizes no gain because making a gift or contribution is not treated as a realization event for the donor. Carlos is entitled

to a deduction of $10,000, the value of the contributed property. Since he is in the 30 percent bracket, this reduces his tax liability by $3,000. If Carlos had sold the stock, he would have realized and recognized a gain of $9,000 and paid a tax of $2,700. This would have left him $7,300 ($10,000 received less $2,700 tax) to spend after taxes. Since Carlos is allowed a deduction worth $3,000 by donating the stock, the after-tax cost of the donation is $4,300.

44.   a.   If the bottle is sold for $1,000, Jin will realize and recognize a gain of $1,000 and pay a $300 tax. Thus, Jin will have an extra $700 to spend.

   b.   If the bottle is donated, Jin will get a deduction of $3,000. This will reduce her tax liability by 30 percent of $3,000, or $900, so she will have an extra $900 to spend. Thus, Jin would be $200 wealthier if she donates the bottle rather than selling it. The keys to this result are: (i) Jin is permitted to deduct the fair market value of the tangible personal property, not just her basis in the property, because the use by the museum relates to its charitable purposes (so that §170(e)(1)(B)(i) does not apply) and (ii) Jin can substantiate the $3,000 value.

   c.   If Jin donates the bottle to a hospital, she will lose her $3,000 deduction. Here, she is donating tangible personal property and the charity donee's use of the property is unrelated to its charitable purpose, so §170(e)(1)(B)(i) applies, limiting her §170 deduction to her basis in the contributed property, which appears to be zero.

   d.   Here, in year one, Jin substantially overstated the value of the bottle. She claimed a $20,000 year one deduction under §170, which reduced her tax for that year by $6,000. Jin is actually allowed a $3,000 deduction for year one (which saves her $900 of tax), so she will have to pay $5,100 of additional tax for year one, plus interest on the deficiency. §6601. The year one deficiency exceeds $5,000 and the value she claimed was more than four times the value of the bottle, so Jin will also be liable for an accuracy-related penalty of $2,040 (40 percent of the $5,100 understatement). §6662(e) and (h).

45.   The limitation of §170(e)(1)(A) applies because the sale of the painting, which Larry owned for less than a year, would have produced short-term capital gain had Larry sold it. Larry's deduction is thus limited to his $10,000 basis in the painting.

46. Kevin can deduct $60,000 unless he elects to be treated under §170(e), in which case he can deduct $80,000. Absent an election under §170(b)(1)(C)(iii), the §170(e)(1)(A) and (B) limitations do not apply because (i) a sale of the property would have produced long-term capital gain, (ii) the property is not tangible personal property, and (iii) Kevin did not donate the property to the type of foundation specified in §170(e)(1)(B)(ii). On the other hand, the §170(b)(1)(C) limitation applies because Kevin donated capital gain property to an "A" charity. Section 170(b)(1)(C) limits Kevin's year one §170 deduction to $60,000, which is 30 percent of his $200,000 adjusted gross income. The $35,000 excess contribution is carried forward to year four. §170(b)(1)(C)(ii). If Kevin elected under §170(e)(1)(C)(iii) to be treated under §170(e), he would deduct $80,000, his basis in the land, in year one.

47. No. Robert is not entitled to a charitable deduction. The transfer benefits the lots in the subdivision, which are still owned by Robert. This substantial benefit received by Robert precludes him from taking a §170 deduction for the contribution. Ottawa Silica Co. v. United States, 699 F.2d 1124 (Fed. Cir. 1983). In addition, the transfer relieves Robert of the legal responsibility of maintaining the transferred property. McConnell v. Commissioner, 55 T.C.M. (CCH) 1284 (1988), aff'd without opinion, 870 F.2d 651 (3d Cir. 1989).

48. Year one. If a taxpayer makes a donation to charity using a credit card, the §170 deduction is taken in the year in which the charge is incurred, not the year in which the charge is later paid by the taxpayer. Rev. Rul. 78-38.

49. Mona is correct. A charitable deduction is more valuable to a high income taxpayer because she is subject to a higher marginal tax rate than a low income taxpayer. A wealthy taxpayer in the 40 percent tax bracket who donates $100 to charity will reduce the amount of tax she owes by $40, so the after-tax cost of the donation is only $60. A low income taxpayer in the 15 percent tax bracket who donates $100 to charity will reduce the amount of tax she owes by only $15, so the after-tax cost of the donation is $85. In addition, the charitable deduction is only available to those who itemize their deductions and many low bracket taxpayers take the standard deduction rather than itemizing.

50. Ned's statement is incorrect. It is true that donations of cash are deductible and donations of services are not deductible. This difference in treatment is necessary, however, to ensure that donors of cash and services bear the same tax burden. Suppose, for example, that Doctor Debby and Lawyer Larry each can earn $1,000 per day providing services. Doctor Debby works for pay four days per week and spends one day providing free medical services to the poor. Debby will have taxable income of $4,000. Lawyer Larry works for pay five days per week and earns $5,000 but he donates one day's earnings, $1,000, to a charitable organization that provides free medical services to the poor. If Larry is permitted to deduct his cash donation, he will have taxable income of $4,000, the same as Debby who donated services.

E. Personal Interest

Reading: §163

The tax treatment of interest paid by a taxpayer varies according to the purpose of the borrowing. Interest on amounts borrowed in connection with a trade or business (*business interest*) and on amounts borrowed for investment purposes (*investment interest*) generally are deductible in calculating net income, subject to certain limitations to prevent tax avoidance. §163(a). (The deduction of business interest and investment interest is discussed in Chapter 5 of this book.)

Prior to the Tax Reform Act of 1986, interest on money borrowed for personal reasons, such as the purchase of a home, automobile, or vacation, also was deductible, although only as an itemized deduction. The 1986 Act eliminated the deduction for personal interest except for *qualified residence interest*. §163(h). Qualified residence interest is defined as interest paid on either "acquisition indebtedness" or "home equity indebtedness" with respect to a "qualified residence" of the taxpayer. §163(h)(3). A *qualified residence* is the taxpayer's principal residence and one other residence of the taxpayer. §163(h)(4)(A). A dwelling that the taxpayer rents to others is a qualified residence only if, during the year, the taxpayer uses the dwelling for personal reasons for longer than the greater of (i) 14 days or (ii) 10 percent of the number of days that it is rented. §§163(h)(4)(A)(i)(II) and 280A(d)(1).

Acquisition indebtedness is any indebtedness that is secured by the residence and was incurred in acquiring, constructing, or substantially improving the residence. §163(h)(3)(B). Acquisition indebtedness also includes any indebtedness, secured by the residence, from refinancing qualified acquisition indebtedness, but only up to the amount that was refinanced. Id. The aggregate amount of acquisition indebtedness for any taxpayer cannot exceed $1 million §163(h)(3)(B)(ii).

Home equity indebtedness is any indebtedness, other than acquisition indebtedness, secured by a qualified residence. §163(h)(3)(C). Home equity indebtedness is subject to two limitations. First, the total of (i) home equity indebtedness plus (ii) acquisition indebtedness cannot exceed the fair market value of the qualified residence. Id. Second, home equity indebtedness cannot exceed $100,000 in any case. Id. Debt secured by a qualified residence and incurred before October 13, 1987, is treated as acquisition indebtedness and is not subject to the $1,000,000 limitation. However, such indebtedness will reduce the $1 million limitation (but not below zero) for any additional loans (other than qualified refinancing). §163(h)(3)(D)(ii).

Points are amounts a lender requires a borrower to pay, usually on the closing of the loan, in lieu of charging the borrower a higher interest rate on the loan. Points paid in connection with a loan generally must be capitalized and are deducted over the term of the loan. §461(g)(1). However, §461(g)(2) provides an exception to that rule for points paid on indebtedness secured by the taxpayer's principal residence and incurred to purchase or improve the principal residence, provided that (i) the payment of points is an established business practice in the area in which the indebtedness is incurred and (ii) the points paid do not exceed the amount generally charged in the area. If the requirements of §461(g)(2) are met, the points are deducted in the year in which they are paid. Note that points paid to refinance an existing home mortgage are not within the §461(g)(2) rule, so they cannot be immediately deducted in the year in which they are paid. Instead, the points are deducted over the term of the loan.

As a policy matter, the home mortgage deduction can be best defended as a method of encouraging home ownership or, more persuasively, as necessary to prevent individuals who have purchased homes in reliance on the deduction from suffering large losses. One important argument against the home mortgage deduction is that it seriously undermines the repeal of the deduction for other personal interest. Homeowners can deduct interest on loans secured by their residence (up to $100,000) even if the amounts are borrowed for purposes unrelated to home ownership such as for the purchase of a new car. More importantly, the home mortgage deduction has been criticized for encouraging individuals to overinvest in housing.

The following questions explore some of the details of the deduction for qualified residence interest. Unless stated otherwise, all debts are incurred after October 13, 1987.

EXAMPLES

51. In year one Alice purchases property to be used as a principal residence for $400,000, using $50,000 of savings and borrowing $350,000 from the Friendly Bank. The loan is secured by the property. In year three the residence is worth $500,000. What portion, if any, of the interest paid on the following alternative loans can be deducted?

   a. Alice borrows an additional $60,000 from the Friendly Bank, secured by her residence. She uses the money to add an additional room to her home.

   b. Assume the same facts as in part (a) except that Alice uses the loan proceeds to purchase a luxury automobile.

   c. Assume the same facts as in part (a) except that the loan is not secured by Alice's home.

   d. Alice borrows $120,000 from the Friendly Bank, secured by her residence, and uses the money to purchase a luxury automobile and take a trip around the world.

   e. Alice borrows $120,000 from the Friendly Bank and uses the proceeds to add a home theater and a pool to her residence.

52. a. In July of year one Jim purchases a home that he will occupy as a principal residence for $220,000, using $20,000 of his savings and borrowing the other $200,000. At the closing, Jim pays $250 in filing fees and $2,000 in "points" on the mortgage. During the remainder of year one, Jim pays $8,000 of interest on the mortgage. What is Jim's deductible interest for year one?

   b. Suppose that by year five interest rates have dropped and Jim's home is worth $400,000. Jim decides to refinance his loan, which has an outstanding principal amount owed of $180,000. He borrows $320,000 and uses $180,000 of the amount to repay the original loan. He also pays $6,000 in "points" on the new mortgage, which runs for 25 years. He uses the remainder of the amount borrowed to purchase an automobile and boat

237

and pay for his daughter's college education. During year five Jim makes monthly interest payments totaling $15,000. What is Jim's deductible interest in year five?

53. Eve has a mortgage of $800,000 on her principal residence, which is worth $1,200,000. What portion of the interest on the following alternative additional loans can be deducted?

   a. In year one Eve purchases a vacation beach house on Cape Cod for $500,000, using $100,000 of savings and borrowing $400,000. The loan is secured by the beach house.

   b. In year one Eve instead purchases a smaller beach house for $250,000 and also purchases a ski chalet in Vermont for $250,000. On each vacation home she puts $50,000 down and borrows $200,000. The loan on the beach house is secured by the beach house and the loan on the chalet is secured by the chalet.

   c. How, if at all, would your answers in parts (a) and (b) change if Eve purchased her principal residence in 1986? If she purchased all the homes in 1986?

54. Fay purchased a home in 1970 for $30,000. The mortgage has been completely repaid and the home is now worth $300,000. In year one Fay borrows $160,000, secured by her home, and purchases a recreational vehicle, boat, and trailer costing a total of $160,000.

   a. What portion of the interest paid in year one on the $160,000 loan is deductible?

   b. Suppose, instead, that in year one Fay sold her home for $300,000, used $160,000 of the proceeds to purchase the RV, boat, and trailer, and at the same time purchased a new home for $300,000, using $140,000 of the proceeds from the sale of her old home and borrowing $160,000. What portion of the interest paid in year one on the $160,000 loan is deductible?

EXPLANATIONS

51. a. Interest on the loan is fully deductible. Qualified residence interest, which includes interest on acquisition indebtedness, is deductible. §163(h)(2)(D) and (3)(A). Acquisition indebtedness includes amounts borrowed to finance a substantial home improvement if the debt is secured by the home. §163(h)(3)(B)(i).

b. Interest on the loan is fully deductible. Qualified residence interest is deductible. §163(h)(2)(D). Here, the interest is qualified residence interest because the debt is home equity indebtedness. The amount borrowed is not acquisition indebtedness because the loan proceeds were not used to purchase, build, or substantially improve her home. However, the loan qualifies as home equity indebtedness because (i) it is secured by her home; (ii) the home equity indebtedness, when added to the acquisition indebtedness, does not exceed the fair market value of her home; and (iii) the total amount of home equity indebtedness does not exceed $100,000. §163(h)(3)(C).

c. Not deductible. The deduction for qualified residential interest is only available for loans secured by the taxpayer's residence. §163(h)(3)(B)(i)(II) and (C)(i).

d. Interest on only $100,000 of the $120,000 borrowed is deductible. Qualified residence interest, which includes interest on acquisition indebtedness and home equity indebtedness, is deductible. §163(h)(2)(D) and (3)(A). The amount borrowed is not acquisition indebtedness because the loan proceeds were not used to purchase, build, or substantially improve her home. However, the interest paid on $100,000 of the debt qualifies as deductible home equity indebtedness because (i) it is secured by her home and (ii) the home equity indebtedness, when added to the acquisition indebtedness, does not exceed the fair market value of her home. §163(h)(3)(C). Section 163(h)(3)(C)(ii) limits the total home equity indebtedness to $100,000, so the interest on the $20,000 of debt in excess of the $100,000 limit is not qualified residence interest and is thus not deductible. §163(h)(1) and (2).

e. Interest on the loan is fully deductible. In this part of the example, unlike part (d), the loan qualifies as acquisition indebtedness because it is used to improve her home substantially. §163(h)(3)(B)(i)(I). Acquisition indebtedness is subject to a $1 million limit, instead of the $100,000 limit imposed on home equity indebtedness, so the interest on the entire $120,000 of debt is deductible qualified residence interest.

52. a. $10,000 ($8,000 interest and $2,000 points). The interest on Jim's principal residence is qualified residence interest. §163(h)(3)(A)(i) and (B). Points paid on the original financing of the purchase of a principal residence are treated as

interest that can be deducted in the year in which they are paid, provided the other requirements of §461(g)(2) are met. Filing fees and similar closing costs do not constitute deductible interest.

b. In year five Jim deducts $13,125 of the $15,000 of monthly interest payments and $240 of the points he paid. Qualified residence interest, which includes interest on acquisition indebtedness and home equity indebtedness, is deductible. §163(h)(2)(D) and (3)(A). Amounts borrowed to refinance a loan on a qualified residence are considered acquisition indebtedness only up to the amount refinanced. §163(h)(3)(B) (flush language). Thus, $180,000 of the amount borrowed is acquisition indebtedness. The other $140,000 borrowed is not acquisition indebtedness. However, $100,000 of that remaining $140,000 of debt is home equity indebtedness. §163(h)(3)(C). Thus, interest on $280,000 of the $320,000 mortgage would be deductible, or 87.5 percent (7/8) of the $15,000 interest paid. In year five Jim will also deduct $240 of the $6,000 of points paid on the refinancing. Although amounts paid for points on the original mortgage on a taxpayer's principal residence are immediately deductible, points on amounts borrowed in connection with refinancings, second mortgages, and purchases of second homes must be amortized over the life of the loan. Thus, on a 25-year loan, 4 percent of the $6,000 paid for points would be deductible each year. See §461(g)(1), Rev. Rul. 87-22, and Rev. Proc. 87-15.

53. a. Interest on $300,000 of the additional $400,000 borrowed is deductible, but the rest of the interest is not deductible. Qualified residence interest, which includes interest on acquisition indebtedness and home equity indebtedness, is deductible. §163(h)(2)(D) and (3)(A). Amounts borrowed to purchase a second home qualify as acquisition indebtedness, provided that the second home is a "qualified residence." §163(h)(3)(B)(i)(I) and (4)(A)(i)(II). However, total acquisition indebtedness is limited to $1 million. §163(h)(3)(B)(ii). Eve already has an $800,000 mortgage on her principal residence, so only $200,000 of the amount borrowed to purchase the beach house is acquisition indebtedness. However, of the remaining $200,000 of indebtedness on the beach house, $100,000 qualifies as "home equity indebtedness" because (i) it is secured by

her home and (ii) the home equity indebtedness, when added to the acquisition indebtedness, does not exceed the fair market value of her home. §163(h)(3)(C). Section 163(h)(3)(C)(ii) limits total home equity indebtedness to $100,000. The interest on the remaining $100,000 of debt (the amount in excess of the $200,000 of acquisition indebtedness and $100,000 of home equity indebtedness) is not qualified residence interest and is not deductible. §163(h)(1) and (2).

b. Deductible qualified residence interest includes acquisition indebtedness on a qualified residence and home equity indebtedness on a qualified residence. The term qualified residence includes the taxpayer's principal residence and one additional residence of the taxpayer's choice. §163(h)(4)(A)(i). Thus, one of the vacation homes is a qualified residence and the other is not a qualified residence. Eve can deduct interest on the indebtedness on the vacation home that is a qualified residence. All of the $200,000 borrowed on that residence will be deductible as acquisition indebtedness since the $1 million limitation is not exceeded. However, none of the interest paid on the indebtedness on the other vacation home can be deducted. §163(h)(1) and (2).

c. A "grandfather clause" exists for indebtedness incurred on qualifying residences purchased before October 13, 1987. §163(h)(3)(D)(i). However, the $1 million limitation on acquisition indebtedness is reduced (but not below zero) by the amount of grandfathered debt. Thus, the results in parts (a) and (b) would not change if Eve had purchased only her principal residence in 1986.

If Eve had purchased all the residences in 1986, however, the result in part (a) would change. On these facts, both Eve's principal residence and her beach house are qualifying residences, so all interest paid on amounts outstanding before October 13, 1987, would be deductible. §163(h)(3)(D). In part (b), on the other hand, only one of the vacation homes would be considered a qualifying residence, so the interest paid on the loan used to purchase Eve's second vacation home would remain nondeductible.

54. a. 62.5 percent (5/8) of the interest paid will be deductible. Qualified residence interest, which includes interest on acquisition indebtedness and home equity indebtedness, is deductible.

§163(h)(2)(D) and (3)(A). Here, none of the amount borrowed is acquisition indebtedness because the loan is not
incurred to acquire, construct, or improve her residence.
§163(h)(3)(B)(i)(I). However, $100,000 of the $160,000 borrowed qualifies as home equity indebtedness because (i) it is
secured by her home and (ii) the home equity indebtedness,
when added to the acquisition indebtedness, does not exceed
the fair market value of her home. §163(h)(3)(C). Section
163(h)(3)(C)(ii) limits total home equity indebtedness to
$100,000, so the interest on the remaining $60,000 of debt in
excess of the $100,000 of home equity indebtedness is not
qualified residence interest and is not deductible. §163(h)(1)
and (2). Fay can deduct 62.5 percent ($100,000 home equity
indebtedness/$160,000 total indebtedness) of the interest she
paid in year one.

b. Here, all of the interest paid in year one is deductible. On these
facts, the entire amount borrowed qualifies as acquisition indebtedness because the debt is incurred to buy the new home.
§163(h)(3)(B)(i)(I). Note that Eve will recognize no gain on
the sale of her principal residence because she purchased a new
principal residence for an equal or greater amount within the
statutory period. §1034.

F. Taxes

Reading: §164; Reg. §§1.164-3, 1.1001-1(b)

A personal itemized deduction is permitted under §164 for state and
local income taxes and taxes on real and personal property. (Section
164 also permits a deduction for certain foreign taxes, but individuals
subject to foreign taxation generally take the §901 foreign tax credit
instead.)

Section 164 does not permit a deduction for state and local *sales*
taxes. Until 1986, §164 allowed a deduction for sales tax, but that
provision in §164 was repealed as part of the Tax Reform Act of
1986. Note that states vary in the degree to which they rely on
income taxes, property taxes, and sales taxes to raise revenue. Following the repeal of the sales tax deduction, a taxpayer who is a resident
of a state that relies heavily on sales tax for revenue pays more federal
tax than a taxpayer with equal income who is a resident of a state that

relies more heavily on income and property taxes. This inequity will be ameliorated if states replace their nondeductible sales taxes with deductible income taxes or property taxes. To date, however, states have generally not taken this course. Taxpayers cannot generally deduct federal taxes paid.

Amounts charged for government services are considered "fees" rather than "taxes." Such fees do not qualify for the §164 personal deduction for state and local taxes. However, they may be deductible as ordinary and necessary business expenses or as expenses incurred in the production of income. Rev. Rul. 72-608. In addition, assessments on real property owners for local benefits, such as sidewalks, are not treated as real property taxes for purposes of §164 and are not deductible. Reg. §1.164-4.

The §164 personal deduction for state and local taxes is taken as an itemized deduction. On the other hand, taxes incurred in a business or in connection with the production of income are deductible under §162 or §212 in the calculation of adjusted gross income. Consistent with the principle that the expenses of earning income should be deductible, state and local excise, sales, and other taxes, as well as income and property taxes, incurred in the production of income, are deductible in the calculation of adjusted gross income. Federal taxes, however, generally remain nondeductible.

A current §164 deduction is not permitted for taxes paid in connection with the acquisition of property. If paid by the buyer, such transfer taxes must be treated as part of the buyer's cost of the property, whether or not incurred in a business context. Similarly, taxes incurred by a seller in connection with the sale of property are not deductible, but instead reduce the amount realized on the sale. §164(a) (flush language).

When real property is sold, the property taxes for the year of the sale must be allocated between the buyer and the seller. §164(d)(1). Under §164(d), the property taxes are allocated based on the part of the year the property was owned by each. For the purpose of making this allocation, the buyer is treated as the owner of the property on the date the property was sold. §164(d)(1). For example, assume that Sela sells Whiteacre to Betty in year one. Sela owns the property for $\frac{1}{4}$ of that year (91 days Sela owned the property/365 days in the year) and Betty owns the property for $\frac{3}{4}$ of that year (274 days Betty owned the property/365 days in the year). If the property tax on Whiteacre for year one is $4,000, Sela is allocated $1,000 of the year one property tax and Betty is allocated the other $3,000 of the property tax. This allocation method determines the amount of property tax that the buyer and seller may deduct under §164.

If the buyer pays property taxes allocable to the seller, the seller's property taxes paid by the buyer increase the seller's amount realized and the buyer's basis in the property acquired. If, on the other hand, the seller pays property taxes allocable to the buyer and is reimbursed for the taxes by the buyer, the property taxes allocable to the buyer and reimbursed by the buyer reduce the seller's amount realized and the buyer's basis in the property acquired. Reg. §1.1001-1(b).

EXAMPLES

55. State whether the following amounts are deductible under §164.
    a. Alice pays a $2,000 per year local real property tax on the home she lives in.
    b. Carlos recently graduated from dental school. He purchases a building to use as an office for $150,000. He is required to pay a state transfer tax of $1,000 on the purchase.
    c. To play tennis on the new public courts of Centerville, residents must purchase an annual pass. Tim pays $100 for a pass.
    d. Ernest must pay a motor vehicle fee of 1 percent of the value of his car each year. The fee in year one is $150.
    e. Karen pays $4,000 of state and local sales tax when she buys a new recreational sailboat for $60,000.
    f. Greta is a cigarette smoker. She calculates that she pays $150 per year in federal cigarette excise taxes and $200 per year in state cigarette excise taxes.

56. On January one of year two, Harry purchases Blackacre from Irving. At the time of the purchase, Irving owes $4,000 in property taxes on Blackacre for year one. Harry pays the year one taxes Irving owes in order to obtain clear title to the property. Can Harry deduct all $4,000 of year one tax that he pays in year two?

57. Jane purchases Whiteacre from Karl on January 31 of year one for $300,000. Karl had already paid $3,650 of property taxes on Whiteacre for all of year one. Will Jane receive a tax deduction for any portion of the taxes paid?

58. The City of Oceanview assesses beachfront property owners for the construction of jetties to protect shoreline property from the destructive effects of ocean storms. Is the assessment deductible by the property owners?

59. What policy justification exists, if any, for permitting a deduction for state and local income and property taxes, but not for state and local sales taxes? What might state governments do in response to the 1986 repeal of the deduction for state and local sales taxes?

EXPLANATIONS

55. a. Alice can deduct the taxes. Local property taxes are deductible as itemized personal deductions. §164(a)(1).

   b. Carlos cannot deduct the taxes in the year in which they are paid. A tax that is paid in connection with an acquisition of property is treated as part of the cost of the acquired property. §164(a) (flush language). Thus, Carlos could not immediately deduct the tax paid, but would include the amount paid in the basis of the property acquired, giving him a basis of $151,000.

   c. Tim cannot deduct the $100 cost of the pass. User fees for state and local services are not considered taxes and thus are not deductible under §164. Rev. Rul. 72-608.

   d. Ernest can deduct the $150 "fee." A motor vehicle fee is a deductible personal property tax under §164(a)(2). Reg. §1.164-3(c).

   e. Karen cannot deduct the sales tax. Sales tax is no longer deductible under §164.

   f. Greta is not entitled to a deduction. Excise taxes are not deductible under §164.

56. No. The §164 deduction for taxes paid is applicable only to taxes owed by the taxpayer. In this case, Irving, not Harry, owed the year one property taxes. Harry would not be able to deduct the $4,000 of Irving's taxes that he paid, but he would be able to add the $4,000 payment to his basis in Blackacre. Irving would include in the amount realized on the sale the $4,000 of tax paid on his behalf by Harry and would take a §164 deduction in the same amount. Reg. §1.1001-1(b).

57. Yes, Jane can deduct $3,350 as year one property taxes. On the sale of property, real estate taxes are allocated between the buyer and seller according to the number of days the property was owned by each. §164(d). Here, the seller would have owned the property for 30 days and the buyer for 335 days. Thus, Jane would be permitted a §164 deduction of $3,350 ($3,650 multiplied by 335/365) for the year one property taxes. Jane's basis in

Whiteacre is $296,650 ($300,000 contract price less $3,350 of property taxes allocable to Jane). Reg. §1.1001-1(b).

58. Probably not. As a general rule, real property taxes do not include amounts assessed for local benefits that increase the value of the assessed property. §164(c)(1) and Reg. §1.164-4. Building jetties will increase the value of the assessed beachfront property. Thus, the amount of the assessment is not deductible, but is added to the adjusted basis of the taxpayer's property.

59. It is difficult to find any policy justification for the different treatment of income, property, and sales taxes. If a taxpayer pays $1,000 of sales taxes, it reduces her "ability to pay" or economic well-being to the same extent as paying $1,000 of property or income tax. It would make sense for states that rely on the sales taxes for revenue to switch to an income tax so that their citizens could deduct state taxes paid. However, few, if any, states have made such a switch.

5

Deductions for the Costs of Earning Income

Business and investment expenses are subtracted from gross income in order to determine net income. Section 162(a) provides that a taxpayer is allowed to deduct "all the ordinary and necessary expenses incurred during the taxable year in carrying on any trade or business." Section 212 also allows a deduction for expenses incurred in connection with investment activities. However, a number of Code sections and judicial doctrines limit the deductibility of certain types of business and investment expenses or require that certain types of expenses be capitalized and deducted over a number of years.

In this chapter, we will first consider the basic statutory framework for deducting the costs of earning income. Second, we will consider the rules for determining whether a business deduction is deducted in the year in which it is incurred or instead is deducted over a number of years. Current expenses of a business can be deducted immediately, while capital expenses — those that create a benefit that extends substantially beyond the close of the year in which the expense is incurred — must be deducted over the time that the expenses produce benefits. As we will see, however, it is often far from obvious whether an expense is a current or capital expense.

Third, we will explore several limitations on the deduction of certain types of business expenses. Fourth, we will consider the rules for determining a taxpayer's deductions for the cost of tangible and intangible depreciable property used in the taxpayer's trade or business or held for investment.

Fifth, we will examine a number of issues that arise in connection with *tax shelters*. A tax shelter is an investment that generates tax losses that can be used to shield other income from taxation. Abusive tax shelters may produce tax losses that greatly exceed the amount of money invested in the shelters. This chapter concludes with an examination of the complex judicial and statutory responses to abusive tax shelters.

A.   The Statutory Framework

Reading: §§62, 63, 67; Reg. §1.62-1T(d)

A basic principle of the federal income tax is that individuals are taxed only on their net income. Thus, individuals generally are permitted to deduct costs associated with earning income.

Section 162 provides a deduction for "ordinary and necessary" expenses incurred in carrying on a trade or business. Under this section, a taxpayer who owns and operates a housecleaning business could deduct, for example, the costs of renting office space, utilities and other office expenses, advertising, and wages paid to employees of the business. The computational effect of a business expense depends, in part, on whether the taxpayer who incurred the expense is an employee because an employee is not considered to be engaged in a trade or business for purposes of computing adjusted gross income under §62. Reg. §1.62-1T(d). If business expenses are incurred by a taxpayer who is not an employee of a firm (for example, a law firm partner who is considered to be self-employed), the business expenses are subtracted from gross income to determine adjusted gross income under §62(a)(1). Deductions taken into account in computing adjusted gross income are referred to as *above the line* deductions because they are taken above the adjusted gross income line on a tax return.

On the other hand, if business expenses are incurred by an employee (for example, an associate in a law firm) and are not reimbursed by the employer, the expenses are subtracted from adjusted gross income to determine taxable income. §§62(a)(1) and 63(a). Deductions taken into account in computing taxable income are called *below the line* deductions because they are taken below the adjusted gross income line on a tax return. Employee business expenses that are not reimbursed by the employer are subject to §67, which generally limits a taxpayer's itemized deductions to her aggregate deductible expenses in excess of 2 percent of her adjusted gross income. §67(a). The 2 percent floor eliminates the business expense deduction for most employee taxpayers. In addition, even if a taxpayer's unreimbursed employee business expenses exceed the 2 percent floor, the taxpayer is allowed to take a deduction for the excess over the floor only if the taxpayer itemizes deductions. A taxpayer taking the standard deduction, instead, is precluded from deducting any of the employee business expenses. Thus, unreimbursed employee business expenses (which are below the line deductions, are subject to the 2 percent floor, and can only be deducted if the taxpayer does not take the standard deduction) are treated less favorably than non-employee business expenses, which are fully deductible and are above the line deductions.

Reimbursed employee business expenses are treated like non-employee business expenses. Thus, they are above the line deductions and thus not subject to §67. §62(a)(2), Reg. §1.67-1T(a)(1). If the amount reimbursed by the employer is equal to the employee business expense, Regulation §1.162-17(b) allows the employee, for reporting purposes, to disregard both the reimbursement (which would otherwise be included in income) and the business expense (which would otherwise be an above the line deduction).

Expenses incurred in earning income from sources other than a trade or business are deductible under §212. For example, this section permits an individual with investment income from stocks and bonds to deduct her brokerage fees and the cost of a subscription to the Wall Street Journal. Section 212 expenses are generally below the line deductions and thus subject to the §67 limitation. An exception is the deduction for §212 expenses attributable to property held for the production of rents or royalties, which is an above the line deduction. §62(a)(4).

EXAMPLES

1. Sally is an employee of Yaba Corporation. She is the chief financial officer of the corporation, so she subscribes to several business and finance newspapers and magazines. The annual cost of these subscriptions is $500. In year one Sally has adjusted gross income of $200,000 and §67 miscellaneous itemized deductions

5. Deductions for the Costs of Earning Income

(determined without regard to the $500 subscription cost) of $1,000. Explain the tax treatment, in year one, of the $500 subscription cost in the following alternative circumstances.

a. Sally pays the $500 cost of the subscriptions and is not reimbursed by Yaba Corporation.

b. Sally pays the $500 cost of the subscriptions and is reimbursed by Yaba Corporation.

EXPLANATIONS

1. a. Sally is allowed to deduct the $500 cost of the subscriptions as an expense of earning income. However, the deduction is not an above the line deduction because (i) Sally is an employee of Yaba Corporation and (ii) Yaba Corporation did not reimburse her for the cost of the subscriptions. Thus, the $500 cost is a below the line itemized deduction and is subject to §67. That section limits Sally's itemized deductions to her deductible expenses in excess of 2 percent of her adjusted gross income. §67(a). The $500 cost of the subscriptions plus her other miscellaneous itemized deductions total $1,500, which is less than 2 percent of her $200,000 adjusted gross income. In effect, the §67 floor eliminates her deduction for the $500 cost of the subscriptions. (In addition, the standard deduction exceeds her itemized deductions.)

   b. Sally is allowed to deduct the $500 cost of the subscriptions as an expense of earning income. Here, the deduction is an above the line deduction because Yaba Corporation reimbursed the expense. §62(a)(2)(A). Thus, the deduction is not subject to the §67 floor. Since the amount reimbursed exactly equals her expense, she does not have to report the amount reimbursed or the expense. Reg. §1.162-17(b).

B. Current Expenses versus Capital Expenditures

Reading: §§263, 263A; Reg. §§1.162-3, 1.263(a)-1, -2, 1.263A-1, -2

Current expenses are deductible in the year in which they are incurred. Business expenses for an asset with a useful life that extends beyond the year in which the expense is incurred, on the other hand,

must be *capitalized*. §263. The object of the capitalization requirement is to accurately reflect the taxpayer's true income for each year
by matching an expense with the income to which it relates. See, e.g.,
Encyclopaedia Britannica v. Commissioner, 685 F.2d 212 (7th Cir.
1982).

The §162 regulations provide several rules for determining
whether certain types of expenses are currently deductible or must be
capitalized. For example, Reg. §1.162-3 provides that a taxpayer may
generally deduct the costs of incidental materials and supplies (for
example, legal pads and pens used in a law firm) in the year in which
the supplies are purchased. Reg. §1.162-4 also provides that a taxpayer does not have to capitalize the cost of incidental repairs that do
not materially increase the value or the useful life of the repaired
property.

The cost of an asset with a useful life that extends beyond the year
in which the expense is incurred is deducted as *depreciation* over the
useful life of the asset, provided that the asset has a determinable useful
life. §167. Suppose, for example, that a donut shop purchases a new
donut-making machine that is expected to produce donuts for 10 years
and then be worthless. Under a theoretically pure income tax, the cost
of the machine would be deducted over the 10-year period with an
annual depreciation deduction equal to the annual reduction in value
of the machine. Under current law, however, annual deductions for the
cost of business assets are determined by reference to bright-line statutory rules rather than by reference to the actual decline in value of the
asset. §§167, 168.

Section 167 allows a deduction for "the exhaustion, wear and
tear" of property used in a trade or business or for the production of
income. Both tangible property, such as a machine or building, and
intangible property, such as a patent, are eligible for the deduction.
Reg. §1.167(a)-2, -3. The term *amortization*, rather than depreciation,
is used to describe deductions for the cost of intangible property.
Under §168, most tangible property with a limited useful life is depreciated under the accelerated cost recovery system (ACRS). ACRS permits a taxpayer to deduct the cost of the asset over a period of time that
is shorter than the actual useful life of the asset. (The rules for calculating a taxpayer's depreciation deductions on business assets are discussed in more detail later in this chapter.)

A depreciable asset is *not* a *capital asset*, despite the fact that the
cost of the depreciable asset must be *capitalized*. §1221(2). Depreciable assets are instead "§1231 assets." Gain or loss from the sale of

§1231 assets may be capital or ordinary. Capital gain and loss, capital assets, and §1231 assets are discussed further in Chapter 8. For now, note that, even if the cost of a business asset must be capitalized, the asset may not be (and, in fact, usually is not) a capital asset. We mention this point because students often incorrectly assume that an asset is a capital asset if the taxpayer has to capitalize the cost of the asset. The confusion is understandable since "capitalization" and "capital asset" sound similar — but remember that the two terms express different concepts in the tax law.

Property with an unlimited useful life, such as land, cannot be depreciated or amortized. Instead, with a few statutory exceptions, the costs of such property may be recovered only when the property is sold (by subtracting the taxpayer's adjusted basis from the amount realized on the sale).

If a taxpayer prepays an expense that is attributable to later years, the expense must be capitalized. For example, in Commissioner v. Boylston Market Association, 131 F.2d 966 (1st Cir. 1942), a cash method taxpayer that prepaid three years of insurance premiums had to allocate that expense over the three years and deduct a portion in each year. Recall that accrual method taxpayers also are generally not allowed to deduct prepaid expenses despite the fact that the all events test may be met in the year in which the expense is prepaid because of the economic performance requirement of §461(h).

Capitalization is required if an expense produces a long-term benefit even if the expense does not create a separate asset. In INDOPCO Inc. v. Commissioner, 503 U.S. 79 (1992), the taxpayer took a deduction for investment banking and legal fees incurred during the year in connection with a friendly takeover. The record indicated that the takeover produced significant long-term benefits for the taxpayer's shareholders, so the court held that the investment banking and legal fees had to be capitalized, despite the fact that the expense did not create a separate asset.

Reg. §1.263(a)-1 and -2 provide that a taxpayer must capitalize certain costs, including the costs of: acquiring or constructing buildings or machinery; making permanent improvements in property; securing a copyright; defending or perfecting title to property; an architect's services; and commissions paid in purchasing securities. If a taxpayer incurs expenses that would otherwise be deductible business expenses (for example, wages paid to employees) in constructing a building or machinery, the otherwise deductible expenses must be capitalized. For example, in Commissioner v. Idaho Power Co., 418

U.S. 1 (1974), a power company had to capitalize expenses for wages and depreciation on trucks used to construct a capital facility with a 30-year useful life. The effect was that the taxpayer was required to recover the cost of the trucks over the 30-year life of the facility, not the shorter useful life of the trucks. The holding in *Idaho Power* was codified in 1986 when Congress enacted the §263A uniform capitalization (UNICAP) rules.

The UNICAP rules apply to manufacturers, wholesalers, retailers, and any other taxpayers who produce real or tangible property for sale or acquire real or tangible property for sale to customers in the ordinary course of their business. §263A(b). *Tangible property,* is defined to include books, films, and sound recordings. §1.263A(b). However, §263A does not apply to freelance authors, photographers, and artists. §263A(h). In addition, §263A applies to a taxpayer who acquires personal property for resale only if the taxpayer's average annual gross receipts from sales, over a three-year period, exceed $10 million. §263A(b)(2)(B).

If §263A applies, it requires the taxpayer to recover the expenses of producing or selling goods when the goods are sold, by including those expenses in the taxpayer's "cost of goods sold" (which is the term for the taxpayer's inventory cost for the year). §263A(a)(1). (Inventory accounting is discussed in more detail later in this chapter.) The UNICAP rules apply to the "direct costs" of producing and selling goods and the portion of "indirect costs" allocable to the goods sold. §263A(a)(2).

The regulations define the terms "direct cost" and "indirect cost" and specify which indirect costs must be allocated to the goods sold. Reg. §1.263A-1(e), (g). *Direct costs* include the cost of materials and wages of employees who produce or sell goods. Reg. §1.263A-1(e)(2)(i), (g)(1), (2). *Indirect costs* include the following costs: the costs of repair and maintenance of equipment or facilities; utility costs; rent on equipment, facilities or land; indirect labor costs; indirect material costs; the costs of tools and equipment, if such costs are not otherwise capitalized; certain taxes; depreciation on equipment or facilities; depletion; the costs of certain administrative or support departments or functions; compensation paid to officers; insurance premiums; contributions to deferred compensation plans; bidding expenses; and certain interest costs. Reg. §1.263A-1(e)(3)(ii). However, the regulations provide that the taxpayer's expenses for marketing, advertising, and general business and financial planning do not have to be capitalized. Reg. §1.263A-1(e)(3)(iii), (4)(iv)(B), (C). As

5.   Deductions for the Costs of Earning Income

you can tell from reading §263A and Reg. §1.263A-1 and -2, the UNICAP rules are complicated.

Most research and experimental expenses do not have to be capitalized even though they provide a benefit extending beyond the taxable year. §§174, 263A(c)(2). However, the costs of researching a book (along with preproduction costs such as editing and illustrating) have to be capitalized. Reg. §1.263A-2(a)(2)(ii)(A)(1). Soil and conservation expenditures incurred by farmers also generally do not have to be capitalized. §175.

EXAMPLES

2.   Briefly explain whether each of the following expenses may be deducted currently or must be capitalized.
   a. Purchase of the copyright to Stormy Weather
   b. Purchase of a copying machine that will be used in law firm
   c. Purchase of paper used in the copying machine described in part (b)
   d. Repair and maintenance of the copying machine described in part (b)
   e. Legal fees incurred in purchasing the property on which the taxpayer's business is located
   f. The costs of a feasibility study on overseas expansion incurred by a chain of fast food restaurants
   g. The commission paid to a stockbroker on the purchase of 100 shares of stock

3.   Pete's Big Business, Inc. outgrows the office building it has occupied for the last several years. Rather than buy or lease an existing structure, Pete commissions an architect to design a new office building. The architect's fees are $120,000. The building costs $15 million to construct. The office furniture and fixtures cost an additional $1.2 million. How much of these expenditures are currently deductible?

4.   In year one the Admiral Byrd Refrigerator Company made the following expenditures: $4 million for materials used in the production of refrigerators, $5 million for labor, and $900,000 of warehousing costs, all of which are allocable to the production and sale of refrigerators. The company had $20 million of gross sales in year one. Will the company be able to deduct all of the year one expenditures in year one?

5. Wilma's Widget Company manufactures widgets that are generally not sold until at least a year after they are produced. Determine which of the following expenditures must be capitalized and included in the cost of the widgets produced.
   a. The company spent $120,000 on salaries for the production line employees.
   b. The company bought a widget manufacturing machine for $1 million.
   c. The company spent $20,000 to insure the widget machine.
   d. The company spent $1,200 on repairs for the widget machine.
   e. The company spent $30,000 on research and development of improved widgets.
   f. The company spent $50,000 on advertising its new line of widgets.

6. Bob's Publishing Company publishes the Surfer's Almanac yearly. The costs of publishing the book are incurred at least a year before the books are sold. For example, in year five the company worked exclusively on the year six edition. The company's year five expenditures included $25,000 for the salary of Cathy, Bob's research assistant, $15,000 for secretarial services, $5,000 for the copyright to a surfer's manuscript, and $10,000 for printing and binding. How much of these expenses must be capitalized?

7. Sarah writes articles and novels that she sells to different publishing companies. In year one she worked on two projects: an article about Portugal for a travel magazine and a romance novel for Jester Romance Books Company. She incurred $5,000 in expenses related to the article and $10,000 in expenses related to the novel. How much of her expenditures must be capitalized and recovered only when she sells the article or the novel?

8. a. Jose has a national chain of balloon retail outlets. He buys the balloons wholesale rather than manufacturing them himself. In year one his business had gross sales of $16 million and incurred the following expenses: $1 million on salaries for his purchasing agents; $50,000 on payroll taxes; $80,000 on general business planning; $2 million on rent for the balloon stores; and $8 million on wholesale balloons. How much of these expenditures must be capitalized?
   b. How, if at all, would your answer in part (a) change if Jose's business had average annual gross sales of $9 million?

EXPLANATIONS

2.   a. The copyright to Stormy Weather has a useful life of more than one year, so the cost of purchasing the copyright must be capitalized. §263 and Reg. §1.263(a)-2.

b. A photocopying machine has a useful life of more than one year, so the cost of purchasing the machine must be capitalized. §263 and Reg. §1.263(a)-2.

c. The cost of the paper may be deducted currently. Supplies that are used up in the taxable year in which they are purchased are immediately deductible because they provide no benefit beyond the current taxable year. Taxpayers who do not keep track of when incidental supplies are used are allowed to deduct the cost of such supplies even if they are not actually used up during the taxable year. Reg. §1.162-3. This rule is designed to simplify matters for taxpayers who do not perform a year-end inventory of supplies.

d. The cost of the repairs and maintenance may be deducted currently. Taxpayers may deduct currently the cost of incidental repairs and maintenance even though the benefit may extend over several years. Reg. §1.162-4.

e. The costs of acquiring the property, including these legal fees, must be capitalized. Reg. §1.263(a)-2(a).

f. The decision to expand overseas might be expected to produce benefits over many years. Costs of planning such an expansion, therefore, might logically be treated as capital expenditures.

   The capitalization of general planning costs, however, would raise a number of difficult issues. Should the restaurant chain be allowed to depreciate the expansion study costs? Should a portion of the costs be allocated to each overseas restaurant and be recovered if and when the restaurant were sold? Or should the costs be recoverable only on the sale of the entire overseas operation? Mindful of these issues, courts generally have allowed a current deduction for the costs of such studies. See, e.g., Young & Rubicam, Inc. v. United States, 410 F.2d 1233 (Cl. Ct. 1969) (permitting current deduction of salaries paid to employees to investigate a possible expansion into foreign markets).

g. The costs of commissions paid to acquire securities must be capitalized. Reg. §1.263(a)-2(a).

3.   None of these expenditures are currently deductible. The costs associated with erecting a building, including architect's fees, and

the cost of furniture and fixtures, must be capitalized. These are all costs associated with the acquisition or construction of property with a useful life that extends beyond the close of the year in which the costs were incurred. Reg. §1.263(a)-2(a). However, beginning in the year in which the building is placed in service, Pete's Big Business, Inc. could recover its investment in the building (for tax purposes) by taking annual depreciation deductions over the useful life of the building.

4.   No. This company is subject to the §263A UNICAP rules because it produces goods for sale to customers. Section 263A requires capitalization of expenditures associated with the production of goods for sale. Such expenses are reflected in the taxpayer's cost of goods sold, so they are deducted when the refrigerators are sold. Unless there are no refrigerators left in the company's inventory at the end of year one, §263A will prevent the company from fully deducting all of the year one expenditures. The costs of materials and labor incurred in producing the goods are "direct costs" and the warehousing costs are "indirect costs" allocable to the production and sale of the goods. §263A; Reg. §1.263A-1(e)(2)(i)(A), (B), (3)(ii)(H).

5.   a. Direct labor costs must be capitalized, so these costs will be part of the taxpayer's cost of goods sold. Reg. §1.263A-1(e)(2)(i)(B).

b. Since the widget machine has a useful life of many years, it must be capitalized under §263(a). The taxpayer will then take depreciation deductions on the machine. The depreciation deductions will be part of the taxpayer's cost of goods sold. Reg. §1.263A-1(e)(3)(ii)(I).

Suppose, for example, that the widget machine costs $100,000 and has a useful life of 10 years. If straightline depreciation were taken over the 10-year period, the company could depreciate $10,000 of the cost each year. The $10,000 of depreciation could not, however, be deducted immediately. Instead, it would be capitalized and recovered as part of the "cost of goods sold" when the widgets are sold.

c. Insurance on machinery or equipment used to produce goods for resale must be capitalized and recovered as part of the taxpayer's cost of goods sold. Reg. §1.263A-1(e)(3)(ii)(M).

d. The costs of repairing machinery used to produce goods for resale must be capitalized and recovered as part of the taxpayer's cost of goods sold. Reg. §1.263A-1(e)(3)(ii)(O).

5. Deductions for the Costs of Earning Income

  e. Research and development costs generally are currently deductible. §§174, 263A(c)(2).

  f. Although advertising seems to be a cost incurred with respect to selling activities, advertising costs do not have to be capitalized and are thus currently deductible. Reg. §1.263A-1(e)(3)(iii)(A). (The cost of advertising is currently deductible even if the purpose of the advertising is to create goodwill.)

6. Section 263A applies only to the production of real or tangible property. §263A(b)(1). Tangible property, however, includes books, films, and sound recordings so all of the expenditures must be capitalized. Although research costs generally are currently deductible, the costs of researching the year six almanac have to be capitalized. The publisher's costs for the copyright, direct labor costs, and direct costs of producing the year six almanac must also be capitalized. §263A(a); Reg. §1.263A-2(a)(2)(ii)(A)(1). Thus, all of the costs will be included in the publisher's cost of goods sold when the year six almanac is sold.

7. Section 263A does not apply to freelance authors, photographers, and artists, so she does not have to capitalize her expenses and can deduct them currently. §263A(h).

8. a. All of the costs except the $80,000 expense for general business planning. Salaries of purchasing agents, payroll taxes, costs of acquiring goods for resale, and rent are all inventory costs. All of these expenditures relating to the resale of the balloons must be capitalized. Reg. §1.263A-1(e)(2), (3)(ii)(K). Costs that are not incurred in connection with the resale of the balloons, such as general business planning costs, can be deducted currently. Reg. §1.263A-1(e)(4)(iv)(B).

  b. Section 263A does not apply to wholesalers and retailers with average annual gross receipts of less than $10 million. §263A(b)(2)(B).

C. Repair and Maintenance Expenses

Reading: Reg. §§1.162-4, 1.263(a)-1

The fundamental principle of capitalization is easily stated: Expenditures that produce a benefit that does not extend beyond the year in which the expenses were incurred do not have to be capitalized, but expenses that produce a benefit that has a useful life that extends beyond the year in which the expenses were incurred must be capitalized. Applying the rule is more difficult.

One of the most perplexing problems is distinguishing between repairs and capital improvements. Suppose a business replaces the leaky roof on its office building with a new one. Is the cost of the new roof a capital expenditure because it will last for many years? Or is it a current expenditure because it restores the building to its prior operating condition?

Reg. §1.162-4 explains that repairs can be deducted currently if the repairs "neither materially add to the value of the property nor appreciably prolong its life, but keep it in an ordinarily efficient operating condition." Repairs are capital expenditures, on the other hand, if the repairs are "in the nature of replacements" that "appreciably prolong the life of the property." Id.; see also Reg. §1.263(a)-1(a), (b).

The determination of whether a particular expenditure is a deductible repair is made on a facts-and-circumstances basis. Expenditures that substantially increase the useful life of an asset, which are large in comparison to the value of the "repaired" asset, and comprise part of an overall plan of remodelling or rehabilitation, are generally treated as nondeductible capital outlays. On the other hand, expenses made to restore property damage are generally deductible. If, in a particular case, some of the factors indicate that current deduction is appropriate, but other factors indicate that capitalization is required, the outcome of the case is uncertain. The case law on this issue (and other capitalization issues) is often inconsistent.

In Midland Empire Packing Co. v. Commissioner, 14 T.C. 635 (1950), acq. 1950-2 C.B. 3, the taxpayer used the basement of its meat packing plant to store and cure meats. In the tax year at issue, oil from a newly constructed refinery began to seep through the walls of the plant basement, creating a health hazard that caused federal meat inspectors to threaten to shut down the plant. In order to avoid a plant shut-down, the taxpayer paid $5,000 to line the basement walls with concrete. The Tax Court concluded that the addition of the concrete wall was a repair, not a capital improvement, because adding the wall merely permitted the taxpayer to keep doing what it had been doing for 25 years before the oil seepage occurred.

In contrast, in Mt. Morris Drive-In Theater Co. v. Commissioner, 238 F.2d 85 (6th Cir. 1956), the taxpayer was denied a current deduction for the cost of a drainage system it installed to stop run-off to nearby land. The run-off had been caused by clearing land during construction of the taxpayer's drive-in theater. The taxpayer argued that installation of the drainage system was a repair and that the cost of the system was therefore currently deductible. However, the court concluded that the need for the drainage system was foreseeable at the time the taxpayer constructed the drive-in theater, so the cost of the drainage system had to be capitalized.

EXAMPLES

9. Determine whether each of the following expenditures incurred with respect to a business office building are currently deductible as a repair or maintenance expense.
   a. The cost of replacing a shingle
   b. The cost of replacing the roof
   c. The cost of replacing a broken window with shatterproof glass
   d. The cost of replacing all of the unbroken windows with shatterproof glass
   e. The cost of repainting the building
   f. The cost of installing aluminum siding (instead of repainting the building)

10. Pursuant to an order of a city building inspector, Syd built a fire passageway in his movie theater at a cost of $30,000. Syd had to tear out seats to build the passageway, so his business was less profitable after the expenditure than it had been before the installation of the passageway. Can the cost of installing the fire passageway be deducted currently or must it be capitalized?

EXPLANATIONS

9. a. The cost of minor repairs, such as replacement of a shingle, is currently deductible. Reg. §§1.263(a)-1, 1.162-4.
   b. The cost of major repairs, such as replacement of an entire roof, generally must be capitalized. Reg. §§1.263(a)-1, 1.162-4.
   c. The cost of a minor repair, such as replacement of a broken window, generally is currently deductible even if the repair makes the broken item better than new. Reg. §§1.263(a)-1, 1.162-4.
   d. The cost of replacing all unbroken windows with shatterproof glass is a capital improvement and must be capitalized. Reg. §§1.263(a)-1, 1.162-4.

   e. The painting simply restores the building to its previous condi-
      tion so the cost of painting the building is an ordinary cost of
      maintaining an office building. Thus, it is currently deductible
      even though it is a fairly large repair. Reg. §§1.263(a)-1,
      1.162-4.

   f. Aluminum siding improves the building — it does not simply
      restore it to its original condition — so the expense must be
      capitalized. Reg. §§1.263(a)-1, 1.162-4.

10. This is a close call, but the cost probably will have to be capital-
    ized. In Midland Empire Packing Co. v. Commissioner, 14 T.C.
    635 (1950), acq., 1950-2 C.B. 3, federal meat inspectors threat-
    ened to shut down the meat taxpayer's packing plant if the tax-
    payer did not install a concrete wall to prevent oil seepage from a
    newly constructed refinery. The taxpayer was permitted to take a
    current deduction for the $5,000 cost of installing the concrete
    wall. However, in Mt. Morris Drive-In Theatre Co. v. Commis-
    sioner, 238 F.2d 85 (6th Cir. 1956), the taxpayer had to capitalize
    the cost of a drainage system installed to stop run-off that had
    been caused by clearing land for a theater. The court concluded
    that the cost had to be capitalized because the need for the drain-
    age system was foreseeable at the time the taxpayer constructed
    the theater.

    Here it appears that Syd's theater was not built to conform
    to the fire code. If that is the case, the facts seem closer to *Mt.
    Morris Drive-In Theatre* because the need for the fire passageway
    was foreseeable at the time the theater was constructed. If, on the
    other hand, the fire code has recently been changed, necessitating
    the construction of a new fire passageway, the facts look more like
    the facts in *Midland Empire Packing Co.* The facts here also resem-
    ble *Midland Empire Packing Co.* in that construction of the pas-
    sageway was necessary to prevent the business from being shut
    down by regulators.

    However, the large cost and size of the construction here
    indicate that it may be a capital expenditure rather than an inci-
    dental repair. In addition, although Syd's profits are reduced as a
    result of replacing seats with the passageway, a court might rea-
    son that the construction increases the value of Syd's business
    because the business cannot be legally operated without the pas-
    sageway. See Trenton-New Brunswick Theaters Co. v. Commis-
    sioner, 13 T.C.M. (CCH) 550 (1954).

D. Inventory Accounting

Reading: §§446, 471, 472; Reg. §§1.446-1, 1.471-1, 1.471-2,
    1.471-3, 1.471-4, 1.472-1, 1.472-2

As we saw earlier in this chapter, Regulation §1.162-3 provides that a taxpayer may deduct the costs of incidental materials and supplies, such as paper for a copying machine, in the year they were purchased. However, a taxpayer who keeps an inventory of goods for sale must capitalize the costs of supplies and materials instead of immediately deducting them; the costs are added to the taxpayer's inventory costs and deducted when the inventory is sold.

Taxpayers must "use inventories" for tax purposes if use of inventories is necessary to clearly reflect the taxpayer's income. §471. The idea is to match income with the expense of producing that income. Reg. §1.471-1 requires a taxpayer to use inventories if (i) the taxpayer produces, purchases, or sells merchandise and (ii) the production, purchase, or sale of such merchandise is an income-producing factor. *Merchandise* is defined as property held for sale to customers. For example, in Wilkinson-Beane, Inc. v. Commissioner, 420 F.2d 352 (1st Cir. 1970), the court held that an undertaker who sold complete funeral packages at fixed prices (around 15 percent of which was attributable to the cost of the casket) had to use inventories to account for his sales of caskets because the caskets were merchandise and the sale of the caskets was an income-producing factor in the taxpayer's business.

Section 471 and Regulation §1.471-1 thus require manufacturers, wholesalers, and retailers to use inventories. Taxpayers who must use inventories are also required to use the accrual method of accounting with respect to purchases and sales. Reg. §1.446-1(c)(2)(i). (However, the taxpayer may still be able to use the cash method of accounting for other types of income or costs or for separate businesses. Reg. §1.446-1(c)(1)(iv), (d).)

Recall that §61(a)(2) provides that gross income includes "gross income derived from business." For a taxpayer who uses inventories, gross income derived from business equals gross receipts from sales less the taxpayer's *cost of goods sold*. Cost of goods sold is equal to the cost of the inventory at the beginning of the taxable year (*opening inventory*), plus the cost of goods purchased during the year (*purchases*), less the cost of the inventory remaining at the end of the year

5. Deductions for the Costs of Earning Income

(*closing inventory*). This matches the cost of the goods sold by the taxpayer with the income from the sale of those goods. Said again, as formulae, cost of goods sold and gross income from inventory sales are as follows:

$$
\begin{array}{l}
 \text{Opening inventory} \\
\underline{+ \text{ Purchases during the year}} \\
 \text{Goods available for sale}
\end{array}
$$

$$
\begin{array}{l}
 \text{Goods available for sale} \\
\underline{- \text{ Closing inventory}} \\
 \text{Cost of goods sold}
\end{array}
$$

$$
\begin{array}{l}
 \text{Gross receipts from sales} \\
\underline{- \text{ Cost of goods sold}} \\
 \text{Gross income from inventory sales}
\end{array}
$$

Opening inventory equals the value of the closing inventory from the previous year. Purchases for the year are taken into account at their cost, determined from purchase invoices. Merchandise is reflected in inventory when the taxpayer has title to the merchandise. Reg. §1.471-1. Inventory costs that are capitalized under the §263A UNICAP rules (for example, warehousing costs, selling costs, direct labor costs, and indirect labor costs allocated to production or sales activities) are also added to the purchase price of the merchandise.

In order to compute the value of closing inventory, a taxpayer must first count the number of units in the inventory at the close of the tax year. The taxpayer can either physically count the units or use "book inventories," provided that the book inventories are verified by physical inventories at reasonable intervals. Reg. §1.471-2(d). The taxpayer must then determine the cost of the units in the closing inventory. If the taxpayer's costs for inventory were constant, the taxpayer could just count the units and multiply the number of units by the constant cost. However, inventory costs fluctuate, so the taxpayer must determine the cost of the units in the closing inventory by using one of several methods.

If a taxpayer can identify its actual cost for the goods in closing inventory, the taxpayer can calculate the cost of the closing inventory on that basis. For example, a fine jewelry store with one-of-a-kind items in their inventory (for example, Tiffany's) may be able to use this method. However, taxpayers cannot typically use the specific identification method because the inventory includes too many fungible items.

Typically a taxpayer determines the cost of its closing inventory by applying either the *first-in-first-out* (FIFO) method or the *last-in-first-out* (LIFO) method. Both of these methods are fictions; they are simply conventions that are used to determine the value of the taxpayer's closing inventory. The FIFO method applies unless a taxpayer makes an election to apply LIFO. §472. A taxpayer who uses LIFO for tax purposes must also use it for financial reporting purposes. §472(c).

The FIFO method assumes that the items sold during the year were the earliest items purchased, and that the items left in closing inventory at the end of the year are the most recently purchased items. A taxpayer using FIFO may compute the value of its closing inventory using the *lower of cost or market* method to value the inventory. Reg. §1.471-2. A taxpayer who uses the lower of cost or market method would (i) first, calculate the cost of the units in the closing inventory, using FIFO, (ii) second, calculate the "market" price (generally replacement cost) of the units in closing inventory, and (iii) use the lower amount as the value of the closing inventory.

What is the effect of using the lower of cost or market method on the taxpayer's cost of goods sold and gross income? If inventory prices have risen, the lower of cost or market will be the cost, so the use of the lower of cost or market method will not have any effect on the taxpayer's cost of goods sold or gross income. On the other hand, if inventory prices have declined so that the market value of the inventory is less than its cost, using the market value reduces the closing inventory, which increases the taxpayer's cost of goods sold, and, in turn, reduces the taxpayer's gross income. In effect, allowing a taxpayer to use the lower of cost or market method, in conjunction with FIFO, permits the taxpayer to anticipate a loss on the inventory before it is sold.

The market value of the inventory is generally the replacement cost of the inventory. Reg. §1.471-4. However, the general replacement cost rule does not apply if (i) goods are defective or obsolete (in which case the goods should be valued at the price at which the goods are actually sold) or (ii) there have been offers to sell and actual sales at a price that is less than replacement cost. Reg. §§1.471-2(c), 1.471-4(b). In Thor Power Tool Co. v. Commissioner, 439 U.S. 522 (1979), the taxpayer valued its inventory using the lower of cost or market method. The taxpayer decided that it had "excess" inventory and reduced its closing inventory to "net realizable value" (in effect, scrap value), which resulted in a $900,000 write-down of the inventory. The write-down amount was calculated by management of the taxpayer, based on their business expertise; it was not based on the replacement cost of the inventory. The taxpayer kept the excess inventory on hand and did not reduce the price at which it sold the inventory. The Service disallowed the inventory write-down, arguing that the taxpayer's inventory method did not clearly reflect income under §§446(b) and 471. The taxpayer offered no objective evidence to support the write-down; in fact, the taxpayer continued to sell the inventory at its original price. However, the write-down taken by the taxpayer did conform to financial accounting principles. After noting that financial accounting rules do not control the tax treatment of inventories, the court held that the Commissioner had not abused his discretion in disallowing the write-down because the write-down appeared to be based on the subjective estimates of management of the taxpayer.

The LIFO method assumes that the items sold were the most recently purchased items, and that the items in closing inventory were the earliest items purchased. A taxpayer using LIFO is not permitted to use the lower of cost or market method; the taxpayer must use cost to determine the closing inventory. §472(b). Using LIFO in a period of rising inventory costs decreases the taxpayer's closing inventory, which increases the taxpayer's cost of goods sold, and, in turn, decreases the taxpayer's gross income. In other words, in a period of rising prices, LIFO produces more favorable tax results than FIFO. However, the vast majority of taxpayers who use inventories use FIFO because §472(c) requires that taxpayers who use LIFO for tax purposes also use LIFO for financial accounting purposes (for example, in reports to shareholders and creditors). For financial accounting purposes, taxpayers want high gross income so they frequently do not want to use LIFO if inventory costs are rising.

If a taxpayer uses LIFO in a period of rising prices, the taxpayer's closing inventory includes the oldest, least expensive units. These old, inexpensive units are often referred to as the *LIFO basket*. If the taxpayer's inventory contracts (so that the number of units in opening inventory exceeds the number of units in closing inventory), the taxpayer's cost of goods sold will include the cost of the inexpensive items in the LIFO basket that were not replaced. This decreases the taxpayer's cost of goods sold, which, in turn, increases the taxpayer's gross income. Said another way, dipping into the LIFO basket inflates the taxpayer's gross income for the year. Thus, a taxpayer who uses LIFO and does not want to inflate gross income should be sure to acquire sufficient inventory during the year to preserve the LIFO basket.

EXAMPLES

11. Is each of the following statements true or false?
    a. Taxpayers who keep inventories generally may use either the cash or accrual method of accounting.
    b. Inventory purchases are currently deductible as a cost of earning income.

12. On January 1, year two, Jack's Piano Palace had $100,000 worth of pianos in inventory. During the year, Jack purchased pianos for $400,000. On December 31, year two, Jack's Piano Palace had $30,000 of inventory left. Jack's gross receipts for year two totaled $850,000. Determine the cost of goods sold and Jack's gross profit for year two.

13. M&M Enterprises, a commodity and institutional food services company, purchases 100,000 bushels of Egyptian wheat for $200,000 in December, year one. In January, year two, M&M Enterprises purchases another 100,000 bushels of wheat for $300,000. In June, year two, M&M Enterprises sells 100,000 bushels of wheat for $350,000.
    a. Assume M&M Enterprises uses the LIFO method of inventory. Determine the amount of M&M Enterprises' cost of goods sold and gross income from sales for year two.
    b. Assume M&M Enterprises uses the FIFO method of inventory. Determine the amount of M&M Enterprises' cost of goods sold and gross income from sales for year two.
    c. Would you advise M&M Enterprises to use LIFO or FIFO?

14. a. In January of year one Products Inc. commences operations and purchases 20,000 widgets for $200,000 ($10 per widget). In March of year one Products Inc. purchases another 20,000 widgets for $300,000 ($15 per widget). In May of year one Products Inc. sells 30,000 widgets for $600,000 ($20 per widget). Developments in the second half of year one cause the value of widgets to fall. The 10,000 widgets left in inventory at the close of the year have a wholesale value of only $50,000 ($5 per widget). Assume that Products Inc. uses FIFO and does not value closing inventory at the lower of cost or market.

5. Deductions for the Costs of Earning Income

Determine the company's year one cost of goods sold and gross income from widget sales.

b. How, if at all, does your answer in part (a) change if Products Inc. uses the lower of cost or market method?

c. What effect does use of the lower of cost or market method have on the year one gross income from sales?

15. Is each of the following statements true or false?

a. The LIFO method of inventory accounting will result in higher taxable income in a period in which the cost of inventory is rising.

b. Taxpayers using either the FIFO or LIFO methods may choose to determine closing inventory using the lower of cost or market method.

c. Taxpayers who use the LIFO method for tax purposes must also use the LIFO method for financial accounting purposes such as in reports to shareholders and creditors.

16. Willie's Widget shop opened early in year one. During year one Willie bought 10,000 widgets for $100,000 ($10 per widget) and sold 5,000 widgets for $75,000. In year two Willie bought 20,000 widgets for $300,000 ($15 per widget) and sold 15,000 widgets for $300,000.

a. Determine Willie's gross income from sales in year one and year two using the FIFO method.

b. Determine Willie's gross income from sales for year one and year two using the LIFO method.

17. Tammy's Thingamajig Emporium opened for business in year one. In January of year one Tammy bought 20,000 thingamajigs for $40,000 ($2 per unit). In March of year one Tammy sold 8,000 thingamajigs for $28,000. After March, a glut in the thingamajig market caused the market value of thingamajigs to fall to $1 per unit, and Tammy sold no more thingamajigs for the rest of the year.

a. Determine Tammy's gross income from sales for year one, assuming she uses the FIFO method.

b. Determine Tammy's gross income from sales for year one, assuming she uses the LIFO method.

EXPLANATIONS

11. a. False. Reg. §1.446-1(c)(2) generally requires the use of the accrual method for taxpayers who keep inventories.

5.   Deductions for the Costs of Earning Income

   b. False. Inventory purchases constitute a nondeductible capital expenditure. The cost of inventory is deductible as an offset against sales proceeds.

12.   Cost of goods sold equals opening inventory plus inventory purchases less closing inventory.

Opening inventory	$100,000
Plus inventory purchases	+$400,000
Less closing inventory	−$ 30,000
Cost of goods sold	$470,000

Gross income from sales equals gross receipts less the cost of goods sold.

Gross receipts	$850,000
Less cost of goods sold	−$470,000
Gross income from sales	$380,000

13.   a. Under the last-in, first-out, or LIFO, method, sales are first attributed to the most recent purchases. Here, the most recent purchase of 100,000 bushels of wheat cost $300,000; M&M Enterprises is treated as having sold that wheat for $350,000. Thus, the closing inventory is the older wheat that was purchased for $200,000. M&M Enterprises' cost of goods sold is therefore $300,000 and its gross income from sales is $50,000. Represented another way:

Opening inventory	$200,000
Plus inventory purchases	+$300,000
Less closing inventory	−$200,000
Cost of goods sold	$300,000
Gross receipts	$350,000
Less cost of goods sold	−$300,000
Gross income from sales	$ 50,000

   b. Under the first-in, first-out, or FIFO, method, sales are first attributed to the earliest purchases. Here, the earliest purchase costs $200,000; M&M Enterprises is treated as having sold that wheat for $350,000. Thus, the closing inventory is the newer wheat that was purchased for $300,000. M&M Enterprises' cost of goods sold is therefore $200,000 and its gross income from sales is $150,000. Represented another way:

Opening inventory	$200,000
Plus inventory purchases	+$300,000
Less closing inventory	−$300,000
Cost of goods sold	$200,000
Gross receipts	$350,000
Less cost of goods sold	−$200,000
Gross income from sales	$150,000

c. It depends on whether M&M would prefer to have (i) higher gross income for both tax and financial accounting purposes or (ii) lower gross income for both tax and financial accounting purposes. As we saw in parts (a) and (b), where the price of inventory is rising, the taxpayer's gross income from sales is lower using LIFO because LIFO increases the cost of goods sold. However, M&M may not want to use LIFO for tax purposes because it would then have to use LIFO for financial accounting purposes. §472(c). A business may prefer to use FIFO in order to show larger gross profits to shareholders, even if it means paying higher taxes.

14. a. Cost of goods sold is determined by adding opening inventory to inventory purchases and subtracting closing inventory. Using FIFO, the earliest purchased items are the ones deemed sold, and the most recently purchased items are the ones deemed to be in the closing inventory. Here, the closing inventory includes 10,000 of the 20,000 widgets Products Inc. purchased in March of year one for $15 per widget.

The closing inventory is $150,000 (10,000 widgets at $15 cost per widget), the cost of goods sold is $350,000 and the gross income from sales is $250,000.

Opening inventory	$ 0
Plus inventory purchases	+$500,000
Less closing inventory	−$150,000
Cost of goods sold	$350,000

5. Deductions for the Costs of Earning Income

Gross receipts	$600,000
Less cost of goods sold	−$350,000
Gross income from sales	$250,000

b. As explained in part (a), the closing inventory is $150,000 (10,000 widgets at $15 cost per widget) if the taxpayer does not use the lower of cost or market method. The market value of the widgets left in closing inventory is $5 per widget, which is less than their $15 per widget cost, so here closing inventory will be determined using the $5 per widget market value.

Here, the closing inventory is $50,000 (10,000 widgets at $5 market value), the cost of goods sold is $450,000, and the gross income from sales is $150,000.

Opening inventory	$ 0
Plus inventory purchases	+$500,000
Less closing inventory	−$ 50,000
Cost of goods sold	$450,000
Gross receipts	$600,000
Less cost of goods sold	−$450,000
Gross income from sales	$150,000

c. Using the lower of cost or market method to value closing inventory reduces the taxpayer's gross income from sales by $100,000. In effect, this method allows Products Inc. to deduct the unrealized decline in the value of their closing inventory before that inventory is sold.

15. a. False. Under LIFO, the more recent purchases are included in the cost of goods sold. In a period of rising prices, recent purchases will be more expensive than prior purchases. The LIFO method will therefore produce a higher cost of goods sold deduction and lower gross income on sales.

b. False. The election to value closing inventory at the lower of cost or market is only available to taxpayers who use the FIFO method of inventory. Reg. §1.471-2.

c. True. §472(c). This is the main reason taxpayers do not use LIFO, even though using LIFO would reduce their gross income from sales in periods of rising prices.

16. a. The FIFO method assumes that the first goods acquired for resale are the first goods sold so that closing inventory consists of the most recently purchased goods.

For year one Willie's cost of goods sold equals $50,000, and his gross income from sales is $25,000.

Opening inventory	$ 0
Plus purchases	+$100,000
Minus closing inventory	−$ 50,000
Cost of goods sold	$ 50,000
Gross receipts	$ 75,000
Less cost of goods sold	−$ 50,000
Gross income from sales	$ 25,000

At the beginning of year two Willie's opening inventory is his closing inventory from year one, $50,000. The FIFO method assumes that these widgets are sold before any widgets that Willie purchased in year two. Therefore, of the 15,000 widgets sold in year two for $20 per widget, 5,000 were purchased in year one for $10 per widget and 10,000 were purchased in year two for $15 per widget. Said another way, the closing inventory at the end of year two is $150,000 (10,000 widgets at a cost of $15 per widget). The cost of goods sold in year two is $200,000 and the gross income from sales in year two is $100,000.

Opening inventory	$ 50,000
Plus purchases	+$300,000
Minus closing inventory	−$150,000
Cost of goods sold	$200,000
Gross receipts	$300,000
Less cost of goods sold	−$200,000
Gross income from sales	$100,000

b. For year one the closing inventory, cost of goods sold, and gross income from sales are the same as in part (a). The LIFO method assumes that the last goods acquired for resale are the first goods to be sold so that closing inventory is assumed to consist of the earliest purchased goods. Willie has no beginning inventory in year one and all of the goods purchased during year one were purchased at the same cost, so his closing inventory using LIFO is the same as his closing inventory using FIFO. This, in turn, means that Willie's cost of goods sold and gross income from sales for year one are also the same using LIFO.

At the beginning of year two, Willie has opening inventory of $50,000 (5,000 widgets in stock, each of which cost Willie $10 per widget). Since the LIFO method assumes that the most recently purchased goods are sold first, the widgets that Willie purchased in year two, at a cost of $15 per widget, are deemed to be sold before any of the widgets purchased in year one are deemed to be sold. Therefore, the 15,000 widgets sold in year two for $20 per widget all come from the stock purchased by Willie in year two for $15 per widget. Said another way, the closing inventory at the end of year two is $125,000 (5,000 unsold widgets that were purchased in year two at a cost of $15 per widget plus 5,000 unsold widgets that were purchased in year one at a cost of $10 per widget). The cost of goods sold in year two is $225,000 and the gross income from sales in year two is $75,000.

Opening inventory	$ 50,000
Plus purchases	+$300,000
Minus closing inventory	−$125,000
Cost of goods sold	$225,000
Gross receipts	$300,000
Less cost of goods sold	−$225,000
Gross income from sales	$ 75,000

17. a. A taxpayer using FIFO may value the inventory using either (i) cost or (ii) the lower of cost or market, provided that the same valuation method is used consistently. Reg. §§1.471-3, 1.471-4.

If Tammy uses cost in valuing inventory, then year one gross income from sales is $12,000.

Opening inventory	$ 0
Plus purchases	+$40,000
Minus closing inventory	−$24,000
Cost of goods sold	$16,000

5. Deductions for the Costs of Earning Income

Gross receipts	$28,000
Less cost of goods sold	−$16,000
Gross income from sales	$12,000

If Tammy uses the lower of cost or market method, then year one gross income from sales is zero.

Opening inventory	$ 0
Plus purchases	+$40,000
Minus closing inventory	−$12,000
Cost of goods sold	$28,000
Gross receipts	$28,000
Less cost of goods sold	−$28,000
Gross income from sales	$ 0

b. Taxpayers using LIFO must use cost; they are not permitted to use the lower of cost or market method. §472(b).

If Tammy uses the LIFO method, then gross income for year one will be the same as in part (a) where cost was used to value the closing inventory, because all of the units purchased or left in closing inventory were purchased at the same price per unit.

Opening inventory	$ 0
Plus purchases	+$40,000
Minus closing inventory	−$24,000
Cost of goods sold	$16,000
Gross receipts	$28,000
Less cost of goods sold	−$16,000
Gross income from sales	$12,000

E. Rent Payments versus Installment Purchase

If a taxpayer makes a series of payments in exchange for the use of business property, the series of payments may be characterized as either (i) an installment purchase of the business property or (ii) rental or lease payments for the property.

If the payments are characterized as an installment purchase of the business property, the purchaser of the property deducts (i) depreciation on the property and (ii) the portion of the installment payments that represents interest. §§167, 168, and 163(a). The seller of the business property includes (i) the income from the sale of the property and (ii) the portion of the installment payments that represents interest. §§1001, 453(b) and (l), and 61(a)(2) and (4).

If the payments are characterized as lease payments, the lessee deducts the lease payment made and the lessor includes the lease payment in income. §§162, 61(a)(5).

Which treatment is more favorable to the taxpayer using the property and the taxpayer providing the property? It depends on a number of factors such as the taxpayers' tax brackets and the period of time over which the property would be depreciated. In some circumstances, installment purchase treatment reduces the combined tax owed by the two taxpayers. In other circumstances, lease treatment reduces the combined tax burden. Taxpayers often label their transaction a "lease" or an "installment purchase" according to which treatment produces the lower tax burden. The Service may challenge the taxpayer's characterization on the theory that the substance, not the form of the transaction, determines the tax consequences of the transaction.

In Starr's Estate v. Commissioner, 274 F.2d 294 (9th Cir. 1959), the taxpayer took the position that it had leased a fire sprinkler system that a sprinkler company had installed in the taxpayer's plant. The "lease" agreement provided that the taxpayer would pay the lessor $1,240 a year in years one through five (for a total of $6,200) and, if the taxpayer renewed the lease, $32 a year in years six through ten. The lease provided that, if the taxpayer did not renew the lease, the lessor would remove the property from the taxpayer's plant. The lease did not say what would happen beginning in the eleventh year. The taxpayer deducted the entire $1,240 of rent paid each year as a §162 expense.

The Service took the position that the "lease" was, in fact, an installment purchase of the sprinkler system and disallowed the taxpayer's deduction for the $1,240 annual lease payments. In the Service's view, the taxpayer was required to capitalize the cost of the property, $6,200, instead of deducting each payment. The useful life of the sprinkler system was 23 years, so under this approach the taxpayer would have been entitled to an annual deduction of around $269 ($6,200 cost of the property/23-year useful life).

The Ninth Circuit Court of Appeals held that the transaction was a sale, based on several facts. First, although the lease did not transfer title to the taxpayer, the court was skeptical that the lessor would ever retrieve the system since sprinkler systems are typically made to fit a specific location and the salvage value of the system would therefore have been negligible. Second, the useful life of the property extended far beyond the original five-year term of the lease. Third, the amount of "rent" to be paid in years six through ten was nominal. (The court characterized the $32 a year payment in those years as a service charge for maintaining the system.)

The court did not, however, agree with the Commissioner that all of the $6,200 of payments had to be capitalized. The court instead concluded that a portion of the "lease" payments represented the purchase price of the system and a portion represented interest on the deferred payments. The sprinkler system typically was sold for $4,960, so the court treated that amount as the purchase price of the system and characterized the remainder of the payments, $1,240 ($6,200 less $4,960), as interest. The $4,960 deemed purchase price for the system had to be capitalized; because the system had a 23-year useful life, the annual depreciation deduction was around $216 ($4,960/23 years).

Since the annual payments were level, each of the payments included a partial payment of the $4,960 of principal owed and interest on the unpaid balance. Taking into account this amortization, the implicit interest rate was 7.93 percent and the year one interest was around $393. Thus, the taxpayer's total deductions for year one were $609 ($393 of interest plus $216 of depreciation), instead of the $1,240 amount that the taxpayer originally deducted as lease payments.

Under the taxpayer's original characterization of the transaction as a lease, the sprinkler company that installed the system would have included the lease payments in income and deducted depreciation based on the 23-year useful life of the property. If the sprinkler company had instead treated the transaction as a sale, it would have been able to deduct its costs for the system over a five-year period instead of over the longer useful life of the property. Thus, the tax benefits to Starr's Estate from characterizing the transaction as a lease were offset, at least to some extent, by a tax cost to the sprinkler company. Tax benefits to a lessee-purchaser and tax costs to a lessor-seller would generally offset each other to some extent, but in many cases they would not fully offset each other. For example, if the lessor/seller and the lessee/purchaser were in different tax brackets, the combined tax burden of the parties could be reduced by characterizing the transaction in the manner that assigns the largest possible tax deductions to the higher bracket taxpayer.

We will further develop this discussion later in this chapter when we examine the tax consequences of sale and leaseback transactions. For now, consider the following examples, which illustrate the principles discussed in this section.

EXAMPLES

18. An exclusive restaurant called Ma Grande Bouche leases a commercial refrigerator from Fanny's House of Refrigerators. The lease contract calls for rental payments of $700 per year for three years, at which time title to the refrigerator will be transferred to Ma Grande Bouche. (Assume that the useful life of the refrigerator is five years.) Will the lease be recharacterized as an installment purchase?

19. At the beginning of year one Frieda's Flowers, Inc. leases a custom-built commercial greenhouse from AgriCo. This type of greenhouse has a useful life of 10 years and costs $40,000 to purchase, so a taxpayer purchasing such a greenhouse would be entitled to take $4,000 a year of straightline depreciation on the greenhouse. The cost of maintaining the greenhouse is $1,000 per year. The lease contract calls for rental payments of $10,000 per year in years one through five with an option to renew the lease for $1,000 a year in years six through ten. Under the lease, AgriCo is responsible for maintaining the greenhouse. If Frieda's Flowers, Inc. does not exercise its option to renew the lease, AgriCo has three weeks to remove the greenhouse. The lease is silent as to what happens after the second five-year term.
    a. How much of the $10,000 of rent would Frieda's Flowers, Inc. deduct in year one if the lease is not recharacterized as an installment purchase?
    b. How much of the $10,000 of rent would Frieda's Flowers, Inc. be able to deduct in year one if the lease is recharacterized as an installment purchase?
    c. Will the lease be recharacterized as an installment purchase?

EXPLANATIONS

18. This purported lease is fairly obviously a sale in substance since title passes to the restaurant at the end of the rental period and the useful life of the refrigerator extends beyond the lease term. Ma Grande Bouche will be deemed to be making an installment pur-

chase and will not be able to deduct the "rental" payments. The restaurant will, however, be able to deduct imputed interest on the installment payment and depreciation on the refrigerator. See Oesterreich v. Commissioner, 226 F.2d 798 (9th Cir. 1955).

19. a. Frieda's Flowers, Inc. would deduct the entire $10,000 of rent as a §162 business expense.

b. The deemed purchase price for the greenhouse is $40,000 and the greenhouse has a 10-year useful life, so Frieda's Flowers could deduct $4,000 a year of straightline depreciation on the greenhouse. The flower company could also deduct interest on the unpaid balance of the purchase price. A portion of the $50,000 of payments to be made in years one through five would be characterized as interest. A greenhouse of this type usually sells for $40,000, so there is $10,000 of interest on the deferred payments. Since the annual payments were level, each of the five $10,000 payments would be deemed to include a partial payment of the $40,000 of principal owed and an interest payment on the unpaid balance. Frieda's Flowers, Inc. would take a total year one deduction of the portion of the $10,000 of interest allocable to year one plus $4,000 of depreciation instead of the $10,000 amount that Frieda's would otherwise deduct as lease payments.

c. Here title does not pass automatically to Frieda's Flowers, Inc. at the end of the rental period. In fact, the contract is silent as to what happens at the end of the rental period. However, some factors weigh in favor of recharacterizing the lease as an installment purchase: First, the entire rental cost is about the same as the purchase price plus interest. Second, the useful life of the greenhouse exceeds the initial five-year term of the lease. Third, the "rent" in years six through ten is nominal and seems to represent a service payment for maintaining the greenhouse. These facts look very similar to the facts in Starr's Estate v. Commissioner, 274 F.2d 294 (9th Cir. 1959), where the lease was recharacterized as a sale. The facts here differ from the facts in that case in one respect. In *Starr's Estate,* the court concluded that, despite the fact that the sprinkler company could remove the system if the lease were not renewed, the sprinkler company would probably not remove the sprinkler system because its salvage value was negligible. Here, it is not clear whether a used greenhouse has a negligible salvage value.

However, the greenhouse here was "custom-built," so it may have little value to another user. On balance it seems likely that the lease would be recharacterized as an installment purchase.

F.   Goodwill and Other Intangible Assets

Reading: §197; Reg. §1.167(a)-3

In the famous case, Welch v. Helvering, 290 U.S. 111 (1933), the taxpayer claimed a §162 deduction when he paid his employer's debts that had been discharged in a bankruptcy proceeding. The taxpayer paid the discharged debts to improve his business reputation so that he could continue to work in the same profession. The court held that the taxpayer could not take a §162 deduction for the amounts paid on the discharged debts. Although much of the opinion is framed in terms of the §162 "ordinary and necessary" requirement, the strongest rationale for the holding in the case is that amounts paid by the taxpayer had to be capitalized because repayment of the discharged debts produced benefits to the taxpayer that extended beyond the year in which the payments were made. In other words, the taxpayer's expenditures were for goodwill.

Before the enactment of the 1993 Tax Act, no deduction or amortization was allowed for the acquisition and maintenance of goodwill. Reg. §1.167(a)-3. One explanation for this was the difficulty in determining the useful life over which goodwill should be amortized. The cost of advertising, on the other hand, traditionally has been immediately deductible even though advertising often increases residual goodwill. See, e.g., Rev. Rul. 92-80.

The 1993 Tax Act provides that "§197 intangibles" acquired after the date of enactment can be amortized ratably over a 15-year period regardless of their actual useful lives. Section 197 intangibles include goodwill, going-concern value, know-how, information bases, governmental licenses, trademarks, covenants not to compete, and similar items. §197(d).

In general, §197 intangibles that are created by the taxpayer (rather than purchased) cannot be amortized unless they are created in connection with a transaction or series of transactions involving the acquisition of assets constituting a trade or business or a substantial portion of a trade or business. §197(c)(2), (d)(1). The rule for self-created intangibles does not apply, however to government licenses, covenants not to compete acquired in connection with the acquisition of a trade or business, or any franchise, trademark, or trade name. Id. The costs of creating a new trade name for an existing business thus could be amortized over a 15-year period. On the other hand, §197 specifically excludes from the definition of a §197 asset interests in a corporation, partnership, or trust, interests in land, certain computer software, and sports franchises. §197(e). Goodwill that is not a §197 asset, such as self-created goodwill, cannot be amortized and is nondeductible. Reg. §1.167(a)-3.

EXAMPLES

20. a. Monroe owns a travel agency. He gives a quote of $800 to his best client, Rich, for a luxury cruise. However, Monroe was looking at an outdated brochure and when he goes to book the cruise, he finds the cruise now costs $2,000. Because he values Rich's patronage, Monroe pays the $1,200 difference to avoid losing Rich as a client. How much of the $1,200 may Monroe deduct?

   b. Suppose that Monroe must capitalize the goodwill expenditure. When, if ever, will Monroe recover his expenditure?

21. Early this year, Global News Company acquired a chain of newspapers for $350 million, $70 million of which was allocable to the cost of the newspaper chain's list of current subscribers and $20 million of which was allocable to goodwill. The useful life of the subscriber list is 20 years. When, if ever, will Global News Company recover the $70 million expenditure for the subscriber list and the $20 million expenditure for goodwill?

22. Kooky Cola is seeking to expand its overall market share by expanding into lemonade. One option is to acquire Snappy, a popular brand of lemonade. Another option is to acquire Tartco, a small regional brand, and use a marketing blitz to increase customer awareness of the brand. What advice would you give Kooky Cola as to the tax consequences of these two alternatives?

EXPLANATIONS

20. a. Courts are split as to the treatment of such "goodwill" payments. The Service may argue that the expenditure is designed to purchase goodwill and that goodwill is a nondeductible

5. Deductions for the Costs of Earning Income

capital asset. Welch v. Helvering, 290 U.S. 111 (1933). On the other hand, Monroe's payment was made to retain existing goodwill rather than to purchase the goodwill of a new business. Thus, Monroe might argue, the expenditure is much like deductible advertising designed to maintain the good reputation of a business. Monroe might also argue that it is common for travel agents to make up the difference if they misquote prices. For cases supporting the deduction of specialized goodwill payments see M.L. Eakes Co. v. Commissioner, 686 F.2d 217 (4th Cir. 1982); Pepper v. Commissioner, 36 T.C. 886 (1961), acq., 1962-2 C.B. 5; Dunn & McCarthy, Inc. v. Commissioner, 139 F.2d 242 (2d Cir. 1943). Monroe's expenditures would not fall under §197 because they were not incurred in connection with the acquisition of assets constituting a trade or business.

b. Unless §197 applies, goodwill cannot be amortized because it does not have a determinable useful life. Reg. §1.167(a)-3.

21. These facts are similar to the facts in Newark Morning Ledger Co. v. United States, 113 S. Ct. 1670 (1993), in which the Supreme Court held that the purchaser of a subscription list could amortize the cost of the list over its expected useful life, which is 20 years here. However, since Global News Company acquired the newspaper chain after the enactment of §197, that section determines the timing and amount of Global News Company's deductions. The subscriber list and goodwill purchased by Global News Company are both §197 assets. §197(c) and (d)(1)(A) and (C)(ii). Global News Company will deduct the $90 million cost ratably over 15 years, or $6 million a year for 15 years.

22. All other things equal, Kooky Cola is probably better off acquiring Tartco. Advertising costs incurred to increase customer awareness of the Tartco brand would be deductible currently. On the other hand, the cost of acquiring Snappy's goodwill would be amortizable over a 15-year period under §197.

G. "Ordinary and Necessary" Expenses

1. The Scope of "Ordinary and Necessary"

Business expenses are deductible under §§162 and 212 only if they are "ordinary and necessary." The complexity and variety of business deal-

80

ings make it impossible to develop clear rules for deciding when an expenditure has met this requirement. In addition, courts are often reluctant to question the business judgment of a taxpayer. Thus, taxpayers generally are permitted to deduct business expenditures even if they appear unusual and unnecessary.

However, in some limited circumstances, the expenses will not be deductible because they are thought to be personal in nature. For example, in Gilliam v. Commissioner, 51 T.C.M. 515 (CCH) (1986), the taxpayer was denied a deduction for expenses incurred to settle lawsuits arising out of a business trip. On that trip the taxpayer, who suffered from a mental condition, had a bad reaction to a prescription drug during an airplane flight, became irrational, tried to exit the plane, and subsequently injured another passenger. The court held that, although the incident would not have occurred but for the business trip, the costs that the taxpayer incurred in connection with the altercation were not ordinary expenses of the taxpayer's trade or business (apparently because the court also thought that the altercation would not have occurred but for the taxpayer's mental condition). Although the *Gilliam* opinion frames the issue in terms of the ordinary or extraordinary nature of the expense, the issue would have been better framed as one involving the distinction between personal and business expenses (which is discussed in more detail in Chapter 6).

(For a discussion of Welch v. Helvering, 290 U.S. 111 (1933), the case typically cited for the "ordinary and necessary" standard, see the last section of this chapter.)

EXAMPLES

23. Jack flies first class to all of his business meetings at a cost of $20,000 per year. He could fly business class for only $10,000 per year. How much of his transportation cost is deductible under §162?

24. Acme Dynamite Company does business in 35 states. The company maintains a private airplane to transport top executives to meetings. Because the president's hobby is flying, the president usually pilots the plane whenever possible. The cost of operating the plane is $50,000 per year. The cost of sending the same employees by commercial airlines would be $40,000 per year. How much of the transportation cost is deductible under §162?

25. The Beverly Hills Dermatology Group, a professional corporation of physicians, owns and maintains a plane in case one of the

doctors has to fly to another city to treat a patient. The plane has not been used for this purpose, but the doctors, who are all licensed pilots, fly the plane to keep up their licenses. The cost of operating the airplane is $50,000 per year. Is the cost of operating the airplane deductible?

26. Ronald owns a chain of 10 donut shops. During the past three years the profits of the shops have declined sharply. Ronald consults a psychic to determine what to do about his reduced profits. On the advice of his psychic he pays $10,000 for 10 custom-made doormats, which he places in front of the entrance to each of his stores. The psychic tells him that the doormats will bring luck to his businesses for the rest of the year. Is the cost of the doormats deductible?

EXPLANATIONS

23. All $20,000 is deductible. If the trip itself has a good business purpose, the entire cost of transportation is deductible even though it is more luxurious than necessary. It is common, moreover, for top executives to travel first class.

24. Businesses are allowed a deduction for "reasonable and necessary" traveling expenses. Reg. §1.162-2(a). The fact that the president is getting a certain amount of personal value from operating the plane is probably irrelevant because the plane is used solely to transport employees to business meetings, that is, for business purposes. The cost of the transportation is $10,000 more than if the company used commercial airlines, which makes it seem that the entire expenditure is not "necessary." However, Acme can argue that the plane is necessary since the meetings are often spur-of-the-moment and commercial airline schedules are often inadequate. The entire $50,000 is probably deductible.

25. In this example, none of the expenditure is deductible. There does not seem to be any business reason for a local medical group to maintain a private airplane. In the event that one of the doctors had to travel to treat a patient, the doctor could fly on a commercial scheduled flight or a charter flight. The doctors, who are licensed pilots, appear to be using the plane for personal reasons, so the expense is not deductible. See, e.g., Harbor Medical Corp. v. Commissioner, 38 T.C.M. (CCH) 1144 (1979) (holding that the expense of purchasing and operating an airplane was not an

ordinary or necessary expense of the taxpayer corporation's medical practice, which was limited to one geographic area).

26. Probably not. Although courts generally do not question the business judgment of a taxpayer, purchasing magic doormats is so unusual that it probably would not be considered a deductible expenditure. Cf. Gilliam v. Commissioner, 51 T.C.M. 515 (1986). Even if Ronald incurred the expense because he genuinely believed that it would help his business, the expense will likely be nondeductible because courts tend to use an objective approach to distinguish between ordinary business expenses and personal expenses. See, e.g., Trebilcock v. Commissioner, 64 T.C. 852 (1975), acq. 1976-2 C.B. 1, aff'd, 557 F.2d 1226 (6th Cir. 1977) (in which the court denied a §162 deduction for the cost of hiring a minister to give the taxpayer and his employees spiritual guidance).

2. Reasonable Compensation

Reading: §162(a)(1) and (m); Reg. §§1.162-7, 1.162-8

Section 162(a)(1) specifically allows a taxpayer to deduct a "reasonable allowance for salaries or other compensation." On the other hand, "unreasonable" compensation paid to an employee is not deductible. Reg. §1.162-7(b)(3). The Service has generally taken the position that compensation is unreasonable and nondeductible only if the compensation arrangement between the employee and employer involves tax avoidance.

For example, a taxpayer may use a compensation arrangement to attempt to convert a nondeductible corporate dividend into deductible compensation. Corporations are generally subject to tax at the entity level. §11. If a corporation pays a dividend to its shareholders, the corporation is not allowed a deduction for the dividend paid. However, if a corporation pays salary to its employees, the corporation is allowed to deduct the salary under §162. If the shareholders of a corporation are also the employees of the corporation, the shareholder-employees may attempt to convert what would otherwise be a nondeductible dividend into deductible salary. In these circumstances, the Service will argue that the excessive compensation should be recharacterized as a dividend.

What standard is used to determine whether compensation is reasonable or unreasonable? The test is a facts-and-circumstances test that takes into account a number of factors, including: (i) the employee's qualifications; (ii) the nature of the employee's work; (iii) the employer's history of paying or not paying dividends; (iv) the compensation paid to comparable employees by comparable employers; (v) the amount the employer has paid the employee in previous years; (vi) the results of the employee's efforts; (vii) general and local economic conditions; and (viii) the profitability of the employer after the compensation has been paid. See Mayson Manufacturing Co. v. Commissioner, 178 F.2d 115 (6th Cir. 1949); Elliotts, Inc. v. Commissioner, 716 F.2d 1241 (9th Cir. 1983).

In addition, a publicly held corporation is allowed to deduct compensation paid to its most highly compensated employees only to the extent that the compensation does not exceed $1 million. §162(m). The $1 million cap does not apply to any portion of the employee's compensation that is based on commissions or the financial performance of the employer.

EXAMPLES

27. Randy is the sole shareholder and president of Randy's Place Inc., a successful country and western music hall in Branson, Missouri. Randy's Place has been in business for six years. Randy has "zeroed-out" the corporation in each of those years, by paying himself compensation in an amount equal to whatever is left after paying all of the corporation's expenses other than his own compensation. The corporation has paid no corporate tax because, after taking into account Randy's compensation, the corporation has had zero taxable income. In addition, the corporation has never paid a dividend. In year six of operations, Randy's compensation was $3.8 million. How much of that compensation will Randy's Place Inc. be able to deduct under §162?

28. Intelligence Inc., an incredibly profitable publicly traded corporation, pays its chief executive officer (C.E.O.) annual fixed compensation of $3 million a year. What advice would you give the company as to the effect of §162(m) on the company's ability to deduct the compensation?

EXPLANATIONS

27. It depends. Two facts indicate that a portion of the $3.8 million of compensation may be nondeductible "unreasonable" compensation: First, the corporation has no profits after paying Randy's

compensation. Second, the corporation has never paid a dividend. Thus, a portion of the compensation may be recharacterized as a disguised dividend, in which case the dividend amount could not be deducted by Randy's Place Inc. See Reg. §§1.162-7, 1.162-8; Elliotts Inc. v. Commissioner, 716 F.2d 1241 (9th Cir. 1983). However, we cannot conclude that a portion of the compensation would be recharacterized as a dividend without considering a number of other factors not mentioned here. For example, if the presidents of other comparable music halls are typically paid compensation in the neighborhood of $3.8 million, that fact would weigh against recharacterization of the compensation. See Mayson Manufacturing Co. v. Commissioner, 178 F.2d 115 (6th Cir. 1949).

The $1 million salary limitation of §162(m) does not apply because Randy's Place Inc. is not a publicly held corporation.

28. I would advise Intelligence, Inc. to pay the C.E.O. a fixed base salary of $1 million and performance-based salary that would make up the rest of the salary usually paid to the C.E.O. If Intelligence, Inc. pays fixed salary in excess of $1 million, the compensation in excess of $1 million is nondeductible under §162(m). However, if the company pays the C.E.O. a fixed salary of $1 million or less, plus performance-based compensation (that is, compensation based on the financial fortunes of the company), §162(m) will not disallow the compensation in excess of $1 million. Using performance-based compensation still enables the company to pay the C.E.O. something on the order of the usual amount of salary because Intelligence, Inc. is very profitable.

3.   Costs Associated with Illegal or Unethical Activities

Reading: §162(c), (f), and (g)

Income obtained illegally is taxable (even if the taxpayer-criminal is required to return the funds to the victim). James v. United States, 366 U.S. 213 (1961). A basic principle of our tax system is that net rather than gross income is taxed. Since the income from illegal or unethical activities is taxable, are the costs of earning that income deductible?

Prior to the passage of the Tax Reform Act of 1969, courts used a frustration-of-public-policy test to determine whether the expenses of an illegal activity were deductible. Under this test, courts allowed a deduction for the expenses of an illegal activity unless allowing the deduction would frustrate a clearly defined state or national public policy, "evidenced by some governmental declaration." The scope of this frustration-of-public-policy test was uncertain and the test fostered a great deal of litigation. For example, in Tank Truck Rentals v. Commissioner, 356 U.S. 30 (1958), the court denied the taxpayer a deduction for the fines it paid for intentionally violating state law that set maximum weight limits for trucks operating in the state. The court concluded that the fines were intended to discourage the behavior in which the taxpayer engaged and that allowing the taxpayer to deduct the fines would dilute their intended effect and frustrate public policy. However, in Commissioner v. Tellier, 383 U.S. 687 (1966), the court allowed a securities dealer to deduct the legal fees he incurred in unsuccessfully defending himself against charges of securities and mail fraud. The court concluded that allowing the deduction would not frustrate public policy severely enough to warrant disallowance.

In 1969 Congress attempted to clarify the law by adding language to §162 that explicitly provides that the following expenses cannot be deducted: most bribes and kickbacks, fines and penalties; and the punitive damages portion of criminal antitrust violations. §162(c), (f), (g). The legislative history of these provisions indicates that they were intended to be all-inclusive and preempt the case law public policy doctrine. S. Rep. No. 91-552, 91st Cong., 1st Sess. 274 (1969), 1969-3 C.B. 423, 597. Thus, expenses of illegal activities are deductible unless §162 explicitly provides that the expenses are nondeductible. (Section 280E provides, however, that expenses incurred in drug trafficking are nondeductible.)

EXAMPLES

29. Tom runs an illegal bookie operation for an organized crime ring. Last year he spent $14,500 on rent and utilities for his gambling operation and an additional $20,000 to hire a thug to break the legs of customers who did not pay their gambling debts. Are these expenses deductible?

30. The delivery trucks of Pizza Shack often have to park illegally to deliver their pizza on time. As a consequence, Pizza Shack pays approximately $7,000 per year in parking fines. Is this expense deductible?

31. Bill ran a moonshining business before the authorities caught up with him. Is he allowed to deduct the following expenses?

5. Deductions for the Costs of Earning Income

   a. The cost of the corn and bottles used in making the moonshine
   b. Bribes paid to local police to let him run his moonshine operation
   c. Fees paid to a local defense attorney who unsuccessfully defended him on the moonshining charges

EXPLANATIONS

29. All $34,500 of Tom's expenses probably are deductible since they do not fall into any of the categories specifically disallowed by §162.

    It is true that the government has repeatedly declared "war" against organized crime, most recently with the enactment of RICO. Hiring a thug to maim people is a very serious crime. For this reason, Tom's deductions probably would have failed the frustration-of-public-policy-test. The Tax Reform Act of 1969, however, has essentially replaced this test with a specific list of nondeductible expenditures.

30. Section 162(f) specifically disallows deductions for fines or similar penalties paid to the government for the violation of *any* law. Thus, it appears that Pizza Shack cannot deduct any fines paid.

31. a. The costs of the glass bottles and corn should be allowed as an ordinary cost of moonshining since they are not disallowed by §162.
    b. Bribes to a government official are nondeductible under §162(c).
    c. Business-related costs of defending oneself against criminal charges are deductible, so Bill is allowed to deduct his legal expenses. The fact that Bill was convicted is irrelevant. Commissioner v. Tellier, 383 U.S. 687 (1966).

H. Depreciation and the Accelerated Cost Recovery System

Reading: §§167, 168, 179, 1016, 1245, 1250

The cost of a business asset with a useful life greater than one taxable year cannot be immediately deducted, but must be capitalized. If the asset declines in value over time, the taxpayer will be entitled to recover the cost of the asset (less the salvage value of the asset when it can no longer be used in the business) by taking depreciation deductions in the years in which the asset is expected to be used in the business. In order to determine a taxpayer's depreciation deductions for an asset, we must determine (i) the useful life of the asset, (ii) the salvage value of the asset, and (iii) the method for allocating the cost of the asset (less the salvage value of the asset) over its useful life.

To illustrate the basic principles (but not the actual rules in §168), assume that a taxpayer who owns a flower delivery service buys a delivery van for $21,000. The taxpayer expects to use the van in her business for five years, then sell it for its salvage value of $1,000. One way to determine the taxpayer's annual depreciation deductions would be to use the *straightline method*. Under this method, we would allocate the $20,000 cost (net of the $1,000 salvage value) ratably over the five years in which the taxpayer expects to use the van in her business. The taxpayer would then deduct $4,000 of depreciation in each of the five years. The depreciation deductions, which represent recovery of the cost of the van, would reduce her basis in the van so that at the end of the five years her adjusted basis would be $1,000. If she sold the van for $1,000, she would have no gain or loss on the sale of the van and would have recovered her entire $21,000 cost of the van (through $20,000 of depreciation and $1,000 of basis, which permitted her to receive $1,000 for the van tax-free). Although this example illustrates the basic concept of depreciation, it does not illustrate the actual §168 depreciation rules that apply to tangible business or investment property. We now turn to those rules.

Section 167(a) provides generally that a taxpayer is allowed to take depreciation deductions for business or investment property, provided that the property has a limited useful life. Depreciation on intangible assets is determined under §167. Depreciation on tangible business or investment property is determined under §168. §§167(b) and 168(a). The §168 system of depreciation, enacted in 1981, is generally referred to as the *accelerated cost recovery system* (ACRS). (Since the rules were substantially modified in 1986, the post-1985 rules are sometimes more specifically referred to as the *modified accelerated cost recovery system* (MACRS).) ACRS accelerates the taxpayer's depreciation deductions in three ways: (i) it uses recovery periods that are substantially shorter than the actual useful lives of the property; (ii) it allows the use of accelerated depreciation methods; and (iii) it assumes that the salvage value of the property is zero, permitting deduction of the entire cost of the property. §168(b), (c), and (e).

Under §168, a taxpayer's annual depreciation deductions are determined using (i) the *applicable depreciation method,* (ii) the *applicable recovery period,* and (iii) the *applicable convention.* §168(a)(1), (2), (3).

The *applicable recovery period* for tangible property is determined under §168(c) and (e). The recovery periods are generally based upon the class life for the property determined by the Secretary of the Treasury. The recovery period specified in §168(c) and (e) for an asset is often shorter than the class life of the asset. For example, property with a nine-year class life has a five-year recovery period.

Section 168(e)(3) gives the classification for certain types of property. For example, it provides that a car or light general purpose truck is "5-year property." §168(e)(3)(B)(i). Section 168(c), in turn, provides that the recovery period for five-year property is five years. Section 168(c) also provides that the recovery period for residential real property is 27.5 years and the recovery period for nonresidential real property is 39 years. If a taxpayer purchases a business asset that is not real property and is not one of the types of assets listed in §168(e)(3), the recovery period of the property is determined under §168(e)(1), based on the class life of the asset as determined by the Secretary of the Treasury.

The *applicable convention* is determined under §168(d). This section determines the date on which the depreciable property is deemed to have been placed in service by the taxpayer. (The date on which the property is placed in service, not the date on which the taxpayer acquires the property, is used to determine when the depreciation deductions begin.) If the asset is not real property, a "half-year convention" applies so the asset is deemed to have been placed in service on the date that is halfway through the year. §168(d)(1) and (4)(A). However, this convention creates some potential for abuse because a crafty taxpayer could place property in service at the end of the year and still take half a year's depreciation. To discourage this type of abuse, a midquarter convention applies (instead of the half-year convention) if a disproportionate amount of depreciable property is placed in service in the last three months of the year. §168(d)(3). If the midquarter convention applies, the property is deemed to have been placed in service on the date that is halfway through the quarter in which the property is actually placed in service. §168(d)(4)(C). A midmonth convention applies to depreciable real property, so real property is deemed to have been placed in service on the date that is halfway through the month in which the property is actually placed in service. §168(d)(2) and (4)(B).

The *applicable depreciation method* is determined under §168(b). The simplest method is the *straightline method*. As we saw in the illustration at the beginning of this section, straightline depreciation allocates the total cost of the asset ratably to each year of the useful life of the property. For example, if the useful life of an asset were five years, 20 percent of the cost could be deducted each year. A taxpayer must use the straightline method to depreciate real property and may elect to use the straightline method to depreciate other types of property. §168(b)(3), (5). If the property is not real property and the taxpayer does not elect to use the straightline method, one of two accelerated depreciation methods will apply: If the property is 15-year property or 20-year property, the *150 percent declining balance method* will apply; if the property is any other type of property, the *200 percent declining balance method* (also known as the *double declining balance method*) will apply (unless the taxpayer elects to apply the 150 percent declining balance method, under §168(b)(2)(C)). §168(b)(1), (2).

Under a *declining balance* depreciation method, the *percentage* deduction that would be allowed for the property under the straightline method is calculated and multiplied by the specified percentage, either 150 percent or 200 percent. This amount of depreciation is then subtracted from the basis of the depreciable property. For example, if a taxpayer places in service five-year property, with a five-year recovery period, the taxpayer would be allowed to deduct 20 percent ($\frac{1}{5}$) of the cost of the property each year (disregarding the conventions) under the straightline method, so the taxpayer would be allowed to deduct 40 percent of the cost of the property under the 200 percent declining balance method. (However, we would then have to apply the appropriate convention to determine the taxpayer's actual year one depreciation deduction.) The taxpayer's basis in the property is then reduced by the amount of depreciation taken in year one, and the taxpayer's year two depreciation deduction equals 40 percent (200 percent of the 20 percent straightline percentage) of that adjusted basis.

If we kept deducting 40 percent of an ever-decreasing adjusted basis, we would never fully depreciate the asset, so §168 provides that we switch over to straightline deductions in the first year in which the straightline deduction is more than the deduction computed using the declining balance method. However, in this context, the straightline deduction in a given year is calculated based on (i) the adjusted basis of the property in that year and (ii) the remaining useful life of the property. (Students often make the mistake of assuming that the straightline amount in this context is the straightline deduction on the original basis determined in the year in which the property is placed in service.)

To illustrate the §168 rules, suppose that Tom pays $20,000 for a delivery van that he will use in his business. He places the van in service in September of year one. The van is five-year property and has a five-year recovery period. §168(c), (e). Under the straightline method, the depreciation deduction would be 20 percent ($\frac{1}{5}$) each year for five years. Under the double or 200 percent declining balance method, the percentage deduction would be 200 percent of 20 percent, or 40 percent, of the $20,000 cost of the van, so the deduction would be $8,000. However, the half-year convention applies to five-year property, so Tom's year one depreciation deduction is $4,000. This reduces Tom's adjusted basis in the van to $16,000.

In year two Tom's double declining balance depreciation deduction equals 40 percent of the $16,000 adjusted basis, or $6,400. Straightline deductions on a cost of $16,000 over a recovery period of 4.5 years (the remaining useful life of the property) would be $3,556, which is less than the $6,400 double declining balance deduction, so Tom deducts $6,400. This reduces Tom's adjusted basis to $9,600.

In year three Tom's double declining balance depreciation deduction equals 40 percent of $9,600, or $3,840. Straightline deductions on a cost of $9,600 over a recovery period of 3.5 years (the remaining useful life of the property) would be $2,743, which is less than the $3,840 double declining balance deduction, so Tom deducts $3,840. This reduces Tom's adjusted basis to $5,760.

In year four Tom's double declining balance depreciation deduction equals 40 percent of $5,760, or $2,304. Straightline deductions on a cost of $5,760 over a recovery period of 2.5 years (the remaining useful life of the property) would be $2,304, which equals Tom's double declining balance deduction, so Tom deducts $2,304. This reduces Tom's adjusted basis to $3,456.

In year five Tom's double declining balance depreciation deduction equals 40 percent of $3,456, or $1,382. Straightline deductions on a cost of $3,456 over a recovery period of 1.5 years (the remaining useful life of the property) would be $2,304, which exceeds Tom's double declining balance deduction, so Tom deducts $2,304. This reduces Tom's adjusted basis to $1,152. Tom will also use the straight-line method to compute his depreciation deduction in year six. He will deduct the remaining $1,152 of adjusted basis in that year. He will then have a zero basis in the property.

Which depreciation method most accurately measures a taxpayer's income? The most accurate method is neither the straightline nor the accelerated method; instead, the most accurate method is the *economic depreciation method.* Under this method the taxpayer would take an annual depreciation deduction equal to the decline, during that year, of the value of the property. How would we determine the decline in the value of the property? In some cases the decline in value could be determined from market transactions, or books or indexes that reflect such transactions. For example, the prices at which used cars sell are compiled and published monthly. We might give a taxpayer a depreciation deduction for a car used in business equal to the decline in the amount for which she could sell the car.

In other cases the decline in value can be determined by discounting expected income streams. To see how this latter approach may be used to determine depreciation, consider the following example: Assume that a taxpayer bought a piece of business equipment for $4,975. The property is expected to produce $2,000 of income a year for three years, and no income thereafter. A $4,975 investment invested at a rate of return of about 10 percent would yield $2,000 a year for three years. If we use this rate to discount to present value the three $2,000 income streams, the sum of the present values must equal $4,975. We can determine the loss in the value of the property in each of the three years by comparing the sum of the present values of the future income streams (i) at the beginning of the year and (ii) at the end of the year, using the 10 percent rate to compute the present values.

Continuing with our example, at the beginning of year one the sum of the present values of the income streams equals $4,975, which is the sum of (i) the $1,818 present value of the $2,000 income stream due in year one,[1] (ii) the $1,653 present value of the $2,000 income stream due in year two,[2] and (iii) the $1,504 present value of the $2,000 income stream due in year three.[3] At the end of year one, the

---

1. Recall from Chapter 1 that the formula for computing present value is:

$$PV = \frac{FV}{(1 + r)^n}$$

Here, $\$1,818 = \$2,000/(1.1)^1$.
2. $\$1,653 = \$2,000/(1.1)^2$.
3. $\$1,504 = \$2,000/(1.1)^3$.

sum of the present values of the income streams equals $3,471, which is the sum of (i) the $1,818 present value of the $2,000 income stream due in year two (that is, one year later) and (ii) the $1,653 present value of the $2,000 income stream due in year three (that is, two years later). The decline in the value of the property in year one thus is $1,504 ($4,975 less $3,471).

The sum of the present values of the income streams at the beginning of year two is $3,471 (as computed in the last paragraph). The present value of the $2,000 income stream due in year three (one year later) is $1,818. The decline in the value of the property in year two thus is $1,653 ($3,471 less $1,818).

At the beginning of year three the present value of the year three income stream is $1,818 (as computed in the last paragraph). The present value at the end of year three is zero, so the decline in the value of the property in year three is $1,818 ($1,818 less zero).

To summarize, the taxpayer in our example would take depreciation deductions of (i) $1,504 in year one, (ii) $1,653 in year two, and (iii) $1,818 in year three. Note that, using the economic method to determine the depreciation for this piece of business equipment, the taxpayer's depreciation deductions are *back-loaded, starting out low and increasing over time*. In fact, economic depreciation will always produce back-loaded depreciation deductions for investments that produce a level stream of income. Recall that straightline deductions are level over time and so-called accelerated method depreciation deductions are front-loaded, starting out high and decreasing over time: For assets that produce a level stream of income, both of those methods overstate depreciation deductions and understate income in the early years of use of the property and have the opposite effect in the later years of the use of the property.

So why do we not require taxpayers to use the economic method to compute depreciation deductions? One reason is that it may be very difficult to estimate the income streams that the asset would produce; if we cannot estimate the income streams, we cannot determine the annual decline in the sum of the present values of the income streams. Even where a market in used equipment exists, valuation may be difficult. This is true in part because businesses may disproportionately sell badly manufactured equipment. If buyers know or suspect this, the used equipment market may undervalue superficially similar equipment not offered for sale. To return to an earlier example, car owners may systematically unload their "lemons." If this is true, and car buyers know this, the price of a used car is to some extent the price of a "used lemon." Cars not offered for sale may be expected to perform better, and to decline in value in a different fashion.

Another reason is that we may want to encourage investment in business assets as a matter of fiscal policy. Allowing taxpayers to use accelerated methods provides an incentive to invest in business assets.

In some limited circumstances, depreciation is computed by reference to the predicted income stream from the property (for example, a motion picture). However, this method is beyond the scope of this book.

Section 168(g) also provides an alternate depreciation system for the types of property specified in §168(g)(1). Property subject to this alternate system has a longer recovery period and is depreciated using the straightline method. §168(g)(2).

As property is depreciated or amortized, its adjusted basis is reduced by the amount of the deductions taken. §1016(a)(2). This increases the gain realized by the taxpayer when the property is sold. Under §1231, gain from the sale of a depreciable asset may be capital gain. §1231(a)(3). However, depreciation deductions are ordinary deductions. Therefore, the portion of any gain on the sale of depreciable property that is attributable to having taken depreciation deductions is recharacterized as ordinary gain under the *depreciation recapture* rules of §1245. For example, if property acquired for $1,000 is fully depreciated, then sold for $1,200, the taxpayer would realize $1,200 of gain on the sale, $1,000 of which would be ordinary gain and $200 of which would be capital gain.

For real property, depreciation is recaptured only to the extent that the depreciation taken is greater than straightline. §1250. This seldom occurs since straightline depreciation is required for almost all real property.

Section 179 permits a taxpayer to elect to deduct up to $17,500 of the cost of "section 179 property" in the year in which the property is placed in service. If the taxpayer places more than $200,000 of "section 179 property" in service during the year, the $17,500 cap is reduced a dollar for each dollar of property in excess of the $200,000 limit. §179(b)(2). In addition, the amount deducted under §179 cannot exceed the taxable income from the taxpayer's business in the year in which the property is placed in service. §179(b)(3)(A). (Any excess deduction is carried over to the next year. §179(b)(3)(B).) *Section 179 property* is defined generally as depreciable tangible personal property. §§179(d)(1), 1245(a)(3). Section 179 only applies if the taxpayer elects to apply it. Making the election reduces the taxpayer's depreciable basis in the property by the amount deducted under §179.

As noted earlier, depreciation deductions also reduce the taxpayer's basis in the depreciable property. §1016(a)(2). The taxpayer's basis is reduced by the amount of depreciation allowed or allowable, so the basis of depreciable property is reduced even if the taxpayer does not take the depreciation deductions permitted under §§167 and 168. The taxpayer's original depreciable basis of property is generally determined under §1012, which provides that the basis is the cost of the property. As we saw earlier, a taxpayer's basis includes the portion of the cost financed with debt. If the taxpayer improves the property, the cost of the improvements increases the taxpayer's basis. §1016(a)(1). There are several exceptions to the general cost basis rule: First, the basis of property acquired by bequest is the fair market value of the property. §1014. Second, the basis of property acquired by gift is the donor's basis or, in some cases, the value of the property at time of the gift. §1015. Third, the basis of property received in a nonrecognition transaction (for example, a transaction subject to §1031) is a substituted basis (potentially with some adjustments).

EXAMPLES

32. A depreciation deduction may be taken for which, if any, of the following assets?
    a. A copyright
    b. An office building
    c. Land on which an office building sits
    d. A valuable original painting placed in the office building lobby
    e. An owner-occupied residence

33. Farmer John bought a tractor for $5,000. He plans to use the tractor for 11 years and then sell it as scrap metal, figuring he will receive about $300 for it. After 11 years, Farmer John scraps the tractor for $400. What is the salvage value of the tractor for purposes of determining Farmer John's depreciation deductions?

34. Is each of the following statements true or false?
    a. Section 168(c) and (e) establish six different recovery periods for tangible personal property and two recovery periods for tangible real property.
    b. The recovery period for an asset generally is based upon the class life for the asset as determined by the Secretary of the Treasury.

c. The recovery period for an asset is frequently shorter than the class life of the asset.

35. State the applicable recovery period for the following types of property.
   a. Residential rental real property
   b. Nonresidential real property
   c. An automobile or light truck

36. Which depreciation method would a taxpayer use to depreciate the following types of property?
   a. Residential or nonresidential real property
   b. An automobile or light truck

37. On December 20, year one, Joan pays $10,000 for an asset that she will use in her business. She places the asset in service on May 5, year two. The asset has a five-year recovery period.
   a. What amount of depreciation will Joan deduct in year one?
   b. What amount of depreciation will Joan deduct in year two?
   c. What amount of depreciation will Joan deduct in years three through seven?
   d. What amount of depreciation would Joan deduct in years two through seven if she elected to use the 150 percent declining balance method instead of the double declining balance method?
   e. What amount of depreciation would Joan deduct in years two through seven if she elected to use the straightline method instead of the double declining balance method?

38. a. In year one Tad buys $195,000 of tangible personal property and places it in service in his business. May Tad elect to expense, rather than depreciate, the first $17,500 of the cost of the property?
   b. How, if at all, would your answer in part (a) change if the property were real property?
   c. How, if at all, would your answer in part (a) change if the cost of the property were $205,000?

39. Assume that patents are granted for 17 years.
   a. Invent Company spends $100,000 to develop a medical patent. May Invent Company depreciate its patent?
   b. Progress Company spends $100,000 to purchase a new patent. What recovery period and depreciation method will Progress Company use to depreciate the patent?

40. In year one Paddy's Pork Rinds Company buys and places in service equipment that costs $20,000. Using the straightline method, the company deducts $1,000 in year one (because of the half-year convention) and $2,000 per year in years two and three. In year four Paddy's Pork Rinds does not take a depreciation deduction because it wants to show a high earnings report to Petunia's Pork Products, which may acquire Paddy's. What is the equipment's adjusted basis at the end of year four?

41. a. Early in year one, Out Damn Spot Company, a laundry business, bought a dry cleaning machine for $10,000. In years one and two the company took total depreciation deductions on the machine of $3,000. At the end of the second year the company sold the machine for $9,000. What are the tax consequences of the sale of the machine?

   b. What are the tax consequences if the company sells the machine for $11,000?

42. a. On January 1, year one, Chubby Candy Company bought and placed in service an office building, at a cost of $936,000. What is the building's basis at the end of year two?

   b. How, if at all, would your answer in part (a) change if Chubby Candy Company placed the property in service on January 1 of year two?

43. Jim, who owns and runs a fine shoe boutique, is an antiques expert. At a yard sale he buys an antique chair worth $10,000 for only $1,000. Jim places the chair in his store. What is Jim's basis in the chair?

44. Carol wishes to purchase Blackacre for use in her business. To pay the $50,000 purchase price, she uses $10,000 of her savings and borrows $40,000 from a bank. What is Carol's basis in Blackacre?

45. Is each of the following statements true or false?
   a. The cost of making improvements in property increases the basis of the property.
   b. The cost of making incidental repairs on property increases the basis of the property.

46. Amy purchases a machine for $100,000 and places it in service in her business at the beginning of year one. Assume that, in year one, Amy takes a $10,000 depreciation deduction for the machine. The actual value of the machine, however, increases by $5,000 during that year so at the end of the year the machine has

a fair market value of $105,000. If Amy sold the machine for $105,000, what would be the tax consequences of the sale? (Disregard the §168(d) applicable convention to simplify the answer.)

47. Is the §168 allowance for depreciation during the first few years of an item's useful life generally less or more than the actual decline in value of the item?

48. Assuming one of the goals of the tax laws is to accurately measure income:
    a. State the reasoning behind the allowance of deductions for depreciation.
    b. Explain the method of determining depreciation that conforms with this goal and state why this method is generally not used.

49. Under a cash-flow consumption tax, individuals would be taxed only on their personal (as opposed to business) expenditures. What depreciation schedule would be consistent with a cash-flow consumption tax?

EXPLANATIONS

32. a. A copyright is an intangible wasting asset and may be depreciated under §167.
    b. An office building is depreciable under §168.
    c. Land is a non-wasting asset and may not be depreciated.
    d. Valuable original artwork would not appear to have a limited useful life and so would not be depreciable.
    e. Only assets used in a trade or business or held for the production of income are depreciable. An owner-occupied residence is treated as an asset that does not produce income and is therefore not depreciable.

33. For purposes of determining depreciation deductions, salvage value is always treated as zero, regardless of the depreciation method used. As this example illustrates, this rule is favorable to the taxpayer. See §168(b)(4).

34. a. True. The "general" rules of §168(c) and (e) establish recovery periods of 3, 5, 7, 10, 15, and 20 years for tangible personal property and 27.5 and 39 years for real property.
    b. True.
    c. True. The recovery periods are *based upon*, but not *equal to*, the class life periods. For example, five-year recovery property is generally defined as property with a class life midpoint of more

than four years and less than ten years. Seven-year property is defined as property with a class life midpoint of more than nine years but less than 16 years. §168(e)(1).

35. a. 27.5 years. §168(c).
    b. 39 years. §168(c).
    c. Five years. §168(c) and (e). The recovery period for automobiles and light trucks is specifically stated in §168(e)(3)(B)(i).

36. a. The straightline method. §168(b)(3).
    b. The double declining balance method, switching to straight-line in the first year in which the straightline deduction for the year exceeds the double declining balance deduction. The property is five-year property. §168(c) and (e)(3)(B)(i). A taxpayer could elect to apply the straightline or 150 percent declining balance method to depreciate the property. §168(b)(2)(C), (3)(D), and (5). If the taxpayer did not elect to apply either of those methods, the taxpayer would use the double declining balance method to calculate the depreciation deductions on the property. §168(b)(1).

37. a. Depreciation does not begin until an asset is placed in service. Thus, Joan will receive no depreciation deduction in year one.
    b. Joan will be allowed to deduct depreciation in year two because the property is placed in service in that year. The applicable recovery period is five years. The property is not real estate and she did not place a disproportionate amount of depreciable property in service during the last three months of year two, so the midmonth and midquarter conventions do not apply. §168(d)(2) and (3). Thus, the applicable convention is the half-year convention, so Joan will be deemed to have placed the property in service halfway through year two. §168(d)(1) and (4)(A). Joan will therefore receive one-half year's depreciation in year two. The other half-year's depreciation is tacked on to the end of the recovery period.

    The applicable depreciation method is the double declining balance unless Joan elects to apply either the straightline or 150 percent declining balance method. §168(b)(1). Applying the double declining balance method and the half-year convention, Joan's year two depreciation deduction equals $2,000. The straightline percentage on five-year property would be 20 percent and 200 percent of that percentage is 40 percent. The double declining deduction thus is $4,000 (40 percent of Joan's

$10,000 basis in the property). However, after applying the half-year convention, Joan's deduction is $2,000 (half of the $4,000 double declining balance deduction). This depreciation deduction reduces Joan's basis in the property to $8,000.

c. In year three Joan's double declining balance depreciation deduction equals 40 percent of the $8,000 adjusted basis, or $3,200. The straightline deduction on a cost of $8,000 over a recovery period of 4.5 years (the remaining useful life of the property) would be $1,778, which is less than the $3,200 double declining balance deduction, so Joan deducts $3,200. This reduces Joan's adjusted basis to $4,800.

In year four Joan's double declining balance depreciation deduction equals 40 percent of $4,800, or $1,920. The straightline deduction on a cost of $4,800 over a recovery period of 3.5 years (the remaining useful life of the property) would be $1,371, which is less than the $1,920 double declining balance deduction, so Joan deducts $1,920. This reduces Joan's adjusted basis to $2,880.

In year five Joan's double declining balance depreciation deduction equals 40 percent of $2,880, or $1,152. The straightline deduction on a cost of $2,880 over a recovery period of 2.5 years (the remaining useful life of the property) would be $1,152, which equals Joan's double declining balance deduction, so Joan deducts $1,152. This reduces Joan's adjusted basis to $1,728.

In year six Joan's double declining balance depreciation deduction equals 40 percent of $1,728, or $691. The straightline deduction on a cost of $1,728 over a recovery period of 1.5 years (the remaining useful life of the property) would be $1,152, which exceeds Joan's double declining balance deduction, so Joan deducts $1,152. This reduces Joan's adjusted basis to $576. Joan will also use the straightline method to compute her depreciation deduction in year seven. She will deduct the remaining $576 of adjusted basis in that year. She will then have a zero basis in the property.

d. The straightline percentage for five-year property would be 20 percent, and 150 percent of that percentage is 30 percent. The depreciation would be calculated using the 150 percent declining balance method until the year in which the deduction using the straightline method exceeds the 150 percent declining balance deduction. However, because of the half-year convention,

Joan's deduction in year two, the year in which the property is placed in service, is half of the amount computed using the 150 percent declining balance method. Applying the 150 percent declining balance method and the half-year convention, Joan's depreciation deductions are as follows:

Year	Basis	150 percent method	S.L. method	Depreciation
2	$10,000	$1,500	$1,000	$1,500
3	8,500	2,550	1,889	2,550
4	5,950	1,785	1,700	1,785
5	4,165	1,250	1,666	1,666
6	2,499	750	1,666	1,666
7	833	250	833	833

e. The straightline percentage for five-year property would be 20 percent. The cost of the property is $10,000, so the annual straightline deduction equals $2,000 a year. However, the half-year convention applies in year two, the year in which Joan places the property in service, so the deduction for that year is $1,000. (On the other end of the recovery period, Joan also deducts $1,000 in year seven.) Applying the straightline method and the half-year convention, Joan's depreciation deductions are as follows:

Year	Basis	S.L. method depreciation
2	$10,000	$1,000
3	9,000	2,000
4	7,000	2,000
5	5,000	2,000
6	3,000	2,000
7	1,000	1,000

38. a. Tad may elect to expense $17,500 of the cost of the property under §179. Tangible personal property is §179 property. §§179(d) and 1245(a)(3).

b. Tad may not make a §179 election with respect to this property because real property is not §179 property. §§179(d) and 1245(a)(3).

c. The option to expense the first $17,500 of §179 property is phased-out, on a dollar-for-dollar basis, as the amount of §179 property placed in service during the year rises above $200,000. §179(b)(2). Here, the amount of §179 property in excess of $200,000 is $5,000. Thus, a taxpayer who places in service $205,000 of §179 property during the year and makes a §179 election may expense $12,500 ($17,500 less $5,000) of the cost of such property. The remaining cost of the property must be capitalized and depreciated.

39. a. Yes. Patents have a limited useful life and are therefore subject to depreciation.

b. The recovery period is not clear, based on the facts given. Intangible assets are not subject to the detailed statutory rules that govern the depreciation of tangible assets. The fact that a patent has a 17-year life might establish a *prima facie* case for a 17-year recovery period. However, the taxpayer might be able to establish a shorter recovery period if it provides evidence that the useful life of a particular patent is likely to be less than 17 years.

Progress Company must use the straightline depreciation method. Section 167 provides taxpayers with a "reasonable" allowance for depreciation. Section 168 provides specific depreciation methods for tangible property, including accelerated declining balance methods for some types of property. There is no authority to use any form of accelerated depreciation for intangible assets, so the patent must be depreciated using the straightline method.

40. The basis is reduced by *allowable* depreciation deductions, even if the deductions are not actually taken. §1016(a). Since Paddy's Pork Rinds is allowed to take a $2,000 depreciation deduction in year four, the equipment's basis must be reduced by that amount. See §1016(a)(2). Therefore, the basis at the end of year four is $13,000, which is the $20,000 cost less allowed or allowable depreciation of $7,000 ($1,000 depreciation in year one and $6,000 of depreciation in years two through four). (Note that Paddy may be violating securities law by misreporting its depreciation on its financial reports.)

41. a. The company's adjusted basis in the machine is $7,000 ($10,000 cost less $3,000 depreciation), therefore, the gain realized on the sale is $2,000 ($9,000 amount realized less $7,000 basis). Gain on the sale of depreciable business assets is often capital. §1231. However, the §1245 depreciation recapture rule states that gain on the sale of depreciable assets is

ordinary income to the extent of the prior depreciation deductions taken with respect to the property. §1245(a)(1), (2)(A). This rule makes sense because depreciation deductions offset ordinary income, not capital gain, and are based on an estimate of the asset's decrease in value. Any gain on the sale of the asset shows that the depreciation was overestimated. By including the gain in ordinary income, the government is, in effect, recovering the excess ordinary deductions taken in the earlier years. §1245. The $2,000 of gain is ordinary because Out Damn Spot Company was allowed $3,000 of depreciation deductions on the machine.

b. The company's adjusted basis in the machine is $7,000 ($10,000 cost less $3,000 depreciation), so the gain realized is $4,000 ($11,000 amount realized less $7,000 basis). Section 1245 mandates the inclusion in ordinary income of the amount by which the lower of (i) original basis (the basis before any depreciation deductions were taken) or (ii) the amount realized exceeds the adjusted basis of the property. §1245(a)(1), (2). In this instance the original basis ($10,000) is lower than the amount realized ($11,000), therefore, Out Damn Spot must include $3,000 as ordinary income ($10,000 original basis less $7,000 adjusted basis). The rest of the gain ($1,000) is probably capital gain. §1231. Put differently, a taxpayer's gain on depreciated property will be taxed as ordinary income to the extent of the depreciation previously taken, but any additional gain will be taxed as capital gain.

42. a. For nonresidential real property, the straightline method over a recovery period of 39 years must be used. §168(b)(3)(A), (c). The annual straightline deduction is thus $24,000 ($936,000/ 39). The applicable convention is a midmonth convention. §168(d)(2). Chubby Candy will be deemed to have placed the property in service in the middle of January, year one, so the company will deduct 23/24 of the annual straightline amount, or $23,000, in year one. In year two the depreciation deduction is $24,000. The total depreciation for years one and two is thus $47,000, which reduces the adjusted basis in the property to $889,000 ($936,000 basis less $47,000 depreciation). §1016.

b. Depreciation begins when property is placed in service. The acquisition date is irrelevant. Therefore, Chubby Candy Company cannot take a depreciation deduction for year one. The year two deduction here is $23,000 (for the same reasons that the year one deduction in part (a) was $23,000). The adjusted basis at the end of year two is $913,000 ($936,000 cost less $23,000 depreciation).

43. $1,000. The basis of a purchased item is equal to the amount paid for the item. §1012.

44. $50,000. It is irrelevant that Carol borrowed part of the funds used to purchase the property.

45. a. True. §1016(a).

   b. False. Incidental repairs are currently deductible under §162, so they do not increase the basis of the property repaired.

46. Her basis at the end of the year is $90,000 ($100,000 cost less the $10,000 of year one depreciation). She would realize and recognize $15,000 of gain on the sale of the machine ($105,000 amount realized less $90,000 adjusted basis), $10,000 of which would be ordinary income under §1245, and $5,000 of which would probably be capital gain under §1231. The depreciation recapture amount is limited to the depreciation taken on the property sold.

47. More. The §168 depreciation deductions allowed are generally much larger than the decline in value of the property, for several reasons. First, the recovery period for most assets is less than the actual useful life of the asset. Second, taxpayers are generally allowed to use accelerated depreciation methods that bunch the deductions in the early years of the asset's useful life. Third, the salvage value of the asset is deemed to be zero.

48. a. If accurate measurement of income is a concern, then income must accurately reflect the cost of assets that produce the income. For this reason, the cost of a "wasting asset" should not be fully deductible in the year of purchase. The asset would still have substantial value at the end of the year and the taxpayer's income would be understated. Since the decline in value of a wasting asset is a cost of earning income, the most accurate reflection of true income requires capitalization of the cost of the asset, then the deduction of depreciation over the useful life of the asset to reflect the decline in value of the asset.

   b. In order to truly measure income, the depreciation method must reflect the asset's *actual* decline in value for the year. This method is referred to as the *economic depreciation* method. This method entails determining the asset's value at the beginning of the year and subtracting its value at the end of the year. The annual cost of the asset equals the decline in the present value of the income that will be earned on the asset in the future. Under this method, depreciation is *back-loaded, increasing* each year. Under the straightline method, depreciation deductions are even. Under the accelerated depreciation methods allowed under §168, depreciation is *front-loaded, decreasing* each year. In other words, both the straightline and accelerated depreciation methods overstate deductions and understate income in the early years of use of the property and have the opposite effect in the later years of the use of the property.

There are a couple of reasons why we do not use the economic depreciation method to compute depreciation for tax purposes. The main reason is that the economic depreciation method is impractical. Often it is impossible to determine an asset's value without selling the asset. We also might prefer to use straightline or accelerated depreciation instead of economic depreciation to encourage capital investments such as investment in equipment and machinery. Many people believe the current accelerated depreciation rules encourage such investment.

49. Deducting the full cost of a business or investment asset in the year in which it is placed in service. The cost of this type of asset is not an item of personal consumption, so the cost should be excluded from the taxable base.

I.   Depletion Deductions

Reading: §§263(c), 611, 612, 613, 613A, 616, 617

Deductions may be taken for the depletion of certain natural resources, including mineral deposits, oil, gas, and timber. §§611-613A. There are two important methods of depletion: cost depletion and percentage depletion.

Cost depletion allocates the cost of the property among the estimated number of units of raw materials that will be recovered from the property. Thus, if the cost of the property were $1,000 and it is estimated that 100 tons of ore will be recovered, $10 of basis will be allocated to each ton.

Percentage depletion, on the other hand, permits a taxpayer simply to deduct a stated percentage of its gross income as a depletion allowance. Under this method, there is no need to estimate the number of recoverable units. Moreover, percentage depletion continues *even after the taxpayer's entire cost has been recovered.* The permitted depletion percentage ranges from 5 percent to 22 percent, depending on the type of natural resource. However, it may not exceed 50 percent (100 percent in the case of oil and gas properties) of the taxable income from the property, computed without allowance for depletion.

EXAMPLES

50. Describe the two main methods of determining depletion deductions.

51. Woody bought 30 acres of timber land for $3 million. He estimates that he will eventually take 500,000 tons of timber on the land. In the first year he cuts down and sells 80,000 tons of timber. Determine Woody's depletion deduction in the first year using the cost method.

52. Mr. Match buys a sulphur mine for $2 million. He estimates that there are about 500,000 tons of sulphur in the mine. In year one Mr. Match recovers 60,000 tons and his gross income is $1.2 million. In year two Mr. Match recovers 90,000 tons and his gross income is $1.8 million. In year three he recovers 30,000 tons and his gross income is $750,000. The depletion percentage for sulphur is 22 percent.
     a. Determine Mr. Match's depletion deductions for year one, year two, and year three under the cost depletion method.
     b. Determine Mr. Match's depletion deductions for year one, year two, and year three under the percentage depletion method.

53. Ursula owns a sulphur mine and uses the percentage depletion method to determine her depletion deductions. The depletion percentage for sulphur is 22 percent. In year one Ursula has $1 million of gross income and $800,000 of expenses (other than the depletion). Determine Ursula's year one depletion deduction.

EXPLANATIONS

50. One method of determining depletion deductions is cost depletion, which is based on the cost of the property being depleted.

5.   Deductions for the Costs of Earning Income

With this method, the taxpayer estimates the number of units of the resource that can be recovered and allocates the adjusted basis of the property to the units as they are sold. The estimate of recoverable units may be revised if it is later ascertained that the estimate was erroneous. §§611 and 612.

The second method of determining depletion deductions is called percentage depletion. With this method, the taxpayer may deduct a percentage of gross income for depletion. Because the same percentage is used each year and there is no limitation on the number of years, the taxpayer may end up taking aggregate deductions that exceed the cost of the property. Section 613(b) lists the percentages applicable to the particular resources. §613.

51. Woody's basis in the timber property is $3 million. Since he estimates that 500,000 tons of timber are recoverable from the land, the cost per ton is $6 ($3 million/500,000 tons). In the first year Woody cuts down and sells 80,000 tons. Therefore his depletion deduction is $480,000 (80,000 tons multiplied by $6/ton).

52. a. Mr. Match's basis in the sulphur mine is $2 million. Since he estimates that 500,000 tons of sulphur are recoverable from the mine, the cost per ton is $4 ($2 million/500,000 tons). In year one Mr. Match recovers 60,000 tons so his cost depletion deduction is $240,000 (60,000 tons multiplied by $4/ton). In year two Mr. Match recovers 90,000 tons, so his cost depletion deduction is $360,000 (90,000 tons multiplied by $4/ton). In year three Mr. Match recovers 30,000 tons, so his cost depletion deduction is $120,000 (30,000 tons multiplied by $4/ton).

   b. Under the percentage depletion method, sulphur mines are allowed a 22 percent deduction from gross income. §613(b)(1)(A). Therefore, in year one Mr. Match's percentage depletion deduction is $264,000 ($1.2 million multiplied by 22 percent). In year two his percentage depletion deduction is $396,000 ($1.8 million multiplied by 22 percent). In year three Mr. Match's percentage depletion deduction is $165,000 ($750,000 multiplied by 22 percent).

53. The maximum depletion deduction is limited to 50 percent of the *taxable* income from the property. §613(a). Since Ursula's gross income is $1 million and her costs are $800,000, her taxable income is $200,000. Ursula's depletion allowance is $220,000

($1 million multiplied by 22 percent). Ursula is only allowed to deduct that allowance to the extent of one-half of her taxable income, or $100,000.

J.   Tax Shelters

1.   *The Tax Shelter Problem*

Not all strategies to reduce tax are "tax shelters." Throughout this book we have noted that various types of investments (for example, deferred annuities and qualified retirement plans) are tax-favored, often as an inducement to invest and save. Taxpayers who make these types of investments are not thought of as engaging in "tax avoidance." On the other hand, taxpayers who structure transactions to generate tax losses (for example, deductions in excess of income) and attempt to use those losses to offset their active business income (for example, from the practice of law or medicine) are often thought of as engaging in tax avoidance. It is often far from clear, however, where "legitimate" tax reduction ends and tax avoidance begins.

How do taxpayers structure transactions that generate tax losses? As we have seen earlier in this book, the tax treatment of capital investment is inconsistent; taxpayers are able to (i) defer realization or recognition of some forms of economic income and (ii) accelerate some forms of economic expense (principally through depreciation deductions). This mismatch in the timing of inclusions and deductions allows taxpayers to defer tax, which has the same effect as either an interest-free loan from the government, in the amount of the tax deferred, or a reduction in the taxpayer's tax rate. Taxpayers have attempted to exploit this mismatch through tax-motivated investments, often referred to as *tax shelters*. Such investments may not produce any real (that is, nontax) economic gain. The tax savings from the accelerated deductions and deferral of income (or conversion of ordinary income into capital gain) may nonetheless make such investments highly desirable.

In the past, many tax shelters involved financial assets. For example, if a taxpayer borrowed at 9 percent to buy a growth stock that was expected to yield an 8 percent return, the transaction produced a real economic loss. However, it could produce tax savings in excess of that economic loss if the interest on the debt was currently deductible, offsetting ordinary income, and gain from the stock was capital and was deferred until the stock is sold.

Many other tax shelters involved real estate. Consider the following simplified example (which does not take into account the judicial and statutory limitations on tax shelters described below): Ivan, who is taxed at the 40 percent rate, decides that he would like to pay lower taxes. In year one he borrows $1 million at 9 percent interest and uses the loan proceeds to buy an apartment building. Ivan's basis in the building includes the $1 million of debt. Crane v. Commissioner, 331 U.S. 1 (1947). Ivan pays $90,000 a year of interest on the debt and receives $90,000 a year of rent from the apartment building, so he does not have any real economic (that is, nontax) gain from the transaction. However, Ivan also takes depreciation on the building of $35,000 a year, which saves him $14,000 (40 percent of $35,000) a year of tax. The $35,000 of annual depreciation reduces his basis in the property. If Ivan fully depreciates the property, then sells it in year 30 for $1 million (or for assumption of the $1 million of debt), he will realize and recognize $1 million of ordinary gain, $35,000 of which is attributable to having taken the $35,000 depreciation deduction in year one. Ivan will pay tax on that gain at his 40 percent rate, so the tax on the $35,000 of gain attributable to the year one depreciation is $14,000. In other words, in year one Ivan saves $14,000 of tax and, as a result, will pay $14,000 in tax in year 30. It is as if the government has made an interest-free 30-year loan of $14,000 to Ivan.

The annual depreciation that may be taken with respect to an asset is determined by reference to the taxpayer's basis in the asset. In many of the more egregious tax shelters, taxpayers attempted to overstate their depreciation deductions by inflating nonrecourse debt on the asset. For example, in Revenue Ruling 77-110, the taxpayers calculated their depreciation deductions for a motion picture on a basis of $2 million, claiming that they had bought the movie for $200,000 in cash and $1.8 million of nonrecourse debt, which was to be repaid out of the income earned from exhibiting the film. The seller of the movie (who was also the promoter of the tax shelter) had recently acquired the movie for $200,000, so the Service ruled that the $1.8 million liability was too contingent to be given effect for tax purposes.

Tax shelters proliferated during the 1970s, but it took some time for Congress to figure out what to do about them. Congress could have limited tax shelter investments by adopting a more uniform approach to capital taxation. Congress could, for example, have moved toward a pure Haig-Simons tax base by taxing all or most forms of annual appreciation and eliminating accelerated forms of depreciation. Instead, Congress has enacted a variety of complex statutory provisions that were crafted to discourage tax shelter investments.

Courts have also lent their judicial voice to the anti-tax shelter chorus by characterizing certain tax-motivated transactions as shams and denying investors anticipated deductions. However, the difficulty of distinguishing between tax and non-tax aspects of an investment and between permissible reliance on tax incentives and impermissible tax arbitrage has rendered some of the judicial approaches to shelters largely ineffective.

2. The Judicial Response to Tax Shelters

Courts have struggled in tax shelter cases to determine whether a transaction should be given effect for tax purposes or disregarded as a "sham." For example, in Knetsch v. United States, 364 U.S. 361 (1960), the Supreme Court considered whether a taxpayer who had borrowed to fund a deferred annuity should be allowed to deduct the interest on the debt. Simplifying the facts of the *Knetsch* case, the taxpayer bought a $4,004,000 annuity from an insurance company for $4,000 of his own money and the proceeds of a $4 million nonrecourse loan from the insurance company. The yield on the annuity was 2.5 percent and the interest rate on the debt was 3.5 percent, so, before taking into account the tax consequences, the taxpayer lost money on the transaction. Each year that the loan was outstanding, the taxpayer was required to prepay $140,000 of interest on the debt. However, the annuity value increased each year and the taxpayer was permitted to borrow (again nonrecourse) the value of the annuity in excess of the $4 million of debt. In year one the taxpayer borrowed $100,000 against the increase in the value of the policy and prepaid $3,500 of interest on that new debt. The taxpayer did not have to include in income the increase in the value of the annuity, but claimed a $143,500 interest deduction for year one.

In the year at issue in the case, the top marginal rate was 91 percent. Assume that the taxpayer's rate was 91 percent, so the claimed interest deduction would have saved the taxpayer around $130,000 in tax. The taxpayer's out-of-pocket cost for year one would have been $47,500 — $40,000 ($140,000 of prepaid interest less the $100,000 the insurance company loaned the taxpayer), plus $4,000 cash paid for the annuity, plus $3,500 prepaid interest on the extra $100,000 borrowed. Thus, the taxpayer's net saving from the transaction in year one would have been $82,500. The Service disallowed the taxpayer's interest deduction and the trial court agreed with the Service, concluding that the purported debt was not true indebtedness.

The Supreme Court affirmed the disallowance of the interest deductions, calling the transaction a "sham." The Court concluded that the form of the transaction was a fiction; that the $100,000 "loan" on the increase in the value of the annuity was "in reality" a rebate of $100,000 of the $140,000 of interest prepaid on the $4 million loan. In addition, the Court characterized the taxpayer's $47,500 out-of-pocket cost as a fee paid to the insurance company for providing the tax shelter.

The outcome in *Knetsch* may be correct, considering the obvious tax avoidance motivation for the transaction and its artificial nature. However, it is not clear where legitimate tax reduction ends and "sham" characterization begins. In many cases in which the Service has urged a court to apply the sham transaction doctrine, the court has refused to do so. For example, in Fabreeka Products Co. v. Commissioner, 294 F.2d 876 (1st Cir. 1961) (and the related cases), the court concluded that taxpayers who had entered into various tax avoidance schemes that involved the deduction of premium paid for bonds were allowed their deductions, despite the fact that the tax avoidance motivation for the transactions was obvious.

The taxpayers in *Fabreeka* and the two companion cases had purchased bonds at a premium, meaning that the price they paid exceeded the amount payable on the debt. At the time of the case, the entire bond premium could be deducted against ordinary income in the year in which the bond was purchased. Fabreeka Products and the two taxpayers in the related cases incorporated the bond premium deduction into various tax avoidance schemes. Fabreeka Products borrowed $100, bought the bonds for $115, deducted the $15 of bond premium, and distributed the bonds to its shareholders. The shareholders then sold the bonds, paid the debt, and were left with $15. The shareholders had to include a $15 dividend on the distribution. A corporation is not allowed to deduct dividends it pays its shareholders, so the scheme effectively converted a $15 nondeductible dividend into a $15 bond premium deduction. Another taxpayer, Sherman, took an ordinary deduction for the bond premium, then sold the bonds six months later, generating capital gain that was taxed at a lower rate than ordinary income. The third taxpayer, Friedman, bought the bonds and donated them to charity. She took a deduction for the bond premium and a charitable contribution deduction for the donation of the bonds. The tax-exempt charity sold the bonds, netting the premium.

The Service argued that the taxpayers' bond premium deductions should be disallowed because the taxpayers had no investment motive when they acquired the bonds; instead, the sole motivation was tax-avoidance. However, the court, noting that the taxpayers bore the economic risk of loss while they owned the bonds, refused to characterize the transactions as shams because the transactions involved "actual investments," instead of "paper proceedings" without any economic substance.

The opinion in *Fabreeka* is difficult to reconcile with the opinion in Goldstein v. Commissioner, 364 F.2d 734 (2d Cir. 1966), cert. denied, 385 U.S. 1005 (1967). In the *Goldstein* case, the taxpayer in 1958 won $140,000 in the Irish Sweepstakes. Her son, an accountant, devised a strategy to minimize the tax due in 1958 on her winnings. Simplifying somewhat, in 1958 the taxpayer borrowed $465,000 from a bank at a 4 percent interest rate, prepaying $52,000 of interest on that debt. With the loan proceeds, she purchased U.S. Treasury notes that yielded 1.5 percent interest and were due in 1961. She repeated these steps with second bank. Her economic (that is, nontax) loss on the bonds was expected to be $18,500. However, the tax savings from the transactions exceeded that economic loss because: (i) in 1958 her interest deductions offset the ordinary income from her winnings, dramatically reducing the tax for that year; (ii) she was in a lower tax bracket when she earned the interest on the notes in later years; and (iii) she converted ordinary income, from her winnings in 1958, into capital gain on the redemption of the bonds in 1961. The Service disallowed the interest deductions for 1958. The Second Circuit noted that, absent tax consequences, a taxpayer would not borrow at 4 percent to buy an investment that yields 1.5 percent. In light of the strong tax avoidance motive and the lack of other business motivation for the transaction, the court concluded that the interest was not deductible under §163.

The *Goldstein* and *Fabreeka* decisions can be reconciled, but not easily. One difference between the facts in the two cases may be significant: The court in *Fabreeka* thought that people would acquire bonds at a premium for reasons other than the current deduction of the bond premium, but the court in *Goldstein* expressed the view that no one would borrow at 4 percent to earn 1.5 percent.

Courts also developed various approaches to deal with taxpayers who artificially inflated the amount of nonrecourse debt on their property in order to increase their depreciation deductions on the property and interest deductions on the debt. Estate of Franklin v. Commissioner, 544 F.2d 1045 (9th Cir. 1976), illustrates one of the judicial approaches to the problem. In that case, a partnership (Associates) "purchased" an inn from the Romneys for $1.2 million purchase money nonrecourse debt (meaning that the sellers took back a note) bearing 7.5 percent interest. At the closing, Associates prepaid $75,000 of interest on the debt. Associates was to make monthly payments to the Romneys of $9,000 (part of which was interest and part of which was repayment of principal). After 10 years, Associates was to make a balloon payment of any remaining balance, approximately $975,000. Associates then leased the motel back to the Romneys in exchange for $9,000 a month of rent. Since the $9,000 monthly payments owed by each party to the other offset each other, no cash (other than the initial $75,000 payment) was to pass between the parties until the balloon payment was due in 10 years. The lease was a net lease, meaning the Romneys paid all of the expenses of owning the motel.

The partners in Associates took interest deductions on the debt and depreciation deductions calculated on $1.2 million of basis, which included the debt, under the *Crane* case. The deductions produced large partnership losses that the partners used to offset their earnings as doctors. The Commissioner disallowed the losses claimed by the partners. The Tax Court held that the transaction was not a debt transaction, but was instead the purchase of an option to acquire the inn. The Ninth Circuit Court of Appeals concluded that, at the time the inn was purchased, the value of the inn (which was in the neighborhood of $600,000) was significantly less than the $1.2 million of nonrecourse debt on the property. Based on that fact, the court further concluded that the nonrecourse debt was not genuine indebtedness, so the debt should not have been included in basis and did not produce interest or depreciation deductions.

Although many courts have followed the *Franklin* approach, some courts have adopted a different approach to inflated nonrecourse debt. For example, in Pleasant Summit Land Corp. v. Commissioner, 863 F.2d 263 (3d Cir. 1988), reh'g denied (1989), cert. denied, 110 S. Ct. 260 (1989), the court allowed the taxpayer basis for the inflated nonrecourse debt, but only up to the fair market value of the property. In that case, a partnership bought property for $500,000 in cash plus $7.2 million of nonrecourse debt. The seller of the property (which was related to the partnership) had paid 4.2 million for the property plus the land it was on just the year before the partnership bought it. The taxpayer, a partner in the partnership, took $760,000 of deductions (for depreciation and interest) with respect to the property, but the Commissioner disallowed the deductions. The Tax Court judge found that the value of the property was not in excess of $4.2 million and concluded that the nonrecourse debt was not real indebtedness, so the debt could not support any of the deductions. On appeal, the court held that, where nonrecourse debt exceeds the value of the property subject to the debt, the nonrecourse debt is includible in basis only up to the value of the property. The court reasoned that a borrower would not default on nonrecourse debt if the debt did not exceed the value of the property, so a taxpayer should get basis credit for that portion of the debt. The court added that any cash paid by the taxpayer should also be included in the taxpayer's basis for the property. In other words, the basis would include both the $4.2 million of nonrecourse debt that did not exceed the value of the property and the $500,000 of cash paid for the property.

As you can tell from this discussion, tax shelters come in myriad forms. However, they have in common the deferral of tax (through interest deductions, depreciation, and possibly tax credits) and conversion of ordinary income into capital gain. The judicial approach to limiting deductions in egregious tax shelters did not stop the proliferation of a kaleidoscope of tax shelters. The fact that many high income taxpayers avoided paying tax by investing in tax shelters annoyed middle and low income taxpayers and threatened taxpayer morale. This was a serious problem because our income tax system relies on self-assessment of tax. Eventually, in the early 1980s, the press began to focus on the public perception that permitting high income taxpayers to avoid tax by investing in tax shelters was unfair. This prompted Congress to launch a frontal assault on tax shelters, which culminated in the enactment, in 1986, of new and expanded statutory limitations on tax shelters.

EXAMPLES

54. Daisy, a highly compensated investment banker, is in the 50 percent tax bracket. In year one she buys a limited edition photograph of a Picasso painting and the worldwide rights to reproduce the photograph in any media (for example, posters and calendars). Two appraisers recommended by the seller, who is a tax shelter promoter, appraised the photograph "package" at around

$700,000, but provided no support for their appraisals. Government experts estimated that the package was worth only $5,000. Daisy paid $550,000 for the package, $50,000 of which was cash and $500,000 of which was from nonrecourse debt. Daisy claimed year one interest and depreciation deductions totaling $90,000. Daisy unsuccessfully attempted to market the package.

The Commissioner disallows Daisy's year one deductions and Daisy has decided to litigate the case. Will a court agree with the disallowance of the deduction?

55. Adam acquired Blackacre in year one for $200,000 of cash and $800,000 of nonrecourse debt. (At the time, Blackacre was probably only worth $700,000). In year one Adam took deductions for $80,000 of interest on the nonrecourse debt and $35,000 of depreciation, which was calculated by reference to a $1 million basis for the property.

The Commissioner disallows Adam's year one deductions and he decides to litigate the case. Will a court agree with the disallowance of the deductions?

EXPLANATIONS

54. A court would probably not allow the deductions. However, this is a tough call because it is impossible to discern a clear standard for determining when a transaction entered into to reduce taxes will be recharacterized for tax purposes.

In Knetsch v. United States, 364 U.S. 361 (1960), the Supreme Court affirmed the disallowance of interest deductions from a "sham" transaction. In that case, the Court concluded that the transaction was a sham because the form of the transaction was a fiction. In the court's view, the transaction had no economic substance; absent tax considerations, no rational person would have entered into such a transaction because, on an economic basis, the transaction lost money. The Court concluded that the $100,000 "loan" made by the insurance company to the taxpayer was "in reality" a rebate of $100,000 of the $140,000 of interest that the taxpayer prepaid to the insurance company on a loan from the insurance company to the taxpayer. The Court also characterized the taxpayer's $47,500 out-of-pocket costs as a fee paid to the insurance company for providing the tax shelter.

However, in many cases in which the Service has urged a court to apply the sham transaction doctrine, the court has refused to do so. For example, in Fabreeka Products Co. v. Commissioner, 294 F.2d 876 (1st Cir. 1961) (and the related cases), the court concluded that the taxpayers, who had entered into various tax avoidance schemes that involved the deduction of premium paid for bonds, were allowed their deductions despite the fact that the tax avoidance motivation for the transactions was obvious. The court noted that people might buy bonds with premium for reasons other than tax avoidance and that buying the bonds exposed the purchasers of the bonds to decreases and increases in the value of the bonds. The court held that the premium deductions should not be disallowed.

Even if Daisy can avoid the sham label, some courts have disallowed deductions from transactions that were not shams because of the taxpayer's patent tax avoidance motive for entering into the transaction. For example, in Goldstein v. Commissioner, 364 F.2d 734 (2d Cir. 1966), cert. denied, 385 U.S. 1005 (1967), the court disallowed the taxpayer's deduction for interest she prepaid on a loan bearing 4 percent interest, which she incurred to acquire bonds yielding 1.5 percent. Although, on an economic basis, the transaction lost money, the transaction was profitable for the taxpayer taking into account the tax savings from the transaction. The Second Circuit noted that, absent tax consequences, a taxpayer would not borrow at 4 percent to buy an investment that yields 1.5 percent. In light of the strong tax avoidance motive and the lack of other business motivation for the transaction, the court concluded that the interest was not deductible under §163.

Here, it is theoretically conceivable that someone could earn substantial amounts by exploiting a photograph of a famous work of art. However, the facts here do not establish the profitmaking potential of the photograph package. It appears that Daisy bought something worth $5,000 on an economic basis, for $50,000 of cash and $500,000 of debt. The $500,000 of debt is also nonrecourse and it seems very likely that Daisy would have defaulted on the debt (which also raises an *Estate of Franklin* issue). In sum, these facts indicate that this transaction is one that people would not enter into for economic reasons, but would enter into for tax avoidance reasons. The facts of this example are loosely based on the facts in Rose v. Commissioner, 88 T.C. 386 (1987), aff'd, 868 F.2d 851 (6th Cir. 1989), in which the court agreed with the Commissioner's disallowance of the deductions from the Picasso photograph tax shelter.

55. A court would probably view this case as distinguishable from Estate of Franklin v. Commissioner, 544 F.2d 1045 (9th Cir. 1976), for the reasons described below, so would not apply that approach to disallow the deductions. However, if a court applies the approach adopted in Pleasant Summit Land Corp. v. Commissioner, 863 F.2d 263 (3d Cir. 1988), reh'g denied (1989), cert. denied, 110 S. Ct. 260 (1989), the basis attributable to the nonrecourse debt will be limited to the $700,000 value of the property so Adam's depreciable basis for the property would be $900,000 instead of $1 million.

    The Service may argue that the nonrecourse debt is not true indebtedness, citing *Estate of Franklin,* so the deductions must be disallowed. The *Franklin* approach is used by a number of circuits, but not all circuits. For example, the Third Circuit would apply the approach adopted in *Pleasant Summit.* In other words, the approach taken by a court might depend on where the taxpayer lives and where the taxpayer litigates. If the taxpayer litigates in the Tax Court or the district court, the court will apply the precedent of the circuit in which the taxpayer resides. If the taxpayer litigates in the Court of Federal Claims, the court will apply precedent from the Federal Circuit Court of Appeals.

    If *Franklin* applies, none of the $800,000 of nonrecourse debt would be included in Adam's depreciable basis for the property. Here, as in *Franklin,* the property subject to the debt has a value that is less than the amount of the debt. However, this case may be distinguishable from *Franklin* for two reasons. First, in *Franklin,* the taxpayers paid only 6 percent of the "purchase price" in cash, so the court concluded that the taxpayers had not made "an investment" in the property, but instead had purchased something akin to an option. Here, on the other hand, Adam paid 20 percent of the purchase price in cash, which may make a difference. Second, in *Franklin,* the nonrecourse debt on the property was twice the likely value of the property. Here, the nonrecourse debt exceeded the value of the property by around 15 percent. In sum, this transaction does not look nearly as egregious as the transaction in *Franklin,* and some courts might view the *Franklin* approach as extreme, so it seems unlikely that a court would hold that the debt was not true debt.

    Under the *Pleasant Summit* approach, Adam's depreciable basis in the property would be $900,000. This would reduce his year one depreciation, but would not reduce it nearly as much as the extreme *Franklin* approach. The basis from the $800,000 of nonrecourse debt would be limited to the value of the property, $700,000. The basis would also include the $200,000 of cash that Adam paid.

3. The Congressional Response to Tax Shelters

As we said earlier, Congress could have limited tax shelter investments by adopting a more uniform approach to capital taxation, but instead enacted a variety of complex statutory provisions that were designed to discourage tax shelter investments. Some of the provisions enacted in 1986 were new and some reinforced older, more specific anti-abuse limitations in the Code (a few of which we will discuss below). The combination of the old and new anti-tax shelter provisions has virtually eliminated the individual tax shelter industry.

In this section, we will consider the following anti-tax shelter provisions: (i) the investment interest limitation of §163; (ii) the passive loss limitation of §469; (iii) the at-risk limitation of §465; and (iv) the interest deduction limitations of §§264 and 265. (In Chapter 6 we will consider another anti-tax shelter provision, the so-called "hobby loss" limitation of §183.)

You can categorize these various limitations by asking yourself two questions: First, what type of *investments* (for example, active business investments, passive business investments, portfolio investments, or investments in insurance products or tax-exempt bonds) are affected by the limitation. Second, what type of *deductions* (for example, depreciation, interest, or other deductions) are affected by the limitation.

a. The Investment Interest Limitation of §163(d)

Reading: §163(d)

The §163 investment interest limitation is designed to prevent the misstatement of income and mismatching of items of income and expense, both of which can result from using borrowed funds to invest in property that is expected to appreciate.

Suppose, for example, that in year one Joan borrows $500 and uses the proceeds to purchase "growth" stock that does not pay a high rate of dividends but is expected to rise in value. During year one the interest on the loan is $50 and the stock appreciates $50, so that its value at the end of year one is $550. The investment does not produce any economic loss since the $50 interest expense is offset by the $50 rise in value. However, because Joan has not realized any gain from the stock through a sale or taxable exchange, the rise in value will not be subject to current tax. If Joan is allowed to deduct the interest expense, the deduction will be offset against her ordinary income for the year, reducing her tax for the year. If Joan sells the stock in year two for $550, she will pay tax on the gain in that year. In other words, Joan will have reduced her tax in year one and increased her tax in year two, which benefits Joan because of the time value of money; the present value of the year two tax payment will be less than the present value of the immediate tax savings.

If Joan retains the stock until her death, the tax treatment of the transaction will be even more favorable. Joan will deduct the loss in year one, but, under §1014, her heirs will receive a basis in the property equal to its fair market value at the time of death. If the property is worth $550 at the time of death, the $50 in gain will never be taxed.

Section 163(d) provides that the amount allowed as a deduction for investment interest shall not exceed net investment income. Investment interest is defined as interest on indebtedness allocable to property held for investment. However, qualified residence interest and interest taken into account in calculating the §469 passive loss limitation are not within the definition of investment interest. §163(d) (3)(B). Investment income is defined, generally, as the net income (gross income less expenses) from investments that produce interest, dividends, annuities, or royalties not derived in the ordinary course of a trade or business. §§163(d)(4) and (5) and 469(e)(1). (Since 1986 rent has not been treated as investment income.) Long-term capital gain (gain on the sale of a capital asset held by the taxpayer for more than a year) from investments is taken into account in computing investment income only if the taxpayer elects to not apply preferential capital gain rates to the gain. §§163(d)(4)(B) and 1222(11). Interest in excess of the §163(d) limitation is carried forward and treated as investment interest in the next year. §163(d)(2). Note that the §163(d) investment interest limitation does not apply to corporations that are subject to the §11 entity level corporate tax.

EXAMPLES

56. What is the purpose of the limitation on the deduction allowed for investment interest?

5. Deductions for the Costs of Earning Income

57. a. On January 1, year one, John borrows $100 and uses the loan proceeds to purchase $100 of Rise Company stock. The loan used to purchase the stock is nonrecourse. On December 31, year one, the value of the Rise Company stock is $110. On that same day, John pays $10 interest on the loan used to purchase the stock. The stock pays no dividends and John has no other investment income or interest expense. How much, if any, of the investment expense may John deduct?

b. How, if at all, would your answer in part (a) change if the loan used to purchase the stock is recourse?

c. How, if at all, would your answer in part (a) change if the value of the stock on December 31, year one, is only $100?

d. How, if at all, would your answer in part (a) change if, on December 31, year one, John sells the stock for $115?

e. Is John allowed to deduct the $10 of interest he paid in year one if, on January 2, year two, he sells the stock for $110?

f. How, if at all, would your answer in part (a) change if, on December 31, year one, John sells the stock for $95?

g. How, if at all, would your answer in part (a) change if, in year one, John includes $6 in interest income from a corporate bond?

h. Assume the same set of facts as in part (a) except that, in year two, John pays another $10 of interest on the loan used to purchase the Rise Company stock and includes $15 of dividends from the Rise Company stock. How much, if any, interest may John deduct in years one and two?

i. Assume the same set of facts as in part (a) except that, in year one, John receives $20 of dividends from the Rise Company stock, and, in year two, John pays $10 of interest but receives no dividends from Rise Company stock. How much, if any, of the interest is John allowed to deduct in years one and two?

j. How, if at all, would your answer in part (a) change if, in year one, John recognizes $10 of rental income?

58. Skip borrows $100,000 from a bank at 10 percent interest, interest only for three years, to buy Pork Belly common stock. The loan is recourse. In year one the stock pays dividends of $8,000. In year two the Pork Belly stock pays no dividends but Skip receives $3,000 in dividends from some Growth Company stock that he inherited. In year three the Pork Belly stock pays $25,000

in dividends. How much of the $10,000 of annual interest can Skip deduct each year?

EXPLANATIONS

56. The §163(d) investment interest limitation is designed to prevent the misstatement of income and mismatching of items of income and expense, both of which can arise from using borrowed funds to invest in property that is expected to appreciate.

57. a. John is not allowed to deduct investment interest in excess of his net investment income. Here, John has $10 of investment interest expense but no investment income. Thus, John will not be able to deduct any of the $10 of investment interest. §163(d).

   b. As in part (a), John will not be able to deduct any of the investment interest. The fact that the loan is recourse is irrelevant.

   c. Recall that the purpose of §163(d) is to prevent the deduction of interest on investments that are expected to produce unrealized gain. Here, there is no unrealized gain: John has suffered an economic loss equal to the amount of the $10 interest payment. Nonetheless, under §163(d), John will not be allowed to deduct any portion of the interest in year one.

   d. John may deduct the $10 of interest. Investment income is defined to include short-term capital gain (gain on the sale of a capital asset held by the taxpayer for a year or less) from the disposition of investment property. (Note that short-term capital gain is not taxed at preferential rates.) John has $15 of net investment income, so he is allowed to deduct the full $10 of investment interest. §163(d)(4)(B)(1).

   e. As in part (a), John cannot deduct the $10 of interest in year one. However, John carries the $10 of investment interest forward to year two. The $10 of long-term capital gain on the sale of the stock is treated as investment income only if John elects to treat it as such and forgoes the capital gains rate on the gain. §163(d)(4)(B)(iii). If John makes this election, he has $10 of investment income and can deduct the $10 of interest in year two. If he does not make this election, he cannot deduct the interest because his investment income is zero.

   f. Here, John has suffered an economic loss on the investment and there is no possibility that the investment will ever produce an economic gain. Nonetheless, John will not be able to deduct any portion of the $10 interest expense since his investment income for year one is zero. John will, however, be able to carry the $10 investment interest deduction forward to year two. He can deduct that interest in year two to the extent of his year two investment income.

g. John may deduct $6 of the interest expense. Interest expense may be deducted in an amount equal to all investment income, including income from investment property that was not purchased with borrowed funds. Here, John has $6 of investment income from the corporate bond and may therefore deduct $6 of investment expense. The other $4 of year one interest is carried forward to year two.

h. As in part (a), John has no investment income in year one and therefore cannot deduct the $10 of interest in that year. The $10 interest expense that cannot be deducted in year one carries forward to year two and is treated as interest expense in that year. In year two John has $15 of investment income and $20 of investment expense ($10 current expense and $10 that is treated as a current expense under §163(d)(2)), so he can deduct $15 of interest in year two. The remaining $5 of interest is carried forward to year three.

i. In year one John may deduct the entire $10 of interest expense, since that amount does not exceed his investment income. In year two John may not deduct any interest expense. Note that, if instead of including $20 of investment income in year one, John had included $10 of investment income in year one and a like amount in year two, he would have been able to deduct both his year one and year two interest payments.

j. John may not deduct any portion of the interest. Prior to 1986, certain forms of rental income were considered investment income. Currently, however, rental income is not treated as investment income. §§163(d)(5), 469(e)(1). Thus, John has no investment income and therefore cannot deduct any of the interest expense.

58. As an anti-tax shelter measure, investment interest is only deductible to the extent of investment income; however, the taxpayer may carry forward any disallowed investment interest to succeeding taxable years. §163(d). In year one Skip may only deduct $8,000 of the $10,000 interest expense because he re-

ceived only $8,000 of investment income (the dividends received). The $2,000 of interest expense that is disallowed is carried forward to year two. In year two Skip has $10,000 of interest expense plus $2,000 from the preceding year. Of the $12,000, Skip may only deduct $3,000, the amount of investment income received from the Growth Company stock. The $9,000 of interest that is disallowed is carried forward to year three. In year three Skip receives $25,000 of investment income so he may deduct the entire $10,000 of year three interest expense plus the $9,000 carried forward from year two. His taxable income from the stocks in year three is $6,000 ($25,000 dividends less $19,000 interest expense).

b. The Passive Loss Rules of §469

Reading: §469

Tax shelters are designed to exploit the mismatching of deductions and inclusions in order to permit the taxpayer to defer tax and, in some cases to convert ordinary income into capital gain. Recall our earlier illustration of a real estate tax shelter, in which a taxpayer buys real estate for nonrecourse debt. The depreciation and interest deductions in excess of the amount of rental income from the property offset the taxpayer's income from other sources (for example, from the active conduct of a trade or business such as the practice of medicine). However, the appreciation in the property is not taxed until the property is sold or exchanged. Even if the tax saved in the early years of the investment exactly equals the tax that will be owed in the later years of the investment, the taxpayer benefits significantly from deferral of tax. For example, in our earlier real estate tax shelter example, Ivan saved $14,000 of tax (from depreciation and interest, net of the rental inclusion) in year one and, as a result of having taken those deductions, owed $14,000 in tax in year 30. It was as if the government had given Ivan an interest-free 30-year loan of $14,000. Section 469 destroys the tax deferral benefit of shelters by disallowing the deductions from the shelter until the income from the shelter is realized.

The §469 passive loss limitation is designed to prevent a taxpayer from using deductions from "passive activities" to offset the taxpayer's income from either portfolio investment or an active trade or business. In order to accomplish this goal, §469 segregates the taxpayer's income and loss for the year into three baskets: (i) *passive*, (ii) *portfolio*, and (iii) *active trade or business*. A passive activity loss is deductible only to the extent of the taxpayer's passive income; it cannot be used to offset the taxpayer's portfolio income (for example, interest or dividends) or active business income. Passive activity losses disallowed under §469 are carried forward to the next tax year and are again subject to §469 in that year. §469(b). When a taxpayer ultimately disposes of her entire interest in a passive activity (in a transaction other than a nonrecognition transaction), the taxpayer can generally deduct the remaining losses from that activity that were carried forward from earlier years. §469(g).

A *passive activity loss* is defined, in general, as the net loss from activities (i) that involve the conduct of a trade or business and (ii) in which the taxpayer does not "materially participate." §469(c), (d). The determination of whether an activity is active or passive usually turns on whether the taxpayer materially participates in the activity. *Material participation* is defined as participation that is "regular, continuous, and substantial." §469(h)(1). Temporary Regulation §1.469-5T(a) provides that a taxpayer is deemed to have materially participated in an activity in a given year only if the taxpayer can satisfy one of the following seven tests set forth in the regulation:

1. The individual participates in the activity for more than 500 hours during the year;
2. The taxpayer's participation in the activity during the year constitutes substantially all of the participation in such activity of all individuals, including non-owners;
3. The individual participates in the activity for more than 100 hours during the year and no one else had greater participation in the activity;
4. The activity is a "significant participation activity" (defined in Temporary Regulation §1.469-5T(c) as a trade or business activity in which the taxpayer "significantly participates") and the taxpayer's aggregate participation in all significant participation activities during the year exceeds 500 hours;
5. The taxpayer materially participated in the activity for any five taxable years in the 10-year period that immediately precedes the current tax year;
6. The activity is a "personal service activity" (defined in Temporary Regulation §1.469-5T(d) as an activity involving the performance of personal services in the fields of health, law,

engineering, architecture, accounting, actuarial science, performing arts, consulting, or any other trade or business in which capital is not a material income-producing factor) and the taxpayer materially participated in the activity for any three taxable years (whether or not consecutive) preceding the taxable year; or

7. The taxpayer participates in the activity over 100 hours during the taxable year and, based on all of the facts and circumstances, the taxpayer participates in the activity on a regular, continuous, and substantial basis during the year. (For purposes of applying this last test, time spent managing an activity counts toward participation only if the taxpayer spends more time than anyone else managing the activity and no other person is paid to manage the activity.)

Section 469(h)(2) provides that a limited partner is not deemed to materially participate in the activities of the partnership. However, Temporary Regulation §1.469-5T(e)(2) provides that, if the limited partner can satisfy the material participation tests of §1.469-5T(a)(1), (5), or (6) (described above) with respect to an activity, the passive loss limitation does not apply to the limited partner's losses from that activity.

A *rental activity*, which is an activity in which payments are principally for the use of tangible property, is generally treated as a passive activity. §469(c)(2). (However, Temporary Regulation §1.469-1T(e)(3)(ii) provides that some activities in which property is rented are not treated as rental activities.) There are several exceptions to the general rule that rental activities are passive. For example, this general rule does not apply to a rental real estate activity if: (i) more than half of the personal services performed in trades or businesses by the taxpayer are performed in real property trades or businesses in which the taxpayer materially participates and (ii) the taxpayer performs more than 750 hours of services during the year in real property trades or businesses in which the taxpayer materially participates.

In addition, if the rental real estate activity is passive, an individual taxpayer who "actively participates" in the rental real estate activity during the year is allowed to deduct up to $25,000 of the taxpayer's passive losses from the activity despite the general disallowance rule. §469(i)(1), (2). This $25,000 exemption is reduced by 50 percent of the taxpayer's adjusted gross income over $100,000. §469(i)(3). The term "active participation" is not defined in the statute, which says only that the active participation standard is not met unless the tax-payer owns at least 10 percent of the value of the activity. §469(i)(6). The legislative history of §469 states that active participation can be established through managerial functions such as deciding on rental terms and approving tenants or capital outlays. Presumably, the standard for active participation is less than the standard for material participation.

If a passive activity involves the use of a dwelling unit and the limitation of §280A(c)(5) (discussed in Chapter 6) applies, the income, deduction, gain, or loss allocable to such use is disregarded for purposes of §469. §469(j)(10). A working interest in any oil and gas property is not a passive activity if the taxpayer has unlimited liability with respect to the property. §469(c)(3).

The term *activity* is defined in Regulation §1.469-4, which provides that trade or business or rental activities may be treated as a single activity if the activities to be grouped together are "an appropriate economic unit" for purposes of applying §469. The determination as to whether activities constitute an appropriate economic unit is based on a facts and circumstances test, but the following factors are given the greatest weight: (i) the similarities and differences in the types of trades or businesses; (ii) the extent of common control or ownership of the activities; (iii) the geographical location of the activities; and (iv) any interdependencies among the activities. Under this test, business or rental activities that are conducted at the same location and are owned by the same person are generally treated as a single activity.

The §469 passive loss rules apply only to individuals, estates, trusts, closely held C corporations, and personal service corporations. §469(a)(2). A *closely held C corporation* is defined as a corporation, 50 percent of the stock of which is held, directly or indirectly, by five or fewer individuals. §§469(j)(1), 465(a)(1)(B), 542(a)(2). A corporation is a *personal service corporation* if its principal activity is the performance of personal services and the services are substantially performed by employees who own stock of the corporation either directly or indirectly. §269A(b).

EXAMPLES

59. On January 1, year one, Ann borrows $80,000 and uses the proceeds of the loan, together with $20,000 of her own money, to open a bicycle shop. The loan is recourse and Ann does not

materially participate in the management of the shop. In year one the bicycle shop shows a net loss on operations of $30,000. In each of the following situations, state the amount of loss that Ann may deduct and the year in which Ann may deduct the loss.

a. Ann has no other investments.

b. Ann receives $20,000 of dividends from stock.

c. Ann also owns a restaurant and works there full-time. Her year one taxable income from the restaurant is $30,000.

d. Ann also owns a restaurant and does not materially participate in the restaurant. Her year one taxable income from the restaurant is $30,000.

e. Ann also owns a restaurant but does not materially participate in the management of the restaurant. In the year before year one, Ann's taxable income from the restaurant is $30,000. In year one the restaurant has no taxable income.

f. Ann also owns a restaurant but does not materially participate in the management of the restaurant. In year one the restaurant has no taxable income. In year two Ann's taxable income from the restaurant is $40,000, and the bicycle shop has zero income or loss.

g. Ann sells the bicycle shop for $130,000 on December 31, year one.

h. Ann sells the bicycle shop for $90,000 on December 31, year one.

i. On December 31, year one, Ann sells a restaurant she owns for $130,000. Ann's basis in the restaurant is $100,000 and Ann does not materially participate in the management of the restaurant. The restaurant shows no taxable income or loss from operations in year one.

j. Assume the same facts as in part (i), except that Ann sells the restaurant for $70,000.

k. Assume the same facts as in part (i), except that the loan is nonrecourse, and in year one Ann recognizes $30,000 of income from another passive activity.

60. Roger's auto repair shop shows a taxable loss of $25,000 in year one. State the amount of that loss, if any, that would be deductible in each of the following situations.

a. Year one is the first taxable year for the repair shop. The shop has five full-time employees. Roger, however, works at the shop for only 450 hours each year.

b. How, if at all, would your answer in part (a) change if Roger works at the shop for 1,050 hours?

c. How, if at all, would your answer in part (a) change if Roger works at the shop for 550 hours?

d. Roger works at the shop for only 150 hours in year nine. The shop has five full-time employees. Roger has owned the store for the past eight years. During four of those years, Roger has worked at the shop for less than 300 hours; during the remaining four years, Roger worked at the shop for over 1,500 hours.

61. On January 1, year one, Shannon starts a consulting business.

a. During year one Shannon works at the business for 150 hours and the only other employee works at the business for 100 hours. Does Shannon materially participate in the activity in year one?

b. During year one Shannon works at the business for 75 hours and there are no other employees who participate in the management of the business. Does Shannon materially participate in the activity in year one?

c. During year one Shannon works at the business for 75 hours and employs two other employees who work full-time at the activity. Does Shannon materially participate in the activity in year one?

d. Shannon works full-time in the business in years one through three. In year four she works at the business 75 hours and employs two other employees who work full-time in the activity. Does Shannon materially participate in the activity in year four?

e. Shannon works full-time in the business in years one through three. In year four she does not work at the business at all. Does Shannon materially participate in the activity in year four?

62. On January 1, year one, Juan purchases an apartment building. The apartment building shows a net loss for the year of $30,000. Juan has a full-time employee manage the building; however, Juan interviews all prospective tenants and makes the final decision on major repairs. Juan spends about 110 hours a year on the building and has no other investments. How much, if any, of the loss may Juan use to offset his salary income?

63. In year one Tissy has an $18,000 loss from an investment in a goat's milk frozen yogurt shop. She did not materially participate

in the business. In the same year, she has $10,000 of income from a limited partnership, made $30,000 in wages as an environmental analyst, and made $15,000 in the stock market. What are the tax consequences?

64. In year one Donna opens up a gas station and an adjoining convenience store located near an off-ramp of an interstate highway. Donna spends 2,000 hours managing the convenience store and approximately 100 hours overseeing the gas station operations. The gas station has a taxable loss of $50,000; the convenience store has taxable income of $40,000. Donna has no other investments. May Donna use her loss on the gas station to reduce the tax due on the convenience store income?

65. Describe the special provisions of §469, if any, that apply to the following investments.
    a. Losses recognized by large, publicly held corporations
    b. Losses recognized by limited partners
    c. Losses recognized by general partners in a limited partnership
    d. Losses recognized by trusts
    e. Losses recognized on working interests in oil and gas properties
    f. Losses recognized on rental of a vacation home

66. Under what circumstances would a taxpayer want to *avoid* material participation in a particular trade or business?

EXPLANATIONS

59. a. Section 469 prevents the deduction of any "passive activity loss." §469(a)(1). A passive activity loss is defined, in general, as the net loss from all activities that involve the conduct of a trade or business and in which the taxpayer does not materially participate. §469(c), (d). Here, Ann has a passive activity loss and so will not be able to deduct any portion of that loss in year one. Instead, that loss may be deducted in subsequent years when and if Ann has passive activity income or disposes of the bicycle shop in a taxable transaction.

   b. Investors with losses from passive activities may offset those losses against gains from other passive activities. However, passive activity losses may not offset portfolio income or trade or business income. The stock dividends constitute so-called "portfolio" income, so no portion of the loss will be deductible in year one.

c. Here, Ann has income from a non-passive activity — the restaurant at which she works on a full-time basis. Ann's passive activity loss from the bicycle shop may only offset passive income. Ann may not use the bicycle shop loss to offset this non-passive income.

d. Here, the restaurant is a passive activity because Ann does not materially participate in the activity. Ann has $30,000 of income from a passive activity, so the entire $30,000 bicycle shop loss may be deducted against that income.

e. The passive loss rules permit taxpayers to carry forward any net passive losses and apply those losses against passive activity income in subsequent years. §469(b). However, the rules do not permit taxpayers to carry back any net passive losses and apply those losses against passive activity income in past years. Here, Ann has past but no current passive activity income and therefore cannot deduct the loss in year one.

f. Ann will not be able to deduct any portion of the year one loss. Instead, that loss will carry over to year two. Since Ann has $40,000 passive activity income in year two, she may deduct the entire $30,000 loss against that income in year two.

g. Ann may deduct the entire year one loss at the time the bicycle shop is sold. §469(g). In addition, Ann will recognize gain or loss on the sale of the shop equal to the difference between the $130,000 sale price and her adjusted basis.

h. Ann may deduct the entire year one loss at the time the bicycle shop is sold. §469(g). The deduction of that earlier loss is not dependent upon the sale price. In year one Ann will also recognize gain or loss equal to the difference between the $90,000 sale price and her adjusted basis.

i. Gain from the sale of a passive activity is treated as passive activity income and can be offset against otherwise unusable passive activity loss. Ann has year one passive income of $30,000, so she will be able to deduct the entire loss from the bicycle shop. Note that while the sale of the bicycle shop would allow Ann to deduct the bicycle shop loss *regardless of whether or not Ann recognized gain on the sale,* the sale of the restaurant allows Ann to deduct the bicycle shop loss only to the extent that gain was recognized on the sale.

j. Ann recognizes a loss on the sale of her restaurant, so there is no passive income from the sale. Since she has no passive activity income in year one, she cannot deduct any of the passive activity loss from the bicycle shop. Note that if Ann had sold the bicycle shop, rather than the restaurant, at a loss, she would have been able to deduct the year one losses from the bicycle shop. To review: Loss from a passive activity may be deducted against gain from other passive activities or at the time *the passive activity that generated the loss* is sold.

k. Section 469 will not prevent deduction of the loss: The fact that the loan used to finance the passive activity is non-recourse does not affect the operation of §469. The use of nonrecourse debt may, however, prevent any loss from being recognized pursuant to the "at-risk" rules of §465, which are discussed in the next section of this book.

60. a. Roger will be able to deduct the loss only if he materially participates in the repair shop. §469(c). The term "material participation" is statutorily defined to require involvement in the activity that is regular, continuous, and substantial. §469(h). Under Temporary Regulation §1.469-5T, a taxpayer is treated as having materially participated only if she meets one of the following tests: (1) she participates in the activity for more than 500 hours; (2) her participation in the activity constitutes substantially all of the participation in the activity of all individuals; (3) she participates in the activity for more than 100 hours and as much as anyone else; (4) she participated in the activity by meeting other participation tests for five of the past ten taxable years; (5) the activity is a personal service activity (such as a law practice) and she has materially participated in the activity by meeting other participation tests for three prior years; or (6) facts and circumstances show material participation.

Finally, there is a class of activities referred to as significant participation activities. These are activities in which the taxpayer participates for more than 100 hours but do not, in themselves, constitute activities in which the taxpayer materially participates. If the sum of the hours of significant participation activities exceeds 500, then the taxpayer is treated as having materially participated in all such activities.

Here, Roger fails the first test because he does not participate for over 500 hours; he fails the second test because he does not participate as much as other employees. Tests based on prior years are not applicable (since this is his first year of operations) and, since he has no other activities, he cannot qualify under the significant participation activity test. The facts and circumstances test is not yet fully defined. Unless he qualifies under this test (which seems unlikely), Roger will not be deemed to have materially participated in the activity, and his loss will be disallowed as a passive activity loss and carried forward to year two.

b. Here, Roger participates in the activity for over 500 hours and so qualifies under the first material participation test of Temporary Regulation §1.469-5T(a).

c. Here, Roger participates in the activity for over 500 hours and so qualifies under the first material participation test of Temporary Regulation §1.469-5T(a).

d. The issue raised here is whether an individual who materially participates in an activity during four of the preceding eight years is treated as materially participating in an activity during the current year. The answer to that question depends on whether the activity is a personal service activity.

If the activity is not a personal service activity, then the material participation standard is met only if the taxpayer materially participated in the activity (as determined under other tests) for five of the preceding ten years. If it is a personal activity, then the material participation standard is met so long as the taxpayer materially participated in the activity (as determined under other tests) for three prior years. Temporary Regulation §1.469-5T(d) defines a personal service activity as an activity in the field of health, law, engineering, architecture, accounting, actuarial science, performing arts, consulting, or any other trade or business in which capital is not a material income-producing factor. If, as seems likely, capital is a material income-producing factor in an auto repair shop, then Roger will not meet the material participation test based on participation in prior years.

61. a. Shannon works at the business for over 100 hours and more than any other employee. Thus, Shannon meets the material participation test of Temporary Regulation §1.469-5T(a)(3).

b. Shannon's participation constitutes substantially all of the participation in the activity and Shannon therefore meets the material participation test of Temporary Regulation §1.469-5T(a)(2).

c. Unless Shannon somehow meets the facts and circumstances

test (which seems highly unlikely), she will not be treated as having materially participated in the activity.

d. The consulting business is a personal service activity under Temporary Regulation §1.469-5T(d). (See the explanation for 60(d).) Shannon has worked full-time at the activity during three previous years and thus met the material participation standard in those years. Because she has materially participated in the activity during three prior years, she will be treated as having materially participated in the activity in year four.

e. Shannon will be treated as having materially participated in the activity in year four because she met the material participation standard (based on over 500 hours a year participation) in three prior years. The fact that she has not participated more than 500 hours a year in the activity in more recent years is irrelevant.

62. Juan does not materially participate in the management of the building. (See discussion of the material participation tests in the explanation for example 60, above.) Moreover, under §469(c)(2), rental activities are treated as per se passive. However, §469(i) permits the deduction of the first $25,000 of losses from rental real estate activities provided the taxpayer actively participates in the activity. The deduction is reduced by 50 percent of the taxpayer's adjusted gross income in excess of $100,000. For example, a taxpayer with an adjusted gross income of $140,000 may deduct a maximum of only $5,000 of such losses, which is $25,000 less $20,000 (50 percent of $40,000).

The term active participation is not defined in the statute, which says only that the active participation standard is not met unless the taxpayer owns at least 10 percent of the value of the activity. §469(i)(6). The §469 legislative history states that active participation can be established through managerial functions such as deciding on rental terms and approving tenants or capital outlays. Presumably, the standard for active participation is therefore less than the standard for material participation. Since Juan owns 100 percent of the value of the building and makes broad managerial decisions concerning the building, it seems likely that Juan will be treated as actively participating in the management of the building. If that is the case, and Juan's adjusted gross income is less than $100,000, Juan will be able to deduct the first $25,000 of the loss. The remaining loss will be treated as a passive activity loss and may be carried forward and deducted against passive activity income in later years or deducted at the time the building is sold.

63. The §469 passive activity loss rules prevent Tissy from offsetting losses from passive activities against gains from active activities or portfolio income. Limited partnerships are presumed to be passive activities; therefore, $10,000 of the $18,000 loss from the yogurt shop may offset the $10,000 income from the limited partnership. The remaining $8,000 of loss is carried forward. Her year one taxable income is $45,000, which includes $30,000 of wages plus $15,000 of portfolio income.

64. The answer to this question depends on whether the gas station is a separate activity or part of the same activity as the convenience store. If the gas station is a separate activity, then it will probably be treated as a passive activity because Donna does not participate in the activity for more than 500 hours and (from the stated facts) does not appear to meet any of the other material participation tests. The loss may not be used to offset the income from the convenience store or any other nonpassive income. If the gas station is treated as part of the same activity as the convenience store, then the loss on the gas station may be netted against the income from the convenience store. Moreover, since the activity is active, the net $10,000 loss may be used to offset any other source of nonpassive income.

Regulation §1.469-4 provides that trade or business or rental activities may be treated as a single activity if the activities to be grouped together are "an appropriate economic unit" for purposes of applying §469. The determination as to whether activities constitute an appropriate economic unit is based on a facts and circumstances test, but the following factors are given the greatest weight: (i) the similarities and differences in the types of trades or businesses; (ii) the extent of common control or ownership of the activities; (iii) the geographical location of the activities; and (iv) any interdependencies between the activities. Under this test, business or rental activities that are conducted at the same location and are owned by the same person are generally treated as a single activity. The convenience store and the gas station would be treated as a single activity. Thus, Donna will be able to use the convenience store loss to offset the gas station income.

65. a. The passive loss rules apply only to individuals, estates, trusts, closely held C corporations, or personal service corporations. §469(a)(2). A closely held C corporation is defined as a corporation, 50 percent of the stock of which is held, directly or indirectly, by five or fewer individuals. §§469(j)(1), 466(a)(1), 542(a)(2). Thus, losses recognized by publicly held corporations are not subject to the §469 passive loss restrictions.

    b. Section 469(h)(2) provides that, unless otherwise stated in the regulations, limited partners are not treated as materially participating in an activity. Thus, limited partners in a trade or business are subject to the passive loss restrictions. However, Temporary Regulation §1.469-5T(e)(2) provides that, if the limited partner can satisfy the material participation tests of §1.469-5T(a)(1), (5), or (6) (described above) with respect to an activity, the passive loss limitation does not apply to the limited partner's losses from that activity.

    c. Losses recognized by general partners in a limited partnership are treated like any other form of losses and are subject to the passive loss rules if the partnership engages in a trade or business and the general partners do not meet the material participation standard.

    d. Losses recognized by trusts are treated like any other form of losses and are subject to the passive loss rules if the trust engages in a trade or business and the beneficiaries do not meet the material participation standard.

    e. Losses recognized on working interests in oil and gas properties may be deducted even if the investor does not materially participate in the activity, provided that the taxpayer has unlimited liability with respect to the activity. §469(c)(3).

    f. Losses recognized on the rental of a vacation home are subject to the limitation of §280A(c)(5) (discussed in Chapter 6) and not §469. §469(j)(10).

66. A taxpayer will want to avoid material participation in a trade or business if the business is profitable and the taxpayer has other passive activities that are unprofitable. Suppose, for example, a taxpayer owns a restaurant and does not participate in the management of the restaurant. The restaurant has a taxable loss of $50,000. Suppose, further, that the taxpayer owns a printing shop that has a taxable income of $50,000. If the taxpayer actively participates in the printing shop, she will have taxable income of

$50,000 from that shop and a passive activity loss that she cannot currently deduct. Her current net taxable income from the two activities will be $50,000. If, instead, the taxpayer does not materially participate in the printing shop, she will have $50,000 of passive income from that shop and $50,000 of passive loss from the restaurant. Now she will be able to net the passive income and passive loss and show no net taxable income from the two activities. Remember, a passive loss cannot be used to offset nonpassive income, but can be used to offset passive income. So taxpayers who already have otherwise unusable passive losses will want future taxable income to be passive rather than active.

c. The At-Risk Rules of §465

Reading: §465

Section 465 limits the deduction of losses from trade or business activities to the amount of the taxpayer's at-risk investment. §465(a)(1). Losses disallowed under §465 are carried forward to the next year. §465(a)(2).

A taxpayer's *at-risk amount* includes cash contributed by the taxpayer to the activity, the basis of property contributed by the taxpayer to the activity, and debt for which the taxpayer is personally liable or that is secured by assets of the taxpayer (other than assets used in the activity). §465(b). The taxpayer's at-risk amount is reduced by any money distributed by the activity to the taxpayer and by the amount of losses that are allowed under §465 based on the taxpayer's at-risk amount. Prop. Reg. §§1.465-22(c)(2) and 1.465-23(c). The at-risk amount is increased by income from the activity that the taxpayer includes but does not withdraw from the activity. Prop. Reg. §1.465-22(c).

A taxpayer's at-risk amount from a real estate activity also includes "qualified nonrecourse financing," which is generally financing (i) borrowed from a "qualified person" and (ii) secured by the real property used in the activity. §465(b)(6). A *qualified person* is defined as an unrelated party who did not sell the taxpayer the property or obtain a fee with respect to the taxpayer's investment in the property. §§465(b)(6)(D), 49(a)(1)(D)(iv). Attribution rules apply to determine whether the taxpayer and lender are related. §§465(b)(3)(C) and (6)(D)(i), 49(a)(1)(D)(iv), 267(b), and 707(b)(1). For example, if a lending bank is owned and controlled by the taxpayer, the taxpayer and the bank are related so the lender is not a qualified person. If a taxpayer borrows from a party that is not a "qualified person," the debt is still qualified nonrecourse financing if the terms of the financing are commercially reasonable and similar to the terms of loans made to unrelated borrowers. §465(b)(6)(D)(ii).

If, at the close of the year, the taxpayer's at-risk amount is a negative number (which could result from distributions being made during the year), the taxpayer must include in income the absolute value of the negative at-risk amount. §465(e). In effect, this rule provides for "recapture" of losses, previously allowed under §465, that would not have been allowed under §465 had the distributions not followed the losses deducted by the taxpayer. The amount included under §465(e) is treated as a deduction allocable to the activity in the next year. §465(e)(1)(B).

Individuals are subject to the at-risk rules of §465. §465(a)(1)(A). The at-risk rules also apply to a C corporation if more than 50 percent of the stock of the corporation is directly or indirectly owned by five or fewer individuals. §§465(a)(1)(B) and 542(a)(2).

The at-risk rules are applied before the §469 passive loss limitation. In other words, the §469 limitation applies only to losses allowed under §465.

EXAMPLES

67. Siskel N. Ebert, a prominent movie critic, buys a motion picture for $500,000. He puts up $50,000 of his own money and $450,000 from a nonrecourse loan. In the first year of distribution, the movie loses $80,000. What are the tax consequences?

68. On January 1, year one, Arnold borrows $100,000 from a local savings and loan. The loan is nonrecourse. Arnold uses the $100,000 of loan proceeds, together with $20,000 of his own funds, to purchase a travel agency that rents space in a downtown office building. In year one, the travel agency has a taxable loss of $30,000; Arnold pays interest on the $100,000 loan but does not make any principal payments on the loan. In year two, the travel agency has a taxable loss of $20,000; Arnold pays interest on the $100,000 loan and makes a $25,000 principal payment on the loan so that at the end of the year the loan balance is $75,000. Arnold materially participates in the travel agency in year one and year two.

    a. How much, if any, of the travel agency loss may Arnold deduct in year one?

    b. How much, if any, of the travel agency loss may Arnold deduct in year two?

    c. How, if at all, would your answer in part (a) change if the travel agency that Arnold purchased were located in a separate building, and if the building, and the land on which the building was located, were included in the purchase price?

69. On January 1, year one, Maria borrows $70,000 from a commercial bank and uses the loan proceeds, together with $30,000 of her own funds, to purchase the food and souvenir concession at a local ballpark. The loan is nonrecourse. In year one the concession has a taxable loss of $40,000. In year two the concession has taxable income from operations of $25,000. Maria does not contribute or withdraw any funds from the operation in year one or year two. Maria materially participates in the activity during both years.

    a. How much, if any, of the concession loss may Maria deduct in year one?

    b. How much, if any, of the concession income must Maria report in year two?

    c. Assume the same facts as in part (a), except that the $70,000 loan is recourse. How much, if any, of the year one loss may Maria deduct?

70. On January 1, year one, David borrows $150,000 from a commercial bank and uses the loan proceeds, together with $50,000 of his own funds, to purchase an apartment building. The loan is nonrecourse. In year one the apartment building has a taxable loss of $60,000.

    a. How much, if any, of the loss may David deduct?

    b. Assume the same facts as in part (a), except that the loan is made by David's brother. How much, if any, of the loss may David deduct?

71. On January 1, year one, Nancy borrows $90,000 and uses the proceeds, together with $10,000 of her own funds, to purchase an apartment building. The loan is nonrecourse and is made by the seller of the property. In year one the building generates a taxable loss of $15,000, and her basis in the building is reduced to $85,000 (for depreciation). On January 1, year two, Nancy sells the building for $95,000; she receives $5,000 and the buyer takes the building subject to the mortgage of $90,000. Describe the tax consequences of the investment in year one and year two.

72. On January 1, year one, wealthy socialite Mary purchases 10 pieces of art from a local artist for $500 apiece. During the next few years, Mary purchases another 20 pieces of art for an average of $500 apiece. On January 1, year four, Mary borrows $40,000 from a bank and uses the proceeds, together with the art she has collected, to open up an art gallery. Mary's basis in the art is $15,000; the fair market value of the art on January 1, year four, is $100,000. The bank loan is nonrecourse and is secured by the artwork. The art gallery shows a taxable loss in year four of $20,000. Mary materially participates in the operation of the art gallery. How much, if any, of the year four loss may Mary deduct?

73. On January 1, year one, publicly traded High Corporation borrows $800,000 and uses $200,000 of its own funds to purchase an apartment building. The loan is nonrecourse and is financed by the seller of the property. In year one High Corporation recognizes a taxable loss on the building of $210,000. What portion, if any, of the loss may the corporation deduct?

EXPLANATIONS

67. Because of the at-risk rules, Siskel may only deduct losses from the activity to the extent of his financial stake in the deal, or the amount which he is personally at risk of losing. Therefore, Siskel may only deduct $50,000 of the first year's loss. Siskel is not at risk for the $450,000 loan because it is nonrecourse. The $30,000 disallowed loss may be carried forward to the next year to offset any income from the movie in that year. §465(a), (c).

68. a. Section 465 limits the deductions from trade or business activities to the amount of the taxpayer's at-risk investment. A taxpayer's at-risk amount includes cash contributed by the taxpayer, here $20,000. §465(b). The $100,000 of debt is not included in Arnold's at-risk amount because Arnold is not personally liable on the debt and the debt is not qualified nonrecourse financing. §465(b)(2). In year one Arnold's at-risk amount is thus $20,000, so Arnold will be able to deduct only $20,000 of the $30,000 loss. The $10,000 of loss disallowed under §465 is carried forward to year two. §465(a)(2).

    b. The $10,000 loss not allowed in year one will carry over to year two. In year two the travel agency loses another $20,000, so the potential loss allowable in year two is $30,000. The deduction of this loss, however, will be limited to Arnold's at-risk amount.

Here, the at-risk investment at the start of the year is zero ($20,000 original at-risk amount less $20,000 of loss allowed in year one under §465). §465(b)(5). The $25,000 of cash Arnold contributes to pay down the loan increases his amount at-risk, so his amount at-risk for year two is $25,000. Thus, he is allowed to deduct $25,000 of the $30,000 of losses. The $5,000 of loss disallowed in year two is carried forward to year three. In years one and two Arnold has contributed $45,000 and has been allowed to deduct $45,000 of losses.

c. Although nonrecourse debt does not generally increase the taxpayer's amount at-risk, nonrecourse debt that is "qualified nonrecourse financing" does increase the amount at-risk "in the case of an activity of holding real property." §465(b)(6). Qualified nonrecourse financing is financing (i) borrowed from a "qualified person" and (ii) secured by the real property used in the activity. §465(b)(6). A qualified person is defined as an unrelated party who did not sell the taxpayer the property or obtain a fee with respect to the taxpayer's investment in the property. §§465(b)(6)(D), 49(a)(1)(D)(iv).

Here, part of the nonrecourse financing was attributable to the real estate that was included in the purchase price. Arnold might argue that, under §465(b)(6), his year one amount at-risk includes some portion of the nonrecourse debt. Neither the statute nor the regulations directly define "an activity of holding real estate." If part of the nonrecourse debt is treated as qualified nonrecourse financing because it is attributable to a real estate activity, that portion of the debt would increase his year one amount at-risk and would allow him to deduct part or all of the $10,000 of year one loss in excess of his $20,000 cash contribution. This would, in turn, reduce the amount of year one loss to be carried forward to year two.

69. a. Maria's at-risk amount is $30,000, the amount of cash she contributed to the activity. The $70,000 of debt is not included in Maria's at-risk amount because Maria is not personally liable on the debt and the debt is not qualified nonrecourse financing. §465(b)(2). In year one Maria's at-risk amount is thus $30,000, so she will be able to deduct only $30,000 of the $40,000 loss. The $10,000 of loss disallowed under §465 is carried forward to year two. §465(a)(2).

b. The $10,000 loss that Maria could not deduct in year one is treated as an allowable deduction in year two, provided that Maria has a sufficient amount at-risk in that latter year. §465(a)(2). The amount at-risk is increased by income included and not withdrawn from the activity. Prop. Reg. §1.465-22(c). Thus, Maria has $25,000 at-risk in year two, and so can deduct the $10,000 of loss carried forward from year one. In year two Maria's net income from the activity will be $15,000—the $25,000 of operating income less the $10,000 loss carried forward from year one. Maria's at-risk amount at the end of year two will be $15,000.

   c. Maria's amount at-risk includes both the $30,000 of cash contributed and the $70,000 of debt for which she is personally liable. §465(b)(1), (2). Since her amount at-risk in year one is $100,000, she is allowed to deduct the entire $40,000 loss in year one.

70. a. David has contributed $50,000 cash; the question here is whether any portion of the borrowed funds will increase his at-risk amount and thereby increase the amount of allowable deduction. As noted above, funds borrowed on a nonrecourse basis generally do not increase a taxpayer's at-risk amount. However, §465(b)(6) provides a special exception for nonrecourse financing used to finance the activity of holding real property. Such borrowed funds increase the taxpayer's at-risk amount provided that the funds are borrowed from a "qualified person." A qualified person is defined as an unrelated party who did not sell the taxpayer the property or obtain a fee with respect to the taxpayer's investment in the property. §§465(b)(6)(D), 49(a)(1)(D)(iv).

     Even if the property is purchased from a related party, such as the taxpayer's sister or controlled business, nonrecourse funds will increase the at-risk amount provided that the loan is commercially reasonable and on substantially the same terms as loans involving unrelated persons. §465(b)(6)(D)(ii). Here, unless the bank is owned by the taxpayer or is the seller of the property, the bank is a qualified person and so the loan will increase David's at-risk amount. Note that even if the bank is a related party (and not a qualified person for that reason), the loan proceeds will increase David's at-risk amount provided that the loan is made at commercially reasonable rates and on substantially the same terms as loans involving unrelated persons.

b. Here, the loan is made by a related party. As a result, the loan will increase the at-risk amounts only if it is made at commercially reasonable rates and on substantially the same terms as loans made to unrelated persons.

71. Nancy's at-risk amount includes the $10,000 of cash she contributed to the activity. As noted above, although funds borrowed on a nonrecourse basis generally do not increase a taxpayer's at-risk amount, §465(b)(6) provides a special exception for nonrecourse financing that is used to finance the activity of holding real property. Such borrowed funds increase the taxpayer's at-risk amount provided the loan is from a qualified person and the debt is secured by the property. Here, the seller of the property is not a qualified person, so the debt here is not qualified nonrecourse financing. §49(a)(1)(D)(iv)(II).

    In year one Nancy is allowed to deduct $10,000 of the $15,000 loss because her at-risk amount is $10,000. In year two Nancy will recognize $10,000 of gain (which may be capital gain, under §1231, discussed in Chapter 8) and deduct a $5,000 ordinary loss. Note that Nancy recognizes a total loss on the transaction of $5,000 — the sum of the $10,000 year one loss allowed as a deduction in year one, the $5,000 year one loss allowed as a deduction in year two, and $10,000 of income recognized in year two. This corresponds to Nancy's out-of-pocket loss of $5,000. At the time an activity subject to §465 is sold, the aggregate tax losses will mirror the out-of-pocket losses.

72. Mary's year four at-risk amount includes the $15,000 basis of the artwork she contributed to the activity. §465(b)(1)(A). Her at-risk amount does not include the nonrecourse debt, which is secured by property used in the activity. §465(b)(2)(B). Since her year four at-risk amount is $15,000, she is allowed to deduct $15,000 of the $20,000 year four loss. The $5,000 of year four loss that is disallowed is carried forward to year five.

73. The at-risk rules apply only to corporations that are closely held. Other corporations are not subject to the at-risk rules. High Corporation is not closely held and therefore may deduct the entire loss unimpeded by the at-risk rules. Note that if the taxpayer here were an individual, the loss would be limited to the $200,000 cash investment. This transaction would not qualify for the qualified nonrecourse financing exception because, while the invest-

ment is in real estate and the loan is commercially reasonable, the lender here is the seller of the property.

d. The Limitations on §§264 and 265

Reading: §§264, 265

A number of anti-abuse provisions prevent taxpayers from deducting interest on debt incurred to purchase certain types of assets on which income is either exempt or deferred. For example, §265(a)(2) provides that a taxpayer is not allowed to deduct interest on debt incurred or carried to purchase obligations that are exempt from tax under §103. This rule prevents a taxpayer in the 40 percent bracket from making an after-tax profit by borrowing at 10 percent (for an after-tax cost of 6 percent) to purchase tax-exempt bonds that yield 7 percent.

As another example, §264(a)(2) provides that a taxpayer is not allowed to deduct interest on debt incurred or carried to purchase a single premium life insurance policy or annuity contract. A policy or contract is treated as a single premium contract or policy if substantially all of the premiums due on the policy or contract are paid within four years of the date on which it was purchased. §264(b).

Similarly, §264(a)(3) disallows a deduction for interest incurred to purchase or carry a life insurance policy pursuant to a plan that contemplates systematic borrowing. However, §264(c) overrides §264(a)(3) and allows deductions for interest paid pursuant to a plan of systematic borrowing if the first four premiums are paid with funds that have not been borrowed.

EXAMPLES

74. On January 1, year one, Xavier borrows $80,000 and uses the proceeds, together with $20,000 of his own funds, to purchase tax-exempt municipal bonds. The loan is nonrecourse. In year one Xavier receives $7,000 of interest on the bonds and pays $8,000 interest on the loan used to purchase the bonds. How much, if any, of the interest expense may Xavier deduct?

75. On January 1, year one, Carol borrows $90,000 and uses the proceeds, together with $10,000 of her own funds to purchase a single premium life insurance policy that pays $1 million upon Carol's death. Carol's life expectancy at the time of the purchase is

35 years. In year one Carol pays $8,100 interest on the loan. How much, if any, of the interest is deductible?

76. On January 1, year one, Carl purchases a so-called "level payment whole life insurance policy" that requires Carl to pay $5,000 a year in return for payment of $500,000 upon Carl's death. If Carl lives to his life expectancy, his total premiums will aggregate $150,000. The $500,000 payment to his beneficiaries will represent a return on investment of about 8 percent.

Carl pays the first 10 premiums with funds that were not borrowed. The $5,000 premium for the 11th year, however, is paid with funds loaned to Carl from the insurance company. If Carl dies before repaying the loan, the insurance company will reduce the amounts paid to Carl's beneficiaries by the amount of the loan. The interest rate on the loan from the insurance company is 10 percent. In the 12th year, Carl again borrows the amount of the premium from the insurance company. Carl borrows an additional amount from the insurance company to cover the $500 of interest owed on the loan from the prior year. Carl continues this practice for the next eight years, so that in years 11 through 20, all funds paid to the insurance company are borrowed. During that time, the principal on his debt continues to grow, as do the interest payments he owes on that debt. The total interest Carl "pays" to the insurance company during those years is about $10,000.

a. How much, if any, of the interest may Carl deduct?

b. Assume the same facts as in part (a), except that Carl borrows the funds needed to pay the premiums and interest on prior loans from savings institutions rather than the insurance company. How much, if any, of the interest is deductible?

EXPLANATIONS

74. In this example, Xavier is paying $8,000 to earn $7,000. This otherwise irrational behavior is tax-motivated. The $7,000 income is tax-free; if Xavier is in the 40 percent marginal tax bracket and can deduct the $8,000 interest expense, his after-tax interest expense will be only $4,800. A before-tax loss of $1,000 would turn into an after-tax profit of $2,200 ($7,000 less $4,800). Unfortunately for Xavier, §265(a)(2) prohibits any deduction for interest on indebtedness incurred to purchase or carry tax-exempt bonds, so he will not be allowed to deduct his interest expense.

75. Section 264(a)(2) prohibits the deduction of any amount paid on indebtedness incurred to purchase or carry a single premium life insurance contract. The reason for this rule is that such contracts present the same kind of mismatching of income and expense as tax-exempt bonds. Each year, as Carol grows older, the value of the life insurance policy increases; at the time of Carol's death, the contract will be worth $1 million. There is no tax on the annual increase in value and, under §101, no tax on the eventual payout of the contract to the beneficiaries of the contract. Some life insurance policies permit the policyholder to borrow some of the increase in value and, in some cases, no tax will be levied on such borrowing. (Section 72(e) will treat certain loans to policyholders as income.)

    Absent §264, Carol could borrow at 9 percent to fund a policy that increased in value (when measured by the difference between purchase price and payout at expected age of death) by 8 percent. The policy would show a before-tax loss and, if the interest were deductible, an after-tax gain. As it turns out, though, §264(a)(2) disallows any deduction for interest incurred or continued to purchase or carry a single premium life insurance, endowment, or annuity contract. Thus, Carol will not be allowed to deduct any of the interest expense associated with the policy.

76. a. Carl is borrowing at 10 percent to earn 8 percent. However, the appreciation of the policy is not taxed. If the interest on the loan is deductible, then Carl will make an after-tax profit on the transaction so long as his tax rate is above 20 percent. If, for example, Carl is in the 28 percent tax rate, the after-tax cost of the loan will be only 7.2 percent, which is 10 percent less 2.8 percent (28 percent of 10 percent). As noted in the previous explanation, §264(a)(2) disallows any deduction for interest incurred in connection with the purchase of a single premium life insurance contract. Carl's contract requires annual payments and is not a single premium life insurance contract. (Note, however, that under §264(b)(1), a life insurance policy on which substantially all of the premiums are paid in the first four years is treated as a single premium policy.)

    Section 264(a)(3) disallows any deduction for interest incurred to purchase or carry a life insurance policy pursuant to a plan that contemplates systemic borrowing. However, §264(c) overrides §264(a)(3) and allows deductions for interest paid pursuant to a plan of systematic borrowing if the first four premiums are paid with funds that have not been borrowed. Since Carl has met this latter condition, the interest on the loans will not be limited by §264.

b. For tax purposes, the fact that Carl borrows the funds from outside sources, rather than the insurance company, is irrelevant. All of the interest will be deductible.

e. The Accuracy-Related Penalties of §6662

Reading: §6662

As part of its efforts to discourage tax shelters, Congress also overhauled the penalty provisions of the Code. Section 6662 imposes a penalty in the case of a "substantial understatement of income tax," which is defined as the greater of (i) an understatement of 10 percent of the tax due for the year or (ii) $5,000. §6662(d)(1)(A). The difference between the correct tax due for the year and the tax shown on the return for the year is the understatement of tax for the year. §6662(d)(2)(A). However, the understatement is reduced by amounts attributable to the tax treatment of an item for which the taxpayer had "substantial authority," provided that, in the case of a tax shelter, the taxpayer reasonably believed that the manner in which the taxpayer treated the item was "more likely than not the proper treatment." §6662(d)(2)(B), (C)(i)(II). The substantial understatement penalty is 20 percent of the understatement. §6662(a).

Section 6662 also imposes an accuracy-related penalty if an underpayment of tax is attributable to the taxpayer overstating the value of property. This penalty is discussed (in the context of the §170 charitable contribution deduction) in Chapter 4.

Various other provisions impose penalties on tax shelter promoters and require additional information reporting by tax shelters. See, e.g., §§6700, 6701, 6111, 6112, 6707, and 6708.

4. Sale and Leaseback Transactions

Suppose that a low bracket or exempt taxpayer plans to buy a significant amount of depreciable property. Since the tax to be saved from depreciation deductions increases as the taxpayer's tax bracket increases, the low bracket taxpayer may attempt to reduce its cost for the property by shifting the depreciation to a higher bracket taxpayer. For example, a low bracket taxpayer might sell depreciable property to a high bracket taxpayer in exchange for the proceeds of a loan incurred by the high bracket taxpayer, and then lease the property back from the high bracket taxpayer. In such a sale-leaseback transaction (also referred to as a "leveraged lease"), the low bracket taxpayer would retain use of the property, but the high bracket taxpayer would nominally own the property and obtain large depreciation deductions.

The taxpayers' characterization of a lease may not, however, be respected. Courts may recharacterize a lease payment as a loan or a conditional installment purchase like the one we saw earlier in this chapter in *Starr's Estate*. Recharacterization is most likely where (i) the length of the lease is greater than the useful life of the property, (ii) the lessee bears the risk of damage to the property, or (iii) the lease payments equal the purchase price, plus interest, of the leased property and the lessee has the option to renew the lease for a nominal amount. However, the lease transaction will usually be respected if there is a business purpose for the transaction and the lessor retains sufficient burdens and benefits of owning the leased property.

Leveraged lease transactions can be quite complex and the characterization of a leveraged lease may turn on a variety of factors. However, the Service will issue an advance ruling that a transaction constitutes a lease if certain requirements, including the following, are met: (i) the lessor must have at least 20 percent of the cost of the leased property at risk unconditionally; (ii) the lessee may not have the option to purchase the leased property for less than the value of the property; (iii) the lessor may not have the right to require the lessee to purchase the property on the expiration of the lease; (iv) the lessee may not furnish any part of the cost of the leased property or loan the lessor any of the funds used to purchase the property; (v) the lessor must expect the lease transaction to generate a positive cash flow without regard to the tax consequences of the transaction; and (vi) the useful life of the leased property must be greater than the term of the lease. Rev. Proc. 75-21 and Rev. Proc. 75-28. However, if the leased property is property that can be used only by the lessee (referred to as "limited use property"), the transaction will not be treated as a lease. Rev. Proc. 76-30.

Even if the transaction cannot meet the advance ruling requirements, the transaction may still qualify as a lease under case law. Courts appear to examine each transaction using a facts and circumstances test and to interpret that test rather loosely in the taxpayer's favor. A transaction that leaves at least some of the indicia of ownership in the hands of the ostensible lessor will be treated as a bona fide lease.

For example, in Frank Lyon Co. v. Commissioner, 435 U.S. 561 (1978), a lessor was allowed to deduct depreciation on property subject to a leveraged lease because the court concluded that the lessor retained some incidents of ownership of the leased property. Simplifying the facts in that case somewhat, Worthen Bank, the lessee, was in a rush to build a new bank headquarters but discovered that bank regulations would not allow it to build the structure as it had planned. The bank then structured the following leveraged lease transaction: Worthen constructed the new building and sold it to Frank Lyon Co. (a home appliance distributor run by a member of the Worthen board) for $7.6 million, $500,000 of which was funded by Frank Lyon Co. and $7.1 million of which was borrowed from a third party lender, New York Life. Worthen then leased the building back from Frank Lyon Co. in exchange for annual rent of $580,000, which equaled the annual amounts Frank Lyon Co. was required to pay New York Life on the building loan. The New York Life loan would be fully repaid after 25 years, at which time the lease payments would drop to $300,000 a year. In addition, Worthen had the option of repurchasing the building for an amount that equaled Lyon's $500,000 investment in the building plus a six percent return on that investment. The lease was a net lease, so Worthen paid the costs of maintaining the building.

Frank Lyon Co. included the $580,000 of rent received from Worthen in income, deducted the interest it paid to New York Life, and claimed large depreciation deductions on the building. The Commissioner disallowed the deductions on the theory that Worthen, not Frank Lyon Co., owned the building. The Commissioner recharacterized the transaction as one in which Worthen borrowed $500,000 from Frank Lyon Co., at 6 percent interest, and borrowed $7.1 million from New York Life, with Frank Lyon Co. acting as a conduit through which the New York Life loan proceeds passed. This recharacterization was based on several factors: (i) the rent due from Worthen to Frank Lyon Co. equaled the amounts Frank Lyon Co. owed New York Life; (ii) Worthen had the option to buy the building by repaying Frank Lyon Co. its investment plus a 6 percent return; (iii) as soon as the New York Life loan was repaid, the rent dropped by almost 50 percent; (iv) the lease was a net lease, so Worthen paid the costs of maintaining the building; and (v) Worthen built the building.

However, the Supreme Court majority refused to recharacterize the sale-leaseback transaction and held that Frank Lyon Co. was entitled to deduct the depreciation on the building. The Court reached this decision based on several factors: (i) bank regulations prevented

Worthen from owning the building itself (so it did not appear that Worthen entered into the transaction for a tax avoidance motive); (ii) the transaction involved three parties (not two parties, as is the case in many sale-leaseback transactions); and (iii) Frank Lyon Co. ran the risk that Worthen would default on the lease before the New York Life loan had been repaid. (The Court also erroneously assumed that Frank Lyon Co. and Worthen Bank were in comparable tax brackets, so that attributing the depreciation to Worthen instead of Frank Lyon Co. would not have raised revenue. Worthen Bank was in fact subject to a lower rate than Frank Lyon Co.)

EXAMPLES

77. Sky Airlines Inc. has significant net operating losses from operations in previous years, so it is taxed at a zero rate. The airline needs to add a new plane to its fleet. If the airline leased the plane directly from the manufacturer, the airline would have to pay the manufacturer $2.1 million a year for 20 years (for a total of $42 million) and, at the end of the 20-year lease term, would have the option to buy the airplane for its value at that time.

    Instead of leasing the plane from the manufacturer, Sky Airlines will lease the airplane from the Top Gun Leasing Partnership, in which the four partners (who each materially participate in the partnership) are in the 40 percent tax bracket. The Top Gun Leasing partnership will acquire the plane from the manufacturer for $25 million, $5 million of which it will fund and $20 million of which will be funded by a recourse loan from an insurance company. Top Gun Leasing will make annual payments of $2 million on the debt for 20 years (for total payments of interest and principal of $40 million).

    Sky Airlines will lease the plane from the Top Gun Leasing on the following terms: (i) the initial term of the lease will be 20 years; (ii) during that lease term, Sky Airlines will pay Top Gun annual lease payments of $2 million (for a total of $40 million during the initial 20-year term of the lease); (iii) on the expiration of the initial lease term, Sky Airlines has the option to renew the lease for another 10 years for an annual lease payment of $50,000 a year; (iv) on the expiration of the initial lease term, Sky Airlines also has the option to purchase the airplane for $30,000; and (v) Sky Airlines will provide all maintenance and insurance on the airplane. The useful life of the airplane is 20 years. Will the partners in the Top Gun Leasing partnership be treated as the owners of the airplane, for purposes of determining who is entitled to depreciation deductions on the airplane?

78. Dennis Company is considering borrowing $10 million and using the proceeds to purchase an office building to house its growing administrative staff. In the first year, interest on the loan will come to $1 million, and the building expenses for property taxes, insurance, and maintenance will be $400,000. Dennis Company expects that these out-of-pocket expenses of $1.4 million will be fully deductible. Dennis Company will also deduct $350,000 of depreciation. Unfortunately, for the next five years Dennis Company does not expect to have annual taxable income in excess of $1.3 million, so $100,000 of the out-of-pocket expenses, and the entire $350,000 depreciation deduction, are likely to be of no use.

For the sake of simplicity, assume that no principal payments are required on the loan for the first five years. After that time the required payments will increase slightly to provide for amortization of the balance of the loan. The term of the loan is 30 years.

Dennis Company arranges with Finance Company for the latter to purchase the office building. Dennis Company agrees to pay Finance Company rent of $900,000 a year. Dennis Company will also pay the $400,000 of property taxes, insurance, and maintenance. The term of the rental agreement is 30 years. The arrangement leaves Dennis Company with out-of-pocket expenses of only $1.3 million—a savings of $100,000.

Finance Company plans to borrow the $10 million and to incur $1 million in annual interest expense. Finance Company will take in $900,000 rent and thus recognize a $100,000 out-of-pocket before-tax loss each year on the investment. However, Finance Company will also take the depreciation of $350,000 and so recognize a tax loss of $450,000. That loss, at Finance Company's tax rate of 34 percent, will produce tax savings of about $150,000. Thus, Finance Company will make an after-tax profit of $50,000 each year (negative cash flow of $100,000 plus tax savings of $150,000). The expenses of operating the building will be borne by Dennis Company.

The term of the rental agreement between Dennis Company and Finance Company is 30 years; however, Dennis Company has an option to purchase the property at the end of five years for

$10 million or at the end of any succeeding year for the amount of the remaining balance of the loan. Will Finance Company be treated as the owner of the building for purposes of determining who is entitled to depreciation deductions on the building?

EXPLANATIONS

77. This is a tough call. This transaction could be characterized as either of the following: (i) a sale of the plane by the manufacturer to Top Gun Leasing and a lease of the plane from Top Gun to Sky Airlines (in which case Top Gun Leasing owns the plane) or (ii) a sale of the plane by the manufacturer to Sky Airlines, with Top Gun acting as a conduit through which the payments from Sky Airlines to the insurance company lender pass (in which case Sky Airlines owns the plane).

The Service will issue an advance ruling that states that a leveraged lease transaction constitutes a lease if certain requirements are met. Rev. Proc. 75-21, Rev. Proc. 75-28. One of the requirements is that the lessor has at-risk at least 20 percent of the purchase price. That requirement is met here because the partners have either paid or assumed personal liability for the full purchase price of the plane. Another requirement is that the useful life of the property must be greater than the term of the leasehold interest. That requirement is not met here. Another requirement is that the transaction generates positive cash flow without regard to the tax consequences of the transaction. This requirement is not met here because the transaction will lose money on a before-tax basis.

The transaction here would not constitute a lease under the advance ruling test since the requirements of the revenue procedures are not satisfied. However, the transaction may still qualify as a lease under case law. Courts appear to examine each transaction on a facts and circumstances test and to interpret that test rather loosely in the taxpayer's favor. A transaction that leaves at least some of the indicia of ownership in the hands of the ostensible lessor will likely be treated as bona fide lease. See Frank Lyon Co. v. United States, 435 U.S. 561 (1978).

The factors indicating that Sky Airlines purchased the airplane, using Top Gun as a financing conduit, are the following: (i) the initial 20-year lease term coincides with the useful life of the airplane; (ii) the lease is a net lease; (iii) the annual lease payments drop significantly after the initial 20-year lease term;

and (iv) Sky Airlines can acquire title to the airplane by paying a nominal amount on the expiration of the initial lease term.

However, some of the facts here are reminiscent of the *Frank Lyon* case, in which the court refused to recharacterize the lease. Here, the Top Gun Leasing Partnership invested $5 million of its own money and assumed personal liability on the entire amount of debt used to finance the purchase of the plane. In other words, Top Gun was exposed to economic risk of loss with respect to the property. As in *Frank Lyon,* the transaction here is not a two-party transaction. (In addition, the seller here is a third party manufacturer, not the lessee, as was the case in *Frank Lyon.*) On the other hand, the motive for the lease transaction here is likely tax avoidance. Taking into account all of the factors here, it is unclear whether a court would recharacterize this lease.

78. The agreement between Dennis Company and Finance Company is obviously motivated by tax savings. The building will produce a taxable loss of $1.75 million each year. Dennis Company cannot use more than $1.3 million of this loss. Thus, $450,000 of annual loss is wasted in that it will not currently reduce Dennis Company's taxes. It would be in Dennis Company's interest to "sell" this loss to someone who could use it currently.

The lease arrangement described here has the effect of a sale of this tax loss. Finance Company receives the benefit of an additional $450,000 annual tax deduction, which produces an after-tax savings of about $150,000. Finance Company gives back $100,000 of this savings by charging Dennis Company only $900,000 in rent when the carrying costs on the loan used to purchase the building are $1 million.

Has anything else changed? Before the transaction Dennis Company paid interest expense and maintenance costs. In return Dennis Company got exclusive use of a new office building. After the transaction Dennis Company pays maintenance costs and rental payments that are approximately equal to the interest expense. Again, Dennis Company gets exclusive use of a new office building. As for Finance Company, it is perhaps best seen as a conduit: Each month it receives a rent payment that it then sends, along with some of its own funds, to the bank as interest on the loan. Finance Company achieves significant tax savings through the arrangement and passes some of those savings back to Dennis Company by charging less rent than the interest it must pay the lender.

Will the lease be recharacterized? In similar cases, the courts have looked to the tax motivation of the parties, and the indicia of ownership possessed by the parties. See Frank Lyon Co. v. United States, 435 U.S. 561 (1978); Swift Dodge v. Commissioner, 692 F.2d 651 (9th Cir. 1982). Here, there does not appear to be any nontax reason for the arrangement. Moreover, the indicia of ownership seem to rest with Dennis Company. Neither Dennis Company nor Finance Company has invested any cash in the property. However, if the property appreciates in value, Dennis Company will exercise the option and purchase the property. If the property depreciates in value, Dennis Company will be obligated under the long-term lease to make payments approximately equal to the payments Finance Company must make to the lender. Thus, the benefits and burdens of changes in value rest with Dennis Company, which is also responsible for the annual maintenance costs.

However, as in *Frank Lyon*, the lessor is obligated to make the interest payments on the debt incurred to purchase the leased property even if the lessee defaults on the lease. In *Frank Lyon*, the Supreme Court accepted the form of the transaction and ruled for the taxpayers, notwithstanding the tax benefits realized by the parties. The Court based its favorable ruling largely upon the fact that the taxpayer was able to point to a nontax motive for the transaction: Federal bank regulators had (at least initially) refused to allow the bank to own its own building. Moreover, the taxpayer in *Frank Lyon* put up $500,000 of its own money (on an investment of about $7.5 million) and so had some of its own funds at risk. Here, Dennis Company has no nontax motive for entering into the transaction and has put up no funds of its own, so it seems likely that the lease would be recharacterized as a financing transaction, in which case Dennis Company, not Finance Company, would be treated as the owner of the building.

5. Alternative Minimum Tax

Reading: §§55-59

The alternative minimum tax, which imposes a lower rate of tax on a base that is broader than the regular income tax base, reflects Congressional ambivalence over the current panoply of tax preferences and deductions. On the one hand, Congress believes the favorable treatment granted charitable donations or investments in depreciable or depletable property serves a valuable purpose. On the other hand, Congress believes that no person of substantial means should be able to eliminate tax liability by taking advantage of these preferences. The alternative minimum tax allows the continued use of tax preferences, but, in effect, prevents taxpayers from using certain tax preferences to reduce their tax liability to zero.

A taxpayer owes alternative minimum tax only if the taxpayer's *tentative minimum tax* for the year is more than the taxpayer's regular tax liability. §55(a). An individual taxpayer's tentative minimum tax equals 26 percent or 28 percent of *alternative minimum taxable income* in excess of the *exemption amount*. §55(b)(1). The alternative minimum tax rate for corporate taxpayers is 20 percent. Id. The exemption amount for individuals is $33,750 or $45,000, depending on the taxpayer's filing status. The exemption amount for corporations is $40,000. §55(d)(1), (2). However, the taxpayer's exemption amount is phased out if the taxpayer's alternative minimum taxable income exceeds $112,500 or $150,000, depending on the taxpayer's filing status. §55(d)(3).

Alternative minimum taxable income (AMTI) is the taxpayer's taxable income for regular tax purposes, adjusted as provided in §§56-59. Some of the adjustments are the same for both individual and corporate taxpayers, and some of the adjustments vary depending on whether the taxpayer is an individual or a corporate taxpayer.

The alternative minimum tax affects many individual and corporate taxpayers and can completely change the tax consequences of a transaction. For these reasons, tax lawyers must always consider both the regular tax consequences and alternative minimum tax consequences of any proposed transaction.

EXAMPLES

79. In year one Sandy and Bob, married taxpayers who file a joint return, have $250,000 of income from wages. For purposes of computing their regular tax liability, their personal exemptions and deductions (including, for example, state income and property taxes, medical expenses above the 7.5 percent floor, and miscellaneous itemized deductions above the 2 percent floor) total $190,000, so their taxable income is $60,000. (Assume, for purposes of computing their regular tax liability, that they are taxed at

5. Deductions for the Costs of Earning Income

a 33.33 percent rate.) For purposes of computing their alternative minimum tax liability, their deductions and exemptions are zero because of various adjustments provided in §§56-59. Assume, for purposes of computing their tentative minimum tax, that they are taxed at (i) a 26 percent rate on the first $175,000 of AMTI in excess of the exemption amount and (ii) a 28 percent rate on any additional AMTI in excess of the exemption amount. How much tax will they owe for year one?

EXPLANATIONS

79. Their regular tax liability for year one is $20,000 (33.33 percent of $60,000 of taxable income). However, under §55, their year one tax liability is $60,900.

Sandy and Bob owe §55 alternative minimum tax if their tentative minimum tax is more than their $20,000 regular tax liability. §55(a). In order to compute their tentative minimum tax, we must first determine their AMTI and exemption amount. Their AMTI equals their $60,000 taxable income, adjusted upward under §§56-59 to $250,000. The exemption amount for married taxpayers filing a joint return is $45,000. §55(d)(1)(A). However, that exemption amount is reduced by 25 percent of the amount of AMTI over $150,000. Their $250,000 of AMTI exceeds $150,000 by $100,000, so the $45,000 exemption amount is reduced by $25,000 (25 percent of $100,000) to $20,000. Their tentative minimum tax equals their $230,000 of AMTI in excess of the exemption amount multiplied by their alternative minimum tax rate. On the first $175,000 of AMTI in excess of the exemption amount, the rate is 26 percent so the tax equals $45,500. §55(b)(1)(A)(i)(I). On the remaining $55,000 of AMTI, the rate is 28 percent so the tax equals $15,400. Sandy and Bob's tentative minimum tax is $60,900 ($45,500 plus $15,400). Their tax liability for year one is that amount, $60,900 because it exceeds their $20,000 regular tax liability for the year.

6. *Additional Review Examples*

80. On January 1, year one, prominent surgeon Leslie purchases Large Company stock for $100,000. On January 2, year one, Leslie borrows $50,000 and uses the proceeds, together with

$50,000 cash, to purchase Small Company stock. The loan is nonrecourse and is secured by the Small Company stock. Leslie is appointed to the Board of Directors of Small Company and maintains a keen interest in her investment in that company. Leslie learns of developments in Large Company only through her broker. Between year one and year ten, Leslie pays $60,000 in interest expense on the debt incurred to purchase the Small Company stock and recognizes $60,000 of dividend income from the Large Company stock. How much, if any, of the interest expense may Leslie deduct?

81. Your client, Daniel, is a doctor who lives and practices in the resort community of Seaview. On January 1, year one, Daniel purchases a restaurant for $400,000. The purchase price includes the real property (land and building) on which the bakery is located. No portion of the purchase price is paid with borrowed funds. On January 5, year one, Daniel completes construction of a bakery and gourmet food shop on a valuable parcel of commercial property that he purchased many years ago for only $10,000. The value of the property is $500,000. The costs of construction total $290,000 and are financed through a nonrecourse loan that is secured by the property. The bakery sells both to the public and to other grocery stores and restaurants, including, of course, the restaurant that Daniel owns. Daniel's sister manages the bakery; Daniel's son-in-law manages the restaurant.

On July 1 Daniel informs you that the restaurant will show a profit of $50,000 for the year but the bakery and food shop will show a taxable loss of $80,000. In order to meet the expenses of the bakery and food shop, Daniel is considering an additional $50,000 nonrecourse loan on the bakery and food shop property. Daniel says that he spends about 10 hours a week supervising restaurant operations and only one or two hours a week supervising the bakery operations. Daniel asks you what portion of the expected loss of the restaurant he may deduct, and what, if anything, he might do to increase his chances of deducting that loss.

EXPLANATIONS

80. The answer to this question turns on whether or not Leslie's investment in Small Company is thought to be subject to the §163 interest deduction limits for portfolio investments, or the §465

and §469 limits on trade or business losses. Sections 163(d) and 469(e) explicitly place interest incurred to carry stock under the ambit of §163 and subject it to the investment interest, rather than passive loss, restrictions. Section 465 does not explicitly address the issue, but it seems that the active management of a personal stock portfolio does not comprise a trade or business activity and so is not subject to §465. Cf. Van Suetendael v. Commissioner, 3 T.C.M. 987 (1944), aff'd, 152 F.2d 654 (2d Cir. 1945). Section 163 would not limit Leslie's $60,000 of interest deduction because she received $60,000 of dividend income during the same period.

81. The deductibility of the bakery loss will be limited by both the §469 passive loss restrictions and the §465 at-risk rules. The at-risk limitation is applied first.

Under §465, losses from a trade or business activity are limited to the amount "at risk" in that activity. The term "activity" is not really defined by statute or regulations; on these limited facts it is not clear whether the bakery-gourmet food store and the restaurant will be treated as a single activity. If they are treated as separate activities, the at-risk rules will limit Daniel's deduction for the $80,000 loss from the bakery-gourmet food store. Daniel has contributed no nonborrowed funds to the food store business and has contributed property worth only $10,000. Further nonrecourse borrowing on the contributed property will not increase the at-risk amount. Thus, absent an increase in the at-risk amount, Daniel's deduction from the food store will be limited to $10,000.

Is there any way for Daniel to get around the at-risk limitation? Daniel could increase his at-risk amount by contributed nonborrowed funds or by obtaining a nonrecourse or recourse loan using his restaurant property as security. Nonrecourse debt secured by property that is not used in the activity will increase the at-risk amount to the extent of the cash investment in the property. Here, Daniel has a $400,000 cash investment in the restaurant property, so a loan secured by the property will be considered a cash investment.

If the bakery-gourmet food shop and the restaurant are treated as one activity, Daniel's amount at risk is $410,000 ($400,000 of cash invested in the restaurant and $10,000 of property contributed to the food shop), and §465 will not disallow his deduction for the $30,000 net loss ($50,000 of income less the $80,000 loss) from the activity.

If Daniel's loss is not disallowed by the §465 at-risk rules, he must still get past the §469 passive loss limitation. His $80,000 loss will be suspended under the passive loss limitation if (i) for purposes of §469, the bakery is considered a separate activity from the restaurant and (ii) Daniel meets the material participation standard for the restaurant and not the bakery.

Daniel might, of course, argue that the restaurant and bakery comprise a single activity. In that case, it looks as if Daniel spends about 12 hours a week on that single activity. That would be sufficient to meet the 500 hours a year material participation test. The loss would then not be a passive loss and Daniel would therefore be allowed to use the bakery loss to offset the restaurant and other sources of income.

Will the bakery and the restaurant be considered a single activity? The term activity is defined in Reg. §1.469-4. That regulation provides that trade or business or rental activities may be treated as a single activity if the activities to be grouped together are "an appropriate economic unit" for purposes of applying §469. The determination as to whether activities constitute an appropriate economic unit is based on a facts and circumstances test, with the following factors having the greatest weight: (i) the similarities and differences in the types of trades or businesses; (ii) the extent of common control or ownership of the activities; (iii) the geographical location of the activities; and (iv) any interdependencies among the activities.

Here, the bakery-food shop and the restaurant are both owned by Daniel. The facts do not indicate whether they are located in the same geographic area. The businesses are similar in that both prepare and sell food; however, the bakery-gourmet food shop probably does not involve serving customers food and drinks at tables on the premises, which the restaurant would involve. There may be interdependencies between the two businesses, for example, if the restaurant buys all of its baked goods from the bakery. The answer is not clear on the facts given in the example.

If Daniel is not able to treat the food store and the restaurant as a single activity, and he continues to work at the restaurant and not the food store, the gain from the restaurant will not be passive and the loss from the food store will be passive. As a result, Daniel will not be able to currently deduct any of the loss.

Daniel could avoid this result by reducing his hours at the restaurant. If, for example, Daniel works only six hours a week at the restaurant, then both the restaurant and the food store will be passive, and Daniel will be able to use the food store loss to offset the restaurant income. If Daniel works nine hours a week at the restaurant and two hours a week at the food store, then both the food store and restaurant will be "significant participation activities." Since the total hours of significant participation activities will exceed 500, neither activity will be considered passive. (Note that if Daniel works more than 500 hours at the restaurant, the restaurant will be nonpassive but will not be a significant participation activity and the hours worked at the food store cannot be combined with the hours worked at the restaurant.)

6

Mixed Personal and Business Expenditures

In contrast to §§162 and 212, §262 provides that no deduction is permitted for personal expenses. The tax law therefore requires that we distinguish between business and personal expenses. It is often difficult to draw a clear line between personal and business expenses. Many expenses are incurred partly for personal reasons and partly for business reasons. For example, a lawyer may purchase art for her office, in part because she enjoys looking at it and in part because she thinks that it will impress her clients.

This chapter will explore the tax treatment of a number of common mixed personal and business expenses. In determining the treatment of some types of mixed personal and business expense, the tax law adopts a black-and-white approach and requires that the mixed motive expense be treated entirely as either a personal expense or business expense. In determining the treatment of other types of mixed motive expense, the tax law requires an allocation of the expense between the business portion and the personal portion. We will see that a number of the rules applicable to mixed motive expenses are anti-abuse provisions designed to prevent taxpayers from converting nondeductible personal expenses into deductible business expenses.

A. Controlling the Abuse of Business Deductions

1. *Hobby Losses*

Reading: §183; Reg. §1.183-1 and -2

Individuals often engage in activities that are enjoyable and offer an opportunity to produce income. The fact that an individual enjoys an income-producing activity generally will not affect the deductibility of the expenses associated with that activity. However, some business activities, such as breeding race horses, painting landscapes, writing books, and farming, tend to combine significant elements of personal pleasure with a low probability of profitability. Although some individuals earn their livelihood from such ventures, others engage in these activities for personal reasons, without regard for whether the activity will be profitable.

The tax treatment of losses generated by such "hobby" businesses is governed, in part, by §183. That section distinguishes between activities that are "not engaged in for profit" and activities that are engaged in for profit.

If an activity is engaged in for profit, §183 does not alter the tax consequences of any of the expenses from the activity. If an activity is not engaged in for profit, the effect of §183 on a deduction depends on whether the deduction is one that is allowed without regard for whether the expense is a personal expense. Recall from Chapter 4 that taxpayers are allowed various personal deductions, including, for example, the §164 deduction for property tax paid. Section 183 does not alter taxpayers' deductions for these types of expenses, which are deductible without regard to whether the activity is personal. §183(b)(1). Some expenses, however, are deductible fully only if the activity is engaged in for profit. If an activity is not engaged in for profit, these expenses are deductible only to the extent that the gross income from the activity exceeds the deductions that are permitted (that is, under §183(b)(1)) without regard to whether the activity was profit-motivated. §183(b)(2). In effect, §183(b)(2) prevents taxpayers from using hobby losses to shield other income.

Section 183(c) defines an *activity not engaged in for profit* as any activity other than one with respect to which deductions are allowable under §162 ("ordinary and necessary" business expenses) or under §212 (expenses related to the production of income). This less-than-helpful definition is fortunately supplemented by §183(d) and the regulations. Section 183(d) creates a rebuttable presumption that an activity is engaged in for profit if, in three or more of five consecutive years, the activity earns a profit (that is, the gross income from the activity exceeds the deductions attributable to the activity). If the activity is horse breeding, the presumption applies if the activity generates a profit in two or more of seven consecutive years.

Under §183(e), a taxpayer can elect to wait to determine whether the presumption is met until the close of the fifth year in which the taxpayer engages in the activity. If the taxpayer makes the election, the statute of limitations on assessment for the first four years in which the taxpayer engages in the activity is extended until two years after the return for year five is due. If the activity is horse breeding, the election defers the determination until the seventh year and extends the statute of limitation for years one through six of the activity until two years after the year seven return is due.

If a taxpayer fails to satisfy the test for the presumption, that failure does not necessarily result in characterization of the activity as a non-profit-motivated activity. The taxpayer may still try to establish that the activity was engaged in for profit. Courts have held that the determination turns on whether the taxpayer engaged in the activity for the purpose of making a profit, not whether, considering the activity objectively, it was likely to make a profit. For example, in Nickerson v. Commissioner, 700 F.2d 402 (7th Cir. 1983), the court stated that taxpayers "need only prove their sincerity rather than their realism." The court articulated this standard despite the fact that Regulation §1.183-2(a) provides that "[i]n determining whether an activity is engaged in for profit, greater weight is given to objective facts than to the taxpayer's mere statement of his intention."

Regulation §1.183-2(b) states that the determination of whether an activity is engaged in for profit is made in light of all the facts and circumstances. The regulation goes on to list nine factors that should be considered:

1.   Whether the taxpayer carries on the business in a businesslike manner and keeps complete and accurate books and records
2.   The degree to which the taxpayer has prepared for the activity, either by study or consultation with experts
3.   The time and effort expended by the taxpayer in carrying on the activity
4.   The likelihood that assets used in the activity will appreciate in value

5.   The success or failure of the taxpayer in carrying on similar activities
6.   The history of income and losses with respect to the activity. (The regulation states that losses in the start-up phase of the activity do not necessarily indicate that the activity is not engaged in for profit.)
7.   The amount of occasional profits, if any, that are earned, as compared with the taxpayer's investment in and losses from the activity
8.   The financial status of the taxpayer. (The regulation provides that the fact that a taxpayer is of modest means may indicate that the activity is engaged in for profit. Conversely, the fact that a taxpayer is wealthy may indicate that the activity is not engaged in for profit, especially if the activity generates substantial tax benefits and involves recreational elements.)
9.   The degree to which the activity is recreational or for personal pleasure

No one factor is dispositive. Instead, they are all considered. For example, in *Nickerson* the court of appeals held that a taxpayer's farming activity was engaged in for profit. In that case, several factors indicated that the activity might not have been engaged in for profit, including the following: (i) The farming activity lost a significant amount of money in the first two years of operation, the years at issue in the case; (ii) during those two years, the taxpayer had a full-time job in a city that was a five-hour drive from the farm, so he visited the farm only on weekends; and (iii) the taxpayer did not have a concrete plan for making the farm profitable and had little expertise in farming. Several factors also indicated that the activity might have been engaged in for profit: (i) The farm was never used for entertainment and lacked recreational facilities; (ii) the taxpayer and his family performed strenuous manual labor when they were at the farm; (iii) the taxpayer was not wealthy; and (iv) during the two years at issue in the case, the taxpayer attempted to learn more about farming by reading magazines and government publications. After weighing all these factors, the court concluded that taxpayer's farming activity was engaged in for profit.

EXAMPLES

1.   Upon retirement from his law firm, Donald purchased a second home and small vineyard in Napa Valley. Donald spends approxi-

mately four months a year working at the vineyard. The simplified tax returns for the years one through five are as follows. (Add
"000" to each of the dollar amounts.)

(All amounts in 000s)	Year 1	Year 2	Year 3	Year 4	Year 5
Gross income	$1	$10	$19	$80	$6
Property taxes	$3	$3	$3	$3	$3
Labor and supplies	$20	$20	$20	$20	$20
Net income (loss)	($22)	($13)	($4)	$57	($17)

a. Is Donald's vineyard presumed to be an activity engaged in for
   profit under §183?
b. If Donald's vineyard is not an activity engaged in for profit,
   which expenses can he deduct in year one?

2. Andi is a successful New York City tax attorney who, believing that
the fast-paced world of tax law is "a young woman's game," decides
to invest some of her free time and money in the manufacture of
chic sweaters for dogs. Although Andi can scarcely conceal her
distaste for all things canine, she feels that dogs will be the trendy
pet of the next decade. Andi derived much greater enjoyment from
her previous successful business producing "designer" cat bowls.

Andi keeps careful records of her dog sweater business operations and looks for ever-cheaper methods of production. She has
taken several classes at the local fashion institute in product design
and merchandising and spends several hours each week looking at
fashion magazines so that she can adapt the latest sweater styles to
dachshund and poodle sizes. Although Andi is optimistic that she
will be able to retire from tax law when the business takes off, she
has lost between $3,000 and $5,000 in each of the four years she
has been in business. Fortunately, earning $250,000 a year as a
lawyer allows her to pay her living expenses and subsidize the dog
sweater business until it becomes profitable. Will Andi be able to
deduct the expenses of her dog sweater activity as business losses?

3. Lita, an accountant for a large corporation, used her weekends
and evenings to write a mystery novel, Blood on the Balance
Sheet, featuring a crime-solving accountant, B. Lance Sheet. After her manuscript was rejected by commercial publishers, she
ignored the advice of her friends and published it herself. "There
are plenty of accountants who would love to read my novel," she

said. Unfortunately, the novel was a critical and commercial failure and Lita lost $15,000 on the venture.

Undaunted, the next year Lita wrote and published a second novel featuring B. Lance Sheet entitled A Cruel Method of Accounting. "The problem with my first novel was that my audience was not aware of it," she reasoned. This time she spent a large sum advertising the novel in the accounting trade magazines. Nonetheless, A Cruel Method of Accounting also failed and Lita lost an additional $25,000. Can Lita deduct the losses she incurred writing, publishing, and advertising the novels?

4. Jasmine raises, shows, and sells Siamese cats as a hobby. In 10 years of raising Siamese cats she has never earned a profit. In year 10, her gross income from the sale of Siamese kittens is $1,600. Although her records of the expenses incurred in the breeding activity are spotty, she can establish that in year 10 she spent $1,000 on transportation and lodging to attend cat shows, $400 on cat food, $700 on veterinary expenses, and $300 on grooming, for a total of $2,400.

a. How much of these costs, if any, can she deduct in year 10?

b. Suppose instead that Jasmine's year 10 gross income from the sale of the kittens is $4,000. How much can she deduct?

5. When Abraham turned 30, he unexpectedly inherited a large sum of money from a rich uncle. Freed from financial worry, he decided to quit his job as a tax associate in a major law firm and become a performance artist. During each of the next five years, he presented an off-Broadway show. The shows received mixed critical reviews and limited commercial success. A summary of the earnings from the shows follows. (Add "000" to each of the dollar amounts.)

Year	Show	Run in Weeks	Gross Income	Costs	Profit/ (Loss)
1	My Best Home Videos	2	$3	$28	($25)
2	Plato and Babe Ruth Go Fishing	10	$22	$21	$1
3	A Pie in the Face	15	$30	$27	$3
4	IRS Follies: A Musical	30	$50	$48	$2
5	An Evening of Mime	1	$1	$26	($25)
	Totals	58	$106	$150	($44)

In year five, will Abraham's performance art be considered an "activity not engaged in for profit" under §183?

EXPLANATIONS

1. a. No, the vineyard is not presumed to be an activity engaged in for profit. Section 183(d) provides that an activity that is profitable in three out of five consecutive years is presumed to be an activity engaged in for profit. In this case, a profit was earned in only one of the five. The fact that the activity has produced a net $1,000 profit over the five-year period does not establish a presumption that it was engaged in for profit.

   b. Section 183 does not alter the taxpayer's deductions for expenses that are deductible without regard to whether the activity is personal. §183(b)(1). Here, the property taxes are deductible without regard to whether the property is used in a profitmaking enterprise. §164. Thus, Donald can deduct the $3,000 of property taxes despite the fact that the activity is not engaged in for profit. If the activity is not engaged in for profit, Donald's deduction for the other expenses will be eliminated under §183(b)(2) because the $1,000 of year one gross income from the activity exceeds the $3,000 of property taxes deducted without regard to whether the activity was engaged in for profit.

2. Andi probably will be permitted to deduct her expenses. She cannot satisfy the §183(d) test for the presumption because her business has not been profitable in any of the four years of operation. However, failure to qualify for the presumption does not establish that the activity was not engaged in for profit. Reg. §1.183-1(c). Even without the advantage of the presumption, Andi may show a profit motive under the nine factors listed in Regulation §1.183-2(b).

   The following factors indicate that Andi may have had a profit motive:

   1. Andi keeps careful records and looks for ways to make production cheaper.
   2. Andi has taken classes to increase her knowledge of merchandising pet products.
   3. Andi spends hours each week studying emerging trends in sweater designs.

4.   Andi has had success in a similar venture.
5.   A profit motive is more likely when the activity is not enjoyable to the taxpayer, and Andi derives little pleasure from making dog sweaters.

The following factors indicate that Andi may not have had a profit motive:

1.   The business has shown steady losses.
2.   There have been no profits.
3.   Andi has high income from working as a lawyer. However, the tax benefits of the losses from the activity are not large compared to her income.

A court weighing these factors would likely conclude that her dog sweater business is an activity engaged in for profit. See Nickerson v. Commissioner, 700 F.2d 402 (7th Cir. 1983).

3.   This is a close case. A good argument can be made that Lita will be able to deduct the losses. Under §183, the test is not whether it was likely that the taxpayer would earn a profit, but whether the taxpayer entered the activity with the *purpose* of making a profit. Dreicer v. United States, 665 F.2d 1292 (D.C. Cir. 1981). Lita apparently believed that her novels would be profitable and changed her advertising strategy for her second novel in an attempt to increase its sales. The fact that her judgment was poor is irrelevant if her intent was to earn a profit. Although Lita may enjoy writing her novels, writing may or may not be an activity that would generally be viewed as recreational. Lita is not wealthy and it seems unlikely that she is publishing the novels primarily for personal reasons unrelated to earning a profit.

Nevertheless, other factors suggest that this is not an activity engaged in for profit. There is no evidence that Lita has writing expertise, although she does have expertise as an accountant. She has no history of making a profit as a novelist and she was advised that the activity would be likely to show a loss. However, on balance (no pun intended), it is likely that Lita will be entitled to a deduction.

4.   a. Jasmine can deduct $1,600. The following factors indicate that Jasmine did not have a profit motive:

1. The business has shown steady losses.
2. There have been no profits.
3. Breeding Siamese cats and attending cat shows is an activity that many cat-lovers enjoy.
4. Jasmine does not maintain complete records in a businesslike manner.

Thus, the activity is not engaged in for profit, so §183(a) and (b) apply. Here, none of the expenses are the type that are deductible without regard to whether the activity was engaged in for profit. All of the expenses here are deductible only to the extent of her gross income from the activity, which is $1,600. §183(b)(2).

b. Jasmine will be allowed to deduct all $2,400 of her expenses. Section 183 does not limit the deduction of the expenses since her gross income from the activity, $4,000, exceeds her expenses. §183(b)(2).

5. The performance art activity meets the §183(d) test since Abraham has earned a profit in three of the five consecutive years in which he has engaged in the activity. The activity is thus presumed to be engaged in for profit even though he has suffered an aggregate loss. The fact that Abraham could have made a larger amount of money by practicing law is irrelevant so long as he intended to make a profit from his performance art. The §183(d) presumption is rebuttable, but the facts here, on balance, do not indicate that the Service could successfully rebut the presumption. Although Abraham does seem to be wealthy, it does not appear that he is engaging in the performance art activity to shelter his other income.

2. *Rental of a Dwelling Used by the Taxpayer*

Reading: §280A

If a taxpayer owns rental property that is not used by the taxpayer for personal purposes at any time during the taxable year, the taxpayer is entitled to deduct all expenses associated with the property, including depreciation, repairs, utilities, property taxes, and interest. (See Chapter 5 of this book for a discussion of business deductions and Chapter

4 for a discussion of the deduction for property taxes.) However, if the taxpayer's property is rented for part of the year and used by the taxpayer for part of the year, allowing the taxpayer to deduct the expenses of the rental property creates potential for abuse. In 1976 Congress enacted §280A to address this potential abuse. Section 280A applies only if the taxpayer uses the rental property for "personal purposes" during the year.

A dwelling unit is deemed used for personal purposes if it is occupied by the taxpayer, certain relatives of the taxpayer (including the taxpayer's spouse, siblings, ancestors, and lineal descendants), or by any person who does not pay a fair rental. §§280A(d)(2), 267(c)(4). A dwelling unit also is deemed used for personal purposes if the use of the unit by another individual gives the taxpayer the right to use another dwelling unit. §280A(d)(2)(B). Rental of the dwelling, at a fair rent, to a relative who uses the dwelling as a principal residence, however, is not considered personal use. §280A(d)(3). Occupation of the dwelling unit by the taxpayer for the purpose of making repairs also is not deemed use for a personal purpose. §280A(d)(2).

Under §280A, a taxpayer's deductions for the expenses of a dwelling unit rented by the taxpayer during the year turn on (i) the number of days during the year that the taxpayer used the dwelling unit for personal purposes and (ii) the number of days during the year that the dwelling unit was rented.

If the taxpayer rents the dwelling and does not use it for personal purposes at all during the year, §280A does not limit the taxpayer's deductions for the expenses of the rental property (although other provisions, such as §469, discussed in Chapter 5, may limit the deductions).

If, during the year, the taxpayer rents the dwelling and uses it for personal purposes on one or more days, §280A(e) and (b) limit the taxpayer's deductions for the expenses of the dwelling to the sum of (i) the deductions that are allowed without regard to whether the dwelling was used in a trade or business or income-producing activity ("non-profit-motivated expenses") such as deductible property taxes and home mortgage interest plus (ii) the portion of the other expenses ("profit-motivated expenses") that are allocable to the period during which the property was rented. The profit-motivated expenses are allocated to the rental period based on the ratio of (i) the number of days that the property was rented to (ii) the number of days that the property was used either by the rental tenant or by the taxpayer for personal reasons. Days on which the property was not used are disregarded. Thus, the profit-motivated expenses allocated to the rental use of the property equal the product of multiplying the profit-motivated expenses for the year by the following fraction:

$$\frac{Number\ of\ Rental\ Days}{Total\ Number\ of\ Days\ Used}$$

What types of expenses constitute non-profit-motivated expenses? In a typical case, they are home mortgage interest and property taxes on the dwelling, both of which are generally deductible without regard to profit motive. §§164 and 163(h)(2)(D). However, note that home mortgage interest is deductible as qualified residence interest only if the debt is acquisition indebtedness or home equity indebtedness on a "qualified residence." The determination of whether a home is a qualified residence is made as the mortgage interest accrues. §163(h)(3)(A). (The deduction for home mortgage interest is discussed in Chapter 4.) A qualified residence is defined as either the taxpayer's principal residence or a second home that the taxpayer uses "as a residence." §163(h)(4)(A). A second home is used as a residence if, during the year, the taxpayer uses it for personal reasons more than 14 days (or, if greater, 10 percent of the days during the year that the home is rented at a fair rental). §280A(d).

If the taxpayer does not use a second home enough to make the home a qualified residence, the mortgage interest on that home is not deductible as qualified residence interest. However, the portion of the mortgage interest allocable to the days during the year that the second home was rented may still be deductible as a profit-motivated expense. In other words, the interest may have to be allocated between personal and rental use of the property.

The property taxes paid by the taxpayer on the rented dwelling are deductible without regard to whether the taxpayer had a profit motive. §164. However, the effect of taking the deduction depends on whether the property taxes were expenses of an income-producing rental activity: Property taxes are taken as an above-the-line deduction to the extent that they are incurred with respect to an income-producing rental activity. Any remaining property taxes are taken as a below-the-line itemized deduction. §62(a)(4). In other words, the property taxes paid during the year must be allocated between the rental use and personal use of the property, despite the fact that the property taxes are non-profit-motivated expenses.

The Service takes the position that the allocation of non-profit-motivated expenses to rental use of the dwelling is done in the same way as the allocation of the profit-motivated expenses, using the formula given above (the "percentage-of-days-used" formula). Prop. Reg. §1.280A-3(d). However, a number of courts have adopted a more pro-taxpayer formula and allocated the non-profit-motivated expenses by comparing the number of days that the property was rented and the number of days in the entire year (the "percentage-of-days-in-the-year" formula). This method allocates a smaller portion of the non-profit-motivated expenses to the rental use and allows the taxpayer to deduct a higher amount of the profit-motivated expenses allocable to the rental use of the property. See, e.g., Bolton v. Commissioner, 77 T.C. 104 (1981), aff'd, 694 F.2d 556 (9th Cir. 1982); McKinney v. Commissioner, 732 F.2d 414 (10th Cir. 1983).

Although §280A(e) generally requires allocation of the profit-motivated expenses if the taxpayer uses the dwelling on one or more days during the year, a special rule in §280A(g) applies if, during the year, the taxpayer uses the dwelling as a residence and rents the dwelling for less than 15 days. If this special rule applies, the taxpayer is not allowed to deduct any of the expenses of the dwelling rented, other than non-profit-motivated expenses, such as mortgage interest and property taxes. §280A(g)(1). In other words, §280A(g)(1) disallows the taxpayer's deductions for the profit-motivated expenses allocable to the rental use of the property. On the other hand, the taxpayer does not have to include in income the rent paid by the tenant. §280A(g)(2).

If the taxpayer rents the dwelling and uses it as a residence during the year (that is, uses it for the greater of 14 days or 10 percent of the number of days on which the property is rented), the taxpayer's deductions for the profit-motivated expenses of the dwelling will be limited both by §280A(e) and (c)(5). In these circumstances, §280A(c)(5) limits the taxpayer's deduction of the dwelling unit expenses in a given year to (i) the gross income from the rental of the dwelling less (ii) the non-profit-motivated expenses allocable to the rental use of the dwelling (under either the percentage-of-days-used formula or the percentage-of-days-of-the-year formula, described above).

Proposed Regulation §1.280A-3(d) also provides an ordering rule for applying the §280A(c)(5) limitation based on whether the profit-motivated expenses allocable to the rental use of the dwelling result in an adjustment of the basis of the dwelling (for example, depreciation) or do not result in an adjustment of the basis of the dwelling (for example, utilities or insurance). Under this rule, depreciation deductions are allowed last, after the deductions for profit-motivated expenses that do not reduce the taxpayer's basis in the dwelling. Any expenses allowed under §280A(e) but limited by §280A(c)(5) are carried forward to the next year. §280A(c)(5) (flush language).

EXAMPLES

6. Jade owns a beach house in South Carolina. She rents the house to her brother Mike year-round for its fair rental value of $1,000 per month. Can Jade deduct the depreciation, repairs, interest, and other expenses of owning and renting the house?

7. Belle lives year-round in a two-bedroom ranch house in Claremont. During July, the International Frozen Yogurt Festival was held in Claremont. Wanting to escape the masses that would converge on the town and knowing that she stood to make a large profit, Belle rented her house to festival-goers and fled Claremont for the duration of the festival. The rent amounted to $3,000 for 10 days. Is Belle allowed to deduct non-profit-motivated expenses (for example, mortgage interest and property taxes) and profit-motivated expenses (for example, insurance, utilities, and depreciation) that are allocable to the period during which her house is rented?

8. Billie owns a beachfront vacation condominium in a resort community in Florida. During year one she uses the condominium for 20 days and rents it for 300 days, for which she receives a fair rent of $15,000. During the year she pays the following expenses with respect to the condo: property taxes of $4,800, mortgage interest of $12,000 (12 percent interest on a $100,000 mortgage), and $1,600 of maintenance charges. The year one depreciation on the condo is $3,200. The mortgage on her principal residence is $500,000.
    a. What is the tax treatment of Billie's year one expenses?
    b. How, if at all, would your answer in part (a) change if she uses the condominium for 60 days and rents it out for 260 days?

EXPLANATIONS

6. Yes. Section 280A limits deductions on a rented dwelling only if the taxpayer has used the dwelling for personal purposes during the year. If the taxpayer has not used the unit for personal

purposes, repair expenses, interest, and other expenses are deductible, subject to the limitations on passive activity and hobby losses.

Although occupancy by a taxpayer's relative usually is considered personal use by the taxpayer, an exception applies where the relative uses the dwelling as a principal residence and pays a fair rental. Note that if Jade visits her brother briefly, her visit will not be considered personal use of the house. Prop. Reg. §1.280A-1(e)(2).

7.   Belle is not allowed to deduct any of the profit-motivated expenses because her house is rented for less than 15 days during the year. §280A(g)(1). But Belle has no reason to complain. She is allowed to deduct the non-profit-motivated expenses such as home mortgage interest and property taxes. In addition, Belle does not have to include in income any of the $3,000 of rent she receives because she rented the home for less than 15 days. §280A(g)(1).

8.   a. During year one the condominium is used for both personal and rental purposes during the taxable year, so §280A will limit Billie's deduction of the year one expenses. Billie is allowed to deduct the $4,800 of property taxes because such property taxes are deductible regardless of profit motive. §164. The property tax will have to be allocated between personal and rental use, despite the fact that it is a non-profit-motivated expense, in order to determine which portion of the tax is an above-the-line deduction and which portion is a below-the-line itemized deduction. §62(a)(4). The Service's position is that non-profit-motivated deductions should be allocated based on the percentage-of-days-used formula. Prop. Reg. §1.280A-3(d)(3). This method has been rejected, however, by the Tax Court and the Ninth and Tenth Circuits, which have held that non-profit-motivated expenses should be allocated based on the percentage-of-days-in-the-year formula. Bolton v. Commissioner, 77 T.C. 104 (1981), aff'd, 694 F.2d 556 (9th Cir. 1982); McKinney v. Commissioner, 732 F.2d 414 (10th Cir. 1983). Here, if we apply the courts' allocation method to the $4,800 of property taxes, Billie will take an above-the-line deduction of $3,945 (300/365 of the $4,800 of property taxes) and a below-the-line deduction of $855 ($4,800 less $3,945) (assuming that she itemizes).

Home mortgage interest is generally deductible under §163(h)(3) as qualified residence interest. However, here the mortgage will not be deductible as qualified residence interest. Mortgage interest can be qualified residence interest only if it is paid with respect to a qualified residence. §163(h)(3)(A). If a dwelling is not used "as a residence," the dwelling is not a qualified residence. §163(h)(4)(A)(i)(II). Section 280A(d)(1) provides that a second home is used "as a residence" only if the taxpayer uses it for the greater of 14 days or 10 percent of the days that the dwelling is rented. Billie does not use the condominium as a residence in year one because she did not use it for more than 30 days (which is the greater of 14 days or 10 percent of the 300 days that the dwelling was rented). The mortgage interest is thus not deductible as qualified residence interest. Recall from Chapter 4 that personal interest other than qualified residence interest is nondeductible. §163(h)(1), (2). Even though the mortgage interest is not deductible as qualified residence interest, the portion of the interest that is allocable to the rental use of the dwelling may still be deductible as a profit-motivated expense allocable to the rental use of the dwelling.

The $12,000 of mortgage interest, $1,600 of maintenance charges, and $3,200 of depreciation are profit-motivated expenses that must be allocated between the personal and rental use of the property. §280A(e). Profit-motivated expenses are allocated to the rental use pro rata by comparing the number of days the property was rented (300 days) to the total number of days the property was used (320). Here, 300/320 or 15/16 of the interest, maintenance, and depreciation expenses are allocable to the rental use of the property. Thus, §280A(e) limits Billie's deduction for the interest, maintenance charges, and depreciation to $15,750 ($11,250 of interest, $1,500 of the maintenance charges, and $3,000 of the depreciation).

Billie's $15,750 year one deduction for interest, maintenance charges, and depreciation is not further limited by §280A(c)(5) because Billie does not use the dwelling as a residence in year one.

b. Here, Billie uses the residence for personal purposes for more than 26 days (which is the greater of 14 days or 10 percent of the 260 days that the dwelling is rented). The dwelling is thus a qualified residence and the mortgage interest is qualified residence interest, which is deductible without regard to profit motive. §163(h)(3) and (4)(A)(i)(II). Because the mortgage interest is a non-profit-motivated expense, it is deductible without regard to the §280A(e) limitation.

As in part (a), the $1,600 of maintenance charges and $3,200 of depreciation are profit-motivated expenses that must be allocated between the personal and rental use of the property. §280A(e). Here, however, the portion of these expenses allocable to the rental use is different than in part (a). Profit-motivated expenses are allocated to the rental use by comparing the number of days the property was rented (here, 260 days) to the total number of days the property was used (320). Thus, 260/320 or 81.25 percent of the maintenance and depreciation expenses are allocable to the rental use of the property. Section 280A(e) limits Billie's deduction for the maintenance charges and depreciation to $3,900 ($1,300 of the maintenance charges and $2,600 of the depreciation).

Billie's $3,900 year one deduction for maintenance charges and depreciation may be further limited by §280A(c)(5). Billie is using the dwelling in year one for more than 26 days (10 percent of the 260 days that the condo was rented), so she is using the condominium as a residence and her year one deductions are thus subject to §280A(c)(5). This will limit her year one deductions for the profit-motivated expenses allocable to the rental use of the property to (i) the year one rental income less (ii) the year one non-profit-motivated deductions allocable to the rental use.

Section 280A does not specify the proper method of allocating non-profit-motivated deductions to the rental use of the dwelling. As noted in part (a), the Service's position is that non-profit-motivated deductions should be allocated based on the percentage-of-days-used formula. Prop. Reg. §1.280A-3(d)(3). This method has been rejected, however, by the Tax Court and the Ninth and Tenth Circuits, which have held that non-profit-motivated expenses should be allocated based on the percentage-of-days-in-the-year formula. Bolton v. Commissioner, 77 T.C. 104 (1981), aff'd, 694 F.2d 556 (9th Cir. 1982); McKinney v. Commissioner, 732 F.2d 414 (10th Cir. 1983). Using this method to determine the §280A(c)(5) limitation allocates a smaller portion of the non-profit-motivated expenses to the rental use and allows the taxpayer to deduct a higher amount of the profit-motivated expenses allocable to the rental use of the dwelling.

Billie has $16,800 of non-profit-motivated expenses ($12,000 of mortgage interest deductible under §163(h)(2)(D) and $4,800 of property taxes deductible under §164, regardless of the taxpayer's profit motive). Assuming that the pro-taxpayer allocation method endorsed by the courts is followed, Billie's non-profit-motivated deductions would be allocated as follows:

Non-profit-motivated deductions:	$16,800
Days of rental use:	260 days
Days in the year:	365 days
Rental use portion:	$260/365 \times \$16,800 = \$11,967$

Billie receives $15,000 of rent. This amount exceeds the $11,967 of non-profit-motivated deductions allocable to rental use of the property by $3,033. Thus, Billie can deduct $3,033 of the $3,900 of year one profit-motivated deductions allocable to rental use of the dwelling. §280A(c)(5). Where the entire amount of profit-motivated expenses cannot be currently deducted, expenses other than depreciation are taken first. In year one Billie will take a $1,300 deduction for the maintenance charges and a $1,733 deduction for depreciation. The portion of the $3,900 expense that cannot be deducted in year one, $867 ($3,900 less $3,033) is carried forward to year two.

3.   *Home Offices, Computers, and Automobiles*

Reading: §§280A, 280F

Many taxpayers work sometimes at home and home computers and personal automobiles are often used part of the time for business purposes. Permitting deductions for these expenses, however, might enable aggressive taxpayers to take deductions for expenses that are primarily personal. On the other hand, denying a deduction would be unfair to individuals who genuinely incur these types of expenses for business reasons. Thus, current law permits deductions for these expenses, but adopts special restrictions to prevent abuse.

6. Mixed Personal and Business Expenditures

Section 280A(a) provides that an individual is not allowed a deduction for use of his dwelling unless one of a number of special rules in §280A applies. Section 280A(c)(1), one of those special rules, allows a deduction for an office in the taxpayer's home (or a separate structure not attached to the home) only where the taxpayer uses the home office exclusively on a regular basis (i) as the principal place of business for any trade or business of the taxpayer; (ii) as a place of business that is used by patients, clients, or customers in meeting or dealing with the taxpayer in his business; or (iii) in connection with the taxpayer's business if the office is in a separate structure that is not attached to the taxpayer's home. In addition, if the taxpayer is an employee (as opposed to being self-employed), he is allowed the home office deduction only if his use of the home office is for the "convenience of the employer." §280A(c)(1). An employee's use of a home office is for the convenience of the employer if the employer does not provide the employee with an office at all, or if the employer has not provided adequate office space in which the employee can effectively carry out employment duties. Weissman v. Commissioner, 751 F.2d 512 (2d Cir. 1984). If the employer has provided the employee with adequate office space, the home office is for the convenience of the employee, not the employer, even if the office is used exclusively for business purposes. Cadwallader v. Commissioner, 919 F.2d 1273 (7th Cir. 1990).

A taxpayer can qualify for one of the three parts of the §280A(c)(1) test only if she is engaged in a "trade or business." If a taxpayer spends most of her time managing her investments from a home office, is the investment activity a trade or business for the purpose of applying §280A(c)? In Moller v. United States, 721 F.2d 810 (Fed. Cir. 1983), cert. denied, 467 U.S. 1251 (1984), the taxpayers deducted the expenses of the home office in which they worked full-time managing their investments. In determining whether the Mollers were engaged in a trade or business, the court distinguished between "investing" and "trading." Investors buy securities for the long-term and their income from investing is primarily dividend and interest income. Traders, on the other hand, invest for the short-term and their income from trading is primarily gain from the sale of securities. Although trading is a trade or business, managing investments, even full-time, is not a trade or business. The court concluded that the Mollers were investors, not traders, and thus were not engaged in a trade or business, so they could not deduct the expenses of their home office.

In Commissioner v. Soliman, 113 S. Ct. 701 (1993), the Supreme Court articulated a standard for determining whether a home office is the "principal place of business" for purposes of applying §280A(c)(1)(A). In that case, the taxpayer was an anesthesiologist who spent 30 to 35 hours a week seeing patients at three hospitals. He did not have any office space at the hospitals, so he spent 10 to 15 hours a week in a home office doing various tasks related to his practice, including billing, professional reading, and speaking on the telephone. The Service took the position that the home office was not the taxpayer's principal place of business and disallowed the deduction he had taken for it. The Supreme Court stated that the "principal place of business" is the most important or significant place for the business. The Court added that the test requires consideration of (i) the relative importance of the activities performed in each of the taxpayer's places of business and (ii) the amount of time spent at each of the places of business. The Court added that great weight must be given to the place of business where the taxpayer delivers goods or services. Dr. Soliman spent 30 to 35 hours a week at the hospitals treating patients and 10 to 15 hours a week in his home office doing ancillary activities related to his practice, so the Court held that the home office was not his principal place of business.

Section 280A(c)(1)(B) allows a deduction for the home office if it is "used by patients, clients, or customers in meeting or dealing with the taxpayer in the normal course of his trade or business." Speaking on the telephone with patients, clients, or customers does not constitute "meeting or dealing" with them. Rather, the clients must be physically present in the office. Green v. Commissioner, 707 F.2d 404 (9th Cir. 1983); Prop. Reg. §1.280A-2(c).

A home office deduction permitted under one of the three parts of §280A(c)(1) is subject to the §280A(c)(5) limitation discussed in the last section of this book. That section limits a taxpayer's home office deduction to the taxpayer's gross income derived from the use of the home office less the deductions allowed for the taxpayer's non-profit-motivated expenses of the home office (such as property taxes and deductible qualified residence interest).

Section 280F imposes additional limitations on a taxpayer's business deductions for certain listed property that is especially subject to abuse. *Listed property* is defined in §280F(d)(4)(A) to include home computers, cars, or other transportation vehicles, cellular telephones, and any property generally used for entertainment or recreation. However, a computer is not listed property if it is used exclusively at a regular business establishment, including a home office that meets the test of §280A(c)(1). §280F(d)(4)(B). Section 280F(d)(4)(C) and

(5)(B) also except from the definition of listed property certain types of cars and vehicles, such as delivery vehicles, moving vans, and cars used in business to transport passengers (for example, by a limousine service).

If a taxpayer does not use listed property for business purposes more than 50 percent of the time, the taxpayer's depreciation deduction for the portion of the cost of the property allocable to the business use of the property is not eligible for accelerated depreciation (discussed in Chapter 5); instead the taxpayer is limited to straightline depreciation deductions on the property. §§280F(b) and 168(g)(1) and (2)(A). This reduces the taxpayer's depreciation deductions in the earlier years in which the taxpayer owns and uses the property.

Additional complications arise if, in an earlier year, a taxpayer took accelerated depreciation deductions on listed property because the taxpayer used the listed property for business more than 50 percent of the time that year, and, in a subsequent year, the business taxpayer's use of the listed property drops to 50 percent or less. If that occurs, the taxpayer must recapture the excess depreciation deduction from the earlier year by including in gross income, in the subsequent year, the difference between the accelerated depreciation deduction taken on the listed property in the earlier year and a straightline deduction on the listed property for the earlier year. §280F(b)(2).

Finally, any use of listed property by an employee (rather than a self-employed individual) is not treated as use in a trade or business (and thus is not eligible for any depreciation) unless such use is (i) for the convenience of the employer and (ii) required as a condition of employment. §280F(d)(3).

EXAMPLES

Assume, in all of the examples below, that the taxpayer uses the home office exclusively for business.

9. Mercedes inherited a $5 million investment portfolio from her parents. She receives almost all of her income from dividends and interest on the securities in the portfolio and spends over 30 hours per week monitoring the portfolio. She maintains an office in her home that she occupies from 9:00 A.M. to 4:00 P.M. each day and that is the principal place from which she manages her investments. Is Mercedes allowed to take a home office deduction?

10. a. June is an employee of Tufftogs, a children's clothing store. She has an office at the Tufftogs store where she performs many of

her duties as the store manager, but she spends only about half of her workday there. The rest of the day is spent at home in a spare room that she has converted into an office where she is required to be available to take business phone calls. There she spends 10 to 15 hours each week on the telephone with customers and suppliers and 10 hours each week performing other work-related duties. Is June entitled to a home office deduction?

b. How, if at all, does your answer in part (a) change if June owns the Tufftogs store and is self-employed instead of being an employee of the store?

11. Alfred, a professor at Eastman University, maintains a laboratory in a detached garage next to his home because the university does not provide laboratory space for him to engage in the scientific experiments that are the subject of his scholarly writing. He spends 20 hours each week working in his home laboratory and 30 hours each week at the university in the classroom and in his university office where he writes and sees students. Is Alfred entitled to a home office deduction?

12. Mabel, who is a lawyer, is an associate in a large urban law firm. One or two days a week and most evenings, Mabel works at home in an office that she set up in a spare bedroom of her home. She uses her home personal computer to research cases through LEXIS and WESTLAW and to write drafts of briefs and memos. Is Mabel allowed to deduct her home office and computer expenses?

13. Bob is an elementary school teacher. On evenings and weekends he operates a mail-order comic book service, buying and selling rare comic books. He sets up an office in his home that he uses exclusively for running the comic book business. His annual gross income from the comic business is $4,000 and his teacher's salary is $40,000. Bob uses a home computer exclusively to maintain customer lists. Is Bob allowed a deduction for his home office and computer?

EXPLANATIONS

9. No. A taxpayer is allowed a home office deduction only if she is engaged in a "trade or business." In Moller v. United States, 721 F.2d 810 (Fed. Cir. 1983), cert. denied, 467 U.S. 1251 (1984), the Federal Circuit held that a couple who managed

their investment portfolio full-time were not allowed to take a home office deduction because long-term investing (as opposed to trading) is not a trade or business. Mercedes, who derives most of her investment income from dividends and interest, not from gain on the sale of securities, is an investor rather than a trader, so she is not engaged in a trade or business and is not allowed a home office deduction.

10. a. June is an employee of the store, so she cannot take a home office deduction unless the home office is maintained for the convenience of her employer. §280A(c)(1) (flush language). She has an adequate office at the store, so the home office is not for the convenience of her employer. Cadwallader v. Commissioner, 919 F.2d 1273 (7th Cir. 1990).

b. June is not an employee of the store, so the limitation discussed in the explanation to part (a) is inapplicable. June can take a deduction for the home office she uses in her business only if either (i) the home office is her "principal place of business" or (ii) she uses the home office "in meeting and dealing" with her customers.

Under the test articulated in Commissioner v. Soliman, 113 S. Ct. 701 (1993), the "principal place of business" is the most important or significant place for the taxpayer's business, taking into account the relative importance of the activities performed in each place of business and the amounts of time spent in each place. In addition, the place where goods are delivered to customers is to be given great weight. June spends half of her time in the store and half of her time in her home office. Although it is not completely clear on these facts, the tasks that June performs at the store are probably more important than, or at least as important as, the tasks she performs in her home office. After giving weight to the fact that the Tufftogs clothes are sold to customers at the store, not in her home, it seems likely that the home office is not her principal place of business.

Is the home office used by customers "in meeting and dealing" with June? No, because a home office is used by customers "in meeting and dealing" with a taxpayer only if the customers actually visit the home office; talking to customers on the phone is not sufficient. Green v. Commissioner, 707 F.2d 404 (9th Cir. 1983); Prop. Reg. §1.280A-2(c).

June cannot satisfy the requirements of §280A(c), so she is not allowed to deduct her home office expenses. §280A(a).

11. Probably yes. The Code provides that an employee may only deduct a home office that is used for the convenience of the employer. §280A(c)(1) (flush language). The Second Circuit has held, however, that where an employer has not provided space in which an employee can effectively carry out his employment duties, a home office is for the convenience of the employer. Weissman v. Commissioner, 751 F.2d 512 (2d Cir. 1984). Although the university provides Alfred an office in which he can talk with students and write, the university does not provide him with laboratory space in which he can perform other essential duties of his employment. Alfred's use of the garage thus is probably for the convenience of his employer.

The garage is a separate structure and is used in connection with Alfred's trade or business, so it satisfies §280A(c)(1)(C). A separate structure need not be the principal place of business or a place where clients are met. Alfred is thus allowed to take a home office deduction.

12. Mabel will not be able to receive any business deductions for either the home office or the computer. Section 280A allows deductions for the cost of a home office only if the office is used exclusively on a regular basis (i) as the taxpayer's principal place of business, (ii) as a place of business where clients meet the taxpayer, or (iii) in a structure separate from the rest of the house. Mabel cannot satisfy any of these three tests because (i) her principal place of business is the law firm, (ii) she does not meet clients in her home, and (iii) the spare bedroom is not a separate structure.

Moreover, §280A(c)(1) states that, for employees, the cost of a home office is deductible only if it is used for the convenience of the employer. Since Mabel presumably has an adequate office at work, the home office would be deemed used for her own convenience and not for the convenience of her employer. See Cadwallader v. Commissioner, 919 F.2d 1273 (7th Cir. 1990).

Computers are "listed property" and thus subject to the limitations imposed under §280F. §280F(d)(4)(A)(iv). A taxpayer is allowed to deduct the cost of a home computer only if the computer is used for the convenience of the employer and is required as a condition of employment. §280F(d)(3)(A). There is no indication that Mabel is required by her law firm to purchase a computer or to work at home, so she will not be able to deduct the cost of her computer.

13. Yes. The office is the principal place of business for the comic book business. Thus, Bob is allowed a home office deduction under §280A(c)(1)(A). Note, however, that §280A(c)(5) could potentially limit Bob's home office deduction since his gross income from the comic business is only $4,000.

    Section 280F does not limit Bob's deduction for his computer, the computer is not "listed property" because it is used for business purposes in a qualifying home office. §280F(d)(4)(B).

B. Travel and Entertainment Expenses

Reading: §§162, 274

Taxpayers are allowed to deduct the ordinary and necessary expenses incurred in carrying on a trade or business. §162(a). Travel and entertainment expenses associated with a business have an inherent element of personal consumption and have been subject to substantial taxpayer abuse. Thus, §§162(a)(2) and 274 place a number of restrictions on the deductibility of such expenses. The goal is to permit deductions for travel and entertainment expenses that serve a genuine business purpose while restricting the deductibility of expenses that are incurred primarily for personal reasons. This section summarizes the §162(a)(2) test and some of the most important provisions of §274.

Section 162(a) provides generally that a taxpayer is allowed to deduct the ordinary and necessary expenses paid in carrying on a trade or business. (For a discussion of the terms "ordinary" and "necessary," see Chapter 5 of this book.) Section 162(a)(2) specifically allows a taxpayer to deduct travel expenses, including the costs of meals and lodging, if the following three requirements are met: (i) the travel expenses are reasonable and appropriate, (ii) the expenses are incurred while the taxpayer is away from home, and (iii) the expenses are motivated by the exigencies of the taxpayer's business, not the taxpayer's personal preferences. For purposes of this test, a taxpayer is "away from home" only if the taxpayer is away overnight. United States v. Correll, 389 U.S. 299 (1967).

Usually, the location of the taxpayer's "home" will be obvious because the taxpayer will live and work in the same area. However, if the taxpayer lives in one location and works in a different location, is the taxpayer's "home" the place where the taxpayer lives or works? A number of courts have refused to adopt a bright-line test on this issue. Instead they have considered all of the facts and circumstances to determine whether the expense is motivated by the exigencies of the taxpayer's business rather than the taxpayer's personal preferences. Hantzis v. Commissioner, 638 F.2d 248 (1st Cir.), cert. denied, 452 U.S. 962 (1981). If a taxpayer maintains two residences and incurs duplicate living expenses because of the exigencies of the taxpayer's business, the expenses are likely to be deductible. On the other hand, if a taxpayer maintains two residences for personal reasons (for example, because the taxpayer must work in one location but simply prefers for personal reasons to live in another area), the duplicate expenses incurred at the work location are not deductible.

For example, in *Hantzis,* the court upheld the Service's disallowance of a law student taxpayer's costs of living in New York City during a 10-week summer law firm clerkship despite the fact that she and her husband lived in Boston. Ms. Hantzis was not engaged in a trade or business in Boston, where she lived and attended law school, but was engaged in a trade or business in New York, where she worked, so the court concluded that her "home," for purposes of §162(a)(2), was New York. The court also concluded that Ms. Hantzis did not meet the "exigencies of the business" test because she chose to live in Boston for personal reasons, not business reasons. Since she could not satisfy the second and third requirements of §162(a)(2), she could not deduct the costs of living in New York as "away from home" travel expenses.

Some taxpayers have no "home" so they cannot be "away from home" for the purposes of §162. In Rosenspan v. United States, 438 F.2d 905 (2d Cir. 1971), the taxpayer traveled for business most of the year. He voted and filed income tax returns from his brother's home, but rarely spent the night with his brother because he feared he would wear out his welcome there. The Second Circuit held that the taxpayer could not deduct his travel expenses under §162(a)(2) because he had no home from which to be away.

Certain meal, recreation, and entertainment expenses incurred in a business setting may be deducted even if the taxpayer is not away from home. However, the costs of such business entertainment or recreation (including meals) may be deducted only if (i) the item was "directly related to" the active conduct of the taxpayer's trade or business (as opposed to the creation of goodwill) or (ii) the item preceded or followed a "substantial and bona fide business discussion" and was "associated" with the taxpayer's trade or business. §274(a)(1). See also Reg. §1.274-2(c)(3) (which sets forth four requirements for establishing that an entertainment expenditure is "directly related" to the active conduct of the taxpayer's business). Under the second part of the §274(a)(1) test, a taxpayer may be able to deduct the cost of taking a client to a concert or sporting event that is not directly related to the taxpayer's business, simply by holding a business discussion at a restaurant before the event.

Section 274(e) provides a number of specific exceptions to §274(a) for certain expenses. For example, §274(e) provides that §274(a) does not limit an employer's deduction for expenses associated with a bona fide business meeting of employees, stockholders, partners, and directors. A meeting held principally to discuss business, not for social purposes, is a bona fide business meeting. §274(e)(5); Reg. §1.274-2(f)(2)(vi).

Even if a business meal deduction is not limited by §274, the deduction will be limited under §162 if the expense of the meal does not appear to be an ordinary and necessary business expense. For example, in Moss v. Commissioner, 758 F.2d 211 (7th Cir.), cert. denied, 474 U.S. 979 (1985), a partner in a law firm was denied a §162 deduction for the expense of daily lunches at a restaurant where the taxpayer and the other partners in his small firm met to discuss and coordinate their work. The court noted that having the partners eat lunch together every day probably fostered camaraderie and facilitated business, but concluded that such frequent lunches were not necessary to coordinate such a small number of partners. The expense of the daily lunches was not, in the court's view, a deductible §162 ordinary and necessary business expense.

All deductions for meal and entertainment expenses are limited to 50 percent of the amount spent. §274(n). If an employer reimburses an employee for such expenses, the employee may deduct the full expense (which, in effect, permits the taxpayer to exclude the reimbursement, which would otherwise have to be included in income), but the employer may deduct only 50 percent of the expense. §274(n)(2)(A), (e)(3). The 50 percent limitation does not apply to expenses for food and beverages that would be excludable by the recipient as a de minimis fringe benefit under §132(e) (discussed in Chapter 2). §274(n)(2)(B).

6. Mixed Personal and Business Expenditures

Except for certain charitable sports events, deductions for entertainment tickets are limited to the face value of the tickets. §274(l)(1)(A). Deductions for luxury skyboxes generally are limited to the cost of seats in non-luxury boxes. §274(l)(2).

Dues or fees paid to athletic or social clubs generally are not deductible. §274(a)(2)(A). In addition, a taxpayer may not deduct fees paid to other types of clubs unless the taxpayer "establishes that the facility was used primarily for the furtherance of the taxpayer's trade or business and that the item was directly related to the active conduct of such trade or business." §274(a)(2)(C). Even if this standard is met, however, no deduction may be taken for membership dues "in any club organized for business, pleasure, recreation, or other social purpose." §274(a)(3). Proposed Regulation §1.274-2 indicates that a club is within the §274(a)(3) limitation if the club's principal function is to entertain its members (for example, country clubs and airline clubs). On the other hand, the §274(a)(3) limitation does not apply to trade or professional organizations (for example, bar associations). Id. Even if the club dues are deductible under §274(a), any portion of the dues that is for meals is also subject to the §274(n) 50 percent limitation.

Business gifts generally are deductible only up to $25 per year per recipient. §274(b).

Business travel often is mixed with personal sightseeing or visiting friends and relatives. If the primary purpose of domestic travel is business-related, then the entire amount of the trip may be deducted except for any additional costs associated with the personal component. On the other hand, for foreign travel exceeding one week, if 25 percent or more of the total travel time is spent on personal activities, then all costs of the trip must be allocated between the personal and business components. §274(c).

To illustrate, if a taxpayer traveled from New York to Alaska on a business trip and spent the first week on business and the second week sightseeing, she would be able to deduct the entire amount of her airfare and the cost of lodging and meals (subject to the §274(n) limitation) for the first week, but not the costs of lodging and meals for the second week. If the destination instead were Paris, meals and lodging would be treated identically, but the cost of the airfare would also have to be allocated between the business and nonbusiness uses. Only half of the cost of the airfare would be deductible.

No expenses for attending a convention outside of the North American area may be deducted unless the taxpayer is able to show that it is reasonable to hold the meeting outside of North America. §274(h)(1). Deductions also are limited for conventions held on cruise ships and for other luxury water transportation. §274(h)(2), (m)(1). No deduction is permitted for travel as a form of education. §274(m)(2).

If a spouse, dependent, or other person accompanies the taxpayer on business travel, the travel expenses of the person accompanying the taxpayer are not deductible unless (i) the person accompanying the taxpayer is an employee of the taxpayer or the taxpayer's employer, (ii) the person accompanying the taxpayer is traveling for a bona fide business purpose, and (iii) the travel expenses of the person accompanying the taxpayer are otherwise deductible. §274(m)(3).

No deduction or credit is permitted for traveling, entertainment, recreation expenses, or business gifts (or for certain listed property such as computers) unless the taxpayer substantiates the expense by adequate records made at or near the time of the expenditure, as specified in the regulations. §274(d); Temp. Reg. §1.274-5T. The regulations allow exceptions to the substantiation requirement for reimbursed employee expenses and expenses of under $25 (other than lodging). Reg. §1.274-5T(c)(2)(iii) and (f)(2). In addition, the regulations permit taxpayers to take specified deductions for certain business expenses such as automobile travel and meals. Reg. §1.162-17(b)(3). For travel by automobile, for example, taxpayers are permitted to deduct a specified amount (which changes from year to year) per mile instead of keeping records of their actual expenses. Reg. §1.274-5T(b)(6)(i)(B). Taxpayers may also take meal deductions based on per diem amounts (subject to the 50 percent limitation of §274(n)) without having to substantiate their actual expenses. Rev. Proc. 92-17.

EXAMPLES

14. Is each of the following statements true or false?
    a. A deduction is permitted for 50 percent of the cost of food and entertainment if the expense is incurred in the active conduct of the taxpayer's trade or business and a business discussion occurs before, during, or after the meal or entertainment.
    b. If an employer reimburses an employee for a business meal, the reimbursement is not included in the employee's income and the employer receives a deduction for 50 percent of the cost of the meal.

6. Mixed Personal and Business Expenditures

15. A management consulting firm holds an annual three-day February "retreat" at an exclusive resort for the employees of the firm. The firm sponsors the following activities: Friday and Saturday night banquets; Saturday and Sunday golf and tennis tournaments; and Sunday horseback riding. A two-hour firm meeting is held from noon to 2 P.M. Saturday. Attendance at the retreat is encouraged, but not required.
    a. Assume that each individual employee pays his or her own expenses. Are the expenses deductible?
    b. Assume that the firm pays all of the employees' expenses. Will those who attend be taxed on their pro rata share of the expenses?

16. Vivien, an executive with Shark Corporation, purchased tickets to Major League Baseball's All-Star Game. During the hour prior to the game and the seventh-inning stretch, she laid the groundwork for a multimillion dollar business deal with the client who accompanied her. Vivien is reimbursed by the firm for the cost of the tickets and the hot dogs and soda consumed during the game. What are the tax consequences to Vivien and Shark Corporation?

17. Ross is a member of the Maple Creek Country Club and pays annual membership dues of $5,000. He plays golf at the club two or three times a week. About twice a month he meets with clients at the club, either for a round of golf or for dinner. Ross says he would have joined a club costing only $2,000 per year if he were only interested in golf, but that the business advantages of Maple Creek justified the additional $3,000 fee. How much of the $5,000 country club dues can Ross deduct?

18. Lou is a college professor of American History and a member of the Society for the Study of United States History. Lou traveled to Venice, Italy, to present a paper at the Society's annual convention. Is the cost of travel to the convention deductible?

19. Kitty is a partner in a Los Angeles law firm with 10 partners and 14 associates. The firm found it convenient to hold meetings during lunch three times a week in a meeting room at the inexpensive Dino's Diner. The meetings consist only of partners and associates at the firm. The luncheon conversation focuses on legal strategy and other topics related to the business of the law firm. Can Kitty deduct the cost of her meals?

20. Laura is assistant manager of Stereo Lab, a Miami, Florida, store selling high quality audio and video equipment. In July she

attends a consumer electronic show in Chicago. She spends six days at the show and the next eight days visiting (and staying) with her parents who live in a Chicago suburb. Her round-trip first class airfare of $1,400 and her $200 per day of meal and lodging expenses while at the show are paid by Stereo Lab. Are all of the expenses deductible by Stereo Lab? Are any of the expenses paid by Stereo Lab taxable to Laura?

21. Wendy owns The Surf Shop, a California store specializing in surfboard and associated clothing and equipment. Wendy is considering whether or not to take a trip to Hawaii to attend a surfing convention at a cost of $1,000. Wendy is in the 40 percent tax bracket. Wendy believes that attending the convention has no business value, but that the personal value of the trip to Hawaii is worth $700 to her.

   a. Will Wendy attend if she can deduct all of the cost of the trip?
   b. Will Wendy attend if she cannot deduct the cost of the trip?
   c. Is it efficient for Wendy to attend the convention?
   d. How, if at all, would your answers in parts (a) through (c) change if Wendy believed that attending the convention would increase the earnings of The Surf Shop by $200?

EXPLANATIONS

14. a. Statement (a) is true. See §274(a)(1) and §274(n).

   b. Statement (b) is true. An employee reimbursed by his employer for a business meal does not have to include the reimbursement (in effect, because the income would be offset by the employee's deduction of that expense). §274(e)(3). The employer will be able to deduct 50 percent of the reimbursed amount. §274(n).

15. a. A deduction is permitted under §274(a)(1)(A) for travel and entertainment expenses only if such expenses directly relate to or directly precede or follow a substantial and bona fide business discussion, including business meetings. Expenses would be deductible under §274(a) only to the extent they directly related to, preceded, or followed the Saturday meeting. It is hard to imagine how the Friday dinner and Saturday horseback riding (among other activities) would meet this standard.

   More generous rules, however, are provided under §274(e) for certain expenses, including those associated with an employee business meeting. Under Reg. §1.274-2(f)(2)(vi) a complete deduction is permitted for expenses associated with "bona fide" business meetings. A business meeting held primarily for social purposes, however, is not considered a bona fide business meeting. The expenses for the firm retreat, therefore, would be deductible under §274(e) only if the weekend is considered to serve primarily a business rather than a social purpose. This seems unlikely.

b. The analysis is identical to that outlined in (a) above. Since the retreat appears to have been held primarily for social purposes, the value of the retreat would be taxable compensation to the employees and would be deductible to the firm like any other form of compensation. In practice, employers and employees seldom report the value of employer-sponsored retreats as income, even where it is clear that the purpose of the retreat is primarily social.

16. Vivien is not taxed on the value of the tickets and meals. §274(e)(3). Shark Corporation can deduct 50 percent of the expenses. Section 274(a)(1)(A) allows a deduction of the cost of entertainment expenses that are "associated with" business and directly precede or follow a "substantial and bona fide business discussion." Because there was a business discussion before the game, the cost of tickets and meals is deductible. However, under §274(n), a deduction for meals and entertainment is limited to 50 percent of the cost.

17. Ross cannot deduct any of the dues. First, dues or fees to a club are deductible only if the club is used by the taxpayer primarily for business purposes. §274(a)(2). Whether a club was used primarily for business purposes is determined by all the facts and circumstances of each case. Under the regulations, an entertainment facility such as a golf club shall be deemed to be used primarily for the furtherance of the taxpayer's trade or business if the taxpayer establishes that more than 50 percent of the total calendar days of use during the taxable year were for business use. Reg. §1.274-2(c)(4)(iii). Ross plays golf at the club 8-12 times a month and meets clients at the club about twice a month, so this test is not met. Under the regulations, the actual use of the club, not the taxpayer's purpose in joining, generally determines its primary use. Thus, Ross's claim that he joined the club for business purposes will be given limited weight. Reg. §1.274-2(c)(4)(i).

Second, even if the Maple Creek Country Club were used

primarily for business purposes, under §274(a)(3) no deduction is permitted for membership dues in any club organized for business, pleasure, recreation, or other social purpose. Since the payments Ross made were membership fees, they would not be deductible.

18. Probably not. Travel to conventions outside the "North American area" is not deductible unless "it is as reasonable for the meeting to be held outside the North American area as within." §274(h)(1). The convention Lou attended was for a society dedicated to United States history, so it probably is more reasonable to hold the convention in North America.

19. Probably not. Under similar facts, the Seventh Circuit in Moss v. Commissioner, 758 F.2d 211 (7th Cir.), cert. denied, 474 U.S. 979 (1985), disallowed a deduction for the expenses of the partner's daily lunch meetings. The court concluded that, although having the eight partners in the firm eat together every day may have facilitated business, the expense of the daily meetings was not an ordinary and necessary expense since the work of eight lawyers could have been coordinated with less frequent meetings. Here, the meetings are less frequent than in *Moss*, and there are more lawyers to coordinate than in *Moss*. However, on balance, the meetings are probably still too frequent to permit deduction of the expense.

20. None of the expenses are taxable to Laura. All of the airfare and lodging and 50 percent of the meal expenses are deductible by Stereo Lab. The primary purpose of the trip seems to be attendance at the consumer electronics show even though more than half of Laura's stay in Chicago was spent visiting her parents. Thus, all of the expenses will be considered incurred for business reasons and will be deductible by Stereo Lab and received tax-free by Laura under §132(d) as a working condition fringe benefit. Stereo Lab's deduction for Laura's meals, however, is limited by §274(n) to 50 percent of the expense. Note that business-related first class air travel and reasonably luxurious hotel accommodations are permitted as ordinary and necessary business expenses.

21. a. Wendy is in the 40 percent tax bracket, so deducting the cost of the $1,000 trip will reduce her taxes by $400. The after-tax cost of the trip is $600 and the trip is worth $700 to her, so she will attend the convention.

    b. If Wendy cannot deduct the cost of the trip, it will have an after-tax cost of $1,000. The trip is only worth $700 to her, so she will not attend the convention.

c. The convention has no business value and a personal value of $700 for a total value of $700. The $1,000 cost of the trip is greater than its total value, so it is not efficient for Wendy to attend the convention. This example demonstrates that inefficiency can result if expenditures with no business value are permitted to be deducted as business expenses.

d. Attending the convention will cost $1,000 and will increase the earnings of The Surf Shop by $200. The net pre-tax cost of the trip is $800. Deducting the $1,000 cost of the trip will reduce her taxes by $400. Taxes on the $200 of additional earnings arising from the trip will be $80. The net tax saving from attending the convention is $320. The after-tax cost of the trip, therefore, is $800 minus $320 or $480. This is less than the $700 personal value of the trip, so Wendy will attend the convention if she can deduct the cost of the trip.

If Wendy cannot deduct the cost of the trip, it will have an after-tax cost of $880. The $1,000 cost of the trip will be offset by the $200 of increased earnings from attending the convention. However, the $200 of increased earnings will be subject to a tax of $80. Since the $700 personal value of the trip is less than its $880 after-tax cost, Wendy will not take the trip.

The convention has a $200 business value and a personal value of $700 for a total value of $900. The $1,000 cost of the trip is still greater than its total value, so it is not efficient for Wendy to attend the convention. This example demonstrates that inefficiency can result from permitting a deduction for expenditures with both a business value and a personal value if the combined business and personal value is less than the cost of the expenditure.

C. Child Care Expenses

Reading: §§21, 129

In Smith v. Commissioner, 40 B.T.A. 1038 (1939), aff'd without opinion, 113 F.2d 114 (2d Cir. 1940), the Board of Tax Appeals held that the child care costs of a two-earner couple were not deductible because such child care expenses were "inherently personal." After *Smith*, a limited deduction for child care costs was added to the Code, but in 1976 the deduction was replaced by a credit.

Under §21, a taxpayer is allowed a credit for certain household and dependent care services incurred to enable the taxpayer to work. Section 21(a) provides that, if the taxpayer's household includes one or more "qualifying individuals," the taxpayer is allowed a credit in an amount equal to the "applicable percentage" of the "employment related expenses" the taxpayer paid during the taxable year.

A *qualifying individual* is (i) a dependent who is under the age of 13 or (ii) a dependent or spouse who is physically or mentally incapable of caring for himself. §21(b)(1). *Employment related expenses* are expenses incurred for the care of a qualifying individual, but only if such expenses are incurred to enable the taxpayer to work. §21(b)(2). The amount of employment related expense that may be taken into account in computing the credit is limited by §21(c) to (i) $2,400 if there is only one qualifying individual in the taxpayer's household or (ii) $4,800 if there are two or more qualifying individuals in the taxpayer's household. Section 21(d) also provides that the eligible employment related expenses cannot exceed the earned income (for example, wages) of the taxpayer, or in the case of a married taxpayer, the lesser of the earned income of the taxpayer or the taxpayer's spouse. §21(d)(1). A special rule permits a credit where the taxpayer's spouse is disabled or a full-time student. §21(d)(2).

The *applicable percentage* is 30 percent but is reduced by one percentage point for each $2,000 (or fraction thereof) by which the taxpayer's adjusted gross income for the year exceeds $10,000. §21(a)(2). For example, suppose a taxpayer's adjusted gross income is $25,000. The taxpayer's adjusted gross income exceeds $10,000 by $15,000. There are eight full or partial $2,000 increments in $15,000. Thus, the applicable percentage will be reduced by eight percentage points, from 30 percent to 22 percent. The percentage cannot be reduced below 20 percent; the applicable percentage for any taxpayer with adjusted gross income in excess of $28,000 is 20 percent because a taxpayer with $28,001 or more of adjusted gross income has at least 10 full or partial $2,000 increments of adjusted gross income in excess of $10,000.

The maximum credit for a taxpayer with one child and adjusted gross income of over $28,000 is thus $480, which is 20 percent of the $2,400 of employment related expenses that may be taken into account. If the taxpayer has a second child, the maximum credit increases to $960, which is 20 percent of the $4,800 of employment related expenses that may be taken into account.

Section 129 also provides an exclusion for employee child care expenses reimbursed by an employer pursuant to a written "dependent care assistance program" as defined in §129(d). The requirements for a §129 program are similar to the requirements under §21 for the child care credit except that, under §129, the employer reimburses the employee for the expense. The amount that may be excluded under §129 is limited to $5,000 a year. §129(a)(2)(A). Any amount excluded under §129 reduces the employment related expenses that may be taken into account under §21(c) for purposes of computing the §21 credit. §21(c). For example, a taxpayer who excludes $5,000 under §129 is precluded from taking a §21 credit. A taxpayer who would prefer to take the credit may do so if she does not avail herself of the employer's dependent care assistance program. In other words, if the taxpayer's employer maintains a dependent care assistance program, the taxpayer must choose between the §129 exclusion and the §21 credit.

Recall that a credit is different from a deduction or exclusion. A credit is a direct reduction in tax while a deduction or exclusion is a reduction in taxable income; the tax saving from a credit is the amount of the credit, while the tax saving from a deduction or exclusion is the amount of the deduction or exclusion multiplied by the taxpayer's tax rate.

Consider the following example, which illustrates this distinction in the context of §§21 and 129. Tom is a single parent and an associate at a big Chicago law firm. He pays a babysitter $20,000 during the year to take care of his three-year-old child. Tom's adjusted gross income is $100,000 and he is in the 30 percent tax bracket. Tom's child is a qualifying individual and his $20,000 of child care expenses are employment related expenses. However, only $2,400 of the employment related expenses may be taken into account in computing the credit. §21(c). Tom earns more than $28,000 a year, so the applicable percentage is 20 percent. Tom's §21 credit equals 20 percent of $2,400, or $480.

Assume instead that Tom avails himself of a dependent care assistance program offered by his employer. His employer reimburses him for $5,000 of his child care expenses, which he excludes from income under §129. That $5,000 exclusion saves Tom $1,500 of tax because he is in the 30 percent tax bracket. The $5,000 exclusion precludes Tom from taking a §21 credit. §21(c). However, the $1,500 of tax saved by taking the §129 exclusion more than makes up for the loss of the $480 credit.

EXAMPLES

22. Leslie and Guy have four children. Leslie earns $65,000 a year as an attorney. Leslie's salary alone places the family in the 30 percent marginal tax bracket. Guy has stayed at home and provided child care, but is now thinking of accepting a job as a secretary. Child care to enable Guy to work will cost $15,000 a year. The secretarial position pays $20,000 a year (after taking into account Social Security taxes and Guy's work-related expenses other than child care). Guy will accept the secretarial position if it increases the family's after-tax income. Which, if any, of the following statements are true?

    a. Guy will accept the secretarial position even if the child care cost is not deductible.

    b. If Guy's secretarial income is exempt from all taxation, Guy will accept the secretarial position.

    c. Guy will accept the secretarial position if the child care costs are eligible for the dependent care credit under §21.

    d. Guy will accept the secretarial position if his employer reimburses him for $5,000 of the expenses and the reimbursement is eligible for the §129 exclusion.

    e. Guy will accept the secretarial position if the child care costs are deductible.

23. Kim and Mike are married with one child. Kim earns $10,000 and Mike earns $5,000 for a total annual income of $15,000. The cost of child care required to enable Mike to work is $2,000.

    a. What amount of tax credit will Kim and Mike be allowed to take under §21?

    b. How, if at all, would your answer in part (a) change if they each earned $20,000 per year?

    c. Suppose that Kim and Mike also care for Kim's mother, who lives with them and is elderly and unable to care for herself. In order to work, they incur $2,000 for the care of their child and $4,000 for the care of Kim's mother. Again, assume that they each earn $20,000. What amount of credit can they claim under §21?

    d. Assume the same facts as in part (c), except that Kim makes

$37,000 and Mike makes $3,000. What amount of credit can they claim under §21?

EXPLANATIONS

22. a. This statement is false. The secretarial position will increase the family's before-tax income by $5,000, the difference between the $20,000 salary and the $15,000 cost of child care. However, if the costs of child care are not deductible, the family's tax burden will increase by $6,000 (30 percent of Guy's $20,000 of income). Thus, the total costs of accepting the secretarial position are $21,000 ($15,000 for child care plus $6,000 of tax). The salary is only $20,000, so the family will be $1,000 poorer, after paying taxes and child care expenses, if Guy accepts the secretarial position. Guy has replaced tax-free imputed household income with taxable income earned as a secretary. The newly created tax burden more than offsets the higher income earned outside of the home.

    b. This statement is true. If Guy's earnings are exempt from taxation, the secretarial position increases the family's income by $5,000 a year, the difference between his $20,000 salary and the $15,000 cost of child care.

    c. This statement is false. Leslie and Guy's combined income is greater than $30,000, so they will receive a 20 percent credit for their child care expenses up to $4,800. §21(a)(2), (c). This produces a $960 credit (20 percent of $4,800) under §21. If Guy accepts the secretarial position, the net change in family income is calculated as follows: $20,000 income from employment less $15,000 child care expenses less $6,000 of tax on the income plus $960 child care credit equals −$40. Guy would suffer a $40 net loss by accepting employment, so he will not take the position.

    d. If the employer reimburses Guy for $5,000 of the family's child care expenses, Guy can exclude the $5,000 reimbursement from income under §129. He will accept the secretarial position because the net change in family income is $4,000, calculated as follows: $20,000 income from employment less $15,000 child care expenses plus $5,000 reimbursed less $6,000 of tax on the $20,000 of income equals $4,000.

    e. This statement is true. If Guy receives a deduction for child care costs incurred while working as a secretary, his taxable income will be only $5,000 a year. If that sum is taxed at a 30 percent rate, his tax liability will be $1,500. He will accept the secretarial position because the net change in family income is $3,500, calculated as follows: $20,000 income from employment less $15,000 child care expenses less $1,500 of tax on the $5,000 of income equals $3,500.

23. a. Kim and Mike are entitled to a tax credit of $540. The child care tax credit is a percentage of expenses, which is reduced from 30 percent (but no lower than 20 percent) by one point for every $2,000 (or fraction thereof) by which the taxpayer's income exceeds $10,000. §21(a)(2). Kim and Mike have a combined income of $15,000, which exceeds $10,000 by $5,000. There are three full or partial increments of $2,000 in that $5,000 amount. Thus, Kim and Mike are entitled to a credit of 27 percent (30 percent less 3 percent). Their §21 credit is $540 (27 percent of the $2,000 of employment related expenses).

b. Here, Kim and Mike are entitled to a tax credit of $400. For taxpayers with income in excess of $28,000, the child care credit is 20 percent of eligible expenses. §21(a)(2). The credit is thus $400 (20 percent of $2,000).

c. Kim and Mike are entitled to a tax credit of $960. Kim's mother is a qualifying individual because she is a dependent unable to care for herself. §21(b)(1)(B). The $4,000 expense of caring for Kim's mother is an employment related expense. §21(b)(2)(A). The maximum amount of employment related expenses that a couple with two or more qualifying individuals can claim is $4,800. Therefore, Kim and Mike are entitled to a credit of $960 (20 percent of $4,800).

d. Kim and Mike are entitled to a tax credit of $400. For purposes of computing the credit, the employment related expenses are limited to the income of the lower-earning spouse. §21(d)(1)(B). Mike's income is $3,000 so the credit is $600 (20 percent of $3,000).

D.   Commuting Expenses

Taxpayers would not incur the commuting expenses of traveling to and from their jobs if they did not work. However, if a taxpayer lives close to the place where he works, he incurs little or no commuting costs. If, on the other hand, the taxpayer chooses to live some distance from the place where he works, he may incur substantial commuting costs. Thus, commuting costs are thought to result from the taxpayer's personal choice of where to live and are generally treated as nondeductible personal expenditures. Reg. §§1.162-2(e), 1.262-1(b)(5), Commissioner v. Flowers, 326 U.S. 465 (1946).

There are a few exceptions to the general rule of nondeductibility of commuting expenses. If a taxpayer has a regular work location but takes a temporary assignment at a different location, the taxpayer can deduct his costs of traveling to and from the temporary job site. Rev. Rul. 90-23. (The deduction is a §162(a) deduction, not a §162(a)(2) deduction.)

In addition, if the taxpayer is "away from home," within the meaning of §162(a)(2), the costs of commuting to and from work (as well as lodging and meals, subject to §274(n)) are deductible if the expense is required by the exigencies of the taxpayer's business. Recall that §162(a)(2) allows a taxpayer to deduct travel expenses if the taxpayer is away overnight and the travel expenses are (i) reasonable and appropriate, (ii) incurred while the taxpayer is away from home, and (iii) are motivated by the exigencies of the taxpayer's business, not the taxpayer's personal preferences. As we saw earlier in this chapter, in the discussion of travel expenses, a taxpayer claiming to be "away from home" has to establish his *business* connection both to the location he calls "home" and the place where he is temporarily working. Hantzis v. Commissioner, 638 F.2d 248 (1st Cir. 1981), cert. denied, 452 U.S. 962 (1981). As we also saw earlier, a taxpayer with no "home" cannot be "away from home." Rosenspan v. United States, 438 F.2d 905 (2d Cir. 1971), cert denied, 404 U.S. 864 (1971).

There is also a limited exception to nondeductibility of commuting expenses if a taxpayer's job requires her to transport job-related tools to and from work. In that case, the taxpayer may be able to deduct her extra commuting costs that are attributable to transporting the tools. Fausner v. Commissioner, 413 U.S. 838 (1973), reh'g denied, 414 U.S. 882 (1973). For example, assume that a taxpayer's work requires her to carry heavy tools to and from work. If the taxpayer did not have to transport the tools, she would commute to and from work on public transportation at a cost of $2 a day. In order to transport the tools, she drives her car to and from work and carries the tools in a trailer attached to the car. If she drove without the tools, her commute would cost $3 a day, but with the tools the commute costs

$8 a day. On these facts, the Service ruled that the taxpayer could deduct $5 a day (the $8 cost of commuting in the car with the trailer less the $3 cost of commuting in the car without the trailer), not $6 a day (the $8 cost of commuting in the car with the trailer less the $2 a day cost of commuting on public transportation). Rev. Rul. 75-380.

In addition, transportation costs while on the job are generally deductible even though the costs of travel between the taxpayer's home and principal place of business are not deductible. Reg. §1.162-2. Thus, an insurance adjuster can deduct the costs of driving to accident sites to assess losses.

EXAMPLES

24. Glen, who lives with his family in Santa Barbara, works full-time for a Los Angeles law firm. When he was hired, the firm wanted him to move with his family to Los Angeles, but he refused. After some negotiations, they worked out an arrangement; Glen works three days a week in the office of the firm and three days a week in office space in Santa Barbara that is sublet from another law firm. Can he deduct his commuting expenses to and from Los Angeles?

25. Regional Manager Barbara spends $10 a day commuting to and from her office in the headquarters of her corporate employer. She spends another $15 a day traveling between the headquarters and branch offices and calling on customers. What portion, if any, of her transportation expenses are deductible?

26. David works as a traveling salesman for a number of clothing manufacturers. David is on the road five months a year; in the remaining months, he works out of his Chicago home.
   a. Are David's "on the road" transportation expenses deductible? Are the expenses of his travel-related meals and lodging deductible?
   b. Assume instead that David is on the road 11 months a year; in the remaining month David rents a vacation home in various locations and spends a week or so visiting his brother and sister-in-law. Are David's business travel expenses for transportation, meals, and lodging deductible?

EXPLANATIONS

24. A deduction is permitted under §162(a)(2) for business expenses incurred while away from home in the pursuit of a trade or busi-

ness. However, case law and regulations deny deductions for commuting expenses incurred while traveling to and from one's principal place of business. Reg. §§1.162-2(e), 1.262-1(b)(5). The facts here are similar to the facts in Commissioner v. Flowers, in which a taxpayer was denied a deduction for the costs of traveling between his home (and part-time work location) in Jackson, Mississippi, and his principal place of business in Mobile, Alabama, because, in the court's view, the expense was motivated by the taxpayer's personal decision to live in Jackson. Here, Glen's costs of commuting to Los Angeles are probably similarly attributable to his personal preference as to where to live, so he would probably be denied a §162(a)(2) deduction.

25. Barbara can deduct only the $15 per day expenses of traveling to branch offices. Commuting expenses to work are nondeductible, but taxpayers are permitted to deduct business transportation expenses other than commuting costs under §162. Reg. §1.162-2.

26. a. David is allowed to deduct his business travel expenses for transportation under §162. He is also allowed to deduct the costs of meals and lodging incurred while away from home and in the pursuit of a trade or business. §162(a)(2). Here, the meal and lodging expenses are incurred in connection with business-related travel to locations other than his principal place of business. David's deductions for meal and entertainment expenses are limited to 50 percent of the expenses. §274(n).

   b. The costs of David's transportation expenses are still deductible under §162(a). However, a deduction is permitted under §162(a)(2) for other travel-related expenses only if they are incurred "away from home" and a taxpayer with no "home" cannot be "away from home." Rosenspan v. United States, 438 F.2d 905 (2d Cir. 1971), cert. denied, 404 U.S. 864 (1971). It seems likely that David has no "home" and is thus not allowed to deduct his other travel expenses such as food and lodging costs.

      Should a taxpayer in Rosenspan's position receive a deduction? The basic policy underlying the deduction is that an individual traveling on business incurs higher expenses than an ordinary individual. Thus, a deduction should be permitted for the additional expenses incurred due to business-related travel, for example, the costs of paying for motel lodging to the extent that they exceed the costs of maintaining a year-round residence. In one sense, the taxpayer here does not face such additional costs; he is not required to maintain two households. In another sense, of course, a taxpayer like Rosenspan does face additional costs since motel lodging and restaurant meals are more expensive than the average taxpayer's food and lodging.

E. Clothing Expenses

An employee is allowed to take an itemized deduction for the unreimbursed cost of clothing worn exclusively at work if (i) the employer requires, as a condition of employment, that employees wear the clothes at work and (ii) the clothing is not suitable for general use. Rev. Rul. 70-474. An objective test is used to determine whether clothing is suitable for general use. In Pevsner v. Commissioner, 628 F.2d 467 (5th Cir. 1980), reh'g denied, 636 F.2d 1106 (5th Cir. 1981), the manager of an Yves Saint Laurent clothing boutique was denied a deduction for the cost of YSL clothes that she bought to wear at work at the urging of her employer. Ms. Pevsner did not wear the YSL clothes when she was not working because she led a simple lifestyle and wanted the clothes to last longer. However, the Fifth Circuit held that an objective approach must be used to determine whether clothing is suitable for general use, so her subjective views about the clothing were irrelevant. The court concluded that the taxpayer could not deduct the cost of the YSL clothes because they were suitable for general use. If the cost of work clothing is deductible and is reimbursed by the employer, the employee does not have to include the reimbursed amount in her gross income. §62(a)(2)(A).

EXAMPLES

27. Sam works at the Enrico Arpaci men's clothing boutique in Beverly Hills, earning $30,000 per year. He is required as a condition of his employment to wear Enrico Arpaci suits, which cost $1,500 each. Sam purchases five new suits each year. He never wears the suits except at work because he does not want to wear them out and because he seldom goes to places where they would be appropriate. Can Sam deduct the costs of the suits?

28. Mary is a tennis pro at a posh country club. Can she deduct the cost of her tennis clothing and tennis shoes?

6. Mixed Personal and Business Expenditures

29. Chuck earned $10,000 per year as a mascot for the Happyville Dogs, a minor league baseball team. He created goodwill for the club by appearing at public events dressed as a bloodhound. He purchased the costume with his own funds at a cost of $1,000. Not only did he wear his costume at public events but, priding himself on being the life of the party, he wore it at private, neighborhood social gatherings. Can Chuck deduct the cost of his costume?

30. Terri is a flight attendant for Northern American Airlines. She is required to wear a uniform to work. The uniform, which is manufactured by a specialty company that makes uniforms, consists of a Navy blue suit jacket, either navy blue slacks or a skirt, a white shirt, and a red scarf. The airline uniform shop charges Terri $1,000 for the uniform. Can she deduct the cost of her uniform?

EXPLANATIONS

27. Probably not. These facts are similar to those in Pevsner v. Commissioner, 628 F.2d 467 (5th Cir. 1980), reh'g denied, 636 F.2d 1106 (5th Cir. 1981). In that case a designer boutique manager who was required to wear expensive designer clothing at work was denied a deduction for the cost of the clothing even though she wore the clothing only at work because she wanted it to last longer and it was not appropriate for her after-work lifestyle. The court denied a deduction because, applying an objective test, the clothing was suitable for general use.

28. Probably not, again because the clothing is suitable for general use. These facts are similar to those in Mella v. Commissioner, 52 T.C.M. (CCH) 1216 (1986). In that case the court denied a deduction for the costs incurred by a nationally ranked tennis pro for clothing and shoes because such apparel is worn for a wide variety of sport and leisure time activities.

29. Probably not. Chuck's costume normally would not be considered adaptable to general use so the cost of the costume would be deductible. However, since he actually did use it outside of his employment, no deduction will be allowed. Pevsner v. Commissioner, 628 F.2d 467 (5th Cir. 1980), reh'g denied, 636 F.2d 1106 (5th Cir. 1981).

30. Yes. An employee is allowed to take an itemized deduction for the unreimbursed cost of clothing worn exclusively at work if (i) the employer requires, as a condition of employment, that employees

wear the clothes at work and (ii) the clothing is not suitable for general use. Rev. Rul. 70-474. No self-respecting flight attendant is going to wear her uniform as street clothes, but, as we saw in the *Pevsner* case, we do not take into account the taxpayer's subjective view as to whether the clothing is suitable for general use; instead, we apply an objective test. Here, Terri's uniform is a navy blue suit, which, at least theoretically, could be worn for general use. However, it is manufactured by a uniform company, not a company that makes clothes for general usage. Ms. Pevsner could have proudly worn her YSL clothes to social events, but she chose not to because of her lifestyle. On the other hand, it would be odd for a flight attendant to wear her navy blue uniform, which many people would recognize as a Northern American Airlines uniform, to a social event, so this case probably is distinguishable from the *Pevsner* case. It seems likely that a court applying the objective test would agree that, even though the uniform may resemble other general use business clothing, a standard, readily identifiable uniform is probably not suitable for general use.

F. Legal Expenses

Reading: §212(3); Reg. §1.263(a)-1 and (a)-2

An individual may deduct legal fees that are incurred in a trade or business or related to the production of income, under §162 or §212 respectively. Legal fees incurred in a business context must be capitalized, however, if they are incurred in connection with the acquisition of property that has a useful life extending substantially beyond the close of the year in which the legal expense is incurred. Reg. §1.263(a)-1.

Personal legal fees, on the other hand, are nondeductible personal expenses. Certain legal fees, such as those arising out of a divorce, can be incurred in part for personal reasons and in part to protect business or investment interests. The deductibility of such legal fees depends on the "origin" of the claim, not on the potential consequences of the claim. If the origin of the claim is personal, legal fees are nondeductible even if they also protect the taxpayer's business or investment interests. For example, in United States v. Gilmore, 372 U.S. 39 (1963), a taxpayer who ran a family business was denied a deduction for legal fees that he incurred, during his divorce, to defend against his wife's claim on his controlling interest in the business. The taxpayer argued that his litigation costs were deductible under §212 because they were incurred to conserve income-producing property. However, the Supreme Court disagreed, holding that the origin of the divorce claim was personal and that the litigation costs were, therefore, not deductible.

Note that §212(3) permits a deduction for expenses incurred "in connection with the determination, collection, or refund of any tax." This provision sometimes allows a taxpayer to deduct legal fees incurred in exchange for personal tax advice, even tax advice given with respect to a divorce. Zmuda v. Commissioner, 79 T.C. 714 (1982), aff'd, 731 F.2d 1417 (9th Cir. 1984).

As the examples in this section demonstrate, however, it often is far from clear how to determine the "origin" of a claim.

EXAMPLES

31. State whether each of the following legal expenses is deductible.
    a. Legal fees incurred by the sole proprietor of a donut shop in connection with a contract dispute with a distributor regarding supplies
    b. Legal fees incurred by an individual taxpayer in obtaining an injunction against a noisy and obnoxious neighbor
    c. Legal fees incurred in defending the taxpayer, who is a clinical psychologist, against an assault claim filed by the taxpayer's neighbor. The taxpayer is spending large amounts to defend himself in the lawsuit because he fears that the charge will damage his business reputation.
    d. Legal fees incurred by a taxpayer, an employee of MaltCo., in defending against a wrongful death action arising out of a car accident after the MaltCo. company Christmas party, which all employees are encouraged to attend. At the time of the accident, the taxpayer, who was very intoxicated, was on his way home from the party and was driving a company car. The plaintiff in the case has filed suit against both the employee and MaltCo.

32. a. Karen had spent years building up a profitable discount jewelry store when her husband George filed for divorce. George claimed he should be awarded a controlling interest in the

store. Karen incurred $100,000 of legal expenses in success-fully fighting George's claim. Can she deduct the legal expenses as a §212 expense incurred for the conservation of income-producing property?

b. Two years later Karen purchased a larger building to house her discount store. The building was expected to last many years and to expand Karen's share of the market. Karen incurred $15,000 in legal expenses in connection with the acquisition of the new building. Can she deduct the legal expenses?

EXPLANATIONS

31. a. These legal expenses are deductible. A taxpayer may deduct only those legal expenses that are deductible under §162 or §212. In other words, legal expenses are deductible only if they arise in connection with a taxpayer's trade or business or in connection with the production of income. Legal fees incurred with respect to a business-related contract dispute are deductible.

b. A dispute with a noisy neighbor is a personal matter, so associated legal expenses are not deductible.

c. The taxpayer may argue that the legal fees are deductible, under §162, because he is defending his reputation for business reasons. However, we must look to the "origin of the claim" in order to determine whether the legal fees are deductible. United States v. Gilmore, 372 U.S. 39 (1963). This standard requires that we focus on the reason that the claim arose, not on whether the claim could harm the taxpayer's business. Here, the alleged assault does not appear to have anything to do with the taxpayer's business, so the legal fees would be nondeductible.

d. This is a close call and the *Gilmore* "origin of the claim" test does not clearly resolve it one way or the other. The taxpayer may argue that the legal fees are deductible as a §162 business expense because the accident occurred in a business context — while he was driving a company car and as a result of drinking at the work-related function. However, the amount that the taxpayer drank at the party was a personal decision, so a court might conclude that these legal fees were nondeductible. Even if the taxpayer can establish that the origin of the claim was business, a court may conclude that this expense is not an "ordinary or necessary" business expense, so is not deductible under §162. (For a discussion of what constitutes an "ordinary and necessary" business expense, see Chapter 5.)

32. a. Karen cannot deduct the legal fees associated with the divorce action. These facts are similar to the facts in United States v. Gilmore, 372 U.S. 39 (1963). As in *Gilmore*, the origin of the claim here is personal because it arises in a divorce proceeding, so no deduction is allowed even though the legal fees are necessary to preserve Karen's business.

   b. Karen's legal expenses are directly related to her business. However, the expenses here must be capitalized (added to her basis in the new building) because the legal expenses are incurred in connection with the acquisition of property having a useful life substantially beyond the taxable year. Reg. §1.263(a)-1 and (a)-2.

G. Educational Expenses

Reading: §274(m)(2); Reg. §1.162-5

The cost of a college education is generally nondeductible because courts consider the cost to be a personal expenditure. See, e.g., Carroll v. Commissioner, 418 F.2d 91 (7th Cir. 1969) (in which a police detective was denied a deduction for the costs of his college tuition because the court concluded that the college education was a personal expense, not an expense of being in the profession of being a detective). On the other hand, an individual is allowed to deduct educational expenses if the education either (i) maintains or improves skills required by the individual in his trade or business or (ii) meets express requirements of the individual's employer or legal requirements imposed by applicable law or regulations as a condition of doing work of the type performed by the taxpayer. Educational expenses incurred to meet the minimum educational requirements of a new trade or business are nondeductible. Reg. §1.162-5(a) and (b).

EXAMPLES

33. Which, if any, of the following educational expenses are deductible?
    a. An individual currently working as an artist pays tuition in connection with earning a graduate degree in business administration.

    b. An individual currently working as a detective incurs expenses in connection with a graduate degree in law enforcement.

34. Teri, a third-year law student, earned $10,000 working as a full-time clerk during the summer prior to her third year and continues to work as a part-time law clerk during the school year. May Teri deduct her third-year law school tuition as a business expense?

35. a. Pierre is hired as an instructor at the Acme School for French Chefs in Cleveland, Ohio. Pierre is considered a member of the Acme School's faculty and has completed the four-year undergraduate course offered by the school. He is working on a graduate degree, specializing in snails and flaming desserts. The school requires that its instructors obtain graduate degrees in some area of French cooking within five years after beginning employment. Can Pierre deduct the expenses for his graduate degree?

    b. The Acme School offers a limited number of graduate courses, and, as a result, the only place that offers the class in snail sauces that Pierre needs to obtain his degree is a cooking school in Paris, France. Can he deduct his tuition costs and travel expenses to attend school abroad?

    c. Suppose Pierre wants to visit France so that he can tour French restaurants and get a better idea of regional variations in French food preparation. Can he then deduct his travel expenses?

36. Doug has finished one semester of his two-semester clown school program. Desperate to fill an unexpected vacancy, the Two-Ring Circus hires Doug, conditioning his continued employment on his completing the second semester of clown school and passing the Twelve Clowns in a Car and Pie Throwing examinations necessary for the state license as a clown. Doug tours with the circus for six months (under a temporary state permit) and then returns to finish clown school. Can Doug deduct his expenses for the second semester of school and for the clown examination review course?

37. Catherine, the managing partner in a major law firm, decides to enter a one-year program leading to a degree as a licensed animal trainer, in the hope that the principles that apply to lions can be used in dealing with other attorneys. Catherine intends to continue practicing law and does not plan to do any work in the

animal training field. Can she deduct the expenses incurred in her animal training education?

38. Richard taught macrame classes at the adult education center, but his heart belonged to folded paper swans, so he took courses that would enable him to teach origami instead. Can Richard deduct his educational expenses?

39. Rita is a clerk in the Woods Department Store. The store encourages its employees to get college degrees and work their way up into management. Rita is getting her bachelor's degree from Eastman University in the hope that the education will help her move up in the company. The course is a general liberal arts curriculum. Can Rita deduct her college expenses?

EXPLANATIONS

33. a. The artist's educational expenses are not deductible because a degree in business administration trains the artist for a new field rather than improving her skills in her current profession. Reg. §1.162-5(b)(3).

    b. The detective will be permitted to deduct the expenses of a degree in law enforcement because it improves or maintains her skills in her current profession. Reg. §1.162-5(a)(1).

34. Only those educational expenses that are incurred primarily for the purpose of maintaining or improving skills in connection with a present occupation are deductible. Reg. §1.162-5; Carroll v. Commissioner, 418 F.2d 91 (7th Cir. 1969). Teri would argue that she meets this test because the educational expenses of her third year in law school are incurred for the purpose of improving her performance at the law firm.

    Unfortunately for the readers of this book, this argument would fail. Education that is necessary to meet the minimum requirements for entry into a trade or business is nondeductible. Reg. §1.162-5(b)(2). An example in the regulations deals explicitly with a situation like Teri's and states that law school tuition is nondeductible because it is required to meet minimum educational requirements for working as a lawyer. Reg. §1.162-5(b)(2)(iii)(Ex.3).

35. a. Pierre's education expenses will be deductible. The minimum educational requirements for a position in an educational institution are considered to have been met once the individual becomes a member of the faculty of that institution. Reg.

§1.162-5(b)(2)(ii). Thus, the additional training would be deductible because it improves Pierre's skills at his current employment.

b. Pierre will be able to deduct both his tuition and travel expenses. His tuition is deductible for the reasons stated in the answer to part (a). He will be able to deduct the travel expenses in spite of §274(m)(2), which specifically disallows any deduction for travel as a form of education. This provision is intended to disallow a deduction, for example, where a French teacher travels to France to maintain a general familiarity with the French language and culture. The rule is not intended to apply to travel in connection with an activity that qualifies for a business deduction. For example, a scholar of French literature who travels to France to take courses offered only at the Sorbonne in Paris would be permitted to deduct her expenses.

c. Pierre will not be permitted to deduct his travel expenses. No deduction is allowed for expenses of travel as a form of education. §274(m)(2).

36. Doug cannot deduct any of his clown school or clown examination preparation expenses. The courses constitute education required to meet the minimum educational requirements for qualification in Doug's trade or business and are not deductible under Reg. §1.162-5(b)(2). The fact that Doug is already employed as a clown does not establish that he has met the minimum educational requirements for clowning.

37. Catherine cannot deduct any of her animal training courses. Expenditures that will qualify the taxpayer for a new trade or business are not deductible even if the taxpayer does not intend to practice in the new field. Reg. §1.162-5(b)(3).

38. Richard will be permitted to deduct the educational expenses associated with learning origami. Although expenditures that qualify the taxpayer for a new trade or business are not deductible, all teaching and teaching-related duties are considered to involve the same general type of work. Even a teacher who takes courses to prepare him for certification as a school administrator is entitled to deduct the costs of the education. Reg. §1.162-5(b)(3)(i).

39. Probably not. There probably is not a sufficient relationship between a general liberal arts education and the particular job skills required of a department store employee. Carroll v. Commissioner, 418 F.2d 91 (7th Cir. 1969).

7

Income Shifting

A. Income from Services and Property

Reading: §1

As we have noted throughout this book, the federal income tax is *progressive*; persons with high income pay a higher percentage of that income to the government in the form of taxes than do persons with low income. (A tax that requires all taxpayers to pay an equal percentage of income is *proportionate* and a tax that requires low income taxpayers to pay a higher percentage of their income is *regressive*.) The progressivity of the income tax encourages high-bracket individuals to shift some of that income to family members, relatives, or close friends in lower tax brackets. Suppose a taxpayer has a combined federal and state marginal income tax rate of nearly 40 percent. She will pay $4,000 of tax on an additional $10,000 of income. Her 16-year-old son, in contrast, may be in the zero percent marginal tax bracket and owe no tax if the $10,000 is attributed to him.

In practice, loss of tax revenue due to income shifting is limited by a number of statutory provisions, three of which deserve special mention. First, virtually all married couples will find their tax liability minimized through filing a joint return, on which all income is combined. The attribution of income between married persons is therefore irrelevant. Compare §§1(a), 1(d).

Second, under §1(g), net unearned income of a child under 14 is taxed at the greater of the child's marginal rate or her parents' marginal rate. Unearned income is that portion of income not attributable to personal services. §§1(g) and 911(d)(2). *Net unearned income* is, to simplify a bit, unearned income in excess of twice the §63(c)(5) limited standard deduction available to an individual who is claimed as a dependent on another taxpayer's return (in 1995, $650). To illustrate the operation of §1(g), suppose that in 1995 a married couple gave their infant daughter a bond that each year paid $10,000 interest, and that the daughter had no other source of income and no itemized deductions. The daughter would have net unearned income of $8,700, which is $10,000 less twice the minimum standard deduction of $650. That $8,700 of net unearned income would be taxed at the parents' rate. The remaining $1,300 of the daughter's gross income would be reduced by the §63(c)(5) $650 standard deduction. The remaining $650 of income would be taxed at the daughter's individual rate. (Note that the daughter is not allowed a personal exemption because her parents are allowed to take a dependent personal exemption for her on their return. §151(d)(2).)

Third, the tax law is less progressive than it once was. For many years the maximum marginal rate on unearned income was 70 percent and the maximum rate on personal service income was 50 percent. The maximum rates are lower today and the payoff for income shifting is less.

Notwithstanding these and other statutory provisions, income shifting is often advantageous. Income shifting can reduce the combined tax liability of unmarried individuals living as domestic partners, parents and children over 14, and wealthy individuals and nonfamily members. And while past marginal rates of 70 percent and upward may be gone forever, the tax law is still progressive and has been getting more so since 1986.

The basic rules governing attempts to shift personal service income are simple enough. Such income is taxed to the person who performs the services and cannot be shifted to a lower bracket taxpayer. Lucas v. Earl, 281 U.S. 111 (1930) (assignment to the taxpayer's wife of half of the taxpayer's income from personal service did not shift that income to his wife); Helvering v. Eubank, 311 U.S. 122 (1940) (assignment to a family trust of commissions to be received in the future for service rendered in the past by the taxpayer did not shift the commission income to the assignees). To illustrate this rule, suppose a high income executive gives her 18-year-old daughter a one-half interest in her next year's salary. Suppose, further, that the gift is legally enforceable. Notwithstanding the gift, the executive will be taxed on her entire salary. The same result would be obtained if the executive gave a one-half interest in payment due for services already performed.

For obvious reasons, the prohibition against shifting income from personal services does not apply to the value of services provided free of charge to a third party. (See the discussion of imputed income in Chapter 2.) Consider a carpenter in the 30 percent marginal tax bracket who gives his cousin $1,000 of his earnings to pay for household improvements. The carpenter is taxed on the $1,000. By contrast, the carpenter would not be taxed on the value of his services if, instead, he builds cabinets for his cousin worth $1,000. Indeed, in this example, no one would be taxed on the $1,000 value. The performance of free services has the same effect as shifting $1,000 of income from the 30 percent to the zero percent tax bracket.

Similar advantages are reaped by contributing services to a §501(c)(3) charity such as the Red Cross. A lawyer is taxed on that portion of her salary she gives to such organizations and may deduct her donation, subject to the annual deduction limitations of §170. Contributions of money to certain other nonprofit organizations, such as political parties, are nondeductible. (See the discussion of §170 in Chapter 4 of this book.) In contrast, the lawyer is not taxed on the value of the services she provides directly to the organization free of charge. Again, working for no pay for the nonprofit organization, as opposed to working for a paying client and donating the proceeds, has the effect of shifting income to a taxpayer in the zero percent bracket.

In the preceding examples, the donee is the end user of the donor's services. Suppose, instead, that the donee sells the services to unrelated parties. For example, suppose a charity holds a benefit concert featuring a popular entertainer who has donated her services. Must the entertainer declare the value of her services as income and then deduct the gift only as permitted by law? In fact, donated services to charitable and political organizations are treated as untaxed imputed income even if the organization sells the services to the public and the value of the service is easy to ascertain. (On the other hand, if the services are donated to an individual and then sold to an unrelated party, the tax treatment is much less clear. For example, a parent who provides legal services to his daughter's law firm, which in turn charges out his services to its clients, may well be thought to be in partnership with his daughter and taxed on the income attributable to his services.)

For taxpayers who wish to offer free services without recognition of income, form is all important. An entertainer avoids taxation on the proceeds from a charity or political benefit only if the benefit is arranged by the organization or its agent. Suppose, instead, that the benefit is arranged by a for-profit promoter not acting as a charitable organization's agent and the entertainer directs the value of her services to a charity. In that event, the entertainer will be taxed on the net proceeds of the event and be left to struggle with the §170 limitations on charitable deductions. A similar emphasis on form is present in gifts of services to family members or friends. A real estate broker can sell her daughter's home free of commission without paying tax on the commission forgone. But a broker who sells her daughter's home, collects a commission, and returns that commission to her daughter the following day will be taxed on that commission.

In contrast to personal service income, which (with the exception of imputed income from services) cannot be shifted, income from property can be shifted by transferring the income-producing property. Thus, a parent with rental property can shift the rental income to his 16-year-old son merely by giving the son the property. A parent with appreciated property can have that appreciation taxed at his 16-year-old son's rate merely by giving him the property prior to sale. (See the discussion of gifts in Chapter 2.)

Here, too, form is important. A transaction in which a donor negotiates a sale of appreciated property and then, a moment before the sale is consummated, transfers the property to a donee who completes the sale, may be recharacterized as a sale of property by the donor, followed by a gift of the sale proceeds to the donee. Under that characterization, it is the donor who must pay tax on the gain.

Perhaps the most difficult set of issues raised in this area concern gifts of partial interests in property. Suppose a parent gives her 15-year-old daughter a one-tenth undivided interest, as a tenant in common, in an apartment building. Has the parent succeeded in shifting one-tenth of the yearly rental income to her daughter? Or suppose a parent gives her daughter the rights to the rental income for the next five years and (to make the examples here parallel) that rental income represents one-tenth of the value of the building. Has the parent here succeeded in shifting rental income to her daughter during the next five years?

It will be useful to begin discussion of these issues on a definitional note. An interest in property that is coterminous in time with the donor's interest is often referred to as a *horizontal interest.* A 10 percent undivided interest in property is a horizontal interest, as it extends as far in time as the donor's remaining interest in the property.

A gift of a horizontal interest in property shifts the income from that interest to the donee. Blair v. Commissioner, 300 U.S. 5 (1937). Thus, if a parent gives her 20-year-old son a half-interest in income-producing property, half the net income from the property and half the proceeds from sale will be taxed to the son.

A gift of property that is not coterminous in time with the interest retained by the donor, but that reverts back to the donor, is often referred to as a *vertical interest*, or a *carved-out interest*. Suppose a donor gives her son the rental income on an apartment building for the next five years, but retains the rental income after the next five years or other incidents of ownership thereafter. The donor has given a vertical or carved-out interest in the property that does not shift income to the donee. Helvering v. Horst, 311 U.S. 112 (1940). The donor will be taxed on the next five years' rental income on the rationale that, notwithstanding the form of the transaction, she has effectively maintained control of the underlying property.

Some gifts may be both horizontal and vertical. For example, a parent might give her son a one-half interest in property for five years with the parent regaining sole control of the property thereafter. Such gifts are taxed in the same manner as gifts of vertical interests: The parent is taxed on the entire income from the property.

The basic rules on income shifting are as follows: Personal service income cannot be shifted except by the performance of gratuitous services. Income from property can be shifted provided there is a complete transfer of the income-producing property, and the donee does not receive a carved-out or vertical interest. One final complication, implicit in the above description, concerns the hazy line between services and property. An artist might use personal efforts to produce a piece of tangible property such as a sculpture. In both a colloquial and legal sense, a composition, patent, or book is also seen as property, albeit property of a more intangible nature. Indeed, even the right to payment for past or future personal services can be seen as property, in the sense that such a right can be bought and sold. For tax purposes, the transfer of tangible self-created property is seen as the transfer of property rather than services and is effective to shift income from the property to the transferee. A sculpture that is transferred by an artist to a relative and then sold by the relative is seen as property of the relative at the time of sale. Gain from the sale is taxed to the relative rather than the artist. At the other extreme, the transfer of the right to payment for personal services by the service provider is not seen as a transfer of property such that the gain is recognized by the transferee. Instead, as noted above, the gain is taxed to the provider of the services.

The transfer of rights to intangibles such as copyrights or patents occupies a middle ground. Here, as elsewhere, form is all important. An author can shift income from a work by transferring her copyrighted manuscript to a donee and having the donee negotiate a contract with the publisher. Suppose, instead, the author signs a publishing contract and then assigns her royalties under the contract to a donee. While the assignment may be legally binding for state law purposes, it is ineffective for tax purposes. The author, and not the donee, will be taxed on the royalty income. Compare Wodehouse v. Commissioner, 178 F.2d 987 (4th Cir. 1949) (novelist P.G. Wodehouse taxed on royalty income notwithstanding assignment of contract rights) with Cory v. Commissioner, 23 T.C. 775 (1955) (assignment of manuscript by philosopher George Santayana effective to shift income to assignee).

EXAMPLES

1. State whether the following taxes are progressive, proportionate, or regressive. Assume all individuals fall into the same filing category (for example that they are all single individuals):
   a. Daniel has taxable income of $50,000 and pays $5,000 of tax. Sarah has taxable income of $40,000 and pays $4,000 of tax.
   b. Daniel has taxable income of $100,000 and pays $8,000 of tax. Sarah has taxable income of $50,000 and pays $5,000 of tax.

2. a. Barbara, who earns $100,000 a year as an attorney, signs a binding contract that requires her to pay half of her future earnings to her 15-year-old daughter. On what portion of her future earnings will Barbara be taxed?
   b. Assume the same facts as in part (a), except that Barbara signs a binding contract to pay her daughter one-half of what she collects from legal work that has already been performed and billed. On what portion of her future earnings will Barbara be taxed?

3. Mary gives 1,000 shares of Bigco stock to her 10-year-old daughter, Nancy. Mary's marginal tax rate is 30 percent; Nancy's is 15 percent. The stock pays an annual dividend of $10 per share. Is each of the following statements true or false?
   a. Nancy will be taxed on the dividends.
   b. The tax on the net unearned income attributable to the divi-

dends will be equal to the tax that would have been paid on the dividends had the stock been retained by Mary.

 c. Unearned income consists of income that is not attributable to wages, salaries, and professional fees.

 d. If Nancy receives stock from her uncle, Tom, the net unearned income attributable to the stock will be taxed at Tom's marginal rate.

 e. If Mary gives the stock to her 15-year-old son, David, the net unearned income attributable to the stock will be taxed at Mary's marginal rate.

4. a. Fred owns 100 acres of rental property. He gives his 18-year-old son, Sam, 50 acres. The 50 acres are worth $50,000. In the year immediately following the gift, the 50 acres are rented out for $5,000, with the rent being paid to Sam. Who pays tax on the rent?

 b. Assume the same facts as in part (a), except that Fred gives his son the right to all of the rental income from all 100 acres for nine years. The present value of that right is $50,000. In the year immediately following the gift, the 100 acres are rented out for $10,000, with the rent being paid to Sam. Who pays tax on the rent?

5. Tom gives Peter the following gifts. State whether each gift creates a carved-out interest.

 a. A 30 percent interest in a business. Tom retains the remaining 70 percent interest.

 b. A five-year right to the income from a 30 percent interest in a business. Tom retains all the other rights to the business.

 c. A five-year right to the income from a business. Tom retains all other rights to income from the business.

 d. The right to the next two years' rent on an apartment building. Tom retains the right to the rentals in succeeding years.

6. Barbara gives her son a sculpture she has just completed. One year later, the son sells the sculpture for $200,000. Who is taxed on the gain from the sale?

7. Real estate broker Ed sells his daughter's home in Redwood City for $200,000.

 a. Ed waives his commission, thereby saving his daughter $4,000. Is Ed taxed on the $4,000?

 b. The total commission on the sale is $12,000 and is collected by the real estate company Ed works for. Ed's share of the commission is $4,000. The company charges Ed's daughter the full $12,000 commission and gives $4,000 of the commission to Ed, who gives a like sum back to his daughter. Is Ed taxed on the $4,000?

8. Discuss the tax consequences of the following transactions:

a. In year one Douglas buys Blackacre for $100,000. On December 30, year four, Tom offers Douglas $200,000 for Blackacre. Douglas immediately transfers the property to his 15-year-old son, Sonny. Douglas then informs Tom that the property is owned by Sonny but that he, Douglas, will negotiate the sale on Sonny's behalf. Douglas next informs Tom that Sonny will agree to sell the property for $210,000. Tom issues a counteroffer at $205,000. Acting on his father's advice, on December 31, year four, Sonny accepts the offer. The terms of the December 31 agreement call for payment and transfer of title on January 30, year five. On January 30, year five, Sonny receives $205,000.

b. Assume the same facts as in part (a), except that Douglas negotiates the sale and signs the December 31, year-four agreement on his own behalf. On January 1, year five, Douglas transfers title to the property to Sonny. Sonny takes title subject to the sale agreement; that is, Sonny is obligated to sell the property on the terms specified in the agreement. The property is in fact sold pursuant to the agreement. On January 30, year five, Sonny receives $205,000.

9. a. Alan accepts a job with Wagner, Inc. which has a long-standing policy to make college more affordable for its employees' children. Under that policy, each year the company pays each college-age child of each employee the lesser of (i) the child's college tuition or (ii) $5,000. Wagner, Inc. pays Alan's child, Donna, $5,000 in year one. Alan received no parental support from his parents and refuses to provide any parental support for Donna. Alan did not know of Wagner's policy when he accepted the job. Discuss the tax consequences of the $5,000 transfer to Donna.

b. Wagner maintains and operates on-premises athletic facilities that are available to its employees, their spouses, and their children. Alan's daughter, Donna, uses those facilities. The cost of similar facilities at a private health club is $500 a year per person. Before accepting his job at Wagner, Alan refused to give his daughter the $500 a year necessary to join a private health club with similar athletic facilities. Is Alan taxed on the value of the facilities made available to Donna?

10. Accountant Amy normally charges $100 an hour for her time. Discuss the tax consequences of the following events:
   a. Amy spends 10 hours preparing her cousin's tax return. Amy does not receive any form of compensation for her work.
   b. Amy spends 10 hours preparing her church's tax returns. Amy does not receive any form of compensation for her work.
   c. Amy spends 10 hours preparing her dentist's tax returns. In return, her dentist provides Amy and her family with approximately $1,000 of dental work.

11. Pop star Paula receives $20,000 per performance from concert promoters. Paula performs at the following events for no compensation. Discuss the tax consequences of these events.
   a. Paula performs at a Democratic Party victory celebration. Seats are free but are available only to party workers, politicians, or past contributors.
   b. Paula performs at a fund-raiser for the Democratic Party. The event nets the Democratic party $20,000.
   c. Paula organizes a concert and gives the net proceeds of $20,000 to the Democratic Party.

EXPLANATIONS

1. a. The tax is proportionate. Daniel faces a higher absolute amount of tax liability, but both taxpayers pay 10 percent of their income to the government. A tax that requires all taxpayers to pay an equal percentage of income is proportionate; a tax that requires high income taxpayers to pay a higher percentage of their income is progressive; a tax that requires low income taxpayers to pay a higher percentage of their income is regressive.

   b. The tax is regressive. Again, Daniel pays more tax. However, Daniel pays a lower percentage of his income to the government than does Sarah. Here, taxes comprise 8 percent of Daniel's income and 10 percent of Sarah's income.

2. a. Barbara will be taxed on all of her earnings. The Supreme Court has held that assignments of personal service income do not shift the tax levied upon that income. Lucas v. Earl, 281 U.S. 111 (1930); Helvering v. Eubank, 311 U.S. 122 (1940).

b. Barbara will be taxed on all of her earnings. Here, the income assigned is attributable to past services. This assignment is in some sense more complete than the assignment discussed in the preceding question because Barbara's work has already been performed. The daughter's interest does not depend on Barbara's willingness to continue work. The Supreme Court has held, however, that assignments of personal service income attributable to past services, like assignments of personal service income attributable to future services, do not shift the tax levied upon that income from the service provider. Helvering v. Eubank, 311 U.S. 122 (1940).

3. a. True. Income from property, unlike income from personal services, can be shifted by transferring the income-producing property. (However, due to the "Kiddie Tax," most of the income will be taxed at the mother's marginal rate. See part (b), below.)

b. True. Although the net unearned income attributable to the stock will be taxable to the daughter, the income will be taxed at the mother's tax rate under the "Kiddie Tax" of §1(g).

c. True. Unearned income is defined in §1(g)(4) as income that is not earned income under §911(d)(2). That latter section states that "[t]he term 'earned income' means wages, salaries, or professional fees, and other amounts received as compensation for personal services actually rendered. . . ."

d. False. The net unearned income will be taxed at her parent's tax rate. §1(g)(1). The fact that the income is attributable to a gift from her uncle is irrelevant.

e. False. Section 1(g) only applies to children under the age of 14.

4. a. Sam. The gift of the underlying property interest shifts the tax from Fred to his son.

b. Fred. The nine-year right to income constitutes a carved-out interest. Fred is regarded as having maintained the underlying property ownership and simply shifted the right to income.

5. a. No carved-out interest is created. The interest assigned is a permanent interest. The 30 percent interest will never revest in, or revert back to, Tom. Thus, although the 30 percent interest is a partial interest, it is not a carved-out interest.

b. A carved-out interest is created. Here, Tom retains a reversionary interest in the 30 percent interest in the business; it is the presence of the reversion which creates a carved-out interest.

     c. A carved-out interest is created because Tom retains a reversionary interest in the business.

     d. A carved-out interest is created because Tom retains a reversionary interest in the rentals.

6. The son. The gift of personally created property will shift the income from such property to the donee. However, *if* the gift had been made immediately prior to the sale, *and* Barbara had arranged the sale, the Service might argue that Barbara controlled the sculpture up to the time of sale and attribute the sale proceeds to Barbara.

7. a. No, here the waived commission would be treated as nontaxable imputed income.

     b. Yes. In similar situations, a number of courts have ruled that taxpayers are taxed on their personal service income even if that income is "rebated" back to the family members.

8. a. As noted throughout this chapter, a high bracket individual may transfer property to a low bracket donee. Gain from the sale of the property is taxed to the donee rather than the donor. On the other hand, a high bracket individual who sells appreciated property and then transfers the proceeds is taxed on the gain. The primary question raised by this example is whether this transaction is properly described for tax purposes as a transfer of property followed by a sale of the property by the donee or a sale of the property followed by a transfer of sale proceeds. The law in this area is far from clear. In general, however, a high bracket individual can shift income from appreciated property by transferring the property prior to the sale, provided that the terms of the sale agreement have not been agreed upon. Here, the property is in fact transferred before an agreement is reached. Most probably, therefore, Sonny, rather than Douglas, will be taxed on the sale proceeds. The fact that Douglas negotiates for his son clouds the issue somewhat but should not alter the final result.

     How much gain does Sonny recognize? As discussed in Chapter 2 of this book, for purposes of computing gain, Sonny receives a basis in property received by gift equal to the donor's basis in the property. §1015. If we assume there are no selling expenses and that Douglas has neither added to the basis of the property since purchase (through improvements) nor reduced the basis (through depreciation), Sonny recognizes gain of $105,000 — the sale price of $205,000 less his basis of $100,000.

This hypothetical raises an interesting — if slightly off topic — timing issue. Is the sale complete in year four, when the sale agreement is signed, or in year five, when the sale "closes"? In fact, property is generally treated as sold for tax purposes in the year in which the sale closes and title is transferred.

b. Here, the terms of the sale agreement are fixed prior to the transfer of the property. Douglas may argue that under state law the sale is not finalized until title passes. Indeed, for some purposes, even the tax law does not treat the sale as final until title passes. For example, as noted in the explanation for part (a), gain is realized in the year in which the transaction closes rather than the year in which the sale agreement is reached. (Whether gain is included in that year depends on the installment sales rules, discussed in Chapter 3 of this book. Here, all payments are received in year five so gain will be included in that year.) Unfortunately for Douglas, a donor who enters into a binding agreement to sell property and then transfers the property subject to the agreement is generally treated as if he had first sold the property and then transferred the proceeds. For this purpose, the tax law treats the donor as the seller of the property, notwithstanding the fact that under state law title to the property has passed to the donee prior to the time the sale is complete.

9.   a. In general, it seems reasonable to assume that most employees feel the $5,000 tuition given their children is as valuable as an additional $5,000 salary. Otherwise, why wouldn't Wagner junk the tuition program and raise salaries? Presumably, Wagner is interested solely in attracting and retaining employees. Of course, some employees, such as Alan, will find the benefit of little value. The tax law is caught in a dilemma. It is impossible to determine and then tax the idiosyncratic value of the tuition benefit to each employee. If the benefit is taxed to the employee at its cost, some employees will be overtaxed. If the benefit is tax-free to employee and child, most or all employees will be undertaxed. If the child, rather than the parent, is taxed on the benefit, the result for most employees, who value the benefit at cost, is that some personal service income is shifted to a lower bracket family member. With respect to this type of benefit, the tax law has chosen the first approach — Alan will be taxed on

the full $5,000. Armantrout v. Commissioner, 67 T.C. 996 (1977), aff'd per curiam, 570 F.2d 210 (7th Cir. 1978).

b. The issue is analytically identical to the issue in part (a). However, this fringe benefit is subject to special legislative treatment. Section 132, discussed in Chapter 2 of this book, excludes from taxation the value of on-premises athletic facilities, provided that substantially all of the use of the facilities is by employees and their spouses and dependents. §132(h)(5). So neither Alan nor his daughter is taxed on the value of the facilities.

10. a. The value of Amy's services provided free of charge to her cousin is not subject to tax.

b. The value of Amy's services provided free of charge to the church is not subject to tax.

c. Here, Amy is receiving valuable compensation for her services. Amy will be taxed on that compensation. The fact that the compensation is in the form of services rather than cash is irrelevant. See, e.g., Rev. Rul. 79-24 (individuals taxed on services or property received under barter arrangements).

11. a. Paula is not taxed on the imputed value of her services.

b. Here, Paula's services are "sold" by the Democratic Party. One might imagine that Paula could be treated as if she had performed for her usual compensation and then given that sum to the Democratic Party. In that event, Paula would be taxed on the $20,000; contributions to political parties are nondeductible. §170(c). In fact, however, Paula will escape taxation on the value of her services so long as she neither receives the profits directly nor organizes the event.

c. Here, Paula has crossed the line between providing free services and contributing personal service income. She will be taxed on the $20,000; the contribution is not deductible. §170(c).

B. Trusts

Reading: §§1(e), 641-643, 651, 652, 661, 662

We saw earlier in this chapter that a gift of property effectively shifts income derived from the property from the donor to the donee. Taxpayers with young or irresponsible family members, however, may not wish to make outright gifts of property. An alternative for such taxpayers is to transfer income-producing property to a trust set up for the benefit of family members.

The trust is a separate legal entity under state law; the transferor-donor is the trust *grantor*; the donee family members are the trust *beneficiaries*. The fiduciary who manages the trust is the *trustee*; the trust property is the *trust corpus*. The taxation of trusts is in many ways quite complicated. The following description of trust taxation is designed to provide students with a brief overview of the subject.

A *simple trust* is a trust that is required to annually distribute current income (and only current income) to the beneficiaries, and that does not distribute or set aside any amounts to charity.[1] Thus, a grandparent who transfers stock to a trust with instructions that all dividends be distributed annually to her son and, upon the son's death, the stock be distributed to her granddaughter has set up a trust that is a simple trust (except in the final year of the trust, during which the corpus will be distributed). Such a trust is (nominally) taxed on its income but receives a deduction for distribution of that income.[2] §651. Thus, a simple trust does not itself generally pay tax. Instead, income from a simple trust is taxed directly to the beneficiaries.[3] §§61(a)(15) and 652(a).

Any trust that is not a simple trust is a *complex trust*. For example, a trust whose governing instrument (the *deed of trust*) allows, but does not require, the trustee to retain income earned in a given year and distribute that income in a later year is a complex trust. A complex trust, like a simple trust, is able to deduct current income that is distributed to the beneficiaries; the beneficiaries are then taxed on that income. §661(a). Suppose, however, a complex trust does not distribute all of its income in one year. In that event, the trust is taxed on its undistributed current income under the rate schedule set forth in §1(e). That rate

---

1. A simple trust may accumulate items such as capital gain and stock dividends that constitute income for tax purposes but for trust purposes are seen as part of the corpus. §643(b).

2. More precisely, the trust receives a deduction equal to the lesser of the taxable income distributed or its "distributable net income." That latter term is defined, generally, as taxable income as determined without regard to the de minimis deduction granted in lieu of the personal deduction or items such as capital gain properly seen as part of the trust corpus. §643(a). For the purposes of this overview, we will assume, somewhat simplistically, that distributable net income is always equal to taxable income.

3. As noted in note 2, above, the trust may accumulate certain items such as capital gains that for trust purposes are treated as part of the corpus. In that case, to simplify just a bit, the trust receives a deduction only for the income distributed, and the beneficiaries are taxed only on the income distributed.

schedule has the same maximum marginal rate as the rate schedule that applies to individuals. However, the maximum marginal rate applies to nearly all of the trust's earnings. Moreover, net income for trusts, unlike net income for individuals, is determined without regard to certain deductions. For example, the trust receives no deduction for medical care and no personal or dependency deductions.[4]

The beneficiaries of a complex trust are taxed on undistributed or accumulated income in the year in which it is finally distributed. §662. The trust in that year receives no deduction for the distribution. However, under a complicated system of "throwback" rules, the tax paid in prior years by the trust on that income is credited to the beneficiaries. §§667(b)(1), 668(b). In most cases, that credit offsets any tax owed by the beneficiary.[5] The tax paid by the complex trust on accumulated income thus bears some resemblance to the tax withheld by an employer on an employee's salary. In both cases the government collects tax first from the paying entity (the trust or the employer). The government then collects tax from the recipient (beneficiary or employee) on the gross amount earned but allows an offset for the tax already paid by the entity.

To summarize, income of a simple or complex trust is taxed only once. In the case of a trust that distributes its entire current income, and only its current income, the income is taxed to the beneficiaries in the year earned. In the case of a complex trust that accumulates income, the income is taxed to the trust in the year it is earned and then taxed again to the beneficiaries when distributed. However, the tax owed by the beneficiaries is offset by the prior tax paid by the trust.

EXAMPLES

12. On January 1, year one, Sandy transfers $100,000 to a trust. The deed of trust appoints Sandy's attorney, Able, as trustee. Able is required by the deed of trust to invest the trust funds in a money market account and to distribute all of the annual income to Sandy's cousin, Max. Upon Max's death, the $100,000 is to be distributed to Max's daughter, Lisa.

    a. Assume that in year one, the trust has interest income of

---

4. The trust does receive a small deduction in lieu of personal and dependency deductions. See §642(b).

5. If the tax paid by the trust exceeds the tax owed by the beneficiaries, the beneficiaries owe no tax but receive no refund. In such situations, the income from the trust is taxed only once, but at the trust's tax rate.

$5,000. Assume further that the trust has no expenses and qualifies for no deductions other than the deduction provided by §651(a). After taking into consideration §651(a), what is the trust's taxable income?

   b. Assume that in year one the trust distributes $5,000 to Max. Is Max taxed on that income?

13. On January 1, year one, Daniel transfers $100,000 to a trust. The deed of trust appoints Daniel's attorney, Able, as trustee. Able is required by the deed of trust to invest the trust funds in a money market account; to accumulate all income for year one, and then, on January 1, year two, to distribute that income, together with the trust corpus of $100,000, to Daniel's son, Greg.

   a. Assume that, in year one, the trust has interest income of $5,000. Assume further that the trust has no expenses and qualifies for no deductions other than the deductions set forth in §§651(a) and 661(a), which may or may not apply. What is the trust's taxable income?

   b. Assume that on January 1, year two, the trust distributes its year one income to Greg, together with the trust corpus. Discuss the tax consequences of that distribution to the trust and to Greg.

EXPLANATIONS

12. a. The trust receives a deduction for the amount distributed so it is left with no taxable income. §651.

   b. Max is taxed on the $5,000 he receives. §652.

13. a. The trust has taxable income of $5,000. Section 651(a) does not apply because the trust is not a simple trust. Section 661(a) does not apply because the trust does not distribute its current income.

   b. The trust receives no deduction because it has not distributed any *current* income. Greg is taxed on last year's income at the time of the distribution but receives a credit for the amount of taxes paid by the trust.

     The computations of the tax liability are somewhat complicated. A portion of the year one income went to pay the taxes due that year. As a result, in year two, the trust will distribute the $100,000 corpus and the $5,000 income less tax paid on that income. Assume that both the trust and Greg are in the 40 percent marginal tax bracket. In that case, the trust pays $2,000 of tax in year one so the total distribution is $103,000. The

$100,000 represents the distribution of the corpus and is tax-free to Greg. For tax purposes, the remaining $3,000 is increased by the $2,000 tax paid by the trust. Greg is treated as having received the entire income included by the trust in year one. In financial argot, the distribution is "grossed up" by the taxes paid by the trust. Greg is taxed on $5,000. His tax liability is $2,000 (40 percent of $5,000) but he receives credit for the $2,000 paid by the trust, so he ends up with no tax liability on the $5,000 deemed distributed — he ends up, then, with after-tax income of $3,000.

The "gross up" feature of the law may be easier to understand if it is compared with the treatment of employer withholding. Assume an employee and an employer are both in the 40 percent tax bracket. The employee earns $5,000; $2,000 tax is withheld by the employer and so the employee receives only $3,000 cash. For tax purposes, however, the employee is treated as having received gross pay of $5,000 — the $3,000 take home pay plus the $2,000 tax withheld by the employer. The employee is taxed on the gross pay but receives a credit for the tax withheld. The net result is that the employee is in the same situation as if he had gotten the full $5,000 and then paid tax directly. The same is true here. Greg ends up with $100,000 corpus and after-tax earnings of $3,000 — the same amount he would have received had the trust paid no tax and made a current distribution of the full income of $5,000, and had that amount been taxed directly to Greg.

Recall from the discussion in the text that if the trust is in a higher tax bracket than the beneficiary, the beneficiary will not get a refund for the difference between the tax paid by the trust and the tax owed by the beneficiary. In this and other ways, the treatment of complex trusts only approximates a single-tax system in which income is taxed only once, and at the beneficiary's tax rate.

C. Grantor Trusts

Reading: §§671-678

In the previous section, we discussed the treatment of complete and unequivocal transfers to a trust. We noted that, in general, income of such trusts is taxed only once, and at the beneficiary's tax rate. We did not discuss, however, situations in which the grantor transfers property to a trust but retains certain controls over the property. Suppose, for example, that the grantor transfers an apartment building to a trust with the income each year to go to his daughter and the building to be transferred outright to his daughter upon his death, but he retains the power to revoke the transfer and reclaim the property. Has the grantor succeeded in shifting the annual income from the building to his daughter? Or is the transfer subject to the common law rules governing partial transfers of property, discussed at the start of this chapter?

In fact, these sorts of partial transfers to trusts are subject to a special set of rules in the Code governing *grantor trusts*. As discussed below, these rules have substantially the same effect as the rules governing partial gifts that do not involve a trust. These rules make trusts a poor vehicle with which to shift income. In cases in which the grantor retains control over property transferred to a trust, it is the grantor, not the beneficiary, who is taxed on the trust income.

Section 673 covers property that is placed in trust for a period of years and then reverts back to the grantor. Under that section, if the value of the reversionary interest exceeds 5 percent of the value of the property, income from the property is taxed to the grantor. (Section 673(b) does not apply to reversionary interests that occur only in the event that a lineal descendant beneficiary dies before attaining the age of 21.) The reversionary interest is valued as of the time of contribution, using federal tables that take into account the prevailing interest rates and, if applicable, life expectancy of beneficiaries. To illustrate the operation of §673, suppose that attorney Able places income-producing property in trust for her niece and the terms of the trust provide that the trust terminates and the property reverts back to Able in 18 years. Assume further, that the appropriate discount rate is 4 percent. In that case, the federal tables will show that Able's reversionary interest is worth about 50 percent of the value of the interest. Accordingly, Able will be treated as if she owns the property outright and she, and not her niece, will be taxed on the income.

As is perhaps evident, §673 is similar in effect to the common law rules governing gifts of carved-out interests. In the first part of this chapter, we discussed the tax treatment of an individual who, outside of the trust context, gives his child the right to income from property for a number of years but retains a reversionary right in the property thereafter. We noted that this form of gift is referred to as a vertical or carved-out interest and does not shift taxes from the donor. Section

673 provides the same result for taxpayers who use trusts to make a temporary gift of property income, but who, in the deed of trust, retain a reversionary interest in the income-producing property.

Section 676 generally provides that a grantor who transfers property to a trust but retains the right to revoke the transfer and regain title to the property is taxed on the income from the property. The same result occurs if a third party is given the power to revest title to the property in the grantor unless the third party has a substantial interest in the trust as beneficiary or power of appointment over the trust. §§676(a), 672.[6]

Section 675 generally treats the grantor as the owner of any property in respect to which he retains certain prohibited administrative powers such as the power to purchase the property at less than full consideration. That section also taxes the grantor on any amounts he has borrowed from the trust unless the loan carries adequate security and interest and meets certain other requirements.

Section 677 generally treats the grantor as the owner of any portion of a trust property the income of which may be distributed or accumulated for the benefit of the grantor's spouse or used to pay life insurance premiums on the life of the grantor or the grantor's spouse.

Section 674 is perhaps the most complex of the grantor trust provisions. Generally speaking, under that section a grantor is treated as the owner of property if, after the initial transfer of the property to a trust, the grantor or her spouse retains the right to change the mix of income received by the trust beneficiaries or to add new beneficiaries. However, a grantor may escape taxation by vesting such power in an independent trustee. An independent trustee is defined, generally, as anyone other than a close relative, employee, or close business relation. §§675(c), 672(c). Thus, a grantor will not be taxed on trust income merely because she gives an independent trustee the power to change the distribution of income among beneficiaries or to add beneficiaries. The same result obtains if such power is given to a non-

---

6. As noted in the preceding text, §673 allows a grantor to retain a reversionary interest in trust property and escape tax on the income from such property, provided that at the time of the original transfer, the reversionary interest represents no more than 5 percent of the value of the property. Section 676(b) provides that the grantor may retain a power to revoke a transfer upon the occurrence of an event, provided that the event is sufficiently distant in the future so that the value of the certain exercise of that power, measured at the time of original transfer, does not exceed 5 percent of the value of the property.

independent trustee (other than her spouse), such as a sister, provided that such power is limited by a reasonably definite external standard. One example of a reasonably definite external standard is an instruction to the trustee that funds are to be distributed in accordance with educational needs.

The grantor trust rules treat the grantor as the owner of property with respect to which she retains certain rights or powers. Suppose that a grantor sets up a trust and gives a third party, as trustee, similar powers. For example, suppose that Grandmother appoints her son, Sonny, as trustee of a trust set up for the benefit of her grandson. The trust instrument provides that grandson is to receive all income but that the trustee, Sonny, has the power to revoke the trust at will; upon revocation, title to the property is to vest in Sonny. Such trusts are often referred to as *Mallinckrodt trusts*. (Mallinckrodt was the taxpayer in an earlier case involving the taxation of such trusts. Mallinckrodt v. Nunan, 146 F.2d 1 (8th Cir. 1945), cert. denied, 324 U.S. 871 (1945).) Under §678, the trust income will be taxed to the trustee rather than the beneficiary.

Taxpayers with modest resources will find trusts a burdensome and expensive way of exercising control over property, the benefit of which they wish to go to their beneficiaries. This is particularly true with respect to small gifts given to minor children. Such taxpayers may instead rely upon the Uniform Transfers to Minors Act, variants of which have been enacted in nearly all states. That Act allows a donor who wishes to give property to a minor to appoint herself or a member of the minor's family as custodian of the property. The custodian is given discretion to use such property, or the income from such property, for the benefit of the minor. The minor receives any remaining property, or income from such property, when she attains the age of 21. The Service has ruled that, generally speaking, the income from the property will be taxed to the minor. However, if and to the extent the property is used to discharge a legal obligation to support the minor, income from the property will be taxed to the person with the support obligation. Rev. Rul. 59-357.

Parents sometimes open up savings accounts in their own name but as trustees for their children (or other individuals). For example, an account may be opened in the name of "Gary Metro as Trustee for Henry Metro." The treatment of such accounts depends on their status under state law. In many states, unless other steps have been taken to evidence a formal trust, the parent-depositor retains the authority to reclaim the funds. In that event, the depositor, rather than the named beneficiary, will be taxed on any interest income. Rev. Rul. 62-148. Savings account trusts that allow the depositor to reclaim funds are sometimes referred to as *Totten trusts*.

EXAMPLES

14. State whether retention of the following powers by the grantor will result in the grantor being taxed on the trust income.
    a. Reversion of the trust corpus to the grantor after 15 years. The value of the reversion at the time the property is transferred to the trust is 30 percent of the value of the property.
    b. The power to change the trust beneficiaries or to select new beneficiaries
    c. The power to switch trust investments

15. Assume a grantor-appointed trustee is given the power to revoke the trust and return the trust corpus to the grantor. Does this power trigger grantor trust treatment?

16. Larry wants to set up a trust for the graduate school education of his children. Larry does not want to earmark any of the income for any particular child; instead he wants the income used as needed to provide educational support. How can Larry achieve his objective?

17. A non-grantor trust that gives a third party the right to revoke the trust and receive the trust corpus is called a Mallinckrodt trust. Is income from such a trust taxed to the grantor?

18. Sam is the grantor of trust *X*. The trust agreement of trust *X* provides that income from the trust is to be distributed to Sam's niece, Jill; however, Jill's father, Bill, is given the power to revoke the trust and take the trust income. Who is taxed on the trust income?

19. Nancy sets up a savings account for her minor daughter. The account is in the daughter's name, but Nancy retains the power to withdraw the funds and use them for her own benefit.
    a. Who is taxed on the annual income?
    b. What name is often used to describe this sort of trust?

EXPLANATIONS

14. a. The grantor will be taxed on the trust income. The grantor's reversionary interest triggers grantor trust treatment where the reversionary interest, measured at the time of transfer, is worth

more than 5 percent of the value of the property transferred. §673.

b. The grantor will be taxed on the trust income. The grantor's retention of the power to switch beneficiaries triggers grantor trust treatment. §674(a). However, if the power to allocate benefits within a class of beneficiaries is lodged in a person not subordinate to the grantor, the trust is not treated as a grantor trust. §674(c). In addition, a power vested in *any* trustee (whether or not subordinate) other than the grantor or the spouse of the grantor to apportion income within a class of beneficiaries will not result in grantor trust treatment if the power to apportion is limited by a reasonably definite standard. §674(d).

c. In general, a grantor may appoint herself as trustee and control trust investments without triggering grantor trust treatment. However, a grantor will be held taxable on trust income if she retains administrative powers proscribed by §675 such as the power to borrow from the trust without giving the trust adequate interest or security. §675(2).

15. Yes. Generally, a power that a non-beneficiary can exercise on behalf of the grantor is treated as a power retained by the grantor. This rule is necessary to prevent grantors from appointing friends or relatives as trustees, and (through such trustees) retaining control over the trust corpus while at the same time escaping tax on trust income.

16. Larry should give the power to distribute income to someone he trusts, such as a close friend, with a stipulation that the funds be used for his children's education. If Larry himself retains the power to control beneficial enjoyment, he will be taxed on the trust income under §674. However, Larry will not be taxed on trust income if the power to control beneficial enjoyment is given to an independent trustee, that is, someone who is not a related party and who is not an employee or otherwise economically subordinate to Larry. §674(c). Larry will also escape grantor trust treatment if the power to control beneficial enjoyment is given to anyone but his spouse, provided that the exercise of that power is limited by a "reasonably definite external standard." §674(d). If Larry gives the power to a close friend, he is doubly secure against grantor trust treatment — he has given the power to an unrelated party and the power is subject to what is arguably a reasonably definite external standard.

7. Income Shifting

17. No. Income from a Mallinckrodt trust is not taxed to the grantor; it is taxed to the third party who controls the trust. §678.

18. Bill. §678.

19. a. Nancy is taxed on the trust income.

    b. Such trusts are often referred to as "Totten" trusts.

D. Family Partnerships

Reading: §704(e)

By this time in the course, most students will have encountered one or two cases involving business operations or investments carried out by partnerships. For example, the real estate in Commissioner v. Tufts, 461 U.S. 300 (1983), was owned and managed by a partnership; Tufts was a partner in that partnership. A partnership is not a taxable entity; although a partnership is required to file tax returns, the partnership does not itself pay tax. Instead, the income or losses of a partnership are allocated to the partners, who report their share of partnership income or loss on their individual tax returns.

Many service businesses are carried out by partnerships. Most law firms are partnerships (as an irrelevant aside, so are most rock bands). Partners in a law firm often are paid no formal salary but instead split the year's profits under some previously agreed upon formula. Suppose a partner in a law firm gives one-half of her partnership interest to her 18-year-old daughter. If the gift were respected for tax purposes, then, under the normal rules of partnership tax, one-half of the income attributable to that interest would be taxed to the daughter. The partner would thus be able to shift one-half of her service income — something she could not do if she realized the income as a salaried employee.

In a series of influential early cases, the Supreme Court developed various standards designed to prevent this sort of income shifting. Under those standards, whether a gift of a partnership interest to a family member succeeded in shifting partnership income to that family member depended on a number of factors, most notably the services or oversight provided by the donee.

Notwithstanding certain ambiguities, the standards generally produced sensible results in cases involving the transfer of interests in service partnerships to family members. The standards would not, for example, respect the transfer of the law firm partnership interest described above. Instead, the lawyer-donor would be taxed as before on the income attributable to her entire interest, including that portion of the interest ostensibly transferred to her daughter.

Suppose, however, the lawyer-parent described above owned a one-half interest in a partnership that itself owned an apartment building, and that the parent provided no services to the partnership. Income from this form of partnership is attributable to capital rather than services. We saw earlier that a parent can shift income from capital simply by making a gift of the income-producing capital. For example, a parent who owns an interest in an apartment building can shift income from that interest by giving away the building. The interposition of a partnership between the parent and the apartment building should not change this result. A parent who owns an interest in a partnership that owns an apartment building should be able to shift income from her partnership interest by giving away that interest. Since the income in question is attributable to capital, rather than services, the fact that the donee performs no services to the partnership should be irrelevant. The parent-donor performed no services, either! Unfortunately, the standards set forth in early cases seemed to apply to all forms of partnerships. Those cases suggested that transfer of a partnership interest did not shift the income from that interest even if the partnership held significant assets, and the transferor himself performed no services to the partnership.

To avoid this latter construction, Congress passed §704(e). That section provides that a transfer of partnership interest to a family member will be respected for tax purposes provided that capital (property) is a material income-producing factor in the partnership. Thus, just as the transfer of property to a low bracket family member will shift income to that family member, so will the transfer of an interest in a partnership that holds property.

What about partnerships whose income is attributable to both capital and the donor's services? The general rule of §704(e) still applies, but under §704(e)(2) the donor is taxed on the share of partnership income that reflects the value of services rendered to the partnership by the donor. Section 704(e) applies only if and to the extent that the interest transferred to the family member is an interest in partnership capital, that is, an interest such that, upon liquidation of the partnership, the family member would receive some portion of the partnership assets.

Suppose that a transfer does not qualify for the safe harbor of

7. Income Shifting

§704(e) because capital is not a material income-producing factor in the partnership. In that case, the standards described at the beginning of this section still apply. As noted above, under those standards, the transfer is generally not respected unless the donee-transferee performs significant services for the partnership.

EXAMPLES

20. Donald is one of 10 partners in an advertising firm. The firm has a number of employees who are not partners. Substantially all of the firm's revenues are attributable to the efforts of its employees. The partnership agreement provides that all items of income and loss are to be divided equally among the partners. Donald gives his son one-half of his partnership interest on January 1, year one. The partnership reports $1 million of income in year one. Donald reports $50,000 of income from the partnership and his son reports the same amount. Each of the other nine partners report $100,000 of income. Is each of the following statements true or false?
    a. The transfer of the partnership interest and the allocation of income to Donald's son will be respected for tax purposes.
    b. The transfer will not qualify for the safe harbor provided by §704(e) because capital is not an income-producing factor in the partnership.
    c. Donald will be taxed on $100,000 of income from the partnership.

21. Monica is a partner in a two-person accounting firm. The partners have agreed, in the partnership agreement, to share equally in all items of income and expense. On January 1, year one, Monica sells her entire partnership interest to her son for $1,000. The partnership earns $80,000 in year one. How much, if any, of the income will be attributed to Monica?

22. Sarah and David are partners in a clothing store. Neither Sarah nor David work in the store. The partnership agreement provides that profit and loss is to be shared equally between them. On January 1, year one, Sarah gives her daughter, Mary, her partnership interest. The partnership earns $100,000 in year one.
    a. Will the transfer of the partnership interest be respected for tax purposes? Will the gift be effective in shifting $50,000 of income to Mary?
    b. Suppose that Sarah and David both work in the store and that the fair market value of each of their services is $30,000 a year.

Neither draws a salary. Discuss the income tax consequences of the transfer.

EXPLANATIONS

20. Statement (a) is false and statements (b) and (c) are true. Section 704(e) provides a safe harbor for transfers of interests in a partnership in which capital is a material income-producing factor. The rationale for this provision is that, as we have seen earlier in this chapter, an individual can shift income from property by transferring ownership of that property. It seems logical, therefore, that a person can shift income from capital investments (or what amounts to the same thing, property) owned by a partnership by transferring her ownership interest in that partnership. This partnership earns its revenue from personal services rather than ownership of property. Thus, this transfer does not qualify for the safe harbor of §704(e).

    Transfers of partnership interests that do not qualify for the safe harbor are subject to the case law and administrative guidelines discussed in the text. In a case such as this one, where the transferee provides no services or management expertise, the putative transfer will be ignored for tax purposes, and the full income will be taxed to the transferor, Donald.

21. The safe harbor of §704(e) applies to sales of partnership interests in addition to donative transfers of those interests. As noted in the text and in the explanation of the previous example, above, that safe harbor does not apply to partnerships in which capital is not a material income-producing factor. It seems clear from the facts that the income of this partnership is attributable to services and capital is not a material income-producing factor. This transfer will not qualify for the safe harbor of §704(e). Moreover, under the case law and administrative rulings, it is almost certain that the transfer would be treated as a sham. Thus, Monica would be taxed on her full share of partnership profits.

    Note: It is not obvious how the $1,000 payment will be treated. It seems most equitable to simply ignore the payment for tax purposes on the assumption that the sum will be returned to the son.

22. a. Capital is a material income-producing factor in this partnership. As a result, under §704(e)(1), the transfer of a partner-

ship interest will be effective for tax purposes. Here, Mary, the donee, will include the $50,000 of income.

b. A significant portion of the income of the store is attributable to capital so capital is a material income-producing factor in this partnership. As noted above, to be consistent with common law rules on income shifting, the law should allow Sarah to shift this income by transferring her interest in the partnership. Here, however, some of the partnership income is attributable to the personal services Sarah rendered to the partnership. It would be inconsistent with other areas of the tax law to allow Sarah to shift this form of income. The value of Sarah's services is $30,000 a year. Section 704(e) provides that where capital is a material income-producing factor, the donee of a partnership interest is allocated all income attributable to that interest except to the extent that such income is determined without allowance of reasonable compensation for the donor's services. Here, that section requires Sarah to include $30,000 of income attributable to services; Mary includes the remaining $20,000 of income from the partnership.

E. Below-Market Loans

Reading: §7872

For many years, high bracket taxpayers with excess cash were urged by their tax advisors to make short-term, no-interest loans to low bracket family members. Interest income attributable to the cash loaned would then be realized by the low bracket family members and taxed to those family members. Section 7872 now severely limits this form of income shifting.

Section 7872 is quite complex. It applies not only to the type of "gift" loan described above (from one family member to another), but to no-interest (or low-interest) loans from corporations to shareholders and employers from employees. We focus here on the application of §7872 to gift loans and, even with that limited focus, ignore some of the complexities of the statute.

Section 7872 applies to a loan if (i) the loan is a *below-market loan*, (ii) the loan is one of the types of loans within the scope of §7872, and (iii) none of the exceptions to §7872 apply. In general, a loan is a below-market loan if it is interest-free or provides for interest at less than the *Applicable Federal Rate*. The Applicable Federal Rate is an interest rate that is set monthly by the Service pursuant to §1274(d) and is based on prevailing interest rates for U.S. government bonds. Under §1274(d), there are different Applicable Federal Rates for short-term loans (with a term of up to three years), mid-term loans (with a term of over three years to nine years) and long-term loans (with a term of over nine years). If a loan is a *demand loan* (that is, a loan payable in full upon demand of the lender), the short-term Applicable Federal Rate applies. If the loan is a *term loan* (that is, a loan with a stated term), the appropriate Applicable Federal Rate (short-term, mid-term, or long-term) depends on the term of the loan.

If the loan is a below-market loan, the next step is to determine whether it is one of the types of loans subject to §7872. Below-market gift loans are within the scope of §7872. §7872(c).

If the loan is a below-market loan, and is one of the types of loans listed by §7872(c), the loan is subject to §7872 unless one of a number of exceptions apply. In the case of a gift loan, a relevant exception might be §7872(c)(2), which excludes from the ambit of §7872 gift loans of less than $10,000 between individuals.

Assume a particular gift loan is covered by §7872. In that event, the statute subjects the loan to three fictions. The first is that the loan bears a market rate of interest. The second fiction is that the lender gives the borrower sufficient funds to enable the borrower to pay the lender a market rate of interest. The third fiction is that the borrower pays the lender a market rate of interest on the loan. The deemed transfer from the lender to the borrower and the deemed retransfer from the borrower to the lender both occur on the last day of the calendar year. The net effect is to leave the generally high bracket lender with interest income and, depending on the nature of the borrower's investment, to possibly give the generally low bracket borrower a corresponding interest deduction.

An example may be helpful here. Wealthy attorney Amy loans her 16-year-old son, Bob, $200,000 on January 1 of year one. The loan is interest-free and must be repaid in two years. The Applicable Federal Rate for such a short-term loan on that date is 10 percent, compounding semiannually. Amy is in the 40 percent income tax bracket; Bob is in the 10 percent income tax bracket. Bob invests the $200,000 in bonds that pay annual interest income of $22,000. Absent §7872, all of the $22,000 would be taxed at Bob's low marginal rate. Amy would pay no tax on the transaction.

7. Income Shifting

Under §7872, the $200,000 loan will be treated as a loan bearing interest at the Applicable Federal Rate of 10 percent, compounding semiannually. The annual interest on the loan is $20,500, which is the sum of $10,000 of interest (5 percent of $200,000) for the first six months of the year plus $10,500 of interest (5 percent of $210,000) for the second six months of the year. At the end of years one and two, the $20,500 of foregone interest on the loan is deemed transferred, as a gift, from Amy to Bob, and is then deemed retransferred, as an interest payment, from Bob to Amy. The deemed transfer does not have any tax consequences here because donors do not deduct gifts and donees do not include gifts. §102. However, Amy will have to include $20,500 of interest income as a result of the deemed retransfer. That amount will be taxed at her 40 percent rate. Bob will be able to deduct the $20,500 of interest deemed retransferred to Amy, subject to the restrictions on "investment interest" discussed earlier in this book. The net result is that Amy will have to include most of the income she would have included had she made the investment in the bonds herself. Thus, §7872, to some extent, prevents taxpayers from using interest-free loans to shift income. A taxpayer who makes an interest-free loan is taxed on the foregone interest (at the Applicable Federal Rate) on that loan. The lender's imputed interest inclusion may be more or less than the actual income earned by the borrower on the loan principal.

EXAMPLES

23. Ed lends his daughter, Sandy, $150,000 on January, year one. The loan has a two-year term and is interest-free. Sandy invests the $150,000 and earns $15,000 interest in year one. The Applicable Federal Rate is 10 percent compounding semiannually. How are Ed and Sandy taxed in year one?

24. Wendy lends her sister, Zelda, $150,000 on January, year one. The loan has a two-year term and is interest-free. Zelda uses the proceeds to speculate in commodities and earns $1.5 million in year one. The Applicable Federal Rate is 10 percent compounding semiannually. How are Wendy and Zelda taxed in year one?

25. A carved-out interest can be thought of as a short-term no-interest loan of income-producing property. Are gifts of no-interest cash loans treated like gifts of carved-out interests?

26. A gift between individuals of an interest-free loan with an outstanding balance of less than $20,000 is not subject to the rules of §7872. True or false?

EXPLANATIONS

23. This term loan is a below-market loan because it is interest-free. It appears to be a gift loan, so it is subject to §7872. The income tax consequences of the loan are determined under §7872(a). Ed and Sandy are treated as if (i) Ed had loaned the money to Sandy at the Applicable Federal Rate of 10 percent compounding semiannually; (ii) Ed had given Sandy enough extra money to pay that market rate of interest; and (iii) Sandy had then used that money to pay Ed interest at the market rate. On the deemed transfer, which is treated as a gift, Ed receives no deduction and Sandy has no inclusion. §102. The deemed retransfer is treated as an interest payment made by Sandy to Ed. The amount of the deemed transfer and retransfer is the amount of foregone interest for the year, computed at the Applicable Federal Rate. Here, the foregone interest is $15,375, which is the sum of $7,500 (5 percent of $150,000) in the first six months of year one plus $7,875 (5 percent of $157,500 in the second six months of year one). (Note that §7872(d)(1) does not apply because the loan exceeds $100,000. If the amount loaned were $100,000 or less, the amount of the deemed transfer would be limited to the borrower's net investment income.)

    On the deemed retransfer: (i) Ed must include $15,375 of constructively received interest and (ii) Sandy has $15,375 of interest expense. Under §163(d), she will be able to deduct only $15,000 of that interest expense. Sandy is then taxed on her investment earnings — here also $15,000. The net result is that in year one Sandy breaks even for tax purposes on the transaction, but Ed is taxed on $15,375.

24. The analysis and calculations are the same as in the explanation of the previous example, except that Zelda has much larger investment income: Wendy is treated as if she had loaned the money to Zelda at the Applicable Federal Rate of 10 percent compounding semiannually. Wendy receives no deduction for the deemed transfer and is taxed on $15,375 of interest income from the deemed retransfer. Zelda has no inclusion from the deemed transfer, which is a gift, and may deduct the $15,375 of interest deemed retransferred to Wendy. Zelda also is taxed on her investment earnings — here $1,500,000.

25. Almost but not quite. A taxpayer who makes a gift of a carved-out property interest is taxed on all income from that interest. A taxpayer who makes an interest-free loan of cash is taxed on the

imputed interest (at the Applicable Federal Rate) on that loan. The imputed interest taxed to the donor may be higher or lower than the actual income earned by the donee on the investment made with the borrowed cash.

26. False. The threshold amount is $10,000, and the exception for no-interest loans below $10,000 does not apply if the loan proceeds are invested in income-producing assets. §7872(c)(2).

8

Capital Gains and Losses

A. The Tax Treatment of Capital Gains and Losses

Reading: §§1(h), 1201, 1211, 1212, 1222

Historically, capital gain has been taxed at lower rates than so-called "ordinary" income (income other than capital gain). Today the maximum marginal rate on capital gain recognized by individuals, estates, and trusts is significantly lower than the maximum marginal rate on ordinary income. §1(h). However, capital gain recognized by corporations does not receive favorable treatment. §1201.

The flip side of favorable treatment for capital gain is unfavorable treatment of capital loss. Both corporate and noncorporate taxpayers can deduct the capital losses they recognize during a given year to the extent of the capital gains they recognize during that year. §1211. Corporate taxpayers are not allowed to deduct their capital losses in excess of their capital gains. §1211. However, they may carry the excess capital loss back three years and forward five years. §1212(a)(1). Noncorporate taxpayers are allowed to deduct up to $3,000 of their capital losses in excess of their capital gains in a given year and carry forward indefinitely the excess capital losses disallowed. §§1211(b) and 1212(b)(1). However, if the capital loss is large, the $3,000 a year allowance may seem paltry. For example, if a taxpayer recognizes a $900,000 capital loss and no capital gain in the current or future years,

§1211 allows the taxpayer to deduct the entire $900,000, but only at a rate of $3,000 a year—at that rate, it would take 300 years for the taxpayer to deduct the full $900,000!

The Code draws a distinction between long-term and short-term capital gain; long-term capital gain is taxed at the favorable §1(h) maximum rate, but short-term capital gain is taxed at ordinary income rates. Capital gain (or loss) is long-term if the taxpayer held the capital asset sold for *more than* one year and short-term if the taxpayer held the capital asset for a year or less. §1223(1)-(4). Both short-term and long-term capital losses are subject to the §1211 limitation described above.

If a taxpayer, in a given year, recognizes more than one type of capital gain or loss, the taxpayer must net the gains and losses as provided in §1222. Suppose a taxpayer has both long-term capital gain and long-term capital loss, short-term capital gain and short-term capital loss. The first step is to compute the taxpayer's *net long-term* capital gain or loss by netting the long-term capital gain and loss, and *net short-term* capital gain or loss by netting the taxpayer's short-term capital gain and loss. §1222(5)-(8). If, after that netting process, the taxpayer has a net long-term gain and a net short-term loss, the second step is to compute the taxpayer's *net capital gain* by netting the taxpayer's net long-term capital gain and net short-term capital loss for the year. §1222(11). If the short-term loss exceeds the long-term gain, a noncorporate taxpayer may deduct the short-term loss to the extent of the long-term gain plus $3,000, under §1211. Any loss in excess of the gain plus up to $3,000 of loss is referred to as a *net capital loss*. If the taxpayer has a net long-term loss and a net short-term gain, the same second-stage netting process occurs.

The following example may help to illustrate the netting system. Taxpayer Dale recognizes a long-term capital gain of $100,000 on the sale of Widget Company stock and a long-term capital loss of $40,000 on the sale of land. Dale recognizes a short-term capital gain of $20,000 on the sale of XYZ stock and a $30,000 short-term capital loss on the sale of Xeno stock. In the first stage of netting, the long-term gains are netted against long-term losses to produce a net long-term gain of $60,000; the short-term gains and losses are also netted to produce a net short-term loss of $10,000. In the second stage of netting, the long-term gain of $60,000 is netted against the short-term loss of $10,000. The result is a net capital gain of $50,000, which qualifies for the preferential capital gains rate.

Now suppose, instead, that Dale had recognized a $130,000 short-term capital loss on the sale of Xeno stock. In that case the first stage of netting would have produced a $60,000 long-term capital gain and a $110,000 short-term capital loss. The subsequent second-stage netting would leave Dale with a net capital loss of $47,000 ($50,000 less $3,000).

One recently adopted capital gain provision deserves brief mention. Under §1202, added to the Code in 1993, 50 percent of the gain from the sale or exchange of "qualified small business stock" held by noncorporate taxpayers for more than five years may be excluded from taxable income. The 50 percent exclusion comes on top of the existing capital gain preference, and cuts the already low tax rate on capital gain in half. Qualified small business stock is defined as stock issued by companies with not more than $50 million in assets. However, stock in corporations engaged in law, accounting, health, farming, banking, mining, and a variety of other activities does not qualify.

EXAMPLES

1. The following is a complete list of capital gains and losses taxpayer Ted recognizes in a taxable year. In each case, state whether the transactions generate a net short-term or long-term capital gain or loss.

   a. Ted recognizes a gain of $10,000 on the sale of a capital asset held 25 months.

   b. Ted recognizes a gain of $10,000 on the sale of a capital asset held 13 months.

   c. Ted recognizes a gain of $10,000 on the sale of a capital asset held three months.

   d. Ted recognizes a loss of $10,000 on the sale of a capital asset held three years.

   e. Ted recognizes a loss of $10,000 on the sale of a capital asset held three years and a gain of $13,000 on the sale of a capital asset held three months.

   f. Ted recognizes a gain of $13,000 on the sale of a capital asset held three years and a loss of $10,000 on the sale of a capital asset held three months.

   g. Ted recognizes a loss of $10,000 on the sale of a capital asset held three months and a gain of $200,000 on the sale of a capital asset held three months.

   h. Ted recognizes a gain of $40,000 on the sale of a capital asset held three months and a gain of $70,000 on the sale of a capital asset held three years.

8. Capital Gains and Losses

      i. Ted recognizes a loss of $30,000 on the sale of a capital asset held four months and a loss of $70,000 on the sale of a capital asset held three years.

      j. Ted recognizes a loss of $10,000 on the sale of a capital asset held eight months, a gain of $70,000 on the sale of a capital asset held six years, and a loss of $40,000 on the sale of a capital asset held four years.

2. In year one Rita recognizes a capital loss of $30,000 on the sale of a capital asset held three years. In year two Rita recognizes a capital gain of $20,000 on the sale of a capital asset held two years. In year three Rita recognizes no capital gains or losses. Discuss the tax treatment in years one, two, and three of the capital gains and losses.

EXPLANATIONS

1. a. Gain on the sale of a capital asset is long-term gain if the taxpayer held the capital asset for more than one year. §1222(3). Ted has $10,000 of long-term capital gain. Since he has no long-term or short-term capital loss, his net capital gain is also $10,000. That gain will qualify for the preferential capital gains rate of §1(h).

    b. Ted has $10,000 of net long-term capital gain, for the same reasons as in part (a).

    c. Ted has $10,000 of net short-term capital gain, which does not qualify for the preferential capital gains rate. Since he held the asset for only three months, the $10,000 of gain is short-term capital gain. §1222(1). The net short-term capital gain is also $10,000 because he did not recognize any short-term capital loss during the year. §1222(5).

    d. Ted has $10,000 of net long-term capital loss. The loss is long-term because he held the asset for three years. §1222(4). The net long-term loss is also $10,000 because he did not recognize any long-term capital gain during the year. §1222(8). Ted, who is a noncorporate taxpayer, will be allowed to deduct only $3,000 of the loss in the current year. §1211(b). The remaining $7,000 loss disallowed is carried forward to the next year. §1212(b). Ted's net capital loss is $7,000. §1222(10).

    e. The $10,000 capital loss is long-term. §1222(4). The $13,000 capital gain is short-term. §1222(1). Ted has a net long-term loss of $10,000 because he has $10,000 of long-term capital loss and no long-term capital gain. §1222(8). Ted has a net short-term capital gain of $13,000 because he has $13,000 of short-term capital gain and no short-term capital loss. The $10,000 net long-term loss and $13,000 net short-term gain are netted to produce a short-term capital gain of $3,000. That gain will be taxed at ordinary income rates.

f. The $13,000 capital gain is long-term. §1222(4). The $10,000 capital loss is short-term. §1222(1). Ted has a net long-term gain of $13,000 because he has $13,000 of long-term capital gain and no long-term capital loss. §1222(8). Ted has a net short-term capital loss of $10,000 because he has $10,000 of short-term capital loss and no short-term capital gain. The net long-term gain and net short-term loss are netted to produce a net capital gain of $3,000. Ted will pay tax on that $3,000 of gain at the preferential capital gains rate of §1(h).

g. Both the gain and the loss are short-term. §1222(1), (2). After netting the short-term gain and loss, Ted has net short-term capital gain of $190,000. §1222(5).

h. Ted has short-term capital gain of $40,000 and long-term capital gain of $70,000. Short-term gains are netted against long-term losses, and short-term losses are netted against long-term gains, but short-term gains are not netted against long-term gains nor are short-term losses netted against long-term losses. Ted has $70,000 of net capital gain, which is subject to the preferential capital gains rate. The $40,000 of short-term capital gain is taxed at ordinary income rates.

i. Ted has short-term capital loss of $30,000 and long-term capital loss of $70,000. Since Ted had no capital gain for the year, he will be allowed to deduct only $3,000 of the loss. His net capital loss for the year is $97,000. §1222(10).

j. Ted has a $10,000 short-term capital loss, a $40,000 long-term capital loss, and a $70,000 long-term capital gain. These transactions require two levels of netting. The first step is to compute Ted's net long-term capital gain, which equals $30,000 ($70,000 long-term gain less $40,000 long-term loss), and net short-term capital loss, which equals $10,000 ($10,000 short-term loss less zero short-term gain). §1222(6), (7). Ted's net capital gain is $20,000, which equals the $30,000 net long-term gain less the $10,000 net short-term loss. §1222(11). That $30,000 of net capital gain is taxed at the preferential capital gains rate.

2. Rita may deduct only $3,000 of the $30,000 long-term capital loss in year one. §1211(b). The remaining $27,000 capital loss carries over to year two. §1212(b). Rita can use $20,000 of that loss to offset the $20,000 of long-term capital gain recognized in year two. §1211(b)(2). This leaves Rita with a $7,000 capital loss in year two. Rita can also deduct $3,000 of that amount in year two. §1211(b)(1). The year two net capital loss, which is the remaining $4,000 of long-term capital loss, is carried forward to year three. §§1222(10), 1212(b). In year three Rita can deduct $3,000 of that loss. The year three net capital loss, which is the remaining $1,000 of long-term capital loss, is carried forward to year four.

B. Policy Rationale for the Treatment of Capital Gain and Loss

Why have we historically taxed long-term capital gain at a preferential rate? Over the years, a number of arguments have been made to support the preferential capital gains rate. (A number of these arguments made more sense when the top marginal ordinary income rate was much higher than it is now.)

One argument in favor of the special capital gain rate is that capital gain should be taxed at a lower rate because the gain included in the year in which the asset is sold may throw the taxpayer into a higher tax bracket than the taxpayer would have been in had the gain been taxed over a number of years. However, most capital gain is realized by taxpayers who are already in the top rate bracket, without regard to their capital gain, and these taxpayers still benefit from the preferential capital gains rate. In addition, allowing income averaging would be a much more precise way to solve the bunching problem for taxpayers who are generally taxed at lower rates.

Capital gain proponents have also argued that capital gain should be taxed at a lower rate because the gain realized on the sale of capital asset reflects both true economic gain from the asset, which should be taxed, and inflationary gain from the asset, which should not be taxed. Suppose, for example that taxpayer Mike bought a share of BigCo stock in year one for $5,000. Fifty years later, Mike sold the share of stock for $205,000. For tax purposes, Mike has a $200,000 realized gain on the sale of the stock. Assume that $160,000 of that gain reflects true economic gain on the stock, but that the remaining

$40,000 of gain is due to inflation (that is, because prices for goods have increased so a dollar buys less than it did 50 years earlier).

The argument is that it is unfair to tax Mike on the full $200,000 of realized gain at the normal tax rates, so we should allow Mike to pay a lower rate of tax on the gain. Extending this argument, the rate should then vary depending on how long the taxpayer held the asset and the inflation rate during the time the taxpayer held the asset. However, the rate applied to capital gain does not reflect the length of time the taxpayer held the property (other than the one-year distinction between short-term and long-term gain) and does not reflect the actual inflation rate during the time the asset was held. In other words, the current capital gain rules are a very gross way of solving the inflation problem. The problem could be solved more precisely by indexing the tax basis of assets to reflect inflation, then taxing gain from the sale of the asset at ordinary tax rates.

Capital gain proponents have also argued that capital gain should be taxed at a lower rate in order to mitigate "lock-in" effect and improve the mobility of capital. The idea is that since taxpayers can defer the tax on gain until the gain is realized, they will refuse to sell assets that they would sell but for having to pay tax on the sale; this lock-in effect causes immobility of capital and inefficient uses of capital. The special capital gain rate may reduce the lock-in effect. However, it does not eliminate the lock-in effect because the realization requirement and §1014 (the stepped-up basis at death rule) both deter taxpayers from selling their assets. If we wanted to improve liquidity of investment assets, we could enact more liberal nonrecognition rules along the lines of §1031. However, the logical extension of taking this approach would be to replace the income tax with a consumption tax.

Another pro-capital gain argument is that capital gain on the sale of stock should be taxed at a lower rate because corporate earnings, unlike most other investments, are double-taxed; corporate income is taxed first at the corporate level and again at the shareholder level when the corporation pays the shareholders dividends or the shareholder sells appreciated stock. Many tax experts believe that corporate income should not be double-taxed, but eliminating the double tax would cost the government a large amount of revenue so it is not politically viable. Taxing gain from the sale of stock at a lower rate at least ameliorates the double tax. However, note that the double tax argument is not applicable to the extent a corporation finances its operations with retained earnings or debt.

Capital gain proponents have also argued that the tax rate for capital gain should be lower than the ordinary rate in order to encourage saving and investment. In order to fund a reduction in rates for capital gain, the rate of tax on income from labor would be increased. The argument is that increased savings and investment would stimulate economic growth, and that the efficiency gains from reducing the rate of tax on investments would more than offset any reductions in efficiency that would result from taxing labor at a higher rate. There may be more precise solutions to this problem. In addition, converting consumption into savings, which shifts consumption to future generations, may deprive poor taxpayers of current consumption.

Capital gain proponents have also argued that the tax rate for capital gain should be lower than the ordinary rate in order to encourage investments in risky start-up businesses that may generate new jobs. If gains from those investments are not taxed at a more favorable rate, investors would require higher pre-tax returns on those investments. However, one might ask whether we should be encouraging businesses that would not survive without special tax breaks. In addition, if we choose to encourage investment in new and risky businesses, we could tax favor those specific types of investments instead of tax favoring all capital gain. We could also encourage investment in risky new businesses by relaxing the §1211 limitation on the utilization of capital losses.

If §1211 discourages investment in risky new businesses, why does the section limit the deductibility of capital losses? The limitation is designed to prevent taxpayers from manipulating the timing of capital gain and loss. Absent such a limitation, a taxpayer with wage income of $100,000, $100,000 of unrealized capital loss and $100,000 of unrealized capital gain could sell the loss asset, eliminating his tax liability for the year in spite of the fact that the taxpayer could defer the gain on the other capital asset until the taxpayer decided to sell it in a later year. However, the loss limitation applies even where such manipulation is impossible because the taxpayer does not own any appreciated capital assets.

C.   The Definition of "Capital Asset"

Reading: §1221

What is capital gain or loss? In common parlance, capital gain is used as a synonym for gain on investment, as opposed to operating income from a business, dividends, interest, or salary income. This simple (and simplistic) definition will give the right answer most of the time but ignores many hard issues that arise in tax practice. As is obvious from the discussion below and the cases assigned for your tax course, the definitional issues surrounding capital gain and loss are complex. Indeed, the distinction between capital and ordinary gains and losses has historically been one of the most troublesome, and hotly litigated, issues in tax law.

The Code defines capital gain or loss as gain or loss on the sale or exchange of a "capital asset." Section 1221 defines the term *capital asset* as "property" that does *not* fall within any of the following five ordinary asset categories:

1. inventory or property held for sale to customers in the ordinary course of business
2. depreciable or real property used in the taxpayer's trade or business
3. certain copyrights or literary properties
4. accounts receivable or notes receivable acquired in the ordinary course of a trade or business
5. certain United States Government publications

We will see in this section of the book that courts have limited the capital asset definition by reading these ordinary income asset categories in §1221 very broadly.

The first category of ordinary assets, listed in §1221(1), consists of "stock in trade . . . or other property of a kind which would properly be included in . . . inventory . . . or property held by the taxpayer primarily for sale to customers in the ordinary course of his trade or business." (whew!) This category encompasses the shoe store's shoes, the smoke shop's cigarettes, and the hamburger shop's hamburgers. Profit from the sale of these items generates ordinary income, not capital gain.

In some cases, determining whether an item falls within §1221(1) can be quite difficult. This is particularly true with respect to real estate, where one can support oneself with just a few sales per year. Consider, for example, a teacher who, in an effort to supplement her income, buys a home on the outskirts of what she feels is a growing vacation area. During weekends she paints and does other minor repairs on the home. She neither uses nor rents out the home but instead allows a college-age child of a close friend to live in the home on a month-to-month basis. She sells the home two years after purchase, and soon thereafter purchases another home in the same area and repeats the process. Over a 10-year period, she makes as much on her real estate activities as she does in salary from teaching. Is the teacher in the trade or business of buying, repairing, and selling old homes? Are the homes held for sale in the ordinary course of that business? If so, the homes are noncapital assets by virtue of §1221(1) and gain on the sale is ordinary income rather than capital gain. Does the answer to these questions change if the teacher retires but continues her real estate activities as before, so that the profits from those activities constitute a predominant source of her income? If some of the homes the teacher purchases after retirement require structural repairs? If the teacher obtains a broker's license to facilitate her real estate activities? If the teacher employs or has long-term working relationships with architects, contractors, and painters?

The best the courts have been able to do with situations similar to this is to agree on a number of relevant factors and, based on those factors, to decide the issue on a case-by-case approach. Factors that point toward inclusion in §1221(1) and hence ordinary income or loss treatment include: (i) frequent or numerous sales, (ii) significant improvements, (iii) brokerage activities, (iv) advertising, (v) purchase and retention of the property with a goal to short-term resale, and (vi) the importance of the activity in relation to the taxpayer's other activities and sources of income. See, e.g., Biedenharn Realty Co. v. United States, 526 F.2d 409 (5th Cir.), cert. denied, 429 U.S. 819 (1976)(ordinary income on the sale of farm property bought as an investment that was later subdivided and sold in lots). In the above example, the teacher's pre-retirement activities probably do not meet the "ordinary course of trade or business" standard of §1221(1) and thus do not preclude capital asset status. But as the relative and absolute importance of the teacher's real estate activities grows after retirement, so does the likelihood the homes will be characterized as noncapital assets by virtue of §1221(1).

One might expect that similar factors would be used to distinguish investment from business activity in stock and commodities so that an individual who spent all of his time, and realized all of his income from, "playing the market" would recognize ordinary income or loss from that activity. In an early case, however, one court held that individual stock trading, no matter how frequent or central to one's livelihood, did not generate ordinary income or loss. Van Suetendael v. Commissioner, 3 T.C.M. 987 (1944), aff'd, 152 F.2d 654 (2d Cir.

1945). The taxpayer in *Van Suetendael* recognized a loss on stocks and bonds and treated the loss as ordinary under §1221(1). The court held that the loss did not fit under that section because the assets were not held primarily for sale to "customers" but were sold through brokers to unknown persons.

The rationale articulated by the court is hard to swallow. In general, the fact that sales are made to regular clients or known parties is irrelevant for purposes of distinguishing between capital and ordinary assets. The holding of the case, however, is now established law. Only securities sales conducted by entities such as commercial brokerages will meet the *Van Suetendael* standard and generate ordinary income and loss under §1221(1).[1] The government's victory in *Van Suetendael* proved Pyrrhic. In the long run, due to inflation and other factors, stock held for investment is generally sold at a gain. The government savings from forcing taxpayers such as Van Suetendael to recognize capital loss on the sale of stock at a loss has been more than offset by the cost to the government of allowing more successful speculators to recognize capital gain when stock is sold at a profit.

One final issue deserves mention before leaving §1221(1). Taxpayers in some industries may experience considerable fluctuation in the cost of inventory or goods used to produce inventory. Such taxpayers may be able to hedge against the risk of a price increase in their raw materials, or hedge against certain other business risks, by buying futures on the commodities market. Are these and similar hedge-related investments capital assets, like investments in other securities? Or are these investments treated as part of the cost of acquiring inventory, and excluded from capital asset treatment under §1221(1)? Most taxpayers who purchase these sorts of hedges are corporations. Such taxpayers will generally prefer noncapital treatment since, as noted above, corporate taxpayers do not qualify for the capital gain preference and cannot deduct capital loss except to the extent of capital gain.

An example may help illuminate the issue. Agri Corp buys oats to process into animal feed. On July 1 oats are selling for $4 a bushel. At that price the company is able to make $1 for every bushel it purchases. To guard against the possibility of an increase in the price of oats, the company buys futures contracts that obligate it to take delivery of a given number of bushels of oats in September at a price of $4 a

---

1. Under §1236, securities dealers can still avoid §1221(1) characterization by segregating securities held for investment, as opposed to business, purposes.

bushel. The price of a bushel of oats falls to $3 a bushel by September 1. If Agri Corp takes delivery of the oats it purchased in July, the oats cost $4 a bushel, so it will earn $1 a bushel from processing the oats into animal feed.

Suppose, however, that Agri Corp finds it somewhat more convenient not to take delivery of the oats but instead to "close out" its futures contract by paying $1 for every bushel it would otherwise have the obligation to purchase. In effect, Agri Corp pays to be relieved of its obligation to purchase oats. This frees up the company to purchase oats at their current market price of $3. At that price the company makes $2 a bushel on the sale of animal feed. However, it loses $1 a bushel on the futures contracts.

Agri Corp earns a net profit of $1 a bushel, regardless of whether or not it takes delivery of the oats. If the company takes delivery of the oats, it obviously earns $1 a bushel of ordinary income. Assume the company does not take delivery of the oats. Must it recognize $2 a bushel ordinary income on the sale of oats and report the loss on the futures contract as a capital loss — deductible only against capital gain?

In a case arising out of a similar fact pattern, Corn Products Refining Co. v. Commissioner, 350 U.S. 46 (1955), the Supreme Court held that these sorts of hedge investments generate ordinary income or loss. In a more recent case, the Court restated *Corn Products* as standing for the following limited proposition: Net proceeds from hedging transactions that are an integral part of a business's inventory-purchase system are treated as proceeds from the sale of inventory and generate ordinary income or loss. Arkansas Best Corporation v. Commissioner, 485 U.S. 212 (1988).

Today the issue is effectively governed by Treasury regulations, which make it somewhat easier for business taxpayers to ensure that hedges are treated as noncapital assets. Under the current regulations, a taxpayer can generally ensure noncapital asset treatment of certain hedges entered into to reduce business risks. Such hedges include contracts entered into to reduce risk due to possible fluctuations in interest rates or currency exchange rates, or in the cost of supplies or inventory. Taxpayers taking advantage of this regulatory provision must, in effect, elect noncapital treatment at the time the hedge is entered into. Reg. §§1.1221-2, 1.446-4.

The second, and most important, statutory exclusion from the category of capital asset is found in §1221(2), which encompasses real or depreciable property used in a trade or business. Such property is excluded from the class of capital assets under §1221(2) only to be subject to a still more favorable set of rules under §1231. Generally speaking, property in this category has the happy quality of generating capital gain when sold at a profit and ordinary loss when sold at a loss. The definition and treatment of §1221(2) property is discussed more fully, in connection with §1231, below.

The remaining statutory exceptions are of minor importance. Section 1221(3) precludes creators of copyrights, literary, musical, or artistic compositions; letters, memoranda, or similar property from treating such property as a capital asset. Section 1221(3) also precludes capital asset status for those who receive such property as gifts or, in the case of letters, memoranda, or similar property, for whom the property was created. Section 1221(4) excludes from capital asset status accounts or notes receivable; §1221(5) prevents persons who receive United States Government publications at a price less than charged to the public from claiming those publications as capital assets.[2]

EXAMPLES

3. Stan spends substantially all of his time buying and selling stocks, bonds, and other securities for his own account. He subscribes to scores of financial newspapers and magazines and has a personal computer with "on line" capabilities from which he is able to make trades through a national brokerage firm. At any given time, Stan may have well over $1 million invested in securities. Last year Stan earned $80,000 in interest and dividends from his securities and $250,000 in profit from the sale of securities. This year Stan has earned $75,000 from interest and dividends from his securities but has lost $150,000 on security sales. Discuss the tax treatment of Stan's current income and losses.

4. Carl Conard owns 8,000 acres of land that is used primarily for raising beef and dairy cattle. Carl also sells a small amount of produce he grows on the land that is not used in his beef and dairy operations. Until year 10, Carl also owned approximately

---

2. Section 1221(5) was adopted in response to reports that several legislators donated their free copies of the Congressional Record to libraries and took a charitable deduction equal to the value of the publications. As discussed in Chapter 4 of this book, taxpayers may claim a charitable deduction equal to fair market value only for capital assets. Otherwise, the charitable deduction is limited to the taxpayer's basis. Since the Congressional Record is received free of charge, the publication has no basis in the hands of legislators, and the donation of that publication would now generate no charitable deduction.

200 acres of land in Sproutsville; the Sproutsville land was used in Carl's dairy operations. Sproutsville was for many years a small, rural town; its character and size changed, however, after the opening of a nearby auto plant in year one. During the next decade, residents of Sproutsville expressed increasing dissatisfaction at the noise and odor generated by the dairy operations.

In year seven a motion to rezone the Sproutsville property to prohibit its then-present use was narrowly defeated. In year eight, after fighting to keep its Sproutsville operations intact for many years, Carl negotiated an agreement with local officials. Under that agreement, Carl discontinued dairy operations and gave 100 acres of his 200 acres of land to the City of Sproutsville. On the 100 acres it received, Sproutsville built roads, parks, and schools. The 100 acres that Carl kept were rezoned; 40 acres were zoned mixed residential and commercial, and the remaining 60 acres were zoned residential. Subdivision into one-acre parcels was allowed. In year 10 Carl sold all 60 acres zoned residential to a single developer for a profit of $1 million. In that same year Carl listed the remaining 40 acres with a local real estate broker. The acres were sold to 40 separate buyers over five years. Carl himself did no promotion or advertising for the parcels and did not improve the land by bringing in utility lines or building roads. Carl recognized $1.5 million of gain from these sales. The $1.5 million of gain recognized from the land sales represented approximately 60 percent of Carl's income over the relevant five-year period. Carl had no other sales or exchanges during that five-year period.

What arguments might Carl make in favor of capital gain treatment of the $1.5 million profit? What arguments might the Service make in favor of ordinary income treatment?

5. Attorney Andy and his law partner Perry purchase a 64-unit apartment building for $3 million. Four years after the purchase, they convert the building to a condominium. The conversion requires $150,000 in improvements. The 64 units are listed with a broker and sell quickly. Each of the two partners realizes a net profit of $1 million on the investment. Neither partner has any other real estate investments or any other sales or exchanges in the year of sale. Discuss the likely tax positions of Andy and his partner, on the one hand, and the Service, on the other hand.

6. Your tax client, Gloria, is a highly successful architect. Gloria pays $1 million for a large, dilapidated, and nearly vacant office build-

ing located near the downtown area. Gloria's purchase was based on the assumption that the downtown area would expand and that, with some renovation, the building would become highly desirable. Unfortunately, in the year following the purchase, the downtown area shrinks and the assessed value of the building falls to $750,000. Gloria tells you that she is not sure what she should do with the property. She may carry out her envisioned but postponed renovations and then sell the building; or she may renovate and then rent the office space in the building. She has asked you to advise her as to the tax consequences of an immediate or future sale of the building. Apart from her home and assets in her pension fund, Gloria owns no other significant assets.

7. Information Inc. publishes a weekly newsmagazine and five daily newspapers. The company owns two large paper mills that it uses to process timber into paper for its magazine and newspapers. In order to guard against an increase in the price of timber, Information Inc. pays $7 million for 70 percent of the stock of Timber Company, a large timber producer. In fact, the price of timber does rise, and so does the price of newsprint. In theory, Information, Inc. could avoid the negative effect of the increase in the price of newsprint by using the timber it has already purchased through the acquisition of Timber Company. In practice, Information Inc. finds it more convenient and slightly more profitable to sell the Timber Company stock at a gain and then purchase newsprint from its regular supplier. Information Inc. sells the Timber Company stock for a profit of $3 million and then pays an additional $2,950,000 for newsprint. The additional cost of newsprint reduces the company's operating income by $2,950,000. Is the stock of Timber Company a capital asset in the hands of Information Inc.?

8. Northern Company is a large shipping company that operates out of 50 ports throughout the world. The company's profits are extremely sensitive to the price of crude oil, which has fluctuated widely over the past two decades. In order to hedge against an increase in the price of fuel, on January 1, Northern Company enters into a contract on a commodities exchange pursuant to which it will take delivery of a certain quantity of crude oil, on July 1, at the January 1 crude oil price. Between January 1 and July 1, the price of oil falls rather than rises. In retrospect, the oil contract is a burden rather than a benefit to the company. In

theory, the company could take delivery of the fuel under the terms of the contract. If it does so, the cost of its oil will be $3 million more than it would have been had they bought it at the July 1 price; this increased oil cost will reduce the company's income from operations to $7 million. In fact, the company finds it more convenient and profitable to pay to get out of the contract and purchase oil more cheaply on the open market. The company pays $3 million to get out of the contract and, due to its lower than expected cost of fuel, earns income from operations (other than the oil contract) of $10 million. Is the $3 million loss on the oil contract capital or ordinary?

EXPLANATIONS

3. The $75,000 of income is ordinary and the $150,000 loss is capital. Stan might consider himself in the trade or business of buying and selling securities. It may seem natural to him to consider the securities a form of "stock in trade" or "property held . . . primarily for sale to customers in the ordinary course of . . . trade or business" and to deduct the $150,000 loss on the sale of securities as an ordinary loss by virtue of §1221(1). In an early case, however, courts held that securities bought and sold by individual investors did fall within the inventory exclusion from capital asset status because they were not sold to "customers." Van Suetendael v. Commissioner, 3 T.C.M. 987 (1944), aff'd, 152 F.2d 654 (2d Cir. 1945); for a more recent application of the "no customer" rationale of *Van Suetendael*, see Swartz v. Commissioner, 876 F.2d 657 (8th Cir. 1989) (where the court held that securities were capital assets in the hands of a full-time commodities trader). The reasoning of the court in that case (and other courts in similar cases) is questionable, but the holding is now firmly established: For all but a handful of taxpayers, securities are capital assets. Securities are a noncapital asset by virtue of §1221(1) only for registered brokers (such as Smith, Barney or Merrill Lynch) that have (or strive for) regular clientele. And brokers can avoid noncapital asset treatment on some or all securities by so electing at the time of purchase, and maintaining such securities in a segregated account. §1236.

4. The issue here is whether the land constitutes "property held primarily for the sale to customers in the ordinary course of his

trade or business" and is therefore a noncapital asset by virtue of §1221(1). Carl will argue that he acquired the land for use in his beef and dairy operations and that he held the land for that purpose for many years until shortly before the ultimate sale. Carl will point out that, apart from the land in question, he is clearly not in the real estate business, that over the years he has earned most of his income from his beef and dairy operations, and that neither he nor any of his employees improved the land or engaged in any sales efforts. Carl would then treat the property as section 1231 property (real property held in a trade or business). Net gain on section 1231 property is capital gain.

The Service may argue that the sheer number of sales, the absolute amount of gain recognized on the sales, and the relative importance of that profit during the years in question to Carl's total income put Carl in the trade or business of selling real estate.

One obvious source of contention is the correct characterization of the deal with Sproutsville. The Service will support its arguments above by stating that Carl applied for and received permission to subdivide the land. The Service will also attribute the improvements to the land (in the form of roads, and perhaps parks and schools) to Carl. While the improvements are nominally constructed by the City, the construction clearly benefits Carl and is in some sense "paid for" by his contribution of land to the City. Carl will argue that the deal was forced upon him by the threat of even less favorable zoning action.

Which party is more likely to succeed? That depends a great deal on the jurisdiction and the trier(s) of fact. For a sense of how the issue plays out in one jurisdiction, compare Houston Endowment, Inc. v. United States, 606 F.2d 77 (5th Cir. 1979) (in which the court held that property was a noncapital asset, under §1221(1), where the taxpayer, a lender, obtained property through foreclosure, did not subdivide the property, but did install utilities, and sold over 200 parcels over 27 years) with Byram v. United States, 705 F.2d 1418 (5th Cir. 1983) (in which the court held that property was a capital asset where (i) the taxpayer made seven sales in a single year, but made no improvements and (ii) there were no sales efforts by the taxpayer or brokers, but the taxpayer had sold 15 other parcels in a three-year period).

Note that it is possible, though unlikely, that the bulk sale of land to the developer would generate capital gain but the sales to individual purchasers would generate ordinary income.

5.   Andy and his partner will argue that the units were either capital assets or §1221(2) property, in which case the units would also be section 1231 property (discussed below); in either case, they would generate capital gain. Andy and his partner may be expected to argue that they did not purchase the building with an eye to selling off the individual units, but instead bought the building either as a long-term investment or in the hope of producing a steady stream of rental income. They are likely to emphasize their lack of other real estate investments, their lack of direct involvement in the sales, and the relatively small cost of improvements made as part of the conversion process.

The Service is likely to argue that, whatever the original motive or other sources of income, the sale of 64 units necessarily puts one in the business of selling units. The Service is likely to see the $150,000 in improvements as significant. It is also likely to impute the efforts of the broker to the taxpayers to buttress its claim of business activity.

There is no obvious "right" way to characterize this transaction. About all one can say is that, in the past, courts have been surprisingly lenient in giving capital asset treatment to gain recognized on condominium conversions. See, e.g., Gangi v. Commissioner, 54 T.C.M. (CCH) 1048 (1987) (gain from the sale of condominiums was capital where the taxpayers constructed an apartment building for rental use, operated it as such for eight years, then converted the apartments to condominiums and advertised the sale of the condominiums, in order to maximize their profit on the liquidation of the investment when the taxpayer and the other investor in the building decided to part company).

6.   Gloria's prime concern should be the limited deductibility of capital losses. An immediate sale would leave Gloria with a loss of $250,000. Under §1211, individuals may deduct capital losses against capital gain. Capital loss in excess of capital gain is deductible only to the extent of $3,000 a year; any remaining capital loss is carried over to the following year, where the same rules apply. Assume the building is sold immediately for its appraised value of $750,000, leaving Gloria with a loss of $250,000. If the building is considered a capital asset and Gloria recognizes no capital gain

in this or future years, at $3,000 a year it will take $83\frac{1}{3}$ years to deduct her entire $250,000 loss.

In the event of an immediate sale, would the building be treated as a capital asset? Gloria could argue that she purchased and held the building with an eye to developing a steady stream of rental income and that the property qualifies as "section 1231 property" (real property used in a trade or business). (Net loss on section 1231 property is treated as an ordinary loss.) Gloria's case would be strengthened by factors that indicate a business (as opposed to investment) motive and operation. The presence of rents, the employment of a professional manager or full-time custodian, advertising for tenants, and development of a plan of renovation would all be helpful.

The possibility of ordinary loss increases if the building is renovated. In general, the more time Gloria herself spends on the project, the greater the extent of renovation, and the more employees directly employed on the project, the more likely that Gloria can claim an ordinary loss on the sale. At some point, the renovation itself becomes a trade or business and the property falls out of the capital asset category through application of §1221(1). If the property is renovated and then rented out, ordinary loss treatment becomes even more likely. Gloria can maximize the possibility of ordinary loss treatment by keeping careful business records of the time she spends on the project and by formally treating the project as a separate enterprise. Maintaining a separate bank account for the building rents, for example, may help to characterize the project as a business.

This question illustrates one of the conundrums of tax planning: the pull between saving taxes and maximizing before-tax income (or minimizing before-tax loss). Obviously, Gloria should not throw good money after bad just to obtain an ordinary loss. On the other hand, if she is uncertain in any event which course to take, it would be foolish not to take the course that offers significant tax savings. There are a host of formalistic actions Gloria might take to make her investment appear more like a business. She might for example, adopt a business name for the building (such as Downtown Towers) and, in accordance with state law, file a "doing business as" notice in a journal of general circulation. She might then order separate stationery for the building, open and maintain a separate bank account in the name of the business, and so on. She could also join associations of real estate professionals and subscribe to periodicals that she will probably never read. There is an obvious air of sham to these actions. An auditor or court may or may not see through these actions. How much guidance should the tax practitioner give?

7. As discussed in the text and in the explanation of example 3 above, securities are almost always capital assets in the hands of anyone who is not a securities dealer. Here, however, the securities act as a sort of an inventory substitute. Information Inc. purchased the securities as a way of assuring itself a steady supply of raw materials at a reasonable cost. Had Information Inc. used the lumber from Timber Company to produce newsprint, it would have saved itself the cost of purchasing newsprint at the market price and increased its operating income by approximately $3 million. For tax purposes, that increase would have been treated as ordinary income. Should the result be different because Information Inc. instead sold Timber Company stock at a profit of $3 million?

In Corn Products Refining Co. v. Commissioner, 350 U.S. 46 (1955), as clarified by Arkansas Best Corporation v. Commissioner, 485 U.S. 212 (1988), the Court stated that for purposes of §1221(1), the term "inventory" includes securities used to assure a steady supply of inventory. Gain or loss on such securities is ordinary gain or loss. Thus, the securities fall within the §1221(1) exception to capital asset treatment. The gain is therefore ordinary income, not capital gain. (If, in the alternative, timber is characterized as a noninventory supply consumed in the taxpayer's business, the result is the same if the purchase of the stock satisfies the requirements of Reg. §1.1221-2(b) and (c)(5).)

Note that Information, Inc. may be indifferent to whether the gain is characterized as ordinary income or capital gain. Capital gain recognized by a corporate taxpayer does not qualify for a reduced tax rate. §1201. Characterization of the gain as capital gain would be advantageous for Information, Inc. only if it had an otherwise unusable capital loss. A corporate capital loss can offset capital gain but not ordinary income. §1211(a). To understand this last point in context, suppose Information, Inc. had a $3 million capital loss. If the gain on the Timber Company stock were treated as capital gain, it could be offset by the capital loss. No tax would be due. If the gain were ordinary income, it could not be offset by the capital loss, and approximately one-third of the gain would go to the government in the form of taxes.

The importance of the *Corn Products-Arkansas Best* exception to capital asset treatment and the hedging regulations is greatest when the security or other inventory-substitute is sold at a loss rather than a profit. In that case, the taxpayer will want the loss to be characterized as an inventory loss, so that it is deductible against ordinary income.

8. This example is analytically quite similar to the previous example. The taxpayer here, like the taxpayer in the previous example, purchases securities to hedge against the price of a commodity used in its operations. If the taxpayer uses its rights under its hedge to take delivery of the commodity in question, gain or loss on the hedge will be incorporated into the gain or loss on its operations. The result will be ordinary income or loss. Here, if Northern Company takes delivery of the oil, the result is an operating profit of $7 million.

In fact, Northern Company does not take delivery of the oil but instead pays to avoid taking delivery on the contract at a cost of $3 million. If the futures contract is treated under "normal" rules governing securities, the loss will be a capital loss. The result will be ordinary income of $10 million and a capital loss of $3 million. Unless Northern Company has capital gain from other transactions, this result will dramatically increase its tax burden because capital losses cannot offset ordinary income.

The theoretically correct result appears to be one that treats the futures contract as a noncapital asset. This will leave the company with ordinary income of $7 million ($10 million less a $3 million ordinary loss) — the same result that would obtain if the company had taken delivery of the oil under the futures contract. An opposite result would force companies in the taxpayer's position to take delivery of commodities under these sorts of futures contracts even under situations in which it is more efficient to liquidate the contract and purchase the needed commodity from other sources.

In the previous example, the correct result was reached under the rationale that the futures contract was an inventory substitute that should be treated as a form of inventory and therefore a noncapital asset by virtue of §1221(1). But in the previous example, the taxpayer had obvious inventory — millions of newspapers and magazines. The taxpayer here has no inventory — it earns its profit by providing shipping services. Thus, if the normal rules governing futures contracts applied, the taxpayer would be left in the unenviable position of recognizing a capital loss that might not be usable. However, under the hedging regulation, §1.1221-2, Northern Company can possibly ensure noncapital asset treatment of the oil futures contract by electing that treatment when it enters into the hedge on January 1.

D.   Section 1231 and Depreciation Recapture

Reading: §§*1231, 1245, 1250*

As noted above, under §1221(2), real or depreciable property used in a trade or business is excluded from the category of capital assets. Instead, such property is characterized as *section 1231 property*, provided the taxpayer has held it for more than one year. Each year, gain or loss on any item of section 1231 property is netted against gain or loss on other items of section 1231 property. If, in a given year, a taxpayer has a net gain on §1231 sales or exchanges, the §1231 gains and losses are capital. (However, the depreciation recapture rules, discussed below, may recharacterize some or all of the §1231 capital gain as ordinary.) On the other hand, if, in the year, a taxpayer has a net loss on §1231 sales or exchanges, the §1231 gains and losses are ordinary. The possibility of recognizing capital gain on favorable outcomes and ordinary loss on unfavorable outcomes gives §1231 a sort of "heads, the taxpayer wins, tails, the government loses" character.

Section 1231 was adopted during World War II in part as a response to arguments that owners of appreciated business property requisitioned for the war effort were "forced" to recognize gain — gain that was then treated as ordinary income. Section 1231 did nothing about the recognition issue but ameliorated the hardship by characterizing gain recognized on all sales and exchanges of qualifying business property (including, quite obviously, on purely voluntarily sales unrelated to the war effort) as capital. Section 1231 has remained largely unchanged since that time, testimony to the staying power of a tax preference.

You should note one technical aspect of the calculation of net gain or loss under §1231: If, in a given year, a taxpayer recognizes a net §1231 gain, but has taken an ordinary deduction for a net §1231 loss within the last five years, the prior ordinary loss deduction is "recaptured" by recharacterizing that portion of the net §1231 gain in the current year as ordinary. §1231(c).

To illustrate the operation of §1231, suppose that in year one, Widgets, Inc. recognizes a gain of $10,000 on the sale of a truck used to transport widgets and a loss of $50,000 on a building used to produce widgets. The result is a net $40,000 §1231 loss, so the gain and loss will both be ordinary.

Now, suppose instead that Widgets, Inc. sells the building at the close of year one and the truck at the start of year two. Can Widgets, Inc. take a $50,000 ordinary loss in year one and a $10,000 capital gain in year two? No. Section 1231(c) prevents taxpayers from timing sales to recognize §1231 (ordinary) loss in one year followed by §1231 (capital) gain in any of the five succeeding years. Here, those rules will characterize the $10,000 of §1231 gain recognized in year two as ordinary so that, over the two years, Widget's Inc. recognizes a $50,000 ordinary loss and a $10,000 ordinary gain for a net $40,000 ordinary loss — the same result that would have been obtained had the two properties been sold in the same taxable year.

Section 1231 is an important provision for corporations and most other enterprises since it applies to virtually all non-inventory property. Section 1231 property includes machinery used to produce goods, cars and trucks used to transport goods, buildings and land owned and used by a taxpayer in its business operations, and any proceeds from the involuntary conversion of property used in the business.

Even if the sale of depreciable property generates capital gain under §1231, some of that capital gain may be recharacterized as ordinary income by the *depreciation recapture* rules of §§1245 and 1250. Section 1245 recharacterizes capital gain from the sale of a depreciable asset (other than real property) as ordinary income, to the extent of prior depreciation on the asset sold. Said another way, on the sale of section 1245 property, a taxpayer includes ordinary income equal to the lesser of (i) the gain recognized on the sale of the asset or (ii) prior depreciation taken on the asset sold. §1245(a)(1), (2). Property is *section 1245 property* if (i) depreciation is allowed on the property under §167 and (ii) the property is one of the types of property specified in §1245(a)(3), including personal and tangible property.

Section 1245 may best be illustrated by an example. Suppose Max pays $10,000 for a car used in a trade or business. Under §§167 and 168, described in Chapter 5 of this book, Max may depreciate the car over five years. The depreciation deduction is treated as a noncapital business expense and reduces the tax Max pays on ordinary income. After the car is fully depreciated and Max's basis in the car is reduced to zero, the car is sold for $2,000. As measured against economic income, the depreciation deduction was $2,000 too generous; the car was treated for tax purposes as having declined in value by $10,000 when in fact it declined in value by only $8,000. Were it not for the recapture provisions, Max would recognize §1231 gain of $2,000 on the sale, which would be capital if Max does not sell any other section 1231 property during the same year. However, under the §1245 recapture provisions, gain to the extent of prior depreciation is characterized as ordinary income. Max therefore includes $2,000 of ordinary income, not capital gain. In effect, the $2,000 "excess" depreciation deduction taken against ordinary income is recaptured by forcing Max to include ordinary income, in the amount of the prior excess deduction, in the year of sale.

Now suppose, instead, that Max sold the car for $13,000. Since Max had taken $10,000 of depreciation on the car, his basis in the car is zero and he recognizes $13,000 of capital gain (via §1231) on the sale of the car, assuming that he does not sell any other section 1231 property in the same year. However, $10,000 of that capital gain (the lesser of the $10,000 depreciation taken on the car or the $13,000 of gain on the sale) is characterized as ordinary income under §1245. The remaining $3,000 of gain is capital under §1231.

If the asset sold is real property, §1250 imposes a limited (and today, illusory) form of recapture. Generally speaking, §1250 requires recapture of gain only to the extent of depreciation in excess of straightline depreciation.[3] Real property placed in service since 1986, however, is depreciable only by the straightline method. §168(b)(3). Thus, there is generally no depreciation in excess of straightline and hence no portion of gain on the sale is subject to recapture.

The Code also includes a host of other, more specialized provisions (for example, §341) that govern the characterization of gain or loss on certain transactions. These various provisions are beyond the scope of this book, but you should know to check for specific characterization rules in practice.

---

3. Section 1250 also applies to all depreciation deductions for property sold or exchanged after being held a year or less; but as this form of property does not generate capital gain in any event, and as such early dispositions are rare, the impact of this provision is modest.

EXAMPLES

9. In year one, Bigco, Inc. sells land on which its computer operations were located for many years at a gain of $300,000. In that same year the company sells some long-held capital assets at a loss of $200,000. Bigco, Inc. has no other sales or exchanges in year one. Discuss the amount, if any, of ordinary income, ordinary loss, capital gain, or capital loss the company recognizes in year one.

10. State whether the following combinations of §1231 gain and loss generate ordinary or capital gain or loss.
    a. Tex recognizes (i) a $10,000 gain on the sale of vacant land used in his trade or business and held for four years and (ii) a $20,000 loss on the sale of tools used in his trade or business and held for five years.
    b. Tess recognizes (i) a $30,000 gain on the sale of vacant land used in her trade or business and held for two years and (ii) a $20,000 loss on the sale of tools used in her trade or business and held for four years.

11. State whether the following combinations of §1231 and §1221 gain and loss generate ordinary or capital gain or loss. State whether any net capital gain or loss is short-term or long-term.
    a. Carlos recognizes (i) a $10,000 gain on the sale of vacant land used in his trade or business and held for four years, (ii) a $20,000 loss on the sale of tools used in his trade or business and held for four years, and (iii) a $30,000 capital gain on stock held for six years.
    b. Carla recognizes (i) a $30,000 gain on the sale of vacant land used in her trade or business and held for two years, (ii) a $20,000 loss on the sale of tools used in a trade or business and held for four years, and (iii) a $40,000 capital gain on stock investment held for six years.
    c. Carmelita recognizes (i) a $30,000 gain on the sale of vacant land used in a trade or business and held for two years, (ii) a $20,000 loss on the sale of tools used in a trade or business and held for four years, (iii) a $30,000 capital gain on stock held for six years, and (iv) a $50,000 capital loss on stock held for five years.
    d. Chuck recognizes (i) a $30,000 gain on the sale of vacant land used in a trade or business and held for two years, (ii) a $20,000 loss on the sale of tools used in a trade or business and held for

four years, (iii) a $50,000 capital loss on stock held for six years, and (iv) a $60,000 capital gain on stock held for two months.

12. State the amount of ordinary income included on the following sales. (Assume that the taxpayers do not sell any other property during the year of the following sales.)

    a. Jan sells the Shady Acres Apartment Building for $320,000. Jan purchased the property in 1990 for $300,000. Her adjusted basis in the property at the time of the sale is $260,000 ($300,000 basis less $40,000 of depreciation taken on the building).

    b. John sells machinery used in his business to build widgets for $150,000. John bought the equipment in 1990 for $400,000. His adjusted basis in the property at the time of the sale is $100,000 ($400,000 basis less $300,000 of depreciation taken on the machinery).

    c. Jen sells equipment used in her auto repair shop business for $60,000. She paid $50,000 for the equipment. Her adjusted basis in the equipment at the time of the sale is zero ($50,000 basis less $50,000 of depreciation taken on the equipment).

    d. Jim sells a copyright for $55,000. He bought the copyright from the person (not related to Jim) who created the copyrighted property in exchange for $50,000. Jim's adjusted basis for the property at the time of the sale is $40,000 ($50,000 basis less $10,000 depreciation taken on the property).

EXPLANATIONS

9. The land is real property used in a trade or business. It is excluded from capital asset status by virtue of §1221(2) but, because it is real property used in a trade or business and because it has been held for more than one year, it qualifies as "section 1231 property" by virtue of (surprise!) §1231. If a taxpayer recognizes a net gain on section 1231 property, the taxpayer's §1231 gains and losses are treated as long-term capital gains and losses. If a taxpayer recognizes a net loss on section 1231 property, the taxpayer's §1231 gains and losses are ordinary. Here, Bigco, Inc. has a net gain on section 1231 property, so the $300,000 of gain on the sale of the land is long-term capital gain and the $200,000 of loss on the sale of the capital assets is long-term capital loss. The $100,000 of net long-term capital gain qualifies for the special capital gain rate of §1(h).

10. a. Tex has a net loss on section 1231 property, so the gain and loss are both ordinary. §1231(a)(2).

    b. Tess has a net gain on section 1231 property, so the $30,000 gain is long-term capital gain and the $20,000 loss is long-term capital loss. §1231(a)(1). Tess has net long-term capital gain of $10,000. §1222(7).

11. a. Carlos has a net loss on section 1231 property, so the $10,000 §1231 gain and the $20,000 §1231 loss are both ordinary. §1231(a)(2). Carlos also has $30,000 of long-term capital gain and the same amount of net capital gain (since he has no long-term capital loss).

    b. Carla has a net gain on section 1231 property so the $30,000 of gain from the sale of the land is long-term capital gain and the $20,000 loss from the sale of the tools is treated as a long-term capital loss. Carla's $70,000 of long-term capital gain ($30,000 from the sale of section 1231 property and $40,000 from the sale of the stock, a capital asset) is netted against the $20,000 of long-term capital loss, so her net capital gain for the year is $50,000.

    c. Carmelita recognizes (i) a $30,000 §1231 gain, (ii) a $20,000 §1231 loss, (iii) a $30,000 long-term capital gain, and (iv) a $50,000 long-term capital loss. Carmelita has a net §1231 gain, so the $30,000 §1231 gain is a long-term capital gain and the $20,000 §1231 loss is a long-term capital loss. Netting the gains and losses, Carmelita is left with a long-term capital loss of $10,000. She can deduct $3,000 of the loss; the remaining $7,000 of loss is carried forward to the next year.

    d. Chuck recognizes (i) a $30,000 §1231 gain, (ii) a $20,000 §1231 loss, (iii) a $50,000 long-term capital loss, and (iv) a $60,000 short-term capital gain. Chuck has a net §1231 gain, so the $30,000 §1231 gain is a long-term capital gain and the $20,000 §1231 loss is a long-term capital loss. Netting the long-term gains and losses, Chuck is left with a long-term capital loss of $40,000. Chuck can deduct the entire $40,000 of long-term capital loss because he recognizes $60,000 of short-term capital gain. The remaining $20,000 of short-term capital gain is taxed at ordinary income rates.

12. a. Jan recognizes $60,000 of gain, which is capital under §1231. None of this gain is subject to depreciation recapture so Jan includes no ordinary income on the sale. Under §1250, capital

gain on real property is subject to recapture only to the extent that the depreciation on the property exceeds straightline depreciation. Since 1986 the only available method by which to depreciate real property is the straightline method. §168(b)(3). Thus, no portion of the gain is subject to recapture.

b. John recognizes $50,000 of gain, which is capital under §1231. However, gain on the sale of tangible physical property such as machinery is subject to recapture in the amount of the lesser of (i) the gain recognized on the sale or (ii) the prior depreciation taken on the property sold. §1245. Here, the total gain recognized is $50,000 and the prior depreciation is $300,000. The lesser of these two figures is $50,000. Thus, all $50,000 of the gain is recaptured as ordinary income. (Another, less mechanical, way to think about the recapture rules is that in this instance the entire gain is due to the reduction in basis caused by accelerated depreciation. The depreciation reduced ordinary income. The taxpayer here must "give back" that reduction in ordinary income by recognizing ordinary income on the sale of the property.)

c. Jen recognizes $60,000 of gain, which is capital under §1231. However, gain is recaptured as ordinary income to the extent of prior depreciation. Here, prior depreciation was $50,000, so $50,000 of gain is ordinary income. The remaining $10,000 of gain is still capital.

d. Jim recognizes $15,000 of gain, which is capital under §1231. Copyrights do not have an indefinite life but instead are valid for a fixed number of years. The value of a copyright thus declines (to zero) as it reaches its expiration date. Holders of a copyright can deduct this form of decline through "amortization" (the form depreciation takes for intangible property). Section 1245 applies to intangible property that has been amortized as well as tangible property that has been depreciated. Here, $10,000 of the $15,000 gain — the portion of the gain equal to prior amortization — is recaptured as ordinary income.

E. Substitutes for Ordinary Income

Capital gain and losses are recognized only on the "sale or exchange" of "capital assets," and, as noted above, capital assets are defined in part as "*property* held by the taxpayer." (italics added) In most cases, whether a transaction involves a sale or exchange of property will be self-evident. In some cases, however, whether a transaction is best characterized as a sale of property (generating capital gain) or the collection of rents, dividends, or salary (generating ordinary income) will be unclear.

Consider, for example, the executive who "sells" her right to the next two dividends payable on stock she owns. The right to collect dividends has value, can be legally sold, and may well constitute a property interest under state law. Perhaps the transaction should be treated as a sale of property; if so, because the "property" does not fall within any of the enumerated exceptions to capital asset treatment, any profit will constitute capital gain. On the other hand, had the executive simply collected dividends in the ordinary course of events, the proceeds would have been taxed as ordinary income. A decision in favor of capital gain in this case would encourage other taxpayers to undertake the same kind of artificial and (once commissions and the like are taken into account) expensive transaction. Dividends would then produce (through anticipatory sales) capital gain rather than ordinary income — a step that seems out of character with legislative intent and common understanding.

Consistent with the intuition expressed in the last paragraph, courts have ruled that transactions such as the one described do not involve "sales" of "property" and therefore do not generate capital gain or loss. Although the stated rationale for the holdings in these cases is murky, the rule the courts have fashioned may be best expressed as follows: For tax purposes, the sale of the right to income from property, for a limited period of time, by a taxpayer who holds the rights to the income from the property thereafter (i) does not constitute a sale or exchange of property, (ii) does not generate capital gain or loss, and (iii) does not allow the taxpayer to offset her basis in the property against the amount received. A temporal interest sold by one who owns the reversionary interest is often referred to as a vertical or "carved-out" interest. Examples of carved-out interests include next year's interest on a bond when sold by one who holds the right to the succeeding years' interest and a building owner's sale of the right to next month's rent.

The careful student may note that carved-out interests were defined earlier, in Chapter 7 of this book. There we were concerned with taxpayers' attempts to shift income to low bracket family members. We noted that income from property could be shifted by transferring ownership of the property. We then posed a similar question: Does a taxpayer who owns an apartment building have a separable property right (for tax purposes) in the right to next month's rental income? If so, the taxpayer could avoid recognizing that income by assigning the right to a low bracket family member. We concluded that, for purposes of income shifting, such a carved-out interest is not treated as property. Income from a carved-out interest is recognized by the taxpayer who assigns that interest. Here, we are interested in the definition of property for purposes of determining whether the taxpayer has capital gain rather than for purposes of determining income attribution, but the answer is the same: For tax purposes, a carved-out interest is not treated as a separate property right. Taxpayers cannot avoid an income inclusion by assigning that interest and cannot convert ordinary income into capital gain by selling that interest.

For example, in Hort v. Commissioner, 313 U.S. 28 (1941), a $140,000 payment received by a *lessor* from a lessee to cancel a lease on commercial property that the lessor continued to own was ordinary income, not capital gain. (The lessor was also not allowed to reduce the $140,000 amount received by any of his basis in the property.) The Court viewed the lease cancellation payment as advance rent; since rent would have been ordinary income, the Court concluded that the lease cancellation payment should also be ordinary income. The lease cancellation payment received by the lessor was for a carved-out interest because the lessor continued to own the lease property. However, note that a lease cancellation payment received by a *lessee* (for example, because the lessor can rent the property at a higher rent) is treated as the sale or exchange of a property interest, so may be capital (either by way of §1221 or §1231); since the payment made to the lessee is for the lessee's entire interest in the leased property, the payment is not received for a carved-out interest. §1241; Commissioner v. McCue Brothers & Drummond, Inc., 210 F.2d 752 (2d Cir. 1954).

In another carved-out interest case, Commissioner v. P.G. Lake, 356 U.S. 260 (1958), the taxpayer assigned to a creditor around $600,000 of oil payments from a working interest owned by the taxpayer. As the parties anticipated, the $600,000 amount was paid over about a three-year period. The Court held that the assignment of the oil payments was not a sale of a capital asset, but was instead ordinary income.

There is another broad category of potential sales that, by virtue of both §1221 and a uniform set of court decisions, does not generate capital gain (or loss). This category consists of sales of what otherwise would be treated as salary or personal service income. Suppose that a taxpayer sells the right to her entire career earnings. While the sale does not fall within any statutory exclusions from capital asset treatment, there is little doubt that a court would rule that the proceeds are ordinary income, and that such a ruling would be consistent with settled understanding and legislative intent.

Attempts by taxpayers to recognize capital gain on less ambitious sales of salary income would also run afoul of the rule governing carved-out interests and various provisions of §1221. For example, the sale of a not-yet-received paycheck for work already performed would generate ordinary income due to §1221(4), which excepts accounts receivable from the capital asset definition. The sale of the right to next month's paycheck is a sale of a carved-out interest and would for that reason generate ordinary income. Copyrights and artistic works held by the person who created such property (or a donee given the property by its creator) are denied capital asset treatment due to §1221(3).

The rule against recognizing capital gain from personal services is not altogether complete. A taxpayer who toils for years to build up the value of his solely owned corporation recognizes capital gain when he sells the stock of that corporation; the same treatment is accorded a taxpayer who sells the goodwill inherent in her non-corporate enterprise.

Section 1235 provides that the transfer of "all substantial rights" to a patent generates capital gain (or loss) to its creator. A taxpayer who is not related to or the employer of the creator of the patent and acquires rights to a patent prior to its reduction to practice may treat amounts received on the sale of the patent as capital gain. §1235. Capital gain (or loss) is the order of the day even if the payments are made over a period of years and are contingent upon the use or productivity of the assigned patent. Other provisions that allow capital asset or §1231 treatment on assets that might otherwise generate ordinary income or loss include §631(a) and (b) (§1231 characterization of certain timber sales) and §631(c) (same for qualifying sales of coal and iron ore).

In some cases, it may be difficult to tell whether a taxpayer has sold salary income or "property." In Commissioner v. Ferrer, 304 F.2d 125 (2d Cir. 1962), the actor José Ferrer entered into an agreement with LaMure, who wrote a book and a play about the artist Toulouse-Lautrec. Ferrer's rights under the agreement included (i) the right to produce the play, (ii) the right to block a movie based on the book until the play was no longer running, and (iii) the right to share in amounts LaMure might receive from a movie based on the book.

LaMure nominally retained all rights in the book and play, except the right to produce the play. John Huston then decided that he wanted to make a movie of the book, so he entered into an agreement with both LaMure and Ferrer. Pursuant to the agreement between Huston and Ferrer, (i) Ferrer was to play the starring role in the movie, in exchange for a salary and (ii) Ferrer assigned the rights he acquired in his agreement with LaMure in exchange for a percentage interest in the movie. The issue in the case was whether the percentage amounts received by Ferrer were ordinary income or capital gain. Ferrer argued, and the Tax Court agreed, that such amounts were received in exchange for the assignment of the dramatic production contract between Ferrer and LaMure, so were capital gain, not ordinary income from personal services.

The Court of Appeals examined each of the contract rights separately. Analogizing to a payment received by a lessee for lease cancellation, the court concluded that amounts Ferrer received for the assignment of the right to produce the play was capital gain. Similarly, the amounts received for the assignment of the right to block a movie were capital gain because they were like a payment received by a lessee to cancel an agreement between the lessee and lessor that would have prevented the lessor from renting adjacent space to the lessee's competitor. However, in the court's view, the right to share in LaMure's movie earnings was not property (since LaMure retained almost all of the rights to the book and play), and the amount Ferrer received for the assignment of the right was an ordinary income substitute, so the court held that the amounts received for assignment of this contract right were ordinary. It is not clear why the court fragmented the rights Ferrer acquired in his contract with LaMure. However, since Huston would probably not have entered into the assignment agreement had Ferrer not starred in the movie, the court may have fragmented the payments because it viewed part of the percentage payments as compensation for Ferrer's personal services.

EXAMPLES

13. Discuss the characterization of the gain or loss recognized in the following transactions.

   a. Attorney Amy agrees to represent Don in a tort suit. In return, Don agrees to pay Amy one-third of any proceeds realized from the suit or settlement of the suit. Shortly before the suit is to come to trial, but after she has done considerable work on the case, Amy receives and accepts an offer to work at a law firm in another state. With Don's approval, Amy sells her right to any share of the contingency award to Dale, an attorney who agrees to carry the case to trial, in exchange for $30,000.

b. Amy also sells to Dale her right to accounts receivable due from other clients for whom she has worked on an hourly, rather than contingency fee, basis.

14. Discuss the characterization of the income or loss recognized in the following sales:

a. Sam owns four large office buildings, which he leases to various commercial tenants. One such tenant is Bank Inc., which has signed a 15-year lease with Sam. Rents have fallen since the lease was signed, so in retrospect the deal looks good to Sam and bad to Bank Inc. Sam sells his right to collect rent under the lease to an unrelated third party for $500,000.

b. Assume the same facts as in part (a), above, except that, instead of selling its right to collect rent under the lease, Sam agrees to cancel the lease. In exchange for that agreement, Bank Inc. vacates the premises and pays Sam $100,000. Sam then leases the property at a somewhat lower rent.

c. Sam enters into a long-term lease with another commercial tenant, Insurance Company, in a different building in a different city. Rents rise dramatically after this lease is signed. In effect, the lease gives Insurance Company the right to premises at below-market rent. The lease is assignable and, two years after signing the lease, Insurance Company assigns its rights and obligations under the lease to an unrelated third party, the law firm of Wagner and Metro. In exchange, the law firm pays Insurance Company $140,000. As part of that assignment, Insurance Company vacates the premises and the law firm moves in and pays the (below-market) monthly rent due under the lease.

15. State whether each of the following sales generates capital gain, §1231 gain, or ordinary income.

a. Inventor Aaron sells all rights to his patent for $1 million cash. Aaron's basis for the patent was $30,000.

b. Inventor Bonnie transfers all rights to her patent for golf balls in exchange for an amount equal to 5 percent of annual sales of the golf balls for the next 10 years.

c. Composer Conrad transfers all rights to a musical composition he has created in exchange for $100,000.

    d. Composer Deborah transfers all rights to a musical composition she has created in exchange for an amount that depends on the number of sales and radio play the song generates.

    e. Famous pop composer Star purchases the copyright to a Beatles tune for $100,000 and later sells all rights to that composition for $250,000.

EXPLANATIONS

13. a. The $30,000 will be treated as ordinary income. Under state law, the contingency fee may well constitute a property interest. For tax purposes, however, the sale of a right to what otherwise would constitute salary or personal service income, even salary or income that has already been earned, is not treated as a sale of a capital asset. There are a few exceptions to this rule (for example, inventors may receive capital gain on the sale of patent rights) but this is not one of them. Note that since Amy has retained the right to later streams of income generated by her legal career, the right sold could also be characterized as a "carved-out" interest and for that reason produce ordinary income rather than capital gain. Finally, capital asset treatment might be denied under §1221(4), discussed in the text and in part (b), below, under the rational that the contingent fee interest is a(n) (odd) form of account receivable.

    b. The proceeds constitute ordinary income by virtue of §1221(4), which excludes accounts receivable from the capital asset definition.

14. a. Sam has sold his right to collect rent for the next 15 years but retained his rights to relet the property after 15 years and keep the rent. Since he has kept a remainder interest in the building, the rights sold constitute a "carved-out" interest. Sale of a carved-out interest produces ordinary income, not capital gain. Hort v. Commissioner, 313 U.S. 28 (1941); Commissioner v. P.G. Lake, Inc., 356 U.S. 260 (1958).

    b. The result is the same as in part (a). Sam has in effect sold his right to collect above-market rents for the following 15 years. Since he has kept a remainder interest in the building, the property sold is a carved-out interest. The proceeds are ordinary income rather than capital gain.

    c. In this example, the taxpayer, Insurance Company, has no remainder interest in the property sold. As a result, the sale is treated as a sale of property and generates capital gain. (The leasehold presumably constitutes "real . . . property held for productive use in a trade or business" and therefore qualifies as "section 1231 property," net gain on the sale of which constitutes capital gain.) See Rev. Rul. 72-85, 1972-1 C.B. 234.

15. a. Section 1235 provides that a sale of all substantial rights to a patent, or an undivided interest therein, shall be treated as a sale of a capital asset. Aaron therefore recognizes $970,000 of capital gain.

b. Bonnie, too, recognizes capital gain on the sale of her patent. The fact that the sale price is contingent upon the successful marketing of the patented product is immaterial. (Note that under the complex rules governing contingent installment sales, some portion of payments received in later years will be treated as interest income.)

c. The $100,000 is ordinary income. Section 1221(3) expressly excludes copyrights and similar artistic property sold by the creator of the copyright or property from the capital asset definition.

d. The amounts that Deborah will receive are ordinary income. §1221(2).

e. The composition does not fall within the §1221(2) copyright exception to the definition of a capital asset because it is not sold by its creator. The asset is thus probably a §1231 asset, so the $150,000 of gain ($250,000 amount realized less $100,000 basis) is capital.

F. The Sale of a Business

Reading: §1060

We noted above that stock is a capital asset in the hands of taxpayers other than brokerage houses and other dealers. The sale of the stock of an incorporated business thus generates capital gain or loss; with one prominent exception,[4] the fact that some portion of the rise (or fall) in

---

4. Under the complicated rules of §341, gain recognized from the sale of stock of a corporation by a shareholder who owns more than 5 percent of the stock in such corporation may in some limited circumstances generate ordinary income, rather than capital gain. Even a brief discussion of this section is beyond the scope of an introductory tax course.

the value of the business may be due to the appreciation (or depreciation) of inventory or other noncapital assets is irrelevant. In other words, the sale of the stock is not treated as a sale of the assets owned by the corporation.

Suppose, however, that a taxpayer operates a business as a sole proprietorship and holds the assets of the business in her own name. The taxpayer then sells all of those assets in a sale of the business to an unrelated party. The assets consist of some capital assets (such as goodwill), some §1231 assets (such as the building in which the business is conducted), and some noncapital assets such as inventory. Consistency would seem to require that this sale be treated like the sale of stock of an incorporated business. If so, the gain or loss would be capital.

In fact, the sale of an unincorporated business is treated as the sale of each of the individual assets of the business, some of which are capital assets and some of which are not. Williams v. McGowan, 152 F.2d 570 (2d Cir. 1945). The purchase price for the business is allocated among the assets of the business based on the classification of the assets and their fair market value. §§1060, 338(b)(5); Temp. Reg. §1.338(b)-2T. The seller then computes the amount of gain or loss on each asset and the character of the gain or loss. For example, the seller might recognize long-term capital gain on the sale of one asset, and an ordinary loss on the sale of another asset.

EXAMPLES

16. Roger Wagner is a California-based concert promoter who specializes in rock and jazz groups appealing to a young audience. Roger rents arenas and other venues in California and the Pacific Northwest, books groups in those arenas, subcontracts out the concessions (beer, soft drinks, and so forth), advertises, and employs security personnel at the concerts. Roger splits ticket sales with the performing artists; his profit is the excess of his share of those sales over the costs involved. Roger has 40 or so full-time employees and hundreds of part-time employees.

   Roger also has two children and is frustrated at the small selection and high prices of most children's clothing stores. Roger decides to sponsor a series of "Kidfests" at exhibition halls in leading cities throughout the nation. The Kidfests will feature hundreds of merchants selling children's clothes and toys — ostensibly at a discount from prices found in stores. The Kidfests will offer live entertainment — saccharine performers who sing about whales, frogs, and ducks. Over the next 14 months, Roger spends hundreds of hours of his and his employees' time planning the Kidfests and spends over $250,000 in advance payments to auditoriums, baseball stadiums, newspapers, and radio stations in order to secure facilities and advertising. A month before the first Kidfest, Roger sells his rights in the events to a promoter of trade shows for $450,000, for a profit (ignoring the value of his and his employees' time) of $200,000.

Is the $200,000 profit ordinary income? Argue the question from the perspectives of both Roger and the government. State any additional facts that might affect those arguments.

17. Donna H. is the sole owner of a bicycle shop. The shop is organized for tax purposes as a sole proprietorship rather than a corporation, so Donna owns all of the assets in her own name and all of the income is taxed at Donna's individual rate. Donna sells the shop for $240,000 in year five. The purchase price is allocated as follows:

Land on which shop is located	$50,000
Building in which shop is located	40,000
Inventory	60,000
Equipment	20,000
Goodwill	70,000

Donna's basis for each of the above-listed assets is as follows:

Land	$10,000
Building	35,000
Inventory	65,000
Equipment	5,000
Goodwill	0

Donna paid $40,000 for the building in year one and has since taken $5,000 of depreciation on the structure. Donna paid $30,000 for the equipment in year four but has depreciated the equipment so that her current basis for it is $5,000. Donna has no other sales or exchanges in the year in which she sells her bicycle shop. Discuss the tax consequences of the sale.

EXPLANATIONS

16. Roger will argue that he has, in effect, sold all of the assets of a separate business — the business of promoting one or more Kidfests. Under case law and established practice, the sale of an unincorporated business is treated as the sale of the assets of a business, so it makes no difference, as a formal matter, if Roger's argument is framed in terms of a sale of a business or a sale of assets. In either event, if the argument is successful, the treatment of the gain will be determined on an asset-by-asset basis. The hypothetical does not tell us, specifically, what particular assets Roger has sold. Presumably, the major asset sold is simply Roger's right to profit from at least the first Kidfest, a right that stems from Roger's advertising and contractual arrangements with arenas and the like. Roger can argue that none of these rights fall into any statutory or judicially created exceptions to capital asset treatment and that the gain is therefore capital gain.

    The Service is likely to characterize the transaction as the sale of the right to ordinary income from Roger's continuing business as a promoter. Since Roger retains a reversionary interest in that business — that is, he retains the rights to income from promoting later events — the right sold is a carved-out interest. For tax purposes, that right is not treated as a property right that generates capital gain. The Service may argue that, if the gain is characterized as capital, Roger would continue to promote events, and then sell out his rights immediately before each event at a profit and claim that any gain is capital. (Of course, at some point a court could rule out capital gain on the grounds that "events" were a form of inventory to Roger.)

    The Service might also argue that the assets sold are noncapital because they are the product of personal services or because a sale so close to the income-generating event is in effect a sale of accounts receivables. These arguments seem weaker than the first argument stated above. (There is also some old authority denying capital gain treatment for the sale of "mere contract rights." The rationale of these cases is fuzzy, however, and at this point we are getting to a level of detail that exceeds what even the most diligent law student should be expected to know.)

    Is the Kidfest a separate business? Roger's argument in favor of this proposition is supported by the new location of the Kidfests and by the new nature of this event. His argument would be enhanced even further if he could argue that Kidfest promotion requires a different set of skills and contacts than concert promotion and that his income in past years has been exclusively from concert promotion. The hypothetical does not state the reason for the sale. Roger's argument that the Kidfests were unrelated to his main occupation would be strengthened if he could present evidence that the rights were sold because he and his organization felt they were getting into an unfamiliar area.

17. The sale of an unincorporated business is treated as the sale of the individual assets. Williams v. McGowan, 152 F.2d 570 (2d Cir. 1945). As a result, some assets may produce capital gain or loss, while other assets may produce ordinary income or loss.

   The equipment is a depreciable asset used in a trade or business and might for that reason be expected to produce §1231 gain or loss. However, the $15,000 of gain from the sale of the equipment is subject to the recapture provisions. Under those provisions, capital gain is converted into ordinary income to the extent of prior depreciation taken on the property. Here, the $15,000 of gain is less than the $25,000 of prior depreciation taken on the equipment, so the recapture amount is $15,000 and Donna must include $15,000 of ordinary income from the sale of the equipment.

   The building and land are also section 1231 property (real or depreciable property used in a trade or business). Gain on real property is subject to recapture only to the extent it has been depreciated on an accelerated, rather than straightline method. Real property placed in service subsequent to 1986 is depreciable only on the straightline method, so recapture will not apply to the sale of the depreciated building. §§1250, 168(b)(3). Land is not depreciable so the issue of recapture does not arise. Thus, the entire $45,000 gain on the sale of the land and building is §1231 gain. Because Donna has no other §1231 gains and losses, the gain is long-term capital gain.

   Inventory is a noncapital asset by virtue of §1221(1). Donna has a $5,000 ordinary loss on the sale of the inventory.

   Goodwill (attributable to the shop's reputation) is a capital asset. Donna recognizes $70,000 of capital gain on the sale of the goodwill.

   Thus, Donna has (i) a $5,000 ordinary loss (on inventory), (ii) a $15,000 ordinary gain (on the equipment, through recapture), and (iii) long-term capital gain of $115,000 (from the building, land, and goodwill).

G.   Connected Current and Prior Transactions

The depreciation recapture rules discussed earlier in this chapter enforce a type of characterization symmetry; since the prior depreciation deductions were ordinary deductions, gain on the sale of the depreciable asset should be ordinary to the extent of the prior depreciation taken on the property. In other situations in which no Code section requires characterization symmetry, courts may impose a judicially created symmetry rule. For example, in Arrowsmith v. Commissioner, 344 U.S. 6 (1952), the taxpayer recognized capital gain on stock when the corporation was liquidated. Four years later, the taxpayer was required to pay a liability of the liquidated corporation and took an ordinary deduction for the payment. However, the Service argued, and the Supreme Court agreed that, despite the absence of a sale or exchange in the year in which the payment was made, the payment made by the taxpayer was characterized as a capital loss because it was connected to the capital gain transaction in the earlier year. The court was of the view that its holding on the characterization issue was not inconsistent with the annual accounting period.

Appendix
Sample Examinations

Introductory Note

This appendix includes seven sample final examinations given in the basic federal income tax class by tax professors from five different law schools. Model answers supplied by the professor follow each exam. (Don't peek at the answers until you take the exam!)

As you will see from these sample examinations, tax professors vary in their approach to examinations. Some professors emphasize policy issues; other professors emphasize technical tax issues. Some professors expect precise answers to their exam questions; other professors are looking for more general answers. Some professors expect students to support their answers by referring to specific Code sections and cases; other professors do not expect students to cite many sources.

Note that some of the model answers are much more detailed than the answers you could write under the time constraints of an exam. Other model answers are brief and approximate the type of answer you would be able to write. A few of the model answers simply sketch the type of answer expected and are briefer than the answer you might be able to write.

We should warn you that these exams include a few idiosyncratic questions on special topics that are not usually covered in the basic tax course and are not discussed in this book. The model answers also include a few citations to cases that were not discussed in this book. However, you should be able to answer almost all of the questions in these sample exams. We have included the professor's instructions for each exam so that you can tell which kinds of materials the professor intended for students to be able to use during the exam.

Good luck!

Final Examination Number One
Professor Blatt
University of Miami School of Law

Instructions

1. This is a closed book examination. You may bring only pens and a calculator. The proctor will give you an appendix with relevant provisions from the Internal Revenue Code. If a relevant provision is missing, explain how it would affect your answer.

2. The exam consists of three parts. You have three hours to complete the exam. I include my estimate of the time required to complete each question.

3. Explain the reasoning behind your answers fully but concisely. State and assume additional facts if needed to answer a question. If appropriate, discuss alternative positions and results. Organize your answers. Feel free to use abbreviations and incomplete sentences.

4. Unless otherwise stated, assume that (i) parties are unrelated, (ii) taxpayers have adopted the calendar year, (iii) corporations report income on the accrual basis, (iv) debt instruments periodically pay market rate interest, and (v) individuals report income on the cash basis.

Appendix

Part I *(60 minutes, allocate as needed over six questions)*

Question 1. Jack and Jill have two children and a taxable income of $40,000. Jack's employer makes available to them $4,000 through a dependent care assistance program. Should they forgo the exclusion under §129?

Question 2. Evaluate the best arguments for and against the deduction for contributions to charity.

Question 3. In 1985, Allen purchased a detached house on a two-acre lot in South Dade for $100,000. In 1988, Allen built an addition to the house at a cost of $50,000. Immediately prior to Hurricane Andrew, the house had a fair market value of $250,000. During Hurricane Andrew, the house was destroyed, leaving a two-acre lot with a fair market value of $75,000. In 1992, Allen received $100,000 in insurance proceeds for the damage to the house. What are the federal income tax consequences to Allen in 1992?

Question 4. Fred owns land with a basis of $200,000. He discovers oil and sells the land to Oil Company for five annual payments equal to $100,000 plus 10 percent of production. The total payments made in each year are as follows:

Year 1	$150,000
Year 2	$150,000
Year 3	$150,000
Year 4	$100,000
Year 5	$100,000

Assume that this transaction is treated as a sale for tax purposes and ignore special rules governing production rights and depletion. How is gain from the sale taxed under the rules governing open transactions, closed transactions, and installment sales?

Question 5. In year one, Hanna is a full-time student in the Stanford University MBA program. She pays $15,000 in tuition each year, and $10,000 for room and board. Prior to entering business school, she earned $50,000 per year as an assistant manager for Chase Manhattan Bank. She does not know what she will do after earning her MBA. How is Hanna taxed in year one under present law? How should she be taxed? How would she be taxed under a consumption tax?

Question 6. Mark is negotiating salaries with two prospective employers: an accrual method for-profit corporation and a tax-exempt charity. Assuming that each is willing to pay the same present value salary, which employer can offer Mark the highest nonqualified deferred compensation? Why?

Part II (60 minutes, 20 minutes per question)

Question 1. Peter works as a lawyer for Miami Legal Services. He purchases the following items: a photograph of Port-au-Prince, which he hangs in his office to make his predominately Haitian clients feel comfortable; a special chair that prevents backaches; a laptop computer, used exclusively for work; and a $50 Christmas gift to his secretary.

How do the expenditures affect Peter's tax liability? Would the items be excluded from Peter's income if Miami Legal Services reimbursed him for them?

Question 2. Richard owns Blackacre, with a fair market value of $4,000, a basis of $1,500, and which is subject to a mortgage of $1,200. Sarah owns Whiteacre, with a fair market value of $2,000 and a basis of $400 and a car with a basis of $400 and a fair market value of $800. Blackacre, Whiteacre, and the car are held for productive use in a trade or business. In a transaction that qualifies under §1031, Richard trades his house (subject to the mortgage) for Sarah's house and car. What are the tax consequences to Richard and Sarah?

Question 3. Betty and Carl are getting divorced. Betty is a songwriter and expects to earn $300,000 per year for the foreseeable future. Carl's expected earnings are $20,000 per year.

Carl will have custody of their nine-year-old child, David. Betty wants to provide for David's college. She is considering transferring to David the following: (i) stock that will pay annual dividends and be sold during David's college years, (ii) the copyright to one of her songs, already licensed and entitled to royalties, and (iii) cash that David would invest and later repay her without interest. What are the tax consequences of each arrangement?

Part III (60 minutes, 30 minutes per question)

Question 1. Tycoon hates paying taxes. His current income is $200,000, half of which is interest on taxable bonds, the other half of which is from a trade or business in which he does not materially participate. To eliminate his taxes, Tycoon concocts the following scheme. First, he converts half his portfolio from taxable to tax-exempt bonds. Next, he purchases a suburban mall for $10,000 and a $10 million nonrecourse note that requires payment of interest only for the first 20 years. He then leases the mall back to the original owner for a rent roughly equal to his interest payments on the note. The projected interest and depreciation deductions from the mall will offset his remaining $100,000 of income. What problems do you foresee for Tycoon's plan?

Question 2. How well does the present law definition of capital asset implement the policies behind the special treatment of capital gains and losses? Be specific.

END OF EXAMINATION

Model Answers

Part I

Answer 1. No. The §21 child care credit reduces their taxes by 20 percent of $4,000. The value of the exclusion to them is 28 percent of $4,000.

Answer 2. The income measurement argument for the deduction is that it reflects reduced wealth. An argument contra is that the donation represents consumption.

The subsidy argument for deduction views charities as performing decentralized governmental functions. Critics of the subsidy might prefer greater oversight and challenge its use for religious purposes. In addition, in a progressive system the deduction operates as an upside-down subsidy, giving the greatest benefit to persons in the highest brackets.

Answer 3. Allen's basis in the house is $150,000. In the absence of insurance his loss would be $75,000 ($150,000 − $75,000). After the receipt of the insurance proceeds, Allen has a $25,000 gain ($100,000 − $75,000). Because his entire loss is compensated by insurance, he is not entitled to a §165 casualty loss. The gain is taxed unless converted into similar property. §1033.

Answer 4. Under the open transaction approach, Fred would recover his basis first. He would have no gain in year one, $100,000 of gain in year two, and the remaining payments would all be gain.

Under the closed transaction approach, Fred would be taxed immediately on the present value of the obligation. His basis would be applied against payments made under the contract.

Under the installment sale approach, Fred would have proportional recovery of basis. Since this instrument is contingent as to the amount but fixed as to the five-year time period, his basis would be allocated $40,000 per year. Treas. Reg. §15A.453-1(c)(3).

Answer 5. Under present law, Hanna has no income or deductions in year one. Her room and board are nondeductible personal expenses. Her educational expenses are not deductible because she is changing professions.

One might argue that (i) she has imputed income for her own work toward the degree, (ii) her imputed and actual costs of obtaining the degree should be deductible, and (iii) these costs should be capitalized because they produce an asset with a useful life exceeding one year.

Under a consumption tax, she would be taxed on her room and board. Amounts spent acquiring the business degree would be deductible if deemed to be investment.

Answer 6. The answer depends on whether the employer will be taxed on the earnings on the deferred payment. Under general principles, the accrual method corporation would not be currently taxed on earnings because it would be able to deduct those earnings when the right to deferred compensation accrued. Section 404(a)(5), however, defers the deduction until the year in which the employee includes the amount in income. The tax-exempt charity can invest the deferred compensation tax free and thus can offer Mark higher deferred compensation.

Part II

Answer 1. Absent other statutory provisions, these expenses are ordinary trade or business deductions under §162(a). The photograph is probably a deductible business expense. Although *Henderson* ruled that a district attorney could not deduct office decorations, Peter has clients, albeit nonpaying ones. The chair may also qualify as a medical deduction (subject to the 7.5 percent floor), although one may question whether it is incurred for the "cure, mitigation, treatment, or prevention of disease." §213(d)(1)(A). Deduction for the computer is probably disallowed under §280F, since there is no evidence that it is "for the convenience of the employer and required as a condition of employment." §280F(d)(3)(A). The gift is deductible only to the extent of $25. §274(b)(1). As assets with a useful life of more than one year, the photograph and chair would ordinarily have to be depreciated, but might qualify for immediate expensing under §179.

The effect of reimbursement: These items would be excludible as working condition fringes to the extent that they would be deductible under §162. §132(d). The laptop computer would likely still be subject to §280F as it is unlikely to be used "exclusively" at the establishment. §280F(d)(4)(B). In addition, the items may be excludible as de minimis fringes. §132(e).

Answer 2. Richard: Richard's amount received is $4,000 ($2,000 Whiteacre plus $1,200 liability plus $800 car). His basis is $1,500. Thus, his realized gain is $2,500. Richard recognizes gain to the extent of the $2,000 of boot received ($800 car plus $1,200 liability assumed). Richard's basis in the car is $800, its fair market value. His basis in the house is $1,500 ($1,500 original basis plus $2,000 gain recognized less $2,000 boot received).

Sarah: Sarah's amount realized on the car is $800, its fair market value. Her basis is $400. Thus, her realized gain is $400. She recognizes the entire gain because the car is not like-kind property. Sarah's amount realized on Whiteacre is its fair market value, $2,000. Her basis in the land is $400. Thus, she realizes a gain of $1,600. Sarah recognizes the gain to the extent of boot received, which here is none. Her basis in the house is $2,400, which is her $400 original basis plus $1,200 liability assumed plus the $800 amount she paid (the car).

Answer 3.   Dividends on the stock are potentially taxed at Carl's marginal rate. §1(g). The proceeds from the stock sale will be taxed at David's capital gain rate, since he will have reached age 14 by the time of the sale. *Heim* suggests that the assignment of the copyright would be respected for tax purposes. Thus, royalties would be taxed to David, but at Carl's top rate. §1(g). Betty will be treated as receiving annual interest on the loan equal to the applicable federal rate. §7872.

Part III

Answer 1.   The interest deduction may be disallowed if the debt is used to "purchase or carry" the exempt bonds. §265(a)(2).

The at risk rules probably do not apply because the note appears to be qualified nonrecourse financing. The passive loss rules do not prevent the offset because both the income and the depreciation are from passive activities.

However, the transaction might be attacked as a sham under *Knetsch.*

The transaction also resembles *Estate of Franklin.* Under the Tax Court's theory in that case, Tycoon would be treated as holding an option. Under the Court of Appeals approach in that case, the debt would be disregarded, eliminating his interest and depreciation deductions.

The minimum tax may be a problem if the bonds are private activity bonds. Although the minimum tax affects ACRS, it does not affect the straightline depreciation for real estate.

Answer 2.   The policies for preferential treatment of capital gains include income measurement (alleviation of bunching and inflation) and economic effect (relief from lock-in and creation of business incentives). The policies for disallowing capital losses include the prevention of paper transactions, cherry picking, and straddles. After describing these policies, an answer would then consider whether they applied in particular situations, such as:

(i)   Stock in trade (trading in stock versus trading in real estate);
(ii) Transactions related to the taxpayer's regular business (*Corn Products* and *Arkansas Best*);
(iii) Bootstrap sales (*Clay Brown*);
(iv) Copyrights and patents (distinction between creators of patents, who are treated as creating a capital asset, and creators of copyrights, who are not treated as creating a capital asset);
(v)   Substitutes for ordinary income (carved out interests); and
(vi) Property used in a trade or business, governed by §1231.

For example, one might justify the stock in trade exception as excluding assets that are unlikely to raise bunching, inflation, or lock-in problems, and do not represent the long-term investments suitable for business investment. It may also be that the expected turnover of these assets makes them unlikely vehicles for loss transactions. The special treatment afforded stock under this exception reflects the ease with which stock can be used in loss transactions.

Final Examination Number Two
Professor Fried
Stanford University School of Law

Instructions

1. Except where otherwise stated, you should assume that all taxpayers are on the cash method of accounting and that all taxpayers report on a calendar year. Any expenses for depreciation of real property should be handled using straightline depreciation over a 10-year life. Any expenses for depreciation of tangible personal property should be handled using straightline depreciation over a five-year life. With respect to tangible personal property, you should assume that the recapture rules of §1245 apply. For all depreciable property, depreciation for the first year of service should be prorated on a daily basis from the date the property is placed in service. Ignore the alternative minimum tax.

2. This examination consists of six (6) questions. You have three and one-half hours to spend on the examination. The suggested time allotted to each of the parts reflects the proportional weight that will be given to your answers.

3. Please write legibly. Any words that I cannot decipher with moderate heroics I will (by necessity) have to disregard.

4. This examination is open book. You may refer to any written material you wish.

5. In answering each question, please be as concise and precise as possible. If you provide numerical answers to any question, make sure you show how the relevant numbers were derived.

6. Although many of the problems posed have clear answers under current law, some do not. If some of the facts necessary to resolve the question are omitted or uncertain, state what those facts are, and what different results will obtain depending on which factual assumptions turn out to be correct.

Appendix

Question 1. (20 minutes) Wendy is a resident dorm adviser at a Stanford undergraduate dorm. As part of her job, she is required to live in the dorm and eat at least one meal a day with the students in the dorm. At no charge to Wendy, Stanford provides Wendy and her domestic partner, Ann, with a four-room apartment in the dorm and gives both of them the right to eat up to three meals a day in the dorm. In addition, Stanford provides Wendy and Ann with free use of the university's athletic facilities and library and the right to buy tickets to University events at a 30 percent discount. In addition, Stanford pays one-half of Wendy's and Ann's medical insurance, at a cost to Stanford of $100 a month for each of them. Which if any of these benefits are taxable to Wendy or Ann?

Question 2. (20 minutes) On January 1, year one, Martha bought an office building in downtown Palo Alto for $150,000 in cash to use as a commercial rental property. At the time of purchase, the building was assessed at $100,000 and the land at $50,000. For the next five years, Martha rented out the building, taking all allowable depreciation deductions on the property. On January 1, year six, when the property was worth $200,000, Martha exchanged it for a vacant lot outside of Fresno worth $150,000, plus $50,000 in cash. The vacant lot was near a site where the state planned to build a new campus for the University of California. Martha planned to develop the land once the campus was built. In year seven, Martha took out a nonrecourse mortgage, secured by the vacant lot, for $50,000. In year eight, California announced it had abandoned its plan for the Fresno campus, and the land became virtually worthless. In year nine, Martha defaulted on the mortgage payments on the loan, and the bank repossessed the land. At the time of repossession, the land was valued at $10,000. What are the tax consequences to Martha in years six through nine of the foregoing events?

Question 3. (30 minutes) Mimi owned 3,000 shares of Corpco stock, which she had purchased at $2 a share in year one. In year 10, when the stock was worth $1 a share, she gave the 3,000 shares to her son, Sam, as a present for his graduation from dental school. In year 12, when the stock was worth $3 a share, Sam gave 1,000 shares to his friend Libby in exchange for Libby's stereo system, which she had bought two years earlier for $4,000; he gave 1,000 shares as a donation to his undergraduate college; and he gave the last 1,000 shares to his dental school classmate Roberto in gratitude for Roberto's having referred a number of patients to Sam to help Sam start up a practice.

What are the tax consequences to Mimi, Sam, Libby, and Roberto from the foregoing events?

Question 4. (30 minutes) In year one, Ben purchased a vineyard in Sonoma for $100,000. In year eight, Ben's upstream neighbor, John, discharged runoff water from his fertilizer processing plant into a stream that ran through Ben's property. The runoff water contained some chemicals that leached into the soil, leaving one-half of Ben's land permanently unfit for cultivation of any sort. Ben filed a tort suit against John for pollution. John's attorney advised John that the chemical discharge did not violate relevant EPA guidelines, and he could probably win the lawsuit. The local agricultural community, however, was among John's biggest clients. In order to avoid any bad publicity within that community, John therefore agreed early in year nine to pay Ben $500,000 in exchange for Ben's dropping all claims against him. Shortly thereafter, John's business hit a downturn, and he never paid Ben anything. Early in year 10, Ben filed a new suit to enforce the settlement agreement. After some negotiations, Ben agreed to accept a $200,000 payment from John in full settlement of John's obligations, which John paid in late year 10. What are the tax consequences to Ben and John of the foregoing events in years eight through 10?

Question 5. (50 minutes) Linda purchased 100 raffle tickets at $1 a ticket for a drawing to benefit the Legal Aid Society. The back of the ticket said that the winner of the raffle would receive a three-day cruise to the Bahamas, with a fair market value of $1,000, and that the Legal Aid Society reserved the right to sell up to 10,000 tickets. By the day of the drawing, the Legal Aid Society had sold only 1,000 tickets.

A week before the drawing, Linda gave all 100 tickets to her full-time childcare person, Jana. One of the tickets ultimately proved to be the winning ticket. Jana went on the cruise. What are the tax consequences to Linda and Jana from the foregoing events?

Question 6. (1 hour) Juan is a lawyer in solo, general practice in San Jose. His clients are mostly small local businesses and individuals of modest means. Juan has a sliding fee scale for his clients, depending upon their financial situation, ranging from $35 an hour to $100 an hour, and generally requires that bills be paid within 30 days of receipt. For clients who cannot afford even the lowest charges, Juan often defers or foregoes payment entirely, or makes other arrangements to accommodate clients' need.

(a) In year one, Alicia's Market, an accrual method taxpayer, retained Juan to defend it in a slip and fall case by a customer. In early October, year one, Juan negotiated a satisfactory settlement on behalf of Alicia's Market and presented Alicia with a bill for $2,000 for work done on the case, payable within 30 days. In late October, Alicia called up Juan and said, "I've got your bill here. I could pay it now if you really want me to, but things are very tight right now, and I'd be grateful if you'd let it ride until early next year." Juan said that was fine, and in February, year two, Alicia sent him a check for $2,000. Early in year three, when Juan's accountants were auditing his books for the previous year, they discovered that Juan's secretary had mistakenly mistranscribed the hours Juan had worked for Alicia's Market, and that Alicia should have been billed $1,500 rather than $2,000. Juan immediately wrote Alicia an apologetic note, explaining what had happened, and enclosed a check for the $500 difference. What are the tax consequences to Juan and Alicia's Market from the foregoing events?

(b) In year one, Juan did about 200 hours of legal work for Betty, in connection with her efforts to buy a restaurant. In lieu of any cash payment, Betty and Juan agreed that Juan would receive a 10 percent interest in the profits of the restaurant for as long as Betty owned it. The restaurant opened in year one, and by year three it became clear to Betty that the restaurant was unlikely to show a profit for a very long time, if ever. Feeling it was unfair not to compensate Juan for his work, in mid-year three, Betty offered to amend their agreement to provide that she would pay Juan $1,000 a year for 10 years, beginning in year four. Juan agreed. What are the tax consequences to Juan of the foregoing events?

END OF EXAMINATION

Appendix

Model Answers

Answer 1. <u>Wendy</u>: As to Wendy, the value of the apartment (at least her allocable share of it — see below) is clearly excluded from income under §119. The apartment meets all of the requirements of §119. The dorm room is on the premises of the employer. It is clearly furnished for the convenience (read necessity) of the employer, as a chief function of a resident dorm adviser is to be *in residence*, and hence available to students at all hours. Although the facts do not explicitly state that Wendy is required to accept the dorm housing as a condition of employment, that seems reasonably implied by the fact that her job is as "*resident* dorm adviser." As to the meals, they also are furnished on the premises of the employer. Unlike lodging, to have meals excluded under §119 employees need not be required to accept meals as a condition of employment. Like lodging, however, the employer must provide meals for its own business necessity. Reg. §1.119-1(a)(2) interprets that requirement to mean that the employer must provide the meals for "a substantial noncompensatory reason." The regulation goes on to state that if "the employee is required to occupy living quarters on the business premises of his employer as a condition of his employment, . . . the exclusion applies to the value of any meal furnished without charge to the employee on premises." That would appear to cover Wendy. Even in the absence of an express provision covering this situation, however, it seems apparent that Stanford has substantial noncompensatory reasons for wishing Wendy to eat in the dorm, so she can fraternize with students. That seems irrefutable as to the one meal a day Stanford *requires* Wendy to eat in the dorm, but almost certainly is the case with respect to the other two as well.

As to free use of the athletic facilities and library: The athletic facilities do not seem to fall within the express exclusion in §132(j)(4). The facilities are on the premises of the employer and are operated by the employer. However, the employees, their spouses and their children do not account for substantially all the use of the facility, given the heavy utilization by students. The provision is probably intended to distinguish between employers that are in the business of selling athletic facilities (for example, private athletic clubs) and those that are not. Technically, Stanford falls in the former category since it "sells" the use of athletic facilities to students as part of the bundled rights they get for their tuition. But clearly it is not Stanford's primary business, and it is doubtful whether the requirement was really intended to apply here. Nevertheless, on its face it does seem to knock out §132(j)(4) here. Happily, this may not matter, as use of the athletic facilities, like the library, is probably excludable under §132(b) (no-additional-cost service). As just noted, Stanford is in the business of providing use of the athletic facilities and libraries for sale to customers (for example, to students and others who purchase day passes) in the ordinary course of business. The requirement that Wendy be in the "line of business" in which the services are provided probably does not present a problem as to either athletic facilities or libraries. In a unitary operation like a university, all services routinely provided to students would probably be considered part of one line of business. (Contrast the case if, for example, Stanford as landlord provided discounts to employees at the Stanford Shopping Center.) Assuming that Wendy is simply using excess capacity in the athletic facilities and libraries (which given the nature of the operations would almost certainly be deemed to be the case), that would meet the requirement that her use impose no additional cost on the university. In the unlikely event that Wendy lost the foregoing argument, she could also seek to exclude these as de minimis fringes. Unfortunately, the benefits are neither small in amount (Stanford charges outsiders a hefty fee, for example, to use the libraries and athletic facilities) nor are they hard to value, given that Stanford has already priced the services for outsiders, and there is (at least in the case of athletic facilities) a well-established market price for private athletic clubs with facilities akin to Stanford's.

As to the right to buy tickets at a 30 percent discount; the value of the discount is excludable if at all under the "qualified employee discount" exception in §132(c). The discount seems to be for services, not property. (While the tickets themselves are in some sense property, they are merely evidencing the right to acquire services, for example, in the form of concerts.) As such, the allowable discount is limited to 20 percent of the normal ticket price. Thus, Wendy will be taxed on 10 of the 30 percent discount provided on any tickets she actually purchases. Does this discount otherwise qualify under §132(c)? Section 132(c)(4) requires that the services be offered for sale in the ordinary course of the line of business of the employer in which the employee is performing services. Although Stanford is not principally in the business of putting on concerts, or athletic events, it clearly seems to satisfy the requirement that it offer tickets to such events for sale in the ordinary course of business. For reasons stated above, it is unlikely the "line of business" requirement will be construed narrowly here to limit it to employees (for example) working in the concert or athletic offices that organize events for which the discount is made available.

Finally, Stanford's contribution to Wendy's medical insurance is clearly excludable under §106.

Ann: First, it should be noted that any benefits provided to Ann that cannot be excluded from income will be taxed to Wendy, not Ann. As Stanford is providing such benefits to Ann because of its employment relationship with Wendy, and as a form of compensation to Wendy, they are treated as part of Wendy's wages. The constructive transfer of such benefits from Wendy to Ann, were they married, would be treated as a form of intrafamily support payment with no tax consequences at all. Since they are not married, the transfer would probably be viewed as a gift (no income tax consequences to either Wendy or Ann, but conceivably gift tax consequences if the amounts were large enough)(cf. Harris).

Which of Ann's benefits will be taxable to Wendy? The use of athletic facilities, libraries, and employee discounts will almost certainly be taxable. The exclusions in §132 for no-additional-cost fringes, qualified employee discounts, and on-premises athletic facilities are limited to employees, their spouses, and their dependent children. For purposes of the Code, "spouse" means anyone to whom a taxpayer is legally married under state law. As no state in the United States currently permits same-sex marriages, Ann and Wendy will not be considered to be married for tax purposes. Ann obviously does not qualify as a "dependent child." Thus, unless Wendy can argue that the portion of the benefits transferred to Ann should be treated as de minimis fringe to Wendy (a doubtful argument, for reasons suggested above), Wendy is in theory taxable on the value of such benefits to Ann. (For valuation, see below.)

As to the lodging, meals, and medical insurance payments: Sections 119 and 106 both extend to spouses and dependents of the employee. Again, Ann cannot qualify as a spouse. Here, however, "dependent" is not limited to dependent children. It includes any individual who is a dependent of the taxpayer for tax purposes under §152. For Ann to qualify, she would have to (among other things) be receiving a substantial amount of her support from Wendy. There are not enough facts provided to know whether Ann would qualify here. If she does not, again they are out of luck: Wendy is taxed on the value of lodging, meals, and medical coverage provided to Ann.

How should the taxable benefits be valued? The general rule is that in-kind benefits should be valued at their fair market value. For the ticket discount and Stanford's contribution to medical insurance, the fair market value is the amount of the discount/contribution. For meals, libraries, and athletic facilities, assuming the latter two are sold separately to outsiders and hence have an established price, fair market value would be equal to that price. That rule may be harsh for Wendy, who might not value them at their full fair market value, but she remains free to decline to accept any benefits if she does not value them at least at the cost of the tax on such benefits. In the case of lodging, however, *if* Stanford would have provided Wendy with a four-room apartment even if she were living alone, then Wendy might well be able to exclude the entire value of the lodging. That is, she would argue that only that portion of incremental housing provided to her only because of Ann's presence should be treated as provided to Ann. Section 119 and the regulations do not explicitly deal with this situation, but common sense suggests it should prevail.

Answer 2. The Palo Alto property is real property used in Martha's trade or business (rental). Hence, the $100,000 of the original $150,000 purchase price allocated to the building is depreciable (under the exam assumptions as to depreciation schedules) straightline over 10 years, leaving an adjusted basis of $50,000 on January 1, year six. The land, which is not depreciable, retains its original cost basis of $50,000. Thus, on January 1, year six, the Palo Alto property has a total adjusted basis of $100,000 in Martha's hands.

Year six. The exchange is a qualified §1031 like-kind exchange. Both the property given up and the property received are real property. Although unlike in many respects, the generous interpretation of "like-kind" for purposes of §1031 would seem to cover even this exchange of a building for undeveloped land. In addition, Martha does not appear to be a dealer in either the property given up or the property received: The one given up was used in a trade or business, and the one received held for investment. Thus, while the change in Martha's economic interests is clearly substantial enough to constitute a realization event under *Macomber* or *Cottage Savings*, she is eligible to defer recognition of a portion of the gain on the exchange under §1031.

Where, as here, like-kind properties of unequal values are exchanged with boot provided to equalize the exchange, §1031 provides that the party receiving boot must recognize any gain (appreciation) in the relinquished property, but only to the extent of boot received. Martha's realized gain on the exchange of the Palo Alto property is $100,000 (fair market value of $200,000 minus an adjusted basis of $100,000). She receives $50,000 of boot (cash). Thus, in year six

Martha must recognize $50,000 of gain. Since the Palo Alto property is §1231 property in Martha's hands (held for use in trade or business), the $50,000 gain would be capital gain.

Under §1031(d), Martha takes a carryover basis in the new property ($100,000 from the old), adjusted upward by the amount of boot received (here, $50,000) and downward by the amount of gain recognized ($50,000). The result: She takes a basis of $100,000 in the land, which has a fair market value of $150,000. This has the effect of preserving for future recognition the $50,000 of the total $100,000 of gain in the Palo Alto property that was realized but not recognized in the exchange pursuant to §1031.

Year seven: Taking out the nonrecourse mortgage has no tax effect for Martha. Loan proceeds are not included in income, since the proceeds are offset by the obligation to repay the loan. The loan also does not increase the basis of the land securing it unless the proceeds of the loan are invested in capital improvements on the land. I will assume for the balance of the question that it was not invested in the land.

Year eight: The only question implicated here is whether Martha can recognize a loss in year eight for the decline in value of the property. The answer is no. To be recognized under §1001, a loss must be "realized" by a closed and completed transaction. In the case of tangible assets, that generally requires a sale or other disposition (including abandonment). A mere decline in value of the property as a result of market forces, where the taxpayer continues to hold such property, would not constitute such a realization event.

Year nine: This scenario poses a *Tufts* problem. Under the nonbifurcated approach adopted by the Court in *Tufts* for property subject to nonrecourse loans, Martha is treated as selling the land to the bank for the outstanding principal amount of the loan. Assuming that Martha has not paid down the principal, that would be the original loan amount, or $50,000. Martha's basis in the land remains $100,000, as land is not depreciable. Result: She recognizes a loss of $50,000 on the repossession. Is it a capital loss or an ordinary income loss? That depends on how we view Martha's investment in the land. The Palo Alto building that she exchanged for the land was a §1231 asset in her hands since she was using it in an active trade or business. As she had not developed the land yet, however, she cannot treat it as a §1231 asset. The only other way to get the loss characterized as ordinary would be if Martha can claim dealer status in land. Since the land was disposed of in one unitary transaction, under the facts and circumstances test for separating investor from dealer status Martha almost certainly cannot claim dealer status on the basis of this one investment. If, however, this was only one of many short-term investments in land in which Martha was engaged, she may well be able to claim dealer status on the strength of all of her dealings in land put together. There are obviously not enough facts to resolve the question here. If Martha can get dealer status, the $50,000 loss is an ordinary loss that she can use to offset ordinary income. If she cannot get dealer status, the land will be treated as a §1221 capital asset in her hand, and the loss will be a capital loss. She would therefore be able to deduct the loss currently *only* against current capital gains, plus $3,000 of ordinary income, with the unused balance carried forward to succeeding taxable years.

Answer 3. *Year 10*: There are no tax consequences in year 10 to Mimi or Sam from the transfer of the Corpco stock. Since the transfer is clearly a gift for tax purposes (the classic case of detached and disinterested generosity), the transfer itself is nondeductible to Mimi and excluded from Sam's income under §102. Mimi does not recognize the depreciation in her stock since the original purchase. Since there is a built-in loss in the stock at the time of transfer, it is subject to the special basis rules in §1015(a), modifying the usual carryover basis rule for inter vivos transfers. Sam's basis in the stock will therefore depend upon the fair market value at the time he disposes of it (see below).

Year 12: First, since the stock has appreciated to $3 a share, above Mimi's cost basis, the special basis rules in §1015(a), which apply only to dispositions where the fair market value is lower than carryover basis, do not apply here. Thus, for purposes of calculating any gain on the year 12 transfers, Sam takes a carryover basis of $2 a share (Mimi's cost basis) under the normal rules of §1015(a).

Transfer to Libby: The 1,000 shares Sam has given Libby are worth $3,000. Although Libby bought the stereo two years earlier for $4,000, a decline in value of $1,000 over two years in this sort of consumer good is not unreasonable. Thus, I will assume for the balance of the question that, notwithstanding the friendship, there is no gift element involved, and this is an arm's-length market exchange of property for property, at a fair market value on both sides of $3,000. (In the event it is not, the same analysis given below would hold, except that Sam, in addition to disposing of the stock for its value ($3,000), would probably be deemed to have received (and Libby would be deemed to have given) a gift of the *excess* value of the stereo above $3,000.)

This exchange of personal property constitutes a realization event for both sides that is not eligible for nonrecognition under §1031 (the stock, as intangible property, does not qualify for §1031, and would in any event not be considered "like" a stereo for purposes of §1031). Thus, Sam will be treated as if he disposed of the stock for its fair market value of $3,000, recognizing a gain of $1,000 ($3,000 minus the carryover basis of $2,000). Since the property exchanged was held by Mimi and Sam for in excess of one year, the gain is treated as long-term capital gain. Sam takes a cost basis in the stereo of $3,000, its effective purchase price for him.

As for Libby, I will assume that Libby used the stereo for personal purposes. If so, the stereo is not depreciable, since any decline in value is treated as personal consumption. Libby thus retains the original cost basis of $4,000 in the stereo at the time of the exchange, disposing of the stereo at a loss of $1,000. Libby is not entitled to claim that loss for tax purposes, however, for the same reason she could not anticipate it through depreciation deductions. Libby takes a cost basis of $3,000 for the stereo (the amount she has paid for it with property worth $3,000).

Donation of 1,000 shares to undergraduate school: Assuming that the school is a qualified, charitable organization for purposes of §170, the donation will be deductible by Sam in year 12 as a charitable contribution. Since the stock is intangible property that would have generated long-term capital gain in Sam's hands (see above), under §170(e)(1), Sam is permitted to deduct against ordinary income the full fair market value of the stock ($3,000) without recognizing the $1,000 in built-in gain in the stock, irrespective of the uses to which the school puts the stock. The $3,000 deduction is subject to the limitations in §170 that it not exceed 30 percent of Sam's contribution base for the year (roughly, AGI), with any excess carried over to the next five years.

Transfer to Roberto: The threshold question is whether this transfer is motivated by detached and disinterested generosity, so as to constitute a gift (with no tax consequences to either side, and a carryover basis to Roberto), or is instead a form of compensation for referral services. This seems very close to the facts in *Duberstein*—Sam has given Roberto something in appreciation for past services rendered to him that were of value, presumably with an eye to encouraging future referrals as well. Thus, notwithstanding the absence of any express quid pro quo, the presence of the word "gratitude," and the possibility that Sam and Roberto may have a genuine friendship, this almost certainly flunks the "detached and disinterested generosity" test, and should be treated by both sides as compensation paid to Roberto.

For Roberto, the stock constitutes property received for services rendered. Under §83 and *Drescher*, Roberto is required to treat the property as current income to him at its fair market value ($3,000), provided that his right to the stock is fully vested and the stock can be valued. Both conditions are clearly met here. Thus, Roberto reports $3,000 of ordinary income in year 12, and takes a stepped-up cost basis in the stock of $3,000.

Sam is treated as having purchased services for appreciated property, which is reconstructed for tax purposes as a two-step transaction: Sam is deemed to have sold his stock for its fair market value of $3,000, recognizing $1,000 of long-term capital gain; and then to have paid $3,000 to Roberto in compensation for referral services. The compensation clearly seems an ordinary and necessary expense of building up a practice, and hence (unless there is some public policy objection to referral fees) should be allowed as an offset against income from the business in some form. The problem for Sam is whether it would be currently deductible, or instead would have to be capitalized in the business, and recovered through amortization deductions or at the back end when the practice is sold or abandoned. Sam is paying Roberto for a number of discrete patient referrals. The question is, is this more like acquiring a patient list (an expense Sam would clearly have to capitalize, subject to possible amortization over the useful life of the referral under *Newark Morning Ledger*) or is it more like an advertising and promotion expense, which is currently deductible notwithstanding the fact that it may create goodwill with a useful life considerably longer than one year. As a practical matter, one suspects such expenses are routinely deducted as current expenses. But as an analytical matter, it is unclear which analogy is stronger. On the side of current deduction, courts may conclude that a bunch of discrete referrals, unlike a patient list, lack a "property-like" quality, and hence do not rise to the level of an intangible asset at all. (The distinction seems more metaphysical than real, but one suspects might be determinative nonetheless.) On the other side, like patient lists and unlike general advertising expenses aimed at the world at large, the goodwill purchased here is embodied in identifiable individuals. If the individuals referred will in most cases become long-term patients of Sam's, courts may well conclude that the referral fees must be capitalized, subject to amortization over the expected duration of the patient relationships if it can be determined with reasonable accuracy.

Assuming that courts opted for the advertising analogy here, there is a further hurdle for Sam to deduct the $3,000 currently. The facts suggest that the referrals were provided prior to the time that Sam had a going practice. If so, under §195 the expense must be capitalized and written off over five years, notwithstanding the fact that it would otherwise (if incurred in an ongoing practice) be currently deductible. Bottom line: Sam probably must capitalize the $3,000, deducting $600 a year for each of the first five years he is in practice.

Answer 4.   <u>Ben</u>: The first question for Ben is whether the pollution of the land itself constituted a realization event for Ben in year eight, permitting him to recognize a loss in that year in the value of his property. The answer is unclear. Under the revenue ruling dealing with airline deregulation and other precedents, this would clearly not qualify as a sale or other disposition of a portion of the property for purposes of §1001. That would probably require that Ben show that the damaged portion was severable from the rest (and hence should be treated as a separate asset), and then either abandon the damaged portion or at a minimum show that it was entirely worthless. He has done neither here. Although the land was rendered permanently unfit for cultivation, it may well have other profitable uses (for example, putting up a fermenting or storage facility, or selling the property to someone else for nonagricultural development). Ben may, however, be able to claim a loss under §165(a). It is unclear what sorts of losses would be covered by §165(a) *other* than casualty losses. This may, however, qualify as a casualty loss, provided that the pollution was sudden and unexpected enough to seem like the sort of "force majeur" contemplated by the IRS and courts. The facts of the case are much like *Midland Empire*. Unfortunately, the decision in *Midland Empire* is little help here, as the court, deciding to treat the expenses of reversing the damage as currently deductible expenses, did not reach the taxpayer's alternative argument that the loss from the oil seepage itself was a currently deductible loss under §165(a). Since Ben is not repairing the property in year eight, the court's theory won't help him.

If Ben were permitted to claim a casualty loss in year eight, he would recognize a loss, equal to the lesser of (i) the decline in the fair market value of the damaged portion of the property as a result of the pollution or (ii) his basis in the damaged portion of the property. (Because the loss is to business property and not personal property, it is not subject to the $100 deductible and 10 percent of AGI floor in §165(c).) It is unclear what either figure is here. (For a discussion of how to allocate basis, see below.) Given what appears to be the substantial appreciation in the property from its original purchase price, indicated by John's generous settlement offer the following year, it is likely that basis will be the lower figure here, even if (as is likely) the fair market value of the damaged portion of the property has not declined to zero. Whatever the total amount of the deductible loss is, for purposes of characterizing the loss Ben would be treated as if he had sold off the portion of the damaged property. Where, as here, the property is §1231 property, that loss would therefore be an ordinary loss and not a capital loss.

For the balance of the answer, however, I will assume that Ben is not eligible for a casualty loss deduction in year eight.

In year nine, John agreed to pay Ben $500,000 in settlement of the suit. Since Ben is a cash method taxpayer (the default assumption in the instructions), that promise itself does not constitute current income to Ben, unless it is fully funded and secured on behalf of Ben. As subsequent events indicate, that is not the case here. Thus, there are no tax consequences to Ben in year nine from the settlement agreement.

In year 10, John actually paid Ben $200,000. The difference between the $500,000 promised and the $200,000 paid is irrelevant for tax purposes for Ben. As he never took the $500,000 into income, he cannot treat John's failure to pay it as a loss for tax purposes. It is at worse a mere expectancy that never came to pass.

The actual $200,000 payment will, however, have tax consequences. The payment is in settlement of a tort suit arising from physical damage to Ben's property. There seems to be no argument under *Roemer* for characterizing this as arising from personal injuries to Ben, and hence no argument for excluding any portion of the $200,000 from income categorically under §104. Instead, the treatment of the $200,000 for tax purposes will depend upon what it is compensating Ben for. See *Glenshaw Glass*. The facts here are reminiscent of *Inaja*, suggesting the payment could be characterized in one of two ways: as the purchase price for an estate in land (a perpetual easement to pollute); or as rental payments for a perpetual license to pollute. In the former case (the characterization the court ultimately opted for in *Inaja*) Ben will be treated as having sold a portion of his land for $200,000, giving rise to capital gain to the extent that the proceeds of sale ($200,000) exceed the allocable share of the original $100,000 basis. In the latter case (the one the IRS argued for in *Inaja*) the entire $200,000 would be ordinary income to Ben, without a basis offset, since it is treated as just prepayment of ordinary rental income.

Obviously, Ben would prefer the former characterization. On the strength of *Inaja*, he appears to have a good shot at it.

Assuming this is treated as a sale of an easement, the remaining problem is how much basis should be allocated to it. This is the second problem in *Inaja*. The answer in theory is that he should allocate a fraction of the $100,000, equal to the fraction of the total fair market value of the property represented by the loss in value from the pollution. The taxpayer in *Inaja*, persuading the court that the fraction was uncertain, was able to get the entire basis of the property frontloaded on the recovery. Ben is unlikely to be treated so generously. Assuming that the whole property is fairly uniform in quality and that the pollution damaged only one-half of it, he could allocate at most $50,000 of the basis to the recovery. If the polluted half retained some value for other purposes, the $50,000 would have to be reduced further.

John: Since John also is a cash method taxpayer, there are no tax consequences to him until year 10, when he actually pays the claim or otherwise sets money aside irrevocably for Ben.

John obviously would like to deduct the amount paid currently as a business expense. There are a number of problems for him. First, it could be argued, pointing to *Welch*, that because John's lawyer advised him he would probably win the suit, any payments he made to settle it were extraordinary and/or unnecessary, and hence are not legitimate business expenses under §162 at all. This argument should lose. It is doubtful that Cardozo's opinion in *Welch* is sound even on the facts of the case. These facts are much stronger for the taxpayer. Taxpayers do routinely make payments to settle nonmeritorious suits against their businesses for a variety of sound, business reasons. Maintaining the goodwill of the plaintiff and others who will hear of the suit is a prime reason. Thus, barring any public policy prohibitions on giving polluters a deduction for damages, or settlements in lieu of damages, John should clearly be able to claim this as a business expense under §162.

Second, is it a currently deductible expense or must it be capitalized? The answer turns on what John has acquired for his money. If he were paying damages in a slip and fall case on his property, he would clearly be entitled to a current deduction: The payment is to erase a liability that generates no asset of lasting value for him. Here, however, one could argue he has purchased an asset of lasting value, on one of two theories. If (as in *Inaja*) the settlement gives him a continuing right to pollute, it creates a valuable business asset with a life as long as his continued use of a fertilizer manufacturing process that throws off pollutants. Alternatively (and more plausibly), he has purchased goodwill in the community of a long and indefinite duration. However, that is often a side benefit of legal settlements that in the first instance are merely removing a liability, and are currently deductible. Should the mere fact that generating goodwill is John's predominant motive change the result? If so, how would we police/establish motives? And doesn't the fact that the payment is made to generate goodwill in the community at large make it more like an advertising or promotion expense that should be currently deductible even if it creates an asset of long life? (See discussion in question 3.) On balance, it seems like this should be a currently deductible expense to John.

Finally, there is the question of whether John recognizes $300,000 in income from discharge of indebtedness under §108, as a result of having settled a legal liability to pay $500,000 for $200,000. The answer is almost certainly no. The agreement to pay $500,000, assuming it was a binding contract, created a legal liability for John. Hence, on the face of it, the partial discharge from that liability falls within §108 (see §108(d)(1)(A)). However, §108(e)(2) provides that no income shall be realized from the discharge of indebtedness to the extent that payment of the liability would have given rise to a deduction. Assuming that whatever payment John does make to Ben is deductible (see above), that fits this case. The logic of the rule is clear: If a deduction is permitted, and if income must be recognized from discharge of indebtedness, the taxpayer should be permitted an offsetting deduction for that amount as if he had constructively paid it (that is, John gets to take a deduction for the full $500,000, but then recognizes income to the extent a portion ($300,000) is not paid). The same result is achieved more directly under §108(e)(2) by not including or deducting the $300,000. Second, even if §108(e)(2) does not cover this case, this seems like the sort of retroactive adjustment of purchase price that is routinely treated as outside the scope of §108 (although there is no express statutory authorization for it, since it does not qualify as a purchase money debt reduction). Third, John could try to argue that the year 10 agreement was merely the settlement of a disputed claim, and hence under *Zarin* does not give rise to §108 income. The problem here is that, unlike the situation in *Zarin*, Ben and John had agreed in year nine to liquidate the debt at $500,000, and hence the amount of the liability (under the logic of the *Zarin* court) was no longer in dispute as of year 10. That difference, however, might not be fatal with other courts. Finally, if John's financial troubles rise to the level of insolvency (no evidence of that on the facts), he could get relief under §108(a)(1)(B). All in all, it seems extremely unlikely John will recognize income under §108, although if §108(e)(2) is not available, the precise theory is uncertain.

Answer 5.   Purchase of raffle ticket by Linda: The first question is, assuming that Legal Aid is a qualified §170 charitable organization, can Linda claim a charitable deduction for any portion of the tickets purchased? Linda has gotten something of value in return: a chance to win a cruise worth $1,000. It is quite plausible that Linda disregarded the possibility of winning entirely when she bought the tickets, and was motivated solely by a desire to make a contribution to Legal Aid. However, unless she renounced any right to win ex ante, it seems likely that the IRS would assume at least a partial self-interested motive. Under *Ottawa Silica*, if this were an implicit quid pro quo, the fact that Linda anticipated getting something of substantial monetary value in return might disqualify the entire purchase from a charitable deduction. But because it is an explicit quid pro quo, as in the case of a mug given to donors to public radio, Linda may be permitted to deduct the price of the tickets ($100), to the extent it exceeds the value of what she is getting in return. If permitted to do that here, how would we value what Linda has gotten in return? It seems clear that, even if Linda had retained the winning ticket herself, she didn't bargain for the cruise in return for the tickets. She bargained for a chance to win the cruise. Thus, the value of what she got in return at first cut should be equal to the *expected* return on the tickets. But as of when? When she purchased the tickets, it was still plausible that Legal Aid would sell all 10,000 tickets it reserved a right to sell. If it did sell them, then Linda's 100 tickets would give her only a 100/10,000 (or one in a hundred) chance of winning a $1,000 cruise. At those odds, the $100 investment had an expected return of only $10. By the time of the drawing, when Legal Aid sold only 1,000 tickets, Linda's odds had increased to one out of 10, for an expected yield of $100. If we go with the former odds, Linda could argue that only $90 of the $100 ought to be deductible; if we go with the latter, none of it is deductible, since Linda is by then engaged in a fair gamble, with an expected return equal to investment. Which is more appropriate? If, as *Ottawa Silica* suggests, what we are after in judging the deductibility of contributions is charitable intent, the former seems fairer to Linda: When she made the decision to purchase the tickets, if she had checked the back of the tickets she had every reason to think that, ex ante, 90 percent of the ticket price was a contribution to Legal Aid.

But is it clear that the quid pro quo to Linda ex ante was limited to the expected financial return on the tickets? Most commercial gambles do not have an expected return equal to investment, although few are at odds as bad as this one (10 percent return). People nonetheless gamble because they irrationally believe they will beat the odds, and for the pure pleasure (consumption value) of gambling. We deny a deduction for gambling losses under §165(d) in part because we believe (given the personal consumption element in gambling itself) that such losses are not real losses. Should that logic carry over to this situation, leading us to conclude that the entire $100 was personal consumption in the form of gambling at very bad odds? Hard to say. These are very bad odds; that fact, combined with the fact that the proceeds are going to a worthy organization, make it likely that most purchasers of charitable raffle tickets in situations like these really are motivated in substantial part by charitable intent.

For the balance of the question, I will assume that Linda is entitled to deduct $90 of the $100 spent on the tickets.[1]

Transfer to Jana: The first question is whether this transfer should be treated as a gift, or as compensation to Jana. As a full-time childcare person, Jana is Linda's employee, not an independent contractor. Section 102(c) creates a categorical rule that *any* transfers from employers to employees cannot be excluded from gross income as gifts. (There is a minor exception in §74(c) for employee achievement awards, an exception that is inapplicable here.) Although the rule is categorical, it seems unlikely it would be enforced where an employer and employee also had an independent friendship, and (purely in a role of friend) the employer gave, for example, a birthday present to the employee. Perhaps excepting such cases could be reconciled with the language of §102(c) by saying the amount is not being transferred by the employer in the capacity of employer at all. Be that as it may, there is no indication here that Linda and Jana do have a friendship wholly independent of their work relationship. If they do not, then the tickets should be treated as compensation to Jana. Thus, they are included by Jana as salary income. Since childcare is a personal expense to Linda, the cost

---

1. In fact (although I did not expect you to know this), courts have consistently held that the cost of raffle and lottery tickets sold by governmental and other charitable organizations is nondeductible. The cases rest on the assumption that the purchaser's intent is to win, not to donate money. That seems plausible as to state lotteries, bingo games run by churches, etc., but less likely with raffle tickets in situations like this. But given the administrative nightmare of trying to distinguish among different sorts of gambles, the utility of a brightline rule is obvious.

is not deductible by Linda, except to the extent it could qualify for a tax credit under §21, or is reimbursable out of Linda's pre-tax earnings through Linda's employer's dependent care assistance program under §129.

How much should be included by Jana/deducted or credited by Linda under §21 or §129? For Jana, this would be treated as property received for services. Under §83, Jana, who has gotten the unrestricted right to these tickets, is treated as receiving compensation in the amount of the tickets' fair market value at the time of transfer. Normally, fair market value would be the cost to Jana of acquiring the same property in an arm's-length exchange — here, $100. But that seems like a harsh rule here, since (due to the charitable element built into the tickets) the property rights Jana acquires by acquiring the tickets, measured solely by the mathematical chance of winning the cruise, are worth considerably less than the cost of the tickets. Under the analysis above, at the time of transfer, when Legal Aid might still have sold all 10,000 tickets, those rights are worth only $10. Moreover, even as to the $10, the tickets are a form of quasi-forced consumption for Jana: If she were given $10 in cash, she might well not choose to spend it on 100 raffle tickets for a cruise to the Bahamas. The normal rejoinder — that she is free to refuse the tickets if she does not value them at least at the tax cost to her — may give somewhat less comfort here, where the personal nature of the relationship between Linda and Jana may make it hard to turn them down. That's probably too bad for Jana — we can't make these sorts of distinctions administratively. But it's still not clear how we ought to value them. Fortunately, it does not matter, since anything not included as income under §83 will be included by Jana as winnings (see below).

As to Linda, the same analysis suggests that what she has given Jana as compensation is really closer to $10 than to $100, with the balance reflecting her own consumption choice to support Legal Aid. In any event, if she has deducted $90 of the $100 previously as a charitable contribution, she may not deduct it again as an expense of childcare.

Cruise: Under *Glenshaw Glass*, all windfall earnings like this are fully taxed to the recipient. Jana is the owner of the winning ticket at the time of the drawing. Thus, the cruise is taxable to her, not to Linda. (One can analogize this to a transfer of stock that appreciates in value after the transfer. Whether the transfer is a gift or compensation, any appreciation in value of the stock post-transfer belongs to the transferee.) There are only two questions. The first is whether Jana can offset the winnings by the cost of the tickets to her, measured by the amount she was taxed on as salary at the transfer. The answer should clearly be yes. Raffle tickets (setting aside the charitable wrinkle) are a form of gambling. Under §165(d), taxpayers may offset gambling gains by gambling losses. The "gain" on the winning raffle ticket would be the proceeds (the cruise) minus the cost of the ticket. All the losing tickets would be gambling losses. Thus, Jana should be able to subtract whatever portion of the ticket price was taxed to her as compensation from the amount taxable as winnings.

What amount is taxable as winnings here? The usual rule under §61 for all in-kind income is that it should be valued at its fair market value. As noted above, that is normally the price at which the recipient could acquire the property in an arm's-length transaction. If Jana can find a better price than $1,000 for the cruise, she can probably use the lower price in valuing it. But if not, she is stuck with the $1,000 value, even if she herself would not pay that much to obtain it.

Answer 6. (a) *Year one*: Juan is a cash method taxpayer (default assumption). Thus, he is normally taxed on income only as received in cash or cash equivalent, subject to two exceptions: the constructive receipt and economic benefit doctrines. The latter does not apply here: There is no indication that Alicia has set the $2,000 aside in a fully funded account secured on Juan's behalf. The problem is constructive receipt. The heart of the doctrine of constructive receipt is that if a cash method taxpayer has it within her volition to obtain cash currently but simply chooses not to exercise that right, she will be treated as if she had received the cash. Notwithstanding some confusing language in *Amend* suggesting that a contract right to current payment creates constructive receipt, it seems clear that Juan did not have constructive receipt of the $2,000 in November year one merely because he sent Alicia a bill in October saying that the bill was payable in 30 days. Even if he and Alicia had agreed in advance that she would pay within 30 days (a reasonable inference from the statement that he "generally requires that bills be paid within 30 days of receipt"), constructive receipt requires more than a legal right to payment currently; it requires also that the payee have the unilateral power to obtain it. The conversation with Alicia in late October, however, raises a more difficult question. Alicia indicated her willingness to pay immediately if Juan insisted. Does that give Juan constructive receipt of the money? Probably not, but it seems a closer question. On the one hand, her offer to pay could be construed to create the unfettered opportunity for Juan to be paid currently if he so chose.

On the other hand, an offer to pay is quite different from actually tendering the cash or making it available in a location where Juan could get it without her cooperation — the classic case of constructive receipt. Maybe Alicia didn't have the cash, or would have reneged on her offer if he had accepted. On balance, no constructive receipt seems like the better answer.

As to Alicia, who is an accrual method taxpayer, the expense (which is deductible as an ordinary and necessary business expense) should be deducted in year one. An accrual method taxpayer may deduct expenses at the *later* of when the "all events" test has been met and there is "economic performance" within the meaning of §461(h). The "all events" test is met as of early October, when Juan completed the work and presented her with a bill, as her liability to pay is fixed at that point, in an amount determinable with reasonable accuracy. As to "economic performance," §461(h)(2)(A)(i) provides that if the liability of the taxpayer arises out of the providing of services to the taxpayer by another person, "economic performance occurs as such person provides such services." Thus, in this case economic performance coincides with meeting the "all events" test.

Year two: Juan takes the $2,000 into income, as the cash is actually paid. There are no tax consequences for Alicia, who has already accrued the deduction in year one.

Year three: Juan's accountants discover the mistake, and Juan returns $500 of the $2,000 to Alicia. Clearly, both sides should account for the return in some fashion for tax purposes. The question is, how? In general, our regime of annual accounting requires that the taxpayer take each year as he or she finds it, irrespective of whether payments made or received may relate back to a transaction reported for other purposes in an earlier year. A taxpayer's right to go back and reopen old returns to recompute tax liability in light of subsequently discovered facts is severely limited generally to arithmetical or other errors that were knowable at the time the original return was filed. As to Alicia, that standard is clearly not met. Like the taxpayer in *Lewis*, she had no way of knowing in year one that the other side had misbilled her. As to Juan (who could have known of the error) it seems a closer question, but on balance it seems like he should not be allowed to amend. He did not merely miscalculate his tax liability; he actually got paid the $2,000, having use of the money for a year, and taking it under a claim of right.

Assuming that neither side may reopen earlier returns to recompute tax liability (with interest owed to or received from the government on the difference), they must take the $500 into account for tax purposes in year three. As to Alicia, the treatment is clear. Under the "inclusionary" wing of the tax benefit doctrine, as limited by §111, she is required to report the $500 as income, taxable at year three rates, to the extent she gained any tax benefit from the deduction in an earlier year (here, year one). Assuming that she had sufficient income to use the full $2,000 deduction in year one, that means she must include the $500 as income in year three. Juan is clearly entitled to deduct the $500 from income in year three. The only question is whether he can avail himself of the special rule in §1341. That section applies only where the taxpayer took an item into income in any early year because it appeared from all facts available that he was entitled to it, and subsequent events establish that he is not. §1341(a)(1),(2); Reg. §1.1341-1(a). It is unclear this would qualify, as Juan could have known in year one, from facts then available to him, that he was not entitled to the $500. But it is not necessary to resolve this question, as the $500 is below the minimum $3,000 necessary to invoke §1341. Thus, Juan claims a deduction in year three for $500, at year three rates.

(b) This fact situation resembles that in *Olmstead*, and raises many of the same problems.

Year one: The 10 percent profits interest in the restaurant that Betty gave Juan is noncash compensation for services. Thus, whether and when it is taxable to Juan is governed by §83 and the deferred compensation rules. Section 83 provides that *property* transferred to someone in compensation for the performance of services is taxable in the first year in which the rights of the transferee to the property are transferable or not subject to a substantial risk of forfeiture. The 10 percent profits interest meets the latter requirement in year one (Juan has an absolute, unconditional right to it, notwithstanding the chance Betty may never pay) and may meet the former as well. The deeper question, however, is whether this interest rises to the level of "property" at all, or is simply an unfunded and unsecured promise for future compensation. This seems arguable, but on balance the latter seems the better answer. The profits interest is an equity interest in the restaurant, and in that sense one could view this like Betty paying Juan with stock in her own company. If Betty's restaurant were IBM, the stock would clearly be taxable to Juan upon receipt at its fair market value. But in the absence of any well-functioning market for such an interest to provide both valuation and liquidity, it is doubtful it rises to the level of "property" for purposes of §83. If not, it is — like the promise in *Minor*—simply an unsecured promise to pay deferred compensation, the amount to be measured by the profitability of the restaurant. On that assumption, Juan, as a cash method taxpayer, will not be taxable until actual receipt of money under the agreement. Since he never receives anything under the original agreement, there are no tax consequences from it.

In the unlikely chance that Juan were held currently taxable in year one on receipt of the 10 percent profits interest, he would be taxed on its fair market value, presumably equal to the present value of the expected future payment stream to Juan. Here, it may be hard to fix that value by reference to either side of the transaction. The future profits of a business like this seem quite uncertain. Consistent with the general presumption that values exchanged in a market transaction are equal, the IRS could seek to value it by looking at the market value of Juan's services. But given that Juan has a sliding scale from $35 to $100, and may make even more generous arrangements than $35 for clients who need it, that value is uncertain as well.

Year three: The new agreement to pay $1,000 a year for 10 years seems unambiguously an unsecured promise to make future payments for services. Assuming that the original agreement is construed to be that as well, we have the *Olmstead* situation: a promise of deferred compensation is exchanged for a somewhat different promise of deferred compensation. Either promise taken alone would not be currently taxable to the recipient. Does the mere fact that one promise is exchanged for the other change that result? The IRS in *Olmstead* argued yes, on the ground that the taxpayer was selling one intangible property right for another, which amounted to a disposition of property under §1001. Since an unsecured promise to pay may well amount to property received for purposes of §1001 (even though it does not rise to the level of property under §83), it argued the taxpayer was taxable on gain at the moment of exchange. As applied to Juan, that argument would mean he is taxed on the present value of the promise to pay $1,000 a year over 10 years. (Since we are assuming he was never taxed on the original promise, he has no basis in that "intangible property" to offset the value received under the new promise.) The IRS's position in *Olmstead* clearly seems wrong, for the reasons we discussed in class. One could argue, as the court did in *Olmstead*, that the exchange of rights is not a sale at all, but merely a novation of a contract. But that argument seemed doubtful in *Olmstead*, and even more doubtful here, where the rights given up are substantially different from those received. A more promising argument, as we discussed in connection with *Olmstead*, would be to say that the original promise of a 10 percent profits interest is not property at all for purposes of §1001, for reasons discussed above, and hence its exchange for a new unsecured promise to pay is not a disposition of property under §1001, but merely a change in the terms of the deferred compensation arrangement. The net result: Juan is not taxed until actual receipt of the $1,000 each year beginning in year four.

In the event we did treat the original 10 percent profits interest as property for purposes of §83, and hence its exchange in year three as a disposition of property under §1001, the exchange would clearly be of materially different enough rights to constitute a realization event under *Cottage Savings*. In the absence of any express nonrecognition provision (§1031 does not apply), Juan would be taxed in year three on the gain or loss on that disposition, equal to the difference between the present value of the $1,000 over 10 years' income stream, and his basis in the 10 percent profits interest (whatever amount he was taxed on in year one based on its then assessed fair market value). [Query whether he could elect installment sale treatment under §453?]

Last point: Given that Juan's 10 percent profits interest may have been worthless in year three, was Betty's offer to give him $1,000 a year over 10 years instead simply a gift? Probably not — although she may have been motivated by fellow-feeling rather than self-interest in preserving her business relations with Juan, the fact that the offer relates back to work done in an unambiguous business relationship would likely require that this be treated as compensation on both sides.

Final Examination Number Three
Professor Griffith
University of Southern California Law Center

Instructions

1. You have three hours to complete this examination. This is a closed book examination. The only written material you may consult is the statutory package distributed with this examination. In addition you may use a hand calculator.

2. There are 15 questions on this exam, many with more than one part. I have listed the *approximate* value of each question next to the question. The lowest score you can receive on any question (or subpart) is a zero. Incorrect analysis of a question may lower your score on that question, but it will not lower your score on other questions.

3. Pace yourself to be sure to finish the examination.

4. Be sure to explain briefly how you reached your answers. If you believe that a question is ambiguous or that relevant information is missing, state the ambiguity or missing information and how the answer would be affected. Some questions may be deliberately "ambiguous" in the sense that the appropriate tax treatment is uncertain because the law is unsettled or because the facts are incomplete. One of the skills being tested is your ability to recognize these situations.

Appendix

Question 1. State whether each of the following statements is true or false. Briefly explain. (3 points each)

a. Under current law an individual's average tax rate generally is higher than his marginal rate.

b. It is possible for an employee to receive a 30 percent discount on goods and services provided by his employer without being taxed on any portion of the discount.

c. No gain is recognized on property transferred incident to a divorce.

d. Under the accrual method of accounting, an attorney would be required to report income for legal services she rendered even if she had not yet received payment.

e. Losses associated with stamp collecting generally are not deductible.

f. If income from a trust can be used to discharge an obligation of the grantor, then the grantor will be taxed on the income.

Question 2. What are the most important policy arguments for *not* taxing unrealized gains on property? (4 points)

Question 3. Which of the following items (if any) generally are included in taxable income? No need to explain your answers. (2 points each)

a. Death benefits received from insurance on the life of your spouse.

b. A full tuition scholarship to U.S.C. law school.

c. Damages received for lost wages resulting from a personal injury.

d. Money received for winning the jackpot in the state lottery.

e. Barter exchanges where the items exchanged have a fair market value less than $100.

f. Embezzled funds.

g. Money withdrawn from a savings account.

Question 4. Janet is a violinist employed by the Cleveland Symphony earning a salary of $40,000 per year. State the likely tax consequences *to Janet* of the following transactions. If additional facts are needed, state them and indicate how they would affect your answer. (3-5 points each)

a. Janet uses one room in her apartment as a practice and listening room. She practices two to four hours per day and usually

517

spends an additional hour listening to music, mostly classical pieces.

b. While on tour, the symphony pays for Janet's hotel room and reimburses her for all meal expenses up to $35 per day.

c. During the two months prior to the new season, rehearsals are held during both mornings and afternoons. During this period, the symphony provides a box lunch to all of the musicians at the rehearsal hall. Janet and about two-thirds of the other musicians typically eat the box lunch. The rest either bring their own lunch or eat at a nearby pizza shop.

d. Janet purchases new violin strings at a cost of $40 per month.

e. During the off-season, Janet travels to Europe. On her trip she attends a classical music concert at least three times a week. The trip costs her $5,000 plus $1,000 for the tickets.

f. Janet purchases a violin for $30,000.

g. The symphony director believes that physically fit musicians generally are better able to endure long rehearsals and will miss fewer days of work. Thus, the symphony reimburses its musicians up to $1,000 per year for a health club membership. Janet joins a health club and is reimbursed for its $800 annual fee.

h. Janet is required to wear a floor-length formal black evening dress at her performances. Most musicians spend about $400 on their dresses. Janet purchases a custom made dress for $2,200. She says the expensive dress looks better and is much more comfortable than cheaper dresses. She only wears the dress during performances.

Question 5. Which one of the following two fringe benefits is subject to the nondiscrimination rules?

a. Working condition fringes
b. Employee discounts

Does the different treatment of these two items with respect to the nondiscrimination rules make any sense? Explain. (4 points)

Question 6. Mary and Ned each have $200,000 to invest. Mary purchases a condominium for $200,000 and lives in it. Ned puts the $200,000 in the bank, earns $20,000 in interest and uses that interest to rent an apartment. Ned's taxable income will be $20,000 more than Mary's taxable income. Make the best case for the position that this result is *not* unfair. (4 points)

Question 7. What are the policy arguments for and against making employer-provided parking tax-free? How do you think employer-provided parking should be taxed? (6-8 points)

Question 8. Alice is a high school English teacher earning a salary of $30,000 per year. For each of the following items, state how Alice would be treated (i) under current law (CL), (ii) under a Haig-Simons (comprehensive) income tax (HS), and (iii) under a comprehensive consumption tax (CT). Explain very briefly. (3-5 points each)

  a. During the summer, Alice tutors the child of her plumber. In return, the plumber installs a new sink at the home of Nellie, Alice's mother.
  b. Alice's friend Mike repays $4,000 he borrowed from her the previous year.
  c. Alice uses $2,000 of her income to purchase two years of karate lessons.
  d. Alice enrolls in a night law school and spends $4,000 of her salary on tuition.

Question 9. Polly purchases an asset that can be depreciated over a five-year period. The asset cost Polly $8,000.

  a. What is the depreciation under the double declining balance method during each of the first two years? (Disregard the half-year convention.) (4 points)
  b. Which depreciation method is closer to the consumption tax ideal, the 200 percent declining balance method or the straight-line method? Why? (3 points)

Question 10. What is the utilitarian argument in favor of a progressive rate structure? Would a utilitarian favor complete equality of income? (5 points)

Question 11. Robert owns Blackacre with a fair market value of $4,000 and basis of $1,500, which is subject to a mortgage of $1,200. Sally owns Whiteacre with a fair market value of $2,000 and basis of $500, plus a rare stamp with a basis of $400 and a fair market value of $800. In a qualifying like-kind exchange, Robert transfers Blackacre (subject to the mortgage) to Sally for Whiteacre and the stamp.

What are the tax consequences to Robert and Sally? (8 points)

Question 12. Jed discovers oil on his land, which has a $120,000 basis. He sells the land to a drilling company for $100,000 immediately plus an additional payment based on the value of any oil produced. Adequate interest will be paid on any additional payment. It is estimated that the additional payment will be $50,000 per year for the next four years, after which the well will be dry. Thus Jed's expected payments will be as follows:

Year 1	$100,000
Year 2	$ 50,000 (estimate)
Year 3	$ 50,000 (estimate)
Year 4	$ 50,000 (estimate)
Year 5	$ 50,000 (estimate)

  a. If the estimated amounts are accurate, what are the tax consequences to Jed if he is taxed on the installment method? (3 points)
  b. How would Jed be taxed if this were taxed as an open transaction? (3 points)
  c. How would Jed be taxed if this were taxed as a closed transaction? (For this part c, do not attempt to calculate the precise numbers.) (3 points)

Question 13. Bill owns a small jewelry shop. He brings his dog Max to work with him. One day a cat follows a customer into the store. Max leaps at the cat and destroys the store's plate glass window. Bill replaces the window with shatterproof glass at a cost of $3,000, double the cost of ordinary glass. How will Bill's $3,000 expense be treated? (4 points)

Question 14. Ed gives Fred a rare coin as a gift. Ed purchased the coin for $5,000; at the time of the gift, the fair market value of the coin was $3,000. Two years later Fred sells the coin for $4,000. (5 points)

  a. What are the tax consequences to Fred on the receipt of the coin?
  b. What are the tax consequences to Fred on the sale of the coin?

Question 15. Jack's store was destroyed in a flood. It had a basis of $400,000 and an estimated fair market value of $600,000.

Jack received $550,000 from insurance. He purchased a new store for $500,000 and used the remaining money to buy two delivery trucks for $25,000 each.

What are the tax consequences to Jack of these transactions? (4 points)

END OF EXAMINATION

Appendix

Model Answers

Answer 1.

  a. False, since marginal rates rise throughout most of the income range.
  b. True for goods, but not for services, where the tax-free discount is limited to 20 percent.
  c. True.
  d. True.
  e. True. Stamp collecting is a hobby, so net losses will not be deductible.
  f. False. The grantor is taxed only if the income is used to discharge her obligation.

Answer 2.

The taxpayer does not have the money yet.
It is hard to determine the gain.
It is consistent with a consumption tax and you think the consumption tax is good.

Answer 3.

  a. Not included.
  b. Not included.
  c. Not included.
  d. Included.
  e. Included.
  f. Included.
  g. Not included.

Answer 4.

  a. This is unlikely to qualify as a home office. A deduction is allowed only where a portion of the home is exclusively used (i) as the principal place of business [not true here] or (ii) as a place of business used by patients, clients, or customers [not true here].
  b. The reimbursement is tax-free to Janet.
  c. Almost certainly taxable. The box lunch is not for the convenience of the employer because the availability and use of the nearby pizza shop suggests there is no business reason to eat lunch at the rehearsal hall.

    d. Deductible as an employee business expense, subject to the 2 percent of AGI floor.

    e. Although not a sure loser, this is unlikely to qualify as a business trip. She would have a better chance if she takes lessons in Europe.

    f. This is a business expense, but Janet must capitalize the cost of the violin and take depreciation deductions.

    g. The reimbursement is taxable to Janet. Under §132, a health club provided by the employer on the premises of the employer is not taxable to the employee. Nothing in the tax code, however, excludes reimbursement for health club memberships. The connection between the club and the job is tenuous.

    h. This is a fairly close call. Uniforms are deductible, but clothing that can be worn in ordinary life is not. The best argument for Janet is that a floor-length formal black evening dress is not usable except at her job and thus should be considered a uniform. If this is correct, it does not matter that she purchased an expensive dress. However, the dress is suitable to wear to very formal events like opening night at the opera, so the cost may not be deductible.

Answer 5. Only employee discounts are subject to the nondiscrimination rules. Nondiscrimination rules do not make sense for working condition fringes because such fringes will vary according to the nature of the job. An office with a view, for example, might serve a business purpose for an attorney, but not for a plumber.

Answer 6. Some of the arguments are:

- Because the tax benefits of the condo would be capitalized into the price, the condo may not be as nice as the apartment.
- Mary is taking a higher risk owning the condo.
- Ned could have purchased the condo if he had wanted to.

Answer 7. For: Parking can be viewed as a business expense. In general, it is desirable to permit a deduction for business expenses.

Against: Parking can be viewed as a personal expense because the individual chooses not to live near work. If parking is provided tax-free, an individual will have less incentive to car pool, thereby increasing pollution. If parking is tax-free, an individual may choose parking rather than cash even if, in a no-tax world, the individual would prefer cash.

Appendix

Answer 8.

  a. *Current Law:* Alice is taxed on the fair market value of the sink. Barter exchanges are taxable.

    Haig-Simons: Either Alice or Nellie is taxed on the fair market value of the sink, since it represents an increase in wealth (and/or consumption). Arguably, both are taxed if the gift is viewed as both consumption to Alice and to Nellie. The taxation of gifts under a Haig-Simons income tax is unclear.

    Consumption Tax: Strictly speaking, the use of the sink is consumption so Nellie would be taxed on the rental value each year. The sink (or the rental value) seems to be consumption to Nellie. You could also argue that Alice received consumption from making the gift.

  b. *Current Law:* Not taxable. Repayments of loans are not taxable.

    Haig-Simons: Not taxable. The increase in consumption is offset by a reduction of the debt.

    Consumption Tax: Taxable (assuming that Alice spends the $4,500 on consumption rather than reinvesting it). Dissaving is taxed under a consumption tax.

  c. *Current Law:* Alice gets no tax deduction for the purchase of the karate lesson.

    Haig-Simons: Alice gets no tax deduction for the purchase of the karate lesson. Lessons taken this year are consumption. The right to lessons next year is a form of wealth.

    Consumption Tax: The purchase of the karate lesson should be viewed as the purchase of an asset and Alice should get a $2,000 deduction. Alice then should take the value of the lessons into income as she uses them.

  d. *Current Law:* Alice gets no tax deduction for the educational expense because it prepares her for a new occupation.

    Haig-Simons: Alice gets no tax deduction because the reduction in consumption is offset by an increase in wealth from the education. Arguably, under a Haig-Simons income tax Alice should be taxed on the value of the education that is derived from the imputed income from her studying.

    Consumption Tax: Alice gets a deduction for the tuition unless the law school cost is viewed as a form of personal consumption. Since night law school is not much fun, the cost is likely to be viewed as an investment in human capital rather than consumption.

Appendix

Answer 9.

    a. Year one: $3,200, leaving a basis of $4,800.
       Year two: $1,920.
    b. The double declining balance method provides faster depreciation than the straightline method. Since under a consumption tax the entire amount would be deducted in the first year, the double declining balance method is more like a consumption tax approach.

Answer 10. The utilitarian argument in favor of a progressive tax is that money is more valuable to the poor than to the rich. A utilitarian would not favor complete equality of income because it would eliminate most work incentives and thus lower total wealth greatly. A utilitarian would balance the utility gain from redistribution against the utility loss from decreasing total wealth.

Answer 11. Robert: He received like-kind property worth $2,000 and boot of $2,000 ($1,200 assumption of liability plus $800 stamp). He has a realized gain of $2,500. He recognizes gain to the extent of the boot, so he recognizes $2,000 of gain. He has a carryover basis of $1,500 in Whiteacre and a fair market value basis in the stamp.

    Sally: She received like-kind property worth $4,000. She received no boot, so she recognizes no gain on the receipt of the property from Robert. She recognizes $400 of gain on the transfer of the stamp, which is not like-kind property, and thus has a tax-basis of $800 in the stamp. Sally's basis in Blackacre is her basis in Whiteacre of $500, plus her $800 basis in the stamp, plus $1,200 of basis from assuming the loan, for a total basis of $2,500.

Answer 12.

    a. Jed's basis is $120,000. The total payments received will be $300,000. Thus, the gain is $180,000. $180,000/$300,000 = 60 percent. Thus 60 percent of each payment will be gain. So Jed will recognize capital gain of $60,000 in year one and $30,000 in each of years two through five. Jed will also recognize ordinary income on the interest payment received.
    b. Jed would not recognize any gain until he recovered his basis. Thus, there would be no gain in year one (basis reduced to $20,000). He would include: (i) interest received (as ordinary income); (ii) $30,000 of capital gain in year two; and (iii) $50,000 of capital gain in years three through five.
    c. First, the present value of the future payments would be calcu-

lated. Then Jed would recognize gain in year one equal to the difference between that present value and his basis. Suppose the present value was $200,000. Then Jed would recognize $80,000 of capital gain in year one. All additional amounts received by Jed would be ordinary income. These amounts would be reduced by amortizing the present value of the future payments.

Answer 13. The issue here is whether this is a capital expense or a repair. This is probably a deductible repair, even though the new window is better than the old since the repair does not significantly improve the shop or extend its useful life.

Answer 14.

a. Donees are not taxed on gifts received. Fred takes a carryover basis of $5,000.

b. Fred realizes no gain or loss. A donee takes a carryover basis for purposes of recognition of gain and the lower of carryover basis or fair market value basis for recognition of loss.

Answer 15. Jack realizes $150,000 of gain on the involuntary conversion. He recognizes capital gain on the $50,000 spent on the trucks because they are not similar use property. Jack will have a basis of $400,000 in the new store and a basis of $25,000 in each of the new trucks.

Final Examination Number Four
Professor Griffith
University of Southern California Law Center

Instructions

1. You have three hours to complete this examination. This is a closed book examination. The only written material you may consult is the statutory package distributed with this examination. In addition you may use a hand calculator.

2. There are 11 questions on this exam, many with more than one part. I have listed the *approximate* value of each question next to the question. The lowest score you can receive on any question (or subpart of a question) is zero. Thus, incorrect analysis of a question may lower your score on that question, but it will not lower your score on other questions. Pace yourself to be sure to finish the examination.

3. Except where otherwise indicated, explain briefly how you reached your answers. If you believe that a question is ambiguous or that relevant information is missing, state the ambiguity or missing information and how your answer would be affected. A few questions may be deliberately "ambiguous" in the sense that the appropriate tax treatment is uncertain because the law is unsettled or because the facts are incomplete.

Appendix

Question 1. Each of the following four problems can be answered in a few sentences or less. (3 points each)

  a. List the following taxes from most regressive to most progressive. (No need to explain.)
    i. Federal "social security" tax
    ii. Federal excise tax on cigarettes
    iii. Federal income tax
  b. List the following items produced by the Treasury in order of the "strength" of their authority in a federal tax case from *weakest* to *strongest*. (No need to explain.)
    i. Regulations
    ii. Private Letter Rulings
    iii. Revenue Rulings
  c. If all individuals, regardless of income, were required to pay a tax of $5,000 per year, the tax structure would be: (Choose one and explain briefly.)
    i. Progressive
    ii. Regressive
    iii. Flat rate
  d. Alice purchases Blackacre which has a fair market value of $1,000. She finances the property as follows: $200 cash, $500 recourse loan, $300 nonrecourse loan. What is her basis in Blackacre?

Question 2. Each of the following four problems can be answered in a few sentences or less. (3 points each except as stated)

  a. Betty is a medical doctor. She spends one day each month working without pay at a free clinic for the poor. If she had worked for pay that day instead, she would have earned $500. Is Betty entitled to a $500 charitable deduction for the donation of her time? Does this rule make sense?
  b. Which of the following exchanges (if any) can qualify for a like-kind exchange. (2 points each) (No need to explain.)
    i. Ford stock for General Motors stock
    ii. Male cattle for female cattle
    iii. Developed real estate for undeveloped real estate
  c. What word or words should be placed in the blank in the following sentence:
    "If there is adequate _____ it will not be necessary to calculate OID." (No need to explain.)

d. Carol is driving home from her law school tax class. Deep in thought about whether a consumption tax is better than an income tax, she runs into the rear end of a taxi that unexpectedly comes to a full stop at a stop sign. Carol's car is destroyed. She has no collision insurance. Assume the 10 percent of AGI floor is met. Can Carol deduct the loss of her car as a casualty loss?

Question 3. Each of the following two problems can be answered in two or three paragraphs. (5 points each)

a. It is a longstanding tradition at Johnson Law School for first-year students to purchase a class gift for each of their professors. Most students contribute $5 for each first-year class, so that professors generally receive gifts worth between $400 and $600 (depending on their popularity and the size of their class). Are the gifts taxable income to the professors under current law?

b. Albert's factory was destroyed in a flood. It had a basis of $500,000 and an estimated fair market value of $900,000. He receives $800,000 from insurance, borrows an additional $200,000 and purchases a new factory for $950,000 and a new steamroller for $50,000. What are the tax consequences to Albert of the transaction?

Question 4. The following questions relate to the proper taxation of our canine friends.

a. Mighty Mutt Dog Food corporation pays a $15,000 fee for the use of the popular beagle "Foam Francis" in dog food commercials. Is Foam required to file a federal income tax return? (2 points)

b. Debbie owns the Six Star Circus. She purchases a piano playing dog, Rex, for $20,000. Food and veterinary expenses for Rex are $1,000 per year. During the season Rex travels with the circus, but during the off-season, Rex lives with Debbie. Discuss the tax treatment of the costs associated with Rex. (5 points)

Question 5. Maria sells her oil rights in Blackacre to the Xenon Drilling Corporation. Her basis in the oil rights is $100,000. Xenon agrees to pay her $50,000 immediately, plus an additional amount, plus interest, depending on how much oil is taken from the well. The parties estimate that payments are likely to vary in amount from $15,000 to $30,000 per year (plus the interest), and that drilling is likely to continue for six to eight years so that she expects to receive six to eight additional payments. In year two, Maria receives a payment of $20,000 plus $1,400 interest.

   a. Under the open transaction approach adopted in Burnett v. Logan, how much taxable income would Maria report from the payments received in years one and two? (4 points)
   b. How much taxable income would Maria report from the payments received in years one and two if the installment method of reporting were adopted? (6 points)

Question 6.   Each of the following two problems can be answered in two or three sentences. (5 points each)

   a. Kirk, Bones & Sulu is a law firm specializing in space law. The firm provides attorneys with free donuts, bagels, cream cheese and Milky Ways in the morning and free Mars bars in the afternoon. Free coffee and soda also are provided. These items are available at the attorneys' lunch room. Secretaries and support staff are provided only with free coffee and must purchase other foods and beverages at vending machines in the building lobby. Discuss the tax treatment of the food and beverages provided to the attorneys.
   b. Carlos, who is 65 years old, purchases a deferred annuity that pays nothing for 10 years (until Carlos is 75 years old) and then pays $2,000 a year for life. The annuity costs $3,000. At the time he purchases the annuity, Carlos has a life expectancy of 15 years. Since during the first 10 of those years, Carlos will receive nothing under the contract, the annuity is expected to pay out $2,000 a year for 5 years.

      In fact, Carlos lives until the age of 81 and thus receives six payments of $2,000. Discuss the tax treatment of these payments.

Question 7.   Bob is assistant manager at the Imperial Bowling Alley and Pool Hall. Like all full-time Imperial employees, Bob is permitted to bowl and play pool at no cost whenever there are open alleys or pool tables. If, however, a paying customer wants to use the facility, Bob is required to leave after finishing his current game (typically about 10 minutes). Under a reciprocal agreement between Imperial Bowling Alley and King's Pool and Pinball World, Bob is permitted to use the pool and pinball machines at King's (under similar restrictions) at no charge.

In addition to playing for free themselves, Imperial employees are permitted to bring their spouses or "significant others" and their children with them at no charge. Pursuant to the "significant other" provision, Bob often brings his longtime companion Carl with him. During the year, Bob plays pool at Imperial Bowling Alley about three hours per week and plays pool and pinball at King's Pool and Pinball World about four hours per week. Carl accompanies Bob about half the time. Neither Bob nor Carl pay any fee for using the facilities.

What are the tax consequences to Bob and Carl of the free use of these recreational facilities? (10 points)

Question 8. For each of the following four problems, state how Zeke would be treated (i) under current law (CL), (ii) under a Haig-Simons (comprehensive) income tax (HS), and (iii) under a comprehensive consumption tax (CT). Explain very briefly. (3-4 points each)

  a. Zeke owns a miniature golf course. The old "Windmill" at hole six of the golf course is in bad shape from years of use. Zeke tears it down (except for the foundation) and constructs a new windmill in its place. The new windmill is of the same appearance and construction as the old one.

  b. During January, when the golf course is closed, Zeke remodeled the basement in his home. The cost for materials is $2,000. Zeke saved $3,000 by doing the work himself.

  c. Zeke is hit by an automobile while crossing the street and suffers a permanent scar on his forehead. He files a claim against the driver of the car and later accepts a settlement of $10,000.

  d. Zeke owes $1,000 to Valerie. She agrees to discharge the debt in exchange for Zeke's baseball card collection. Zeke purchased the baseball cards 15 years ago for $50.

Question 9. The Middletown Savings and Loan Company learns that maintaining a flower garden in front of the bank and decorating the interior of the bank building with plants and fresh flowers would cost $1,200 per month. It is estimated that the new decorations would increase the number of bank customers by an amount that would generate $800 of profit (not considering the cost of the decoration). Under what circumstances, if any, is it efficient for the bank to redecorate? (4 points)

The last two questions on the examination are policy questions. A fairly good answer to each question can be made in one to four short paragraphs (or in a

Appendix

list) and the points indicated would be awarded for such an answer. If, however, you have extra time and wish to write a more comprehensive essay, you may receive a few additional points. You should do this, however, only if you have completed the rest of the examination.

Question 10. Under current law, taxpayers receive a personal exemption of about $2,200 for each dependent. What are the best arguments *for and against* replacing the exemption with a tax credit? (9 points)

Question 11. State the best arguments *against* the current deduction for charitable contributions. Please present both arguments in favor of entirely eliminating the deduction and sensible suggestions for limiting the deduction. (11 points)

END OF EXAMINATION

Appendix

Model Answers

Answer 1.

    a. Order is: (ii), (i), (iii).

    b. Order is: (ii), (iii), (i). (But if a PLR was issued to the taxpayer herself, it is the strongest authority.)

    c. Regressive. Although each taxpayer would pay the same absolute amount, the poor would pay a higher percentage of their income in taxes.

    d. $1,000. The debt is included in basis.

Answer 2.

    a. Betty is not entitled to the deduction. The rule makes sense because Betty is not taxed on the imputed income she would have earned from practicing medicine. Betty is in the same position as if she had worked for pay and donated the money.

    b. i. No.

       ii. No.

      iii. Yes.

    c. Stated interest.

    d. Carol can deduct the loss. Ordinary negligence will not prohibit a casualty deduction, but gross negligence or willfulness will disallow a deduction. Here Carol's negligence appears ordinary.

Answer 3.

    a. The answer is uncertain.

       Arguments in favor of taxation:

       • For most students the gift is not from love and affection.

       • Gift arises out of employment relationship, like "tokes" and tips.

       • Tradition may lead professors to expect gifts.

       Arguments against taxation:

       • Apparently, professors who are not first-year professors do not get a gift. They probably are paid the same.

       • Gifts are not mandatory. The size of the gift depends in part on the popularity of the professor.

       • There is no indication that such gifts are a normal part of the compensation for professors.

    b. No gain is recognized on the involuntary conversion because all of the insurance proceeds were reinvested in similar use property. Albert will have a basis of $650,000 in the new factory and $50,000 in the steamroller.

Answer 4.

a. No. Foam's owner will pay the tax. Dogs cannot own property and do not pay taxes. Animals are not persons under the Internal Revenue Code.

b. Rex would be a business asset. Debbie could deduct the cost of the food and vet expenses. The cost of Rex would be capitalized since Rex is an asset with a useful life greater than one year. Debbie would be able to "depreciate" Rex over his useful life as a performer. Since it probably is less costly to keep Rex in her home during the off-season than anywhere else, it would be reasonable for Debbie to deduct the cost of keeping Rex at her home even though he might have a "pet" value.

Answer 5.

a. Maria reports zero in year one. In year two Maria includes only the $1,400 of interest. Under the open transaction doctrine basis is recovered first.

b. Maximum total receipts are: $50,000 + (8 × $30,000) = $290,000. Basis is $100,000. ($290,000 − $100,000)/ $290,000 = $190,000/$290,000 = .655. Thus, 65.5 percent of each payment is taxable and Maria has taxable income as follows: Year one, $32,750; year two, $13,100 plus $1,400 of interest.

Answer 6.

a. This probably is excluded as a de minimis fringe benefit. Nondiscrimination rules do not apply to de minimis fringe benefits.

b. Carlos paid $3,000 for the annuity and is expected to receive $10,000 if he lives the expected 15 years. $3,000/$10,000 = $.30. Thus, 30 percent of each of the first five payments is recovery of basis; 70 percent is income. After five years Carlos has used all his basis so the entire payment in year six is taxable income.

Answer 7. This is a no-additional-cost fringe. Probably the 10-minute wait will not disqualify the use of the alleys, unless it appears likely that business is lost because of the delay. The reciprocal agreement (if in writing) is okay if the businesses are the same. Probably the availability of pinball would not disqualify the agreement. Significant others (same sex or different sex) are not allowed to receive no-additional-cost fringes tax-free. Bob (not Carl) would be taxed on the value of Carl's play because Bob is performing the services to the bowling alley. Carl's use would be a gift from Bob to Carl.

Answer 8.

a. *Current Law*: It is not clear whether this would be characterised as a repair or capital expenditure. If capital, depreciate. If repair, deduct.
Haig-Simons: Capitalize and depreciate. The decline in value of the old windmill was already deducted in prior years under a Haig-Simons tax.
Consumption Tax: Deduct immediately as a form of investment.

b. *Current Law*: No taxation of imputed income, no deduction for cost of materials. Add the cost of materials to the basis of the home.
Haig-Simons: Taxed on the amount by which the value of the home increased, less the cost of material. Presumably this is $3,000 ($5,000 increase in value less $2,000 cost of materials).
Consumption Tax: Deduct the cost of materials. There is no tax on the value of labor. However, Zeke will be taxed annually on the consumption value of the new room.

c. *Current Law*: Not taxed on the personal injury recovery.
Haig-Simons: Unclear. Under Haig-Simons, Zeke would be taxed on the receipt of the recovery, but it is unclear if the permanent scar would constitute an off-setting change in wealth. Henry Simons probably would not have permitted the deduction for the scar.
Consumption Tax: Taxed on the cash received, unless it is saved. Unclear if the scar would reduce his consumption (of good looks) each year.

d. *Current Law*: Zeke is taxed on the $950 of unrealized gain in the cards.
Haig-Simons: No tax. Zeke would have been taxed in earlier years on the growth in value of the cards.
Consumption Tax: No taxation. Zeke has neither increased nor decreased his consumption.

Answer 9. When the total value of the flowers is greater than $1,200. Thus, when the value to the employees is greater than $400.

Answer 10. The basic argument for a credit is that a credit is more progressive than a deduction. For example, a $3,000 deduction is worth $1,200 to a 40 percent bracket taxpayer, but only $450 to a 15 percent taxpayer.

The argument for a deduction is that the personal exemption is designed to make the tax base more accurately reflect a family's true economic circumstances. A family with children is likely to be less well-off financially than a family with an identical income without children. In addition, the cost of raising a child generally increases as a family's income increases.

Answer 11.

   a. Some of the main arguments against the deduction are listed below.

     i. The charitable deduction often supports causes like fine arts rather than the truly needy.

     ii. The deduction is an upside-down subsidy. It costs the rich 60 cents or less to give a dollar to charity while it costs the poor a dollar to give a dollar since the poor do not itemize deductions.

     iii. Donors often get benefits for their gifts such as prestige, invitations to meet stars, buildings named for them, and so on. Spending money on charitable contributions can be viewed as just another form of consumption and should thus be taxed.

     iv. Fund raising for charities is very expensive — taxation is a much cheaper way of raising money for worthy causes.

     v. The deduction is an indirect support for religion that violates the principle of separation of church and state.

     vi. The government should fund worthwhile activities directly, rather than indirectly through the tax system. Direct expenditures are subject to better oversight.

     vii. There is a lot of fraud associated with the charitable deduction. Individuals often lie on their tax returns about the size of their charitable donations. In addition, individuals often overvalue gifts of property, particularly art or other items that are difficult to value.

   b. Here are some ways the charitable deduction might be limited.

     i. Limit the tax deduction for property donations to the basis of the property donated.

     ii. Permit a charitable deduction only for donations to institutions that help the poor, such as the Salvation Army or college scholarship funds for the needy.

iii. The charitable deduction might be replaced by a tax credit. This would eliminate the so-called upside-down subsidy.

iv. Deductions for charitable contributions might also be made subject to a floor.

Final Examination Number Five
Professor Kaufman
Saint Louis University School of Law

Instructions

1. Materials permitted: any materials other than another person. Calculators are expressly permitted.

2. This examination consists of one question with several parts.

3. You have two hours and fifteen minutes to complete the exam.

4. Identification and analysis of issues are the substance of this exam. If the facts relating to a particular issue are ambiguous (which is sometimes intentional), it would be wise to answer in the alternative. Purely computational errors are of little consequence unless a failure to address or appropriately analyze one or more issues results. Please thoroughly label any numerical computations so that the grader will be able to distinguish a computational error from a substantive one.

5. Please think before writing. The premium is on the quality of your response, not the quantity.

6. Thank you and good luck.

Appendix

Question 1. (2 hours and 15 minutes)

Anne is a cash basis, calendar year taxpayer, who has been employed as Vice President and General Manager for Blue Inc. for the last 10 years. Blue Inc. operates a chain of convenience stores. On average, the products in Blue Inc.'s stores are marked up 20 percent over cost.

Blue Inc. pays Anne a hefty salary. Like all Blue Inc. employees, Anne is also entitled to a 20 percent discount on all items sold by Blue Inc. in its stores. In addition, Blue Inc.'s benefit package, which is available to all Blue Inc. employees, allows Anne to choose one of the following fringe benefits: group health insurance; a $50,000 term life insurance policy; or cash. Anne has always chosen the health insurance.

In year one, Anne purchased a house in the City suburbs for $250,000. Anne paid $25,000 in cash and financed the remainder of the purchase of the house with a $225,000 recourse loan from her employer with interest payable at the market rate. The loan from Anne's employer was secured by a mortgage on the house. Anne lived in the house in the City suburbs and, of course, paid for all repairs and maintenance on the house.

In year three, Anne drove to a beach resort on the Atlantic on vacation. Along the way, Anne stopped overnight at a motel. In the drawer of the bedside table in her motel room, Anne found a copy of the Bible. Leafing through it, she found a $100 bill folded inside a piece of paper. A note that had been written on the paper said, "This $100 is for the needy. Whoever finds it may keep it." Not feeling any particular need for additional money, Anne left the $100 bill and the note in the Bible in the motel room.

a. Please discuss the tax consequences of the foregoing to Anne.
b. Please discuss how your answer to (a), above, would change if, instead of living in the house in the City suburbs herself, Anne rented the house to an unrelated person for $24,000 per year and used the rent payments from her tenant to rent an apartment for herself. Anne did not occupy the house at any time.
c. The facts are the same as in (a), except that in year four, Anne sold the house in the City suburbs for $220,000. Although Anne had made timely payments of interest on the mortgage loan on the house, the amount of principal outstanding on the loan was still $225,000 when the house was sold. Anne's employer agreed to take the $220,000 sales proceeds in complete satisfaction of the mortgage loan on the house. Please discuss the tax consequences of the foregoing to Anne.

Appendix

Model Answer

Answer 1a

Anne's salary. Unless otherwise provided, gross income includes income from. whatever source derived, including compensation for services. §61(a). Cash method taxpayers take income into account when received and take deductions into account when paid. Anne's salary is compensation for services and is therefore included in her gross income in the year in which it is received.

The employee discount. Gross income does not include any fringe benefit that qualifies as a qualified employee discount. §132(a)(2). A qualified employee discount includes any employee discount with respect to *qualified property* to the extent such discount does not exceed the *gross profit percentage* of the price at which the property is being offered by the employer to customers. §132(c)(2). The gross profit percentage is generally the employer's profit margin determined on the basis of all property offered to customers in the ordinary course of the line of business of the employer in which the employee is performing services and the employer's experience during a representative period. §132(c)(2). Qualified property is property offered for sale to customers in the ordinary course of the line of business of the employer in which the employee is performing services. §132(c)(4). The exclusion for qualified employee discounts is available for highly compensated employees only if the availability of the benefit does not discriminate in favor of highly compensated employees. §132(j)(1).

Anne's discount is for qualified property since the discount is on items sold by Blue Inc. (to the public) in its stores. Her discount does not exceed the gross profit percentage, since Blue Inc.'s profit margin is 20 percent and Anne's discount is 20 percent. Although Anne, as Vice President and General Manager, is probably highly compensated, the discount is available to all Blue Inc. employees, and therefore does not appear to discriminate in favor of highly compensated employees. Anne's discount is thus a qualified employee discount and is excludable from her gross income.

Employer-provided health insurance. Gross income of an employer does not include employer-provided coverage under an accident or health plan. §106. However, under the doctrine of constructive receipt, a taxpayer is treated as receiving cash when the taxpayer has an unrestricted right to receive cash. Since the fringe benefit package offers Anne the unrestricted right to receive cash, then, absent another exclusion, Anne would be required to include in gross income the value of the group health insurance, even though it would otherwise be excluded from income. However, no amount is included in the gross income of a participant in a cafeteria plan solely because, under the plan, the participant may choose among the benefits of the plan. A cafeteria plan is a written plan under which all participants are employees and the participants may choose among two or more benefits consisting of cash and qualified benefits. §125(d). Qualified benefits include group health insurance and group term life insurance not exceeding $50,000 (see §79(a)). §125(f). Blue Inc.'s fringe benefit plan is a cafeteria plan (assuming it is written) because all of the participants are employees and they may choose among two or more benefits consisting of cash and qualified benefits (life insurance or health insurance). Therefore, the cost of Anne's health insurance is excluded from her gross income.

Acquisition and maintenance of house: Basis equals cost. §1012. Anne's basis for the house is its cost of $250,000. Loan proceeds are not includible in gross income because they are offset by a corresponding liability and therefore do not increase wealth. Anne borrowed $225,000, which is excluded from her gross income. Although the loan is an employer-employee loan, it is not subject to §7872 because it bears a market rate of interest and is thus not a "below market loan."

Section 262 disallows deductions for personal living or family expenses. The interest Anne pays on the mortgage loan, as well as her repair and maintenance expenses on the house, are personal expenses and therefore would generally not be deductible. However, the interest on the mortgage loan will be deductible to the extent it constitutes qualified residence interest within the meaning of §163(h).

Anne does not have to include the imputed income from occupying her house.

The cost of the trip: Anne's expenses for her trip are also personal and therefore not deductible.

The $100 she found: Gross income includes windfalls. The $100 would be a windfall and therefore includible in gross income unless it were excluded, for example, as a gift. A gift arises when a transfer of money or property is motivated by the donor's detached and disinterested generosity, out of affection, charity, or like impulse. The person who left the $100 in the drawer appears to have acted out of detached and disinterested generosity (the donor did not have a pecuniary interest in the payment), and on a charitable impulse (the donor left the $100 for the needy). Therefore, the $100 found by Anne is excluded from her gross income.

The $100 she left: Gifts are personal expenses and therefore are not deductible by the donor. The fact that Anne left the $100 in the drawer may be viewed as a gift from her which would be a nondeductible personal expense. Another way to approach the same facts is to say that Anne was not entitled to the money she found because she was not needy. Since it was not her money, she would not have to include it in gross income.

Answer 1b

Renting the home: The $24,000 rental income is includible in gross income. §61(a). Anne's interest payments would no longer be personal expenses and would be deductible. §163(a). Anne would be allowed depreciation deductions on the house. §§167, 168. Her depreciation deductions would reduce her basis in the house. §1016. Section 162(a) allows a deduction for ordinary and necessary expenses incurred in trade or business; §212 allows a deduction for ordinary and necessary expenses incurred for the production of income. Anne's expenses for repairs and maintenance would now be ordinary and necessary business expenses and would therefore be deductible under §162(a) or §212. The rent Anne pays on her apartment would not be deductible because it would be a personal expense. Overall, Anne's taxable income would probably be greater. This problem highlights the benefit Anne would have if she lived in the house herself in which case the imputed income from occupying her house is not taxed.

Answer 1c

The sale of the house: The loss realized on the sale of property equals the taxpayer's adjusted basis in the property less the amount realized by the taxpayer on the sale. §1001. Here, Anne realizes a loss of $30,000 because her adjusted basis in the house is $250,000 and she realizes $220,000 on the sale. However, loss deductions for individuals are limited to trade or business losses, losses on transactions entered into for profit, and certain casualty losses. She will not be able to deduct the $30,000 loss on the sale of the house because it was her personal residence.

The discharge of the debt: A taxpayer must include cancellation of indebtedness income, which is the amount of debt owed less the amount the taxpayer paid to discharge the debt. *Kirby Lumber* and §61(a)(12). Here, Anne's cancellation of indebtedness income is $5,000; the $225,000 debt owed less the $220,000 paid to discharge the debt. Debt discharge income is excludable if the taxpayer qualifies for one of the exclusions in §108 (for example, if the taxpayer is insolvent). Here, we do not have sufficient facts to determine whether Anne qualifies under §108. In addition, the IRS could view the debt discharge income as additional compensation paid to Anne by her employer, includible under §61(a)(1), in which case the §108 exclusion might not be available.

Final Examination Number Six
Professor Kaufman
Saint Louis University School of Law

Instructions

1. Materials permitted: any materials other than another person. Calculators are expressly permitted.

2. This examination consists of two questions.

3. You have three hours to complete the exam.

4. Identification and analysis of issues are the substance of this exam. If the facts relating to a particular issue are ambiguous (which is sometimes intentional), it would be wise to answer in the alternative. Purely computational errors are of little consequence unless a failure to address or appropriately analyze one or more issues results. Please thoroughly label any numerical computations so that the grader will be able to distinguish a computational error from a substantive one.

5. Please think before writing. The premium is on the quality of your response, not the quantity.

6. Thank you and good luck.

Question 1. (2 hours)

Thelma is 33 years old. She has one son, Jerome, who is in the fourth grade. Jerome is a good boy and does well in school. Thelma works as a dry cleaner for True Blue Cleaners, Inc. (hereinafter "True Blue"). True Blue operates a local laundry and dry cleaning establishment.

Thelma owns the house in which she and Jerome reside. Jerome has his own room. Thelma's ex-husband, Abe, purchased the house for $55,000 prior to his marriage to Thelma. He financed the purchase with $5,500 in cash and the proceeds of a $49,500 loan secured by a mortgage on the house. While Abe and Thelma were married, Abe remained the sole owner of the house. When they divorced on January 1, year one, Abe transferred the house to Thelma pursuant to the divorce decree. The house was then worth $63,000. Thelma assumed the then outstanding balance of $41,500 on the mortgage loan. Thelma paid interest of $4,000 on the mortgage in year one.

The divorce decree ending Thelma's marriage to Abe also requires Abe to pay Thelma $150 per month until Jerome is eighteen. To fulfill this obligation, Abe paid Thelma a total of $1,800 in year one.

Thelma owns an automobile, a Ford, which she purchased shortly after she and Abe divorced. The Ford gets pretty good gas mileage but seems to eat oil. Thelma drives the Ford to and from work and to run personal errands.

True Blue, Thelma's employer, pays Thelma an hourly wage. In addition, Thelma and her son participate in True Blue's group accident and health insurance plan. True Blue pays the health insurance premium.

Since Thelma is on good terms with her co-workers who run the washroom and presses, she usually gets her laundry and dry cleaning done for nothing. True Blue has a written policy against using company facilities and time for this purpose. However, the management has found it impossible to stop the practice entirely. In year one, the free laundry and dry cleaning services Thelma took advantage of would have cost a customer $950.

The people in the dry cleaning trade in St. Louis know Thelma to be just about the best dry cleaner in the metropolitan area. The stain has not yet been found that Thelma cannot remove. Thelma maintains her expertise by subscribing to a journal for the dry cleaning industry. The journal regularly has articles describing the latest techniques for efficient dry cleaning and the pros and cons of the chemicals currently available on the market for removing spots. Thelma's subscription to the journal cost her $35 in year one.

Thelma is a calendar year, cash method taxpayer. Please discuss the federal income tax consequences of the foregoing to Thelma.

Question 2. *(1 hour)*

Collectible Inc. (hereinafter, "Collectible Inc.") is a corporation formed under the laws of one of the fifty United States. Collectible Inc. is engaged in the business of buying and selling baseball cards and other collectible baseball paraphernalia. Collectible Inc. rents store space in which it operates a small shop.

Collectible Inc. had been in business for many years, and the shop had come to look a little dingy. In October year one, Collectible Inc. obtained a commercial loan for $6,000 from Friendly Bank to finance a complete redecoration of the shop. The loan required repayment with interest at market rates on May 31, year two. Among other things, Collectible Inc. purchased three new display counters. It also hired a painter to do a very fancy paint job in red, white, and blue, the colors worn by the local professional baseball team. All of the work was completed by the end of year one. However, Collectible Inc. did not get around to paying the painter until January of year two.

Business was not as good as anticipated. By the end of April, year two, Collectible Inc. had serious cash flow problems. The value of its assets still exceeded its liabilities but Collectible Inc. simply did not have the cash to pay back the $6,000 borrowed from Friendly Bank in year one. Fortunately, all of the Bank's customers were avid baseball fans and loyal patrons of Collectible Inc.'s shop. Besides, Collectible Inc. had been a customer of Friendly Bank for years. Upon learning of Collectible Inc.'s cash flow problems, Friendly Bank agreed to accept $4,000 in full satisfaction of the loan. Collectible Inc. paid the $4,000, plus all accrued but unpaid interest on May 31, year two.

Collectible Inc. maintains its books and records using the accrual method of accounting and uses the calendar year as its taxable year. Please discuss the federal income tax consequences of the foregoing to Collectible Inc.

END OF EXAMINATION

Model Answers

Answer 1

Transfer of the house from Abe to Thelma: The transfer is covered by §1041 since it is to a spouse or former spouse incident to their divorce (related to the cessation of the marriage). §1041(a), (c). Thelma is treated as if she received a gift. §1041(b)(1). The receipt of the house is excluded from Thelma's gross income. §102(a). Thelma takes a transferred basis in the house. §1041(b)(2). Assuming no capital expenditures, Abe's basis in the house at the time of the transfer is $55,000. §1012. His cost was:

(a)   the $5,500 cash he paid for it, plus
(b)   the $49,500 loan proceeds he used to pay for it. *Crane.*

The interest on the mortgage: Interest is generally a deductible expense. §163(a). However, it may not be deducted if it is personal interest. §163(h)(1). It is not personal interest if it is "qualified residence interest." §163(h)(2). The interest paid by Thelma is qualified residence interest because it is paid with respect to "acquisition indebtedness":

(a)   it is paid with respect to debt used to acquire the residence;
(b)   the amount of the debt does not exceed $1 million; and
(c)   the debt is secured by a mortgage on the house. §163(h)(3).

Although it is an itemized deduction, it is not subject to the 2 percent floor. §§62(a), 67(b)(1). It could be subject to §68's overall limitation if Thelma's AGI exceeds $100,000 as adjusted for inflation. §68.

The imputed income from the house: Imputed income is the value of goods and services one provides to oneself and one's family. The imputed income equals the fair rental value of the house. Imputed income has been excluded from gross income as a matter of practice.

The $1,800 she received from Abe: The payment is for child support so Thelma excludes it from income. §71(c). It is not an alimony or separate maintenance payment subject to §71(a). The child support payment is not an accretion to Thelma's wealth but the fulfillment of Abe's obligation to support Jerome.

Appendix

The cost of maintaining and operating Thelma's car: These costs are nondeductible personal expenses. §262. Commuting expenses are also nondeductible personal expenses. *Flowers*.

Wages: Thelma's wages are includible in her gross income. §61(a)(1).

The accident and health insurance plan: As a general rule, the fair market value of the plan would be includible in gross income. §61(a). However, it is excluded under §106.

The value of Thelma's free dry cleaning and laundry service: This might be a gift because the dry cleaning and laundry service were provided by Thelma's co-workers out of benign and disinterested generosity having been motivated by their affection for Thelma. *Duberstein*. However, Thelma's co-workers did not own the services they transferred to her so they could hardly give them away.

The value of the services would normally be included in Thelma's gross income as compensation for services. §61(a)(1). However, they might be excluded under §132(a)(1) as a no-additional-cost service because:

a. True Blue provides dry cleaning services to customers in the ordinary course of its business (§132(b)(1));
b. True Blue incurred no substantial additional cost (including foregone revenue) in providing the service to Thelma (§132(b)(2)) (this might also be the case since the fact that True Blue cannot keep track of the practice might indicate that the employees are using excess capacity); and
c. The services were "provided by" True Blue to Thelma (§132(b)) (although this may be a tough one since True Blue has a written policy against the practice).

In the alternative, the value of the services might be excluded under §132(a)(2) (qualified employee discount), but only to the extent the employee discount (100 percent) does not exceed 20 percent of the retail price. §132(c)(1). This exclusion is available only if the service (dry cleaning) is offered for sale to customers (which it is) in the ordinary course of the line of business of the employer in which the employee works. §132(c)(4). However, were the services "provided by" True Blue? If not, §132(c) may not apply. §132(c)(3).

The value of the services might also be excluded under §132(a)(4) as a de minimis fringe benefit since True Blue finds it impossible (administratively impracticable?) to keep track of the exchange of services among employees. §132(e)(1). On the other hand, $950 during the year might be too large for "de minimis."

Since True Blue may not intend to transfer the value of the services to Thelma, the value of the services might be included in Thelma's gross income as a windfall (an accretion to wealth, clearly realized, and over which Thelma has complete dominion and control). *Glenshaw Glass.*

Reasons for deciding one way or another: It may violate public policy to exclude free services gotten dishonestly (*Blackman* in the exclusion context?). However, one of the purposes of §132 was to legitimize the exclusion from gross income of amounts employees exclude from their gross incomes as a matter of practice.

The cost of Thelma's subscription to the trade journal: The cost is an ordinary expense because one could reasonably expect someone in her trade or business to purchase such a publication. *Guilliam.* Also, it is a recurring expense that will not give rise to income substantially beyond the current taxable year. §§162(a), 262(a); *cf. Encyclopaedia Britannica.*

It is a necessary expense because it is helpful to Thelma's trade or business of being an employee engaged in dry cleaning.

Thelma's §162 deduction for the subscription cost is an itemized deduction because True Blue does not appear to reimburse her that expense and the performance of services as an employee is not a "trade or business" for purposes of §62. §62(a)(1), (2).

Unreimbursed employee business expenses are not on the list of itemized deductions exempt from the 2 percent floor; hence this cost is deductible only to the extent it and Thelma's other itemized deductions subject to the floor exceed 2 percent of her adjusted gross income. §67.

If Thelma's AGI exceeds $100,000, as adjusted for inflation, her itemized deductions (including the cost of the journal) will also be subject to the §68 limitation on itemized deductions.

Thelma should try to get her employer to reimburse her for the cost of the journal. Then the cost would be excluded from her gross income as a working condition fringe benefit. §132(a)(3), (d).

Answer 2

Entity tax: As a corporation, Collectible Inc. is a separate taxable entity. See §11.

Appendix

Rent paid: The rent Collectible Inc. pays is currently deductible. §162(a).

The loan proceeds: The loan proceeds are excluded from Collectible Inc.'s gross income on the premise that loan proceeds are offset by a corresponding obligation to repay. Loan proceeds are not an accretion to wealth. *Glenshaw Glass.*

Interest in the loan: The interest is deductible under §163(a).

The cost of the three new display counters: The cost is a capital expenditure because the counters are equipment with a useful life that extends significantly beyond the taxable year. Reg. §1.263(a)-2(a); see *Encyclopaedia Britannica.* The cost is thus not currently deductible. §263. The cost will instead be recovered through depreciation deductions because the display counters are (i) property used in a trade or business and (ii) subject to wear and tear. §167(a). Section 168 will permit Collectible Inc. to use an accelerated depreciation method to compute its depreciation deductions. The basis of the display counters will be reduced by the amount of the depreciation deductions. §1016(a)(2).

The cost of the paint job: The cost of a paint job is generally deductible as an ordinary and necessary business expense because it is more like a repair not significantly adding to the useful life of the shop or increasing its value. §162(a).

When does Collectible Inc. deduct the cost of the painting? Accrual method taxpayers deduct an expense when (i) the fact of the liability for expense has been established, (ii) the amount of the expense can be determined with reasonable accuracy, and (iii) the "economic performance" requirement of §461(h) is met. Here, the first two requirements are met in year one. The third requirement is also met in year one; the expense relates to services provided to the taxpayer, so the economic performance requirement is met in the year in which the services are provided to Collectible Inc., year one. §461(h)(2)(A).

However, the deduction in year one may not be allowed because the expense arguably is a capital expenditure. The fancy paint job here may go beyond the maintenance type of paint job contemplated by the regulations.

The paint job will increase the value of the shop, in terms of the amount of business it does, and may also significantly increase the life of the store space as a shop.

Appendix

The debt discharge: Collectible Inc. settled its $6,000 debt for $4,000. The discharge results in cancellation of indebtedness ("COD") income in the amount of $2,000, which is the $6,000 amount owed less the $4,000 Collectible Inc. paid to discharge the debt.

Under the tax benefit theory of COD income, the discharge for less than the amount owed is an event that is fundamentally inconsistent with the exclusion of the $6,000 loan proceeds in the first instance. See the dissent in *Zarin*.

Under the *Kirby Lumber* theory of COD income, the discharge creates COD income because the discharge freed $2,000 of Collectible Inc.'s assets from debt. The $2,000 of COD income is includible in gross income. §61(a)(12).

The COD income could not be excluded under §108(a). Collectible Inc.'s liabilities did not exceed the value of its assets so it was not insolvent at the time of the discharge. §108(a), (d). There is nothing in the problem indicating that Collectible Inc. had filed a bankruptcy petition prior to the discharge.

The bank's discharge of Collectible Inc.'s debt was probably not a gift. Whether the discharge could be considered a gift is a question of fact to be decided based on all of the relevant facts and circumstances indicating that the bank was not acting with detached and disinterested generosity, out of affection, charity, or like impulse. The discharge might have resulted from detached and disinterested generosity since the bank's shareholders and customers were regular customers of Collectible Inc. On the other hand, they may not have been motivated by detached and disinterested generosity. They may have forgiven the debt so (i) they could have easy access to baseball paraphernalia, (ii) the bank would have profitable patronage from Collectible Inc. in the future, or (iii) the bank would not alienate its other customers by playing hard ball (no pun intended!) with Collectible Inc. Any of these motivations would cut against gift treatment.

Final Examination Number Seven
Professor Katherine Pratt
Loyola Law School, Los Angeles

Instructions

1. Allowable materials: A calculator and the exam addendum of Code and regulation sections assigned in this course.

2. The exam period is three hours (180 minutes). Time allocations are given for each question. These time allocations reflect the points allocated to each question. Be careful to adhere to the time allocations. Accurate answers may be short. Do not waste time paraphrasing the Code. You may use common abbreviations (for example, AR, AB, FMV, and so on).

3. Provide authority (for example, Code, regulations, cases) for your answers and explain each step in your answers in order to receive maximum credit.

4. If an answer is more than a few lines long, please be sure to concisely state and underline your conclusions at some point in your answer.

5. Read the facts and the questions carefully. Do not assume un-stated facts. If you think that a question is ambiguous or unclear, explain why in your answer.

6. Make the following assumptions, unless otherwise indicated:

    a. All individual taxpayers are calendar year, cash method taxpayers and all corporate taxpayers are calendar year, accrual method taxpayers.

    b. Apply the taxpayer's marginal rate to any income or gain and assume that the marginal rate is 40 percent for ordinary income and 28 percent for capital gain.

    c. If §83 applies to a transfer of property, the taxpayer may or may not make a §83(b) election. (Explain what would happen with and without an election and whether you would advise the taxpayer to make the election.)

    d. The taxpayer has not made any other elections.

    e. In order to simplify your calculations, assume (unrealistically) that:

       i. A market rate of interest is 10 percent compounding *annu-*

ally (for purposes of making any present value or future value calculations) and

ii. The "applicable federal rate" (AFR) is 10 percent compounding *semiannually*.

7. California is in the Ninth Circuit, Illinois is in the Seventh Circuit, and Pennsylvania is in the Third Circuit.

8. If three asterisks (***) appear between two questions, that means that the question following the asterisks begins a new fact pattern that is unrelated to the previous question.

GOOD LUCK!

Appendix

Part I (60 minutes)

Question 1. (5 minutes) *T* pays $150,000 for an annuity that will pay *T* $20,000 a year for 10 years. In the year in which *T* receives the first $20,000 annuity payment, how much of the payment will *T* *include* in income?

* * *

Question 2. (5 minutes) *T* owes $10,000 to a bank, and owes $35,000 to other creditors. He cannot pay all of his debts because he lost his job and his assets are worth only $40,000. The bank agreed to discharge *T*'s $10,000 debt for $4,000. What amount must *T* include in income as a result of this debt discharge?

* * *

Question 3. (5 minutes) *T* was awarded the Nobel Prize for literature. The prize included a check for $825,000. *T* plans to donate the entire prize to charity. She has asked for your advice as to the tax consequences of receipt of the prize. What do you advise?

* * *

Question 4. (5 minutes) In year one, *W* bought a condominium apartment in New York City for $100,000 of cash. In year 20, *W* gave her goddaughter, *D*, the apartment so that *D* could live in the city and afford to take an interesting but low paying job. At the time of the transfer to *D*, the apartment was worth $300,000. *D* lives in the apartment. What amount, if any, must *D* include in income, as a result of receiving and living in the apartment and what is *D*'s basis in the apartment?

* * *

Question 5. (8 minutes) On August 1, year one, *T* paid $30,000 for a delivery van, which she will use in her flower delivery business. Assuming that *T* uses the 200 percent declining balance method, what amount of depreciation deduction will she be allowed to take in year one and year two?

* * *

Question 6. (12 minutes) In year one, *T*, a resident of Philadelphia, purchased an office building for $1.4 million of nonrecourse debt and $100,000 cash. At the time of the purchase, the building was worth

$500,000. During the period from year one to year four, T took depreciation deductions with respect to the building and interest deductions on the debt. In year four, when the property was still worth $500,000, B purchased the building from T in exchange for assuming the debt on the building. What is T's original year one basis in the building? What is the amount realized on the sale of the building to B in year four?

***

Question 7. (10 minutes) On January 1 of year one, T purchases a bond issued by ABC Inc. for $7,000. The redemption date is December 31 of year three. The face amount payable at maturity is $9,930. The bond bears no stated interest, but the yield to maturity (YTM) on the bond equals 12 percent per annum, compounding semiannually. T will hold the bond until maturity. What are the tax consequences of the foregoing, in year one, to T (a cash method taxpayer) and ABC Inc.?

***

Question 8. (10 minutes) Mom and Pop are wealthy taxpayers who are taxed at a 40 percent marginal rate. Son, age 25, is a struggling musician who is taxed at a very low rate. Mom and Pop plan to loan Son $200,000 interest-free for two years so he can invest it and use the earnings from the investment for living expenses. They believe that this plan will reduce the family's overall tax burden because the earnings on the $200,000 will be taxed at Son's low tax rate instead of Mom and Pop's high tax rate. What advice would you give Mom and Pop about the income tax consequences of their plan?

Part II (45 minutes)

You are a staff attorney for U.S. Senator Strom. He is introducing "pro-family" legislation and wonders whether his piece of legislation should include any tax proposals. He has asked you to prepare a memo for him in which you do the following:

i. Describe the current law as to the tax treatment of child care expenses (explaining any deductions, credits, or exclusions to which taxpayers may be entitled),

ii. Give a policy critique of the existing rules, and

      iii. Describe and critique possible legislative proposals that would change the existing rules.

You should consider the treatment of single-parent families and two-parent families (both families with one income earner and families in which both parents work outside the home).

In order to make your description a little more concrete, Senator Strom would like you (at a minimum) to be sure to include in your memo a description of the tax consequences to the following taxpayers of paying for child care or providing it themselves:

- Taxpayer *T1* is a single mother whose annual AGI is $30,000. She is in the 15 percent rate bracket. Her annual child care expenses (for one child) are $5,000.

- Taxpayer *T2* is a single mother whose annual AGI is $100,000. She is in the 30 percent rate bracket. Her annual child care expenses (for one child) are $20,000.

- Taxpayer *T3* is a married couple in the 30 percent rate bracket. The husband's annual AGI is $50,000 and his wife's annual AGI is $50,000. Their annual child care expenses (for one child) are $20,000. They file a joint return.

- Taxpayer *T4* is a married couple in the 30 percent rate bracket. The husband's annual AGI is $100,000 and his wife's annual AGI is zero. The wife works in the home, taking care of the house and their child. They file a joint return.

(This assignment involves a number of issues and your memo is limited to five pages, so you should organize your answer before you begin to write.)

Part III (75 minutes)

Biotech Breakthroughs Inc. ("BB Inc.") is a small but highly profitable privately owned biotechnology company based near Palo Alto, California. As part of long range plans for expansion of its headquarters, BB Inc. in year one purchased real property all around its headquarters, including a mansion (for which BB Inc. paid $1.5 million), which was located on the edge of the BB Inc. grounds. BB Inc. in year one also recruited Dr. Teresa Thomas (*T*), a world famous research biochemist and senior University of Chicago professor. *T* decided that she would like to work for BB Inc. and she began negotiating the terms of her employment with the company in November, year one. The company agreed to pay T a salary of $100,000 in her first year of employment. In addition, the company agreed to allow T, in the first year of her employment, to purchase up to 200 shares of BB Inc. stock (valued at that time at $900 a share) for $25 a share. The company also agreed to pay T an annual salary of $300,000 in all subsequent years of her employment.

T was concerned that she could not afford the extraordinarily expensive housing near Palo Alto, especially since her first year cash compensation would be only $100,000, before taxes. In order to help T solve her housing problem, BB Inc. agreed to sell the mansion to her for $100,000, subject to certain terms (described below). BB Inc. also arranged to have a local bank loan T the $100,000 purchase price on a nonrecourse basis, secured by the property. The loan required T to pay interest only, of $700 per month, during years one through 10, and to repay the $100,000 principal at the end of year 10.

BB Inc. wanted T to stay near the headquarters throughout her long work day, in case of any emergencies involving her research. The company asked her to eat her lunch at the headquarters, and offered to cater in anything that she wanted to eat. T did not want to have to stay at the headquarters all day and suggested a compromise. T agreed to eat her lunch every weekday at her nearby home, if BB Inc. would cater in food for T's lunch. BB Inc. agreed to this suggestion.

In December, year one, T and BB Inc. signed the employment agreement that they had negotiated. When T arrived in Palo Alto on January 1, year two, to begin working for BB Inc., she borrowed $100,000 from the local bank and purchased the mansion from the company in exchange for the $100,000. T's $100,000 note to the bank was nonrecourse and was secured by the mansion. The note provided that T was to repay the bank the $100,000 on January 1 in year 10. T also had to pay the bank $700 per month of interest on the loan during years 1 through 10.

The mansion was worth $1.6 million when BB Inc. sold it to T in year two. Since the company was giving up a valuable piece of appreciating real estate in order to induce T to work for it, the company required T to agree to sell the property back to BB Inc. for what she paid for it if T stopped working for BB Inc. before January 1, year seven. BB Inc.'s finance people expected the property to be worth around $2.1 million on that date. T planned to sell the property in year seven or eight and reinvest the money.

During year two, BB Inc. also paid $7,000 for a gourmet catering company to deliver *T*'s lunch to her at her home each weekday.

In December, year two, *T* purchased 200 shares of BB Inc. stock for $25 a share. The stock was worth $1,000 a share at that time.

In June, year six, the president of BB Inc., Mr. Petersen, retired and his nephew, Harry Hacker, became the new president of BB Inc. Mr. Hacker was overtly bigoted. He especially disliked *T* because she was an assertive older woman and he repeatedly made derogatory remarks about *T*'s age and gender in front of other employees. When *T* confronted Mr. Hacker about these remarks during a company meeting, on January 2, year seven, he screamed at her that there was no room in his company for "geriatric biddies" and fired her on the spot, to the horror of everyone else at the meeting.

Later in January, year seven, *T* moved back to Chicago. At that time, the Palo Alto mansion was worth $2.1 million. She was not sure whether she wanted to sell the house, so she rented it. Converting the mansion to rental use allowed *T* to deduct depreciation on the property. (Assume that *T* was allowed total depreciation deductions in years seven and eight of $300,000.)

T also hired a law firm and sued BB Inc. for sex discrimination under Title VII of the Civil Rights Act, and for age discrimination under the Age Discrimination in Employment Act.

In December, year seven, *T* went to work for a competing biotechnology firm in Chicago, at a salary of $400,000 a year.

In December, year seven, a jury awarded *T* $1.5 million in compensatory, backpay, and punitive damages in her sex and age discrimination suit against BB Inc. BB Inc. paid the judgment immediately, but in late December appealed the trial court decision.

In January, year eight, *T* exchanged the Palo Alto mansion for a Chicago apartment building. In exchange for her mansion plus assumption of a $1 million nonrecourse liability on the Chicago property, *T* received (i) $500,000 in cash, (ii) the Chicago apartment building (which she rented to tenants), and (iii) the buyer's assumption of the $100,000 nonrecourse debt on the Palo Alto mansion. At the time of the year eight exchange, the Palo Alto property was worth $2.2 million and the Chicago property was worth $2.6 million.

In year eight, an appellate court affirmed the decision of the trial court in *T*'s discrimination suit in part, but remanded the case for reconsideration of the punitive damage award. On remand, later in year eight, the punitive damage award was reduced by $300,000, which *T* repaid BB Inc.

Appendix

Assume that T retained you as her tax lawyer in year one and that you have represented her since that time. What advice would you have given T, *for years two, seven, and eight,* regarding the tax consequences to her of the foregoing events and transactions? Since this question involves a number of issues, please be careful to think through the question and organize your answer before you start writing.

END OF EXAMINATION

Appendix

Model Answers

Part I

Answer 1. $5,000, which is the $20,000 payment less the $15,000 ($20,000 times $150,000/$200,000) excluded under §72(b). §72(a).

Answer 2. $1,000. Although the discharge results in $6,000 of cancellation of indebtedness income, under *Kirby Lumber* and §61(a)(12), *T* excludes $5,000 (the $45,000 of debts less the $40,000 of assets) of that COD under the §108(a) insolvency rule.

Answer 3. If *T* is paid the prize money, then donates it, she will have to include the full $825,000. §74(a). Section 170 permits taxpayers to deduct charitable contributions. However, the deduction is capped at 50 percent of AGI. Unless *T*'s other income for the year totals $825,000 or more, this limitation will apply. If *T* arranges for the payor to pay the prize money directly to the charity, *T* can exclude all of the prize money. §74(b).

Answer 4. If the transfer of the apartment is a gift, *D* excludes the value of the apartment. §102(a). Here, the transfer is probably a gift; focusing on the donor's intent, it appears that *W* gave her goddaughter the apartment out of detached and disinterested generosity. *Duberstein*. *D*'s basis in the apartment is $100,000. §1015. *D* is not taxed on the income from living in the apartment she owns. The United States does not tax imputed income from property owned by a taxpayer.

Answer 5. The recovery period is five years. Before applying the half-year convention, the year one deduction equals $12,000 — under the double declining balance method, the cost recovery deduction equals 40 percent (200 percent of the 20 percent straightline percentage) of the $30,000 basis (since *T* did not make a §179 election). §168(e)(3)(B). However, the half-year convention applies so the year one deduction equals $6,000. §168(d)(1).

The year two deduction is $9,600, which is 40 percent (200 percent of the 20 percent straightline percentage) of the $24,000 adjusted basis (the $30,000 basis less the $6,000 year one depreciation deduction).

Answer 6. *T*'s adjusted basis equals her §1012 basis plus or minus the §1016 adjustments. A taxpayer's basis generally includes nonrecourse debt (*Crane, Tufts*), but here the nonrecourse debt far exceeds the value of the property and cash investment is small. Apply *Pleasant*

Appendix

Summit, under the *Golsen* rule, because *T* lives in the Third Circuit. Include the nonrecourse debt up to the value of the property, $500,000. Also include the $100,000 cash investment in basis, so *T*'s original basis is $600,000.

Amount realized equals the cash the taxpayer received plus the fair market value of any property received. §1001(b). Debt relief is included in amount realized regardless of the fair market value of the property at the time of debt relief (*Tufts*). However, debt relief is limited to debt included in basis at the time of acquisition, here $500,000.

Answer 7. The total original issue discount ("OID") on the bond equals $2,930 ($9,930 stated redemption price at maturity less $7,000 issue price). §1273.

The OID for the first six-month accrual period equals $420, which is 6 percent (12 percent YTM/2 accrual periods in the year) of the $7,000 issue price. The OID for the second six-month accrual period equals $445, which is 6 percent of the $7,420 adjusted issue price ($7,000 issue price plus $420 of prior accrued OID). In year one, *T* will include $865 ($420 plus $445) of interest, even though *T* is a cash method taxpayer. §1272(a)(1). ABC Inc. will deduct the same amount. §163(e). The §163(d) limitation does not apply to corporate taxpayers like ABC Inc.

* * *

Answer 8. Section 7872 will prevent the interest-free loan from completely shifting the investment income from Mom and Pop to Son. The planned interest-free loan is a below-market loan because it does not bear interest at the applicable federal rate. It appears to be a gift loan, which is one of the types of below-market loans to which §7872 applies. The loan is too large to be within the §7872(c)(2) exception. Under §7872(a), on the last day of the calendar year, the foregone interest on the loan (interest on the $200,000 loan at the AFR) would be deemed transferred from Mom and Pop to Son as a gift. Son would not be taxed on the gift. §102. Mom and Pop would not be able to deduct the gift. On the same day, the foregone interest would be deemed retransferred from Son to Mom and Pop. Son may be able to deduct the interest deemed retransferred, depending on how he invests the loan proceeds. Mom and Pop will have an interest inclusion in the amount of the foregone interest. The net effect is that Mom and Pop will pay tax at a 40 percent rate on the foregone interest. The return Son earns on the $200,000 loan proceeds may be more or less than the foregone interest. If Son earns more than the foregone interest, the loan will shift some income from Mom and Pop.

Part II

[Note to students: Your discussion of current law will either be right or wrong. However, there is no one "right" answer to the policy discussion. The answer below is intended as an example of what a student might write.]

The big issue here is this: Are child care expenses a cost of earning income or a personal consumption expenditure? If the child care expenses are a cost of earning income, the appropriate tax treatment would be to allow those parents who pay their own child care expenses to deduct them and those parents whose employers pay their child care expenses to exclude them. If, on the other hand, child care expenses are not a cost of earning income, perhaps we should not allow a deduction/exclusion. If we still wanted to provide a subsidy to parents with small children in need of child care, a credit or direct subsidy program might be more appropriate, since it would allow us to target the benefit and provide it to those most in need.

Current law and a critique of it.

Child care costs are not deductible because the cost is a mixed personal-business expense that is treated as an inherently personal expenditure. *Smith.* The decision to have children is regarded as an inherently personal choice. Just as taxpayers who decide to live far from where they work cannot deduct the costs of commuting, parents cannot deduct the costs of child care. However, commuting expenses may not be a perfect analogue. Most commuters could live near their workplace, but decide not to for personal reasons. However, once a person becomes a parent (either by chance or by choice), they must care for the child.

T1 and *T2* must incur child care expenses if they are to work. As to the *T3* family, either one spouse (typically the wife because of societal pressures) must stay home and care for the child or *T3* must incur child care costs. In two-parent families, the current tax treatment exacerbates the other incentives in the Code (for example, treatment of imputed income and payroll tax and income tax rates applied to the wages of the secondary wage earner) that encourage secondary wage earners to not work outside the home.

561

The fact that taxpayers' child care costs are highly variable (*T1*'s costs ($5,000) are lower than *T2*'s and *T3*'s ($20,000)) raises another issue: Are these taxpayers' costs different because *T2* and *T3* live in a more expensive area—or are they buying better care for their child? Even if child care costs are properly deductible "business" costs, is there a personal consumption element to the cost if it exceeds a certain amount? This is something that we should consider if we decide to allow parents a deduction for child care costs. If we are to propose a deduction for child care expenses, we may want to provide a ceiling on the amount that can be deducted.

Section 21 provides a credit for child care expenses. The percentage equals 30 percent if the taxpayer's AGI is $10,000 or less, 20 percent if the taxpayer's AGI is over $28,000, and between 20 percent and 30 percent between those AGI numbers. However, the amount of child care expenses against which that percentage may be applied is limited to $2,400 for one child. Taxpayers *T1*, *T2*, and *T3* would each be entitled to a $480 credit (20 percent of $2,400) with respect to their child care expenses, despite the fact that *T1*'s child care expenses were $5,000 and *T2* and *T3*'s were $20,000. *T4* would not be entitled to a credit.

If we use a credit, we are implicitly assuming that child care costs are not costs of earning income and are a subsidy. If we adopted a direct expenditure program, would we allocate the funds as the credit allocates them here? Should we be giving taxpayers *T1*, *T2*, and *T3* the same benefit, or should the lower income taxpayer, *T1*, receive more assistance? Note that, although *T4* does not receive a credit, *T4* benefits from other Code provisions that encourage secondary wage earners to work in the home.

Section 129 provides an exclusion for employer-provided dependent care assistance programs. The exclusion is limited to $5,000. The tax saving from the exclusion equals the taxpayer's tax rate multiplied by the amount excluded, so a $5,000 exclusion would save *T1* $750 and both *T2* and *T3* $1,500. *T4* would not have any child care expenses to exclude. A taxpayer must choose between the §21 credit and §129 exclusion. §21(c). The exclusion is worth more than the credit to taxpayers *T1*, *T2*, and *T3*, so they will opt for the §129 exclusion if it is available. A minority of employers (primarily large employers) have §129 qualified dependent care assistance programs. This raises a potential equity issue because the greatest dollar benefit of the exclusion is going to high income taxpayers who work for the large employers that can offer dependent care assistance programs. Again, higher tax savings for higher income taxpayers is appropriate if we conceptualize child care expenses as a cost of earning income. If that is thought to be the correct approach, then the Code should provide for both deduction (by taxpayers paying their own child care expenses) and exclusion (by employees whose employers pay their expenses).

Subsidizing child care through the Tax Code raises another significant issue: What if a single parent is too poor to pay for child care? Unless she can pay for child care, a deduction or credit would be of no value to her. Perhaps we could make the credit refundable (i.e., a voucher) that could be used to pay for child care. In addition, since the credit is a large revenue loser, perhaps the credit should be phased out as AGI increases.

Possible proposals:

1. Increase the credit for child care expenses. In addition, perhaps we should make the credit refundable to assist low income taxpayers.

2. Give a credit for each child irrespective of the taxpayer's child care expenses (so that *T4* would receive the same credit as taxpayer's *T1*, *T2*, and *T3*). This is not advisable since it would further exacerbate the current incentives in the Code that encourage secondary wage earners to work in the home.

3. Eliminate the exclusion because (i) not all employers have it, which raises an equity issue, and (ii) it operates like a deduction, benefiting the highest bracket taxpayers the most. If we were to keep the exclusion, then consistency might require that we also allow an equivalent deduction for taxpayers who pay their own child care expenses.

4. If we allow a deduction/exclusion, perhaps it should be capped, so that taxpayers do not add a personal consumption element to their child care costs as a result of the deduction/exclusion.

There are many children of working parents in this country. How would we fund new child care assistance in the Code? In the current deficit-cutting environment, it is hard to imagine how we would pay for significant new child care assistance in the Code.

Part III

Year two consequences:

1. The $100,000 of cash wages are included in income. §61(a)(1).

2. *The $7,000 of free catered lunches at T's house.* Compensatory in-

kind benefits provided to employees are included in the employee's income. §61(a)(1); Reg. 1.61-1(a). Does the §119 exclusion apply? *T* was required to eat at home for the convenience of her employer (to be near labs), but were the meals provided "on the business premises of the employer"? *T*'s home was adjacent to BB Inc.'s headquarters, and some courts have interpreted the "business premises of the employer" broadly. *E.g.*, *Lindeman*. But the house is *T*'s, so a court may say lunch was not on the business premises. This is a close call — it may or may not be excludable.

3. *The purchase of the stock.* A compensatory bargain purchase of property by an employee from an employer triggers inclusion under §§61 and 83. *T* must include the bargain element in income in year two because the stock is not subject to a substantial risk of forfeiture. *T* includes $195,000, which is the $200,000 fair market value of the stock less the $5,000 *T* paid for stock. The income is ordinary.

4. *The purchase of the mansion.* A compensatory bargain purchase of property by an employee from an employer triggers inclusion under §§61 and 83. BB Inc. transferred $1.6 million of property to *T* for $100,000. The transfer was in connection with the performance of services because *T* had to work for BB Inc. until year seven to keep the house. *T* is not required to include the bargain purchase compensation until the substantial risk of forfeiture ends in year seven. However, *T* could elect to include the bargain purchase compensation in year two, under §83(b), in order to convert future appreciation on the property from ordinary income to capital gain. *T* would decide whether to make the §83(b) election by comparing the present value of the tax due with and without the election.

If *T* does not make the election, *T* will include in year seven $2 million, the $2.1 million value of the property at the time it vests less the $100,000 *T* paid for the property. The inclusion is ordinary income, so *T* would pay $800,000 of tax (40 percent of $2 million) on the inclusion. *T* would then take a $2.1 million basis in the property. *T* would also be taxed on any gain realized on the subsequent sale of the property, but the gain would probably be capital. (If *T* does not make an election, there may also be collateral tax consequences. For example, *T* may also have income from utilizing the house while it is owned by BB Inc., under the §83 regulations. However, these consequences are beyond the scope of most basic tax courses, so they are not included in this model answer.)

If *T* makes the §83(b) election, she will include in year two $1.5 million, which is the $1.6 million value of the mansion less the $100,000 she paid for it. That inclusion is ordinary income so she would owe $600,000 of tax (40 percent of $1.5 million) on the inclusion. Her basis in the mansion would then be $1.6 million. If she sold the property in year seven, after it vested, she would also pay tax on any gain realized on the sale, but the gain would probably be capital.

5. The interest *T* pays on her $100,000 loan to the bank is deductible qualified residence interest. §163(h).

Year seven consequences.

1. *The $1.5 million recovery in her lawsuit against BB Inc.* The recovery looks like income, under *Glenshaw Glass.* Although BB Inc. has filed an appeal, *T* must include in year seven under *North American Oil* and the claim of right doctrine. May *T* exclude all or a part of the judgment, under §104(a)(2)? *T* cannot exclude punitives, because her case does not involve physical injury.

    T may be able to exclude the compensatory damages if the suit was based on tort or tort type rights. Reg. §1.104-1(c). In *Burke*, the Supreme Court held that Title VII damages were not excludable under §104(a)(2) because the remedial scheme of Title VII did not include traditional tort remedies. However, Title VII has been amended since the facts in *Burke* arose so compensatory damages received under Title VII may now be excludable. In *Schleier*, the Supreme Court held that an ADEA age discrimination claim is not a personal injury claim. Thus, compensatory damages received on the ADEA claim are not excludable, but compensatory damages received on the sex discrimination claim may be excludable. However, even if the Title VII sex discrimination claim is a personal injury, *T* can exclude the damages only if she can establish that the damages were received "on account of" the personal injury. In *Schleier*, the Court's analysis of the "on account of" language seems to create a distinction between physical and nonphysical injury, so it is not clear whether *T* could exclude any of the damages received.

2. *The mansion "vests."* Absent a §83(b) election in year two, *T* must include in income, under §83, $2 million (the $2.1 million

fair market value of property at the time it vests less the $100,000 T paid for the property). T's basis in the property is $2.1 million.

3. The interest T pays on her $100,000 loan to the bank is deductible qualified residence interest, per §163(h).

4. T includes rental income from the Palo Alto rental property and takes depreciation deductions on it. §§61(a)(5) and 168.

5. The compensation paid by the Chicago firm is included in T's income. §61(a)(1).

Year eight consequences:

1. As to the award affirmed, T included the damages in year seven so there is no inclusion in year eight. As to the $300,000 that T must repay, T is entitled to a deduction under *Lewis*. Under §1341, she can elect to either (i) deduct the amount in year eight or (ii) reduce her year eight tax by the amount of tax that she would have saved had she not included the repaid amount in year seven.

2. *The exchange of the mansion for the new property in Chicago.* Gross income includes gains from dealings in property. §61(a)(3). The exchange of the two properties is a realization event, because the exchange changes T's legal entitlements. *Cottage Savings.*

    Realized gain equals amount realized less adjusted basis plus adjustments. The amount realized equals $3.2 million, which is the $2.6 million fair market value plus the $500,000 of cash T received plus the $100,000 of debt relief (under *Crane* and *Tufts*). The adjusted basis plus adjustments total $2.8 million, which is T's $100,000 original basis, plus the $2 million T included in year seven when the mansion vested, less the $300,000 of depreciation deductions T took in years seven and eight, plus the $1 million liability on the new property. T's realized gain is $400,000, which is the $3.2 million amount realized less the $2.8 million adjusted basis plus adjustments.

    The recognized gain equals $400,000. Realized gain is recognized unless otherwise provided in the Code. §1001(c). The mansion and the Chicago properties are "like-kind" business properties, so §1031 will apply to the exchange. The $400,000 of realized gain is recognized up to the amount of boot received, here the $500,000 of cash T received. (T received a larger liability than she gave up, so she does not have boot from net debt

Appendix

relief for the purpose of computing her recognized gain.) §1031(b) and Reg. §1.1031(d)-2.

T's basis in the Chicago property equals $2.6 million:

$1,800,000	AB in the old property
+$1,000,000	liability on the new property
−$ 600,000	money received ($500,000 cash plus $100,000 of debt relief)
+$ 400,000	gain recognized
$2,600,000	

Table of Cases

Table of Cases

Table of Cases

Table of Internal Revenue Code Sections

Table of Internal Revenue Code Sections

Table of Treasury
Regulations

Table of Revenue Rulings

Table of Revenue Procedures

Topical Index

Index

Index

Index

Index